Third
Edition

TAXES AND BUSINESS STRATEGY

A Planning Approach

Myron S. Scholes

Mark A. Wolfson

Merle Erickson

Edward L. Maydew

Terry Shevlin

PEARSON
Prentice
Hall

Upper Saddle River, NJ 07458

Library of Congress Cataloging-in-Publication Data

Taxes and business strategy : a planning approach / Myron S. Scholes . . . [et al.].—3rd ed.
    p. cm.
  Includes bibliographical references and index.
  ISBN 0-13-146553-8
    1. Business enterprises—Taxation—Law and legislation—United States. 2. Tax
planning—United States. I. Scholes, Myron S.

KF6450.S33 2004
343.7305'268—dc22

                                  2003069004

Managing Editor: Alana Bradley
Editorial Director: Jeff Shelstad
Assistant Editor: Sam Goffinet
Senior Editorial Assistant: Jane Avery
Marketing Manager: Beth Toland
Marketing Assistant: Melissa Owens
Managing Editor (Production): John Roberts
Production Editor: Kelly Warsak
Production Assistant: Joe DeProspero
Manufacturing Buyer: Michelle Klein
Cover Design: Bruce Kenselaar
Composition/Full-Service Project Management: Rozi Harris, Erika Kauppi/Interactive Composition Corp.

Cover Printer: Phoenix Color Corp.

Credits and acknowledgments borrowed from other sources and reproduced, with permission, in this textbook
appear on appropriate page within text.

Pearson Prentice Hall™ is a trademark of Pearson Education, Inc.
Pearson® is a registered trademark of Pearson plc
Prentice Hall® is a registered trademark of Pearson Education, Inc.
Pearson Education LTD.
Pearson Education Singapore, Pte. Ltd
Pearson Education, Canada, Ltd
Pearson Education—Japan
Pearson Education Australia PTY, Limited
Pearson Education North Asia Ltd
Pearson Educación de Mexico, S.A. de C.V.
Pearson Education Malaysia, Pte. Ltd

10 9 8 7 6 5
ISBN 0-13-146553-8

CONTENTS

PREFACE

This book was written primarily for MBA students and graduates, specifically for those embarking on (or already in) careers in investment banking, corporate finance, strategy consulting, money management, or venture capital. Executives and finance professionals in such careers are typically not aiming to become tax specialists but do recognize the competitive advantage that comes from a solid understanding of the decision contexts that give rise to tax planning opportunities, how to integrate tax strategy into the bigger picture of corporate decision making, and the dramatic impact that changes in transaction structure can have on after-tax cash flows.

Every top MBA program teaches its students the fundamentals of corporate finance, financial statement analysis and valuation, and investments. Every MBA graduate knows how to perform a discounted cash flow analysis and apply the NPV criterion—valuable skills, but not something that differentiates oneself. MBA programs historically have been deficient, however, at teaching their students about the pervasive role taxes play in decision making. Each of the authors has taught taxes and business strategy at the MBA level. Their courses have been, and are, uniformly popular at their respective institutions. Former students have reported back that they possess a competitive advantage over those MBA graduates who know little or nothing about tax strategy. The material in this book draws from and builds on the authors' classroom and business experiences, as well as the experiences of colleagues around the country, and is not duplicated in any other text.

The book's MBA focus comes from integrating the tax law with the fundamentals of corporate finance and microeconomics. Through integration with traditional MBA topics, the book provides a framework for understanding how taxes affect decision making, asset prices, equilibrium returns, and the financial and operational structure of firms. Relative to legal-based tax books, this text focuses more on the economic consequences of alternative contracting arrangements than on the myriad details and exceptions of the tax laws governing the arrangements. It is not meant to imply that the details of the tax laws are unimportant; they certainly are important. In fact, students new to the tax law will find that this text provides them with significant tax legal knowledge in certain key areas where taxes play a big role in decision making and areas MBAs are likely to encounter in their careers (e.g., mergers and acquisitions, employee stock options, international tax). In addition, the book integrates tax with financial accounting by emphasizing differences and trade-offs between the taxation and the financial accounting of a transaction.

CHANGES IN THE THIRD EDITION

The text retains the same chapter and topic structure as the prior edition.
Our objectives for the revision include:

- Updating the text to reflect major changes in the tax laws.
- Adding analyses of selected tax law changes.
- Replacing some old analyses with new more relevant analyses.
- Updating the lists of additional readings, which should be particularly useful to faculty and doctoral students.

The financial accounting for corporate taxes is explained and illustrated in a new appendix to Chapter 2 for those wishing to relate tax planning to corporate financial statements. Discussion of College Savings Plans (529 plans) was added to Chapter 3. Chapter 4 (organizational form choice) was updated to reflect the new tax rates on dividends and capital gains. A discussion of corporate/individual tax integration using the Australian system as a vehicle for illustration was added as an appendix to this chapter.

Additional material clarifying corporate marginal tax rates was added to Chapter 7. New material on restricted stock and employee stock options was added to Chapter 8. A new appendix explaining and illustrating the accounting for the income tax benefits received by corporations on employee stock options was added to Chapter 8, with discussion of how this accounting affects estimates of corporate taxable income and marginal tax rates.

Chapters 10 and 11 (international tax) reflect the repeal of the Foreign Sales Corporation and provide discussions of the current controversies over export subsidies and corporate inversion transactions.

Chapter 12 primarily reflects the 2003 changes in dividend taxation and changes in the accounting treatment of trust preferred stock.

Chapters 13–17 (mergers and acquisitions) were updated to reflect tax law changes and the change in the financial accounting rules for mergers and acquisitions where the pooling method of accounting is no longer allowed and goodwill is no longer amortized.

Chapter 18 (estate and gift planning) was updated for the major changes in estate and gift taxation that were enacted in 2001 and are being phased-in over the decade.

Acknowledgments

We would like to thank the following people for their help in reviewing drafts of the second and third editions:

Jennifer Blouin, University of North Carolina
Debra S. Callihan, Virginia Polytechnic Institute and State University
Xia Chen, University of Chicago
Anthony P. Curatola, Drexel University
Dan S. Dhaliwal, University of Arizona
Courtney Edwards, University of North Carolina
Mary Margaret Frank, University of Virginia
John Graham, Duke University
Paul A. Griffin, University of California—Davis

Michelle Hanlon, University of Michigan
Steven J. Huddart, Pennsylvania State University
Stacie Kelley, University of Washington
Kimberley G. Key, Auburn University
Mike R. Kinney, Texas A&M University
Michael Knoll, University of Pennsylvania
Barry Marks, University of Houston—Clear Lake
Gary L. Maydew, Iowa State University
Jeffrey Maydew, Baker and Mackenzie
Lil Mills, University of Arizona
Gil B. Manzon Jr., Boston College
Robert McDonald, Northwestern University
Kaye J. Newberry, University of Arizona
Sonja L. Olhoft Rego, University of Iowa
Thomas C. Omer, University of Illinois—Chicago
John R. Robinson, University of Texas—Austin
Richard C. Sansing, Dartmouth College
Jim A. Seida, University of Notre Dame
Douglas A. Shackelford, University of North Carolina
Keith Smith, Arkansas State University
William D. Terando, Iowa State University
Ralph B. Tower, Wake Forest University
Shiing-wu Wang, University of Southern California
Ira Weiss, Columbia University
Craig White, University of New Mexico
Jeffrey Wong, University of Cincinnati
Ronald Worsham Jr., Brigham Young University
Robert W. Wyndelts, Arizona State University
Robert J. Yetman, University of California—Davis

ABOUT THE AUTHORS

Myron S. Scholes is a Partner of Oak Hill Capital Management and a Principal of Oak Hill Platinum Partners. He is also involved in the private and public investment activities of the Robert M. Bass organization. Professor Scholes has been the Frank E. Buck Professor of Finance Emeritus at the Stanford University Graduate School of Business since 1996.

Professor Scholes is widely known for his seminal work in options pricing, capital markets, tax policies, and the financial services industry. He is co-originator of the Black–Scholes options pricing model, which is the basis of the pricing and risk management technology that is used to value and to manage the risk of financial instruments around the world. For this work, he was awarded the Alfred Nobel Memorial Prize in Economic Sciences in 1997.

He was the Frank E. Buck Professor of Finance at the Stanford University Graduate School of Business from 1983 to 1996 and a Senior Research Fellow at the Hoover Institution from 1987 to 1996. He received a Ph.D. in 1969 from the University of Chicago where he served as the Edward Eagle Brown Professor of Finance in the Graduate School of Business from 1974 to 1983 and Director of the Center for Research in Security Prices from 1976 to 1983. He was an Assistant and Associate Professor of Finance at Sloan School of Management, MIT, from 1969 to 1974.

Professor Scholes is a member of the Econometric Society and served as President of the American Finance Association in 1990. Professor Scholes has honorary doctorate degrees from the University of Paris, McMaster University, and Louvain University.

Professor Scholes has consulted widely with many financial institutions, corporations, and exchanges. He was a Principal and Limited Partner at Long-Term Capital Management LP, an investment management firm, from 1993 to 1998. From 1991 to 1993, he was a Managing Director at Salomon Brothers, a member of Salomon's risk management committee, and Co-Head of its Fixed Income Derivatives Sales and Trading Department, where he was instrumental in building Salomon Swapco, its derivatives intermediation subsidiary, and in expanding its derivative sales and trading group.

Mark A. Wolfson is a Managing Partner of Oak Hill Capital Management (OHCM) and has played instrumental roles in the establishment of Oak Hill Strategic Partners, Oak Hill Venture Partners, Oak Hill Platinum Partners, Oak Hill Investment Management, and the Oak Hill Special Opportunities Fund. OHCM manages Oak Hill Capital Partners, a private equity partnership founded by Robert M. Bass and his longtime team of investment professionals. Mr. Wolfson serves on the Boards of

Directors of 230 Park Investors, Accretive Healthcare, Caribbean Restaurants, DaVinci I, LLC (Japan real estate), eGain Communications, Financial Engines, and Investment Technology Group. Mr. Wolfson holds the title of Consulting Professor at the Stanford Graduate School of Business, where he has been a faculty member since 1977, including a three-year term as Associate Dean, and formerly held the title of Dean Witter Professor. He has also taught at the Harvard Business School and the University of Chicago and has been a Visiting Scholar at the Sloan School of Management at Massachusetts Institute of Technology and the Hoover Institution at Stanford University. Mr. Wolfson has been a Research Associate at The National Bureau of Economic Research since 1988 and serves on The Board of Trustees of Menlo School as well as the Board of Advisors and Executive Committee of The Stanford Institute for Economic Policy Research.

Merle Erickson is an Associate Professor of Accounting at the Graduate School of Business at the University of Chicago where he teaches a tax strategy course in the MBA program and executive education courses that focus on tax-related valuation issues in mergers, acquisitions, and divestitures. He received his Ph.D. from the University of Arizona in 1996. Professor Erickson's research focuses on tax-related valuation issues, earnings and balance sheet management, and various aspects of accounting fraud. His research has been published in *The Accounting Review, Journal of Accounting Research, Journal of Accounting and Economics, Journal of the American Taxation Association,* the *National Tax Journal,* and *Tax Notes.* He is also the author/editor of *Cases in Tax Strategy* (Pearson/Prentice Hall). Professor Erickson has received awards for his teaching and research, and he consults periodically with both private and governmental entities. He is an associate editor of the *Journal of Accounting Research* and is currently on the editorial boards of *The Accounting Review* and the *Journal of the American Taxation Association.*

Edward L. Maydew is Chair of the Accounting Area and the David E. Hoffman Term Professor of Accounting at the University of North Carolina, Kenan-Flagler Business School. He also serves as Director of Research at the UNC Tax Center. Professor Maydew formerly served on the faculty of the University of Chicago and earned his Ph.D. from the University of Iowa. His research and teaching interests span a variety of tax and accounting topics, and he has received a number of awards for research and teaching. He has published in *The Accounting Review, Journal of Accounting Research, Journal of Accounting and Economics, Journal of Public Economics, National Tax Journal,* and *Journal of the American Taxation Association.* He has assisted firms in a variety of complex accounting and tax matters. He is an Associate Editor at the *Journal of Accounting and Economics* and serves or has served on the editorial boards of *Review of Accounting Studies, Accounting Horizons,* and *Journal of the American Taxation Association.*

Terry Shevlin is Deloitte & Touche Professor of Accounting at the University of Washington. He received his Ph.D. from Stanford University in 1986. He teaches or has taught financial accounting at the undergraduate level, taxes and business strategy at the graduate level, and seminars in empirical tax research and capital markets research at the Ph.D. level. He has presented talks on research in taxation at the American Accounting Association Doctoral Consortium on three separate occasions and has given presentations at both the Big 10 and PAC 10 Doctoral Consortiums.

Professor Shevlin's research has been published in *The Accounting Review, Journal of Accounting Research, Journal of Accounting and Economics, Contemporary Accounting Research, Journal of the American Taxation Association, Journal of Accounting, Auditing and Finance, Review of Accounting Studies,* and *Accounting Horizons.* In addition to his interest in taxation, his research interests include earnings management, capital markets, and employee stock options. He has twice won both the American Accounting Association Competitive Manuscript Award and the American Taxation Association Tax Manuscript Award. He served as editor of the *Journal of the American Taxation Association* from 1996–1999, currently serves as Senior Editor of *The Accounting Review* (2002–2005), and serves on a number of journal editorial boards. He also serves as the Faculty Director of the Ph.D. Program at the University of Washington Business School.

1

INTRODUCTION TO TAX STRATEGY

After completing this chapter, you should be able to:

1. List and briefly explain the three key themes underlying our approach to effective tax planning.

2. Briefly explain the concept of implicit taxes.

3. Briefly explain the concept of tax clienteles.

4. Explain the difference between effective tax planning and tax minimization.

5. Understand that explicit taxes affect pretax rates of return.

6. Understand that tax planning is a tax-favored activity.

Our broadest objective in this book is to provide you with a framework that is useful for thinking about how taxes affect business activities. Although we will not stress this point very often, we also hope that it becomes apparent that the framework also applies to the analysis of how business is affected by many other nontax regulatory policies. Examples of other nontax regulatory policies include international trade agreements, monetary policy, rate regulation for public utilities, currency restrictions, and regulation of the securities markets, the banking industry, the pharmaceutical industry, and a host of other government programs not reflected in the tax law, such as agricultural subsidies.

The framework we develop is highly integrative: **investment strategies** and **financing policies** within firms are linked through taxes. That is, the investments that a firm undertakes depend on how they are financed. In addition, financing decisions depend on the investments that the firm undertakes. By investments we mean not only the actively managed assets the firm uses to run its business but also passive assets such as bonds, stocks, and direct investments in other entities. Our approach differs from that of others in that much of our focus is on the evolving strategies applicable to existing firms. These firms make incremental investment and financing decisions that depend, in part, on past investment and financing decisions. New strategies depend on past strategies because it is costly to adjust investment and financing decisions once they have been made. From this brief introduction, it is obvious that we take a rather broad look at what we call the economic balance sheets of firms and the factors that affect firms' asset and financing positions.

1.1 WHY DO TAX RULES INFLUENCE INVESTMENT DECISIONS?

Tax rules affect the **before-tax rates of return** on assets. By before-tax rate of return, we mean the rate of return earned from investing in an asset before any taxes are paid to domestic and foreign federal, state, and local taxing authorities. We explain why some firms select investments with high before-tax rates of return while others select assets with low before-tax rates of return even when both types of investments are available to all firms. On the assets side of the ledger, we emphasize that before-tax rates of return differ because (1) the returns on different types of assets are taxed differently; (2) the returns on similar assets are taxed differently if they are located in different tax jurisdictions; (3) the returns on similar assets located in the same tax jurisdiction are taxed differently if they are held through different legal organizational forms (such as a corporation versus a sole proprietorship); and (4) the returns on similar assets located in the same tax jurisdiction and held through the same legal organizational form are taxed differently depending on such factors as the operating history of the organization, the returns to other assets held by the organization, and the particular characteristics of the individual owners of the organization.

Tax rules also influence the financing decisions of firms through their effect on the cost of financing the firms' activities. A firm is said to make a "capital structure decision" when it decides how it will finance its activities. The capital structure of a firm is composed of various types of ownership claims, some called debt and others called equity. We emphasize that the cost of issuing a capital structure instrument depends on the tax treatment it is accorded, which, in turn, depends on whether the instrument (1) is *debt, equity,* or a *hybrid;* (2) is issued to an *employee,* a *customer,* a *related party,* a *bank,* or a number of other special classes of suppliers of capital; and (3) is issued by a *corporation, partnership,* or some other legal *organizational form.* It also depends on the tax jurisdiction in which the capital structure instrument is issued.

1.2 STRUCTURE AND THEMES OF THE BOOK

This book contains two parts. In the first part, Chapters 1–7, we develop the fundamental concepts that represent the building blocks of our framework. Then, in Chapters 8–18, we consider how this framework applies to specific decision settings.

Three key themes run throughout the building-block chapters:

1. Effective tax planning requires the planner to consider the tax implications of a proposed transaction for all parties to the transaction.
2. Effective tax planning requires the planner, in making investment and financing decisions, to consider not only **explicit taxes** (tax dollars paid directly to taxing authorities) but also **implicit taxes** (taxes that are paid indirectly in the form of lower before-tax rates of return on tax-favored investments).

3. Effective tax planning requires the planner to recognize that taxes represent only one among many business costs and all costs must be considered in the planning process: to be implemented, some proposed tax plans may require exceedingly costly restructuring of the business.

Traditional approaches to tax planning fail to recognize that effective tax planning and tax minimization are very different things. **Effective tax planning** involves considering the role of taxes when implementing the decision rule of maximizing after-tax returns. In a world of costly contracting, implementation of **tax minimization** strategies may introduce significant costs along nontax dimensions. For example, suppose an employer's tax rate is expected to increase while the employee's tax rate is expected to remain constant in the next period. Deferring payment of compensation to the employee until a later period saves taxes but subjects the employee to the risk of non-payment if the firm goes bankrupt. The employee may require an additional payment (a risk premium) to compensate her for the increased risk. Therefore, the tax-minimization strategy may be undesirable. A particularly easy way to avoid paying taxes is to avoid investing in profitable ventures, but this does not maximize after-tax returns.

We view effective tax planning as part of the larger problem of the efficient design of organizations. In developing this organizational design theme, we adopt a **contractual perspective.** Contracts specify the rights of various parties to make decisions and to receive cash flows in differing circumstances. We focus on how the tax-related cash flows specified by contracts affect the prices at which assets are traded. We further stress how these cash flows affect the ways in which production is organized by business units.

A Planning Approach

As the subtitle of the book suggests, we adopt a planning approach to taxes and business strategy. More precisely, we adopt a *global* planning approach. The key themes we have just described suggest that there are three aspects of planning globally:

1. *Multilateral approach: All* contracting parties must be taken into account in tax planning. This is a global or multilateral, rather than a unilateral, approach.
2. *Importance of hidden taxes: All* taxes must be taken into account. We are interested in a global measure of taxes, not simply explicit taxes.
3. *Importance of nontax costs: All* costs of business must be considered, not just tax costs.

Taxing Authority as Investment Partner

All of the interesting problems in tax planning arise because, from the standpoint of individual taxpaying entities, the taxing authority is an uninvited party to all contracts. The taxing authority brings to each of its "forced" ventures with taxpayers a set of contractual terms (tax rules). Unlike other contracting parties, the taxing authority generally does not negotiate these terms separately for each venture. Such a policy would simply be too expensive. Instead, it announces a standard set of terms taxpayers must accept. In addition, although the taxing authority claims a partnership interest in taxpayer profits, it exercises no voting rights. Nor does it directly monitor taxpayer performance to determine whether taxpayers are violating the contractual terms. Of course, the taxing authority does conduct audits. Moreover, being a partner in all firms enables the taxing authority to determine when taxpayers are reporting results far out of line with what other taxpayers are reporting in similar situations (information that is used to select returns for audit).

The specific contractual rules (the Tax Code) that the taxing authority imposes on its joint venturers result from a variety of socioeconomic forces. Among other things, taxes are designed (1) to finance public projects (such as national defense and a legal system that enforces property rights), (2) to redistribute wealth (high-income individuals pay tax at higher rates than do low-income individuals), and (3) to encourage a variety of economic activities deemed by Congress to be in the public interest (such as research and development and oil and gas exploration).

From a social policy standpoint, tax rules are most controversial when they are designed to discriminate among different economic activities. Success is achieved when the tax rules subsidize activities that benefit society as a whole more than they benefit the individuals engaging directly in the activities. For example, Congress subsidizes research and development (R&D) through a tax credit based on R&D spending by the firm. Society benefits to the extent that the tax credit stimulates additional R&D. But this desirable outcome is by no means guaranteed since it is possible that special tax favors are bestowed undeservedly on taxpayers that mount successful lobbying efforts.[1]

For better or for worse, **tax-favored treatment** is granted to a variety of activities by taxing authorities around the world. Common examples include the favorable treatment accorded charitable organizations and educational institutions, energy-related investments, research and development activities, agricultural production, investments in productive equipment, foreign export activities, retirement-oriented savings vehicles, and entrepreneurial risk-taking activities.

Noble as the objectives listed earlier might be (finance public projects, redistribute wealth, and encourage economic activities), any tax system designed to achieve a variety of social goals inevitably provides considerable private incentives to engage in tax planning. Any tax system that seeks both to redistribute wealth as well as to subsidize certain economic activities gives rise to marginal tax rates that may vary widely from one contracting party to the next, for a given contracting party over time, and for a given contracting party over different economic activities.

Most taxpayers around the world pay no more tax than they believe they must and they spend nontrivial resources to arrange their affairs to keep the tax bite as painless as possible. It is precisely this behavior that provides tax policy with so much potential as a means of achieving a variety of social goals.

To illustrate, consider the case of low-income housing that U.S. citizens, through their elected representatives, have chosen to subsidize for many years through various tax benefits. If taxpayers were not responsive to these tax incentives (and refused to

---

[1]Often special tax treatment is included in legislation to obtain the vote of particular legislators. Hulse (1996) provides evidence that $10.6 billion of such provisions were included in the Tax Reform Act of 1986. He refers to these provisions as rifle-shot transition rules because they are written to benefit single taxpayers. The beneficiaries are not specifically named but can be inferred by interested parties from the specific details of the tax rule.

build low-income housing to garner the tax benefits), subsidizing low-income housing through tax policy would be ineffective. Instead, the government would have to enter on the expenditure side, engaging directly in the construction and management of the low-income housing itself. Both tax subsidies and direct government expenditures to increase the supply of low-income housing generate deadweight costs. This suggests that we must be careful in criticizing tax subsidies if we desire to achieve our social objectives. The direct government expenditure alternative might be far more costly than a tax system that favors private construction of the properties.

While the deadweight costs associated with time spent in tax planning may seem socially wasteful, the relevant question is how much waste would exist using alternative means to achieve the same social goals. In other words, how does the net benefit of the altered economic activity brought about by the tax system compare with the net benefits of the next best alternative? Obviously, if we could implement social policy through a mechanism that would result in zero waste, we would do so, but this is not a realistic goal.

Tax planning (or tax avoidance, as it is sometimes more pejoratively labeled) has long earned the blessing of the United States courts. For example, in a famous 1947 court opinion, Judge Learned Hand wrote (and similar statements appear in official documents of other countries as well):

> Over and over again courts have said that there is nothing sinister in so arranging one's affairs as to keep taxes as low as possible. Everybody does so, rich or poor, and all do right, for nobody owes any public duty to pay more than the law demands: taxes are enforced exactions, not voluntary contributions. To demand more in the name of morals is mere cant. (*Commissioner v. Newman,* 159 F.2d 848 (CA-2, 1947))[2]

The Importance of a Contractual Perspective

Morality issues aside, let us now return to the first of the three key themes that run throughout the building-block chapters: namely, that to organize production to maximize after-tax return requires that the tax positions of all parties to the contract be considered, both at the time of contracting and in the future. To avoid operating at a competitive disadvantage, managers must understand how changes in tax rules influence the behavior of their customers, their employees, their suppliers, and their competitors. Among other things, this observation exposes the naiveté of distinguishing between business tax planning and personal tax planning, or of tax planning for one type of business in isolation from tax planning for all other types of business.

For example, as we will see in later chapters, it is costly to prescribe an effective compensation policy for a firm without simultaneously conducting some personal tax planning analysis for each of its employees. Similarly, it is costly to prescribe an effective capital structure policy for a firm (that is, determining whether operations should be financed with debt, preferred stock, common stock, or other financial instruments)

---

[2]This is the standard citation for the court case. For further information on the format of court case citations, see Pope, Anderson, and Kramer (2001), Chapter 15, especially pp. 15–17 to 15–22.

without simultaneously considering how the returns to prospective lenders and share-holders of the firm will be taxed.

To be more concrete, consider the decision whether business equipment should be bought or leased. In the United States, as in most countries around the world, the government encourages capital investment by permitting rapid depreciation on buildings, equipment, and machinery. That is, the business can deduct the cost of the investment from its taxable income using a schedule in which the write-off rate exceeds the rate of economic depreciation of the investment. Alternatively, if a business entity rented plant and equipment over its economic life, the rental payments could be deducted only as they were made. The present value of rental deductions is often far less than the present value of depreciation deductions.

We cannot conclude, however, that owning assets minimizes the taxes of all firms using machinery and equipment in their businesses. Once we analyze the tax positions of both low-tax-bracket and high-tax-bracket taxpayers, we might find low-tax-bracket taxpayers are better off passing up tax savings and renting. The reason is that low-tax-bracket and high-tax-bracket businesses will find it desirable to enter into a contract that arranges property rights so that the low-tax-bracket businesses effectively sell their tax benefits to high-tax-bracket businesses. This is accomplished by reducing the rental rate to the low-tax-bracket taxpayer in exchange for the right to take rapid depreciation, for tax purposes, on the equipment.

Implicit Taxes and Tax Clienteles

The leasing example illustrates two very important concepts we will encounter time and time again throughout the text:

1. Implicit taxes
2. Tax clienteles

Implicit taxes arise because the before-tax investment returns available on tax-favored assets are less than those available on tax-disfavored assets. In the rent or buy example, a reduction in the rental rate is required to induce renters to forego the tax benefits of ownership, and this decreases the pretax investment return garnered by property lessors. Another example of implicit taxes is the reduced yield available on tax-exempt municipal bonds in the United States relative to taxable corporate bonds of equal risk. Here, the reduced yield represents an implicit tax paid to the issuing municipalities rather than to the federal government.

The **tax clienteles** and implicit tax concepts are closely related. Tax clienteles arise because of cross-sectional differences in tax rates. Certain taxpayers are more likely than others to own various kinds of assets or to organize production in particular ways. Examples of tax clienteles are high-tax-bracket taxpayers who are more likely to hold tax-exempt municipal bonds rather than taxable corporate bonds and who are more likely to be lessors and owners of depreciable equipment rather than lessees. With every topic we cover throughout the book we will encounter implicit taxes, tax clienteles, or both concepts.

Tax Planning as a Tax-Favored Activity

One reason Congress uses the Tax Code to encourage (or discourage) a variety of economic activities is that tax planning itself is a tax-favored activity. Specifically, money spent on tax planning is tax deductible while any tax savings arising from the tax plan-ning are effectively tax exempt because they reduce taxes payable.

Suppose a taxpayer could invest $10,000 in fully taxable corporate bonds for 1-year that yield 10% per annum before taxes. If the taxpayer faces a marginal tax rate of 28%, the after-tax rate of return is 7.2% (calculated as .10 × (1 − .28)). Alternatively, suppose the taxpayer could invest in tax planning services for $10,000 to save $11,000 in taxes in the current year. The pretax rate of return is 10%. However, the after-tax rate of return is 13.89%, calculated as the tax savings net of the tax plan-ning cost, $1,000, divided by the after-tax cost of the tax planning services, $10,000 × (1 − .28) or $1,000/$7,200. Note that the tax-favored treatment of tax plan-ning results here in an after-tax rate of return higher than the pretax rate of return. In this case, tax planning is more tax-favored than is **tax exemption** (a situation in which an asset escapes explicit taxation such that the after-tax rate of return equals the pretax rate of return). Note also that the after-tax return to tax planning depends on the taxpayer's marginal tax rate. For a taxpayer facing a marginal tax rate of 15%, the after-tax rate of return is 11.76%, calculated as $1,000/[$10,000 × (1 − .15)]. For a taxpayer facing a 35% marginal tax rate, the after-tax rate of return is 15.38%, or $1,000/[$10,000 × (1 − .35)]. The after-tax returns are largest for high marginal tax rate investors, so these taxpayers tend to be most responsive to tax rule changes and tend to spend the most on the services of tax accountants and tax lawyers.

Why Study Tax Planning?

We answer this question with the following simple example. Suppose there were two skills that you could acquire: tax planning and investing expertise. Further suppose you could only learn one. You are faced with the following fact pattern. You are endowed with $5,000 of after-tax cash, have a 20-year investment horizon, face a current mar-ginal tax rate of 35% that also is the rate you expect to face over the next 20 years. You expect that investing passively in an index fund will generate a 10% pretax return each year for the next 20 years.

You choose to learn tax planning skills and invest passively. You invest in a pen-sion plan (such as a 401(k) plan, discussed in more detail in Chapter 3) such that the after-tax cost of the investment is $5,000. The investment is tax deductible while tax on the returns in this plan are deferred until the end of the investment horizon. The after-tax accumulation from this investment is[3]

$$\frac{\$5,000}{(1 - .35)}(1 + .10)^{20}(1 - .35) = \$33,650$$

Suppose instead you choose investing expertise and behave as a day trader actively moving in and out of stocks. You hold stock no longer than one month and thus there is no deferral of taxes on your annual returns. How much would you have to earn pretax to match the returns to the basic tax planning above? Since the basic tax planning above earns 10% after-tax per year, you would need to earn 15.38%

---

[3]The formula used to calculate the accumulations are developed and discussed in more detail in Chapter 3. Our purpose here is simply to show the after-tax accumulations under the various alternatives and the advantages (or returns) to tax planning skills.

pretax per year on your actively managed portfolio to earn 10% after-tax per year [$15.38\%(1 - .35) = 10\%$].

But what if, more realistically for most taxpayers, you just *thought* you could beat the market but really could not and your active portfolio management yielded a 10% pretax return per year? In this case you would accumulate after-tax after 20 years

$$\$5,000[1 + .10(1 - .35)]^{20} = \$17,618$$

which is substantially less than the return to basic tax planning.

But, of course, tax planning and investing expertise are not mutually exclusive. Consider now what happens if you can beat the market *and* be a good tax planner. That is, you invest in a pension plan such as a 401(k) plan *and* actively manage the investment in the plan, earning a 14% annual pretax rate of return for the next 20 years. Because the investment is in a 401(k) plan, the tax on the annual returns are deferred until the funds are withdrawn in 20 years. The after-tax accumulation at the end of 20 years is now

$$\frac{\$5,000}{(1 - .35)}(1 + .14)^{20}(1 - .35) = \$68,700$$

Firms spend billions of dollars on tax planning activities and on tax compliance, which refers to record-keeping and return preparation activities. For example, Slemrod and Blumenthal (1993) report that the 1,329 active firms in the Internal Revenue Service's Coordinated Examination Program spent approximately $1.4 billion on federal-tax related activities in 1991.[4] These firms paid $51 billion in taxes, or over 50% of the total corporate tax revenues, in 1991. Mills, Erickson, and Maydew (1998) estimate that large corporations save, on average, $4 for every $1 spent on tax planning activities. Thus not only is tax planning a big business but the returns on investment in tax planning can be very large.

1.3 TOPICS COVERED IN THIS BOOK

We have outlined some of the major themes of the book, so let us now describe how the book develops. In the next chapter, we cover some fundamentals on the structure and evolution of tax laws, including a discussion of how tax laws are changed in the United States. This material is important if we are to appreciate current and future tax-rule uncertainty. An appendix explains the accounting rules for corporate income taxes. Knowledge of these rules can help tax planners interpret firms' disclosures and possibly glean information about their tax planning activities. In Chapters 3 and 4, we illustrate how *identical production and investment strategies* can be undertaken by taxpayers through a variety of different legal organizational forms, each of which is taxed very differently. We go on to show how the after-tax returns from investing through some organizational forms dominate the returns from investing through other organizational forms.

---

[4]Firms are included in the Coordinated Examination Program based on their size and complexity of return: the larger and more complex the return, the greater the likelihood of inclusion in the program. The tax returns of most of these firms are audited by the Internal Revenue Service each year.

In Chapter 5, we focus on *different investments* undertaken within a *given organization.* Differences in the tax treatment of investment returns give rise to implicit taxes that bring after-tax returns of these differentially taxed assets into closer alignment with one another. We also demonstrate that when there are no costs to implementing certain tax planning strategies, the availability of alternative legal organizational forms and investment projects that are taxed differently provides an opportunity to eliminate all income taxes through simple **arbitrage techniques** (generating positive after-tax returns by buying one asset while simultaneously selling another asset with neither investment cost nor risk). In addition, we show that when there are no costs to implementing certain tax planning strategies, differentially taxed assets force all taxpayers in the economy to pay taxes on their last dollar of income at identical tax rates, no matter how wealthy they are and no matter how progressive the legislated tax rate schedule is. Again, the availability of simple arbitrage techniques ensures this outcome. A corollary here is that there will be no distinct tax clienteles. At the margin, all taxpayers will be indifferent to whether they hold tax-favored or tax-disfavored investments.

But these results have miserable predictive power. Even the most casual empiricists can confirm two counterpropositions: (1) the government collects substantial tax revenues and (2) taxpayers do not all face the same marginal tax rate; tax clienteles not only exist, they are pervasive.

Obviously, some important economic forces have been omitted from the analysis in the first five chapters. We complete Chapter 5 by incorporating the importance of frictions and tax-rule restrictions. By **frictions,** we mean transaction costs incurred in the marketplace that make implementation of certain tax planning strategies costly. By **tax-rule restrictions,** we mean restraints imposed by the taxing authority that prevent taxpayers from using certain tax arbitrage techniques to reduce taxes in socially undesirable ways. It is these frictions and restrictions that make the potential returns to tax planning so high. Once tax planning strategies have been implemented, they may be very costly to reverse or change as economic circumstances, including the tax rules themselves, change. We complete the development of the conceptual framework in Chapters 6 and 7 by exploring tax planning in the presence of (1) uncertainty concerning pretax investment returns and tax rules, (2) nontax costs, and (3) difficulties of estimating taxpayers' marginal tax rates.

In the second part of the book, we apply the concepts developed in the first seven chapters to a variety of organizational settings. We begin in Chapters 8 and 9 with compensation and pension planning, respectively, where we emphasize the importance of considering the tax consequences of compensation alternatives to both the employer *and* the employee. We also stress the importance of nontax factors in designing efficient compensation policies.

In Chapters 10 and 11 we add a crucial dimension to the tax planning problem by introducing different tax jurisdictions and multinational tax planning. In multinational businesses, a given taxpayer may face different tax rates in different tax jurisdictions. Such a taxpayer may have an incentive to enter into transactions that transfer income out of highly taxed pockets and into modestly taxed pockets in the same pair of trousers. But one need not own pants with differentially taxed pockets to exploit differences in tax rates across taxpayers. Unrelated taxpayers facing different tax rates can also contract with one another to shift taxable income from those facing high tax rates to those facing low tax rates.

In Chapter 12, we apply the framework to an analysis of corporate capital structure decisions. Here we see that taxes encourage two kinds of marriages between firms and capital suppliers: those between high-tax-rate firms and low-tax-rate capital suppliers and those between low-tax-rate firms and high-tax-rate capital suppliers. Moreover, the kinds of financial instruments issued in the two relationships are very different. This chapter also emphasizes that financing decisions cannot be made without simultaneously considering the tax characteristics of the asset side of the firm's balance sheet. We describe a number of legal organizational forms that have arisen to effect a repackaging of claims to both tax deductions and different types of taxable (and nontaxable) income.

Chapters 13 through 17 are devoted to corporate reorganizations and restructurings. Among the distinctive features of these chapters is the way we model the effect of taxes on acquisition and divestiture structures and pricing. These analyses explicitly incorporate the tax preferences of buyers and sellers of corporate ownership rights.

In Chapter 18, our final chapter, we emphasize the importance of integrating estate and gift tax planning considerations into the income tax planning problem. We consider the degree to which tax laws encourage both charitable and noncharitable gifts. Moreover, we assess the extent to which the tax laws encourage charitable transfers relative to noncharitable transfers. We further analyze the trade-offs between lifetime transfers of wealth and bequests. We examine the most common estate planning techniques including family limited partnerships, life insurance trusts, bypass trusts, and charitable remainder trusts. As in most of the other applications chapters, we pay considerable attention to the nontax aspects of the tax planning problem.

1.4 INTENDED AUDIENCE FOR THIS BOOK

This book is appropriate for two categories of people:

1. Tax planners: Those who wish to avoid being beaten by other tax planners and by social planners.
2. Social planners: Those who wish to participate in the design of effective social policies, while at the same time avoid being beaten by other social planners and by tax planners.

We believe that a course built around the ideas developed in this book differs fundamentally from traditional courses offered in business schools, law schools, and economics programs. These other courses tend to focus on: (1) tax policy, with the objective of exploring macroeconomic effects of existing or proposed tax systems, or (2) tax law, concerned with principles of tax laws and judicial doctrines or with the details of the tax rules themselves and the ways to minimize taxes for a given set of transactions. Neither of these courses focuses on planning which transactions ought to take place, and our book falls into neither of these camps. We develop neither a macro tax policy approach nor a transactional tax law approach. Instead we adopt a *micro*economic perspective. Our interest is in the implications of tax rules for individual and firm behavior.

Similarly, our primary goal is neither to evaluate the welfare effects of various tax rules nor to provide narrow training to exploit "tax loopholes." It is true that we will occasionally appear to take much pleasure in describing clever tax planning techniques. And while our objective is certainly *not* to teach you how to "beat" the tax system, we will occasionally provide you with the tools necessary to build better organizational mousetraps where taxes play an important role. But this means that we are providing you with the tools to evaluate whether the tax system is meeting its various legislative objectives without giving rise to excessive distortions in economic activity. And perhaps most important, we hope that you will come away from reading this book recognizing that our framework applies to far broader issues than simply how taxes factor into business decisions.

The last major restructuring of the U.S. Tax Code was in the Tax Reform Act of 1986. However, the Tax Reform Act of 1986 is unusual only in the *degree* of change it introduced into the U.S. Tax Code; congressional bills that introduce major changes in tax rules are by no means unusual. Congress passed bills that changed the Tax Code in 20 of the 25 years preceding the 1986 restructuring and in 12 of the 17 years since 1986. In light of the frequency of tax law changes, you may well ask, "What is the half-life of the knowledge gained by investing time to read and to understand this book?" We expect many more legislative changes in the years to come. Moreover, it is naive to restrict attention to changes in tax laws in a given tax jurisdiction. For example, every time any country changes its tax regime, it changes the terms of trade U.S. investors face. Once we recognize this, we realize that many changes in tax rules take place every year both in the United States and abroad.

For these reasons, tax books and related tax courses that stress mastery of current tax rules become obsolete rather quickly. Absent a framework to determine the implications of the rules for business decisions, the knowledge gained in a rules-oriented course represents little more than accumulated trivia. This is precisely what led us to develop this book. We think that the basic tool-kit we provide you is appropriate to deal with virtually any tax regime we are likely to experience in the future. Moreover, we believe you can use these tools just as appropriately to study non-U.S. taxes as to study U.S. taxes.

All changes in tax regimes involve turning two kinds of dials:

1. Levels of tax rates
2. Relative tax rates:
   - Across different tax paying units,
   - Across different tax periods for the same taxpayer, and
   - Across different economic activities for the same taxpayers and same time period.

Our framework is designed to deal with just such differences; our intent is to make you leaders rather than followers in understanding how business activities inevitably become reorganized as the rules of the game evolve.

Table 1.1 presents the top tax rates faced by individuals and corporations over the last 25 years.[5] This table illustrates the incentives faced by individual taxpayers to have income taxed at more favorable capital gains tax rates, to shift income across periods, and to organize their investment activities in corporate form. The table also illustrates how these incentives change over time as both the level and relative tax rates change.

---

[5]Table 1.1 is reproduced on the inside back cover of this book.

TABLE 1.1 Historical Top Statutory Tax Rates

Time Period	Individual		C Corporation	
	Ordinary Income	*Capital Gains*	*Ordinary Income*	*Capital Gains*
Pre-1981	.70	.28	.46	.28
1982–1986	.50	.20	.46	.28
1987	.39	.28	.40	.28
1988–1990	.28	.28	.34	.34
1991–1992	.31	.28	.34	.34
1993–1996	.396	.28	.35	.35
1997–2000	.396	.20	.35	.35
2001–2002	.386	.20	.35	.35
2003–	.35	.15	.35	.35

Prior to 1981, individual taxpayers faced a top tax rate of 70% on ordinary income compared with corporations facing a tax rate of 46% on ordinary income. As we will see in Chapter 4, this can favor the corporate form as a means to shelter income from the high tax rates faced by individuals. The top individual tax rate declined in 1981 and again in 1986 but since that time has gradually increased until lowered in 2001. The Economic Growth and Tax Relief Reconciliation Act of 2001 enacted reduced tax rates for individuals that were to be phased in over the following 5 years. However, the Jobs and Growth Tax Relief Reconciliation Act of 2003 (JGTRCA 2003) accelerated these phase-ins to reduce the top rate for individuals to 35%. This Act also reduced the top tax rate on corporate dividends to 15%.[6] Except for a short period after the Tax Reform Act of 1986, individuals faced a lower tax rate on capital gains compared with the rate on ordinary income.[7] To qualify for the favorable capital gains tax rate, the gains must be classified as long-term capital gains, which simply means that the asset giving rise to the gain must be held for some minimum period. Whenever we refer to capital gains we will be implicitly assuming long-term capital gains. Except for a short period in 1998, this holding period has been 12 months. Short-term capital gains are taxed at ordinary income rates.[8] For tax years beginning after December 31, 2000,

---

[6]To achieve a target revenue cost of the tax rate reductions, many of the changes in the JGTRCA 2003 have sunset provisions, meaning that the reduced rates are terminated at some future date. For example, the 15% top capital gains tax rate reverts to 20% in 2009 and the 15% top rate on dividends reverts to 35% in 2009. As we will see, such sunset provisions further complicate (or offer incentives for effective) tax planning.

[7]Prior to 1986, the tax rate on capital gains for individuals was estimated as $(1 - d)$ times the taxpayer's statutory tax rate on ordinary income, where d was the percentage of the capital gains excluded from taxable income. The percentage was set at 60%, implying 40% of the gain was included in taxable income. Thus in 1982–86, the top capital gains rate was $(1 - .60).50 = .20$. After 1986, the top rate on capital gains has been set as a specific rate in the Tax Code.

[8]This is a simplification. There are somewhat complex rules for netting short-term capital gains and losses and long-term capital gains and losses. We do not need to know these rules for our purposes but the interested reader is referred to Pope, Anderson, and Kramer (2001), Chapter 5.

the top capital gains tax rate is reduced to 18% for assets held longer than 5 years. The 2003 Tax Act lowered the capital gains rate to 15% for assets held longer than 12 months. There have been fewer changes in the top corporate tax rate, with the last major change occurring in 1986 when the top rate decreased from 46% to 34%. Since 1986, corporations have faced the same tax rate on capital gains and ordinary income.

Although this is not a rules-oriented book, you will still learn a good deal about current tax rules. This is necessary for three reasons: (1) to breathe life into the basic framework through illustrations, (2) to test the basic framework's ability to explain economic activities that are going on around us, and (3) to help you to apply the basic framework to specific decision contexts that many of you now face or will be facing in short order. For readers with little background in taxes, we present a simple introduction to the calculation of both individual taxpayers' and corporate taxpayers' tax liability in the appendix. We also define some common tax terms in this appendix.

Finally, some of the empirical academic literature we cite to provide evidence on issues raised in the framework refers to results gathered around the 1986 Tax Reform Act. At first, this evidence might seem dated. However, the 1986 Act provided an outstanding laboratory for academics to subject tax predictions to empirical tests. Academics continue to examine data from around the 1986 Act to test their theories. Our justification for including these references to the 1986 Act, and for academics continuing to use these data, is that the evidence collected and cited is timeless. It speaks to the framework's predictive power rather than to the specific tax rules analyzed in a particular study. This quality is consistent with our focus on a framework for analysis rather than on the specifics of sometimes highly technical but constantly changing tax rules.

Summary of Key Points

1. Tax rules are pervasive in their effect on the investment and financing decisions of businesses.
2. Because it is costly to recontract, investment and financing decisions that have been made in the past influence current and future investment and financing decisions.
3. Tax rules influence investment and financing decisions because they affect the before-tax rates of return on investment and financing alternatives. More highly explicitly taxed investments require higher before-tax rates of return compared with alternatives that bear low explicit taxes. Investment and financing alternatives that face low explicit taxes (due to favored treatment under the tax law) bear high implicit taxes.
4. Firms that find themselves with low marginal tax rates are encouraged by the tax system to contract with firms that face high marginal tax rates.
5. All tax planning actions are tempered by the nontax costs of achieving tax savings.
6. Effective tax planning means considering (a) the tax implications of a proposed transaction to all parties of the contract; (b) explicit taxes, implicit taxes, and tax clienteles; and (c) the costs of implementing various tax planning strategies.
7. Tax planning is a tax-favored activity in that the investment is tax deductible while the payoffs (reductions in tax payable) are tax exempt. The higher the taxpayer's marginal tax rate, the higher the returns to tax planning.

Appendix 1.1

OVERVIEW OF CALCULATION OF INCOME TAX LIABILITY

The basic tax formula for determining federal income tax liability for corporations and individual taxpayers is presented in Exhibit 1.1. We start our description with economic income, which is defined as income from whatever source (wages and salaries, dividend and interest income, sales revenue, appreciation in assets owned, etc.). Economic income includes both realized and unrealized increases in the taxpayer's wealth. Unrealized income is (generally) excluded from taxation until realized via the sale of the underlying asset. Taxation is deferred until realization because at that point the taxpayer presumably has the cash from the sale to pay the taxes due. This leaves realized income, but not all realized income is taxable. The Tax Code specifically excludes from taxation some types of income. Major items of income excluded are gifts and inheritances, life insurance proceeds, social welfare payments, certain payments for injury and sickness, certain employer-provided fringe benefits, interest

EXHIBIT 1.1	Basic Tax Formula
<u>Corporation</u>	<u>Individuals</u>
Economic income	Economic income
− <u>Unrealized income</u>	− <u>Unrealized income</u>
= Realized income (§61)	= Realized income (§61)
− <u>Exclusions</u>	− <u>Exclusions</u>
= Gross income	= Gross income
− <u>Deductions</u>	− <u>Deductions for AGI</u>
	= Adjusted gross income (AGI)
	− <u>Deductions from AGI</u>
	1. Max (itemized deductions or the standard deduction)*
	2. Exemptions*
= Taxable income	= Taxable income
× <u>Tax rate</u>	× <u>Tax rates**</u>
= Gross tax	= Gross tax
− <u>Credits</u>	− <u>Credits</u>
= Regular tax	= Regular tax
+ Excess (if any) of tentative <u>minimum tax over the regular tax***</u>	+ Excess (if any) of tentative <u>minimum tax over the regular tax</u>
= Federal income tax liability	Federal income tax liability

*Phase-outs apply as AGI increases.

**Different tax schedules apply depending on filing status (single, married filing jointly, married filing separately, head of household).

***The Tax Code refers to this as the alternative minimum tax.

on state and local government (municipal) bonds, and gain from sale of a personal residence (up to $500,000 per couple every 2 years). After these exclusions, we are left with gross income.

Taxpayers then deduct allowable items to arrive at taxable income. Note that all income is included in gross income unless specifically identified in the Tax Code as an allowable exclusion. In contrast, expenditures are not deductible unless specifically identified in the Tax Code. For corporations, all costs incurred in carrying on a trade or business are allowed as deductions. Examples include wages and salary paid to employees, cost of goods sold, depreciation on plant and equipment, interest on borrowings, and state and local taxes. A percentage of dividends received on investments in other companies is also allowed to be deducted (the so-called corporate dividends received deduction discussed in further detail in later chapters). Note that, while interest on borrowings is deductible, dividends paid to the firm's shareholders are not tax deductible to the paying corporation.

The calculation of taxable income for individual taxpayers is slightly more complex because deductions are partitioned into two categories: deductions for adjusted gross income and deductions from adjusted gross income. Deductions for adjusted gross income (AGI) are generally expenses associated with the individual taxpayer carrying on a trade or business. Deductions from AGI are personal expenses that Congress has chosen to allow as deductions. The major deductions from AGI, also known as itemized deductions, are home mortgage interest expense, charitable contributions, and medical expenses (with limits). In an effort to simplify taxpayers' tax return preparation and record-keeping, Congress allows a standard deduction for each taxpayer with the amount varying with the taxpayer's filing status and age. Taxpayers

itemize only if the claimed deductions exceed the standard deduction. In addition to itemized deductions, individual taxpayers are allowed a dollar amount exemption for themselves and their dependents. (The amount of the exemption is adjusted each year for increases in the cost of living. In tax year 2003, the amount of the exemption was $3,000.) Adjusted gross income is used in numerous tax calculations related to limitations on the amount allowed as a deduction from AGI (such as setting a minimum below which medical expenses are not deductible—medical expenses have to exceed 7.5% of AGI before they are deductible—or a maximum above which the expenditure is not deductible, such as charitable contributions).

Given taxable income, the taxpayer then calculates the gross tax that is due, by applying the tax rate schedule applicable to that taxpayer's filing status. The taxpayer then deducts from the gross tax due any allowable tax credits, which include any tax prepayments, to arrive at the regular tax due or tax refund. Tax credits can be classified as refundable tax credits and nonrefundable tax credits. Refundable tax credits can give rise to a tax refund. As noted, tax prepayments (such as withholding taxes on wages paid by the taxpayer to the government during the tax year) are a tax credit and thus are a refundable tax credit if the taxpayer has overwithheld. Nonrefundable tax credits are credits created by Congress to achieve goals such as encouraging certain desirable economic activities (R&D tax credit for businesses) and social goals (child and dependent care credit). The excess of nonrefundable tax credits can be carried forward—the excess is the amount by which the tax credit exceeds the gross tax liability. It should be obvious that tax credits, which reduce the gross tax dollar for dollar, are more valuable than deductions, which reduce taxable income dollar for dollar but reduce the gross tax liability by the taxpayer's tax rate.

Finally, the taxpayer performs an alternative calculation (known as the alternative minimum tax (AMT) calculation) and compares the alternative tax due to the regular tax due and pays the larger of the two. We do not discuss the AMT calculation but note that it is intended to make sure taxpayers with a large economic income pay some taxes (thus the AMT includes some extra income items and disallows some deductions—the specifics are beyond our discussion here).

Discussion Questions

1. Why is tax minimization different from effective tax planning?
2. Under what circumstances should social planners encourage taxpayers to engage in costly tax planning?
3. List five examples of tax-favored investments.
   a. Do these investments bear high implicit taxes?
   b. Who should undertake these investments? Do they?
   c. Who receives the implicit taxes?
4. Which of the following statements accurately describes an efficient tax plan?
   a. High-tax-bracket investors should invest in municipal bonds.
   b. It is rarely a good strategy to pay explicit taxes.
   c. Renting durable business assets is more efficient than owning for low-tax-rate investors.
   d. Employees prefer to defer receipt of their compensation (assuming this succeeds in postponing the recognition of taxable income) whenever they expect their tax rates to fall in the future.
5. Refer to Exhibit 1.1. For an individual prepare a list of
   a. Income items that are taxed (specifically items included in realized income).
   b. Items excluded from realized income.
   c. Deductions and exemptions.
   d. Credits.
6. Refer to Exhibit 1.1. For a regular corporation prepare a list of
   a. Income items that are taxed (specifically items included in realized income).
   b. Items excluded from realized income.
   c. Deductions and exemptions.
   d. Credits.
7. Why is it important for the tax planner to know the tax consequences of a particular transaction not only to the entity employing the tax planner but also to the other party (or parties) to the transaction? Provide a real-world example to illustrate your answer.
8. We generally think that taxes lower returns, which means that after-tax returns are lower than pretax returns. Is this always true, or can you provide counterexamples?
9. Explain the difference between tax avoidance and tax evasion. Provide an example of each activity.

Exercises

1. Taxpayer A purchased $100,000 of corporate bonds yielding 12.5% per annum; the interest income from these bonds is taxed at a rate of 28%. Taxpayer B purchased $100,000 of municipal bonds yielding 9% per annum. The interest from these bonds is tax exempt. The bonds have similar maturities and risk. What is the

after-tax rate of return earned by each taxpayer? Is taxpayer B paying taxes in any sense here?

   a. Who are the taxes being paid to?

   b. What is the implied tax rate?

2. A taxpayer is considering buying a fully taxable corporate bond. The bond has a remaining maturity of 5 years, promises to pay 6% interest annually (assume the coupon interest is payable annually), and has a face value of $1,000. The taxpayer faces a 31% tax rate on the interest income and requires a pretax rate of return of 6% to invest. What price is the taxpayer willing to pay for this bond? The same taxpayer is also considering buying a tax-exempt municipal bond. The municipal bond has a remaining maturity of 5 years, also promises to pay 6% interest annually (again the coupon interest is payable annually), and has a face value of $1,000. Assume the corporate and municipal bonds are equally risky. At what price is the taxpayer indifferent between the corporate and municipal bond? (Alternatively stated, what price is the taxpayer willing to pay for the municipal bond assuming he requires a pretax rate of return of 6% and faces a marginal tax rate of 31%?) How does this example relate to the discussion of implicit taxes in the text? (This exercise assumes the reader is familiar with present value techniques and the pricing of bonds.)

3. A taxpayer is considering two mutually exclusive alternatives. Alternative A is to hire a tax accountant at a cost of $20,000 to research the tax law on a tax-avoidance plan. If successful, the plan would save the taxpayer $21,000 in taxes. The probability of success is estimated to be 75%. Alternative B is to hire a marketing firm at a cost of $18,000, whose task would be to develop a marketing plan for the taxpayer's product. If successful, the plan would reduce other advertising costs by $25,000 without affecting sales revenue. The probability of success is estimated at 80%. Which alternative should the taxpayer choose if she faces a tax rate of 15%? Of 35%? Comment on your results. Is tax planning a tax favored activity? For whom?

4. A taxpayer works at a corporation nearing the end of its fiscal year. The company has had a very successful (profitable) year and has decided to award the employee a cash bonus of 20% of her annual salary (a bonus of $30,000). The firm has announced that employees can take the cash bonus this year or defer it until next year. The taxpayer faces a current tax rate of 39.6%, but because she plans to work only a 50% schedule next year, she expects to face a tax rate of 31%. Assuming she can earn 5% after tax on her personal investments, should she accept the bonus this year or next year? Suppose she can earn 15% after tax on her personal investments. Would you change your recommendation?

Tax Planning Problems

1. A large corporation hires you as a consultant. The firm has accumulated tax losses and it expects to be in this position for a number of years. The firm needs a new distribution facility on the West Coast to service its West Coast customers more efficiently. The facility has an estimated cost of $10 million. The firm is considering three alternative plans. Under plan A, the firm can borrow the $10 million and purchase the facility. Under plan B, the firm can issue common stock to raise the $10 million and purchase the facility. Under plan C, the firm can lease the facility from the current owners. The firm asks you to prepare a brief report outlining the tax consequences of each plan. Your report should also contain your recommendation as to the most tax-efficient plan.

2. The compensation committee of a large public corporation engages you to help design a tax-efficient compensation plan for the current chief executive officer (CEO). In a preliminary interview with the compensation committee, you ask for the opportunity to meet with the CEO to discuss her personal financial and tax situation. A member of the compensation committee questions why you would want to meet with the CEO. Prepare a response to this question.
3. Refer to problem 2. What nontax considerations might you consider in designing a tax-efficient compensation contract for the CEO?
4. The ABC Corporation is a large multinational company that has facilities (both manufacturing and distribution) located in many states and in overseas countries. The firm's long-serving chief financial officer just retired and his replacement is reviewing the firm's economic balance sheet. She discovers that the firm leases many of its distribution facilities and relies heavily on long-term debt for financing. She vaguely recalls having heard about implicit taxes and tax clienteles and would like these concepts explained and then applied to her observations to determine if the firm is bearing implicit taxes and whether the firm is in the right clientele.

References and Additional Readings

Hulse, D., 1996. "The Timing of the Stock Market Reaction to Rifle-Shot Transition Rules," *Journal of the American Taxation Association* (Fall), pp. 57–73.

Mills, L., M. Erickson, and E. Maydew, 1998. "Investments in Tax Planning," *Journal of the American Taxation Association* (Spring), pp. 1–20.

Pope, T. R., K. E. Anderson, and J. L. Kramer, (Editors), 2001. *Federal Taxation 2001 Individuals.* Upper Saddle River, NJ: Prentice Hall.

Slemrod, J., and M. Blumenthal, 1993. *The Compliance Costs of Big Business.* Washington, DC: The Tax Foundation.

CHAPTER

2 | TAX LAW FUNDAMENTALS

After completing this chapter, you should be able to:

1. Describe how tax rules are designed to achieve socially desirable outcomes.

2. List and provide examples of the three broad types of tax planning.

3. Explain why there are broad legal restrictions on taxpayer behavior.

4. Outline the legislative process leading to tax-rule changes.

5. Explain the role of revenue rulings, court cases, and secondary authorities in tax planning.

6. Explain how tax law ambiguity might affect tax planning.

In the introductory chapter, we discussed how the tax system seeks to achieve a variety of social goals and how this naturally gives rise to:

- Tax rates varying across different economic activities,
- Tax rates varying across different individual taxpaying units, and
- Tax rates varying for a given taxpaying unit over time.

These differential tax rates, in turn, provide strong incentives for taxpayers to engage in tax planning. These incentives are the key ingredients that allow the tax system to be used to implement desired social policy.[1]

---

[1]This view of the tax system is admittedly rather rosy. We adopt this perspective at this stage more for peda-gogical convenience than for descriptive validity. We acknowledge that private parties have incentives to seek legislation that is beneficial to them, even if it leads to reduced social welfare. We do not mean to deny the existence of legislative "capture" on the part of certain groups of taxpayers, even when the public debate takes on a "public interest" melody. The interested reader might wish to browse two interesting and enter-taining articles discussing proposed tax cuts by Dan Morgan in *The Washington Post* entitled "Whale of a Tax Break for Eskimos" (July 22, 1999, p. A21) and "Business Gets Big Breaks in Tax Bills: Surpluses Allow Lobbyists to Win Billions in Relief from Capital Hill GOP" (July 24, 1999, p. A01). The second article con-tains the following quote: "If you're a business lobbyist and couldn't get into this legislation, you better turn in your six-shooter," said a Democratic lobbyist. "There was that much money around."

A problem with this approach, however, is that tax rules adopted for the purpose of achieving certain social goals are generally too broad and the rules themselves encourage some taxpayers to exploit their ambiguity and, as a result, lead to some **socially undesirable economic activity.** Socially undesirable economic activities are activities undertaken in response to the tax laws by taxpayers that were unanticipated or not intended by legislators. These activities are undertaken with the major (or sole) purpose of reducing the taxpayers' tax bill without any real nontax benefits to society. The response to the broadness is to fine-tune the tax system. In particular, when taxpayers have gone "too far" in their efforts to avoid taxes, the Congress or the Treasury (or both) fight back by establishing legislative restrictions (tax bills), judicial restrictions (court cases), or administrative guidelines on what taxpayers can do.[2]

To combat socially undesirable tax planning, Congress imposes two classes of restrictions. These include (1) very broad restrictions that apply to a great variety of transactions, and (2) very specific restrictions that respond to particular abuses of the tax system. Of course, Congress must be careful not to impose *too* many restrictions or to make enforcement of the rules *too* uncertain. Tax rule and enforcement uncertainty may discourage precisely the transactions that Congress wishes to encourage. In other words, restrictions can be too broad as well.

Moreover, the costs associated with imposing many specific restrictions can be quite high. These include (1) legislative costs, such as the cost of elected representatives and their research and administrative staffs, and the cost of lobbyists; (2) the cost to the general public of becoming informed so that they can participate in the legislative process; and (3) compliance costs, which increase with the complexity of the tax system and the number of restrictions.

Life would be simple, indeed, if tax rules were unambiguous. But tax rules, like all other areas of the law, are far from clear. **Tax law ambiguity** implies that even if you could claim to have committed to memory the entire Internal Revenue Code, you would be able to resolve only a small degree of ambiguity in how a tax return should be prepared. As technically detailed as the Tax Code may seem to be, it still contains rules that are far too general to indicate clearly how particular transactions are to be taxed.

The inherent ambiguity in the tax law gives rise to numerous disputes between taxpayers and the taxing authority, since these parties have opposing interests regarding the assessment of tax liabilities. In turn the judicial branch of government (the court system) must resolve disputes. And as disputes are resolved by the courts, the tax rules take on greater and greater detail—that is, the courts help to interpret the rules.

Contrary to the incessant calls for system overhaul that we commonly read about in the press, our current tax system is unlikely to change dramatically in structure.

---

[2]Of course, legislative changes are designed to do much more than simply plug tax loopholes. As noted in Chapter 1, Congress also uses them to change the distribution of wealth in the economy, to raise revenue, and/or to change the degree to which certain economic activities are subsidized in light of changes in the economy.

Consider an alternative system in which rules exist for each and every type of transaction. The scope of the rule-writing problem becomes obvious when we consider that taxpayers may enter into an infinite variety of contracts. Determining how the tax laws apply to each possible contractual arrangement would be prohibitively expensive. Instead, we adopt a more sensible approach. We codify the general rules and allow the courts, or negotiation between taxpayers and the taxing authority, to resolve ambiguities on an *exception* basis.

We can make the tax system simple only if we abandon using it as a means of achieving desired social policies. In fact, the Tax Reform Act of 1986 was a clear move in this direction. Many tax-rule changes brought about by this major piece of legislation were designed to "level the playing field," so to speak—that is, they removed or reduced tax subsidies for many economic activities. But as we mentioned earlier, it is not obvious that these tax rule changes are desirable, since the alternative means of implementing policy may well be both more costly and less effective. In the years since the 1986 Tax Act, Congress has re-introduced substantial complexity into the Tax Code via complex phase-out rules,[3] special capital gains rates, and a myriad of tax credits, among other items.

In this chapter, we consider some of the difficulties associated with using the tax system to achieve social goals. In particular, we identify a few classes of tax planning games that aggressive taxpayers might naturally be inclined to play, and we provide examples of the broad restrictions that are imposed when such tax planning games lead to socially undesirable outcomes.

In later chapters we elaborate on the importance of more specific tax-rule restrictions. We also consider how transaction and information costs affect taxpayers' abilities to engage in socially unacceptable tax planning, and we will see that Congress need not impose as many tax-rule restrictions where transaction costs are high.

2.1 TYPES OF TAX PLANNING

Over the years, taxpayers have displayed considerable ingenuity in their attempts to have their income (1) converted from one *type* to another, (2) shifted from one *pocket* to another, and (3) shifted from one *time period* to another. Briefly, we consider each of these types of tax planning activities.

Converting Income from One Type to Another

"Capital gains" are typically realized on the sale of capital assets such as common stock or a house. Wages, interest on bonds, and royalties are items that are typically considered "ordinary income." In most countries, capital gains are taxed favorably relative to ordinary income. Table 1.1 presented the top statutory tax rates for each income type over the last 25 years. Attempts to convert income into capital gains have probably accounted for more tax planning abuses than any other activity.

---

[3]For a discussion of the phase-out rules and the difficulties they introduce into tax planning see Enis and Christ (1999).

Besides the capital gains/ordinary income distinction, tax liabilities are often affected by whether income is classified as:

- Interest, dividend, or operating income,
- Earned domestically or abroad,
- Derived from a profit-seeking business or from an activity engaged in as a hobby.

For example, whether income is classified as interest or operating income may determine the amount of deductible interest expense. Whether income is deemed to be U.S.-sourced or foreign-sourced may affect not only the tax rate that applies to the income but also the foreign taxes paid that the United States will permit as a credit against U.S. income tax liability. Whether income is judged to come from an actively managed business or a passive investment may affect whether losses from such activities are currently tax deductible. Whether income is considered to come from an activity engaged in for profit or an activity that is a hobby may affect whether losses from such activities will ever be deductible. These examples are by no means exhaustive. Many other labeling distinctions are important to taxpayers, particularly in the foreign tax area.

EXAMPLE 1:
Corporations are entitled to a dividends received deduction (DRD) on their holdings of stock in other corporations. The purpose of the DRD is to avoid triple (or more) taxation on the original corporation's earnings (once at the original corporation when earned, again at the second corporation when dividends are received, and third at the shareholder level when the second corporation distributes dividends to its shareholders). The DRD allows the firm to exempt a fraction of the dividends received from other corporations. This fraction is currently 70% if the corporate shareholder owns less than 20% of the corporate stock. The fraction increases to 80% (100%) if the corporate shareholder owns more than 20% (80%) of the corporate stock. Thus if a corporation's marginal tax rate is 35% and it owns more than 20% of the stock of another company, the effective tax rate on dividends is $.35 \times .20$ (amount of dividends included in taxable income) = .07, or 7%. This deduction gives corporate stockholders an incentive to attempt to classify proceeds from the sale of stock that would be taxed as capital gains (for corporations this rate equals the tax rate on ordinary income, 35%) as a dividend effectively taxed at a 7% rate. However, to obtain dividend treatment on redeeming (selling back) stock to the issuing company requires that the redemption not be "substantially disproportionate." Hence *failing* the substantially disproportionate test is necessary for dividend treatment. Thus if the shareholder simply sells back its shareholdings, this will be treated as disproportionate (because no other shareholder sold stock) and thus trigger sale treatment with gains taxed at 35%. However, if the shareholder after the "sale" still holds approximately the same percentage of equity instruments in the issuing company then the "sale" is not disproportionate and dividend treatment is allowed. One way to "sell" and keep the same approximate ownership interest is to receive warrants to buy the issuing corporation's stock as part of the proceeds of the "sale." These warrants count as equity instruments

thus maintaining the ownership percentage. Seagram did this in 1995, saving $1.7 billion in taxes in its redemption of its stockholdings in DuPont. For its part in the transaction, DuPont received about $700 million of the tax savings.[4]

Shifting Income from One Pocket to Another

All other things being equal, high-tax-bracket taxpayers would prefer to have their income earned through a tax-exempt pension fund rather than on personal account, where it is fully taxable. They also prefer to have their income earned by their low-tax-bracket children or by their low-tax-bracket business (perhaps one located in a low-tax foreign jurisdiction), rather than earned by themselves.

> **EXAMPLE 2:**
> Several years ago, banks advertised generous interest rates on individual retirement accounts (IRAs), on which the earnings are tax exempt if the depositor also purchased a fully taxable certificate of deposit at below-market rates of interest. If permitted by the taxing authority, this is clearly a smart idea: The tax-exempt pocket of the taxpayer obtains a return in excess of market rates while the taxable pocket obtains a below-market rate of return. Like most loopholes, the IRS eventually caught on and, using its broad powers, cracked down. However, it took several years of abuse before the IRS announced its policy to impose penalties on such tie-in arrangements.

Shifting Income from One Time Period to Another

If tax rates are constant or declining over time, taxpayers prefer to delay recognizing income until it can be taxed at as low a rate as possible. It is also desirable to defer paying taxes as long as interest is not being charged on the tax liability. If tax rates are increasing over time, it pays to accelerate recognizing income unless interest rates are very high.

For example, if tax rates are 28% today and expected to be 33% in 1 year, it makes sense to accelerate paying the tax unless the taxpayer can invest 28 cents today to return more than 33 cents after-tax in 1 year. Such an investment would have to yield nearly 18% *after tax* in 1 year to warrant postponing paying the tax.[5] Of course, nontax factors (such as financing current consumption) might also figure importantly in the taxpayer's decision whether or not to defer income recognition.

---

[4]This transaction is analyzed in Erickson and Wang (1999). As one might expect, Congress quickly reacted to this transaction. Sale treatment is now required when a corporate shareholder takes part in a redemption that is not pro rata as to all shareholders or is a partial liquidation.

[5]The 18% return can be, in this case, simply calculated as $(.33/.28) - 1$. But more formally, the after-tax return is calculated by solving first for R, the pretax rate of return, in the following equation $\$1(1 - .28)[1 + R(1 - .33)] = \$1(1 + R)(1 - .33)$ and then recognizing that the after-tax rate of return $r = R(1 - t)$. The left-hand side represents the taxpayer paying the tax today and investing the after-tax amount of 72 cents for one year at R, the pretax rate of return, and paying tax on R at 33% in period 2. The right-hand side represents the taxpayer waiting one year to receive the $1 so that tax in the second period is on the entire amount $(1 + R)$. The equality represents the taxpayer being indifferent between the two choices. Solving for R gives .2665 and thus $r = R(1 - .33) = .178$ or 18%.

The U.S. tax system, as in most systems around the world, taxes income based on a **realization principle.** That is, income is not typically taxed until certain types of exchanges take place. For example, income from the appreciation of most assets is not taxed until the assets are sold and, even then, the income *might* not be taxed until cash is received from the sale (for example, the seller may accept a note receivable or promissory note from the buyer delaying the receipt of cash to the seller—an installment sale). This relief feature of the tax law (deferral of taxation until gains/losses are realized) is motivated by a desire by Congress to avoid forcing taxpayers to liquidate assets or borrow money to pay their accrued tax liability. Such relief would be unnecessary if it were costless to liquidate assets or to borrow money—that is, if there were no market frictions. But in many circumstances, such frictions are very important and, without the relief provisions, taxpayers would be forced to engage in economically wasteful transactions to meet their tax liability. Alternatively, they might choose to forego socially desirable activities (such as the sale of an asset with a note to a buyer that can better utilize the asset) in anticipation of possible problems with making tax payments. Conversely, the granting of tax relief of this sort has drawbacks as well. Such relief offers tremendous potential for abuse, especially when the cost to liquidate certain assets is low. Although it may be socially inefficient for them to do so, taxpayers can and do incur real costs in timing their asset sales to shift income from one period to another.

We illustrate two of the many ways in which income can be shifted across time periods. We will see that taxpayers could (possibly permanently) defer the payment of all income taxes if transaction costs were low enough and if tax-rule restrictions were absent. This is a theme we revisit more fully in later chapters as well.

EXAMPLE 3:

Many firms in the mid-1990s shifted income through corporate-owned life insurance (COLI). In this transaction, a corporation purchases a number of cash value life insurance policies on lives of employees and either uses borrowed funds to pay the premium or borrows the premium directly back from the insurance company. The life insurance policy builds up in value over the term of the policy and when cashed out is subject to tax. Basically, this strategy exploits the fact that interest on the borrowings is deductible each period as it accrues (even if not paid) while the "inside buildup" on the insurance policy (the investment returns credited to the policy each year) are not taxable each year. Because the inside buildup is approximately equal to the accrued interest, there is little nontax benefit to the corporation from the policy.

These policies have been around for a long time and Congress limited a corporation's interest deduction on the debt that was incurred to purchase or carry these policies in 1986, but the interest was only limited on borrowings that exceed $50,000 per insured life. Corporations responded by reducing the amount of insurance per employee but increased the number of employees covered (some firms insured all employees). The corporations made up in volume what they lost in size per contract.

In 1996, Congress limited a corporation's interest deductions on all debt that was directly traceable to COLI investments to interest on $50,000 of borrowing for up to 20 policies. Corporations were not yet beat. Some firms planned to have COLI contracts on the lives of their customers and to use general business borrowings rather than traceable indebtedness to finance these investments. Congress responded by disallowing interest deductions to the extent that the policies did not insure the lives of the corporations' employees.

EXAMPLE 4:

Some large stockholders, in an effort to defer the taxation of the gains on their appreciated stock while at the same time obtaining cash, undertake transactions known as "shorting against the box." This strategy involves the taxpayer borrowing shares of stock equal to the number already owned. The taxpayer then sells the borrowed shares, thus realizing cash, but no taxes are owed because there was no taxable gain on the shares sold. The loan is repaid at a later date by delivering the original appreciated stock. Delivery of the stock also triggers tax on the gain at this later date. The cost to the taxpayer of deferring the tax is the interest due on the value of the shares borrowed. And note that the taxpayer has locked in the gain because the borrowed shares are repaid by delivering the original shares, no matter what their value. The ability to undertake this transaction was curtailed in 1997.[6]

To summarize, these illustrations provide examples of taxpayer attempts to reduce taxes by having their income (1) converted from one *type* to another, (2) shifted from one *pocket* to another, and (3) shifted from one *time period* to another.[7]

2.2 RESTRICTIONS ON TAXPAYER BEHAVIOR

Many of the illustrations in Section 2.1 clarify why it is desirable to build restrictions into the law. The *broad legal restrictions* on taxpayer behavior essentially give the taxing authority the right to ask whether transactions "pass the smell test." In other words, the tax collector can question whether there is a **valid business purpose** for the taxpayer's transactions other than tax avoidance. If a taxpayer engages in a set of transactions deemed to have no valid business purpose other than tax avoidance, and if a similar economic outcome could have been achieved using simpler transactions, the taxing authority often is allowed to recharacterize the transactions, leading to a less favorable tax treatment. And if there *is* some business purpose to the transactions, is it sufficient? The courts play an important role in interpreting these elusive concepts and in allowing their definition to evolve over time as the socioeconomic environment changes. Let us take a closer look at some of the broad restrictions that are involved.

---

[6]Estee Lauder of the Estee Lauder company undertook this strategy as part of her estate plan to save over $100 million in taxes. The Estee Lauder case is discussed in more detail in Chapter 18 on Estate Planning. For a teaching case on this topic, see E. Maydew, "Turning a Tax Liability into a Tax Refund: The Case of Estee Lauder," University of North Carolina Teaching Case, February 2000.

[7]The reader interested in more complex examples of aggressive tax-avoidance strategies is referred to Appendix A of the report by the Department of the Treasury (1999). These transactions include the fast-pay or step-down preferred transaction, liquidating real estate investment trusts, and lease-in, lease-out (LILO) schemes.

Examples of Broad Restrictions on Taxpayer Behavior in the U.S. Constructive-Receipt Doctrine

The Internal Revenue Service (IRS) has the authority to adjust a taxpayer's tax accounting method to ensure that it "clearly reflects income." Most accounting method abuses involve postponing taxable income. A related consideration comes under the **constructive-receipt** label. This doctrine basically prevents taxpayers from turning their backs on income they have already earned and could collect easily. Examples include (1) interest credited on bank accounts where funds are available for withdrawal at any time and (2) year-end paychecks that can be picked up at the payroll department.

Substance-Over-Form and Business-Purpose Doctrines

Among the most powerful tools at the IRS' disposal to discipline aggressive tax planners are the closely related substance-over-form doctrine and the business-purpose doctrine. The challenge of proving a business transaction's validity is termed the **business-purpose doctrine.**[8] The **substance-over-form** doctrine allows the IRS to look through the legal form of transactions to their economic substance.

The landmark case of *Gregory* (a taxpayer) *v. Helvering* (an IRS Commissioner) illustrates these doctrines well. In that case the aggressive taxpayer tried to transform a dividend into a capital gain as follows: Gregory (1) split the corporation in two in a tax-free reorganization and (2) liquidated one of the two new corporations.

Prior to the 1986 Tax Act, the complete liquidation of a U.S. corporation (whose balance sheet included no inventories or depreciable assets) was a nontaxable event at the corporate level. The liquidation gave rise to a capital gain to shareholders, taxed at well below ordinary income tax rates, and much of the sale proceeds was received by shareholders as a nontaxable return of capital. Dividends, though, have always been taxed at ordinary rates to individual shareholders.

The court viewed the economic substance of Gregory's two transactions as equivalent to a dividend. Moreover, because it saw no business purpose for the two transactions other than tax avoidance, it ruled that the less favorable dividend treatment be applied for tax purposes.[9]

Of course, there are ways to transfer property out of a corporation and into the hands of shareholders at capital gains rates, or as a nontaxable return of capital,

---

[8]Revenue Canada, the Canadian counterpart of the IRS in the United States, has access to a similar weapon, the "general anti-avoidance rule" (GAAR) introduced in 1988. As indicated by Ernst & Whinny (*Tax News International,* December 1988), "Revenue Canada can apply (the general anti-avoidance rule) to eliminate any form of tax advantage resulting from one transaction or a series of transactions, where any step in the series is undertaken primarily to obtain a tax benefit . . . and it represents a misuse of any one provision of the Income Tax Act, or an abuse of the Act overall" (p. 5). KPMG (*TaxFacts,* Canada, January 1998) states "It is still too early to know how effective this rule will be in dealing with tax-motivated transactions as only a few transactions to date have been challenged by GAAR. To the extent planned transactions could be construed as a 'misuse' or 'abuse' of the provisions of the Income Tax Act, however, taxpayers should be aware of the possible application of GAAR" (p. 30).

[9]Similarly in the United Kingdom, "the case of *Furniss v. Dawson* . . . established that a pre-ordered series of transactions should be regarded as a single composite transaction for U.K. tax purposes where one or more steps were introduced with no business purpose other than U.K. tax avoidance" (Price Waterhouse, *International Tax Review,* January/February 1989, p. 11).

without liquidating. The simplest way is to repurchase shares of stock in the open market.[10] If share repurchases are proportional to shareholder interests, however, the share repurchases will be considered to be an ordinary dividend. This is another example of the substance-over-form doctrine. The requirement that share repurchases be disproportionate to avoid being classified as dividend distributions can be much more of a problem in closely held firms than in widely held public corporations. In closely held firms, disproportionate share repurchases can have a substantial impact on the voting control of the firm. This nontax cost can greatly reduce the attractiveness of implementing the tax plan.

The IRS has also tried (often unsuccessfully) to use the substance-over-form argument when taxpayers essentially manufacture riskless assets from portfolios of risky assets. While the returns on risky assets are generally taxable at capital gains rates, the returns on riskless assets are taxable (or tax deductible) at ordinary income tax rates. Consider the possibilities when capital gains tax rates are below ordinary tax rates. Suppose that taxpayers could borrow at the riskless interest rate, take an ordinary tax deduction for the interest, and then use the proceeds to purchase a portfolio of risky assets that, together, are not risky. If the portfolio of risky assets earns the riskless interest rate before tax but is taxed at favorable capital gains tax rates, such taxpayers could wipe out their tax bills. We expand on this tax arbitrage notion in Chapter 5.

The substance-over-form and business-purpose doctrines have been codified in several parts of the Internal Revenue Code (IRC). By codified, we mean that Congress has passed tax bills transforming the judicial support for these doctrines into statutes or laws. The IRS's broadest ability to recharacterize transactions from their legal form into their economic substance is granted in IRC Section 482. This section has been used most extensively by the IRS in cases involving international transfer pricing (for example, interest rates on loans, or sales prices on transfers of goods or services between parent and subsidiary corporations operating in different countries). The motivation for playing games with transfer prices is that the parent and subsidiary may face very different tax rates. Section 482 has also been applied to a variety of transactions among related individuals who are taxed at different rates within the same tax jurisdiction (such as parents and children).[11]

Congress' motivation for allowing the IRS to invoke Section 482 and to recharacterize transactions is to prevent taxpayers from taking unreasonable advantage of situations where their left pocket and right pocket are taxed differently. Other Code sections that give the IRS broad powers include:

Section 269	Grants authority to disallow certain acquired losses.
Section 446(b)	Allows the IRS to adjust a taxpayer's accounting method when the method chosen by the taxpayer "does not clearly reflect income."

---

[10]"In 1998, U.S. corporations announced plans to buy a record-setting $220 billion worth of their own shares, according to Securities Data Co.", from Ed McCarthy, "Stock Buybacks: The Rules," *Journal of Accountancy* (May 1999, p. 91).

[11]For readers wanting more discussion (history and application over time) of the economic-substance doctrine and its potential application to current corporate tax avoidance schemes, see the article by Battle (1997). The Department of the Treasury report (1999) also discusses the application of existing doctrines to corporate tax shelters and the difficulties of arriving at broad new rules to curb these shelters.

Section 7701(1)   Grants authority to prescribe regulations recharacterizing any multiple-party financing transaction as a transaction directly among any two or more parties where it is determined that such recharacterization is appropriate to prevent avoidance of tax.

In its 2000 budget, the administration included several proposals designed to limit the growth of corporate tax shelters (such as those discussed in Appendix A of the Department of Treasury (1999) report). These proposals focus on the following areas:

1. Increasing disclosure of corporate tax shelter activities,
2. Increasing and modifying the penalty relating to substantial understatement of income tax,
3. Changing the law to disallow the use of tax benefits generated by a corporate tax shelter, and
4. Providing consequences to all the parties to the transaction (promoters, advisers, and tax-indifferent accommodating parties).

These proposals did not go unchallenged by various bar associations and the American Institute of Certified Public Accountants (AICPA). The Treasury Report provides more discussion of the preceding proposals and of the challenges and counterproposals offered by the bar associations and the AICPA.

Related-Party versus Arms-Length Contracts

It is worth noting that the IRS worries much less about form-over-substance problems in contracts between parties with opposing interests than it does between **related parties.** Why? Parties with opposing interests cannot always afford to write a contract in which the legal form differs much from the economic substance. Otherwise, if one party fails to perform as promised under the contract, the courts may not enforce the other party's property rights in the desired way.

For example, suppose a manufacturer buys steel from several suppliers to use in his manufacturing operations. For tax purposes, he determines that it would be very advantageous for him to reduce his taxable income this period and increase it next period. He could arrange for a supplier to ship some steel at a very high price this year with the understanding that the price will be correspondingly lower next year.

The problem with such an arrangement is that once the supplier has received above-market payment for this year's shipments, there is little incentive for her to keep the manufacturer happy for next year's shipment. Or the supplier might claim that the agreement was to deliver materials of inferior quality next period. If the contract is very explicit, so as to deter contractual breach by the supplier (because the breach of an explicit contract may be remedied by bringing legal action), the tax plan will fail if audited by the IRS. So it is not surprising that the IRS worries about related-party contracting more so than arm's length contracts.

Assignment-of-Income Doctrine

The courts have enabled the IRS to invoke another related doctrine, **assignment of income.** Here the taxpayer instructs one party to pay income on the taxpayer's behalf to a third party, transferring the tax liability to the third party as well (the third party is presumably in a lower tax bracket). As an example, a taxpayer may wish to give a child an interest in partnership income (the fruit of the tree) but not an interest in partnership capital (the tree itself).[12] By the assignment-of-income doctrine, the taxpayer must give away the whole tree to be successful in shifting taxable income. Because taxpayers have devised numerous ways to skirt this doctrine, the Tax Code contains some restrictions to attack these income-shifting plans between parents and children. In particular, all but a small amount of passive income earned by children under 14 years of age is taxed as if it were earned by the parent.

The landmark case in the "assignment of income" area is *Lucas v. Earl.* In this case, a husband and wife entered into a contract providing the wife with a claim to 50% of the husband's income. The taxpayer resided in a noncommunity property state. (In a community property state, the wife automatically is deemed to earn 50% of the husband's income.) The couple then filed separate tax returns and, given the progressive income tax schedule (tax rates increase with the level of taxable income), the total tax bill was less than it would have been had they filed a joint tax return. When the court agreed with the IRS Commissioner that this was unacceptable, the assignment-of-income doctrine was born.

Interestingly enough, several Tax Court cases involving baseball players have clarified the assignment-of-income doctrine. One involves Randy Hundley, a Chicago Cubs catcher [48 TC 339 (1967)]. His father trained him as a youth, and Hundley agreed as a teen to give his father half of any bonus he might receive later. The Tax Court blessed this arrangement, claiming that Hundley's father had earned his share of the bonus.

By contrast, consider the case of Philadelphia Phillies ballplayer Richie Allen [50 TC 466 (1969)]. Although Allen arranged for his employer to pay his mother half of his bonus, the Tax Court ruled this to be an assignment of income and taxed the full bonus to Allen. In reaching its conclusion, the Tax Court emphasized that Allen's mother knew nothing about baseball.

2.3 THE LEGISLATIVE PROCESS AND SOURCES OF TAX INFORMATION[13]

Despite the many broad restrictions that exist, numerous opportunities for abuse remain. Moreover, they will exist as long as the tax system encourages particular economic activities. Such restrictions also clearly make tax planning more difficult. As we mentioned in the introductory chapter, effective tax planning requires that the tax and nontax implications of proposed transactions be considered for all parties to the transaction. But as we just discussed, simply determining the tax implications of proposed transactions is not a trivial undertaking: It requires knowledge of tax rules that are inherently ambiguous.

---

[12]This is similar to the situation that arose in the court case of *Helvering v. Horst,* where a father sought to make a gift of detachable bond coupons to his son and have the son be taxed on the interest income. The Supreme Court ruled that it was the father who was taxable on the interest income.

[13]For a more technical discussion of what follows, see Pope, Anderson, and Kramer, (2001, Chapter 15).

A crucial step in minimizing the ambiguities of the tax implications of proposed transactions is seeking the proper authority for applying a particular tax rule. The remainder of this chapter reviews how one does just this for U.S. tax rules. This should provide some idea of how the tax professionals you may hire spend their time. It will also help make it feasible for you to research your own tax problems and it should give you a better idea of how the tax system is laid out.

Primary and Secondary Authorities

We can distinguish between primary and secondary types of authority for determining the appropriate tax treatment for a transaction. The most important **primary authority** is the Internal Revenue Code (IRC). The Code provides statutory authority. Gathering authoritative support for the proper tax treatment of a particular transaction should always begin here. Other primary authorities include Treasury Regulations, judicial decisions, administrative pronouncements (for example, by the IRS), and Congressional Committee Reports. Secondary authorities consist primarily of tax professionals (for example, accountants and lawyers), commercial tax services, and tax journals. We now discuss each of these authorities.

To develop an understanding of how the primary authoritative sources can help clarify the way a transaction should be treated for tax purposes, we must understand the legislative process, the means by which tax bills are enacted. The passage of such legislation gives rise to the most dramatic changes in tax rules.

The Legislative Process

Figure 2.1 traces a tax bill's route from origin to final enactment. With minor exceptions, all tax bills originate in the House of Representatives and then are forwarded to the House Ways and Means Committee (arrow 1 in Figure 2.1). If the bill is a major one, the Ways and Means Committee will hold public hearings. Then the Ways and Means Committee prepares a report that it sends back to the floor of the House (arrow 2). This committee report, which may provide important authoritative support by indicating the legislative intent of the bill, is often considered in court cases to help resolve taxpayer and IRS disputes.

The bill is then debated on the floor of the House, typically under "closed rule," where debate is limited and no amendments are permitted (see Graetz 1972). If the House bill is passed, it is sent to the Senate (arrow 3), where it is forwarded to the Senate Finance Committee (arrow 4). After public hearings, the Senate Finance Committee sends its report, along with proposed amendments to the House bill, back to the floor of the Senate (arrow 5). There it is debated under "open rule" with unlimited debate and amendment and under intensified lobbying pressure. If passed, both House and Senate Committee Reports are forwarded to a Conference Committee (arrow 6).

The Conference Committee is composed of members of both the House and the Senate. Its task is to iron out House and Senate disagreements. The Conference Committee Report contains recommendations for resolving differences between the House and Senate versions of the bill. In effect the Conference Committee creates a compromise bill. The report is sent back to the House and then the Senate for a vote (arrow 7). If both houses approve, the bill is sent to the president for signature or veto (arrow 8). If the president vetoes the bill, the veto can be overridden by a two-thirds override vote of the House and Senate members.

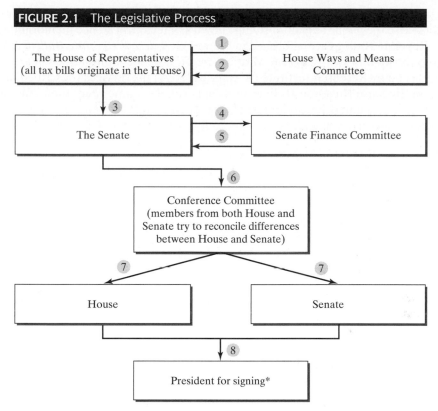

FIGURE 2.1 The Legislative Process

*If president vetoes, bill goes back to the House and Senate, 66% vote overrides presidential veto.

Regulations and Revenue Rulings That Result from the Passage of a Tax Act

Once a bill is passed, the Treasury is generally the first to interpret it. It issues **Treasury Regulations,** which provide general interpretations. Interested parties (such as tax lawyers, tax accountants, and other affected taxpayers) can request hearings on proposed regulations. The Treasury Department also issues **Revenue Rulings,** which are specific interpretations of existing or new laws. These result from a request for rules clarification from a taxpayer with a particular set of actual or proposed transactions. For example, a rulings request might be made when two corporations planning a tax-free reorganization wish to obtain IRS assurance that their merger will not be taxable to the target company's shareholders; that is, the IRS will bless the merger, in advance of the transaction, as being a tax-free reorganization.

Revenue Rulings represent official IRS policy. The Treasury will publish a rulings request from a taxpayer as a Revenue Ruling if it is of sufficient general interest. Otherwise it issues a **private letter ruling.** Private rulings are available to the public under *The Freedom of Information Act,* but they cannot be cited as precedent in a court of law. Still, they may be valuable as an indicator of IRS policy. Another form of letter rulings are **technical advice memoranda.** When auditing a technical tax matter, the IRS district or appeals office may refer the matter to the IRS national office in Washington, D.C., for technical advice concerning the appropriate tax treatment. The answer is made available to the public as a letter ruling known as a technical advice memorandum.

Revenue Rulings are published in the weekly *Internal Revenue Bulletins.* They are also published in the "Current Matters" section of the Commerce Clearing House (CCH) and by Research Institute of America (RIA) tax services (described more fully below). Because Revenue Rulings may be revoked or amended, their current status must be determined before relying upon them. Merten's *Law of Federal Income Taxation* contains a convenient current status table, as do the CCH and RIA tax services.

The Role of Judicial Decisions

Judicial decisions also play an extremely important role in interpreting the tax rules. The two court levels are courts of original jurisdiction and courts of appeal. Courts of original jurisdiction include the U.S. Tax Court, U.S. district courts, and the U.S. claims court. Only U.S. district courts offer jury trials. The U.S. Tax Court hears only tax cases, and the presiding judge is more familiar with the tax law than is the typical judge presiding in other courts.

Courts of appeal include the 13 circuit courts (numbered 1 through 11 plus the District of Columbia plus the Federal Circuit Court) and the Supreme Court. Legal precedent is circuit-specific—that is, different circuits can hand down different decisions based on identical facts. When this happens, the Supreme Court is often called upon to provide a final, overarching answer.

Decisions of the U.S. Tax Court for the more important cases are published in the *Tax Court Reporter.* Memorandum decisions of the U.S. Tax Court (dealing primarily with questions of fact with only one judge writing the decision) are published in CCH's *Tax Court Memorandum Decisions* and in RIA's *TC Memorandum Decisions.* All tax-related cases from all of the other courts (district courts, claims court, circuit courts of appeal, and the Supreme Court) are published in CCH's *U.S. Tax Cases* and RIA's *American Federal Tax Reports,* among other places.

Secondary Authorities

To this point we have discussed almost exclusively sources of *primary* authority: statutory (Internal Revenue Code); administrative (Treasury Regulations, Treasury Rulings); and judicial (cases from the U.S. Tax Court, district courts, claims court, circuit courts, and Supreme Court). For the nonexpert, **secondary authorities** are probably more useful, particularly the commercial tax services. The two most popular tax services are CCH's *Standard Federal Tax Reporter* and RIA's *United States Federal Tax Reporter.* Each section of these services begins with a layperson's discussion of an area of the Tax Code, introducing the subject in general terms. This is followed in turn by (1) the text of the IRC section (the statutes established by the passage of tax legislation); (2) the text of Treasury Regulations (Treasury's interpretation of the Code); (3) editorial explanations (sometimes including tax planning tips); and finally (4) synopses of court decisions, Revenue Rulings, and other Treasury pronouncements that pertain to the Code section, along with citations to complete documents.

Another extremely useful reference is the Bureau of National Affairs *Tax Management Portfolios,* of which there are several hundred. Each portfolio, 50–200 pages long, deals with a specific tax topic (such as sale-and-leaseback transactions or corporate acquisitions planning). The material proceeds from the general to the specific and offers excellent bibliographies. Also useful are the frequent excerpts from the Congressional Record that pertain to the enactment of relevant legislation. Note, too, the helpful sample contracts or wordings to be included in the corporate minutes. These are likely to pass muster with the taxing authority to secure the desired tax treatment.

Another useful reference is CCH's *Tax Articles,* which lists articles and their abstracts, by Code section number, by topic, and by author. In addition, the RIA tax service offers its "Index to Tax Articles," organized by Code section numbers.

Summary of Key Points

1. Tax rules designed to motivate socially desirable activities often motivate transactions that reduce taxpayers' tax liabilities but serve no social purpose. This gives rise to tax-rule restrictions that serve to limit exceedingly aggressive tax planning behavior.
2. Ambiguity in the tax law is pervasive. As a result, numerous disputes arise between taxpayers and the taxing authority, two groups with opposing interests regarding the assessment of tax liabilities. The courts may be used to resolve these disputes.
3. Several common classes of tax planning strategies include attempts to convert tax-disfavored types of income into more favorably taxed types, to shift income from a highly taxed pocket to a lower taxed pocket, and to shift income from a time period of high tax rates into one of lower tax rates.
4. The business-purpose doctrine and the substance-over-form doctrine are broad restrictions on taxpayer behavior. The taxing authority often has the right to recharacterize transactions in a way that affects the tax outcome if the transactions can be shown to have had no other purpose than tax avoidance and a simpler set of transactions could have been undertaken. The taxing authority can also look through a transaction's legal form to its economic substance. As a result, the taxing authority can deny tax benefits or recharacterize a transaction in a way that is less favorable to the taxpayer.
5. The business-purpose and the substance-over-form doctrines have been codified in the Tax Code. That is, judicial support for these doctrines has been transformed into statutes or laws. For example, Section 482 allows the IRS to recharacterize transactions from their legal form into their economic substance. This section is used heavily in cases involving transfer-pricing transactions among related parties.
6. Assignment of income is another important doctrine. The taxing authority uses this doctrine to prevent high tax-bracket taxpayers from assigning their income to related low tax-bracket taxpayers for the sole purpose of reducing their joint tax bill.
7. Handling transactions on an individual basis is expensive, and many tax-rule restrictions are created by Congress out of a desire to close down certain socially undesirable tax planning avenues before taxpayers have a chance to use them. For example, the "at risk" rules require that taxpayers be exposed to the risk of economic loss before they may deduct any tax losses resulting from a transaction. The "passive activity loss" rules restrict the deduction of these losses to the extent the taxpayer has passive activity income.
8. Tax laws are ambiguous. Ambiguity can frustrate legitimate tax planning and taxpayers must be aware of primary and secondary authorities for determining appropriate tax treatment for a transaction. Understanding the legislative intent of Congress provides additional guidance in interpreting the tax rules. The intent of Congress may play an important role in the court's interpretation of the tax rules.
9. Various sources of information can provide guidance to taxpayers in predicting how transactions will be treated for tax purposes. Some of these sources appear in this chapter. Others are listed in an appendix to this chapter.

Appendix 2.1

SOURCES OF INFORMATION ON TAX LEGISLATION

Several excellent publications follow the evolution of proposed tax legislation and document the dates on which certain legislative events take place. These include:

- BNA (Bureau of National Affairs) *Daily Tax Report*
- BNA *Weekly Tax Report*
- *Tax Notes Today:* a daily electronic newsletter available on LEXIS, an electronic news retrieval service (also available in print)
- *Tax Notes:* a weekly tax service. Each issue contains:
  - a summary of bills introduced
  - a description of change in the status of bills, by day
  - a description of public hearings on proposed legislation
  - a calendar of future congressional hearings
  - a summary of lobbying letters sent to Treasury, organized by IRC section number
  - a complete report of developments, all organized by IRC section number, relating to:
    - Treasury Regulations
    - Judicial decisions
    - Administrative pronouncements
  - a list of recently published tax articles by Code section number

An especially interesting feature of *Tax Notes* is the document retrieval service. For a modest cost the company will rush you complete texts of any documents to which they refer (they will even deliver within 24 hours if you pay the Federal Express charges).

Copies of Committee Reports (House Ways and Means, Senate Finance, or Conference) can be found in:

- The government documents section of most law libraries
- *Weekly Internal Revenue Bulletin,* which is bound into *Cumulative Bulletins* every 6 months
- U.S. *Code Congressional and Administrative News*
- Parts of the major acts appear in the Research Institute of America (RIA) and Commerce Clearing House (CCH) tax services under the titles *United States Federal Tax Reporter* and *Standard Federal Tax Reporter,* respectively

Sometimes it is important to know the date on which a particular rule that now appears in the Code first became effective. Two good sources for laws passed prior to 1954 are:

- *Federal Tax Laws Correlated* (Walter Barton and Carol Browning; Warren, Gorham, and Lamont; 1969)
- Seidman's *Legislative History of Federal Income Tax and Excess Profits Tax Law, 1939–1953* and Seidman's *Legislative History of Federal Income Tax Laws, 1861–1938*

Two additional sources that are useful for tracking down legislative histories of more recent changes in the Tax Code are:

- RIA's *Federal Taxes Cumulative Changes*
- BNA's *Primary Sources*

WEB SITE ADDRESSES

There are many Web site for tax information searches. (These Web site addresses were valid at the time of writing, but Web site addresses can change.)

IRS
http://www.irs.ustreas.gov/prod/cover.html

Commerce Clearing House (CCH)
http://www.cch.com/

Research Institute of America (RIA)
http://www.riahome.com/

Bureau of National Affairs (BNA)
http://www.bna.com/

Tax Analysts, publisher of *Tax Notes*
http://www.tax.org

A site with extensive links is maintained by Professor Dennis Schmidt
http://www.taxsites.com/

Big 4 accounting firms:
Deloitte & Touche
http://www.us.deloitte.com

Ernst & Young   *http://www.ey.com*

KPMG   *http://www.kpmg.com*

PricewaterhouseCoopers
http://www.pwcglobal.com/

Appendix 2.2

ACCOUNTING FOR CORPORATE INCOME TAXES

After reading this appendix, you should be able to:

1. Explain why tax rules differ from accounting rules.
2. Define and give examples of temporary differences.
3. Define and give examples of permanent differences.
4. Interpret corporate disclosures relating to income taxes.

Publicly traded corporations face two separate sets of rules for tax and financial reporting. These two sets of rules arise because of the differing purposes underlying each set of rules. As explained in Chapter 1, the Tax Code is the outcome of multiple, sometimes conflicting, objectives: raise revenue to fund government activities, to redistribute wealth, to encourage (or discourage) certain economic activities, and as a macroeconomic policy tool to stimulate the overall economy. In contrast, the financial accounting rules used by corporations to report the results of their activities to shareholders and other interested parties, have a different objective: to provide information useful to investors and creditors in making investment and other decisions about the firm.[14] We will refer to the financial accounting rules as book or generally accepted accounting principles (or GAAP) to differentiate from the tax rules. The primary determinant of GAAP is the Financial Accounting Standards Board, or FASB.

We discuss the accounting for corporate income taxes because a knowledgeable reader can sometimes learn a great deal from the corporate income tax disclosures about the company's tax situation. Tax returns are not publicly available, and investors, analysts, tax planners, governmental agencies, and academics can use financial statements to address a variety of issues. Is the firm paying taxes? If not, why not, especially if it is reporting large profits to shareholders in its publicly released financial statements? Does it have an NOL carryforward? Does it expect to realize the future tax benefits of the NOL carryforwards, etc.? We can sometimes also learn about the firm's tax planning activities. However, meaningful interpretation of these disclosures requires knowledge about how the tax and book numbers differ and how the accounting disclosures are prepared.[15] The difference between book and taxable income has attracted much political, academic, and financial press attention in recent years arising from a perceived explosion in corporate tax shelters (reducing taxable income but not book income), in employee stock options, and from recent financial accounting scandals (such as Enron).

There are three primary financial statements: an income statement, a

---

[14]See Objectives of Financial Reporting of Business Enterprises, Statement of Financial Accounting Concepts No. 1. Financial Accounting Standards Board, 1978.

[15]For a more detailed and technical discussion of the accounting for income taxes, see Revsine, Collins, and Johnson (2002) and Knott and Rosenfeld (2003). For further discussion of limitations that restrict what can be learned from financial statements, see Hanlon (2003a).

statement of cash flows, and a balance sheet. The income statement presents a summary of the results of operations of the corporation for the period using **accrual accounting.** The summary measure of performance is referred to as net income (or more generally book income or GAAP earnings). The statement of cash flows provides a summary of the cash inflows and outflows for the period and explains the change in the balance of the corporate cash account from the start to the end of the period. The operating section of the statement of cash flows calculates the cash flows from operations and can be thought of as a cash-based measure of the operating performance of the firm in contrast to net income, which uses the accrual basis. Under a cash basis method, sales revenue is recognized when the cash is received and expenses are recognized when paid whereas, under the accrual basis, sales revenue can be recognized before the cash is received (a credit sale) provided the firm is reasonably confident of collection and expenses can be recognized in periods different than when the cash is paid (for example, facilities rent might be paid in advance for the period). Cash flow from operations generally starts with net income calculated under the accrual system, then makes adjustments to derive the cash flow from operations. The balance sheet lists the assets, liabilities, and shareholders' equity of the corporation at the end of the accounting period.

Given the different objectives of the Tax Code and GAAP, the same transaction is often accounted for differently in calculating taxable income versus net income. To achieve the objectives of the Tax Code, the rules generally allow less choice and are closer to a cash basis system of realization than those in the accrual-based income statement measurement of net income.[16] The difference can be substantial—Table A2.1 reports the total pretax book income and estimated taxable income (estimated as described below in equation A2.4) for all firms (other than financial firms) on Compustat with available data (Compustat is an electronic data base compiled by Standard and Poors containing current and past years' financial statement data for most publicly traded U.S. corporations). The tabled numbers are graphed in Figure A2.1. In the mid-1980s book exceeded taxable income, with the difference reduced after the Tax Reform Act of 1986 broadened the corporate tax base such that taxable income exceeded book income in the early 90s. The early 90s also reflects a major change in the book accounting for postretirement benefits which moved to an accrual basis from the prior cash basis.[17] In the late 90s, book income again exceeded taxable income with a maximum difference of $65 billion in 1999. This large difference motivated the Treasury Department's concern with corporate tax shelters (U.S. Department of Treasury 1999). Somewhat surprisingly, book income fell below taxable income by $137 billion in 2001 reflecting a large decline in corporate profits (and note, as discussed below, taxable income here is over-estimated because we ignore the large tax deductions enjoyed by firms arising from employee stock options).

---

[16]The Internal Revenue Code (Section 446(a)) states that "Taxable income shall be computed under the method of accounting on the basis of which the taxpayer regularly computes his income in keeping his books." The Code (446b) further states taxable income must "clearly reflect income." Thus it appears as though taxable income and book income should be very similar; however this is not the case.

[17]See "Employers' Accounting for Postretirement Benefits Other Than Pensions," Statement of Financial Accounting Standards No. 106, 1990. For example, General Motors recorded a $20.8 billion one-time book charge on the adoption of SFAS 106 in its 1992 fiscal year.

TABLE A2.1	Pretax Book Income and Estimated Taxable Income by Year Summed Across N Firms with Available Compustat Data. $Millions			
Year	*N*	*Pretax Book Income*	*Estimated Taxable Income*	*Difference*
1983	2,225	$140,838	$90,633	$50,205
1984	2,866	$161,175	$113,585	$47,590
1985	2,984	$150,862	$107,937	$42,925
1986	2,933	$130,835	$80,857	$49,978
1987	3,048	$169,191	$137,779	$31,413
1988	3,188	$193,722	$191,251	$2,471
1989	3,182	$194,764	$188,238	$6,526
1990	3,140	$194,539	$200,432	−$5,894
1991	3,180	$148,620	$181,861	−$33,241
1992	3,238	$163,241	$178,071	−$14,830
1993	3,454	$191,141	$208,131	−$16,990
1994	3,741	$280,040	$246,715	$33,325
1995	3,999	$328,002	$287,780	$40,222
1996	4,233	$370,307	$328,735	$41,572
1997	4,544	$386,431	$363,329	$23,102
1998	4,449	$357,993	$344,815	$13,178
1999	4,258	$452,647	$387,665	$64,981
2000	4,077	$484,323	$450,896	$33,427
2001	3,939	$106,144	$243,233	−$137,089
Total	66,678	$4,604,816	$4,331,944	$272,871

Pretax book income as reported.

Estimated taxable income = current tax expense/top corporate statutory tax rate (ignores the ESO tax deduction).

Source: Hanlon, Kelley, and Shevlin 2003.

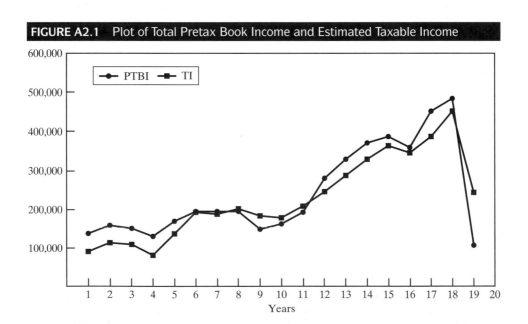

FIGURE A2.1 Plot of Total Pretax Book Income and Estimated Taxable Income

The differences between tax and book income can be partitioned into two major types: temporary differences and permanent differences.[18]

Temporary differences: The transaction is included in both sets of books (i.e., in calculating taxable and net income) but in different time periods (thus these differences are sometimes also referred to as timing differences).

Permanent differences: The transaction is included in one set of books (i.e., taxable or net income) but never the other.

Examples of Temporary Differences

Some typical examples of temporary differences are summarized in Table A2.2. Income is the difference between revenues and expenses. For book purposes, revenue is recognized (included in the calculation of book income) when earned (when the firm has substantially completed its obligations to provide the goods or services) *and* the buying firm has either paid or agreed to pay for the goods or services (these are referred to as the revenue recognition criteria). For tax purposes, revenue is recorded when earned or cash received, whichever occurs earlier. Thus, firms receiving cash in advance, for example, a magazine publisher, will defer revenue recognition (as unearned revenue) for book purposes until the good or service is provided but will include the amount as income in taxable income.

For book purposes, expenses are recognized in the period in which they can be matched to revenue (for example, cost of goods sold, depreciation) or the period in which they are incurred (head office expenses and CEO salary) whereas, for tax purposes, an item cannot be deducted until it satisfies the "all events" test which is

(a) all of the events that determine the taxpayer's liability for the expense must have occurred, (b) the amount must be determined with reasonable accuracy, and (c) economic performance must have occurred—that is, the goods or services must have been provided to the taxpayer. Because of the all events test, oftentimes expenses are recognized in the books before they are deducted for tax purposes. For example, warranty expense, bad debt expense, loan losses, and deferred compensation, are included in book income on an accrual basis but are deducted only when paid (which usually occurs in a later period). Firms restructuring operations (closing down a plant, laying off employees) often recognize the expense for book purposes in advance of the actual cash outlay or losses associated with the restructuring whereas, for tax purposes, the expense is recognized when the cash is paid out (severance pay) or when the assets are sold at a loss.

Another temporary difference arises when tax losses that cannot be carried back and which are expected to be used as a deduction against future taxable income give rise to a deferred tax asset and thus a deferred tax benefit reducing total tax expense in the year of the loss. We discuss the net operating loss carryforward rules in more detail later in the text.

Recent accounting rules no longer allow the pooling of interests method of accounting and changed a major difference between book and tax relating to mergers and acquisitions.[19] We defer this discussion to Chapters 13–17. A terse discussion is included in the table because the accounting and tax treatment of a merger can give rise to either a temporary difference or a permanent difference.

---

[18]Current GAAP does not use the term permanent difference but earlier statements did and we continue to use the term as a convenient label for these types of differences.

[19]See "Business Combinations," Statements of Financial Accounting Standards No. 141 (2001) and "Goodwill and Other Intangible Assets," Statements of Financial Accounting Standards No. 142 (2001).

TABLE A2.2 Typical Temporary Differences

Item	Book Treatment	Tax Treatment
Unearned revenue (cash received in advance)	Revenue deferred until earned—by firm providing the good or service for which it has been paid.	Deferral not allowed, thus income recognized when cash received.
Long-term construction contracts	Percentage of completion or completed contract allowed (income recognized at completion of contract)	Percentage of completion (income recognized during contract life)
Gain on installment sale (where customer promises to pay over a number of future periods)	Entire gain included upon sale	Gain deferred until cash received
Bad debts	Expense based on management's estimates of uncollectibles, recorded in same period as the credit sale giving rise to the accounts receivable	Deductible when specific receivable actually written off
Warranty expenses	Expense based on management's estimates of future warranty costs associated with current period's sales	Not deductible until paid
Deferred compensation	Expensed when liability is incurred (when employee earns the deferred compensation)	Not deductible until paid
Postretirement benefit obligations (other than pensions)	Expensed when liability is incurred (when employee earns the deferred benefits) and based on actuarial assumptions	Not deductible until paid
Inventory valuation allowances	Application of lower of cost or market could result in write-downs	Reserves not allowed, loss recognized when inventory sold at lower price
Prepaid expenses (rent, insurance)	Expensed when benefit received	Deductible when paid
Depreciation	Method, useful life, and salvage value as determined by management	Accelerated depreciation under MACRS-prescribed lives by asset class
Intangible assets—goodwill*	May exist on both sets of books (purchase accounting and tax basis step-up in basis after merger), may exist on balance sheet but not tax books (purchase accounting but no tax step-up in asset basis—thus a permanent difference). Prior to FAS 144, different amortization schedules. Post-FAS 144, goodwill no longer amortizable for book purposes but subject to write-down if value impaired. The latter two give rise to a temporary difference.	
Intangible assets—purchased in-process R&D	For accounting purposes, R&D is expensed as incurred. In a merger accounted for as a purchase, the amount of the purchase price allocated to the likely payoffs from the target's past R&D efforts (labeled purchased in-process R&D) is immediately expensed for book purposes. If no step-up in tax basis, then, for tax purposes, no purchased in-process R&D, so a permanent difference. If tax basis step-up, then temporary difference as write-off for tax likely is later.	

*A terse summary is presented here. For more details, see later Chapters 13–17. While it is possible for goodwill to be on the tax books (arising from a step-up in basis merger) and not on the accounting books (pooling of interests), this is an unlikely scenario.

Examples of Permanent Differences

The classic example of a permanent difference is the interest on tax-exempt municipal bonds. The interest is included in book income but excluded from taxable income. To avoid multiple levels of taxation on dividends between corporations, corporations can exclude from their taxable income a percentage of dividend income received on their holdings of stock in other corporations—this is referred to as the corporate dividends received deduction and is discussed in more detail later in the text. However, depending on how the stock holdings are accounted for, dividends are included in income (if the investor company owns less than 20% of the outstanding stock of the investee). For stock holdings greater than 20%, the investor's proportionate share of investee earnings (rather than dividends) are included in the investor firm's income. Other permanent differences include some fines and penalties, portion of meal and entertainment expenses, excess nonperformance-based compensation, and life insurance premiums are not deductible for tax purposes but can be treated as expenses for book purposes. Life insurance death benefits are included in book income but excluded from taxable income.

Corporate Accounting for Income Taxes

The accounting for income taxes is set out in SFAS 109 "Accounting for Income Taxes."[20] The income tax expense reported on the corporate income statement reflects the application of accrual accounting.

Specifically,

Total income tax expense
$$= \text{(pretax book income less permanent differences)} \times \text{the corporate statutory tax rate (str)} \quad \textbf{(A2.1)}$$

Pretax book income is also referred to as income from operations before income taxes. Total income tax expense is also referred to as provision for income taxes. The total income tax expense can be decomposed into

Total tax expense
$$= \text{current tax expense} + \text{deferred tax expense} \quad \textbf{(A2.2)}$$

where current tax expense is an estimate of the current taxes due on the firm's taxable income for the period, and deferred tax expense is an estimate of the tax effects arising from items included in the current period calculation of net income but will be taxed (i.e., included in taxable income) in a future period. That is, deferred tax expense arises from temporary differences. Specifically,

Current tax expense
$$= \text{taxable income} \times \text{str} \quad \textbf{(A2.3)}$$

Thus to derive an estimate of the firm's current period taxable income from publicly available reports we can rearrange (A2.3) to

Estimated taxable income
$$= \text{current tax expense/str} \quad \textbf{(A2.4)}$$

This is only an estimate because as we will see in Chapter 8 a major adjustment for many firms that we must make is for the tax benefits of employee stock options.[21] Using equation (A2.4), results in an overstatement of estimated taxable income due to the ESO tax deduction.

---

[20]"Accounting for Income Taxes," Statement of Financial Accounting Standards No. 109, Financial Accounting Standards Board, 1992. SEC Regulation S-X Rule 4-08(h) also requires some additional disclosures for firms subject to SEC regulation.

[21]Note also that an examination of Chapter 1, exhibit 1.1 shows that the firms tax liability (= taxable income × str) is reduced by any tax credits (which are a dollar for dollar reduction in the tax liability). We ignore the effects of tax credits here.

Deferred tax expense (benefit)
= temporary differences × str   **(A2.5)**

Example Illustrating Corporate Income Tax Disclosures

A simple numerical example illustrates the above concepts. Suppose the following as facts:

Sales revenue	$1000
Cost of goods sold	−400
R&D	−200
Depreciation − book	−120
Interest expense	−100
Municipal bond interest income	+50
Pretax book income	230

Other information:

Corporate statutory tax rate = 35% = str.
Depreciation for tax purposes = $200.
Municipal bond interest income is tax exempt (that is, excluded in the calculation of taxable income).

From (A2.1),

total income tax expense
= (pretax book income less permanent differences) × the corporate statutory tax rate (str)
= (230 − municipal bond interest which is tax exempt) × .35
= (230 − 50) × .35
= $63.

Total tax expense can also be partitioned into current and deferred tax expense as per equation (A2.2). Current tax expense is calculated as taxable income × str per equation (A2.3). Taxable income in this example is:

Sales revenue	$1000
Cost of goods sold	−400
R&D	−200
Depreciation − tax	−200
Interest expense	−100
Taxable income	100

Thus current tax expense = 100 × .35 = $35.

Deferred tax expense (benefit) = temporary differences × str per equation (A2.5). The only temporary difference in this example is the differing amount of depreciation recognized for book versus tax in this period. Thus,

deferred tax expense (benefit)
= (tax depreciation less book depreciation) × str
= (200 − 120) × .35
= 80 × .35 = $28

As noted in equation (A2.2), the sum of current and deferred tax expense equals total tax expense: $35 + $28 = $63.

An alternative way to estimate taxable income is

pretax book income +/− temporary differences +/− permanent differences
= 230 − 80 − 50 = $100   **(A2.6)**

SFAS 109 requires firms to provide reasonably detailed disclosures about the income tax expense, and financial statement users with a reasonable understanding of the accounting for income taxes can sometimes learn much from the disclosures. Firms are required to explain (via a rate reconciliation) why the firms effective tax rate, defined under GAAP as total tax expense/pretax book income, differs from the top corporate statutory tax rate (currently 35%). Reference to equation (A2.1) shows that any difference must be due to the effects of permanent differences:

Total income tax expense = (pretax book income less permanent differences) × str   **(A2.1)**

In our simple example, the only permanent difference is the $50 of tax-exempt municipal bond interest. Firms present the reconciliation either in % terms or in tax effect dollar terms. In our example, the $50 of tax-exempt municipal bond interest reduces the firm's effective tax rate by 7.6%, from 35%

to 27.4%, or reduced income taxes in the amount of $17.50.

	%	$
Top statutory tax rate	35.0	.35 × $230 = $80.50
Municipal bond interest	7.6	.35 × $50 = $17.50
Effective tax rate (63/230)	27.4	$63.50

Permanent differences that cause book income to exceed taxable income (e.g., tax-exempt municipal bond interest) result in an effective tax rate lower than the top U.S. statutory tax rate (as does the earning of income in lower taxed jurisdictions). Permanent differences that cause book income to be lower than taxable income (e.g., nondeductible fines, expensed purchased in-process R&D which is not deductible) result in an effective tax rate higher then the top statutory tax rate. The level of detail varies across companies, limiting what we might learn from the disclosures. Not surprisingly, firms have incentives to mask their use of corporate tax shelters and we might expect the ideal tax shelter (reduced taxable income with no effect on book income in the current or future periods—a permanent difference) to show up in the effective tax rate reconciliation. An examination of the income tax note, and specifically the tax rate reconciliation, of firms named by the financial press and Treasury as having entered into tax shelters fails to provide any evidence of such tax shelter activity.

Temporary differences give rise to either future tax liabilities or future tax deductions. Future tax deductions save future taxes and thus are referred to as deferred tax assets while future tax liabilities are referred to as deferred tax liabilities

because they represent future tax payments. (Note that because permanent differences do not give rise to either future liabilities or future tax deductions, they do not give rise to deferred tax liabilities or assets.) In our simple example, if this were the first year of operations, the deferred tax assets and liabilities at the start of the period would be zero and, at the end of the period, would be the difference between the book and tax basis of the depreciable asset times the statutory tax rate. If we assume the firm paid $1,000 for the asset, the tax basis at the end of the period is $1,000 less accumulated tax depreciation of $200 = $800; the book basis is $1,000 less accumulated book depreciation of $120 = $880. The difference in the book and tax basis of the asset is $80 and represents future book depreciation which has already been deducted for tax purposes—a temporary difference which will reverse in the future when book depreciation on the asset exceeds tax depreciation. Thus in the current period pretax book income exceeds taxable income but, in some future periods, taxable income will be higher, resulting in a higher tax liability. Thus the depreciation temporary difference gives rise to a future tax liability, which is shown as a deferred tax liability in the accounting books. The deferred tax liability is $80 × .35 = $28. In this example, the change in the deferred tax liability is $28 and we have no deferred tax assets, so the total change in the deferred tax assets and liabilities is $28 which equals the deferred tax expense calculated in equation (A2.5).[22]

Under SFAS 109, firms are required to present a summary of their deferred tax assets and deferred tax liabilities; however, the level of detail and hence the usefulness of the disclosures varies across companies. When a firm has deferred tax assets, it is

---

[22]Thus total tax expense can also be written as equal to current taxes payable plus (increase in deferred tax liabilities and decrease in deferred tax assets) less (decrease in deferred tax liability and increase in deferred tax asset).

required to assess whether future taxable income will be sufficient to realize the tax savings represented by the deferred tax asset. If the firm believes it is more likely than not that some portion of the deferred tax asset will not be utilized (for example, deferred tax assets arising from past and current tax losses), the deferred tax asset must be reduced by a valuation allowance. Because the valuation allowance reduces the net book value of the deferred tax asset at the end of the period, the change in the net deferred tax asset is reduced, which affects the deferred tax expense component of the tax expense number on the income statement. That is, the deferred tax benefit of the deferred tax asset is reduced, resulting in an otherwise higher tax expense and lower reported book income (because the tax benefits are not recognized this period).[23]

The above discussion focuses on U.S. federal income taxes. U.S. corporations also pay state income taxes, which are deductible at the federal level. In addition, many large corporations also have foreign operations on which they pay taxes to foreign tax jurisdictions. Detailed discussion of the taxation of foreign operations is deferred until Chapters 10 and 11. Further, most large public corporations are organized as a parent corporation with divisions or segments of the business organized into wholly owned or partially owned subsidiaries. The tax and book rules differ on consolidation of subsidiaries—for tax purposes, firms can elect to consolidate U.S. subsidiaries if they own at least 80% of the stock of the subsidiary. U.S. firms do not consolidate their foreign subsidiaries for tax purposes even if wholly owned. For financial reporting purposes, U.S. firms consolidate U.S. and their foreign subsidiaries if they have control over the assets and operations of the subsidiaries. One criteria to assess control is the extent of ownership and thus 50% ownership is often used as a cutoff to determine whether to consolidate a subsidiary for financial reporting purposes. Under SFAS 109, firms are required to disclose, if material, both current and deferred tax expense partitioned into U.S. federal, state and local, and foreign portions. Because of the differing consolidation rules, the reported tax expense and any resulting estimate of taxable income is only for the entities included in the consolidated financial reporting entity.[24]

In summary, the required corporate income tax disclosures include (1) the current and deferred portions of the tax expense, broken down into the U.S., foreign, and state portions; (2) a listing of deferred tax assets and deferred tax liabilities; and (3) a reconciliation of the tax computed at the federal rate on pretax book income to the firm's effective tax rate. Using these disclosures, the astute financial statement reader can:

1. Estimate current taxable income from the disclosure of current tax expense.
2. Infer the firm's major temporary differences.
3. Infer the firm's major permanent differences.

---

[23]An increase in the valuation allowance decreases deferred tax benefit, increasing total tax expense, thus reducing book income. By similar reasoning, a decrease in the valuation allowance increases book income. Because determining the valuation allowance is subjective, management has the ability to manage reported book income via the valuation allowance. However, Miller and Skinner (1998) find little evidence of firms managing reported book income via the valuation allowance.

[24]There are several other points we should note. First, the total tax expense relates only to income from continuing operations. Items reported below this line item on the income statement are usually reported net of their specific tax effects (which tax effects are sometimes specifically disclosed). Second, because publicly traded corporations file their financial statements with the SEC before preparing and filing their tax returns with the IRS, the current tax expense is actually an estimate of the actual tax liability. Third, firms sometimes include a "tax cushion" in current tax expense to allow for the possibility of disallowance of aggressive tax positions or disagreements between the IRS and the company on the appropriate tax treatment of an item.

Knowledge of these three items can help the external reader assess how aggressive the firm is in its tax planning, what major tax-favored activities the firm is entering into (as reflected in the permanent and temporary differences because these differences often arise from tax-favored treatment under the Tax Code), and the amount by which, and the reasons why, its taxable income differs from its net income. These book-tax differences, especially the temporary differences can also be used to infer how aggressive the firm might be in its accrual accounting choices in calculating net income.[25]

Example of Actual Corporate Disclosure

At the end of this appendix are extracts from the Microsoft Corporation 2002 Annual Report. Per GAAP, the 2002 Income Statement presents 3 years of results for comparison purposes. Microsoft reports pretax book income (labeled as Income before taxes by Microsoft) of $11,513 (in millions) in 2002 down from $11,525 in 2001. The total tax expense (labeled Provision for income taxes by Microsoft) is $3,684 for 2002 and $3,804 for 2001. These imply a GAAP effective tax rate:

	2000	*2001*	*2002*
Provision for income taxes	$4,854	$3,804	$3,684
Income before taxes	14,275	11,525	11,513
GAAP effective tax rate (%)	34.00	33.00	32.00

The income tax note disclosures (Note 12 in the Microsoft Annual Report) partitions the total tax expense in 2002 into a current tax expense of $4,219 and a deferred tax benefit of $535, resulting in the total tax

expense of $3,684 reported on the income statement. Microsoft presents a terse description of its deferred tax assets and deferred tax liabilities. Recall that deferred tax assets and liabilities arise from temporary differences—items that are recognized in both sets of books but in different time periods. With respect to deferred income tax assets, the 2002 $2,261 amount for revenue items likely arises from Microsoft classifying some sales dollars as unearned revenue on software sales, thus delaying revenue recognition for book purposes, however 100% of the sales dollars are likely included as revenues for tax purposes. For further discussion, see Note 3 Unearned Revenue of the Microsoft 2002 Annual Report available at http://microsoft.com/msft/ar.mspx. The $945 for expense items represents expenses that have been recognized for book purposes but not yet deducted for tax purposes. The $2,016 for impaired investments indicates that Microsoft has written down the book value of investments that have declined in value (recognized the losses for book purposes) but cannot deduct the losses for tax purposes until the investments are sold and the losses realized.

With respect to deferred income tax liabilities, the 2002 $887 unrealized gain on investments represents gains recognized for book purposes but not yet recognized for tax purposes. The gain will be included in taxable income when the investments are sold and the gain realized. The $1,818 for international earnings reflects the different consolidation rules between tax and book. The earnings of foreign subsidiaries are included in book income (because book consolidates the foreign subs) but will only be included in taxable income when the foreign earnings are repatriated to the United States via dividend payments (see

---

[25]For example, see Phillips, Pincus, and Olhoft Rego (2003) who examine the ability to detect earnings management behavior by firms from deferred tax expense; and Hanlon (2003b) who examines whether large temporary differences indicate less persistent net income arising from short-term earnings management.

Chapters 10 and 11 for further discussion of this point). It is anybody's guess as to what constitutes the $803 Other, although it does represent a future tax liability.

In 2002, deferred tax assets increased by $1,992 (from $3,230 to $5,222) and deferred tax liabilities increased by $1,391 (from $2,117 to $3,508) for a net increase in deferred tax assets of $601. A net increase in deferred tax assets represents a deferred tax benefit in the calculation of the total tax expense on the income statement—however, the deferred tax benefit component of the total tax expense for Microsoft is $535 and there is no explanation as to the difference (the existence of such a difference is not that unusual, and our speculation is that it is due to merger activity by Microsoft resulting in a different set of deferred tax assets and liabilities at the end than at the start of the period).

The difference between deferred tax assets and deferred tax liabilities at the end of 2002 is $1,714 (assets of $5,222 less liabilities of $3,508). Net deferred tax assets is thus $1,714. However, for presentation on the balance sheet, the current and noncurrent portions of the deferred tax assets and deferred tax liabilities are netted separately. The current (noncurrent) portion refers to those temporary differences associated with current (noncurrent) assets and liabilities. Microsoft discloses current deferred tax assets of $2,112 and, in the long-term liabilities section, deferred income tax liabilities of $398, which nets out to $1,714 ($2,112 − $398), which equals the net total deferred assets in the income tax footnote. For many firms, the totals are not traceable to the balance sheet usually because the netted amount is combined with other items in that section of the balance sheet under the rubric Other (for example, Other current assets, if a current deferred asset, or Other current liabilities, if a current deferred tax liability).

The income tax note contains no discussion of the existence of a valuation allowance, indicating that Microsoft is confident that it will realize all the tax benefits of the deferred tax assets (that is, lower future taxes than otherwise). The income tax note also indicates that International taxes represent $575 of the total current tax expense of $3,684. The note also discloses the U.S. and international components of Income before taxes.

Finally, Microsoft presents an explanation of why the GAAP effective tax rate differs from the top U.S. statutory tax rate. Recall, the explanation takes the form of a tax rate reconciliation and arises from permanent differences. We present it here in tabular form:

	2000	*2001*	*2002*
Top statutory tax rate	35.00%	35.00%	35.00%
Tax credits	(2.5)	(3.1)	
Other items	1.5	1.1	(0.6)
Extraterritorial income exclusion tax benefit*			(2.4)
GAAP effective tax rate (etr)**	34.00%	33.00%	32.00%
Dollar amount***	(143)	(231)	(345)

*Income that is included in book income but excluded from taxable income because of tax-favored treatment under the Tax Code.

**As calculated above and as reported by Microsoft.

***Dollar amount = (str − etr) × income before taxes; represents the total permanent differences in terms of taxes (reduction in taxes here because the effective tax rate is lower than the statutory tax rate).

Based on the Microsoft disclosures, we can estimate the firm's U.S. and worldwide taxable income as follows (using equation A2.4, estimated taxable income = current tax expense/str) ignoring the tax benefits of employee stock options (which are substantial for Microsoft), which we will discuss in Chapter 8. We are also ignoring tax credits here.

	2000	*2001*	*2002*
U.S. current tax expense/.35	$4,744/.35	$3,243/.35	$3,644/.35
= estimated U.S. taxable income	13,554	9,266	10,411
Worldwide (total) current tax expense/.35	5,279/.35	3,757/.35	4,219/.35
= estimated worldwide taxable income	15,083	10,734	12,054
Reported worldwide income before taxes	14,275	11,525	11,513
Total difference	808	−791	541
Temporary differences*	+1,214	−134	+1529
Permanent differences**	−406	+657	−988

*Temporary differences = deferred tax expense/.35

**Permanent differences = tax reductions (+ tax increase) due to permanent differences/.35
$$= [(str - etr) \times \text{income before taxes}]/.35$$

In 2002, U.S. taxable income is estimated to be approximately $10,411 (ignoring the effects of any tax deduction from employee stock options) and worldwide taxable income is estimated to be $12,054 compared with reported pretax book income of $11,513. Recall from equation (A2.6) that

Difference between taxable and book
  income = temporary and permanent
  differences.

For 2002, the above table shows that taxable income exceeds book income ($12,054 − $11,513 = $541) because of temporary differences increasing taxable income relative to book income of $1,529 and permanent differences reducing taxable income relative to book income by $988.

Microsoft Corporation (extracts from 2002 Annual Report)
INCOME STATEMENTS

In millions, except earnings per share

Year Ended June 30	*2000*	*2001*	*2002*
Revenue	$22,956	$25,296	**$ 28,365**
Operating expenses:			
Cost of revenue	3,002	3,455	**5,191**
Research and development	3,772	4,379	**4,307**
Sales and marketing	4,126	4,885	**5,407**
General and administrative	1,050	857	**1,550**
Total operating expenses	11,950	13,576	**16,455**
Operating income	11,006	11,720	**11,910**
Losses on equity investees and other	(57)	(59)	**(92)**
Investment income/(loss)	3,326	(36)	**(305)**
Income before income taxes	14,275	11,525	**11,513**
Provision for income taxes	4,854	3,804	**3,684**
Income before accounting change	9,421	7,721	**7,829**
Cumulative effect of accounting change (net of income taxes of $185)	—	(375)	—
Net income	$ 9,421	$ 7,346	**$ 7,829**

Microsoft Corporation
BALANCE SHEETS

In millions

June 30	2001	2002
Assets		
Current assets:		
Cash and equivalents	$ 3,922	**$ 3,016**
Short-term investments	27,678	**35,636**
Total cash and short-term investments	31,600	**38,652**
Accounts receivable, net	3,671	**5,129**
Inventories	83	**673**
Deferred income taxes	1,522	**2,112**
Other	2,334	**2,010**
Total current assets	39,210	**48,576**
Property and equipment, net	2,309	**2,268**
Equity and other investments	14,361	**14,191**
Goodwill	1,511	**1,426**
Intangible assets, net	401	**243**
Other long-term assets	1,038	**942**
Total assets	$58,830	**$67,646**
Liabilities and stockholders' equity		
Current liabilities:		
Accounts payable	$ 1,188	**$ 1,208**
Accrued compensation	742	**1,145**
Income taxes	1,468	**2,022**
Short-term unearned revenue	4,395	**5,920**
Other	1,461	**2,449**
Total current liabilities	9,254	**12,744**
Long-term unearned revenue	1,219	**1,823**
Deferred income taxes	409	**398**
Other long-term liabilities	659	**501**
Commitments and contingencies		
Stockholders' equity:		
Common stock and paid-in capital— shares authorized 12,000; Shares issued and outstanding 5,383 and 5,359	28,390	**31,647**
Retained earnings, including accumulated other comprehensive income of $587 and $583	18,899	**20,533**
Total stockholders' equity	47,289	**52,180**
Total liabilities and stockholders' equity	$58,830	**$67,646**

Microsoft Corporation
NOTE 12   INCOME TAXES

The provision for income taxes consisted of:

In millions

Year Ended June 30	2000	2001	2002
Current taxes:			
U.S. and state	$4,744	$3,243	**$3,644**
International	535	514	**575**
Current taxes	5,279	3,757	**4,219**
Deferred taxes	(425)	47	**(535)**
Provision for income taxes	$4,854	$3,804	**$3,684**

U.S. and international components of income before income taxes were:

In millions

Year Ended June 30	2000	2001	2002
U.S.	$11,860	$ 9,189	**$ 8,920**
International	2,415	2,336	**2,593**
Income before income taxes	$14,275	$11,525	**$11,513**

In 2000, the effective tax rate was 34.0% and included the effect of a 2.5% reduction from the U.S. statutory rate for tax credits and a 1.5% increase for other items. In 2001, the effective tax rate was 33.0% and included the effect of a 3.1% reduction from the U.S. statutory rate for tax credits and a 1.1% increase for other items. The effective tax rate in 2002 was 32.0% and included the effect of a 2.4% reduction from the U.S. statutory rate for the extraterritorial income exclusion tax benefit and a 0.6% reduction for other items.

Deferred income taxes were:

In millions

June 30	2001	2002
Deferred income tax assets:		
Revenue items	$ 1,469	**$ 2,261**
Expense items	691	**945**
Impaired investments	1,070	**2,016**
Deferred income tax assets	$ 3,230	**$ 5,222**
Deferred income tax liabilities:		
Unrealized gain on investments	$ (395)	**$ (887)**
International earnings	(1,667)	**(1,818)**
Other	(55)	**(803)**
Deferred income tax liabilities	$ (2,117)	**$ (3,508)**

Microsoft has not provided for U.S. deferred income taxes or foreign withholding taxes on $780 million of its undistributed earnings for certain non-U.S. subsidiaries, all of which relate to fiscal 2002 earnings, since these earnings are intended to be reinvested indefinitely.

On September 15, 2000, the U.S. Tax Court issued an adverse ruling with respect to Microsoft's claim that the Internal Revenue Service (IRS) incorrectly assessed taxes for 1990 and 1991. The Company has filed an appeal with the Ninth Circuit Court of Appeals on this matter. Income taxes, except for items related to the 1990 and 1991 assessments, have been settled with the IRS for all years through 1996. The IRS is examining the Company's 1997 through 1999 U.S. income tax returns. Management believes any adjustments which may be required will not be material to the financial statements. Income taxes paid were $800 million in 2000, $1.3 billion in 2001, and $1.9 billion in 2002.

Discussion Questions

1. Provide an example of a tax rule designed to motivate a socially desirable activity that also motivates transactions that reduce a taxpayer's tax liabilities but serve no social purpose.
2. True or False? Discuss.
   a. Congress drafts very tight and specific tax rules to prevent taxpayers from misinterpreting them.
   b. Most tax legislation originates in the Senate.
   c. The Treasury drafts regulations and issues Revenue Rulings to clarify the tax rules.
   d. Revenue Rulings issued by the Treasury can be relied upon by taxpayers, while private letter rulings are valid only for the taxpayer who requested the ruling.
   e. The courts cannot change the substance of tax laws through their judicial rulings.
3. Why might Congress and the Treasury avoid drafting tax rules that are very specific? What costs would such rules impose on the Internal Revenue Service? What benefits might they bestow on certain taxpayers?
4. Outline the path of a tax bill through Congress from proposal to passage. Why might a final tax bill differ from the original proposal?
5. What are the sources and causes of complexity in our tax system? Which, if any, of these causes are correctable?
6. How do such judicial doctrines as substance-over-form and business-purpose affect taxpayer behavior? Is it socially beneficial to have such doctrines?
7. What incentives exist for taxpayers to shift income from one party to another? Are there costs associated with such income shifting? Give examples of such costs in a family-planning situation. How would the elimination of the assignment-of-income doctrine affect the costs of shifting income? What could taxpayers do to ease these costs?
8. Why do the tax laws sometimes discriminate against related-party contracts? Is this always in society's best interest?
9. Should the taxing authority always agree to provide a Revenue Ruling requested by a taxpayer to clarify the tax treatment of a proposed transaction? Should taxpayers requesting rulings be assessed a fee to cover the taxing authority's cost of responding?
10. Suppose the United States were to convert its tax system from an income tax to a national sales tax on sales of goods and services. Certain necessities, like food, would be exempted from taxation, and low-income households would be granted

tax refunds. Would such a tax system eliminate incentives to shift activities (a) from one period to the next, (b) from one type to another, and (c) from one pocket to another?

11. Suppose the United States were to convert its tax system from an income tax to a flat tax. For individuals there would be no itemized deductions allowed, a high standard exemption (thus low-income taxpayers would not have to file returns), and tax exemption for dividend and interest income. Businesses could deduct all expenditures on salaries and immediately expense asset acquisition costs. Would such a tax system eliminate incentives to shift activities (a) from one period to the next, (b) from one type to another, and (c) from one pocket to another? Do you believe a flat tax with no itemized deductions is politically feasible in the United States?

12. Assume you are an individual taxpayer. If you expected your marginal tax rate to decline in the next period, what tax planning might you undertake in the current period?

13. Below is an extract from Cisco Systems 2002 Annual Report. What is the firm's GAAP effective tax rate? Why does it differ from the top statutory tax rate? What are deferred taxes? What are the major deferred tax items for Cisco?

11. Income Taxes

The provision for income taxes consisted of the following (in millions):

Years Ended	July 27, 2002	July 28, 2001	July 29, 2000
Federal:			
Current	$929	$581	$1,843
Deferred	(480)	(697)	(652)
	449	(116)	1,191
State:			
Current	117	157	282
Deferred	(68)	(199)	(118)
	49	(42)	164
Foreign:			
Current	344	326	332
Deferred	(25)	(28)	(12)
	319	298	320
Total	**$817**	$140	$1,675

The Company paid income taxes of $909 million, $48 million, and $327 million in fiscal 2002, 2001, and 2000, respectively.

Income (loss) before provision for income taxes consisted of the following (in millions):

Years Ended	July 27, 2002	July 28, 2001	July 29, 2000
United States	**$1,550**	$(1,727)	$2,544
International	**1,160**	853	1,799
Total	**$2,710**	$ (874)	$4,343

The items accounting for the difference between income taxes computed at the federal statutory rate and the provision for income taxes consisted of the following:

Years Ended	July 27, 2002	July 28, 2001	July 29, 2000
Federal statutory rate	35.0%	(35.0)%	35.0%
Effect of:			
State taxes, net of federal tax benefit	1.8	(2.4)	1.9
Foreign sales corporation	(1.5)	(1.8)	(1.9)
Foreign income at other than U.S. rates	(4.9)	(1.7)	(1.6)
Nondeductible in-process R&D	0.9	30.3	7.6
Nondeductible goodwill	—	20.9	0.5
Nondeductible deferred stock-based compensation	1.9	8.0	—
Tax-exempt interest	—	(1.0)	(1.8)
Tax credits	(3.4)	(2.5)	(1.6)
Other, net	0.3	1.2	0.5
Total	**30.1%**	16.0%	38.6%

U.S. income taxes and foreign withholding taxes were not provided for on a cumulative total of $1.2 billion of undistributed earnings for certain non-U.S. subsidiaries. The Company intends to reinvest these earnings indefinitely in operations outside the United States.

The components of the deferred tax assets (liabilities) are as follows (in millions):

	July 27, 2002	July 28, 2001
ASSETS		
Allowance for doubtful accounts and returns	$ 247	$ 466
Lease reserves	281	325
Loan reserves	249	284
Inventory allowances and capitalization	340	706
Investment reserves	476	274
In-process R&D, goodwill, and purchased intangible assets	436	400
Deferred revenue	968	478
Credits and net operating loss carryforwards	391	414
Other	497	230
Total deferred tax assets	3,885	3,577
LIABILITIES		
Purchased intangible assets	(192)	(266)
Unrealized gains on investments	—	(1)
Other	—	(187)
Total deferred tax liabilities	(192)	(454)
Total	**$3,693**	$3,123

The following table presents the breakdown between current and noncurrent deferred tax assets (in millions):

	July 27, 2002	July 28, 2001
Current	$2,030	$1,809
Noncurrent	1,663	1,314
Total	$3,693	$3,123

The noncurrent portion of the deferred tax assets is included in other assets.

As of July 27, 2002, the Company's federal and state net operating loss carryforwards for income tax purposes were $83 million and $14 million, respectively. If not utilized, the federal net operating loss carryforwards will begin to expire in fiscal 2010 and the state net operating loss carryforwards will begin to expire in fiscal 2003. As of July 27, 2002, the Company's federal and state tax credit carryforwards for income tax purposes were $255 million and $164 million, respectively. If not utilized, the federal tax credit carryforwards will begin to expire in fiscal 2005 and state tax credit carryforwards will begin to expire in fiscal 2003.

The Company's income taxes payable for federal, state, and foreign purposes have been reduced, and the deferred tax assets increased, by the tax benefits associated with dispositions of employee stock options. The Company receives an income tax benefit calculated as the difference between the fair market value of the stock issued at the time of exercise and the option price, tax effected. These benefits were credited directly to shareholders' equity and amounted to $61 million, $1.8 billion, and $3.1 billion in fiscal 2002, 2001, and 2000, respectively. Benefits reducing taxes payable amounted to $61 million, $1.4 billion, and $2.5 billion in fiscal 2002, 2001, and 2000, respectively. Benefits increasing gross deferred tax assets amounted to $358 million and $582 million in fiscal 2001 and 2000, respectively.

The Company's federal income tax returns for fiscal years ended July 31, 1999, and July 25, 1998, are under examination and the Internal Revenue Service has proposed certain adjustments. Management believes that adequate amounts have been reserved for any adjustments that may ultimately result from these examinations.

Exercises

1. Suppose a taxpayer can time when he is to receive $100,000 of income that is fully taxable. Current interest rates are 10% on fully taxable securities and the taxpayer faces a current tax rate of 31%. If the taxpayer delays receipt the amount will grow to $110,000 at the end of year 2. The taxpayer must decide whether to receive the money today at the end of year 1 or at the end of year 2.
   a. When should the taxpayer elect to receive the income?
   b. Is there an interest rate at which the taxpayer is indifferent between the two options?
   c. The taxpayer expects tax rates to increase to 35% in year 2. Now when should he elect to receive the income?
   d. At what tax rate in period 2 is the taxpayer indifferent between the two options?
2. Suppose a taxpayer invests $100,000 in a partnership. The taxpayer faces a personal tax rate of 70% and a tax rate on capital gains of 28%. In the first year, the partnership spends the entire $100,000 on research, which the taxpayer can claim as a deduction against her other income. In the second year, the partnership sells the developed technology, and the taxpayer's share of the sale price is $50,000,

which is taxed as a capital gain. (Ignore the time value of money in your answer.)

    a. What is the pretax rate of return to the taxpayer?

    b. What is the after-tax rate of return to the taxpayer?

3. A taxpayer is the sole owner-employee of a small corporation that prepares tax returns. Before paying himself any salary or dividends or taking fringe benefits, the corporation has taxable income of $100,000. Summarize the tax consequences to both parties (the corporation and the taxpayer) of:

    a. paying a salary of $50,000.

    b. paying no salary but dividends of $50,000.

    c. providing $10,000 of fringe benefits and $40,000 of salary.

4. A taxpayer owns two separate companies. Company A is in the 35% marginal tax bracket and company B is in the 15% tax bracket. Company A sells all its output to B at cost, and B sells to outsiders at a markup of 50%. Company A's revenues total $2 million, while company B's revenues total $3 million. What are the tax implications of this arrangement? How will the IRS react?

5. A taxpayer owns and operates an art gallery with a large inventory of paintings held for sale to customers. She took one of the paintings home and hung it in her dining room. A week later, a dinner guest liked the painting so much that he purchased it at a large profit to the taxpayer. The taxpayer believed, since the painting was displayed at home, that it was a personal investment and therefore a capital asset with the profit treated as a capital gain. The painting cost the taxpayer $50,000 and was listed for sale while at the gallery for $90,000. The dinner guest paid $80,000 for the painting. As an IRS agent, how might you react? What tax do you think the IRS agent will assess the taxpayer (assuming the taxpayer faces the top statutory tax rates)?

6. Suppose a corporation (the investor company) owns 164 million shares in another corporation (the investee company). The investor company wishes to liquidate the majority of its holdings. The average basis per share of the investor company's holdings is $17.62, and the investee company is currently trading at $61 per share.[26]

    a. Assume that the investor company's tax rate is 35%. What are the tax consequences of an open market sale of 95% of its holdings in the investee company (that is, a sale of 156 million shares)?

    b. Note that the after-tax gain to the investor is the same if, instead of an open market sale, the investor sold the stock back to the investee company directly. Now instead of selling the stock back to the investee company, suppose the transaction could be structured such that the "sale proceeds" would be taxed as a dividend to the investor company. Further suppose the investor company could exclude from taxable income 80% of the dividend received (since the investor company owned approximately 25% of the investee company prior to this transaction). What are the tax consequences of dividend treatment of the "sales proceeds"?

    c. Which tax treatment is better for the investor company? What are the tax effects, if any, to the investee company? Are there any nontax costs to the dividend treatment?

---

[26]This problem is based on a real-world transaction. For an excellent analysis of the transaction, see Erickson and Wang (1999). Erickson and Wang discuss the rules that control dividend treatment for this transaction and how the two parties structured the transaction to satisfy the rules. Erickson and Wang also provide estimates of how the tax savings arising from dividend treatment were shared between the two parties. The interested reader is also referred to an article in *Forbes* entitled "The high cost of Hollywood" (*Forbes,* April 1997, pp. 44–45) which discusses the use to which Seagrams put the proceeds from liquidating its position in DuPont.

7. A taxpayer owns 100,000 shares of Microsoft Corporation that is currently valued at $10 million. The taxpayer purchased the stock for $10 per share and thus has an unrealized gain of $9 million. The taxpayer faces a tax rate of 20% on capital gains. He has heard about a tax deferral strategy called "shorting against the box." Explain this strategy to the taxpayer.

Tax Planning Problems

1. A taxpayer suffered a $20,000 capital loss early this year (from selling some securities) and is considering two alternatives for generating extra income. The first alternative is to find part-time employment at the local university teaching taxes. The second alternative is to purchase a "fixer-up" bungalow and to spend his evenings and weekends cleaning, repairing, and painting it, then selling the fixed-up property. The taxpayer estimates that his income before taxes would be about $45,000 from either alternative. Evaluate the taxpayer's options.

2. Taxpayer A earned $50,000 working as a carpenter during the year. Taxpayer B, also a carpenter by trade, worked the entire year renovating her house. Comment on the after-tax position of both carpenters. Does it matter if taxpayer B plans to live in her house one more year versus 10 more years?

3. A taxpayer is forming a new corporation and has $500,000 to invest in her company. Following the advice of her tax consultant, the taxpayer designated $300,000 for the purchase of corporate stock and $200,000 as a loan to the corporation. Comment on this tax plan.

4. A taxpayer is currently saving for his 14-year-old daughter's college education (out of his after-tax college salary). He faces a marginal tax rate of 28%. His daughter faces a marginal tax rate of 15%. How might the taxpayer increase the after-tax dollars available for his daughter's college bills? Are there any incentive problems (that is, nontax costs) with your plan?

5. A taxpayer uses borrowed funds to acquire non-dividend-paying corporate stock. Note that interest on borrowed funds may be deducted in the period paid, up to the amount of net investment income from other stocks or investments (that is, interest and dividend income). Comment on the tax consequences of this plan.

6. Firms that incur a tax loss are allowed to carryback the tax loss to obtain a refund of taxes previously paid. To the extent the losses cannot be carried back to obtain a refund (because past taxable income is less than the current tax loss) the losses can be carried forward to be deducted against future taxable income. The Taxpayer Relief Act of 1997 reduced the carryback period to 2 years from 3 years and extended the carryforward period to 20 years from 15 years beginning in 1998. Thus a firm with tax losses in 1997 could elect to carryback the losses to obtain a refund of 1994 taxes paid, then of 1995 taxes paid, and then of 1996 taxes paid (up to the point that the losses are fully offset).

   a. In general what effect will the shortening (lengthening) of the carryback (carryforward) period have on firms that incur a tax loss?

      Assume a firm in November 1997 expects to report a tax loss of $250,000 for the tax year 1997. The CFO argues that the firm should defer recognition of $50,000 of income until 1998, thus increasing the tax loss to be carried back to $300,000. The firm reported an annual taxable income of $100,000 in each of the past 5 years. The firm expects to earn $500,000 in 1998 (before any shifting of income). The firm uses an after-tax discount rate of 6% to discount cash flows. The statutory tax rate is expected to remain unchanged at 35%.

    b. Evaluate the CFO's plan. How much in taxes will the firm save if the CFO's plan is implemented?

    c. How much in taxes would the firm save if the statutory tax rate in the carryback period were 45% rather than 35%?

    d. Under what conditions would you advise a firm to carryforward a tax loss rather than carryback the tax loss to obtain an immediate tax refund?

7. The CEO of ABC Corporation is a dog lover. He and his spouse like cocker spaniels and have a pure-bred male cocker spaniel. Because of their love for dogs, they decide to breed and sell cocker spaniel pups. In the first year, they spend $25,000 building some kennels, $5,000 on veterinarian fees, $5,000 buying breeding females, and $1,000 on food and sundry supplies. By the end of the first year, they have successfully produced their first litters but have not yet sold any puppies. They would like to deduct their losses (which they calculate by simply summing all their expenditures, a total of $36,000), but they have heard something about hobby-activity loss rules. Under the IRC, for activities classified as hobbies, only losses up to any income generated by the activity can be deducted. If, however, the activity is classified as a trade or business, and the taxpayer is actively engaged in the business, the losses are deductible against the taxpayer's other income.

    a. Why might Congress distinguish between hobby activities and trade or business activities?

    b. If you were writing the Tax Code, what rules (or tests) would you write to distinguish an activity as a hobby versus a trade or business? Explain the purpose of each rule (or test).

    c. Would the CEO's dog breeding activity be classified as a hobby or business under your rules?

    d. Refer to one of the sources listed in Appendix 2.1 to ascertain the IRC rules for classification. Would the CEO's dog breeding activity be classified as a hobby or business under IRC rules?

    e. If the dog breeding activity was classified as a business, how much would the CEO be allowed to deduct against his other income?

References and Additional Readings

Anderson, K. E., T. R. Pope, and J. L. Kramer (Editors), 2001. *Federal Taxation 2001 Corporations, Partnerships, Estates and Trusts.* Upper Saddle River, NJ: Prentice Hall.

Battle, F., Jr., 1997. "Corporate Tax Shelters, Financial Engineering, and the *Colgate* Case," *Taxes* (December), pp. 692–705.

Enis, C., and L. Christ, 1999. "Implications of Phase-Outs on Individual Marginal Tax Rates," *Journal of the American Taxation Association* (Spring), pp. 45–72.

Erickson, M., and S. Wang, 1999. "Exploiting and Sharing Tax Benefits: Seagrams and Dupont," *Journal of the American Taxation Association* (Fall), pp. 35–54.

Frankel, M., and R. Trezevant, 1994. "The Year-End LIFO Inventory Purchasing Decision:

An Empirical Test," *The Accounting Review* (2), pp. 382–398.

Graetz, M., 1972. "Reflections on the Tax Legislative Process: Prelude to Reform," *Virginia Law Review* (November), pp. 1389–1450.

Guenther, D., 1994. "Earnings Management in Response to Corporate Tax Rate Changes: Evidence from the 1986 Tax Reform Act." *The Accounting Review* (1), pp. 230–243.

Hanlon, M., 2003a. "What Can We Infer About a Firm's Taxable Income from Its Financial Statements?" *National Tax Journal* (December), forthcoming.

Hanlon, M., 2003b. "The Persistence and Pricing of Earnings, Accruals and Cash Flows

When Firms Have Large Book-Tax Differences," Working paper. Ann Arbor, MI: University of Michigan, pp. 831–863.

Hanlon. M., S. Kelley, and T. Shevlin, 2003. "Evidence on the Possible Information Loss of Conforming Book Income and Taxable Income," Working paper. Seattle, WA: University of Washington.

Klassen, K., M. Lang, and M. Wolfson, 1993. "Geographic Income Shifting by Multinational Corporations in Response to Tax Rate Changes," *Journal of Accounting Research* (Supplement), pp. 141–173.

Klassen, K., and D. Shackelford, 1998. "State and Provincial Corporate Tax Planning: Income Shifting and Sales Apportionment Factor Management." *Journal of Accounting and Economics* (3), pp. 385–406.

Knott, A., and J. Rosenfeld, 2003. "Book and Tax (Part One): A Selective Exploration of Two Parallel Universes," *Tax Notes* (May), pp. 685–899.

Lightner, T., 1999. "The Effect of the Formulatory Apportionment System on State-Level Economic Development and Multijurisdictional Tax Planning," *Journal of the American Taxation Association* (Supplement), pp. 42–57.

Lopez, T., P. Regier, and T. Lee, 1998. "Identifying Tax-Induced Earnings Management around TRA 86 as a Function of Prior Tax-Aggressive Behavior," *Journal of the American Taxation Association* (2), pp. 37–56.

Manzon, G., and G. Plesko, 2002. "The Relation Between Financial and Tax Reporting Measures of Income," *Tax Law Review*, Vol. 55., pp. 175–214.

Maydew, E., 1997. "Tax-Induced Earnings Management by Firms with Net Operating Losses," *Journal of Accounting Research* (1), pp. 83–96.

Miller, G., and D. Skinner, 1998. "Determinants of the Valuation Allowance for Deferred Tax Assets under SFAS-109," *The Accounting Review* (April), pp. 213–234.

Mills, L., and K. Newberry, 2000. "Cross-Jurisdictional Income Shifting by Foreign-Controlled U.S. Corporations." Working paper. Tucson, AZ: University of Arizona.

Mills, L., K. Newberry, and W. Trautman, 2002. "Trends in Book-Tax Income and Balance Sheet Differences," *Tax Notes* (August), pp. 1109–1124.

Murray, A., and J. Birnbaum, 1987. *Showdown at Gucci Gulch*. Random House.

Phillips, J., M. Pincus, and S. Olhoft Rego, 2003. "Earnings Management: New Evidence Based on Deferred Tax Expense," *The Accounting Review* (March), pp. 491–521.

Plesko, G., 2002. "Reconciling Corporation Book and Tax Net Income, Tax Years 1996–1998," *SOI Bulletin* (Spring), pp. 1–16.

Pope, T. R., K. E. Anderson, and J. L. Kramer (Editors), 2001. *Federal Taxation 2001 Individuals.* Upper Saddle River, NJ: Prentice Hall.

Revsine, L., D. W. Collins, and W. B. Johnson, 2002. *Financial Reporting & Analysis.* Upper Saddle River, NJ: Prentice Hall.

Scholes, M., P. Wilson, and M. Wolfson, 1992. "Firms' Responses to Anticipated Reductions in Tax Rates: The Tax Reform Act of 1986," *Journal of Accounting Research* (Supplement), pp. 161–191.

U.S. Department of Treasury, 1999. *The Problem of Corporate Tax Shelters: Discussion, Analysis and Legislative Proposals* (July).

Weber, R., and J. Wheeler, 1992. "Using Income Tax Disclosures to Explore Significant Economic Transactions," *Accounting Horizons* (September), pp. 14–29.

Wheeler, J., and E. Outslay, 1986. "The Phantom Federal Income Taxes of General Dynamics Corporation," *The Accounting Review* (October), pp. 760–774.

CHAPTER 3

RETURNS ON ALTERNATIVE SAVINGS VEHICLES

After completing this chapter, you should be able to:

1. List six alternative savings vehicles and describe their differing tax treatment.

2. Calculate the after-tax accumulations and after-tax rates of return to the six savings vehicles.

3. Explain and illustrate the advantage of an investment's tax deductibility.

4. Explain and illustrate the advantage of deferring taxation.

5. Explain and illustrate the effect of tax rate changes over time on the various savings vehicles.

6. Compare investment in a deductible IRA with a Roth IRA pension account.

7. Evaluate the rollover decision from a deductible IRA to a Roth IRA.

In this chapter, we begin by discussing different legal organizational forms through which individuals save for the future. To facilitate comparisons, the same underlying investment will be held in each of the savings vehicles. As a result, the before-tax rates of return will be identical in each case. The investment returns will be taxed quite differently across the alternatives, however, so the after-tax rates of return will differ widely. Examples of organizational forms used as savings vehicles include money market mutual funds and pension fund accounts. In the next chapter we discuss alternative organizational forms, such as corporations and partnerships, through which goods and services are produced. Our major objective is to introduce some basic algebra that we will exploit throughout subsequent chapters. Algebra offers a powerful tool to capture and present the differences in taxation across different savings vehicles and organizational forms.

In the absence of transaction and information costs (or frictions) and/or explicit restrictions imposed by the taxing authority, different after-tax returns across the savings vehicles would allow investors to eliminate their taxes by employing tax arbitrage strategies. By tax arbitrage, we mean earning a relatively high after-tax rate of return by investing through a tax-favored organizational form, financed at a relatively low after-tax cost by borrowing through a different organizational form. We defer a discussion of the nature of existing restrictions and frictions that keep the system in check until we cover some preliminaries. At this stage, our objective is simply to demonstrate the sensitivity of investment performance to differences in the tax treatment across alternative savings arrangements. This is why we assume that the before-tax rates of return are identical across the alternatives. It allows us to turn only one dial at a time. With differing underlying investments, after-tax returns would differ because of both risk and tax differences, and, as a result, it would be difficult to separate the effects of the different tax treatments on after-tax returns.

We begin in Section 3.1 by comparing the relative attractiveness of six differently taxed savings vehicles when tax rates are constant year to year. In Section 3.2, we demonstrate how changes in tax rates over time can affect the relative attractiveness of the six savings arrangements. Finally, in Section 3.3, we apply the concepts to an analysis of deductible IRAs and Roth IRA pension accounts.

3.1 INTERTEMPORALLY CONSTANT TAX RATES

We assume in this section that tax rates are constant over time. We also assume that our investor cannot affect the before-tax rates of return on the investment by buying more or less of it. In other words, the market for investment is perfectly competitive. We begin by considering some relatively straightforward ways to save for future consumption. In particular, suppose that the only investment that can be held in each organizational form is an interest-bearing security such as a fully secured (virtually riskless) corporate bond.

Table 3.1 lists six categories of savings vehicles that are distinguished by their tax attributes. Tax treatments across the six savings vehicles differ along three dimensions:

1. Whether deposits into the savings accounts give rise to an immediate tax deduction (only Vehicle VI does).
2. The frequency with which investment earnings are taxed (annually as in Vehicles I and III; only when the investment is liquidated as in Vehicles II, IV, and VI; or never as in Vehicle V).
3. The rate at which the investment earnings are taxed (ordinary rates as in Vehicles I, II, and VI; capital gains rates as in Vehicles III and IV; or complete tax exemption as in Vehicle V).

Each of these different organizational forms has existed in the United States as well as in many foreign tax jurisdictions. Examples of Savings Vehicle I include corporate bonds and money market accounts offered by mutual funds, banks, and savings and loan associations. A common example of Savings Vehicle II in the United States is a single premium deferred annuity contract (SPDA) offered by insurance companies (explained below). Vehicle III includes certain mutual funds, and Vehicle IV includes shares in certain corporations located in tax jurisdictions where the interest on investment is tax exempt. While Savings Vehicles III and IV are relatively rare, Savings

TABLE 3.1 Six Different Legal Organizational Forms (Savings Vehicles) Through Which Investors Can Hold Riskless Bonds

Savings Vehicle (Example)	*Is the Investment Tax Deductible?*	*Frequency That Earnings Are Taxed*	*Rate at Which Earnings Are Taxed*	*After-Tax Accumulation per After-Tax Dollar $I Invested*
I (Money market fund)	No	Annually	Ordinary	$\$I[1 + R(1 - t)]^n$
II (Single premium deferred annuity)	No	Deferred	Ordinary	$\$I(1 + R)^n(1 - t) + t\$I$
III (Mutual fund)	No	Annually	Capital gains	$\$I[1 + R(1 - t_{cg})]^n$
IV (Foreign corporation)	No	Deferred	Capital gains	$\$I(1 + R)^n(1 - t_{cg}) + t_{cg}\$I$
V (Insurance policy)	No	Never	Exempt	$\$I(1 + R)^n$
VI (Pension)	Yes	Deferred	Ordinary	$\left[\frac{\$I}{(1-t)}\right](1 + R)^n(1 - t)$ or $\$I(1 + R)^n$

where: R = before-tax rate of return

n = number of time periods

t = tax rate applicable to ordinary income

t_{cg} = tax rate applicable to capital gains income

Vehicles V and VI are used heavily. Examples of Savings Vehicle V include 529 College Savings Plans (named after the Tax Code section), Roth Individual Retirement Accounts, Education Savings Accounts, the savings portion of certain life insurance policies in the United States, and postal (so-called *maruyu*) accounts in Japan. An example of Vehicle VI is a pension account (including the Traditional, or Classic, Individual Retirement Account). Note, however, the label attached in parentheses to each savings vehicle is for convenience only. It is the tax characteristics of the vehicles we wish to stress and the effects on the after-tax rates of return.[1] Thus instead of thinking in terms of savings vehicles, the reader could think in terms of what happens to the after-tax rate of return as we vary the taxation of the investment, holding constant the pretax rate of return on the investment.

In the following discussion, we elaborate on the examples presented in the parentheses, but we avoid technical nuances that apply to each of them. Discussing these nuances would simply cloud the general points and obscure the taxonomy we are

---

[1]For example, Savings Vehicle III is labeled a mutual fund but this mutual fund should not be confused with a common stock mutual fund. Investors in a common stock mutual fund will be taxed annually on any dividends received on stock held by the mutual fund even though such dividends are not distributed to the mutual fund investors. Similarly, the mutual fund investors will be taxed annually on any capital gains realized by the mutual fund as it trades stock in its portfolio. See Bergstresser and Poterba (2002) for a discussion of taxation of mutual funds and how this affects investors' choice of which funds to invest in. We will see in the next chapter that Savings Vehicle IV represents the tax position of investors in non-dividend-paying corporations such as Cisco Systems and Amazon.com.

developing in this chapter. We do look at each of these investment alternatives more fully in subsequent chapters. Throughout the text we will use capital R to denote the pretax rate of return and lowercase r to denote the after-tax rate of return. For a 1-year investment in a simple interest-bearing savings account, the after-tax rate of return $r = R(1 - t)$.

In Table 3.1, we show the after-tax accumulations per after-tax dollar of initial investment ($\$I$) of six different legal organizational forms through which investors can hold our riskless asset.[2] The after-tax accumulations are a function of their respective tax treatments, the before-tax rate of return on the investment, the number of periods the investment is held, and the tax rates on ordinary income and capital gains. Examples of ordinary income include wages earned from employment and interest earned on bonds, while examples of capital gains income include the realized gain on the sale of common stock or other investments.

Review of Compound Interest

An understanding of the algebraic expressions in Table 3.1 requires an understanding of the simple principle of compound interest. If $\$I$ is invested at (an after-tax) rate r per period, and the principal plus interest is reinvested for n periods, the accumulation after n periods is

$$\$I[(1+r)(1+r)\ldots(1+r)], \quad \text{or} \quad \$I(1+r)^n \tag{3.1}$$

For example, if the after-tax rate of return on investment is 12% per year, the after-tax accumulation per dollar invested for 10 years is $(1 + .12)^{10} = \$3.11$. We denote this accumulation as F (for future value of the investment). If we wish to know the annualized rate of return, r, we start by noting that $F = \$I(1 + r)^n$. Solving for r, we get $r = (F/\$I)^{1/n} - 1$. For example, if we know that a $1 investment today accumulates to $3.11 in 10 years, we compute the annualized rate of return as 12% per year $(\$3.11/\$1)^{(1/10)} - 1 = .12$, or 12%.

In the case of Savings Vehicle I, tax at rate t must be paid each period on the interest earned at the before-tax rate R. The after-tax interest rate earned each period r, then, is $R - tR$, or $R(1 - t)$. Substituting $R(1 - t)$ for r in expression 3.1 above yields

$$\$I[1 + R(1 - t)]^n$$

which is the expression given in Table 3.1.

Investments in Savings Vehicles I and II

Savings Vehicle I: Deposits into a **money market savings account** are not tax deductible. Earnings on the investment are typically taxed fully each year at ordinary tax rates. Savings Vehicle I is the least tax advantageous of our savings vehicles in the sense that it produces the lowest after-tax accumulation when individual tax rates are assumed to be constant over time.

Savings Vehicle II: Deposits into a **single premium deferred annuity** (SPDA) contract through an insurance company in the United States are not tax deductible. The taxes on the investment earnings, however, are deferred and taxed at ordinary income tax rates only when the investor takes money out of the contract.

---

[2]Table 3.1 is reproduced on the inside back cover of this book.

Although slightly oversimplified, the mechanics of an SPDA investment follow. The investor turns over cash to an insurance company, which in turn invests in interest-bearing securities. The insurance company pays no taxes on the interest it accumulates from holding the securities on behalf of its policyholders. In this way, the insurance company effectively acts as a conduit through which investors save. Another example of Savings Vehicle II that might be more familiar is the nondeductible individual retirement account (nondeductible IRA). Contributions are not tax deductible (that is, contributions are made with after-tax dollars), and earnings are not taxed until withdrawn in retirement when they are taxed as ordinary income.

The value of deferral (and hence the attractiveness of Vehicle II over Vehicle I) can be considerable. In Savings Vehicle II, the investment earnings compound at the before-tax rate of return R rather than at the after-tax rate of return, $R(1 - t)$, as in Vehicle I. Just prior to liquidation of the investment, then, each dollar invested in Vehicle II grows to $(1 + R)^n$. Tax at rate t is paid only on the earnings $[(1 + R)^n - 1]$ at the end of time period n when the account is liquidated. This leaves the investor with

$$\$I(1 + R)^n - t[\$I(1 + R)^n - \$I]$$

where the first term is the pretax accumulation and the second term is the tax due on the earnings. This equation can be simplified to

$$\$I(1 + R)^n - t\$I(1 + R)^n + t\$I = \$I(1 + R)^n(1 - t) + t\$I \qquad \text{(3.2)}$$

which is the expression given for Savings Vehicle II in Table 3.1. Another way to look at this result is to note that investors pay tax on the entire accumulation except the initial investment of $\$I$.

In Table 3.2 we illustrate the after-tax accumulation and the after-tax annualized rate of return achieved by investing in Savings Vehicles I and II for different holding periods, assuming that $R = 7\%$ and $t = 30\%$. The after-tax accumulations are plotted in Figure 3.1. The after-tax rate of return on Savings Vehicle I, a money market account, would be $7\% \times (1 - .30) = 4.9\%$ per year after tax. This is true no matter how long the investment horizon is. In contrast, the after-tax rate of return on Savings Vehicle II, an SPDA, changes with its holding period. To calculate the after-tax rate of return per year on Savings Vehicle II, we must first find the after-tax accumulation for a given holding period. Let us suppose that an investor deposits $1 in Savings Vehicle II

TABLE 3.2 After-Tax Accumulation per Dollar Invested and Rates of Return for Different Holding Periods for Savings Vehicles I and II When $R = 7\%$ and $t = 30\%$

Holding Period (n):	1	5	10	20	40	100	1000
			After-Tax Accumulation ($)				
Savings Vehicle							
I	1.05	1.27	1.61	2.60	6.78	119.55	5.96×10^{20}
II	1.05	1.28	1.68	3.01	10.78	607.70	1.69×10^{29}
			After-Tax Rates of Return per Period (%)				
Savings Vehicle							
I	4.90	4.90	4.90	4.90	4.90	4.90	4.90
II	4.90	5.09	5.31	5.66	6.12	6.62	6.96

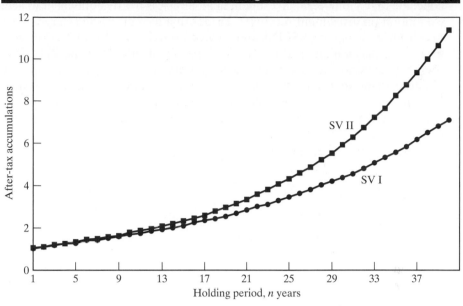

FIGURE 3.1   After-Tax Accumulations to Savings Vehicles I and II: $R = 7\%$, $t = 30\%$

for 5 years. This $1 accumulates to $1.28 after tax (as shown in Table 3.2, under a holding period of 5 years). To show how $1.28 was derived, note that an investment of $1 for 5 years at 7% grows to $1(1.07)^5$, or $1.40 before tax. At the end of 5 years, on withdrawing the accumulated sum from the account, tax is owed on the amount withdrawn in excess of the initial investment. In this example, the excess is equal to $.40, and the tax on the excess is .30 × $.40, or $.12, leaving $1.28 after tax (or $1.40 − $.12).

Alternatively, using equation (3.2), we can derive the same after-tax dollar amount directly:

$$\$1(1.07)^5(1 - .30) + \$1(.30) = (\$1.40 \times .7) + \$.30 = \$1.28$$

Notice that except for investment horizons of only one period (when an SPDA becomes equivalent to a money market account), the after-tax accumulation in an SPDA (Vehicle II) always exceeds that in a money market account (Vehicle I)—remember, we are assuming here that the taxpayer faces constant across time tax rates. Moreover, the longer the holding period, the greater the difference in the accumulation. After 40 years, for example, $1 accumulates to $10.78 after tax in an SPDA, or 59% more than the $6.78 in a money market account.

The after-tax annual rates of return are shown in the bottom panel of Table 3.2. For example, after 5 years an investment of $1 in Vehicle I grows to $1.27, which translates to an annual rate of return of $(1.27)^{(1/5)} - 1$, or 4.9%. All of the after-tax annualized rates of return are 4.9% in a money market savings account, but these rates increase in an SPDA with the number of holding periods. In fact, as the number of periods becomes large, the after-tax rate of return per period approaches the before-tax rate of 7%.

Although 7% is equal to the before-tax rate of return, we must be careful not to conclude that a long-term investment in an SPDA is nearly equivalent to achieving tax exemption on investment returns. Consider that as n grows very large, the accumulation from investing in an SPDA approaches a fraction of $(1 - t)$ (or 70% in our example) of the accumulation from investing tax-free at rate R per period.[3] The reason is that as the investment horizon becomes very large, nearly all of the return to the SPDA is interest (the original dollar deposited becomes relatively unimportant over long investment periods), and when the SPDA is cashed out, the earnings (which represent almost the entire contract when n is very large) will be taxed fully at ordinary rates.[4]

Hybrid Savings Vehicles

Although not listed in Table 3.1, certain savings vehicles permit tax deferral on only a part of the earnings until the investment is liquidated. Previously untaxed earnings are then taxed at ordinary rates. This savings vehicle is taxed as a hybrid of Vehicles I and II. With some important exceptions that we discuss in the chapters on multinational tax planning, some foreign income is not taxable in the investor's home country until it is repatriated. Since the interest earned is taxed at a lower rate than in the home country, it compounds faster than if the same investment were made at home. The after-tax return available through this hybrid vehicle will always be between that available in Vehicle I (no deferral) and Vehicle II (100% deferral). Certain trusts can also give rise to this hybrid tax treatment.[5] Still another example is a contingent interest bond, where part of the interest is paid at maturity as a function of some performance index.

Differences in After-Tax Accumulations in Savings Vehicles I and II as a Function of Pretax Rates of Return

The advantage of an SPDA over a money market account increases with the level of pretax rates of return. For example, if R were 12% rather than 7%, Vehicle I would accumulate to $5.02 in 20 years, and Vehicle II would accumulate to $7.05 for each dollar invested. Vehicle II returns just over 40% more than does Vehicle I when $R = 12\%$, whereas Table 3.2 indicates that Vehicle II beats Vehicle I by less than 16% ($3.01 versus $2.60) when $R = 7\%$.

Investments in Savings Vehicle III

Deposits into Vehicle III are nondeductible, as in Vehicles I and II. Unlike Vehicles I and II, however, investment earnings are taxed periodically at capital gains tax rates. There is generally a distinction between the rates at which capital gains income and ordinary income are taxed. Most countries exclude a substantial portion of capital

---

[3]Suppose $n = 40$ years and you invest at 7% tax-free per year ($R = .07$). The investment will accumulate to $(1 + .07)^{40} = \$14.97$ compared with the accumulation of $10.78 reported in Table 3.2 for an SPDA invested for 40 years with $R = .07$ and $t = 30\%$. Note that $10.78 is $(1 - t)$, or 70% of $14.97.

[4]SPDAs are available to individual taxpayers. An additional excise tax of 10% is levied if the SPDA is surrendered, in part or in whole, prior to age 59.5, unless withdrawals take the form of a life annuity.

[5]A trust is a legal entity through which property is managed by one party for the benefit of another. For U.S. income tax purposes, the undistributed earnings of a trust are often taxed to the trust rather than to the beneficiary. The hybrid tax treatment discussed in the text can be achieved in certain cases when the tax rate of the trust is below that of the beneficiary.

gains from taxation. Capital gains and losses arise from the sale or exchange of capital assets, including such passive investments as common stocks, bonds, and real estate. Between 1921 and 1987, U.S. tax laws distinguished between capital gains and ordinary income rates. The distinction in rates disappeared in many circumstances in 1988 with the top statutory capital gains rate and ordinary income rates being set at 28% from 1988–1991. The capital gains rate remained at 28% through 1996, with the top tax rate on ordinary income rising to 31% in 1992 and 39.6% in 1993–1996. In 1997, the top capital gains tax rate was reduced to 20%, but the holding period required for capital gains treatment increased from 12 to 18 months. The holding period was reduced to 12 months in 1998. The top capital gains tax rate was further reduced to 15% in 2003. Thus the top capital gains rate is now less than half that of the top rate on ordinary income. In addition, the difference between capital gain and ordinary income treatment is particularly important in the United States in several other circumstances:

- If property is transferred by bequest, the capital gains rate remains zero;
- If property is transferred by gift to a lower tax-bracket taxpayer, the effective capital gains tax rate becomes the donee's lower tax rate;
- If a taxpayer has sold other capital assets at a loss, the capital gains tax rate could vary between 0% and the ordinary rate, depending on how binding the so-called capital loss limitations are.

At this point you need not understand these specific sources of difference between ordinary income rates and capital gains rates. You should simply be aware that in many circumstances the distinction is important. You should also be aware that the difference between ordinary income and capital gains tax rates are likely to change numerous times in the future. We address some of the implications of the likelihood of future changes in tax rates in Section 3.2.

The Vehicle III category includes arrangements where capital gain is recognized annually through "mark-to-market" rules or annual "sale." Mark-to-market means that the asset is marked up to its market value at year-end. Mark-to-market rules apply to futures contracts in the United States, where they are classified as capital assets and where assets still held at year-end are taxed *as if* they were sold at that time. The annual sale treatment would apply to certain mutual funds that invest exclusively in our fully taxable bonds and that distribute annual income by repurchasing mutual fund shares from fundholders. The share repurchase triggers capital gains treatment equal to the income on the underlying bonds held in the fund.

Comparison of Savings Vehicles II and III

Savings Vehicle III may be more or less attractive than Savings Vehicle II depending on n, the length of time the investment is held, and t_{cg}, the tax rate on capital gains. For example, if $t_{cg} = 0$, Vehicle III always dominates Vehicle II, even for $n = 1$. In this case, the returns on the investment are tax exempt. For $0 < t_{cg} < t$, Vehicle III dominates Vehicle II for short investment horizons, but Vehicle II dominates Vehicle III for long investment horizons.

Assume, for example, that $t_{cg} = .5t$, that is, the capital gains rate is half the ordinary rate. At the end of year 1, then, \$1 grows to $[1 + R(1 - .5t)]$. When $R = 7\%$ and $t = 30\%$ (implying $t_{cg} = 15\%$), the after-tax return is 5.95% (or $7\%(1 - .5 \times 30\%)$) per year. This return exceeds the money market savings account return by 1.05% per year (or $5.95\% - 7\%(1 - 30\%)$). The 15% tax rate reduction on capital gains (relative to ordinary income) multiplied by the 7% pretax return yields the 1.05% after-tax return difference. Earning 5.95% per year after-tax in Savings Vehicle III dominates the after-tax return from investing in SPDAs (Savings Vehicle II) for holding periods of up to 31 years. Beyond 31 years, SPDAs provide the superior after-tax investment returns.[6]

Investments in Savings Vehicle IV

In Savings Vehicle IV, as with the preceding vehicles, deposits are not tax deductible. However, the tax on the earnings is deferred and taxed at capital gains rates when the investment is liquidated. Examples of this vehicle include investments in the common stock of an investment company located in a tax-haven country (that is, one in which the tax rate is near 0%)[7] and bond investments held by corporations in tax-haven countries.[8]

Note from the formula given in Table 3.1 that the accumulation in Vehicle IV is similar to that for Vehicle II except that income from Vehicle IV is taxed at the more favorable capital gains rate t_{cg} rather than at the ordinary rate t. Vehicle IV is superior to Vehicles II and III except for special cases: $t_{cg} = 0$ (capital gains are tax exempt, as they have been for many taxpayers in a number of countries) and $t_{cg} = t$ (capital gains are taxed at ordinary rates as in the United States in 1988–1990). When $t_{cg} = 0$, Vehicles III and IV both yield after-tax returns equal to before-tax rates of return (of 7% in our example). When $t_{cg} = t$, Vehicle IV becomes equivalent to an SPDA (that is, Vehicle II). Table 3.3 illustrates the superiority of Vehicle IV over Vehicles I and II

TABLE 3.3 After-Tax Accumulation per Dollar Invested and Rates of Return for Different Holding Periods for Savings Vehicles I, II, and IV When $R = 7\%$, $t_{cg} = .5t$, and $t = 30\%$

Holding Period (n):	5	10	20	40	100	1000
			After-Tax Accumulation ($)			
Savings Vehicle						
I	1.27	1.61	2.60	6.78	119.55	5.96×10^{20}
II	1.28	1.68	3.01	10.78	607.70	1.69×10^{29}
III	1.34	1.82	3.44	12.88	737.71	2.06×10^{29}
			After-Tax Rates of Return per Period (%)			
Savings Vehicle						
I	4.90	4.90	4.90	4.90	4.90	4.90
II	5.09	5.31	5.66	6.12	6.62	6.96
III	6.06	6.18	6.37	6.60	6.83	6.98

---

[6]Specifically, for $n = 31$ years, the SPDA earns 5.95% per year, which equals the annual after-tax return on the mutual fund, and for $n = 32$ years, the SPDA earns 5.97%.

[7]This opportunity is no longer available for investors in companies that invest only in passive investments such as stocks and bonds. These companies are classified as "passive foreign investment companies" and income is *de facto* taxed as earned at ordinary tax rates (as Savings Vehicle I). This opportunity still exists, however, for investors resident in a number of other countries.

[8]The corporation holding bonds in tax-haven countries must be engaged in real economic activities, rather than just holding passive investments, if the U.S. shareholder is to qualify for Vehicle IV tax treatment. For the qualifying corporation, interest income is tax-free to the tax-haven corporation. For U.S. shareholders, income is subject to capital gains taxation when shares are sold or when the corporation is liquidated, as long as the corporation is not a so called "controlled foreign corporation"—that is, it does not have five U.S. shareholders that together own more than 50% of the common stock.

FIGURE 3.2   After-Tax Accumulations to Savings Vehicles I, II, and IV. $R = 7\%$, $t = 30\%$, $t_{cg} = 15\%$

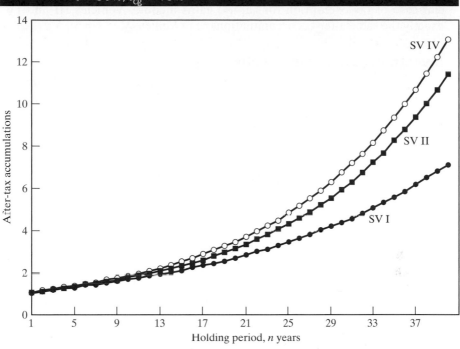

when capital gains are taxed at half the ordinary rates. The after-tax accumulations are plotted in Figure 3.2.

Investments in Savings Vehicle V

While deposits into Savings Vehicle V accounts are not tax deductible, the earnings on the investment are entirely tax exempt. An example of this investment vehicle is the 529 College Savings Plan. After-tax dollars are contributed and for tax years after December 31, 2001, distributions are tax-free provided they are used for qualified college-related education expenses. A second example is the Education Savings Account where distributions to fund education (not just college) related expenses are tax-free. Contributions however are limited to $2,000 per beneficiary per year. A third example is the savings portion of a whole life (or universal life) insurance contract. As we discuss more fully in later chapters, a whole life policy consists of term (or pure) insurance plus a savings account. Earnings on bonds held in the saving account are tax exempt, so the pretax return is also equal to the after-tax return. Insurance companies typically invest the savings portion of the portfolio in ordinary interest-bearing securities.[9]

---

[9]If the insurance policy is surrendered prior to death, a portion of the interest may be taxable as ordinary income. In particular, if withdrawals from the policy exceed the premiums paid into the policy (including both the savings and the insurance components of the premiums), the excess is taxed as ordinary income. In this case, the insurance policy becomes an example of Savings Vehicle II. Why? Because only a portion of the interest income is taxable (only that portion of the interest that exceeds the term insurance premiums), and even this is taxable only when and if the policy is surrendered for cash.

Note that the after-tax accumulation in Savings Vehicle V dominates that for Savings Vehicles I through IV as long as the capital gains tax rate is not 0%. In the special case of tax exemption for capital gains income, Vehicles III and IV generate exactly the same after-tax accumulations as in Vehicle V.

Investments in Savings Vehicle VI

In Savings Vehicle VI, the investment is tax deductible, and investment earnings are tax deferred. An example is a pension plan. While contributions to the plan are tax deductible and earnings on investments in the plan are not taxed, distributions from the plan are fully taxable to the pensioner.[10]

Each dollar deposited into the pension fund grows to $(1 + R)^n$ dollars in n periods before the pension assets are distributed to the taxpayer and to $(1 + R)^n(1 - t)$ dollars after tax if the entire accumulation is taxed at rate t at time n when it is withdrawn.[11] Because each dollar invested in the pension fund costs only $(1 - t)$ dollars after tax, the after-tax return per after-tax dollar invested is

$$\frac{\$1}{(1 - t)}(1 + R)^n(1 - t) = (1 + R)^n$$

When tax rates are constant over time, Vehicles V and VI are equivalent; that is, pension savings are equivalent to tax exemption. Think of the pension fund as a tax-free partnership with the government. For every $(1 - t)$ dollars you invest in the partnership, your partner (the government) invests t dollars. Collectively, the partnership has $1 invested. This dollar grows at rate R each period for n periods. Before liquidating, the partnership has accumulated $(1 + R)^n$ dollars. You are entitled to a fraction $(1 - t)$ of the partnership assets, and your partner takes the remaining fraction t. So you take home $(1 + R)^n(1 - t)$ dollars on an initial investment of $(1 - t)$ dollars. Your return per dollar invested is simply $(1 + R)^n$.

Dominance Relations and Empirical Anomalies

Up to this point, we have demonstrated that investors realize different after-tax rates of return on identical assets held through different legal organizational forms. We have shown several strict dominance relations among the savings vehicles—that is, investors would always prefer to avoid some of the savings vehicles. In the absence of frictions and restrictions, we would never observe such tax-disfavored savings vehicles as ordinary money market savings. And yet, in the real world, money market savings command a larger share of our savings than most tax-favored forms of savings. The reasons, as we have suggested earlier, stem largely from frictions and restrictions.

---

[10]We initially ignore here the penalties for early withdrawal from pension plans (that is, a 10% non-deductible excise tax penalty on withdrawal before age 59.5).

[11]Note that the earnings in the pension account are taxed as ordinary income when withdrawn even if the investment in the account generated capital gains (or were even tax exempt if the pension invested in tax-exempt municipal bonds). This raises the question as to what types of assets taxpayers should put in their pension accounts. We defer this question to Chapter 9 where we discuss pensions in greater detail. We are also assuming here for simplicity that the earnings in the pension account are taken as a lump-sum payment and not spread out as an annuity.

3.2 CHANGES IN TAX RATES OVER TIME

In this section we relax the assumption of constant tax rates through time. Note however for pedagogical reasons we assume here that future tax rates are known. We relax this assumption in later chapters. Even without frictions and restrictions, the dominance relations derived in Section 3.1 disappear when we introduce intertemporal changes in tax rates. In such a setting, Vehicles V and VI are no longer equivalent; tax-exempt saving through an insurance account is no longer equivalent to saving through a pension account. In particular, when tax rates are rising over time, pensions (and single premium deferred annuities) become less attractive, and when tax rates are falling over time, they become *more* attractive.

Vehicle V returns $(1 + R)^n$, irrespective of tax rates, but Vehicle VI returns:

$$\frac{\$1}{(1 - t_0)}(1 + R)^n(1 - t_n) \tag{3.3}$$

where the subscript on each tax rate refers to the time at which taxes are saved or paid. A subscript of 0 indicates the tax rate in the period when the contribution is made, assumed here to be the current period, and the subscript n indicates the tax rate in the future period n when withdrawals are made. When $t_n > t_0$ (that is, tax rates in retirement at time n are relatively high), Vehicle V is superior. Conversely, if $t_n < t_0$ (that is, tax rates today are relatively high), Vehicle VI is superior.

As mentioned previously, we can view a pension plan as a tax-exempt partnership with the government in which the taxpayer puts up a fraction $(1 - t_0)$ of the capital in exchange for a fraction $(1 - t_n)$ of the liquidation proceeds from the partnership. The taxpayer does better than tax exemption when t_n is lower than t_0, and worse than tax exemption when t_n is higher.

For example, consider a situation faced by many high-income taxpayers following the passage of the Tax Reform Act of 1986. Suppose the marginal tax rate in 1986 was 50%, but the rate was expected to fall to 28% in retirement. With this configuration of tax rates, a pension provides an after-tax accumulation of 44% more than complete tax exemption! Using equation (3.3):

$$\frac{1}{(1 - t_0)}(1 + R)^n(1 - t_n) = \frac{1}{(1 - .50)}(1 + R)^n(1 - .28) = 1.44(1 + R)^n$$

Conversely, in 1992, many high-income taxpayers, facing tax rates of 31%, expected tax rates to increase by the time they retired. If they expected rates to increase to 40% at the time of retirement (recall the top tax rate increased to 39.6% in 1993), then pensions would accumulate to

$$\frac{1}{(1 - .31)}(1 + R)^n(1 - .40) = .87(1 + R)^n$$

or 13% *less* after tax than complete tax exemption. In this case, investing in the pension plan is exactly the same as investing in a tax-exempt insurance policy that imposes a back-end termination fee of 13% on all distributions.

In fact, when tax rates are increasing, the pension plan is even worse than investing in a money market savings account over short investment horizons. If current tax rates are 28% and will increase to 40% in 5 years ($n = 5$) and $R = 7\%$, a pension investment accumulates at a rate of only 3.2% per year after tax, or 1.7% less per year than ordinary money market savings.[12] By comparison, an SPDA contract would yield 4.4%, well above the pension return but still below the 4.9% available on ordinary money market savings.[13]

Conversely, for $n = 10$, the after-tax return from investing in a pension plan is 5.1% per year, which is better than investing in money market savings. Moreover, it now beats the 4.7% return available through SPDAs. The best after-tax return among all of the alternatives when tax rates are expected to rise in the future is the 7% available through investing in Savings Vehicle V such as universal life insurance policies.

The best alternative among the savings vehicles depends not only on how a particular organizational form is taxed but also on how tax rates in the future are expected to differ from current rates. While one particular organizational form may dominate another when tax rates remain constant, the ranking could change if tax rates increase or decrease in the future. When we add frictions and restrictions, the rankings change further and in ways that differ across taxpayers, even when they face the same set of statutory tax rates over time.

3.3 MORE ON PENSION PLANS

In this section we provide some institutional detail on pension plans and apply the savings vehicles concepts to a comparison of deductible individual retirement accounts (IRAs) with Roth IRAs. Taxpayers have a variety of pension plans to use in saving for retirement. Employers often set up pension plans for their employees, and the employer often matches the employee's pretax contributions dollar for dollar. That is, for every pretax dollar the employee contributes, the employer also contributes a dollar. An example of such a plan is the **401(k) plan.** For many taxpayers this investment will represent a major asset at retirement. For small employers (or employers wishing to avoid the complexities of the above plans), there are the alternative **simplified employee pension plan (SEP)** and **savings incentive match plan for employees (SIMPLE).** A SEP is a program in which the employer opens IRAs for its employees (but is limited to 25 or fewer employees) and can contribute, similarly to regular corporate pension plans, up to the maximum of the lesser of $30,000 a year or 15% of the employee's income. A SIMPLE plan is also available to small employers wishing to avoid the complexities of other pension plans. A SIMPLE plan can be adopted by firms with fewer than 100 employees and can be set up as an IRA for each employee. Employees were allowed to make elective contributions of up to $8,000 pretax per year in 2003 ($9,000 in 2004 and $10,000 in 2005) which are then matched by the employer.

Individuals with self-employment income can establish and make tax-deductible contributions to so-called **Keogh plans** (up to $40,000 per year). Self-employment income includes income earned from a sole proprietorship or from a partnership, income earned as an independent contractor or as a consultant, and book royalties.

---

[12]After tax, the individual invests $1/(1 − .28)$ at a 7% rate of return for 5 years and then pays tax on the accumulated amount at a 40% rate. At the end of 5 years, the after-tax accumulation is $1/(1 − 28) \times (1.07)^5 \times (1 − .40) = \$1.1688$. The annualized rate of return is $(1.1688)^{(1/5)} − 1 = .0317$, or 3.2%.

[13]The SPDA annualized after-tax rate of return is calculated as $\$1[(1.07)^5(1 − .40) + .40] = \$1.24153$, implying $r = (1.24153)^{(1/5)} − 1 = .0442$ or 4.4%. The 4.9% after-tax rate of return on the money market savings account is calculated as $[1 + .07(1 − .28)]^4[(1 + .07(1 − .40)] = \$1.2685$, implying $r = (1.2685)^{(1/5)} − 1 = .0487$ or 4.9%.

Individuals can also contribute to individual retirement accounts (IRAs). There are three different types of IRA accounts: (1) traditional deductible IRAs, (2) Roth IRAs, and (3) nondeductible IRAs.[14]

Traditional Deductible IRAs

An eligible taxpayer may contribute up to $3,000 (or 100% of compensation if less than $3,000) per year to a **traditional deductible IRA.** Contributions are tax deductible and, as with most other pension plans, earnings in the pension account are tax deferred until the taxpayer makes withdrawals in retirement. Thus, the deductible IRA belongs to the Savings Vehicle VI category. Since 1997, nonworking spouses may also contribute up to $3,000. For taxpayers participating in a pension plan offered by their employer, the tax deductibility of the IRA contribution is phased out depending on the taxpayer's income and filing status. For example, for 2002, the phase-out range for joint filers is between $54,000 and $64,000. That is, if the taxpayer earns above $64,000, none of the contribution is tax deductible.

Roth IRAs

Beginning in 1998, taxpayers can contribute to a **Roth IRA.** Contributions are not tax deductible but withdrawals are tax-free if taken after age 59.5. That is, earnings in a Roth IRA are not tax deferred but tax exempt (provided the withdrawals meet certain conditions). Thus, the Roth IRA fits in the Savings Vehicle V category. Taxpayers may contribute up to $3,000 each with the contribution limit phased out depending on the taxpayer's income and filing status. For example, the limit is phased out for joint filers with income between $150,000 and $160,000. That is, joint filers with income above $160,000 cannot contribute to a Roth IRA. The $3,000 limit is reduced by the amount, if any, the taxpayer contributes to a deductible IRA.

Nondeductible IRAs

If the taxpayer does not or cannot make (because of the income limitations) a deductible contribution to an IRA or Roth IRA account, the taxpayer may make nondeductible contributions of up $3,000 per year. The earnings in the pension account are tax deferred until the taxpayer makes withdrawals in retirement. Thus, the nondeductible IRA belongs to the Savings Vehicle II category.

Comparison of the Deductible and Roth IRAs—New Contributions

As indicated in Table 3.1, the Roth IRA (Savings Vehicle V) will accumulate over n years to $\$I(1 + R)^n$, and the deductible IRA (Savings Vehicle VI) will accumulate to

$$\frac{\$I}{(1 - t_0)}(1 + R)^n(1 - t_n) = \$I^*(1 + R)^n(1 - t_n)$$

where $\$I^*$ denotes pretax dollars invested. Suppose the taxpayer wishes to contribute $1,000 of after-tax dollars to an IRA and she expects no change in her current tax rate of 30% between now and retirement in 30 years, when she plans to withdraw the funds.

---

[14]Beginning in 2002, taxpayers 50 and over can make additional catch-up contributions designed to boost their retirement accumulations.

Assume she can earn 8% per year pretax in either IRA account. The Roth IRA will accumulate to $1,000(1 + .08)^{30} = \$10,063$. The deductible IRA will accumulate to $\frac{\$1,000}{(1-.30)}(1 + .08)^{30}(1 - .30) = \$10,063$. The accumulations are the same because the tax rate is expected to be unchanged between the contribution date and the withdrawal date. The government is contributing t percent of the (pretax) investment to the deductible IRA but then taking t percent of the accumulation. If the taxpayer expects her tax rate to increase to 35% when she retires, the deductible IRA will accumulate to $\frac{\$1,000}{(1-.30)}(1 + .08)^{30}(1 - .35) = \$9,344$. Thus the Roth IRA is favored (disfavored) if the taxpayer expects her tax rate to be higher (lower) in retirement than the tax rate during the contribution period.

Note that these conclusions are the same as we reached earlier comparing Savings Vehicles V and VI. We compared alternative vehicles earlier both by using the after-tax accumulation and by converting the after-tax accumulation F to an annualized rate r, or $r = (F/\$I)^{1/n} - 1$. A third way of comparing alternatives is to find the difference in the algebraic expressions and simplify as follows.

$$\text{Roth IRA Accumulation} - \text{IRA Accumulation}$$

$$= \$1,000(1 + R)^n - \frac{\$1,000}{(1 - t_0)}(1 + R)^n(1 - t_n)$$

$$= \$1,000(1 + R)^n - \$1,000(1 + R)^n \frac{(1 - t_n)}{(1 - t_0)}$$

$$= \$1,000(1 + R)^n \left[1 - \frac{(1 - t_n)}{(1 - t_0)}\right] \tag{3.4}$$

If the expression in equation (3.4) is positive, the Roth IRA is preferred. We can analyze which investment alternative is preferred simply by analyzing the last term in square brackets (because the sign of the expression in (3.4) depends only on the sign of the last term). Thus, as the numerical example illustrates, if $t_0 = t_n$, then the accumulations are the same (the difference in the accumulations is zero as per equation (3.4)). If $t_0 < t_n$ (3.4) is positive, and the Roth IRA is preferred. For example, if $t_0 = .30$ and $t_n = .40$, the Roth IRA accumulates to $\left[1 - \frac{1-.40}{1-.30}\right] = .1428$, or 14.3% more than the deductible IRA. Finally, if $t_0 > t_n$ (3.4) is negative, and the deductible IRA is preferred (since the future tax rate is lower the government is extracting a smaller percentage than it contributed).

It is important to note that a taxpayer can contribute a maximum of $3,000 after tax to a Roth IRA account but only $3,000 maximum pretax to a deductible IRA account. The equivalent after-tax amount depends on the taxpayer's tax rate. If the taxpayer's tax rate is 30%, the maximum $3,000 pretax contribution is equivalent to a maximum $2,100 after tax. Thus, we must be careful in comparing investments in deductible IRAs with Roth IRAs. For a valid comparison we must have equal after-tax amounts invested in each alternative. In the example above this was not a problem since the taxpayer was contributing less than the maximum. For the taxpayer with a tax rate of 30% wishing to contribute the maximum to either IRA, it is important to recognize the taxpayer has an additional $900 after tax to invest if she chooses the deductible IRA. For comparison purposes we will assume this excess is invested in an SPDA. (The reader can conduct the comparison assuming the excess is invested in one of the other savings vehicles listed in Table 3.1.) Thus the accumulation in a deductible

IRA with the excess in an SPDA is the sum of the accumulation in each account (the sum of Savings Vehicles V and II):

Deductible IRA/SPDA Accumulation

$$= \frac{\$3,000(1 - t_0)}{(1 - t_0)}(1 + R)^n(1 - t_n) + \$3,000t_0[(1 + R)^n(1 - t_n) + t_n] \qquad \textbf{(3.5)}$$

The numerator in the first term—$\$3,000(1 - t_0)$—equals the after-tax investment amount, and the denominator grosses the amount back up to the pretax quantity since the contribution is deductible. Alternatively stated, because the two $(1 - t_0)$ terms cancel out, the $\$3,000$ is in pretax dollars.

Again to compare an investment in a Roth IRA with the deductible IRA/SPDA alternative we can find the difference in the accumulations and simplify as follows:

Roth IRA Accumulation – Deductible IRA/SPDA Accumulation

$$= \$3,000(1 + R)^n - \{\$3,000(1 + R)^n(1 - t_n) + \$3,000t_0[(1 + R)^n(1 - t_n) + t_n]\}$$

$$= \$3,000(1 + R)^n t_n - \$3,000t_0[(1 + R)^n(1 - t_n) + t_n] \qquad \textbf{(3.6)}$$

The Roth IRA is preferred if (3.6) is positive. If the taxpayer's tax rate is expected to remain constant through retirement, then (3.6) simplifies to $\$3,000t^2[(1 + R)^n - 1]$, which is greater than zero, and so the Roth IRA is favored. The math shows that the Roth IRA earns $R\%$ on the entire $\$3,000$. However, in the deductible IRA/SPDA alternative, only the deductible IRA component earns $R\%$ while the SPDA component earns less than $R\%$.

If $t_0 < t_n$, then (3.6) > 0 and the Roth IRA is favored. If $t_0 > t_n$, then (3.6) is positive or negative depending on the relative magnitude of the two tax rates (and this scenario is the most likely for most taxpayers because they expect to face lower marginal tax rates in retirement).

Comparison of the Deductible and Roth IRAs—The Rollover Decision

Taxpayers with balances in deductible IRAs can, beginning in 1998, rollover the balance into a Roth IRA. The amount rolled over is included in the taxpayer's taxable income in the year of the rollover.[15] To analyze the decision to rollover we assume that any taxes due on the rollover are paid by non-IRA funds and that the tax payment avoided by not rolling over is invested in an SPDA. If a rollover is not made, then the deductible IRA will accumulate to

$$\text{Deductible IRA accumulation} = V(1 + R)^n(1 - t_n) \qquad \textbf{(3.7)}$$

where V is the market value of the accumulation in the deductible IRA at the decision date.

With a rollover, the after-tax accumulation in a Roth IRA will be

$$\text{Rollover Roth IRA accumulation} = V(1 + R)^n - Vt_0[(1 + R)^n(1 - t_n) + t_n] \qquad \textbf{(3.8)}$$

---

[15]Note that the taxpayer includes in taxable income the difference between the accumulated value of the funds in the deductible IRA less any basis. We assume here that the basis is zero. For rollovers in the 1998 tax year, the taxpayer can elect to spread the gain (and hence the tax) over 4 years.

The first term in (3.8) is the accumulation in the Roth IRA (the entire amount V is invested in the Roth IRA since we assume taxes are paid from non-IRA rollover funds). The second term in (3.8) is the tax due on the rollover plus the lost SPDA earnings on the tax paid. To determine whether a rollover is preferred we subtract the deductible IRA accumulation from the rollover accumulation[16]

$$\text{Roth IRA} - \text{deductible IRA}$$
$$= V(1+R)^n - Vt_0[(1+R)^n(1-t_n)+t_n] - V(1+R)^n(1-t_n)$$

This equation simplifies to[17]

$$V(1+R)^n - Vt_0[(1+R)^n(1-t_n)+t_n] - V(1+R)^n + V(1+R)^n t_n$$
$$= V(1+R)^n t_n - Vt_0[(1+R)^n(1-t_n)+t_n] \tag{3.9}$$

If $t_0 = t_n = t$, then (3.9) simplifies to $Vt^2[(1+R)^n - 1]$, which is greater than zero, and so the rollover is tax preferred. If $t_0 < t_n$, then (3.9) > 0 and again the rollover is preferred. Finally, if $t_0 > t_n$ then (3.9) is positive, zero, or negative, depending on R, n, and the relative change between t_0 and t_n. Specific cases can be easily analyzed using (3.9), or the sensitivity of the decision can be assessed via spreadsheet analysis. As mentioned at the start of the comparisons, equations (3.5) and (3.8)—and the equations derived from them—can be easily modified to incorporate alternative investment vehicles (such as a money market account or mutual fund). We selected the SPDA because it is often the next most tax-favored savings vehicle after pensions.[18]

Recent Events

Finally, in Spring 2003, President Bush proposed two new savings plans and a plan to consolidate many employer-sponsored retirement accounts with the objective to both simplify the existing Tax Code in this area and to stimulate additional savings. The two new savings accounts are

Retirement Savings Accounts (RSAs): consolidate all the current IRAs into one savings account that is very similar to the Roth IRA with an annual contribution limit of $7,500 per year.

Lifetime Savings Accounts (LSAs): again similar to a Roth IRA, contributions not deductible, but earnings and distributions would be tax-free, with an annual contribution limit of $7,500 per year.

Employer Retirement Savings Accounts (ERSAs): designed to simplify the Tax Code by merging various types of employer pensions into a plan similar to the 410(k) plan.

---

[16]It is evident from the math that it does not matter whether the second term in (3.8)—representing the taxes due and the earnings lost on the taxes—is subtracted from the Roth rollover accumulation or added to the deductible IRA accumulation alternative.

[17]The observant reader should notice the similarity between equations (3.6), used when evaluating a new contribution and equation (3.9), used when evaluating the rollover decision. The only difference is the substitution of V, the value of the funds to be rolled over, for I, the after-tax new contribution amount.

[18]For more discussion on the choice between the deductible IRA and Roth IRA and for more detailed discussion of other tax aspects (such as early withdrawal and estate tax planning opportunities available with a Roth IRA) see Seida and Stern (1998). Hulse (2003) analyzes the initial contribution choice incorporating the option allowed as to the timing of any rollover from the traditional to Roth IRA—the option is the flexibility to rollover in a future low-tax year.

Summary of Key Points

1. Numerous organizational forms are available for savings. We considered a number of alternative savings vehicles that were distinguished by the tax treatment of investment returns. While investments made in most savings vehicles do not give rise to immediate tax deductions, investments in pensions do. While the earnings on some investments are taxed annually, the earnings on others are partially or fully tax deferred or may be tax exempt altogether. Earnings in some vehicles are taxed at ordinary rates while earnings in other vehicles attract tax at capital gains rates. Because of these differing tax treatments, the after-tax accumulation and rate of return from holding a fully taxable bond in each of these savings vehicles varies dramatically across the alternatives.

2. With constant tax rates, pension savings and tax-exempt savings through insurance contracts dominate money market accounts and such other savings vehicles as single premium deferred annuities.

3. Without frictions and restrictions, the dominant returns available from some organizational forms would result in tax arbitrage opportunities. Investors would save only through the dominant organizational forms.

4. If tax brackets change through time, the dominance relations can disappear. For example, when tax rates are increasing over time, money market accounts (the least tax-advantageous organizational form when tax rates are constant) can provide higher after-tax rates of return than pension accounts (the most tax-advantageous organizational form when tax rates are constant).

5. The introduction of frictions and restrictions further alters the rankings of the alternatives. Empirically, we find that investors use all of the organizational forms that we analyzed.

6. There are a variety of retirement savings vehicles available to taxpayers. In addition to corporate sponsored pension plans, individuals can contribute to individual retirement accounts (IRAs), subject to income limits. Self-employed individuals can set up Keogh accounts to save for retirement. Under most pension plans contributions are tax deductible and plan asset earnings are tax deferred until withdrawn during retirement. Two exceptions are the Roth IRA and the nondeductible IRA. Contributions to both these accounts are not tax deductible and earnings are not taxed during the life of the plan. However, withdrawals from the Roth IRA account are tax-free but withdrawals from the nondeductible IRA are taxed. Thus the Roth IRA dominates the nondeductible IRA.

7. Depending on the configuration of current and future tax rates, the Roth IRA often dominates the deductible IRA even though contributions are not tax deductible. Beginning in 1998, taxpayers were allowed to rollover the balances in their deductible IRAs into Roth IRAs. The rollover requires taxpayers to pay income tax on the amount rolled over. Provided the tax is paid from non-rollover funds, the Roth IRA generally dominates the deductible IRA unless the taxpayer expects to face lower tax rates in retirement.

Discussion Questions

1. Identify three tax characteristics that differ among alternative savings vehicles.

2. The interest income on bonds issued by tax-exempt organizations is often exempt from federal taxation in the United States. In comparing savings vehicles, why is it inappropriate to view these bonds as perfect substitutes for such savings accounts as tax-exempt life insurance contracts?

3. With constant tax rates over time, why does a single premium deferred annuity contract (SPDA) provide greater after-tax rates of return than does a money

market account? How is the difference in after-tax accumulations in these two vehicles affected by the level of interest rates? Why does the length of the holding period affect the after-tax rates of return per period on SPDAs and not on money market accounts?

4. Under what circumstances is an investment that is taxed each period at capital gains rates preferred to an SPDA contract (taxed at ordinary rates on investment income but only at the point of liquidation)? When is Savings Vehicle IV (income deferred and taxed at capital gains rates at the point of liquidation) preferred to an SPDA?

5. Why do a pension account and the savings portion of a life insurance product provide the same after-tax rates of return if tax rates are constant over time? In comparing these two savings vehicles, is it appropriate to have the same number of dollars invested in both alternatives?

6. If tax rates are constant over time, why might a taxpayer prefer to save through a money market account rather than a pension account or a tax-exempt insurance policy?

7. If tax rates are changing over time, do pension accounts dominate tax-exempt savings accounts?

8. Why do rising tax rates make single premium deferred annuities and pension accounts less attractive relative to ordinary money market accounts than when tax rates are falling?

9. In analyzing whether to contribute to a deductible IRA or a Roth IRA in equation (3.6) we assumed a single lump-sum contribution (of $$I$). How would the choice change if the taxpayer were considering contributing $$I$ every year from the current period to the last year before retirement?

10. In analyzing the rollover decision in equation (3.9) we assumed that any tax due on the rollover would be paid in the year of the rollover. For 1998 only, the taxpayer could elect to spread the tax (more specifically, include equal portions of the rollover amount in taxable income) over 4 years. Under what conditions does this election *not* make sense?

Exercises

1. A taxpayer can invest $1,000 in a money market fund that yields an annual pretax rate of return of 8%, or buy an acre of land for $1,000 that appreciates at a 7% annual rate. The taxpayer plans to sell the land after 20 years and faces a 25% tax rate each year.
   a. What is the after-tax accumulation at the end of 20 years from each investment?
   b. What is the annualized after-tax rate of return from each investment?
   (Exercise adapted from problem written by Richard Sansing, Dartmouth College.)

2. A taxpayer can invest $5,000 in a common stock that pays no dividends but appreciates at a rate of 8%. The taxpayer's tax rate is 30%. He plans to sell the stock after 30 years.
   a. Find the after-tax accumulation and the annualized after-tax rate of return for this investment.
   b. What would have been the annualized after-tax rate of return on the stock if there were a special tax rate of 20% on capital gains?
   (Exercise adapted from problem written by Richard Sansing, Dartmouth College.)

3. A corporation can invest $10,000 in preferred stock that pays a 6% dividend and does not appreciate in price. The corporation faces a 40% tax rate. Dividends from the stock are eligible for the 70% corporate dividends received deduction. That is, the corporation has to include only 30% of the dividend in its taxable income. This

results in an effective tax rate on the dividend of 12%(= .30 × .40). Assume dividend income is reinvested in more 6% preferred stock.
a. Find the after-tax accumulation for this investment after 10 years.
b. Find the annualized after-tax rate of return on this investment after 10 years.
(Exercise adapted from problem written by Richard Sansing, Dartmouth College.)

4. Suppose a taxpayer, when 25 years old, made one tax-deductible $2,000 contribution of her after-tax salary to a deductible IRA. Her investment (taxable corporate bonds) earned a 12% annual return, and she liquidates the investment 10 years later when she retires. Her tax rate is 35%, but she must pay an additional 10% excise tax because she liquidates the IRA before she reaches the age 59.5.
a. After taxes, how much cash does she have when she liquidates the IRA?
b. Was it a mistake for the taxpayer to have set up an IRA? What would she have earned had she invested her after-tax salary in the taxable corporate bonds directly instead of through an IRA?

5. A taxpayer has some spare cash sitting in his checking account and would like to put $1,000 into a retirement account. He has come to you for advice as to whether he should put the $1,000 into a traditional deductible IRA or a Roth IRA account. You learn that he faces a current marginal tax rate of 28% and expects to face the same rate in 40 years, when he plans to withdraw the funds at age 70. He expects to earn a pretax rate of return of 10% in either retirement account by investing the funds in corporate bonds. Advise the taxpayer as to what he should do.

6. Assume the same facts presented in exercise 5 with the exception that the taxpayer expects his tax rate to be 20% when he retires in 40 years. What should the taxpayer do now?

7. A taxpayer wants to invest the maximum allowed in his retirement account. He has come to you for advice as to whether he should contribute to a traditional deductible IRA or to a Roth IRA account. You learn that he faces a current marginal tax rate of 28% and expects to face the same rate in 40 years when he plans to withdraw the funds at age 70. He expects to earn a pretax rate of return of 10% in either retirement account by investing the funds in corporate bonds. Advise the taxpayer as to what he should do. Be explicit about any assumptions you need to make when comparing the two alternative retirement accounts.

8. Assume the same facts presented in exercise 7 with the exception that now the taxpayer expects his tax rate to increase from its current 28% level to 35% when he retires in 40 years. Again, be explicit about any assumptions you need to make when comparing the two alternative retirement accounts.

9. A taxpayer currently has $20,000 in a traditional deductible IRA account. She comes to you for advice about whether to roll the $20,000 into a Roth IRA account. The taxpayer faces a current tax rate of 28%, and she expects to face the same rate when she retires in 40 years. She is currently earning 12% per year pretax in the deductible IRA, and she expects to continue to earn this pretax rate of return regardless of whether she is invested in a deductible IRA or a Roth IRA. Should the taxpayer rollover into a Roth IRA? Assume any taxes due on the rollover are paid from non-IRA funds. Be explicit about any assumptions you make in advising the taxpayer.

10. Assume the same facts presented in exercise 9 with the exception that the taxpayer elects to pay the taxes on the rollover from the IRA funds. Should the taxpayer rollover into a Roth IRA?

11. Assume the same facts presented in exercise 9 with the exception that the taxpayer expects her tax rate to decline from the current 28% to 20% when she retires in 40 years. Should the taxpayer rollover into a Roth IRA?

12. Many taxpayers that elected to rollover the funds in their traditional deductible IRA to a Roth IRA in the summer of 1998 converted back to a traditional IRA in September 1998 after the stock market fell (the Dow Jones Industrial Average fell from approximately 9300 to 7500). Many of these taxpayers after converting back to the traditional IRA then rolled over into the Roth IRA at the lower stock market levels.[19] Note that Treasury Regulations allow taxpayers to undo a rollover and to re-rollover at a later date.

   a. Explain the rationale for reversing the original rollover and then making the re-rollover at the lower stock market level. In your explanation, assume that a taxpayer facing a marginal tax rate of 39.6% rolled over $100,000 from a traditional IRA into a Roth IRA at the start of the summer of 1998. After the rollover, the stock market declined 20% (that is, the value of the assets in the pension account declined in value by 20% since the taxpayer had invested the plan assets in the stock market). Assume also that the taxpayer has a 20-year investment horizon and faces a tax rate of 39.6% currently and in retirement.

   b. Does your answer to part (a), depend on the future performance of the stock market (that is, on R)?

Tax Planning Problems

1. Assume that fully taxable bonds yield 10% per year before tax, tax-exempt bonds yield 6.5%, and the pretax return on single premium deferred annuities (SPDAs) is 9.5%.

   a. What are the after-tax rates of return per period (for holding periods of 3, 5, 10, and 20 years) for an investment in (1) tax-exempt bonds; (2) taxable bonds; (3) SPDAs cashed out after age 59.5 (no excise tax); and (4) SPDAs cashed out *before* age 59.5, requiring a 10% nondeductible excise tax (in addition to the normal tax) on the accumulated interest, for an investor facing (i) a 40% ordinary tax rate each period and (ii) a 30% ordinary tax rate each period?

Holding Period	Tax-Exempt Bonds	Taxable Bonds	SPDAs (with no penalty)	SPDAs (with penalty)
3 years				
30% taxpayer				
40% taxpayer				
5 years				
30% taxpayer				
40% taxpayer				
10 years				
30% taxpayer				
40% taxpayer				
20 years				
30% taxpayer				
40% taxpayer				

   b. How do optimal investment strategies change as a function of tax rates, lengths of investment horizon, and age?

---

[19]See the *Wall Street Journal,* (May 4, 1999) p. B9, Your Money Matters column entitled "IRA Holders do Flip-Flops Over Accounts" for financial press discussion of Roth IRA rollovers.

    c. At age 34.5, you deposited $50,000 into an SPDA yielding 9.5% pretax. Ten years later, to finance the purchase of a second home, you require a mortgage exceeding the cash-out value of your SPDA. As an alternative to liquidating your SPDA, you can borrow funds at an annual interest rate of 11%, tax deductible, for 15 years. Your current tax rate is 30%, and you expect it to remain at that level. How much better or worse off, after tax, will you be at age 59.5 if you invade your SPDA today (and incur the 10% excise tax) to reduce the size of the required mortgage?

    d. How does your answer to part (c) change if the interest expense incurred on the debt used to finance the expenditure is not tax deductible (for example, you purchased a flashy, expensive personal automobile)?

2. Equation (3.6) analyzes the choice between a deductible IRA and a Roth IRA for new contributions when the taxpayer wishes to contribute the maximum allowed. Equation (3.6) indicates that if the taxpayer expects his future tax rate to decline, the contribution choice depends on the relative magnitude of the taxpayer's current and future tax rates t_0 and t_n, the holding period n, and the pretax rate of return expected R to be earned on plan assets. (Note also that equation (3.6) assumes that any excess funds under the deductible IRA are invested in an SPDA.) Assume the taxpayers current tax rate t_0 is .40. Complete the following spreadsheet, first assuming that $R = 10\%$. Then repeat the spreadsheet for $R = 5\%$ and $R = 15\%$.

Holding Period n	$t_n = .40$	$t_n = .35$	$t_n = .30$	$t_n = .25$
5 years				
10 years				
20 years				
30 years				

Interpret the results of your analysis. How does the rollover decision vary as a function of the pretax rate of return, holding period, and relative magnitudes of tax rates?

3. Equation (3.9) indicates that the choice as to whether to rollover from a deductible IRA into a Roth IRA when the taxpayer expects his future tax rate to decline depends on the relative magnitude of the taxpayers current and future tax rates t_0 and t_n, the holding period n, and the pretax rate of return expected R to be earned on plan assets. (Note also that equation (3.9) assumes that any taxes due on rollover are paid in the rollover year from non-rollover funds that would otherwise be invested in an SPDA.) Assume $V = \$50,000$ and $t_0 = .40$. Complete the following spreadsheet, first assuming that $R = 10\%$. Then repeat the spreadsheet for $R = 5\%$ and $R = 15\%$.

Holding Period n	$t_n = .40$	$t_n = .35$	$t_n = .30$	$t_n = .25$
5 years				
10 years				
20 years				
30 years				

Interpret the results of your analysis. How does the rollover decision vary as a function of the pretax rate of return, holding period, and relative magnitudes of tax rates?

4. In comparing the deductible IRA with the Roth IRA, we assumed that any excess funds left after investing the maximum pretax dollars in a deductible IRA were invested in an SPDA. How would the comparison change if the excess funds were invested instead in Savings Vehicle III (a special type of mutual fund)?

5. In analyzing the rollover decision in equations (3.8) and (3.9), we assumed that any taxes due would be paid from non-rollover funds that would otherwise be invested in an SPDA. How would these equations and thus the relevant comparisons in the rollover decision change if
   a. any taxes due were paid from the rollover funds (ignore the 10% excise tax penalty due on early withdrawals).
   b. instead of paying the taxes from funds invested in an SPDA, the taxes were paid from funds invested in Savings Vehicle III (a special type of mutual fund).

References and Additional Readings

Bergstresser, D., and J. Poterba, 2002, "Do After-Tax Returns Affect Mutual Fund Inflows?" *Journal of Financial Economics,* pp. 381–414.

Hulse, D., 2003, "Embedded Options and Tax Decisions: A Reconsideration of the Traditional Vs Roth IRA Decision," *Journal of the American Taxation Association* (Spring), pp. 39–52.

Seida, J., and J. Stern, 1998, "Extending Scholes/Wolfson for Post-1997 Pension Investments: Application to the Roth IRA Contribution and Rollover Decisions," *Journal of the American Taxation Association* (Fall), pp. 100–110.

4

CHOOSING THE OPTIMAL ORGANIZATIONAL FORM

After completing this chapter, you should be able to:

1. Explain and calculate the after-tax rate of return to investment via the partnership form.

2. Explain and calculate the after-tax rate of return to investment via the corporate form.

3. Explain and illustrate the importance of deferral of shareholder-level taxation in the corporate form.

4. Explain and illustrate the importance of capital gains treatment for shareholders.

5. Estimate the required corporate pretax return that results in equal after-tax returns to the corporate and partnership forms.

6. Discuss how the relative tax disadvantage of double taxation of the corporation has changed over the last 25 years as Congress has changed tax rates.

7. List alternative legal entities through which production activities can be organized.

8. Explain the tax and nontax costs of the alternative organizational forms.

In Chapter 3 we considered how differences in the tax treatment of earnings across alternative savings vehicles affect after-tax investment returns. In this chapter, we focus on the taxation of the returns on businesses that produce goods and services. Sole proprietorships, partnerships, and corporations are a few examples of organizational forms in which such activities are undertaken. As we will see, significant differences in tax treatment can result from undertaking identical investment projects that generate the same before-tax cash flows through different legal organizational forms. Such tax treatment differences can have an important influence on the organizational form selected to conduct business.

To illustrate the nature of these tax differences, let us consider a few important tax rules affecting corporations and partnerships in the United States. Corporations must pay an **entity-level tax** on their taxable income. They file tax returns and pay tax on corporate taxable income in ways very similar to individuals. Shareholders pay additional tax (at their own statutory rates) on dividends that are paid out of corporate earnings and profits, and they pay tax on gains from the sale of their shares. This gives rise to the phrase that corporate profits are subject to **double taxation.** This means that corporate stockholders are effectively taxed twice on income, once at the corporate level and again when profits are distributed as a dividend or when shares are sold.[1] In contrast, partners and sole proprietors are subject to only one level of taxation, at their own personal rates. Rather than pay an entity-level tax, partnerships and proprietorships act as **conduits** through which income flows to their owners. For example, partners record their share of partnership profits and losses on their own tax returns, whether the profits are distributed or not.

It is worth emphasizing that only corporate income attributable to stockholders, the residual claimants, is subject to double taxation. Income distributed to creditors, employees, and suppliers, in the form of interest, compensation, and other costs to produce and sell goods and services, is *not* taxed at the corporate level (since these items are deductible in computing corporate taxable income). Instead, this income is taxed exclusively to its recipients, just like partnership income.

In this chapter, we begin by analyzing the effects of taxes on the returns from productive activities that corporations and partnerships undertake. We employ a simplified model where there are no transaction or information costs (frictions). The model's primary implication is that an investor's choice between the corporate form of organization (two levels of taxation) and the partnership form (one level of taxation) depends on the length of the investment horizon as well as three tax parameters: (1) the investor's personal tax rates on ordinary income, (2) corporate-level tax rates, and (3) the shareholder-level tax rates on the returns to investing in corporate shares. The model provides insights into how a specific investor might choose an organizational form. It does not explain, however, how partnerships and corporations can compete successfully against each other in the marketplace. In fact, one implication of this model is that if all investors faced exactly the same three tax parameters, we would not expect to observe both partnerships and corporations producing the same goods and services.

Moreover, in the absence of frictions and restrictions, even if investors initially faced differences in these three tax parameters—leading some investors to produce goods and services in partnership form and others to produce identical goods and services in corporate form—tax arbitrage opportunities would prevent these initial differences in taxes from being an equilibrium situation (see Chapter 5). As investors exploited the arbitrage possibilities, their tax positions would be altered, and the activity would continue until all investors faced the same three tax characteristics. As a result, once again we would not expect to observe both partnerships and corporations producing the same goods and services.

---

[1]In many countries, corporate and personal taxes are *integrated,* in that shareholders are granted a tax credit for the corporate taxes they pay indirectly as owners. In fully integrated systems, this arrangement results in single taxation of income earned through corporations. We present an example of integration in the appendix to this chapter. Note that double taxation can also be avoided if distributions of corporate income (dividends and capital gains) are deductible at the corporate level or are exempted from taxation to owner-recipients. This situation is approximated in countries where capital gains are exempted from taxation and dividend yields are low.

In the real world, partnerships and corporations *do* compete head to head. This can occur quite naturally when market frictions and tax-rule restrictions are present. As we have emphasized before, to maximize after-tax returns, investors must consider both tax and nontax factors. In this chapter, we consider special tax provisions for both partnerships and corporations that reduce the differences in after-tax rates of return that the model otherwise predicts. Similarly, we touch on market frictions that might prevent one organizational form from dominating another. That is, while one organizational form may enjoy less favorable tax treatment than another, the tax-disfavored entity may still be able to compete effectively against its rival if nontax factors cause its *before*-tax profitability to be greater. For example, if tax rules favor partnerships over corporations, the corporate form may still be preferable, because corporate owners enjoy limited liability, easy transferability of ownership, and a relatively active market for management control. In contrast, it is relatively expensive to limit partnership liability, to trade partnership interests, and to change control of the partnership.

A reduced rate of shareholder-level or corporate-level taxation makes corporations more competitive relative to partnerships. This is important to corporate strategists because reducing either corporate or shareholder tax rates lowers the corporate cost of capital—that is, the rate of return that the corporation must earn on investment projects of a designated risk if it expects to cover its costs of financing the projects. Moreover, as with the analysis of savings vehicles in Chapter 3, changes in tax rates across time might affect taxpayers' preference for corporations or partnerships.

We concentrate in this chapter on the standard partnership and corporate form, leaving for later chapters special considerations regarding the taxation of such institutions as universities and charities (that is, tax-exempt organizations). Multinational corporations, as well, face unique tax considerations, which we address in later chapters.

4.1 ORGANIZATIONAL FORMS FOR PRODUCING GOODS AND SERVICES

We begin with a brief overview of the taxation of several organizational forms used to produce goods and services. The income statement of sole proprietorships in the United States is filed along with the owner's personal tax return. The profits of the business are taxed only once at the personal level. In this regard, the sole proprietorship serves as a conduit through which the income of the business is passed through to the tax return of its owner.

A U.S. **partnership** is another legal organizational form that serves as a tax conduit between the business and its partners. The partnership files its own information tax return, including an income statement, a balance sheet, and a schedule of specific allocations to each partner. These allocations are broken down by type of income and expense (for example, depreciation, interest, rent, and capital gains); partners report their designated share of income and expense on their own tax returns. The partnership entity does not pay any income tax. Partnerships may have two classes of partners: **general partners** and **limited partners.** As with a sole proprietor, general partners' personal liability is limited only by their personal resources and the bankruptcy laws. A limited partner, on the other hand, like a corporate stockholder, faces a more **limited liability:** The investor usually is at risk for only the amount he has invested in the business. As with most shareholders in widely held corporations, a limited partner typically does not participate actively in the operations of the business.[2]

Unlike partnerships, regular U.S. corporations (also known as **C corporations**) are taxed directly on their taxable income.[3] In addition to corporate-level taxes, stockholders are also taxed on dividend income and realized capital gains at their own personal rates. If corporate taxable income is $1 and the corporate marginal tax rate is 40%, corporate after-tax profits are $.60, or $1(1 − .40). If the corporation then pays a cash dividend of $.60 (its entire after-tax profits), shareholders pay tax on this dividend at their own personal tax rates. Until recently, dividends, like wages or interest receipts, were typically taxed at ordinary rates. For example, if shareholders face a 30% marginal tax rate, they retain only $.42, that is, $.60(1 − .30) of the initial $1 of corporate before-tax earnings, a 58% total rate of tax. These calculations are shown graphically:

Pretax corporate earnings of $1:

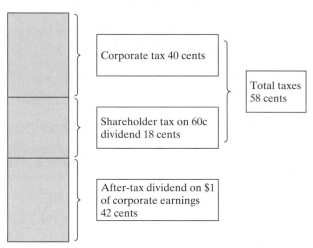

Shareholders also realize capital gains and losses on the sale of their stock. Such income is granted special treatment. It is taxed only when realized under the tax laws, which ordinarily occurs on a sale. Capital gains (losses) on the sale of stock are computed as the difference between the sale price and the **basis** of the asset (usually the purchase price).[4] As discussed in Chapter 1, for individuals, except for the period

---

[2]Indeed, active participation in the management of the business may void the limited liability protection of "limited" partners.

[3]Regular corporations are referred to as *C corporations* to distinguish them from *S corporations* (discussed below). The letters *C* and *S* are derived from the subchapters of the Tax Code defining the structure of each type of corporation. Most corporations listed on U.S. stock exchanges are organized as C corporations. Examples include Microsoft Corporation, Amazon.com, IBM, General Motors, etc.

[4]The basis of the asset at the time of sale often differs from the initial purchase price because the company may have declared a stock dividend or a stock split. For example, a 10% stock dividend results in a 10% increase in the number of shares held and a corresponding reduction in the basis per share of 1/11, or 9.09%. If the initial purchase price and basis of a stock was $55, then after a 10% stock dividend, the new basis per share would be $50, or $55/1.1. Another common circumstance in which the basis of a share of stock falls below its purchase price occurs when dividends are distributed in excess of "accumulated earnings and profits." Such dividends are treated for tax purposes as a nontaxable return of capital—that is, as a refund of part of the purchase price.

1988 through 1990, and starting again in 2003, capital gains have been taxed at a lower rate than dividends in the United States. Further, capital gains are taxed at lower rates in most countries.

Although income earned by U.S. corporations is subjected to two levels of tax, the common reference to the corporation as a "double tax" system can be misleading for several reasons. First, shareholders are taxed only on the after-tax profits earned by the corporation. The taxes paid by the corporation are effectively deducted in determining the income taxed at the shareholder level. Second, the after-tax income earned at the corporate level is not taxed instantly to shareholders unless the corporation immediately pays out all of its after-tax earnings as a dividend or shareholders sell their shares each period. Other sources of reduction in the two-level tax include:

- An ability to distribute corporate profits in a tax-deductible way via interest, rent, royalty, compensation, and other payments, rather than by way of nondeductible dividends to stockholders
- Reduced tax rates at the shareholder level (for example, as discussed earlier, capital gains in most countries are taxed at lower rates than ordinary income such as dividends)
- Reduced corporate-level tax rates for certain entities (for example, U.S. savings and loan associations) and
- Deferral of corporate income taxes (for example, income earned abroad by certain majority-owned foreign subsidiaries and not repatriated by way of dividend income)

After-Tax Returns to Pass-Through and Non-Pass-Through Forms of Organization

Pass-through entities are not taxed at the entity level. The income earned by the entity is passed through to be taxed in the hands of the owners. In non-pass-through entities, income is taxed at the entity level and then in the hands of the owners when distributed. We develop a simple model to compare the after-tax returns from investing in a pass-through organizational form such as the partnership or sole proprietorship form to those from investing in non-pass-through forms such as corporations. We assume initially that the before-tax rate of return on a project is constant at a rate of R per year whether the project is undertaken in corporate or partnership form. The project lasts for n years, at which point the organization is assumed to liquidate. All after-tax income generated in the interim that is not distributed is reinvested in the business at rate R per period before tax.

If the project is undertaken in partnership form, partners pay tax at their marginal personal tax rates, t_p, each year, as income is earned. We assume distributions at rate $t_p R$ are made each period from the partnership to enable partners to pay their personal tax. A partner's after-tax accumulation for an initial $\$I$ investment is[5]

$$\$I[1 + R(1 - t_p)]^n \tag{4.1}$$

---

[5]Note that this assumes there is no capital gain or loss on the liquidation of the partnership interest. At time n, partners receive a liquidating distribution of all after-tax partnership income generated over n periods, plus their initial dollar invested.

Note that we have already seen this equation in Chapter 3 as the money market fund, or Savings Vehicle I. Assume, for example, that $R = 20\%$, $n = 5$ years, and $t_p = 40\%$. A partner's after-tax accumulation for a $1 investment is

$$\$1[1 + .20(1 - .40)]^5 = \$1.76$$

This provides an annual after-tax rate of return of 12% (or $1.76^{1/5} - 1$, or more simply $.20(1 - .40)$).

Now consider if the project is undertaken in corporate form. We assume initially the corporation pays no interim dividends. In this case, shareholders pay tax at their capital gains rate, t_{cg}, when the firm liquidates or when shareholders sell their shares. In addition to the shareholder-level tax, the corporation must pay taxes each year at rate t_c on the before-tax return, R. Combining the annual corporate-level tax and the shareholder-level tax, the after-tax accumulation to the owners in a corporation for an initial $1 investment is as follows

$$\$I\{[1 + R(1 - t_c)]^n - t_{cg}[(1 + R(1 - t_c))^n - 1]\}$$

where the first term is the proceeds from the liquidation (or sale of shares) and the second term is the shareholder-level tax due on the liquidation (or sale). This equation can be rearranged to

$$\$I[1 + R(1 - t_c)]^n(1 - t_{cg}) + t_{cg}\$I \qquad \textbf{(4.2)}$$

We have already seen a form of equation (4.2) in the previous chapter. More specifically, the accumulation in (4.2) is exactly the same as that on a single premium deferred annuity (or Savings Vehicle II) for n periods in which the account grows at rate $R(1 - t_c)$ each period, and all earnings are taxed at time n at rate t_{cg}.

Assuming that $t_c = 30\%$ and the shareholder faces a capital gains rate of 15%, the 5-year after-tax accumulation in corporate form for an initial $1 investment is

$$\$1[1 + .20(1 - .30)]^5(1 - .15) + .15\$1 = \$1.79$$

This provides an annualized after-tax rate of return of 12.31% ($1.79^{1/5} - 1$), or 0.31% more than the partnership. Ignoring nontax considerations, a taxpayer will prefer to invest in a partnership (or proprietorship) rather than a corporation whenever the accumulation in equation (4.1) exceeds that of equation (4.2), or

$$\$I[1 + R(1 - t_p)]^n > \$I[1 + R(1 - t_c)]^n(1 - t_{cg}) + t_{cg}\$I \qquad \textbf{(4.3)}$$
$$\text{Partnership (P)} \qquad\qquad \text{Corporation (C)}$$

For what values of t_c, t_p, and t_{cg} in relation (4.3) will investors prefer the partnership form to corporate form? Before considering the question at this level of generality, let us consider the case of $n = 1$. When $n = 1$, relation (4.3) simplifies to

$$(1 - t_p) > (1 - t_c)(1 - t_{cg}) \qquad \textbf{(4.4)}$$

For example, for a one-period investment, if $t_p = 40\%$, $t_c = 30\%$, and $t_{cg} = 10\%$, the corporate form is preferred to the partnership form because

$$(1 - .40) = .60 < (1 - .30)(1 - .10) = .63$$

Although there are two levels of taxation on corporate income, the product of one minus the corporate-level tax rate and one minus the shareholder-level tax rate happens to be higher than one minus the ordinary personal tax rate in this example. If policymakers had set the shareholder capital gains tax rate at 14% rather than 10%, investors facing a 40% marginal tax rate would be about indifferent between investing in partnership and corporate form (as can be seen by substituting for $t_{cg} = 14.3\%$, $t_p = 40\%$, and $t_c = 30\%$ in inequality (4.4)).

Once we leave the world of one-period investments, whether the partnership is preferred to the corporation depends also on the value of deferring the payment of the shareholder-level capital gains tax. The value of the deferral is greater (a) the higher the after-tax accumulation in the corporation, $R(1 - t_c)$, and (b) the *longer* the deferral period, n. Since shareholders accumulate more after tax if they can defer the payment of shareholder-level taxes, the firm's dividend policy also affects the after-tax accumulation. Shareholders who receive dividends pay tax earlier than shareholders who do not receive dividends. Moreover, if $t_{cg} < t_p$, omitting dividends is an optimal policy, since paying tax at rate t_{cg} is superior to paying tax at rate t_p on dividends.[6]

The Choice of Partnership or Corporate Form in Special Cases—Assuming Zero Dividends

As already indicated, whether the partnership form provides greater after-tax rates of return than does the corporate form depends on four factors:

1. The ordinary tax rate, t_p
2. The corporate tax rate, t_c
3. The taxes paid at the shareholder level, t_{cg}
4. The length of the investment horizon, n

Let us consider the following cases (using equation (4.3) for the analyses):

1. The corporate tax rate, t_c, is equal to the ordinary tax rate, t_p, and after-tax corporate income is tax exempt at the shareholder level (that is, $t_{cg} = 0$). In this setting, investors are indifferent between producing in partnership or corporate form. Both provide investors the same after-tax rate of return. In effect, corporate income is taxed only once and at the same rate as if generated in partnership form.
2. The corporate tax rate, t_c, is equal to the ordinary tax rate, t_p, but $t_{cg} > 0$. Because shareholders pay additional tax on the same level of after-tax profits as is earned in partnership form, a partnership is preferred to a corporation. To illustrate the advantage of the partnership form over the corporate form, assume that $t_c = t_p = .35$, $t_{cg} = .15$, and $R = 10\%$. Partnership investments return $10\% \times (1 - .35) = 6.5\%$ after tax, while corporate investments return $10\% \times (1 - .35) \times (1 - .15) = 5.525\%$ after tax for 1-year investments. If shareholders can defer, but not eliminate, the

---

[6]Suggesting that a non-dividend-paying policy is optimal may sound counterintuitive. After all, we usually think of announcements of an increase in the dividend as good news that increases the value of publicly traded shares of stock. Such increases in value, however, stem from investors interpreting the announcement as managers having favorable information about the future profitability of the firm, and this is beyond the scope of the present model. The fact remains that declaring dividends is an expensive way to signal this private information in that it exacts a tax cost, as we have illustrated.

payment of shareholder-level taxes, the advantage of the partnership over the corporation is reduced.

3. The corporate tax rate, t_c, is less than the personal tax rate, t_p, and after-tax corporate income is tax-exempt at the shareholder level (that is, $t_{cg} = 0$). In this case, investing through the corporation dominates investing through a partnership for any length of the investment horizon. For example, with a 10% before-tax rate of return on investment, a corporate tax rate, t_c, of 35%, and a personal tax rate, t_p, of 40%, investors earn a 6.5% after-tax rate of return on investment in the corporate form but only 6% in the partnership form.

4. The corporate tax rate, t_c, is less than the personal tax rate on partnership income, t_p, and the shareholder-level tax is positive (that is, $t_{cg} > 0$). With this configuration of corporate and personal tax rates, there is no clear-cut tax preference for organizational form. Depending on shareholder-level taxes, either the corporate form or the partnership form could be preferred. We will explore this case in more detail below.

4.2 CHANGING PREFERENCES FOR ORGANIZATIONAL FORMS INDUCED BY TAX RULE CHANGES

As presented in Table 1.1 in Chapter 1, the relations between the top corporate tax rate, tax rates on individuals' ordinary income, and tax rates on individuals' capital gains have changed a number of times over the last 25 years. These changes influence the choice of organizational form from a purely tax view. However, before we analyze the effect of specific tax rate configurations on the choice of organizational form over the last 25 years, we need to develop several more concepts.

The Required Before-Tax Rates of Return on Corporate and Partnership Activities

The corporate sector of the economy has dominated (in terms of capital under control) and continues to dominate the partnership form as the vehicle through which goods and services are produced. For this dominance to persist, the cost of converting from corporate form to partnership form or the nontax advantages of corporate form must be considerable. In this section, we determine how large the before-tax return of corporations must be (because of the nontax advantages) to preserve indifference between the partnership and the fully taxable corporation.

Let us denote the before-tax rate of return in corporate form as R_c and in partnership form as R_p. Previously we assumed that the before-tax rate of return (R) was the same in corporate and partnership form. In this section, we allow for the possibility that, for nontax reasons, it might be less costly to produce identical goods and services in a corporation than in a partnership. For example, partners might not enjoy as well-defined property rights (due to relatively sparse case law) as corporate stockholders. Partnerships might have poorer access to capital markets and might face higher administrative costs.

After corporate taxes, *but before shareholder-level taxes,* the corporation realizes a return of r_c, where $r_c = R_c(1 - t_c)$. After personal taxes, the partnership realizes a return of r_p, where $r_p = R_p(1 - t_p)$. Let us assume that both R_c and R_p are constant across time, so we need not employ a second subscript to denote time.

What level of corporate after-tax return, r_c, will make a tax planner indifferent between corporate and partnership form? We will denote this particular level of return as r_c^*. To find r_c^*, we continue to assume that the corporation pays no dividends and that shareholders pay tax on realized capital gains at tax rates below the personal tax rate $(0 < t_{cg} < t_p)$. Suppose the typical shareholder holds stock for n years. To be competitive, the after-tax rate of return on shares must be equal to the after-tax rate of return on undertaking the same investment in partnership form. By starting with equation (4.3) and equating the after-tax returns from an initial investment of $\$I$ in both corporate and partnership form we can derive the following

$$\$I[1 + R_p(1 - t_p)]^n = \$I[1 + R_c(1 - t_c)]^n(1 - t_{cg}) + t_{cg}\$I \qquad \textbf{(4.3)}$$

$$(1 + r_p)^n = (1 + r_c^*)^n(1 - t_{cg}) + t_{cg}$$

$$[(1 + r_c^*)^n(1 - t_{cg}) + t_{cg}]^{1/n} - 1 = r_p \qquad \textbf{(4.5)}$$

The left side of equation (4.5) has the following interpretation. A stock investment appreciates at rate r_c^* per year for n years. At time n, the firm buys back all of its shares and a shareholder-level tax is paid at rate t_{cg} on the entire value of the repurchased shares, except for the initial I dollars invested, which are returned tax-free to the investor. The after-tax accumulation at time n is $[(1 + r_c)^n(1 - t_{cg}) + t_{cg}]$. As previously noted, accumulation in non-dividend-paying common stock is exactly the same as accumulation in a single premium deferred annuity that accrues interest at rate r_c and is taxed at rate t_{cg} on surrender. The annual rate of return is determined by taking the nth root of the after-tax accumulation per dollar invested and then subtracting 1.

We can rearrange equation (4.5) to solve directly for r_c^*, the after corporate tax— but before shareholder-level taxes—rate of return that will make a tax planner indifferent between corporate and partnership form

$$r_c^* = \{[(1 + r_p)^n - t_{cg}]/(1 - t_{cg})\}^{1/n} - 1 \qquad \textbf{(4.6)}$$

Even armed with equation (4.6), the tax planner has a difficult task to determine r_c^*. The tax planner must know the holding period and the personal tax rate of the firm's shareholders. And the task is complicated further because shareholders face different tax rates and investment horizons.

Still, equation (4.6) holds the key to determining before-tax required rates of return. Consider current tax rules. Assume that the typical shareholder has a personal tax rate, t_p, of 35%, has a capital gains rate, t_{cg}, of 15%, and holds shares for 5 years $(n = 5)$. Assume further that projects undertaken in partnerships return 10% before tax (that is, $R_p = 10\%$). Then after-tax partnership returns are 6.5%, or $10\%(1 - .35)$. To be competitive, stocks must appreciate at a rate exceeding 6.5% but less than 10%. The upper bound arises because shareholders face a tax on share appreciation but the tax is at favorable capital gains rates, giving rise to the lower bound. The required return is given by solving for r_c^* in equation (4.6). The stock must appreciate at a rate of 7.5% per year (after corporate-level tax but before shareholder-level tax)

$$r_c^* = \{[(1 + .065)^5 - .15]/(1 - .15)\}^{1/5} - 1 = .075$$

A 7.5% appreciation rate on stock results in a 6.5% after-tax rate of return to shareholders. That is, if shareholders pay tax on their realized capital gains at the end of 5 years, they realize exactly the same after-tax rate of return as if they had invested in a partnership that yields 10% pretax and 6.5% after tax. Each dollar invested in stock at a before-tax return of 7.5% per year grows to $1.436 in 5 years. After paying tax at a capital gains rate of 15% on the $.436 of realized gain, shareholders retain $1.37. Accumulating $1.37 after-tax in 5 years per dollar of initial investment is equivalent to an after-tax rate of return of 6.5% per year $[(1.37)^{1/5} - 1 = .065]$. Table 4.1 gives the required annual before-tax rate of return on corporate shares, r_c^*—highlighted by boldface type—for various holding periods and marginal tax rates. The required returns are plotted in Figure 4.1.

TABLE 4.1	Required Annualized Corporate After-Tax—but Before Shareholder-Level Tax—Return on Shares, r_c^*, for Different Investor Marginal Tax Rates (t_p and t_{cg}) and Holding Periods (n), with a Partnership Before-Tax Return (R_p) of 10%						

Shareholder Tax Rates		R_p	**Before Shareholder-Level Tax Required Rates of Return on Stocks (%), r_c^* (after corporate tax but before shareholder tax)[a]**					**After-Tax Return[b]**
t_p	t_{cg}		$n = 1$	5	10	20	50	
50%	20%	10%	**6.25**	**6.11**	**5.97**	**5.76**	**5.43**	5.0
40%	16%	10%	**7.14**	**7.00**	**6.86**	**6.65**	**6.35**	6.0
30%	12%	10%	**7.95**	**7.82**	**7.70**	**7.52**	**7.27**	7.0

[a]r_c^* is calculated using equation (4.6). The numbers in boldface are calculated based on the parameter values in normal typeface.

[b]This is the after-tax rate of return on both stocks and partnerships.

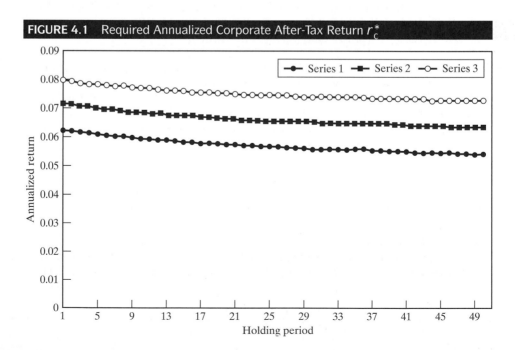

FIGURE 4.1 Required Annualized Corporate After-Tax Return r_c^*

Note that for any level of the personal tax rate, t_p, the required before share-holder-tax rate of return, r_c^*, falls as the holding period increases. As n increases without limit, r_c^* approaches the after-tax return on partnerships. The reason that the required return on shares before shareholder-level tax decreases as the investment horizon lengthens is that holding onto the shares allows the capital gains tax to be deferred. Therefore, for any given rate of annual appreciation on shares, r_c^*, the after-tax return on shares increases with the length of the holding period, just as was true for a single premium deferred annuity contract. We can view this as a reduction in the shareholder-level tax rate as the holding period on shares increases. As this tax rate decreases, so does the level of the before-tax return on shares required to achieve a target level of after-tax return. Also, because of the favorable capital gains tax rates, the required return to shares before shareholder-level tax is below the before-tax rate of return to partnerships (of 10% in Table 4.1) even for short holding periods. Investors require higher before-tax rates of return on investments that are taxed less favorably.

The Required Rate of Return on Stocks in the Presence of Dividends

In establishing the required rate of return on shares in equation (4.6), we assumed that all returns were taxed as capital gains. If, instead, shares pay a dividend at rate d, and such dividends are taxed at rate t_{div}, the required return on shares over a *single* period, r_c^*, satisfies[7]

$$[(1 + r_c^* - d)(1 - t_{\text{cg}}) + t_{\text{cg}}] + d(1 - t_{\text{div}}) = 1 + r_p \qquad \textbf{(4.7)}$$

That is, the after-tax capital gain on shares (the first term in (4.7)) plus the after-tax dividend return on the shares, $d(1 - t_{\text{div}})$, (the second term in (4.7)) must be equal to the after-tax partnership return. Again solving for r_c^*, we find that

$$r_c^* = [(1 + r_p) - d(1 - t_{\text{div}}) - t_{\text{cg}}]/(1 - t_{\text{cg}}) + d - 1$$

If dividends are taxed less favorably than are capital gains to individual shareholders, as we initially assume here, the required return on shares is increasing in the dividend yield. For example, when total stock returns are taxed at capital gains rates, a taxpayer facing tax rates of $t_p = t_{\text{div}} = 40\%$ and $t_{\text{cg}} = 16\%$ requires a before-tax return on stocks of 7.14% over a 1-year horizon to yield the 6% after-tax return available in partnerships. (See the 40% row of Table 4.1.) That is, $7.14\% \times (1 - .16) = 6\%$. But when the dividend yield is 3%, the required r_c^* is

$$r_c^* = [(1 + .06) - .03(1 - .40) - .16]/(1 - .16) + .03 - 1 = .08$$

The total required return before shareholder-level tax, then, is 8%, consisting of 5% in capital gains and 3% in dividends.

Table 4.2 reports the required before-tax rates of return, for various investor tax rates and holding periods, for a stock that pays a 3% dividend. In calculating the values in Table 4.2, we assume that dividends distributed to shareholders are taxed at the

---

[7]In Chapter 5, we will explore arbitrage strategies that may allow dividends to be taxed more favorably than at rate t_{div}.

TABLE 4.2 Required Annualized Corporate After-Tax—but Before Shareholder-Level Tax—Return on Shares, r_c^*, *Paying a 3% Dividend Rate* for Different Investor Marginal Tax Rates (t_p and t_{cg}) and Holding Periods (n), with a Partnership Before-Tax Return (R_p) of 10%

Shareholder Tax Rates		R_p	Before Shareholder-Level Tax Required Rates of Return on Stocks (%), r_c^* (after corporate tax but before shareholder tax)[a]					After-Tax Return[b]
$t_p = t_{div}$	t_{cg}		$n = 1$	5	10	20	50	
50%	20%	10%	**7.38**	**7.28**	**7.17**	**7.02**	**6.76**	5.0
40%	16%	10%	**8.00**	**7.90**	**7.80**	**7.64**	**7.40**	6.0
30%	12%	10%	**8.57**	**8.48**	**8.38**	**8.24**	**8.04**	7.0

[a]r_c^* is calculated using the equation in footnote 8. The numbers in boldface are calculated based on the parameter values in normal typeface.

[b]This is the after-tax rate of return on both stocks and partnerships.

investors marginal tax rate, that is, $t_{div} = t_p$, and the after-tax dividends are reinvested in the partnership sector at rate r_p.[8]

Compare required returns in Tables 4.1 and 4.2. Table 4.2 indicates that required returns before shareholder-level tax are higher when dividend yields are positive. In addition, the required returns fall off more slowly in Table 4.2 as the length of the investment horizon increases. The reason, of course, is that when dividends are paid, a smaller fraction of the total return on shares comes from capital gains, and it is only the tax on capital gains that is reduced as the investment horizon increases.

The Effective Annualized Tax Rate on Shares: t_s

Tables 4.1 and 4.2 show the required rates of return on stocks before shareholder-level tax necessary for corporations to compete with partnerships. These returns depend on the length of the investment horizon. We find it convenient to define a variable that captures the hypothetical annual tax rate that shareholders could pay *each year* on their pretax stock returns that would be equivalent to paying the shareholder-level tax they actually pay when they sell their shares. Call this variable the **effective annualized tax rate on shares,** and denote it t_s. If shareholders paid tax at rate t_s each year on their total stock returns (dividends plus capital gains), they would end up with the same after-tax accumulation as they actually achieve. The effective annualized tax rate on shares is found from

$$r_c^*(1 - t_s) = r_p \qquad (4.8)$$

Thus,

$$t_s = 1 - r_p/r_c^* \qquad (4.9)$$

---

[8]The table values for r_c^* satisfy (solved by iteration):

$$(1 + r_c^* - d)^n(1 - t_{cg}) + t_{cg} + d(1 - t_{div})\sum_{t=1}^{n}(1 + r_c^* - d)^{t-1}(1 + r_p)^{n-t} = (1 + r_p)^n$$

For example, in Table 4.1, we find that for a personal tax rate of 50% and a 10-year holding period, the annual required before shareholder-level tax rate of return, r_c^*, is 5.97%. Thus, $t_s = 1 - .05/.0597$, or 16.2%. If investors paid tax at a rate of 16.2% on accrued gains each year, this would be equivalent to paying tax at a 20% capital gains rate on selling their shares in 10 years.

Required Before-Tax Rate of Return: Corporations versus Partnerships

Having defined r_c^*, we can now express easily the required before-tax return on projects undertaken by corporations, R_c^*.

$$R_c^*(1 - t_c) = r_c^* \tag{4.10}$$

Substituting r_c^* from (4.10) into (4.8)

$$R_c^*(1 - t_c)(1 - t_s) = r_p$$

and noting that $r_p = R_p(1 - t_p)$, we can now determine the required before-tax return, R_c^*, on corporate projects relative to partnership projects:

$$R_c^*(1 - t_c)(1 - t_s) = R_p(1 - t_p)$$

or

$$\frac{R_c^*}{R_p} = \frac{(1 - t_p)}{(1 - t_c)(1 - t_s)} \tag{4.11}$$

Note that if the effective annualized tax rate on shares, t_s, is low and the corporate tax rate is somewhat below the personal tax rate, the required rate of return on corporate projects could be approximately equal to that on partnership projects. For example, if the corporate tax rate is 35%, the personal tax rate is 39.6%, and the effective shareholder-level tax rate is 7%, the required pretax return on corporate projects is approximately equal to that on partnership projects.

However, if the personal tax rate is only 28% rather than 39.6%,

$$\frac{R_c^*}{R_p} = \frac{(1 - .28)}{(1 - .35)(1 - .07)} = 1.191$$

In other words, the pretax return on corporate projects must exceed that on partnership projects by 19%. If partnership projects yield 10% pretax, corporate projects must yield 11.9% ($.10 \times 1.191$) to provide the same after-tax return. In the absence of a nontax advantage of corporations over partnerships of at least 1.9% pretax, corporations could not compete with partnerships for the same investments under these circumstances.

Armed with the above relations we can now quickly determine how the relative attractiveness of the corporate form versus the partnership form has fluctuated over the last 25 years as Congress has changed tax rates. We summarize the comparisons in Table 4.3. In generating this table, we assume investments in the partnership form yield a 10% pretax rate of return, that the investor holds the investment for a 10-year period, that the corporation pays no interim dividends, and that the investor faces the top statutory tax rate each year. We plot the results in Figure 4.2.

TABLE 4.3	Required Annualized Corporate After-Tax—but Before Shareholder-Level Tax—Return on Shares, r_c^*, Effective Annualized Tax Rate on Shares, t_s, and Required Pretax Corporate Return, R_c^*, for Corporation to Earn Same After-Tax Return as Partnership Form Over the Past 25 Years.[a] (Assumes Investor Holding Period (n) of 10 Years and Partnership Before-Tax Return (R_p) of 10%)						

Period	R_p	t_c	t_p	t_{cg}	r_c^*	t_s	R_c^*
Pre-1981	10.0	.46	.70	.28	**3.98**	24.7	**7.37**
1982–1986	10.0	.46	.50	.20	**5.97**	16.3	**11.06**
1987	10.0	.40	.39	.28	**7.81**	21.9	**13.02**
1988–1990	10.0	.34	.28	.28	**9.12**	21.1	**13.82**
1991–1992	10.0	.34	.31	.28	**8.77**	21.3	**13.29**
1993–1996	10.0	.35	.396	.28	**7.77**	22.0	**11.91**
1997–2000	10.0	.35	.396	.20	**7.16**	15.7	**11.02**
2001–2002	10.0	.35	.386	.18	**7.14**	14.0	**10.99**
2003–	10.0	.35	.35	.15	**7.34**	11.5	**11.30**

[a]r_c^* is calculated using equation (4.6), t_s is calculated using equation (4.9), and R_c^* is calculated using equation (4.11). The numbers in boldface are calculated based on the parameter values in normal typeface. The 18% capital gains tax rate in 2001–2002 applied to assets held longer than 5 years.

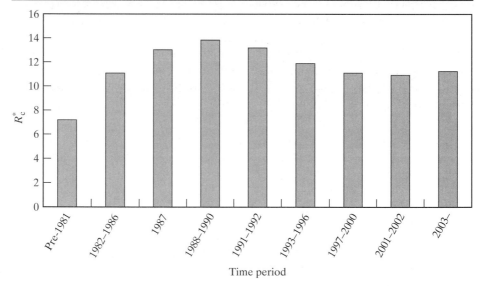

FIGURE 4.2 Required Pretax Corporate Return R_c^*, $R_p = 10\%$, Holding Period 10 Years, 0 Dividends

Pre-1981 Economic Recovery Tax Act (ERTA 1981)

Prior to the 1980s, the maximum personal tax rate, t_p, at 70% was far greater than the corporate tax rate, t_c, at 46%, and capital gains were taxed at rates substantially less than ordinary income tax rates. This favored the corporate form (unless for nontax reasons current corporate profits were distributed as dividends and shareholders were unable to convert dividends into capital gains by using arbitrage strategies).[9] For example, as reported in Table 4.3, the required corporate return, R_c (before all taxes, corporate- and shareholder-level), for an investor to be indifferent between the partnership form earning 10% pretax and the corporate form is 7.37%. Thus even though the corporate form is subject to double taxation, the deferral of taxation, the lower capital gains tax rate at the shareholder-level, and the lower corporate tax rate relative to the personal tax rate all combine to make the corporate form tax advantaged during this period. Recall, that these results are for a non-dividend-paying stock and an investor holding period of 10 years. For a dividend-paying stock, the required pretax corporate return will be somewhat higher than 7.37%. Why? The shareholder-level tax will be higher because there is no deferral for the dividend portion, which is taxed at the higher ordinary-income tax rate. For holding periods longer than the 10 years assumed in Table 4.3, the effective shareholder-level tax is lower, and thus the required pretax corporate return is even lower than 7.37% (tabulated in Table 4.4 below).

Post-1981 Economic Recovery Tax Act (1981–1986)

The Economic Recovery Tax Act of 1981 lowered both the maximum personal income tax rate from 70% to 50% and the capital gains rate from 28% to 20%. As indicated in Table 4.3, these changes lowered the effective shareholder tax rate from approximately 25% to 16%. This might appear to increase the tax advantage of the corporate form even more. However, lowering the personal tax rate increased the after-tax return to the partnership from $.10(1 - .70) = 3\%$ pre-1981 to $.10(1 - .50) = 5\%$ post-1981. To be competitive, the required pretax corporate rate of return increased from 7.37% pre-1981 to 11.06% post-1981. Thus, the corporate form became tax-disfavored.

Post-1986 Tax Reform Act (1987, 1988–1990)

With the 1986 Tax Reform Act, the top personal tax rate fell below the top corporate tax rate. When personal tax rates are below corporate tax rates, the after-tax rate of return in partnership form is greater than the after-tax rate of return in corporate form. Thus, as a result of the 1986 Tax Act, partnerships became even more tax-favored relative to corporations as a way to minimize taxes. The 1987 tax year was a transition year as the new lower statutory tax rates were phased in over 2 years. Nevertheless, even in 1987, it is evident that the corporate form became more tax-disfavored relative to the partnership form. In the period 1988–90, the required pretax corporate return of 13.82% indicates that the pretax return on corporate projects needed to exceed that on partnerships by at least 38% for the corporation to earn the same after-tax return. This is a large tax disadvantage. But as we will explain in more detail later in this chapter, the nontax advantages of the corporate form and the cost of converting from one form to another may have been enough to overcome the tax disadvantages of continuing to operate in corporate form. As we stress throughout the text, good tax planning strategies do not always result in minimizing taxes: Tax minimization may be sacrificed because of nontax costs and benefits that differ across the tax planning alternatives.

---

[9]We will investigate such arbitrage strategies in Chapter 5.

Post-1990 Revenue Reconciliation Tax Acts (1991–1996)

The Revenue Reconciliation Tax Act of 1990 increased the top tax rate on ordinary income to 31% for the tax year 1991. Because of this impact on the after-tax return to the partnership form, the required corporate pretax return declined slightly from 13.82% to 13.29%. The Revenue Reconciliation Tax Act of 1993 increased both the corporate tax rate (from 34% to 35%) and the ordinary tax rate (from 31% to 39.6%). Since the corporate rate was now lower than the ordinary income tax rate, the corporate form offered a deferral advantage thus reducing the relative tax disadvantage of the corporate form: The required corporate pretax return decreased from above 13% to 11.91%.

Post-1997 Tax Payer Relief Act (1997–2000)

The Taxpayer Relief Act of 1997 reduced the capital gains rate to 20% from 28% (and the IRS Restructuring and Reform Act of 1998 clarified and simplified the holding period and capital gains rules). This reduced the effective shareholder-level tax to 15.7% for the 10-year holding period illustrated in Table 4.3. This change further reduced the relative tax disadvantage of the corporate form.

Post-2000 Economic Growth and Tax Relief Reconciliation Act (2001–2002) and the Jobs and Growth Tax Relief Reconciliation Act of 2003 (2003 on)

The Economic Growth and Tax Relief Reconciliation Act of 2001 enacted reduced tax rates for individuals that were to be phased in over the following 5 years and the top capital gains tax rate on assets held longer than 5 years was reduced to 18%. However, the Jobs and Growth Tax Relief Reconciliation Act of 2003 (JGTRCA 2003) accelerated these phase-ins and reduced the top capital gains tax rate to 15% and the top individual tax rate to 35%. This act also reduced the top tax rate on corporate dividends to 15% (analyzed below). While a reduction in the long-term capital gains tax rate lowers the required corporate pretax return, a decrease in the individual tax rate on partnership income increases the required corporate pretax return. In 2001–2002, the 2% reduction in capital gains tax offset the 1% reduction in the top marginal rate, resulting in a decrease in the required corporate pretax return. With the further reduction in the top capital gains tax rate in 2003, the effective shareholder-level tax rate is reduced but the further reduction in the top individual tax rate to 35% (increasing the after-tax return to partnerships) more than offsets the benefit of the 3% reduction in the top capital gains tax rate to 15% such that the required corporate pretax return increases.

Our comparisons between the corporate form and partnership form assume a 10-year holding period for the investor. Table 4.4 presents the required pretax corporate rates of return for various holding periods again assuming zero dividends. In calculating the 1-year holding period results we assume that returns to shareholders are taxed at capital gains rates.

The results in Table 4.4 indicate, as expected, that as the holding period increases, the required corporate pretax rate of return declines. The longer holding period allows investors to defer the shareholder-level tax in a non-dividend-paying stock. For investors with relatively long holding periods, under the current configuration of top statutory tax rates, there is only a slight tax disadvantage to the corporate form.

TABLE 4.4 Required Pretax Corporate Return, r_c^*, for Corporation to Earn Same After-Tax Return as Partnership for Different Holding Periods.[a] (Assumes Partnership Before-Tax Return (R_p) of 10%)

					Required R_c^*, for n-Year Holding Period				
Period	R_p	t_c	t_p	t_{cg}	$n = 1$	5	10	20	50
Pre-1981	10.0	.46	.70	.28	**7.72**	**7.55**	**7.37**	**7.09**	**6.56**
1982–1986	10.0	.46	.50	.20	**11.57**	**11.32**	**11.06**	**10.67**	**10.06**
1987	10.0	.40	.39	.28	**14.12**	**13.56**	**13.02**	**12.29**	**11.28**
1988–1990	10.0	.34	.28	.28	**15.15**	**14.46**	**13.82**	**13.00**	**11.95**
1991–1992	10.0	.34	.31	.28	**14.52**	**13.88**	**13.29**	**12.51**	**11.49**
1993–1996	10.0	.35	.396	.28	**12.91**	**12.40**	**11.91**	**11.24**	**10.32**
1997–2000	10.0	.35	.396	.20	**11.62**	**11.31**	**11.02**	**10.60**	**9.99**
2001–2002	10.0	.35	.386	.18	**11.52**	**11.25**	**10.99**	**10.61**	**10.06**
2003–	10.0	.35	.35	.15	**11.76**	**11.53**	**11.30**	**10.98**	**10.51**

[a]R_c^* is calculated using equation (4.11). The numbers in boldface are calculated based on the parameter values in normal typeface. In 2001–2002, for simplicity we assume the 18% top capital gains tax applies to all holding periods.

Further Analysis of the 2003 Tax Act

As previously noted, the Jobs and Growth Tax Relief Reconciliation Act of 2003 (JGTRCA 2003) reduced the top capital gains tax rate to 15% and the top individual tax rate to 35%. However, in a radical departure from prior policy, the act also reduced the top individual tax rate on corporate dividends to 15%.[10] With the reduction in the tax rate on dividends and the equating of the tax rates on dividends and capital gains, dividends are now less tax-disfavored relative to capital gains although capital gains still offer the advantages of deferral. We illustrate this in Table 4.5. With 100% payout of all taxable earnings, the after-tax accumulation to shareholders is calculated as

$$\$I[1 + R_c(1 - t_c)(1 - t_{\text{div}})]^n \tag{4.12}$$

and the annualized after-tax rate of return is

$$r_c = \$I[1 + R_c(1 - t_c)(1 - t_{\text{div}})]^{n(1/n)} - \$I$$

which because of no deferral simplifies to

$$r_c = R_c(1 - t_c)(1 - t_{\text{div}}) \tag{4.13}$$

Thus because of no deferral of shareholder taxation, the after-tax rate of return is a constant regardless of the holding period. In contrast, with zero dividends, capital gains offer the advantage of deferral thus the after-tax rate of return to shareholders

---

[10]President Bush initially proposed a 0% tax rate on dividends and an indexing of the taxpayers' basis in their stock for purposes of calculating capital gains for stocks paying out less than 100% of their taxable earnings (which would have resulted in adding more complexity to the Tax Code). The reduced dividend tax rate applies only to dividends that are paid from corporate earnings on which corporate taxes have already been paid. Also instead of a 0% tax rate on dividends, an alternative is to (a) allow firms to deduct dividends in calculating their taxable income or (b) include dividends in the taxpayers' taxable income while allowing a credit for the corporate taxes paid on their personal tax returns. The latter alternative is referred to as an integrated or dividend imputation system. We analyze such a system in the appendix to this chapter.

TABLE 4.5 After-Tax Return to Shareholders Assuming Corporate Pretax Rate of Return of 10%. Dividends and Capital Gains Both Taxed at 15%[a]

| Dividend Policy | R_c | t_c | t_{div} | t_{cg} | *After-Tax Return to Shareholders r_c* | | | | |
					$n = 1$	5	10	20	50
100% payout	10.0	.35	.15	.15	**5.53**	**5.53**	**5.53**	**5.53**	**5.53**
0% payout	10.0	.35		.15	**5.53**	**5.56**	**5.72**	**5.90**	**6.17**

[a]The numbers in boldface are calculated based on the parameter values in normal typeface.

increases as the holding period increases. The 0% payout line in Table 4.5 is calculated using equation (4.2).

An alternative way to present these comparisons is to calculate the pretax rate of return required to be earned by corporations, R_c^*, to give the same after-tax return as investing in a partnership. With 100% payout, we calculate R_c^* by equating the accumulations to each organizational form: that is, equating equations (4.1) and (4.12)

$$\$I[1 + R_p(1 - t_p)]^n = \$I[1 + R_c(1 - t_c)(1 - t_{div})]^n$$
$$(1 + r_p)^n = [1 + r_c^*(1 - t_{div})]^n \qquad (4.14)$$

Solving for r_c^* we get

$$(1 + r_p)^{n(1/n)} = [1 + r_c^*(1 - t_{div})]$$
$$(1 + r_p) - 1 = r_c^*(1 - t_{div})$$
$$r_c^* = [(1 + r_p)^n - 1]/(1 - t_{div}) \qquad (4.15)$$

And R_c^* then is given by $R_c^* = r_c^*/(1 - t_c)$. For the zero-dividend-paying corporation, the required pretax rates of return are given by equation (4.6) and (4.10) and can also be found in the last line of Table 4.4. The required corporate pretax rates of return are reported in Table 4.6 for different holding periods. Because there is no deferral of any taxes with a 100% dividend payout, the required corporate pretax rate of return is a constant regardless of the holding period whereas capital gains continue to offer deferral. When dividends are taxed at a lower rate, the required corporate pretax rate of return is correspondingly lower.

The required corporate pretax rate of return can be thought of as a cost of equity capital *assuming* the next best alternative for investors is the 10% pretax partnership

TABLE 4.6 Required Pretax Corporate Return, R_c^*, for Corporation to Earn Same After-Tax Return as Partnership for Different Holding Periods.[a] (Assumes Partnership Before-Tax Return (R_p) of 10%)

| Dividend Policy | R_c | t_c | t_{div} | t_{cg} | *Required R_c^*, for n-Year Holding Period* | | | | |
					$n = 1$	5	10	20	50
100% payout	10.0	.35	.35		**15.38**	**15.38**	**15.38**	**15.38**	**15.38**
	10.0	.35	.15		**11.76**	**11.76**	**11.76**	**11.76**	**11.76**
0% Payout	10.0	.35		.20	**12.50**	**12.16**	**11.82**	**11.35**	**10.70**
	10.0	.35		.15	**11.76**	**11.53**	**11.30**	**10.98**	**10.51**

[a]The numbers in boldface are calculated based on the parameter values in normal typeface.

return. Thus lowering the tax on dividends from 35% to 15% for a firm paying out 100% of earnings reduces the firm's cost of capital from 15.38% to 11.76%. Lowering the capital gains rate for a non-dividend-paying firm also lowers its cost of capital. Further, the cost of capital is still lower for non-dividend-paying firms even when $t_{\text{div}} = t_{\text{cg}}$ because of the effects of tax deferral on capital gains (for $n = 20$ years, 100% payout, the required pretax corporate return is 11.76% compared with 10.98% with 0% payout). When a firm pays out some dividends but less than 100% of its earnings, the required corporate pretax rates of return (or its cost of capital) lie between the 100% and 0% payout required returns.

In summary, Tables 4.3 to Table 4.6 indicate that pre-1981, corporations, even though subject to double taxation, were generally tax-favored over partnership forms. During the early 1970s, many professional organizations were incorporated. Although they faced a shareholder-level tax when they liquidated their corporations, many doctors, lawyers, and consultants incorporated to escape the high personal tax rate and to shelter income at the lower corporate tax rate of less than 50%.[11] After the Economic Recovery Tax Act was passed in 1981, many of these corporations converted back to partnerships (or alternative organizational forms in which profits are taxed directly to owners rather than taxed first at the entity level). This movement accelerated with the 1986 Tax Reform Act as the corporate tax rate was set above the personal tax rate. The tables indicate that the 1986 Act substantially increased what the nontax advantage of corporations over partnerships had to be for corporations to overcome partnerships' tax advantage. In the years succeeding the 1986 Tax Act through 2000, Congress has gradually increased the tax rate on ordinary income, thus decreasing the after-tax return to partnerships. More recently Congress lowered the top capital gains tax rate and both individual income and dividend tax rates. For non-dividend-paying stocks, the lowering of the top ordinary income tax rate favored the partnership form relative to corporations, but for dividend-paying stocks, the relative tax disadvantage declined. However, it is still beneficial for firms to defer dividends to obtain deferred capital gains tax treatment for shareholders.

Cross-Sectional Variation in Corporate, Personal, and the Shareholder-Level Tax Rates

Our discussion shows that tax rules can lead to a preference for producing goods and services through a particular type of legal entity. To compare investing in the partnership and corporate forms, we used a very simple model in which the corporate tax rate, t_c, the personal tax rate on ordinary income, t_p, and the personal capital gains rate, t_{cg}, were given and each party was taxed at the top statutory tax rate. We now relax some of the assumptions of this simple model to recognize that:

1. The corporate tax rate is not constant across corporate organizations or over time.
2. The shareholder-level tax varies across individual investors.
3. With progressive income tax rates, the ordinary rate, t_p, also varies among investors.

---

[11]Another important factor contributing to the decision to incorporate was the generous opportunities to postpone the payment of tax by making tax-deductible contributions to pension accounts on behalf of corporate owner-managers. We will explore this consideration further in Chapter 9.

Net Operating Losses and the Corporate Tax Rate

The corporate tax rate is not the same for all corporations. Start-up companies might generate **net operating losses** for many years before becoming profitable. With net operating losses, a corporation does not pay tax currently. Prior to the 1997 Tax Act losses could be carried back for 3 years and carried forward for a period of 15 years. For example, if the corporation experienced a net operating loss in 1988 when the statutory tax rate was 34%, and it paid taxes in 1985 at a 46% marginal tax rate, it would receive a rebate of $.46 on every dollar of net operating loss in 1988, up to the taxes it paid in 1985. Once the 1985 taxable income is exhausted, further net operating losses in 1988 would result in rebates of taxes paid in 1986 and then 1987. This opportunity did not go unnoticed by corporate America. Numerous companies sold or closed plants at a loss following the drop in corporate tax rates to secure tax refunds at a 46% rate.[12] The 1997 Tax Act reduced the carryback period to 2 years and increased the carryforward period to 20 years.[13]

Because a start-up firm might take several years to generate taxable profits, if it ever turns profitable at all, a start-up company's marginal tax rate is often far less than the statutory corporate tax rate. This might appear to make the corporate form relatively more attractive than a partnership. But if start-up losses can be deducted against other income earned by a partner, operating in partnership form might prove advantageous: A personal tax rate higher than a corporate tax rate makes the loss deduction more valuable for the partnership.[14] If the partnership becomes profitable, it could convert to a corporation. As we discuss later, there are restrictions on the deductibility of losses generated from so-called passive partnership activities. A partner must be actively involved in the operations of the business to deduct its losses against other income.

Further Complications in Determining the Shareholder-Level Tax Rate, t_s

We have seen that evaluating and ranking the corporate and partnership forms based on tax costs is difficult when investors face different shareholder-level tax rates, which arise because investment horizons and personal tax rates differ. The analysis becomes even more complicated if the returns on stock is held in different organizational forms which are taxed differently. Then the after-tax rates of return for stock depend not only on investor and project characteristics but also on the choice of organizational form in which the stock investment is held. For example, consider the following five investor

---

[12]For further discussion and empirical evidence of firms' incentives to report tax losses in the post TRA-86 years, see Maydew (1997). Note also that we discuss the estimation of corporate marginal tax rates in more detail in Chapter 7.

[13]Most countries allow tax losses to be carried forward, but a number of countries do not allow losses to be carried back to offset previously taxed income. In addition, while many countries allow losses to be carried forward for only a few years, some allow indefinite carryforwards.

[14]Note that deducting start-up losses was a major motivation for the use of (limited) partnerships by the tax shelter industry in the 1970s and early 1980s. Individuals with high personal tax rates invested as limited partners and were allocated the losses that they could deduct against their other income. With top personal tax rates of 70%, the deductions were quiet valuable. Over the years Congress has reduced the attraction of such tax shelters. In particular, as we discuss in Chapter 6, the passive income activity rules introduced in the 1986 Tax Act severely curtailed this type of tax shelter activity.

groups that hold common stock:

1. *Fully Taxable Investors:* Wealthy investors hold a large fraction of the market value of common stock. Such high-income investors typically defer realization of capital gains. Their effective tax rate on shares depends partly on how long they defer capital gains and the rate at which capital gains are taxed. As we will discuss in later chapters, their tax rate also depends on the characteristics of other investments they hold in their portfolio. For these investors, the shareholder-level tax could be very low.

2. *Tax-Exempt Organizations:* **Tax-exempt organizations** include pension funds, universities, hospitals, charities, and religious organizations. They escape tax on both dividend and capital gains income. For this group, the before-tax rate of return on shares is the same as the after-tax rate of return on shares (that is, $t_s = 0$).

    Tax-exempt organizations might appear to be natural candidates for investing in partnerships. But the earnings from active participation in such investments are classified as "unrelated business income" and are taxed at corporate rates.[15] The corporate tax can be avoided if tax-exempt entities invest passively in limited partnership interests, but the presence of debt in the partnership's capital structure taints the passive income, subjecting it once again to corporate tax on unrelated business income. So in many circumstances, tax-exempt organizations face the same tax burden whether investing in corporate entities or partnerships. Tax-exempt organizations are more naturally suited to passive investment in assets like taxable bonds, for which the income they earn escapes taxation.

3. *Corporations:* When a corporation owns a partnership interest, the partnership income is subjected to double taxation (that is, at the corporate- and shareholder-level), just as if the project were undertaken directly by the corporation. When a corporation invests in the stock of other corporations, the income may be subjected to *triple* taxation, twice at the corporate level and once at the personal shareholder level, although some relief may be granted at the corporate level.[16]

---

[15]Even though tax exempt (and not-for-profit—discussed below) organizations are taxed on unrelated business activity many still engage in these unrelated business activities. Given the differential taxation across the related (tax-exempt) and unrelated (taxable) activities, these organizations have incentives to shift costs into the unrelated activity because the costs are then deductible. Yetman (2002) provides evidence consistent with this shifting and provides estimates on the magnitude of costs shifted and taxes saved. He estimates that these organizations shifted $2 to $4 billion of costs annually, saving approximately $700 to $1,400 million in taxes.

[16]U.S. corporations are exempt on a fraction of dividend income received from other U.S. corporations. This fraction currently is 70% (80% exempt if the shareholder owns at least 20% of corporate stock and 100% exempt if the shareholder owns at least 80% of the corporate stock). Canadian corporations receive a 100% exemption for dividends received from other Canadian corporations. If taxes were the only consideration, U.S. corporations should not invest in the stock of other U.S. corporations if they can undertake the same investments directly, even if the corporation they invested in had a policy of paying out 100% of its after-tax profits as dividends that are 70% tax exempt. An investment in the stock of another corporation would simply result in *triple,* rather than double, taxation of corporate income. To see this, note that a direct investment in a project that yields R before tax, yields $R(1 - t_c)$ after corporate tax. An investment in the stock of a corporation that undertakes the same project and distributes a dividend yields only

$$R(1 - t_c)(1 - dt_c)$$

where d is the fraction of the dividend that is taxable to the corporate investor (for example, 30% after 1987). As long as $d > 0$ (some dividend tax is paid), direct investments in the project dominate an investment in the same project through another corporation.

4. *Foreign Investors:* Foreign nonresident investors do not pay U.S. taxes on realized capital gains on common stock of corporations they do not control. They may, however, face home-country tax on such gains. Depending on the jurisdiction of residency, the tax rate could be well above or well below the rate faced by U.S. investors. U.S. corporations are required to withhold a tax of from 0% to 30% of the dividends they pay to foreigners depending upon the foreigners' countries of residence and the treaties between the United States and the respective countries.

Under certain circumstances, foreign investors can have a strong preference for undertaking passive investment in the United States through a U.S. corporation rather than a partnership, even though a U.S. investor may prefer the partnership form. This could occur if the foreign investor's home country assessed a high tax rate on partnership income earned in the United States but exempted capital gains.

5. *Broker-Dealers:* Broker-dealers make markets in common stock. They hold inventories of stock to facilitate their market-making activities. Like gains and losses on inventory holdings in other businesses, all broker-dealer income (both dividends and capital gains and losses) is taxable at ordinary rates. Unlike other businesses, however, broker-dealers must mark their inventory of securities to fair market value at year-end (known as mark-to-market) and must include in taxable income any unrealized gains and losses. That is, broker-dealers recognize gain or loss each year as if the security is sold on the last day of the tax year. For broker-dealers, the shareholder-level tax rate is typically the corporate or personal marginal tax rate depending on whether the business is organized as a corporation or a partnership. Note that a broker-dealer is indifferent between a dollar of capital gain and a dollar of dividend income. Although this is also true for tax-exempt entities, it is not true of all investors. For example, individual investors typically prefer capital gain income, and those corporate investors eligible for a substantial tax exemption on dividend income typically prefer dividend income.

Progressive Personal Income Tax Rates, t_p and t_{cg}

Finally, not all individuals face the same marginal tax rates on ordinary income and capital gains. The tax rate schedules for individuals (and corporations) are progressive: The statutory tax rate increases as a function of the taxpayer's taxable income. The schedule depends on filing status (single, married filing jointly, married filing separately, and head of household). Not all individuals face the top statutory tax rate and, for example, dividends and partnership income could be taxed at rates lower than the top statutory rate assumed in our model. Also, for lower income individuals, the tax rate on capital gains is 5% instead of 15%.

These complications do not invalidate the basic points illustrated in our model but do require the tax planner to exercise caution when conducting tax planning for individual taxpayers (what rates do they face?) or when making statements about the tax costs of different organizational forms. The actual tax costs will differ depending on the profitability of the business (and hence on t_c), on the identity of the investor (individual, tax-exempt organization, or another corporation), and on the investor's own marginal tax rate.

4.3 OTHER ORGANIZATIONAL FORMS THROUGH WHICH TO ORGANIZE PRODUCTION ACTIVITIES

Hybrid Corporate Forms

Although many corporate stockholders are subject to double taxation on corporate income, several corporate organizational forms enable shareholders to avoid some or all of the entity-level tax and still retain some of the nontax advantages of the corporate form. As a result, these corporate forms may be more competitive with the partnership form in appropriate circumstances.

1. **S Corporations:** S corporations are limited liability corporations that are taxed as pass-through entities. Stockholders report their pro rata share of income (loss) on their own income tax return just as if they were taxed as partners. Prior to 1996, an S corporation was limited to a maximum 35 stockholders, only one class of stock, and no foreign or corporate shareholders. These requirements limited the ability of S corporations to raise large amounts of capital. For tax years beginning in 1996, the limit on the maximum number of shareholders increased to 75 shareholders, and some trusts (small business trusts), some exempt organizations (qualified retirement plan trusts, as described in IRC Sec 401(a), and some charitable organizations, as described in IRC Sec 501(c)(3)), are now allowed to be S corporation shareholders.

   As we have discussed, the 1986 Tax Act favored organizational forms, like S corporations, that avoid an entity-level tax. In 1985, there were approximately 75,000 S corporation elections. In the 5 weeks spanning the end of 1986 and the beginning of 1987 there were approximately 225,000 S corporation elections, or three times as many (over this 5-week period) as occurred throughout all of calendar 1985.[17] This suggests that the costs of operating as an S corporation relative to a regular corporation did not outweigh the advantages of avoiding an entity-level tax subsequent to the 1986 Tax Act for a large number of businesses.

2. **Limited Liability Companies (LLCs):** LLCs are hybrid entities that under state law are neither partnerships nor corporations. Under state law, they offer shareholders limited liability (that is, protection from personal liability for entity debts). Under current federal tax law, these entities can elect to be taxed as a partnership. Prior to 1997, determining whether the LLC qualified for partnership tax treatment was very complex, but the 1997 "check-the-box" regulations simplified the entity classification process.[18] The **check-the-box regulations** allow eligible entities that are not automatically treated as a corporation to elect (check-the-box) to be treated as a corporation for

---

[17]Tax Notes, 2/1/88, p. 434, quoting Ronald Perlman. See also Plesko (1999) for evidence on S conversions after 1986.
[18]Prior to 1997, to be taxed as a partnership, the tax law required that a partnership differ in economically significant ways from a corporation. Any association (including a partnership) was taxed as a corporation unless it failed to exhibit at least two of the following characteristics: (a) continuity of life, (b) centralization of management, (c) easy transferability of ownership, (d) limited liability, and (e) an economic purpose to the organization.

federal tax purposes.[19] Those not electing corporate tax treatment are treated as flow-through entities.

If treated as a partnership for tax purposes, the LLC offers the advantages of single-level taxation with limited liability and avoids some of the restrictions on ownership that the S corporation faces. Note, however, as with any new organizational form, there is the general uncertainty of the LLC rules governing formation and operation as well as many specific tax issues not yet settled. Further, if LLC's begin to cost the Treasury too much in lost tax revenue, we might expect to see Congress (or Treasury) introduce rules restricting their tax-favored treatment.

3. **Small Business Corporations (Section 1244):** Original stockholders that collectively contribute up to $1,000,000 of equity in such an entity are permitted to deduct realized capital losses against their other income without regard to the usual annual limitation that applies to the sale of regular stock (currently $3,000). The annual Section 1244 deduction limit is $50,000 per taxpayer ($100,000 for a joint return). To qualify, the corporation must be essentially an operating company rather than engaging primarily in passive investment.

4. **Foreign Subsidiaries:** Many U.S. corporations' foreign subsidiaries earn business income in countries where marginal tax rates are below those of the United States. Only when the U.S. parent repatriates these profits are they taxable at the higher U.S. tax rates. At that time, the United States also provides a credit for the foreign taxes that have been paid. By initially paying lower taxes to a foreign government, the U.S. corporation defers the payment of the incremental tax due to the U.S. government compared with what would have been paid had the same activity been carried out in the United States. This deferral reduces both the present value of the tax and the annualized corporate marginal tax rate.[20]

5. **Closely Held Corporations:** Closely held corporations are corporations owned by just a few shareholders, which is common in family or small business concerns. Relative to widely held firms, there tends to exist considerable trust among the owners and employees of closely held firms. In fact, closely held firms are typically managed by their owner. By paying themselves generous salaries and bonuses, owner-managers can avoid part of the corporate-level tax. Unlike dividend payments and capital gains to owner-managers, compensation payments are a tax-deductible expense to the corporation. Many incorporated consulting firms pay out most of their before-tax profits as year-end bonuses to avoid the corporate-level tax. There are limits here, however. The taxing authority may seek to treat part of compensation as a disguised dividend.

---

[19]Basically, entities automatically treated as corporations for tax purposes include firms incorporated under federal or state law, joint-stock companies, insurance companies, and banks. The check-the-box election is also not available to trusts, real estate investment trusts, real estate mortgage investment conduits, or publicly traded partnerships. These organizations are discussed below.

[20]But investing in low-tax foreign jurisdictions may give rise to reduced before-tax rates of return on investment. This is the essence of implicit taxation that is the focus of the next chapter.

A special category of close corporations is personal service corporations. The principal activity of such an entity is personal services performed by owner-employees. For example, a business school professor who provides consulting services might incorporate her consulting business, with her as the sole shareholder, as a personal service corporation.

6. **Not-for-Profit Corporations:** A tax-exempt entity can produce certain goods and services and avoid the corporate tax on the earnings. Prominent examples include not-for-profit hospitals, universities, and religious organizations. In addition, prior to the 1960s, most savings and loan associations were effectively exempt from the corporate tax. The "owners" of all of these tax-exempt enterprises are effectively taxed as a special type of partnership. For example, doctors in not-for-profit hospitals may draw larger salaries as hospital income increases, and such income is taxed only at the personal level. Moreover, although the same opportunity exists in for-profit corporations, deferred salary in tax-exempt entities may be invested at rates of return that are not reduced by entity-level taxation.[21]

7. **Corporations Subject to a Progressive Tax Rate:** Many countries have a progressive corporate tax-rate system. The marginal tax rate of corporations with low levels of taxable income is below that of those with higher levels of taxable income. Because of a progressive corporate tax in the United States, aggressive taxpayers have, in the past, established multiple small corporations. This enabled some entrepreneurs to earn substantially higher returns after paying both the U.S. corporate- and shareholder-level tax than was possible by operating as a partnership. This "loophole" has been closed, and all commonly controlled corporate businesses are now consolidated for tax purposes; the progressive corporate rate remains for only a very limited amount of corporate taxable income.[22]

Other Noncorporate Organizational Forms

1. **Master Limited Partnerships (MLPs):** MLPs are basically partnerships with two types of partners: general partners and limited partners. Provided the limited partners do not actively participate in the management of the partnership, their liability for partnership debts is limited to their invested capital. General partners manage the partnership and have unlimited liability for the partnerships debts. To provide limited liability to the general partner, the general partners are often organized as corporations. MLPs were the backbone of the tax shelter industry in the 1970s and early 1980s. Wealthy individuals contributed capital as limited partners to fund, for example, research and development or oil and gas exploration, which gave rise to losses in the first few years of the business that the limited partners could deduct against

---

[21]The likelihood is great that before-tax rates of return are lower in activities that are tax exempt than in activities that are taxed at the corporate level. Once again, we will discuss this in the next chapter on implicit taxes.

[22]As we will discuss at greater length in Chapter 6, the fact that net operating losses can yield tax savings only if they offset other taxable income also gives rise to progression in corporate tax rates. But then the progression encourages corporate mergers to minimize the chance of generating losses.

their other income.[23] As previously noted, the 1986 Tax Act curbed these activities by limiting the ability of investors to take such losses. Many financial press commentators argued that this change adversely affected the U.S. real estate market. The LLC form tends to be a better choice than the MLP form because investors in an LLC can have both flow-through taxation and limited liability without giving up an active voice in management activities.

2. **Publicly Traded Partnerships (PTPs):** One of the limitations of the partnership form is the difficulty a partner faces in trying to exit from the business. Partnership interests are not easily transferable since there is not an active secondary market for these interests. This lack of transferability represents a major nontax cost of this organizational form. In the early 1980s, some partnerships, especially oil and gas entities, listed their partnership interests on organized stock exchanges, which made it easier for partners to sell or expand their partnership holdings. However, with the 1997 Tax Act, easy transferability of partnership interests (for example, interests traded on an organized exchange such as the New York Stock Exchange) results, with some exceptions, in the partnership being taxed as a corporation. PTPs are specifically excluded from being able to elect partnership treatment under the check-the-box election.

3. **Limited Liability Partnerships (LLPs):** The LLP is a modified general partnership designed specifically for professional service organizations, such as the Big 4 accounting firms, to operate as a partnership with some personal liability protection. The partners are not protected for breaches of professional responsibility. Many but not all states recognize LLPs, which offer advantages similar to the LLC: namely limited liability with a single level of taxation.

4. **Real Estate Investment Trusts (REITs):** This entity is organized as a trust or corporation that receives most of its earnings from real estate activities. If all of the earnings are distributed each year to beneficiaries or shareholders, the REIT avoids an entity-level tax. To qualify for pass-through treatment, the REIT must satisfy such constraints as having a minimum of 100 shareholders, no significant concentration of ownership, and, satisfy two income tests (known as the 95%/75%, but basically income must be generated from real estate–related activities) and an asset test (at least 75% of its assets invested in qualified real estate).

5. **Real Estate Mortgage Investment Conduits (REMICs):** This is another pass-through entity. Substantially all of the REMIC assets must consist of qualified mortgages and mortgage-related assets. REMICs have two classes of owners: owners of "regular" interests and owners of "residual" interests. The former are like bondholders and the latter are like stockholders (except that REMICs do not pay an entity-level tax).

Many of these noncorporate entities are pass-through entities. Distributions from pass-through entities are often referred to as dividends. However, such dividends are subject to tax at the taxpayers marginal tax rate on ordinary income, not the 15% tax rate on corporate dividends, because the earnings from which the "dividends" are paid have not been taxed at the entity level.

---

[23]We will discuss these activities in more detail in Chapter 6.

To compare investing in partnership and corporate forms, we began our analysis with a very simple model in which the corporate tax rate, t_c, the personal tax rate, t_p, and the capital-gains rate, t_{cg}, were given. In some circumstances, even though there is double taxation of corporate income, investors achieve higher after-tax returns in corporate form than in partnership form. When we relaxed the assumptions of this simple model, we found many differences in tax treatment within the corporate form and among different shareholders. This expands the set of circumstances in which corporations may be tax preferred. Note that in selecting an organizational form for a start-up, if losses are expected, then a flow-through entity might be tax-favored because the owner-manager may be able deduct the losses against his other personal income. If small profits are expected, the owner-manager can pay out all profits as compensation effectively converting the C corporation to a flow-through entity. For larger, more profitable entities the algebra in Section 4.2 and tables present the required pretax returns for the C corporation to be competitive with a flow-through entity. Finally, if the owners of the business plan on eventually selling the business, a flow-through entity (such as the S corporation) could result in a higher sales price to the owners. As shown in Chapter 15 and in Erickson and Wang (1999b) the purchase of a flow-through entity, in contrast to a freestanding C corporation, is more likely to be structured for the buyer to obtain a step-up in basis making the acquired business more valuable to the buyer thus leading to a higher price for the flow-through entity in a competitive bidding setting.

We now briefly discuss some frictions and tax-rule restrictions that allow the same activities to coexist in both partnership and corporate form even when tax rates differ across the alternatives.

4.4 NONTAX ADVANTAGES OF OPERATING IN CORPORATE FORM

As we will indicate in subsequent chapters, corporations do enjoy significant nontax advantages over partnerships. Moreover, there can be significant tax and nontax costs to convert from one form to another.[24] These tax and nontax factors make it undesirable for many organizations to operate as partnerships, particularly if they are already "stuck" in corporate form.[25] Some of the more important nontax factors include:

1. *Transaction costs of operating as a large partnership.* Reorganization costs, underdeveloped case law, uncertain property rights in various

---

[24]For example, Code Section 336 requires taxable income to be recognized on the termination of corporate life to the extent the fair market value of the assets exceeds the "basis" (cost for tax purposes) in the stock. Also a converting corporation that uses the LIFO inventory basis must pay a corporate-level recapture tax on the amount by which the FIFO valuation exceeds the LIFO value (called the LIFO reserve).

[25]Guenther (1992) provides evidence on the incremental tax costs and nontax costs of the corporate form versus the master limited partnership form for large publicly traded firms. He also provides evidence on how corporations responded to the increase in the tax costs of the corporate form arising from the changes in the 1981 Tax Act (as indicated in Table 4.3). He found, consistent with the discussion in the text, that firms (a) increased long-term debt, (b) increased non-dividend distributions such as share repurchases, and (c) decreased dividend payout ratios. All three responses reduce the effect of double taxation. Interested readers are also referred to Wolfson (1985) who discusses oil and gas limited partnerships; Shelley, Omer, and Atwood (1998) who discuss restructuring a business as a publicly traded partnership; Omer, Plesko, and Shelley (2000) who examine conversions from C corporations to S corporations in the natural resource industry following TRA 86; and Petroni and Shackelford (1995) who examine the organizational structure of property-casualty insurers.

circumstances, lack of limited liability, and greater operating costs increase the costs to operating as a partnership.

2. *Access to capital markets.* Large corporations traded on organized exchanges typically have easier access to markets for both debt and equity capital. Likewise, shareholders value the right to acquire or sell their assets in liquid markets, a right that is typically absent in the market for partnership interests.

3. *Control of management.* It is more difficult for limited partners to control the actions of managers (the general partners) than it is for stockholders to control managers of corporations.

Even with these corporate nontax benefits, the double taxation of corporate profits cannot be too onerous. Otherwise, costly changes in organizational form will occur or hybrid forms such as the LLC will emerge. Still, tax rules change over time, and it is costly to switch back and forth between partnership and corporate form. Fewer corporations will convert to partnership form if the tax rules are expected to change in favor of the corporate form in the future (as they have gradually over the last 10 years). Finally, we have not yet analyzed fully the investment and financing strategies that corporations may undertake to mitigate the effects of double taxation. We do so in the chapters on capital structure and corporate reorganization.

Summary of Key Points

1. Different organizational forms can produce the same goods and services. Due to differences in tax treatment, conducting identical activities in different organizational forms can result in different after-tax rates of return.

2. Regular corporations are subject to double taxation in many countries, once at the corporate level and then again at the shareholder level. In contrast, partnerships (and other pass-through entities) are taxed only at the investor level.

3. With equal before-tax rates of return on investment, the partnership is tax-favored over the corporate form if the corporate and the ordinary tax rates are the same but there is a non-zero tax on corporate profits at the shareholder level, $t_c = t_p$, and $t_s > 0$.

4. With equal before-tax rates of return on investment, the corporate form is tax-favored over the partnership form if the corporate tax rate is below the ordinary tax rate, $t_c < t_p$, and the tax at the shareholder level, t_s, can be kept sufficiently low.

5. More generally, the corporate form is tax-favored over the partnership form if one minus the corporate tax rate, multiplied by a factor of one minus the effective annualized tax rate on income from holding shares of corporate stock, exceeds one minus the tax rate on partnership income—that is:

$$(1 - t_c)(1 - t_s) > (1 - t_p)$$

6. If the partnership form is tax-favored over the corporate form, and both forms undertake similar investments, some combination of market frictions, tax-rule restrictions, and nontax benefits of operating in corporate form would be necessary to prevent arbitrage.

7. Cross-sectional differences in ordinary and shareholder-level tax rates create opportunities for tax arbitrage in the presence of both corporate and partnership forms of organization. Without frictions or restrictions, if some investors were indifferent between producing in either organizational form, other investors with different tax rates would strictly prefer to invest through one organizational form

and finance the investment by borrowing claims against the returns to the other organizational form.

8. When personal tax rates exceed corporate rates, there exists a unique tax rate on shares, t_s, for a given holding period for stock investment that makes it equally attractive to produce through partnerships as through corporations. Investors with longer investment horizons prefer corporate investments; investors with shorter horizons prefer partnerships.

9. Prior to the 1981 Tax Act, with maximum personal tax rates set well above the corporate tax rate and shareholder-level tax rates set well below personal rates on ordinary income, the corporate form was tax-favored relative to partnerships for many businesses. This was less true of service businesses due to the presence of a 50% maximum personal tax rate on earned income (versus a 70% top rate for unearned income). In the decades preceding the 1970s, earned income was not only taxed at the same high rate as unearned income, but was also taxed at rates as high as 90%. Corporations faced a 50% tax rate and there was a maximum 25% capital gains tax rate on shares, which could be reduced further through tax deferral privileges. Thus, corporations were especially tax-favored during this earlier period.

10. While the required before-tax rates of return at the corporate level might have been quite close to the required before-tax rates of return at the partnership level between the Economic Recovery Tax Act of 1981 and the Tax Reform Act of 1986, this is unlikely to be true subsequent to the Act. This is so because (1) the corporate tax rate exceeded the top personal tax rate and (2) the shareholder-level tax on after-tax corporate profits increased dramatically.

11. From 1998–2002, top individual tax rates were above corporate rates, and capital gains were taxed at rates lower than ordinary income. These changes combined to lower, but not completely remove, the tax disadvantage to the corporate form.

12. Since 2003, capital gains and dividends have been taxed at a top rate of 15% to individuals, thus lowering the relative tax cost of the corporate form. Capital gains continue to offer the advantage of deferral although such advantage is lowered relative to when dividends were taxed at the top rate of 39.6%.

13. In recent years, several organizational forms, such as limited liability companies and limited liability partnerships, have emerged that combine the benefits of limited liability and single-level taxation. A relaxation of the rules for S corporations has also made this organizational form more attractive. However, each alternative organizational form is subject to common law and tax uncertainties relative to the traditional corporation and general partnership forms. Thus we continue to observe the corporate form as the dominant form for business entities requiring large amounts of capital.

14. When there exist tax disadvantages to the corporate form, unless there exist nontax benefits to operating through the corporate form, or unless there are nontrivial costs to corporate liquidation, the tax rules would lead corporations to dissolve or convert to some other form.

15. Nontax benefits of the corporate over partnership form include limited liability, better established corporate case law, a more effective market for corporate control than for partnership control, superior corporate access to capital markets, and the ease of transferability of corporate ownership interests, which enhances investor liquidity.

Appendix 4.1

DIVIDEND IMPUTATION IN THE CORPORATE FORM

A number of countries have a "dividend tax imputation" system that converts part of the corporate-level tax into a partnership-level tax which is intended to mitigate or eliminate the double taxation of corporate dividends, which is inherent in a classical tax system. For example, Australia, France, Italy, Germany, and Canada allow partial or full imputation. By imputation we mean that if the corporation pays a dividend to its stockholders resident in that country from its after-tax corporate income, stockholders (a) receive a credit (as compensation for the corporate taxes that are imputed to have been paid by them) equal to some fraction of the dividend they receive and (b) declare as dividend income (on which ordinary tax rates are levied) the dividend received plus the tax credit amount. For example, if the corporate tax rate were 35%, $100 of before-tax profits results in $65 of profits after corporate tax. In a full imputation system, if the corporation pays a $65 cash dividend, it issues to its stockholders $35 in tax receipts along with a form instructing them to declare $100 of dividend income on their personal tax returns. The shareholder in a 40% tax bracket, for example, records $100 of income on which tax of $40 is due but this is partially offset by the dividend tax credit resulting in $5 additional tax. The shareholder in a 30% tax bracket, for example, records $100 of income on which tax of $30 is due. The $35 tax receipt leaves a net credit of $5 to be used to offset any tax due on other income. Dividends on which a credit is attached are referred to as franked dividends. With 100% dividend payout, the imputation system converts the corporate form to the partnership form of taxation for those investors with sufficient taxable income to use the tax credit. The corporate income attracts only one level of taxation, at personal tax rates. As a result of the imputation system, tax-exempt shareholders such as pension funds are forced to pay tax at high corporate marginal tax rates. For them, the $35 tax receipt has no value unless they generate "unrelated business income" that is otherwise taxable.

More formally, the shareholder is taxed as follows on a fully franked dividend

$$\text{Div} - [t_p\text{Div}/(1 - t_c) - t_c\text{Div}/(1 - t_c)] \quad \textbf{(A4.1)}$$

where the middle term is the amount of personal tax due on the grossed-up dividend before credit for corporate taxes paid, which credit is calculated as per the final term. This equation can be rearranged as

$$\text{Div}[1 - t_p/(1 - t_c) + t_c/(1 - t_c)]$$
$$= \text{Div}(1 - t_p)[1 + t_c/(1 - t_c)] \quad \textbf{(A4.2)}$$

To check, we insert our example from above $65(1 - .40)[1 + .35/(1 - .35)] = $65(.60)[1 + .53846] = 60 after-tax dividend.[26]

---

[26]The mechanics of the dividend tax imputation system, taxpayers receiving a credit for corporate taxes, is similar to the mechanics of the foreign tax credit for U.S. multinationals, which we discuss in Chapters 10 and 11. Further our description here closely resembles the Australian system introduced in 1987.

In some cases, shareholders can receive dividends that are not franked. That is, for example, when the dividends are paid from profits that have not been taxed at the corporate level, profits earned and taxed overseas, and profits earned prior to the introduction of the imputation system. To illustrate this situation, suppose a corporation pays a dividend of $100 of which $70 (70%) consists of franked dividends. In this case the shareholder faces the following

the unfranked dividend of $30
+ the franked dividend of $70

$30(1 − .40) + $70(1 − .40)
  $\times [1 + .35/(1 − .35)]$
  = $18 + $64.62
  = $82.62 dividend after
    shareholder-level taxes.

This solution can also be derived more simply as

$$= \text{Div}(1 − t_p)[1 + kt_c/(1 − t_c)] \quad \textbf{(A4.3)}$$

where k = the percentage of the dividend that is franked. Substituting our numerical example

$100(1 − .40)[1 + .70(.35)/(1 − .35)]
  = $100(.60)[1 + .37692] = $82.62

We can now adjust the equation used in Table 4.2 for dividend imputation. If shares pay a dividend at rate d of which k percent are franked, and dividends are taxed at rate t_p, the required return on shares over a *single* period, r_c^*, satisfies

$$[(1 + r_c^* − d)(1 − t_{cg}) + t_{cg}] + d(1 − t_p)$$
$$\times \{1 + k[t_c/(1 − t_c)]\} = 1 + r_p \quad \textbf{(A4.4)}$$

which is equation (4.7) of the text adjusted for dividend imputation (by including the term $\{1 + k[t_c/(1 − t_c)]\}$ on $d(1 − t_p)$). Solving for r_c^*, we find that

$$r_c^* = \{(1 + r_p) − d(1 − t_p)$$
$$\times [1 + k(t_c/(1 − t_c))] − t_{cg}\}/(1 − t_{cg})$$
$$+ d − 1 \quad \textbf{(A4.5)}$$

Assume $d = .03$, $R_p = 10\%$, $t_p = 40\%$, $t_{cg} = 20\%$, $t_c = 35\%$, and k (the percentage of dividends that are fully franked) = 100%, then

$$r_c^* = \{(1 + .06) − .03(1 − .40)$$
$$\times [1 + 1.00(.35/(1 − .35))] − .20\}/$$
$$(1 − .20) + .03 − 1 = .0704$$

With $k = 70\%$,

$$r_c^* = \{(1 + .06) − .03(1 − .40)$$
$$\times [1 + .70(.35/(1 − .35))] − .20\}/$$
$$(1 − .20) + .03 − 1 = .0740$$

Similarly, the multi-period equation can be easily adapted.

$$(1 + r_c^* − d)^n(1 − t_{cg}) + t_{cg} + d(1 − t_p)$$
$$\times [1 + k(t_c/(1 − t_c))]\sum_{t=1}^{n}(1 + r_c^* − d)^{t−1}$$
$$\times (1 + r_p)^{n−t} = (1 + r_p)^n \quad \textbf{(A4.6)}$$

We use this equation to generate the numbers in Table A4.1.

The first line of the table is repeated from Table 4.2 of the text and indicates that required returns before shareholder-level tax are higher when dividend yields are positive compared with the 0 dividend case in Table 4.1. In addition, the required returns fall off more slowly in Table 4.2 than in Table 4.1 as the length of the investment horizon increases. The reason, of course, is that when dividends are paid, a smaller fraction of the total return on shares comes from capital gains, and it is only the tax on capital gains that is reduced as the investment horizon increases. With full dividend tax imputation ($k = 100\%$), the required pretax corporate returns are lower. Further, because we model less than 100% dividend payout, and $t_p > t_c$ there is still an advantage to deferral. With less than 100% franking on any dividends paid, the required pretax corporate return is between the required returns of the 100% imputation and zero imputation.

TABLE A4.1 The Effects of Dividend Imputation on the Required Annualized Corporate After-Tax—but Before Shareholder-Level Tax—Return on Shares, r_c^*, *Paying a 3% Dividend Rate* for Different Holding Periods (n), with a Partnership Before-Tax Return (R_p) of 10%

Shareholder Tax Rates			Before Shareholder-Level Tax Required Rates of Return On Stocks (%), r_c^* (after corporate tax but before shareholder tax)[a]					After-Tax Return[b]
t_p	t_{cg}	R_p	$n = 1$	5	10	20	50	r
No dividend imputation, $k = 0\%^c$, $t_c = 35\%$.								
40%	20%	10%	**8.25**	**8.15**	**8.06**	**7.95**	**7.88**	**6.0**
With dividend imputation at $k = 100\%^c$, $t_c = 35\%$.								
40%	20%	10%	**7.04**	**6.93**	**6.82**	**6.66**	**6.40**	**6.0**
With dividend imputation at $k = 70\%^c$, $t_c = 35\%$.								
40%	20%	10%	**7.40**	**7.29**	**7.17**	**6.99**	**6.71**	**6.0**

[a]The numbers in boldface are calculated based on the parameter values in normal typeface.
[b]This is the after-tax rate of return on both stocks and partnerships.
[c]k = percentage of dividends that are fully franked.

Discussion Questions

1. Explain the phrase "corporations are subject to double taxation." Is this true for all corporate forms? Explain the phrase "taxed as a pass-through entity."
2. What role do corporate dividends play in comparing the relative tax positions of investors in corporations versus partnerships?
3. What are the major variables that affect the magnitude of the required after-corporate tax—but before shareholder-level taxes—rate of return r_c^*? Give examples to illustrate the importance of each variable. Is it possible to rank the importance of each variable?
4. What are the major variables that affect the magnitude of the shareholder-level tax, t_s? Give examples to illustrate the importance of each variable. Is it possible to rank the importance of each variable?
5. What are the major variables that affect the magnitude of the pretax corporate rate of return, R_c? Give examples to illustrate the importance of each variable. Is it possible to rank the importance of each variable?
6. The data presented in Table 4.3 suggest that the corporate form suffered a tax disadvantage relative to the partnership form from 1987 to 1992. List and explain the factors that caused this outcome. Why did not more firms convert from the corporate form to partnership form during this time?
7. What factors might lead to cross-sectional and time-series differences in corporate tax rates, personal tax rates, and shareholder-level tax rates? How do these differences affect tax planners? How do these differences affect tax policymakers?
8. Why might one group of investors prefer the corporate form while another group of investors prefers the partnership form?
9. If corporations face tax disadvantages relative to partnerships, why might we continue to observe the corporate form, especially for large public businesses?
10. Explain the "check-the-box" election. Prior to this election, how did the IRS determine whether a business was taxed at the entity level or as a pass-through entity?

11. Give five examples of organizational forms used to produce goods and services. What tax characteristics distinguish one from the other?
12. Compare and contrast the S corporation, the general partnership, and the limited liability company.
13. Explain how a dividend tax imputation system works.
14. What is the effect of dividend imputation on the r_c^*, the required corporate after-tax—but before shareholder-level taxes? What is the effect of dividend imputation on r_c^*, as k (the percentage of dividends that are franked) declines towards zero?
15. Compare and contrast a policy of
    a. Excluding dividends from taxation for individual taxpayers.
    b. Allowing firms a tax deduction for dividends paid.
    c. A dividend tax imputation system where taxpayers receive a tax credit for corporate taxes paid.
    d. Setting the corporate tax rate to zero.

Exercises

1. Suppose that the tax rate on personal income, t_p, is equal to 40%, the corporate tax rate, t_c, is equal to 35%, and the capital gains tax rate, t_{cg}, is 20%. Also assume that the before-tax rate of return on investment to both the corporate and partnership form is 15% per year. These tax rates and investment returns are constant over time. On the basis of these facts, identify the following as true or false. (Support your answer with numerical examples.)
    a. The annualized after-tax rate of return to investing in the corporate form increases with the length of the investor's holding period. Explain.
    b. The annualized after-tax rate of return to investing in the partnership form increases with the length of the partner's holding period. Explain.
    c. If a corporation paid out its entire after-tax profits as fully taxable dividends each year, shareholders would realize a lower before-tax rate of return than if the corporation retained the after-tax profits. Explain.
    d. Because the corporate tax rate is below the personal tax rate, the corporate form is always preferred to the partnership form.
    e. Because corporate income is subject to two levels of taxation, the partnership form is always preferred to the corporate form.
2. Following the 1986 Tax Act, the corporate tax rate of 34% was set above the personal tax rate of 28% on ordinary income, and 100% of realized capital gains became taxable at investors' ordinary rates. What are the required before-tax rates of return (that is, the cost of equity capital) to corporations and to partnerships if investors require that the after-tax rate of return on investments of similar risk be equal to 15% per year and the typical shareholder holds shares for 8 years? Under what circumstances might we see both a corporation and a partnership producing the same goods and services in light of these required before-tax rates of return?
3. A taxpayer capitalizes a wholly owned corporation with $100,000. The corporation invests in a project that earns an annual pretax rate of return of 15% and faces a 15% corporate tax rate. The taxpayer faces a personal tax rate of 39.6% and expects to liquidate the corporation after 20 years.
    a. What is the after-tax rate of return on this investment?
    b. Do you recommend that the taxpayer make this investment via an S corporation to avoid double taxation? Assume the corporation distributes enough cash to the taxpayer each year to allow him to pay his taxes on the S corporation income.
    (Exercise adapted from problem written by Richard Sansing, Dartmouth College.)

4. Suppose Congress was to reduce the top capital gains tax rate, t_{cg}, to 10% from 15%. How would this affect the required pretax corporate return, R_c^*, calculated in the final line of Table 4.4? That is, recalculate the required pretax corporate return for the holding periods and other parameter values as listed for the 2003 line in Table 4.4.

5. Suppose Congress were to increase the top personal tax rate, t_p, to 45% from 35%. How would this affect the required pretax corporate return, R_c^*, calculated in the final line of Table 4.4? That is, recalculate the required pretax corporate return for the holding periods and other parameter values as listed for the 2003 line in Table 4.4.

6. Suppose Congress were to reduce the top corporate tax rate, t_c, to 30% from 35%. How would this affect the required pretax corporate return, R_c^*, calculated in the final line of Table 4.4? That is, recalculate the required pretax corporate return for the holding periods and other parameter values as listed for the 2003 line in Table 4.4.

7. What rate k, the percentage of dividends that are franked in a dividend tax imputation system, would equate to a tax rate of 15%? If necessary, assume the 2003 top tax rates.

Tax Planning Problems

1. With the Tax Reform Act of 1986, corporate tax rates fell from 46% in 1986 to 40% in 1987 and to 34% for income earned subsequent to 1987. Since the Tax Code allowed a 3-year carryback for net operating losses during this period, would it be tax advantageous for those firms that were profitable during 1984–1986 to generate net operating losses during 1987–1989 by: (1) selling certain assets at a loss, (2) postponing the recognition of income, and (3) accelerating certain tax-deductible expenditures? If the after-tax discount rate is 7%, how tax advantageous is this strategy? What specific actions might a firm have undertaken to generate net operating losses in 1987–1989?

2. Because U.S. corporations are allowed to exclude from taxable income 70% of the dividends they receive from other U.S. corporations, it is sometimes suggested by tax planners that they should invest in dividend-paying common or preferred stock. Is it tax advantageous for a U.S. corporation to buy dividend-paying stock? Is it tax advantageous for a U.S. corporation to buy adjustable-rate preferred stock (short-term dividend-paying preferred stock, with a dividend yield that floats in direct proportion to short-term treasury yields) instead of dividend-paying stock? Is it tax advantageous for a corporation to issue the preferred stock? Canadian firms can exclude 100% of the dividends they receive from other Canadian corporations. Is it tax advantageous for Canadian companies to buy common stock in other Canadian corporations?

3. An established corporation currently pays out 50% of earnings as dividends. The CFO asks you whether it is tax advantageous for the corporation to pay dividends to shareholders other than corporations. How did the 1986 Tax Act affect these calculations?

4. Let us assume, as was true of wealthy individuals in the United States in the 1960s, that the personal tax rate is 70% and that realized capital gains are taxed at half the top personal tax rate—that is, $t_{cg} = 35\%$. Assume that the top corporate rate is 48%. The before-tax rate of return on investments is 15%. You are asked to advise a doctor as to whether she should incorporate. What would be the

tax-advantageous strategy for 5-year, 10-year, and 15-year investment horizons? Suppose that she did incorporate and that 5 years later the personal tax rate falls unexpectedly to 50%. Should she then liquidate her corporation and start a new partnership?

5. A U.S. corporation has a wholly owned foreign subsidiary in a low-taxed country. The subsidiary returns 20% a year before tax. The foreign country tax rate is 25%, and the U.S. corporate tax rate is 35%. Corporate tax in the United States is assessed only when profits are repatriated, and the profits are taxed at a rate equal to the difference between U.S. and foreign rates—that is, 10%. Compare the after-tax rates of return of a U.S. corporation that repatriates profits each year against a U.S. corporation that defers repatriation of after-foreign-tax profits for 10 years. Assume that funds invested in the United States also earn 20% a year before tax.

6. A wealthy taxpayer is planning to start an Internet-based business. The taxpayer expects to generate tax losses for at least the first 5 years of the business. The tax-payer also hopes to cash out of the business within 10 years by either going public or selling to another business. Discuss the pros and cons of starting out as a regular C corporation versus a sole proprietorship (or some other pass-through entity). In your discussion, indicate whether it matters that the investor:
   a. cashes out via going public or by selling to another business.
   b. is actively involved in the operations of the business.
   How might your answers to (a) and (b) differ if the investor were not so wealthy?

7. Suppose you are advising a college basketball coach on whether to organize his summer basketball camps for high school students as a C corporation versus an S corporation. The taxpayer plans to operate the camps for 5 years, then wind up the corporation by simply paying any retained earnings as a dividend in the final year. The taxpayer faces a marginal tax rate of 35% while the corporate tax rate is a flat rate of 35%. The expected pretax rate of return on the camps is 12% per year (before any compensation or dividends to the taxpayer).
   a. Assuming zero dividends are paid each year, which corporate form would you advise the taxpayer to select?
   b. Assuming 50% of taxable income is distributed each year as dividends, which form would you advise the taxpayer to select? Explain your answer in words (no algebra is required here).
   c. Again assuming a zero dividend payout each year, what shareholder-level tax rate, t_s, in the C corporation form would equate the after-tax return to the tax-payer in both corporate forms?
   d. Explain, in words, how it might be possible to lower the shareholder-level tax to the required rate in (c) such that the after-tax rate of return to the taxpayer is the same in both corporate forms.

8. The ABC Corporation is considering a joint venture with another company to start an Internet-based business. The new business will tap into the expertise ABC has developed in writing the complex software algorithms the firm uses to schedule and manage its complex manufacturing and distribution processes. Each entity is required to initially contribute $20 million for a 50% share in the joint venture. As with most Internet-based businesses, the joint venture partners do not expect to earn positive profits in the foreseeable future.
   a. Discuss the pros and cons of the alternative organizational forms that the joint venture might take. In your discussion consider both the tax and nontax costs and benefits of the alternatives. Note that to file a consolidated tax return (that is, to include another company on ABC's tax return), a corporation must own at

least 80% of the voting shares of the other corporation (compared to only 50% for financial accounting purposes). Which organizational form would you recommend the joint venture use?

b. In contributing the $20 million, ABC is considering two options:

   i. the entire amount contributed as equity, or

   ii. $10 million treated as equity with the remaining $10 million being treated as a note payable with annual interest rate of 10%.

Evaluate these two options.

When the joint venture eventually becomes profitable (in year 10), the business is expected to earn approximately 20% pretax per year. The joint venture is not expected to pay any dividends, and ABC expects to liquidate its position 20 years from today. It also expects to face the top corporate tax rate of 35% in each of the next 20 years. Finally, assume ABC's investment of $20 million in the joint venture was all equity.

c. If the joint venture is organized as a C corporation, what is the expected annual after-tax return to ABC?

d. If the joint venture is organized as a limited liability company, what is the expected annual after-tax return to ABC?

References and Additional Readings

Ayers, B., C. Cloyd, and J. Robinson, 1996. "Organizational Form and Taxes: An Empirical Analysis of Small Businesses," *Journal of the American Taxation Association* (Supplement), pp. 49–67.

Beatty, A., P. Berger, and J. Magliolo, 1995. "Motives for Forming Research & Development Financing Organizations," *Journal of Accounting and Economics* (2&3), pp. 411–442.

Carroll, R., and D. Joulfaian, 1997. "Taxes and Corporate Choice of Organizational Form," *U.S. Department of the Treasury, Office of Tax Analysts Working Paper 73.* Washington, D.C.: U.S. Department of Treasury.

Erickson, M., and S. Wang, 1999a. "Exploiting and Sharing Tax Benefits: Seagrams and Dupont," *Journal of the American Taxation Association* (Fall), pp. 35–54.

Erickson, M., and S. Wang, 1999b. "The Effect of Transaction Structure on Price: Evidence from Subsidiary Sales," *Journal of Accounting and Economics* (April), pp. 149–176.

Gentry, W., 1994. "Taxes, Financial Decisions, and Organizational Form: Evidence from Publicly Traded Partnerships," *Journal of Public Economics* (February), pp. 223–244.

Goolsbee, A., and E. Maydew, 2002. "Taxes and Organizational Form: The Case of REIT Spin-Offs," *National Tax Journal* (September), pp. 441–456.

Goolsbee, A., 1998. "Taxes, Organizational Form, and the Dead Weight Cost of the Corporate Income Tax," *Journal of Public Economics* (July), pp. 143–152.

Gordon, R., and J. Mackie-Mason, 1994. "Tax Distortions to the Choice of Organizational Form," *Journal of Public Economics* (October), pp. 279–306.

Gordon, R., and J. Mackie-Mason, 1997. "How Much do Taxes Discourage Incorporation?" *Journal of Finance* (June), pp. 477–505.

Guenther, D., 1992. "Taxes and Organizational Forms: A Comparison of Corporations and Master Limited Partnerships," *The Accounting Review* (January), pp. 17–45.

Maydew, E., 1997. "Tax-Induced Earnings Management by Firms with Net Operating Losses," *Journal of Accounting Research* (Spring), pp. 83–96.

Omer, T., G. Plesko, and M. Shelley, 2000. "The Influence of Tax Costs on Organizational Choice in the Natural Resource Industry," *Journal of the American Taxation Association* (Spring), pp. 38–55.

Petroni, K., and D. Shackelford, 1995. "Taxation, Regulation, and the Organizational Structure of Property-Casualty Insurers," *Journal of Accounting and Economics* (3), pp. 229–253.

Plesko, G., 1999. "The Role of Taxes in Organizational Choice: S Conversions After the Tax Reform Act of 1986," Working paper, Boston, MA: MIT.

Scholes, M., and M. Wolfson, 1990. "The Effects of Changes in Tax Laws on Corporate Reorganization Activity," *Journal of Business* (January), pp. 141–164.

Shelley, M., T. Omer, and T. Atwood, 1998. "Capital Restructuring and Accounting Compliance Costs: The Case of Publicly Traded Partnerships," *Journal of Accounting Research* (2), pp. 365–378.

Shevlin, T., 1987. "Taxes and Off-Balance-Sheet Financing: Research and Development Limited Partnerships," *The Accounting Review* (3), pp. 480–509.

Terando, W., and T. Omer, 1993. "Corporate Characteristics Associated with Master Limited Partnership Formation," *Journal of the American Taxation Association* (Spring), pp. 23–45.

Willens, R., and H. Wright, 2002. "Tax-Free Real Estate Spin-Offs: Will They Catch On?" *Tax Notes* (February 4), pp. 619–627.

Wolfson, M., 1985. "Empirical Evidence of Incentive Problems and their Mitigation in Oil and Gas Tax Shelter Programs" in *Principals and Agents: The Structure of Business* edited by John W. Pratt and Richard J. Zeckhauser (Harvard Business School Press), pp. 101–125, 221–224.

Yetman, R., 2002. "Tax-Motivated Expense Allocations by Nonprofit Organizations," *The Accounting Review* (July), 297–311.

5

IMPLICIT TAXES AND CLIENTELES, ARBITRAGE, RESTRICTIONS, AND FRICTIONS

After completing this chapter, you should be able to:

1. Explain and calculate the implicit tax rate on a variety of assets.

2. List assets that are tax-favored and so bear implicit taxes.

3. Explain why it is necessary to adjust for risk differences among assets when calculating implicit taxes.

4. Explain and illustrate the concept of tax clienteles.

5. Explain the concept of tax arbitrage and why it is important.

6. Explain and provide examples of organizational-form-based tax arbitrage.

7. Explain and provide examples of clientele-based tax arbitrage.

8. Discuss the importance, and provide examples, of market frictions and tax-rule restrictions.

In Chapter 3, we discussed how different tax treatments of investment returns influence the after-tax rates of return to alternative savings vehicles. To facilitate comparisons, we held the same investment in each savings vehicle. In Chapter 4, we discussed how different tax treatments of the returns to productive activities undertaken in different organizational forms affect their after-tax rates of return. To facilitate these comparisons, we assumed that the same goods and services were produced in these alternative organizational forms.

In the first half of this chapter, we hold the organizational form constant but vary the tax treatments for different economic activities. We stress how taxing activities unequally influence the relative pricing and the *before-tax rates of return* on investments. For example, if we buy a building to rent space to others, we can deduct from rental income not only the costs of running the business but also part of the building purchase price each year ("depreciation") before paying taxes on any remaining income. Conversely, an investment in equipment that generates the same pretax cash flows as the rental building might give rise to more liberal depreciation allowances and, as a result, higher after-tax cash flows than the real estate investment. Because the equipment's after-tax cash flows exceed those for the rental property, investors are willing to pay more for the equipment.

More generally, when two assets give rise to identical pretax cash flows, but the cash flows from one asset are taxed more favorably than those from the other asset, taxpayers will bid for the right to hold the tax-favored asset. As a result, the price of the tax-favored asset will increase relative to the price of the tax-disfavored asset. And because the before-tax cash flows for the two investments are identical, the pretax rate of return to the tax-favored asset will fall below that for the tax-disfavored asset. In important special cases, their prices will change, with the result that the after-tax rates of return will be the same to some investors (the marginal investors). In fact, as we explain in more detail below, without further tax-rule restrictions or market frictions, the equalization of after-tax rates of return is a necessary condition for market equilibrium.

Given differences in tax treatment, if after-tax returns are to be equalized, then before-tax rates of return must differ across the assets. More lightly taxed investments require lower before-tax rates of return than do more heavily taxed investments. As a result, investors pay taxes *explicitly* on heavily taxed investments and they pay taxes *implicitly* on lightly taxed investments through lower before-tax rates of return. Moreover, taxing investments differentially gives rise to tax clienteles. That is, the proper investors ("clientele") for lightly taxed assets will often be a different set of investors than for the more heavily taxed investments.

Throughout most of this chapter we assume that markets are perfect. In this setting, no transaction costs are incurred to undertake investments or to manage them. All investors are assumed to possess identical information regarding the future cash flows from investment alternatives. Moreover, investors act as though their behavior has no influence on the prices at which assets can be bought and sold. For example, renting a house or a car is assumed to provide the same service flows as owning a house or a car. A renter is assumed to manage property in exactly the same manner as would an owner. As a result, property owners incur no monitoring costs or other informational costs as a consequence of renting property to others. Moreover, if investments must be sold, it is easy and costless to establish their market value. The assumption of perfect markets is as convenient as it is a poor description of the world.

In the second half of the chapter, we initially assume that frictions (that is, brokerage fees and other information-related costs required to buy or sell assets in imperfect markets) and tax-rule restrictions do not exist. Under these conditions, if one savings vehicle or organizational form dominated another savings vehicle or organizational form, taxpayers could eliminate all of their taxes. They would accomplish this by holding negative quantities of wealth through the inferior vehicles (that is, borrow or promise to pay the after-tax rate earned on the inferior vehicle) and positive amounts of wealth through the superior vehicles. This is a form of **tax arbitrage.**

We then move to a consideration of the forces that prevent tax arbitrage from effective implementation—namely, tax-rule restrictions and market frictions. In

Chapter 2, we discussed some of the broad tax law restrictions that prevent taxpayers from engaging in socially undesirable tax planning, such as the business-purpose doctrine and the substance-over-form doctrine. In this chapter, we consider some of the more specific restrictions in the tax law that are designed to prevent taxpayers from being too successful in reducing their taxes by exploiting differential taxation of organizational forms and by exploiting differences in tax rates across taxpayers and over time. We briefly introduce the effect of frictions on the ability of taxpayers to conduct tax arbitrage. We then expand the analysis of frictions in Chapter 6. Both forces, tax-rule restrictions and market frictions, play a central role in preventing arbitrage and, in some respects, they are substitutes. In fact, as frictions are reduced or eliminated by the creation of new markets or transaction-enhancing technologies, the imposition of new tax-rule restrictions may be required to prevent the forms of arbitrage that we discuss in this chapter. As will become clear shortly, in the absence of frictions, the tax-rule restrictions that we observe are simply insufficient to eliminate arbitrage opportunities. This implies that the more costly it is to implement tax planning strategies, the fewer are the number of explicit restrictions required to prevent implementing those strategies considered to be socially undesirable.

5.1 TAX-FAVORED STATUS AND IMPLICIT TAXES

Implicit taxes arise because the prices of investments that are tax-favored are bid up in the marketplace. As a result, the *before-tax* rates of return on tax-favored investments are lower than are those on tax-disfavored investments. Taxes are paid implicitly through lower before-tax rates of return on investment. To calculate implicit taxes requires a **benchmark asset** against which to compare pretax returns. Suppose our benchmark asset is an asset whose returns are taxed fully each year at ordinary rates. That is, tax is not deferred on any part of the economic gain that accrues from holding the asset. A fully taxable bond that is default-free, with its interest rate set to market rates each period, is such an asset. Moreover, there are no changes in the economic value of the bond over time with which to contend. We would then refer to investments that are taxed more lightly than fully taxable bonds as *tax-favored* investments and those that are taxed more heavily as *tax-disfavored* investments.

Investments may enjoy one or more of several types of tax-favored status, including:

- Full tax exemption (for example, municipal bonds in the United States)
- Partial exemption or lower marginal tax rates (for example, capital assets in most countries)
- Tax credits (for example, investment tax credit, targeted jobs credit, alcohol fuel credit, research and experimental credit, low-income housing credit, energy investment credit, payroll tax credit, and rehabilitation investment credit)
- Tax deductions permitted at a rate faster than the decline in economic value of the asset (for example, accelerated depreciation on business property, immediate expensing of research and experimental costs and advertising expenditures)
- Taxable income permitted to be recognized at a rate slower than the increase in the economic value of the asset's cash flows (for example, most assets that appreciate in value)

Similarly, there are many sources of tax-disfavored treatment, including:

- Special tax assessments (for example, windfall profits tax on oil, import duties, and excise taxes)
- Taxable income recognition at a rate faster than income is earned (for example, risky bonds, where the high coupon rate received is fully taxable even though it includes a default premium that, economically, represents a return of capital rather than interest income)
- Tax deductions at a rate slower than the decline in economic value (for example, non-amortizable trademarks that have finite economic lives)

The lower before-tax rates of return on municipal bonds, relative to fully taxable bonds of comparable risk, provide the most direct and vivid illustration of the concept of implicit taxes. Municipal bonds are issued by state and local authorities and the interest earned on most of these bonds is exempt from federal taxation in the United States.[1] For this reason, they are called tax-exempt bonds and investors bid up the prices of these municipal bonds such that their before-tax return is lower than the before-tax return on fully taxable bonds.

The residents of certain states are exempt from tax not only at the federal level but also at the state level if they hold municipal revenue or general obligation bonds issued by authorities within their own state. These instruments are called doubly tax exempt. If residents of a given state hold municipal bonds of out-of-state issuers, however, they pay state income taxes on the interest earned on these out-of-state bonds. State taxation also affects the prices of municipal bonds. Certain states (for example, California and New York), tax their residents at high marginal tax rates and exempt their residents from paying tax on interest from state and local bonds issued within their own borders. Municipal bonds issued by such states are priced to yield a lower rate of return relative to municipal bonds issued by states with low marginal tax rates, such as Texas (which has no state individual income tax) or states that tax the interest on bonds issued by municipalities within their own borders.

Interest derived from an investment in corporate bonds is fully taxable at both the federal and state level. Interest earned on obligations issued by the federal government (like Treasury bills, bonds, and notes) and certain authorities (such as Federal Farm Credit Bank System, which includes the Banks for Cooperatives and Federal Land Banks, Federal Home Loan Bank System, Financing Corporation, and Resolution Funding Corporation) is fully taxable at the federal level but exempt from all state income taxes. Puerto Rico also issues bonds that are exempt at the federal level and in all 50 states. Even after controlling for differences in risk, the before-tax returns to Treasury securities tend to be lower than the returns to non-Treasury securities. A California resident facing a 10% state and a 30% federal marginal tax rate would be indifferent between holding Treasury securities yielding 9% and equally risky non-Treasury securities yielding 10%. Both securities yield 6.3% after all relevant taxes.[2]

---

[1]Bonds issued by local governments are not exempt from taxation at the national level in all countries. Provincial bonds in Canada, for example, are fully taxable at the federal level.

[2]The after-tax returns are calculated as follows: For the Treasury security, $.09(1 - .30) = .063$ or 6.3% after-tax. Because state taxes are deductible at the federal level, the California resident here faces an effective state tax rate of $.10(1 - .30) = .07$ or 7%. The total tax rate faced by the California resident is $30\% + 7\% = 37\%$, implying an after-tax rate of return on non-Treasury securities of $.10(1 - .37) = .063$ or 6.3%.

Let us now consider how tax credits and accelerated depreciation deductions affect before-tax required rates of return and thus give rise to implicit taxes on investments. Depreciation allowances on property, plant, and equipment reduce taxable income. Different schedules of allowable deductions apply to different classes of property. The more accelerated the depreciation schedule, the closer the taxpayer comes to expensing the cost of the investment immediately and the more tax-favored the investment. For example, if the cost of an investment is $100,000 and the taxpayer's marginal tax rate is 40%, an immediate deduction of the entire cost of the investment would reduce taxes by $40,000 (or $100,000 × .40). With a slower rate of depreciation, the present value of the deduction depends on the after-tax discount rate. For a given depreciation schedule, the higher the discount rate, the lower the present value of the depreciation tax shelter. For a given (positive) discount rate, the slower the rate of depreciation, the lower the present value of the tax shelter, and the less tax-favored the investment. For example, assume a straight-line depreciation schedule over 2 years and a 9% after-tax discount rate. That is, the taxpayer is allowed to deduct $50,000 in the first year and an additional $50,000 in the second year from taxable income. Assuming that the deductions can be used immediately to reduce taxes (in other words, the taxpayer reduces estimated tax payments when the equipment is acquired), the after-tax present value of the depreciation deductions is

$$\$38,349 = \$50,000 \times .40 + \frac{\$50,000 \times .40}{1.09}$$

which is $1,651 less than an immediate ($40,000) deduction of the full cost.

In many countries, taxpayers have been granted investment tax credits on the purchase of certain types of equipment equal to a fraction of the asset's purchase price. A tax credit is like a tax receipt. For example, if equipment costs $20,000 and a 10% tax credit is available, the tax credit would be $2,000. If the taxpayer owed $15,000 in taxes on other income, the $2,000 tax credit reduces the required tax payment from $15,000 to $13,000. Generally, a tax credit is more valuable than a deduction. Whereas tax credits reduce taxes dollar for dollar, deductions reduce taxes by a fraction equal to the tax rate. With the 1986 Tax Reform Act, investment tax credits were eliminated in the United States, although a number of other types of tax credits were retained.

Liberal depreciation allowances and tax credits on equipment affect the required before-tax rates of return on investment. The more liberal the depreciation allowances or investment tax credits, the lower the required before-tax rate of return on investment (and as we will see below, the higher the implicit tax). To illustrate the effects of liberal depreciation and investment tax credits on the implicit tax rate, assume that the taxing authority allows very fast write-offs of the cost of certain equipment. In fact, the deduction allowances (coupled with investment tax credits) are so liberal as to be equivalent, in present value, to an immediate expensing of the cost of the investment. Research and development investments and advertising expenditures are accorded this treatment. Also assume that all of the returns resulting from the investment are fully taxable. We can define the investor's marginal tax rate as t_{p0} today and t_{pn} in n years. For simplicity, suppose that our project generates no cash flows until time n, at which time it generates $(1 + R)^n$ dollars (so the before-tax rate of return on investment per period is R). The after-tax return per dollar of after-tax investment can be expressed this way

$$(\text{After-tax return})/(\text{After-tax investment}) = \frac{\$1(1+R)^n(1-t_{pn})}{\$1(1-t_{p0})} \qquad \textbf{(5.1)}$$

Because the taxpayer deducts the investment cost, a \$1 investment today has an after-tax cost of $\$1(1-t_{p0})$. For example, if the investor's marginal tax rate were 40%, the after-tax investment cost would be \$.60 per dollar invested. If the investment is held for n years and returns $(1+R)^n$ before tax for every dollar invested, the tax-payer retains $\$1(1+R)^n(1-t_{pn})$ after tax, because tax at rate t_{pn} is paid on the entire dollar return. Thus, if the project returns 8% per year before tax for 5 years, and the taxpayer's marginal tax rate remains 40%, the taxpayer retains \$.882 after tax $[(\$1.08)^5(1-40\%)]$ per dollar invested. Because the taxpayer earned \$.882 after tax on an after-tax investment of \$.60, the 5-year return per dollar invested is \$1.469 or (\$.882/.60). The return per year is 8% or $1.469^{1/5} - 1$.

In the special case of constant across time tax rates ($t_{pn} = t_{p0}$), the before-tax return and the after-tax return on investment are the same (that is, 8% in the above illustration). We can see this from equation (5.1). With constant tax rates, equation (5.1) simplifies to $(1+R)^n$. This means that the after-tax rate of return per period is R. But R is also the before-tax rate of return on investment, so the before-tax and the after-tax rates of return on investment coincide—the return is tax exempt.

If we assume that marginal tax rates are constant, then, in equilibrium, the required before-tax rate of return, R, on this project must be equal to the after-tax bond rate, r_b. Note that this is exactly the required return on tax-exempt municipal bonds as well. If investors could earn rates of return higher than r_b, they could profit by borrowing at rate r_b after tax and investing at the higher rate. As a result, they would bid up the prices of the inputs necessary to undertake the tax-sheltered investment. In addition, with more investment, they might reduce the output prices of goods and services to consumers. This would continue until the expected after-tax rate of return on the last dollar of investment is equal to that on the next best alternative, the after-tax bond rate or the municipal bond rate.

Equation (5.1) is familiar to us because we used the same algebra when describing the returns to investing in pension funds in Chapter 3. In both the investment here and pension fund investing, we deduct the cost of the investment and the returns are fully taxable. The major difference, however, is that the pension fund can invest in fully taxable bonds to return the before-tax bond rate, but competition causes the before-tax return on our tax-favored investment to be equal to the after-tax bond rate (assuming equal risk or, as discussed below, on a risk-adjusted basis). The difference between the pretax rate of return on fully taxable bonds and that on the tax-sheltered investment represents an implicit tax paid to customers (by way of reduced prices) and/or factor suppliers (by way of increased prices for inputs).

In equation (5.1), we allowed for the possibility that marginal tax rates change over time. If tax rates were expected to fall (that is, $t_{pn} < t_{p0}$), the required before-tax rate of return on investment would be less than the after-tax bond rate, r_b. If tax rates were expected to increase (that is, $t_{pn} > t_{p0}$), the converse would be true. To illustrate the power of tax rates changes, consider the following example. Assume that $t_{p0} = 40\%$, $t_{pn} = 30\%$, $n = 5$ years, and the after-tax bond rate, r_b, is 7%. We know that on a risk-adjusted basis, in equilibrium, the cumulative n-year after-tax return for this investment and a fully taxable bond must be the same

$$\frac{(1 + R)^n (1 - t_{pn})}{(1 - t_{p0})} = (1 + r_b)^n \tag{5.2}$$

Solving for the required risk-adjusted before-tax rate of return per period, R, we find that

$$R = \left[\frac{(1 + r_b)^n (1 - t_{p0})}{(1 - t_{pn})} \right]^{1/n} - 1$$

Substituting the values for r_b, t_{p0}, and t_{pn} from our example, we find that

$$R = \left[\frac{1.07^5 (1 - .40)}{(1 - .30)} \right]^{1/5} - 1 = 3.75\%$$

A before-tax required rate of return of 3.75% is well below the after-tax rate of return on bonds of 7%. Because the government puts up 40% of every dollar invested but requires only 30% of the resultant returns, investors bid up the investment price of the project (or reduce prices for goods and services) such that the before-tax rate of return falls below the tax-exempt bond rate. By construction, the pretax return of 3.75% per year for 5 years provides exactly the same after-tax return per dollar of after-tax investment as investing in fully taxable (or tax-exempt) bonds—that is, 7%.

Conversely, if tax rates are expected to increase in the future, the required before-tax rates of return on the project would exceed the after-tax bond rate, and the project would bear some explicit tax. An analogous result occurs when tax rates remain constant over time but the depreciation and tax credit allowances are less than an immediate expensing of the cost of the investment. Explicit taxes will be paid on the project's returns, and the before-tax required rate of return on the project will exceed the municipal bond rate.

Favorable tax treatment (such as liberal depreciation allowances or investment tax credits) stimulates demand for investments. Increased investment exerts upward pressure on factor prices (for example, labor costs and equipment costs), unless the supply of such factors is perfectly elastic.[3] Increased investment also exerts downward pressure on consumer prices unless consumer demand is perfectly elastic. For example, accelerating depreciation rates on buildings (referred to as real property in the Tax Code) encourages the production of more rental units. But the increase in supply of rental units puts downward pressure on rental rates. This, in turn, encourages people to rent the units from the increased supply. Because of the anticipated increased supply of rental units and lower rental rates, the resale prices of existing rental units do not increase by the full value of the increase in present value of the depreciation-related tax savings.

If we had a capital stock that could be redeployed instantly to new uses, the capital stock and the prices of goods and services would adjust immediately to unanticipated

---

[3]Elasticity refers to the ratio of the proportionate change in quantity as price changes. A demand function with unit elasticity implies that as price changes the quantity demanded changes such that total revenue is unchanged. An inelastic demand function implies no change in quantity demanded as price changes (thus demand quantity is not a function of price). A perfectly elastic demand curve implies a small price change leads to a large change in quantity demanded (the demand curve is relatively flat). A perfectly elastic supply curve implies a small change in price leads to a large change in the quantity supplied.

changes in depreciation allowances and the prices of underlying assets would not change. With adjustment costs to change the capital stock, neither the supply of capital nor prices would adjust as quickly, and an unanticipated liberalization of tax allowances would generally create capital gains for the holders of capital assets. Conversely, the owners of the capital stock would experience capital losses on an unanticipated elimination of a tax shelter (for example, less liberal depreciation allowances).

5.2 THE IMPLICIT TAX RATE, THE EXPLICIT TAX RATE, AND THE TOTAL TAX RATE

Holding taxes constant, the required rate of return on a risky bond exceeds that of a less risky bond because, for the same amount of promised coupons and principal repayment, the prices of bonds with a high risk of default are lower than the prices of bonds with a low risk of default. Because we wish to isolate the effects of differential tax treatments on required before-tax rates of return, we must adjust the before-tax rates of return on bonds for differences in risk. We use the term **risk-adjusted** to indicate that we are comparing the returns on alternative investments after adjusting for risk differences. After isolating the effects of differential taxation on before-tax returns, we introduce risk and nontax-cost differences into the analysis.

Computing the Implicit Tax

The implicit tax on the returns to any asset is defined as the difference between the before-tax return on a fully taxable bond (our benchmark security) and the risk-adjusted before-tax return on an alternative asset (such as a tax-favored municipal bond). For example, assume that the pretax return on fully taxable bonds is 10% and that the risk-adjusted return on tax-exempt bonds is 7%. The implicit tax on tax-exempt bonds would then be 3%, simply 10% less 7%. The implicit tax on the fully taxable bond is zero.

The **implicit tax rate**, t_{Ia}, on a particular investment, a, is that tax rate that, if applied explicitly to fully taxable bonds, would leave a return equal to the *before-tax* rate of return on the alternative investment. If we define R_b as the risk-adjusted before-tax return on fully taxable bonds (the **benchmark** asset) and R_a as the risk-adjusted before-tax return on the **alternative** investment, the implicit tax rate is given by

$$R_b(1 - t_{Ia}) = R_a$$

or

$$t_{Ia} = (R_b - R_a)/R_b \qquad \textbf{(5.3)}$$

Substituting for $R_b = 10\%$ and $R_a = 7\%$ in equation (5.3), we find that the implicit tax rate on municipal bonds is 30% [or $(10\% - 7\%)/10\%$].[4] Thus, paying tax at a rate of 30% on fully taxable bonds would result in a return of 7%, the same as the before-tax rate of return on tax-exempt bonds. Although investors do not pay any explicit tax on

---

[4]Although our discussion will concentrate on pretax return differences between fully taxable bonds and tax-favored assets, we could also calculate implicit taxes on assets whose returns are taxed less favorably than fully taxable bonds. These assets would yield a pretax premium. They would be priced to yield a *negative* implicit tax.

the interest earned from holding municipal bonds, they pay the tax implicitly at a tax rate of 30% through a lower before-tax rate of return.

To whom is the implicit tax paid? In our tax-exempt municipal bond example, it is paid to the issuers of the tax-exempt securities. The issuing municipalities receive an implicit subsidy by way of a lower cost of capital. In the example, the subsidy is at the rate of 30% of normal (that is, fully taxable) borrowing costs. This taxing scheme, which uses implicit taxes to subsidize municipal spending programs, is similar to an alternative scheme in which all bonds (including municipal bonds) are fully taxable at the federal level and the federal government remits the tax collected on municipal bonds to each issuing authority. In this alternative setting, the before-tax returns on municipal and fully taxable bonds would be 10%. Whether the bond was labeled a municipal or a taxable bond would make no difference to investors.

Total Tax Rates in a Competitive Market

The total taxes paid on any investment is the sum of implicit taxes plus explicit taxes, where implicit taxes are measured relative to some benchmark asset. In a competitive equilibrium (with no tax-rule restrictions and frictions), the risk-adjusted after-tax return on all assets must be equal. Otherwise, there will exist arbitrage profit opportunities. We denote this common after-tax return as r^*.

In the preceding section, we defined the implicit tax on any asset (say, asset a) to be the difference between the pretax return on our benchmark asset (say, asset b, which we take here to be fully taxable riskless bonds) and the pretax return on the asset in question—that is, $R_b - R_a$. The explicit tax on any asset is the difference between its pretax and after-tax return—that is, $R_a - r_a$, In a competitive equilibrium, the explicit tax can be expressed as $R_a - r^*$. The total tax, then, is equal to

$$\text{Implicit tax} + \text{Explicit tax} = (R_b - R_a) + (R_a - r^*)$$
$$= R_b - r^* \tag{5.4}$$

In other words, the total tax is the same for all assets in a competitive equilibrium.

Just as we defined the implicit tax rate by stating the implicit tax as a fraction of the pretax return on our benchmark asset—that is, $(R_b - R_a)/R_b$—we define the **explicit tax rate** by stating the explicit tax as a fraction of the pretax return on our benchmark asset—that is, $(R_a - r^*)/R_b$. This definition ensures that the **total tax rate**—that is, the implicit tax rate plus the explicit tax rate—is the same for all assets. (It is important to note that once we introduce market imperfections, the total tax rate may vary among assets as we will see, for example, in our discussion of tax clienteles.) More formally,

$$\text{Total tax rate} = \text{Implicit tax rate} + \text{Explicit tax rate}$$
$$= (R_b - R_a)/R_b + (R_a - r^*)/R_b$$
$$= (R_b - r^*)/R_b \tag{5.5}$$

Suppose that fully taxable bonds yield 10% before tax, partially taxable bonds yield 8% before tax, and tax-exempt bonds yield 7%. Each security is riskless. As Table 5.1 shows, while the mix of implicit and explicit taxes differs across the three assets, the total tax rate is the same (30%) for each asset. This implies that the statutory tax rate on ordinary taxable income is 30%.[5]

---

[5]The interested reader can verify that the fraction of income, g, from the partially taxable asset that is taxable at the statutory rate of 30% is 41.67%. You can determine this by noting that $.08(1 - .30g) = .07$.

TABLE 5.1   Implicit, Explicit, and Total Tax Rates for Differentially Taxed Assets

	Fully Taxable Bond	*Partially Taxable Bond*	*Tax-Exempt Bond*
Pretax return	$R_b = 10\%$	$R_p = 8\%$	$R_e = 7\%$
Implicit tax	$R_b - R_b = 0\%$	$R_b - R_p = 2\%$	$R_b - R_e = 3\%$
Implicit tax rate = Implicit tax/R_b	0%	20%	30%
Explicit tax	$R_b - r^* = 10\% - 7\% = 3\%$	$R_p - r^* = 1\%$	$R_e - r^* = 0\%$
Explicit tax rate = Explicit tax/R_b	30%	10%	0%
Total tax = Implicit tax + explicit tax	3%	3%	3%
Total tax rate[a]	30%	30%	30%

[a]Total tax rate = Implicit tax rate + Explicit tax rate or (Implicit tax + Explicit tax)/R_b

To avoid confusion, we wish to reemphasize that our measure of the explicit tax rate for any asset requires that the pretax return of the benchmark asset appear in the denominator. So, for example, the explicit tax rate on the partially taxable asset is 1%/10%, or 10%, and *not* 1% divided by the pretax return on the partially taxable asset, which would be 12.5%. Using this definition ensures that total tax rates will coincide for all assets.

5.3 THE IMPORTANCE OF ADJUSTING FOR RISK DIFFERENCES

Earlier in this chapter we assumed the assets being compared were equally risky (or that the returns were already risk-adjusted). It is important to adjust for differences in risk to avoid incorrect calculation of the tax effects on the returns to assets. Alternatively stated, the tax planner could incorrectly estimate the implicit and explicit tax rates on assets, leading to incorrect decisions about, for example, which assets to invest in.

The focus here is on the question of why to adjust for risk, not how to derive the adjustment for risk. In practice, we require a model to adjust for differences in risk. Such models as the capital asset pricing model or the arbitrage pricing model, for example, could be used to compute before-tax risk premiums. Adjusting for risk using the **capital asset pricing model (CAPM)** is illustrated in Appendix 5.1. We assume here that we know the required pretax risk premium (derived, for example, from the CAPM).

To facilitate the discussion of risk adjustment we introduce some more notation. We continue to use R to denote pretax rate of return and r to denote after-tax rate of return. We use the following notation and definitions:

R^o = required (or observed) pretax total rate of return (includes risk and tax effects),

R^{rp} = required pretax risk premium on some risky asset,

R^{ra} = risk-adjusted pretax rate of return on some risky asset = $R^o - R^{rp}$,

r^{rp} = required after-tax risk premium on some risky asset, where g is the percentage of the pretax return from the asset that is included in taxable income and, because $r^{rp} = R^{rp}(1 - gt)$, then $R^{rp} = r^{rp}/(1 - gt)$,

r^{ra} = risk-adjusted after-tax rate of return on some risky asset = r^* in equilibrium, which further implies that because $r^{\mathrm{ra}} = R^{\mathrm{ra}}(1 - gt)$, then $R^{\mathrm{ra}} = r^*/(1 - gt)$.

In these definitions, g defines the tax treatment for the asset under consideration. For a fully taxable bond, $g = 1$ (all the income is taxable at ordinary rates). For a tax-exempt municipal bond, $g = 0$, and thus none of the return on the bond is taxable. For a partially taxable asset, $0 < g < 1$. With these definitions we are now ready to illustrate the importance of adjusting returns for risk before calculating the implicit tax rates (or more generally, in comparing differentially taxed assets, because risk differences can mask tax differences).

Table 5.2 presents calculations of the implicit and explicit tax rates for three assets, a fully taxable asset (asset b, denoted by subscript b), a partially taxable asset (asset a, denoted by subscript a), and a tax-exempt asset (asset m, denoted by subscript m). The

TABLE 5.2   Implicit, Explicit, and Total Tax Rates for Differentially Risky and Differentially Taxed Assets

	Fully Taxable Bond	Partially Taxable Bond	Tax-Exempt Bond
	(Asset b)	(Asset a)	(Asset m)
Required pretax return R^o	20%	12%	12%
Ignoring risk differences			
$R_m = r^* = 12\%$, implies			
Explicit tax rate t_e	(20% − 12%)/20% = 40%	(12% − 12%)/20% = 0%	(12% − 12%)/20% = 0%
Implicit tax rate t_i	(20% − 20%)/20% = 0%	(20% − 12%)/20% = 40%	(20% − 12%)/20% = 40%
Total tax rate	40%	40%	40%
Adjusting for risk differences			
Required pretax risk premium R^{rp}	5%	2%	3%
$R^{\mathrm{ra}} = R^o − R^{\mathrm{rp}}$	15%	10%	9% = r^*
Explicit tax rate t_e	(15% − 9%)/15% = 40%	(10% − 9%)/15% = 6.7%	(9% − 9%)/15% = 0%
Implicit tax rate t_i	(15% − 15%)/15% = 0%	(15% − 10%)/15% = 33.3%	(15% − 9%)/15% = 40%
Total tax rate	40%	40%	40%
Other calculations:			
g (% of return taxable)[a]	100%	25%	0%
$r^{\mathrm{ra}} = R^{\mathrm{ra}}(1 − gt)$	.15(1 − 1 × .40) = 9%	.10(1 − .25 × .40) = 9%	.09(1 − 0 × .0) = 9%
$r^{\mathrm{rp}} = R^{\mathrm{rp}}(1 − gt)$	.05(1 − 1 × .40) = 3%	.02(1 − .25 × .40) = 1.8%	.03(1 − 0 × .0) = 3%

[a]g is the fraction of income from the asset that is taxable at ordinary income tax rates (40% in this example). We estimate g by noting that $R^{\mathrm{ra}}(1 − g × .40) = r^*$. Thus, for the partially taxable asset, substituting $R^{\mathrm{ra}} = 10\%$ and $r^* = 9\%$ and solving gives $g = 25\%$.

required pretax total rates of return for each asset, R^o, are 20%, 12%, and 12%, respectively. What happens if we ignore any risk differences? In this case, the return on the tax-exempt asset of 12% represents the required after-tax return for all assets to be held in equilibrium, or r^*. Using the required pretax total returns (and ignoring risk differences) we can quickly calculate the explicit and implicit tax rates for each asset. For the fully taxable asset, the explicit tax rate is 40% (calculated as $(R_b - r^*)/R_b = (.20 - .12)/.20$). This equals the total tax rate because the fully taxable asset bears no implicit tax $[(R_b - R_b)/R_b = (.20 - .20)/.20 = 0]$. For the tax-exempt asset, the implicit tax rate is 40% (calculated as $(R_b - R_m)/R_b = (.20 - .12)/.20$). This equals the total tax rate because the tax-exempt asset bears no explicit tax $[(R_m - r^*)/R_b = (.12 - .12)/.20 = 0]$. For the partially taxable asset, the implicit tax rate is also 40% (calculated as $(R_b - R_a)/R_b = (.20 - .12)/.20$). This also equals the total tax rate because the explicit tax rate on the partially taxable asset is zero $[(R_a - r^*)/R_b = (.12 - .12)/.20 = 0]$. Thus, ignoring risk differences leads us to conclude that the implicit tax rate is the same on both the partially taxable asset and the tax-exempt asset—even though one asset is partially taxable and the other is tax exempt!

When we incorporate differences in risk among the three assets, a different picture emerges. Table 5.2 reports that the (given) required pretax risk premium R^{rp} on each asset is 5% for fully taxable, 2% for partially taxable, and 3% for tax exempt. We can now calculate the pretax risk-adjusted return R^{ra} by subtracting the pretax risk premium from the required (or observed) pretax total return ($R^o - R^{rp}$). Given the pretax risk-adjusted returns for each asset, it is now simple to calculate the explicit and implicit tax rates. For the fully taxable asset, the explicit tax rate continues to be 40% (and the implicit tax rate to be 0%). For the tax-exempt asset, the implicit tax rate continues to be 40% (and the explicit tax rate to be 0%). For the partially taxable asset, the explicit tax rate is calculated as $(10\% - 9\%)/15\% = 6.7\%$. The implicit tax rate is $(15\% - 10\%)/15\% = 33.3\%$, which is, as expected, less than the implicit tax rate on the tax-exempt asset.

There are several other calculations of interest in Table 5.2. The tax treatment, denoted by g (the percentage of income from the asset that is taxed at the statutory tax rate), of each asset is reported in the table. For the fully taxable asset, $g = 1$, as expected. For the tax-exempt asset, $g = 0$ by definition. Note that 25% of the income from the partially taxable asset is taxed at the statutory tax rate. Thus this asset is tax-favored (has a lower g) relative to the fully taxable asset. Also reported in the table is the after-tax risk-adjusted rate of return for each asset. For each asset to be held in equilibrium, this rate must be the same for each asset. Finally, and very importantly, the after-tax risk premiums are reported for each asset. Consistent with pretax returns reflecting tax differences, pretax returns also reflect risk differences, and thus the pretax risk premiums incorporate not only risk differences but also tax differences among assets. To assess which assets are more (less) risky we must compare the after-tax risk premiums. In our example in Table 5.2, the partially taxable asset with an after-tax risk premium of 1.8% is the least risky of the three assets. The other two assets both have after-tax risk premiums of 3% indicating that they are equally risky. However, the pretax risk premiums on these two assets are markedly different at 5% for the fully taxable asset and 3% for the tax-exempt asset. This difference arises from the differential tax treatment of the two assets. Further, because these two assets are equally risky, we could have compared the required total pretax returns of 20% and 12% to compute the implicit and explicit taxes for these two assets. However, to correctly calculate the implicit and explicit taxes on the partially taxable asset, it is necessary to risk-adjust the returns of all three assets.

In summary, unless we adjust properly for risk differences in comparing assets, we can be misled as to the rates of implicit taxes and explicit taxes that an asset bears. Further, the risk differences can mask differences in the tax treatment of assets, as in the case of the 12% pretax return on the partially taxable and tax-exempt assets in Table 5.2.

5.4 CLIENTELES

Taxpayers bear a total tax burden equal to the sum of explicit and implicit taxes. Taxpayers in a 30% statutory tax bracket would be indifferent between investing in taxable bonds yielding 10% before tax and municipal bonds yielding 7% (as well as any other investment in the economy that returns 7% after tax on a risk-adjusted basis). Such taxpayers are indifferent between paying all implicit, all explicit, or any combination of explicit and implicit taxes that totals 30%. Taxpayers who are indifferent between purchasing two equally risky assets, the returns to which are taxed differently, are called the **marginal investors.** Investors with explicit tax rates different from the explicit tax rate marginal investors face are *not* indifferent to the choice of differently taxed assets and are called **inframarginal investors.** We now turn to a consideration of investment strategies for these inframarginal investors.

Taxpayers in the same tax brackets are attracted to investments that are taxed similarly. Returning to our tax-exempt and taxable bond example, investors with high marginal explicit tax rates prefer tax-exempt bonds, and investors with low marginal explicit tax rates prefer fully taxable bonds. Taxpayers that prefer one investment over another (inframarginal investors) are referred to as the *tax clientele* for the preferred investment. Unless investors correctly identify their proper tax clienteles, they will not maximize their after-tax rates of return.

For example, assume that the implicit tax rate on municipal bonds is 30% and that taxable bonds yield 10% before tax. The clientele for fully taxable bonds are taxpayers with marginal explicit tax rates below 30%. A taxpayer with a 20% marginal explicit tax rate will earn 8% after tax by investing in fully taxable bonds, 1% greater than in municipal bonds. The investor is better off paying explicit taxes of 20% by investing in taxable bonds than paying implicit taxes of 30% by investing in municipal bonds.

Analogously, an investor whose marginal explicit tax rate is 40% is better off investing in municipal bonds. Paying an implicit tax rate of 30% is less expensive than an explicit tax rate of 40%. While the implicit tax rate on a given asset is the same for all investors, explicit tax rates vary among investors. Taxpayers with high explicit tax rates are led to invest in assets that bear high implicit taxes. It is only the marginal investors who lack any "brand loyalty." In the absence of transaction costs, they would jump back and forth between taxable and municipal bonds as relative prices change.

Tax clienteles are pervasive, and they apply to organizations as well as individuals. For example, if a corporation faces a lower statutory tax rate than the implicit tax rate on tax-exempt assets, holding fully taxable bonds is a superior investment to holding municipal bonds. With different clienteles, market frictions or tax-rule restrictions are required to prevent arbitrage opportunities. We will develop this theme below.

Evidence on the Existence of Implicit Taxes and Clienteles

We have predicted that tax-favored treatment leads to lower pretax rates of return on the tax-favored assets as taxpayers bid up the prices of the tax-favored assets. Tax-favored treatment results in lower explicit tax bills for the taxpayer and lower pretax returns. We label this as the implicit tax model.[6] If U.S. individual investors are the marginal holders of stock, we would expect (1) stocks to bear implicit taxes relative to bonds and (2) low-dividend-paying stocks to bear more implicit taxes than high-dividend-paying stocks. In other words, we would expect the before-tax risk-adjusted returns on stocks to be below those of bonds and the risk-adjusted returns of low-dividend-paying stocks to be below those for high-dividend-paying stocks. The empirical evidence is generally inconclusive regarding these propositions. In part, this is because the expected magnitude of the tax effects on stock returns relative to bond returns is small compared with the variability of returns. That is, current empirical methods are not powerful enough to control for risk differentials between stocks and bonds so that the unique effect of taxation can be isolated (see Fama and French (1998) for a good discussion of the issue).

One stream of empirical research examines stock returns around unexpected announcements of tax law changes affecting the taxation of corporate dividends or capital gains. Erickson and Maydew (1998) examine the stock price reaction to a proposed reduction in the corporate dividends received deduction (DRD). In a surprise announcement in December 1995, the Treasury proposed reducing the corporate DRD from 70% to 50%. Recall from Chapter 4 that the DRD allows corporations to deduct (or exclude) from their taxable income 70% of any dividends they receive on stock they hold in other corporations. If this tax-favored treatment is incorporated in the prices of high-dividend-yield stock, then the implicit tax model predicts that an unexpected proposal to lower the amount of the DRD lowers the price of the stock. Erickson and Maydew report that the prices of preferred stock declined but that the prices of high-dividend-yield common stock did not. These results are consistent with preferred stock but not common stock bearing corporate DRD-related implicit taxes. Alternatively stated, the results are consistent with corporations being the marginal investors in preferred stock but not in common stock. It is not too surprising that common stocks might not bear corporate DRD-related implicit taxes because there are many reasons to invest in stocks with varying dividend yields (with diversification being an important one). Erickson and Maydew also provide an excellent discussion of the problems facing researchers in testing for implicit taxes in equity securities including common stocks. Ayers, Cloyd, and Robinson (2002) examine stock returns around the increase in individual tax rates in 1993 and report evidence that stock prices declined more for high-dividend-yield firms but the decline was mitigated by the level of institutional holdings in the firm. Dhaliwal, Li, and Trezevant (2003) also report evidence consistent with dividend tax capitalization—they find that a firm's dividend yield has a positive impact on its pretax return that is decreasing in the level of institutional

---

[6]The effect of taxation on asset prices has also been labeled as tax capitalization. There is a large empirical literature addressing this issue, far too voluminous to summarize here. See Shackelford and Shevlin (2001) and Hanlon, Myers, and Shevlin (2003) for a discussion of the current debate and empirical evidence on whether dividend taxes or capital gains taxes are incorporated in common stock returns and/or stock prices.

and corporate ownership, their proxy for whether the marginal investor is an individual facing a high dividend tax rate.

Several studies have documented that prices paid by acquiring firms incorporate the tax effects of the acquisition to the selling firm—that is, the higher the purchase price, the higher the tax costs to the selling firm (see, for example, Hayn 1989, Erickson 1998, and Erickson and Wang 1999). Also, any tax benefits to the acquiring firm (such as a step-up in basis of the acquired assets or the tax deductibility of goodwill after 1993) are also associated with higher purchase prices (see, for example, Henning, Shaw, and Stock 2000; Ayers, Lefanowicz, and Robinson 2000; and Weaver 2000). That is, buyers bid up the price to reflect the tax-favored treatment of the assets acquired.

One approach that has been somewhat successful in documenting the existence of implicit taxes is to examine price changes of assets affected by tax-rule changes. Guenther (1994) examines the change in prices (more specifically, the yields) of Treasury bills around the time of statutory tax rate reductions. Treasury bills have a zero coupon rate and are thus sold at a discount. The interest income from the discount is not taxable to a cash-basis taxpayer until the bill matures. Thus the interest from two different Treasury bills maturing across a year-end that also coincides with a change in tax rates is taxed at different rates depending on whether the Treasury bill matures in December or January. If the decrease in tax rates results in a decrease in the pretax return required by investors from debt securities, the implicit tax model predicts that yields will decrease from December of the high-tax year to January of the low-tax year. Guenther finds such a difference when examining yields after the tax rate reductions in 1981 and 1986, providing evidence consistent with the existence of implicit taxes.

Other researchers have examined the relation between corporations' reported pretax accounting returns and the level of explicit taxes. For example, Wilkie (1992) documents a consistent (across years) and statistically significant negative relation between tax subsidies and pretax rates of return. (Wilkie uses tax subsidy, which we can think of as the reduction in explicit taxes due to investments in tax-favored assets: It is the difference between (1) what explicit taxes would be if the firm's income were taxed at the top statutory tax rate and (2) actual taxes.) However, the negative relation is weaker than predicted for a perfectly competitive and frictionless economy suggesting the presence of nontrivial market frictions.

Callihan and White (1999) extend Wilkie's study to examine the effect of the potential market power of the firm on the relation between implicit taxes and pretax rates of return. Firms operating in less than competitive markets are predicted by Callihan and White to capture more of the benefits of tax-favored treatment on assets, resulting in higher pretax returns and lower implicit taxes. This implies a weaker relation between explicit taxes and pretax rates of returns for these firms. Callihan and White provide evidence consistent with this prediction.

Finally because detailed data on ownership of securities is difficult to obtain, most researchers elect to test for the existence of implicit taxes rather than clienteles because data on prices, returns, and yields are easier to obtain. One study that does examine shareholdings directly is Dhaliwal, Erickson, and Trezevant (1999). They find that when non-dividend-paying stocks initiate dividend payments, the shareholder base of the firm shifts from individuals to institutions. This shift is consistent with individual investors selling their shares to investors who pay lower rates of tax on dividends, such as tax-exempt entities like pension funds. Such a result is consistent with the existence of dividend clienteles.

5.5 IMPLICIT TAXES AND CORPORATE TAX BURDENS

Over the years, some corporations have not paid explicit taxes. The primary reasons for this include the availability of generous depreciation deductions, tax credits, immediate write-offs of certain investments (like advertising, research and development, and certain personnel costs), and interest expense deductions, along with myriad opportunities to postpone the recognition of taxable income. Some industries enjoy special tax rules. The oil industry receives very rapid write-offs of the cost of drilling wells; timber companies may treat much of their profits as capital gains; and defense contractors prior to the Tax Reform Act of 1986 were able to postpone substantial sums of income on long-term contracts by using the "completed contract method of accounting" to reduce explicit taxes.[7]

Not paying explicit taxes can have political costs. For example, Citizens for Tax Justice published a study in 1985 entitled "Corporate Taxpayers and Corporate Freeloaders." The study highlighted those corporations that paid little or no explicit taxes. This group's mission is to make public that certain corporations use "loopholes" to avoid paying taxes. During the period of their 1985 study, the federal corporate tax rate was 46% on pretax profits. The study claims that "129 of the companies—or almost half—managed to pay absolutely nothing in federal income taxes, or to receive outright tax rebates, in at least one of the 4 years from 1981 to 1984 . . . The 129 companies earned $66.5 billion in pretax domestic profits in the years they did not pay federal income taxes . . ." Nine companies paid no federal taxes in each of the 4 years: Boeing, ITT, General Dynamics, Transamerica, First Executive, Mitchell Energy and Development, Greyhound, Grumman, and Lockheed.[8] The study lauds those corporations that pay explicit taxes, claiming that it is inherently unfair that some corporations avoid paying their share. Many in Congress believe that because of tax loopholes, corporations avoid paying taxes and, as a result, fail to pay their fair share of the tax. For this reason, Congress passed an Alternative Minimum Tax (AMT) provision to replace a weaker "add-on" corporate tax as part of the Tax Reform Act of 1986. The AMT has as its goal that every corporation should pay some explicit taxes.

The debate continues today: "Thirteen years after Congress passed a tax-reform law intended to make every company pay its fair share, government and corporate records show that many profitable U.S. corporations are again paying little or no federal

---

[7]Long-term contracts are contracts to build and supply some plant or equipment (for example, 100 jet fighters) over a number of years. The completed contract method of accounting allows firms to delay recognition of revenue and profits on the contract until the contract is completed, for example, when the last jet fighter is delivered.

[8]Consider the case of General Dynamics. By using the completed contract method of accounting, General Dynamics was able to postpone the payment of all explicit federal taxes for many years. To the extent that General Dynamics must bid competitively against other firms for the right to supply goods to the Defense Department, however, it may pay substantial sums of implicit taxes. If the defense contract market were perfectly competitive, General Dynamics would pay a full implicit tax. The recipient of the implicit tax in this case would be the Defense Department. Because of this accounting method, the Defense Department is charged lower prices for goods and services through the competitive bidding process. However, some people might argue that the defense market is not very competitive. As a result, General Dynamics might have been able to capture a large fraction of the explicit tax savings for itself and the studies by Wilkie (1992) and Callihan and White (1999) discussed earlier, provide evidence consistent with firms in less competitive industries capturing some of the benefits of the tax-favored treatment of investments. Note that the completed contract method of accounting for tax purposes was eliminated in the TRA 1986.

income tax."[9] Both Congress and Treasury are currently concerned that corporations are unfairly avoiding explicit taxes via aggressive use of corporate tax shelters. These concerns are based on data that indicate (explicit) corporate tax receipts are falling as a percent of reported book income. (See U.S. Congressional Research Service, Average Effective Tax Rates (2000); U.S. Department of Treasury, The Problem of Corporate Tax Shelters (1999); Manzon and Plesko (2002); Desai (2002); and Table A2.1 in Chapter 2.) Treasury and Congress have proposed rules to limit the use of corporate tax shelters (increased disclosure, penalties for all parties to the shelter including the promoter, and increased taxes). However, these studies ignore implicit taxes and the benefits of these proposals might not exceed their costs.[10]

It is not only politicians or others with political motives who ignore implicit taxes in discussing tax burdens across taxpayers. Most academic studies also omit implicit taxes in calculating tax burdens and assessing the distributions of tax burdens across taxpayers.[11] However, most of these studies recognize this omission. The reason implicit taxes are omitted from these studies is the difficulty in estimating them for each taxpayer, whether a corporate taxpayer or an individual taxpayer. Nevertheless, implicit taxes are important in assessing tax burdens and the distribution of taxes across taxpayers, and future research should attempt to estimate and incorporate implicit taxes into their analyses; otherwise the analyses are incomplete and could lead to misleading conclusions and flawed policy recommendations.

5.6 TAX ARBITRAGE

We next demonstrate that in the absence of market frictions and tax-rule restrictions, if one savings vehicle or organizational form dominated another savings vehicle or organizational form—that is, provided higher after-tax rates of return—taxpayers could eliminate all of their taxes through **tax arbitrage.** As with any type of arbitrage, tax arbitrage is the purchase of one asset (a "long" position) and the sale of another (a "short" position) to create a sure profit despite a zero level of net investment. We also consider the forces that prevent tax arbitrage from being implemented effectively—namely, tax-rule restrictions and market frictions.

We distinguish between two types of tax arbitrage: (1) organizational-form arbitrage and (2) clientele-based arbitrage. **Organizational-form arbitrage** is the taking of a long position in an asset or a productive activity through a *favorably* taxed organizational form and a short position in an asset or a productive activity through an *unfavorably* taxed organizational form. Although **clientele-based arbitrage** may also involve taking a long position in a tax-favored asset and a short position in a tax-disfavored asset, the nature of clientele-based arbitrage depends on whether the taxpayer starts out with a relatively high or a relatively low marginal tax rate. For the high-tax-rate taxpayer, clientele-based arbitrage is taking a long position in a relatively

---

[9]Quote from an article entitled "As Congress Ponders New Tax Breaks, Firms Already Find Plenty," *Wall Street Journal,* (August 4, 1999), p. A1, by Michael Phillips.
[10]In addition to ignoring implicit taxes, the problem of corporate tax shelters might be overstated because of the increasing use of employee stock options and their accounting and tax treatment. See Yin (2000) for a discussion of this issue. Employee stock options are discussed in Chapter 8.
[11]See for example studies by Shevlin and Porter (1992) and Kern and Morris (1992).

tax-favored asset (one that bears a relatively high implicit tax) and a short position in a tax-disfavored asset (one that bears relatively more explicit tax). For the low-tax-rate taxpayer, clientele-based arbitrage is taking a long position in a tax-disfavored asset and a short position in a tax-favored asset.

5.7 ORGANIZATIONAL-FORM ARBITRAGE[12]

Immediate Tax Rebates When Taxable Income Is Negative

Suppose that the same asset could be held in two differentially taxed organizational forms and that the asset bears no implicit tax.[13] Further suppose that taxpayers' marginal tax rates are always positive—that is, when taxable income is negative, the government shares in the loss by sending a check to the taxpayer. In such circumstances, the taxpayer could create infinite wealth. For example, assume that a taxpayer invests in a single premium deferred annuity (SPDA), which in turn invests in the riskless bond that appreciates in value at the rate of R per period before tax for 2 years. Tax on the appreciation is deferred until the end of year 2. Also suppose that the investment is financed by borrowing (via issuing bonds) at before-tax rate R. Interest payments are deductible at the end of each year, resulting in an annual after-tax rate of $R(1 - t)$. The taxpayer undertakes an additional loan at the end of the first period equal to the after-tax interest that accrues in the first period. For marginal tax rate t, each dollar employed in the strategy gives rise to an after-tax dollar return of

$$\text{After-tax SPDA accumulation} - \text{After-tax loan repayment}$$
$$= [(1 + R)^2(1 - t) + t] - [1 + R(1 - t)]^2$$
$$= R^2 t(1 - t) > 0 \tag{5.6}$$

and without restrictions or frictions, the taxpayer would continue to borrow to increase wealth without limit as long as t remains positive.

For example, if we assume $R = 10\%$ and $t = 40\%$, the taxpayer accumulates $\$1000(.10)^2.40(1 - .40) = \$2.40$ after tax on a zero net-investment position per thousand dollars borrowed and invested in a 2-year SPDA contract. That is, a $\$1,000$ investment in the SPDA accumulates to $\$1,126$ after tax [or $\$1,000(1.10^2 \times .60 + .40)$] and is financed at an after-tax cost of $\$1,123.60$ (or $\$1,000 \times 1.06^2$) for a net benefit of $\$2.40$. The government provides a rebate of tR on the interest expense in the first year and collects tax on the cumulative SPDA interest in year 2.

Note that this illustration of organizational-form arbitrage shows a long position in bonds invested through a favorably taxed organizational form (the SPDA or nondeductible IRA) and a short position in bonds invested through an unfavorably taxed organizational form (a loan that generates ordinary taxable income to the lender and a corresponding deduction for the borrower each period). This is not consistent with investor equilibrium. To prevent unlimited arbitrage of this form, most tax systems, including that of the United States, do not provide tax rebates for negative taxable

---

[12]Example 3, corporate-owned life insurance (COLI), and Example 4, "shorting against the box," discussed in Chapter 2 are examples of organizational-form arbitrage.
[13]Examples include riskless corporate bonds (our benchmark asset) and depreciable assets that give rise to income taxed at ordinary rates and depreciation deductions for tax purposes that are equal in present value to the path of economic depreciation.

income. Instead, such amounts are carried forward to offset positive amounts of taxable income that may be generated in the future. We consider this tax structure next.

No Tax Rebates on Negative Taxable Income

Suppose that a taxpayer generates taxable income of Y and faces a marginal tax rate of t. If the taxpayer were to pay tY of tax, she would be left with $Y(1-t)$ after tax. Now suppose that the taxpayer can invest in an organizational form that provides complete tax exemption on investment returns (such as the savings portion of a life insurance policy). If the taxpayer could borrow at a tax-deductible rate R per period and invest the proceeds of the loan in the tax-exempt organizational form at the same rate R per period, the taxpayer could wipe out all tax on the Y dollars of taxable income (but could not increase wealth by more than tY because of the absence of tax rebates on negative taxable income). We now illustrate this organizational-form arbitrage.

> **EXAMPLE**
> Suppose our taxpayer will earn $100,000 in salary over the forthcoming year. Before any tax arbitrage activity, she would pay tax at a 40% rate on this income, producing a tax of $40,000. Suppose that the before-tax interest rate on riskless fully taxable bonds is 10%. The taxpayer's $40,000 tax liability can be reduced to zero by borrowing, at the beginning of the year, an amount equal to $100,000/.10, which is $1,000,000, and investing the proceeds of the loan in a tax-exempt insurance product through a life insurance company that holds risk-free taxable bonds yielding 10%. The $100,000 in salary is used to pay the $100,000 of interest (or $1,000,000 × .10) on the loan. As a result, taxable income becomes zero because it is computed as salary minus the interest that is paid on the loan. But this is not troubling to the taxpayer because the savings portion of the insurance policy has now grown to $1,100,000 (or 1.10 × $1,000,000), $100,000 more than the $1,000,000 loan. On surrendering the tax-exempt insurance policy and paying off the loan, our taxpayer is left with $100,000 after tax, an amount equal to her before-tax salary.[14]

Note that this illustration of organizational-form arbitrage shows a long position in bonds invested through a favorably taxed organizational form (life insurance) and a short position in bonds invested through an unfavorably taxed organizational form (a loan that generates ordinary taxable income to the lender and a corresponding deduction for the borrower each period). As a result of this arbitrage activity, salary income becomes tax exempt. Moreover, this process can be repeated with respect to future income as well.

Of course, if the tax-exempt savings vehicle were literally a life insurance policy, some amount of "term" (or pure) insurance must be purchased that may be of no value to someone lacking a bequest motive. But in the absence of tax-rule restrictions, an

---

[14]Under U.S. tax rules, if taxpayers surrender life insurance policies, they are taxed at ordinary rates on the excess of what they realize from the policy (that is, policyholder dividends and surrender proceeds) over the premiums that they paid into the policy. Instead of surrendering their policies, however, investors have had the opportunity to borrow desired funds, using the accumulated amounts in their policies as collateral for the loan. This transaction was not taxable. Because the loan is fully secured by the insurance policy, the borrowing rate on the loan can be the same as the earning rate in the policy, so borrowing on the accumulated earnings in the policy has succeeded in creating tax exemption on the investment income. The 1988 Tax Act added several new restrictions on borrowing the savings portion of insurance policies issued after 1988.

arbitrarily small amount of term life insurance would be sufficient to take advantage of tax-free savings in the policy. Moreover, in the absence of frictions, taxpayers could offset their purchase of term insurance on their lives by selling insurance policies on their lives to other investors or investment intermediaries. In more realistic settings, however, this would prove to be quite difficult and costly.

Restrictions on Organizational-Form Arbitrage

Arbitrage of the type we just described could be prevented by placing limits on taxpayers' ability to deduct interest from their taxable income. For example, if taxpayers were permitted to deduct interest only to the extent of other taxable investment income earned (that is, no net interest deduction), the organizational-form arbitrage we discussed would fail to eliminate tax on salary income. Such restrictions would prevent the taxpayer from making the after-tax cost of borrowing lower than the after-tax return available on the exempt savings vehicle. The U.S. Tax Code provides a similar restriction in Code Section 163(d). This section allows a tax deduction for interest only to the extent that the taxpayer generates taxable investment income, which includes interest, dividends, rents, royalties, and capital gains (if the taxpayer elects the capital gains to be treated as ordinary income).

An exception to the interest deduction limitation is provided for home mortgage interest in the United States. But taxpayers cannot really exploit this exception in a way that enables them to effect organizational-form tax arbitrage. After all, one must actually buy a house to qualify for a mortgage. Any arbitrage opportunity available through home ownership should affect the purchase price of the home, creating an implicit tax. Moreover, the Tax Code contains restrictions on the deductible amounts of home mortgage interest.

A second set of restrictions to limit organizational-form arbitrage relates to the types of life insurance policies that allow tax-free buildup of savings. Recall that an insurance policy has two components: a pure insurance (or term) component that protects against loss of life and a savings component. The savings component helps ensure that funds are available to pay future insurance premiums, although they can be withdrawn from the policy. Section 800 of the U.S. Tax Code requires a minimum ratio of term insurance to savings in the policy.[15] The restrictions ensure that if a taxpayer wishes to use the tax-free savings feature of cash value life policies to a substantial extent, a nontrivial portion of additional savings deposits must be allocated to the purchase of additional term insurance.[16]

So, in the absence of restrictions and market frictions, if taxpayers invest through a tax-exempt organizational form, financed by loans that generate tax-deductible interest expense, they could eliminate all income taxes.[17]

---

[15]As mentioned earlier, in the absence of frictions, this would not be a binding constraint. The taxing authority can exploit the presence of frictions in choosing its restrictions.

[16]As the popularity of using cash-value life insurance policies has grown, so has the frequency with which legislators have proposed changes in the tax laws that would eliminate the tax-favored status of this organizational form.

[17]Note that it is not necessary that the investment give rise to complete tax exemption of returns to enable the elimination of taxes on income. Organizational-form arbitrage can be achieved with a partially tax-exempt savings vehicle. Using g to denote the inclusion rate of income that is taxable, instead of borrowing Y/R as in the earlier example, arbitrage involves borrowing the larger amount $Y/[R(1-g)]$. This strategy works for any $g < 1$.

Full Taxation with Deferral and Organizational-Form Arbitrage

Next, we demonstrate that when the tax-favored organizational form includes deferral of taxation but investors are eventually taxed fully on all investment income (as with a SPDA), taxpayers can reduce but not eliminate the tax on their salary income. To illustrate, assume that a taxpayer will earn income of $100,000 in the forthcoming year and the before-tax interest rate is 10%. She now borrows $1,000,000 and invests in an SPDA. The interest deduction in the first year is $100,000, which, in the absence of restrictions on the deductibility of interest, eliminates taxable income. If the SPDA were cashed out at the end of the first year, however, the $100,000 in taxable income would reappear from the interest earned through the SPDA. So the SPDA must be held for at least 2 years to succeed in postponing any tax payments. The tax on the first year's income is postponed until such time as the SPDA and the loan position are cashed out. In the extreme (that is, when the SPDA and the loan position are maintained indefinitely), this strategy results in the elimination of the tax on salary income.[18]

The Effects of Frictions on Organizational-Form Arbitrage

Let us now reconsider opportunities to engage in organizational-form arbitrage in the presence of market frictions (but without tax-rule restrictions), using savings vehicles that allow full exemption of investment earnings (such as the savings portion of a life insurance policy). Suppose that, because of special costs incurred to invest in a particular savings vehicle, the taxpayer loses a fraction, f, of the before-tax rate of return, R, from the vehicle—that is, the taxpayer realizes only $R(1 - f)$ of the before-tax return in the savings vehicle. Alternatively, the frictions might relate to special costs incurred to borrow funds to finance other investments, in which case the before-tax borrowing rate becomes $R(1 + f)$, even when the loan is a riskless one. In the case of investing in life insurance policies, the special costs arise, in part, from the presence of sales people who are paid to teach taxpayers how life insurance policies work; from administrative personnel, who are necessary to keep track of policies as well as file reports; and from auditors, who are necessary to assure policyholders that their money really is being invested in riskless bonds (or in whatever types of securities the insurance company advertises).

Suppose that a taxpayer with current taxable income of Y dollars seeks to effect organizational-form arbitrage by borrowing at rate R to invest in a tax-exempt savings vehicle. The tax-exempt savings vehicle, however, yields a return of only $R(1 - f)$ due to the presence of frictions. The taxpayer must borrow Y/R at the start of the year to generate sufficient interest deductions to reduce taxable income to zero. This generates RY/R, or Y dollars of interest expense, an amount equal to the income to be sheltered. The Y-dollar amount of income is just sufficient to pay the interest on the loan and reduce taxable income to zero. The investment made with the loan proceeds generates a return of only $R(1 - f)Y/R$, or $Y(1 - f)$, in the tax-favored savings vehicle. Note that fY of the original Y dollars of income has been lost, not due to the tax payment, but due to market frictions. It is as if the taxpayer paid an explicit tax at rate f. We can see that frictions have the same effect on investment returns as implicit taxes.

---

[18]For an 11-year period (that is, 10 years of deferral beyond the receipt of salary), a 40% tax rate, and a 10% before-tax interest rate, the tax is reduced in present value terms by nearly 50%.

Suppose that administration costs require the insurance company to reduce the rate of interest offered on the savings account to 9% when the rate on equally risky fully taxable investments yield 10%. As a result, f would be equal to 1% (because $10\%(1 - f) = 9\%$). By borrowing at a tax-deductible rate of 10% and investing at a tax-exempt rate of 9%, the taxpayer can convert $100,000 of taxable income into $100,000 × .9, or $90,000, of after-tax insurance-related interest income.

We just considered an example that incorporates frictions on the *borrowing* side of the transaction. Suppose that cash cannot be borrowed at the 10% riskless rate because the lender incurs administrative costs. If the $100,000 of prospective taxpayer income comes from salary, the lender may worry that the taxpayer will quit his job and never receive the salary, which represents an important part of the lender's collateral. The lender may run a credit check on the taxpayer to ease this concern, but such information is costly to obtain and to process. For this reason, suppose the lender charges a 12% interest rate on the loan even though the taxpayer knows that the loan is riskless.

At a 12% interest rate to borrow funds, the taxpayer now need only borrow $100,000/.12, or $833,333, to create sufficient interest deductions to eliminate the taxable salary income, rather than $1 million as before. At a before-tax rate of investment return of 9%, the $833,333 in life insurance savings earns $75,000 of interest. So although explicit income taxes are eliminated, these market frictions act as "implicit taxes." The $100,000 salary is transformed into only $75,000 of after-tax life insurance savings. It is as if the taxpayer incurs an "implicit tax" of $25,000. The "implicit tax rate" is 25%. It is equal to the 12% borrowing rate minus the 9% lending rate, divided by the 12% borrowing rate. Alternatively, it is equal to the before-tax salary of $100,000 minus the "after-implicit tax" life insurance investment income of $75,000 divided by the before-tax $100,000 salary. This is exactly the same formula used to compute implicit tax rates earlier in the chapter (equation (5.3)).

Where does the "implicit tax" go? In this case, it goes two-thirds to the lender and one-third to the insurance company. Unlike the earlier implicit tax examples, however, the implicit tax collected here is allocated to the lender and the insurance company to cover transaction-related business costs and may be to no one's benefit. That is, society would be better off if these costs could be avoided, although this might not be possible.

Note that for taxpayers with explicit marginal tax rates below 25%, natural market frictions are sufficient to prevent organizational-form arbitrage from reducing taxes, and tax-rule restrictions become unnecessary. A taxpayer with $100,000 in salary income and an explicit tax rate of 20% retains $80,000 after tax by not using the organizational-form arbitrage strategy and only $75,000 by employing the strategy.

Bankruptcy Rules and Organizational-Form Arbitrage

We have assumed full exemption of the returns to investing in an insurance policy. To achieve this in the United States requires that the taxpayer never cancel the insurance policy and that the policy be held until death. At that time, all income tax is forgiven on the tax-free accumulation (so-called "inside buildup") in the policy. If the policy were cashed out, however, it would be taxed in a manner similar to an SPDA (except that interest income would be forgiven on amounts paid to cover term insurance premiums). As discussed earlier, the effects of borrowing and investing the proceeds in a savings vehicle that eventually is taxed on some of the interest income reduces the scope for organizational-form arbitrage relative to the case in which interest income is forever exempt from tax.

Can a pension account be used successfully to effect organizational-form arbitrage as an alternative to using insurance accounts? Recall that organizational-form arbitrage requires a short position in a relatively tax-disfavored organizational form and a long position in a relatively tax-favored organizational form. In the absence of restrictions on the tax deductibility of pension plan contributions, taxpayers could eliminate taxes on salary income by depositing their salary into a pension account. While funds are invested in the pension account, no taxable income is recognized. During retirement, however, taxpayers must pay tax on amounts they withdraw from their pension accounts.

If instead of withdrawing funds taxpayers borrow during retirement to finance their consumption, they would continue to avoid paying tax on any of the accumulated pension earnings in retirement. In fact, if taxpayers were to pledge the assets in the pension fund as collateral for the loan, the borrowing rate should, in the absence of frictions, be equal to the before-tax return on assets held in the pension fund. If taxpayers plan it just right, on the date of their deaths, the amount of their loan (including accumulated interest) would be exactly equal to the accumulation in the pension fund. The secured creditors would then receive the assets in the pension fund to pay off the loan, leaving no assets to pay the tax liability to the taxing authority.

Not surprisingly, because of the availability of the pension fund as a savings vehicle, other restrictions have been introduced that do prevent the arbitrage from taking place. These include (1) limitations on the amount of compensation that can be deposited into a pension fund each year (as under Code Section 415 in the United States) and (2) limitations on how long pension funds can be left to accumulate tax-free without being withdrawn. In particular, rules have been added over the years that require taxpayers to remove pension assets from their pension accounts during retirement. For example, under current rules, taxpayers must begin to draw down pension assets no later than April 1 of the calendar year following the one in which they become 70.5 years old or in the calendar year in which they retire if still working at age 70.5, at a rate no slower than the annuity rate for their life expectancy at the attained age.

Beyond these two restrictions, the IRS would probably contest in bankruptcy court a situation in which the taxpayer's estate had no assets to pay the tax due on the accumulated pension assets because the taxpayer had pledged all of the pension assets as collateral on loans to finance consumption. In fact, to retain the tax deductibility of the pension contribution, restrictions prevent the taxpayer from assigning the pension assets as collateral on a loan. As a result, the lender's property rights become unclear: Without collateral guarantees, the lender would have to charge a higher rate than the before-tax riskless rate of interest on the loan. As we saw with insurance savings, such frictions act as an implicit tax on taxpayers who employ this particular strategy.

SPDA treatment is similar. Complete tax exemption could be achieved if an account holder could borrow on the SPDA and never cash it in. This would require that the SPDA and the loan on the SPDA be of equal size at the time of the taxpayer's death and, once again, that the lender could seize the assets in the SPDA to satisfy the loan ahead of the claims of the taxing authority. Alternatively, complete exemption could be achieved if the IRS were to forgive any income tax owed by the taxpayer on death. Such forgiveness is expressly granted for life insurance policies but not for SPDAs.

Buying and Selling Implicitly Taxed Assets to Effect Organizational-Form Arbitrage

In the preceding examples, organizational-form arbitrage was effected by taking positions in an asset that bore no implicit tax (except possibly through market frictions). But organizational-form arbitrage can also be undertaken with assets that bear implicit taxes, as long as the asset is held long and short in ways that give rise to differential tax treatment. For example, absent any restrictions, taxes on salary income could be eliminated by holding both a long and a short position in the same capital asset, such as a common stock.

In a frictionless market setting, a taxpayer could sell stock short and use the cash proceeds from the short sale to purchase an offsetting long position in the stock. The net investment position is zero, and the pretax investment returns are perfectly hedged. The strategy requires taking sufficiently large positions so that the stock will either increase or decrease in value, before the tax year ends, by the amount of taxable income—say $100,000—that the taxpayer wishes to shelter.

If the stock increases in value, the short position can be "closed out" by purchasing additional shares and tendering them to the broker who lent the shares to the taxpayer in the first place. This results in recognizing a $100,000 loss from the short position, which wipes out the salary income. If the stock decreases in value, the long position can be closed out simply by selling the stock to recognize a $100,000 loss, which again wipes out the salary income. Of course, the taxpayer has an offsetting gain of $100,000 on the remaining long (or short) position in the stock, but this is not taxed until the position is closed out.

If the tax rules provide that only fraction L of the loss is deductible against ordinary income, then the magnitude of the arbitrage transactions need only be scaled up by a factor of $1/L$ to preserve the outcome of zero taxable income. Either way, after the loss is taken, the position that was sold can be repurchased to restore the investor to a perfectly hedged position. This position can then be held until death. This locks in a $100,000 (or $100,000/L$) unrealized gain. If capital gains realized at death are tax exempt, as they are in the United States, the taxpayer escapes the tax.[19] Thus, capital assets can lead to complete tax exemption via organizational-form arbitrage transactions, just as with life insurance accounts.[20]

As in previous examples, market frictions and several tax-rule restrictions prevent taxpayers from taking advantage of the fact that gains and losses are typically recognized for tax purposes only when sales occur. First, capital loss limitations prevent taxpayers from offsetting excessive amounts of ordinary income with capital losses. The current restriction in the United States is $3,000 per year for individuals, and any unused losses can be carried forward indefinitely to be used against future gains. The restriction on corporations is even tighter: Capital losses are deductible only against

---

[19]If capital gains were taxable at death, but taxpayers consumed all income as it was earned, the taxing authority would once again be in a position in which there would be no assets in taxpayers' estates with which to satisfy the claim.
[20]In countries where capital gains are taxable at death at the same rate as the losses are deductible, capital assets can be used to achieve organizational-form arbitrage in exactly the same way as we used SPDAs. Losses are recognized "early and often," and gains are deferred.

capital gains, and while such losses can be carried *back* for 3 years, they can be carried forward for only 5 years before the carryforwards expire. Second, under the so-called "wash sale rules" (Code Sections 1091(a) and 1256) capital losses are not deductible currently if substantially similar assets are repurchased within 30 days of sale. This means that the investor's position must probably be exposed to a nontrivial degree of risk for a 30-day period to permit the deduction of the capital loss. Third, hedging rules preclude losses from being deducted unless the taxpayer's investment positions differ substantively from perfectly hedged positions—that is, there must be nontrivial risk of overall gain or loss. Fourth, in response to the Lauder family using this strategy to save over $100 million in taxes (as discussed in Chapters 2 and 18), Congress created the constructive sale rules of Section 1259. This rule requires taxpayers to recognize gain (but not loss) upon entering into the constructive sale of an appreciated financial position.

In summary, although organizational-form arbitrage strategies are theoretically possible in many cases, market frictions often, for all practical purposes, prevent their implementation. And where market frictions are insufficient, tax-rule restrictions are often introduced to prevent most of these arbitrage opportunities.

5.8 CLIENTELE-BASED ARBITRAGE

Clientele-based arbitrage strategies mean reducing explicit tax liabilities at the expense of increasing implicit tax liabilities, or *vice versa.* Such strategies arise when (1) taxpayers can take both long and short positions in differentially taxed assets, at least one of which bears some implicit tax, and (2) taxpayers face different marginal tax rates. In most tax regimes, statutory tax rates are progressive, with marginal tax rates rising with taxable income. Progression in the tax rate schedule is an attempt to achieve an equitable distribution of tax burdens (or to redistribute income). At the same time, because Congress uses the tax system to encourage various economic activities, assets are taxed differentially. As we have discussed, the result of taxing assets differentially is the creation of a system of implicit taxes, where the prices of tax-favored assets are bid up such that their before-tax rates of return fall below those of equally risky but less tax-favored assets. Without frictions or restrictions, we demonstrate below that clientele-based arbitrage results in all taxpayers facing the *same* marginal tax rates in equilibrium (which could very well be zero!). In addition, all assets would bear the same total (implicit plus explicit) tax rate. To preserve the ability to redistribute income through progressive marginal tax rates, the federal government has set up many tax rules to prevent clientele-based arbitrage.

Absent tax-rule restrictions, a particularly simple example of clientele-based tax arbitrage is the purchasing of tax-exempt bonds with a loan that gives rise to tax-deductible interest. While this strategy can succeed in eliminating explicit taxes, it also creates an implicit tax liability. Let us again assume a situation in which $100,000 of salary income is expected over the forthcoming year, and the statutory tax rate is 40%. Taxable bonds yield 10% before tax and taxpayers can borrow at this rate in unlimited quantities. Finally, suppose that municipal bonds yield 7% tax-free. Note that municipal bonds bear an implicit tax of 30% [or $(.10 - .07)/.10$].

To eliminate income tax on $100,000 of salary income, we borrow $1,000,000, or $100,000/.10, and invest the proceeds in municipal bonds to earn $70,000, or

$1,000,000 × .07, after tax. Note that we have converted salary income taxed explicitly at 40% into municipal bond interest income taxed implicitly at 30%. As the example illustrates, clientele-based arbitrage enables high-tax-bracket taxpayers to convert income that would be taxed at high explicit marginal rates into income that is taxed at lower implicit tax rates. If low-tax-bracket taxpayers can take short positions in tax-favored assets, they could profitably pursue the opposite strategy.

In our example, when taxpayers face tax rates below 30%, they would not want to borrow for the purpose of purchasing municipal bonds. For example, if taxpayers face tax rates of 25% on the first $50,000 of salary income and 40% on the next $50,000, the optimal strategy would be to borrow enough to reduce taxable income, not from $100,000 to $0, but only to $50,000. This is achieved by borrowing $500,000 at a 10% rate of interest and investing the proceeds in municipal bonds at a 7% rate of interest to yield $35,000 in tax-exempt interest. The net position after tax is

$$\$50,000(1 - 25\%) + \$35,000 = \$72,500$$

By contrast, a strategy of no borrowing would leave

$$\$50,000(1 - 25\%) + 50,000(1 - 40\%) = \$37,500 + \$30,000 = \$67,500$$

and borrowing $1 million to eliminate all explicit taxes would leave $70,000, or $1,000,000 × 7%.

In an attempt to preserve a more progressive tax rate structure, Congress imposes restrictions on such clientele-based arbitrage. In addition to the interest deduction limitations we discussed earlier, Code Section 265 prevents the deduction of interest on loans used to purchase certain assets that yield tax-exempt income, like municipal bonds.[21] Note that for taxpayers facing explicit tax rates less than the implicit tax rate on municipal bonds (the cutoff point is 30% in our illustration), this restriction has no effect. Moreover, the restriction may have no effect on more highly taxed taxpayers if there is a positive spread between the riskless interest rate and the rate at which taxpayers can borrow. For example, if taxpayers must pay interest at a rate of 12% to borrow when equally risky taxable bonds earn only 10%, the implicit tax rate becomes 41.67%, or (.12 − .07)/.12. Because this implicit tax rate exceeds the explicit tax rate of 40% on the last $50,000 of salary income, market frictions are sufficient to prevent this clientele-based arbitrage strategy from being profitable.[22]

As indicated earlier, it is unprofitable for taxpayers with low marginal tax rates to borrow to purchase tax favored assets. But the reverse strategy would be profitable if permitted. These taxpayers would prefer to issue municipal bonds, for example, and invest the proceeds in taxable bonds. If they could issue the bonds at a 7% before-tax rate of return and buy fully taxable bonds that return 10% before tax, their taxable

---

[21]A generous *de minimus* rule applies, however. Corporations may hold up to 2% of their total U.S. assets in tax-exempt securities or receivables without running afoul of Section 265. Still, this limit can be a problem for businesses that sell goods or services on credit to tax-exempt entities.

[22]For many years banks and insurance companies were allowed to engage in clientele-based arbitrage; they could deduct interest on loans used to buy municipal bonds. As long as the implicit tax rate on municipal bonds was below their explicit tax rate on fully taxed income, these firms could profit by engaging in clientele-based arbitrage. Various tax acts during the 1980s restricted these activities. For further discussion of these tax-rule changes and their impact on banks' holdings of municipal bonds, see Scholes, Wilson, and Wolfson (1990).

income would increase until their marginal tax rate was equal to 30%. The clientele-based arbitrage opportunity disappears at that point.

Clientele-Based Arbitrage with Investments in Tax-Favored Assets Other Than Tax-Exempt Bonds

While restrictions exist on borrowing to finance the purchase of municipal bonds, no such restrictions exist on borrowing to buy such tax-favored investments as stocks,[23] land, equipment that is eligible for accelerated depreciation, or a host of other tax-favored investments. If the marginal total tax rate (implicit plus explicit) reflected in market prices for tax-favored investments is below a taxpayer's explicit tax rate on other fully taxed income, the taxpayer can borrow to purchase such assets to effect clientele-based arbitrage. Because U.S. corporations are not subject to limitations on interest deductions, such clientele-based arbitrage activities are especially advantageous for them. This is particularly so for the years following the passage of the Tax Reform Act of 1986, when the top corporate marginal tax rate was above that for individuals.

Note, however, that assets that are tax-favored due to accelerated tax deductions are not as effective in bringing about clientele-based arbitrage as are tax-exemption-type shelters such as municipal bonds. This type of arbitrage requires other taxable income against which to deduct the accelerated tax deductions. And because municipal bond investments do not require deductions against other taxable income to achieve tax exemption, taxpayers can shift much larger amounts of taxable income from explicit to implicit taxation. This helps to explain why special restrictions apply to the deductibility of expenses incurred to generate tax-exempt interest income that do not apply to these other types of tax-favored assets.

Market Equilibrium with Tax-Exempt Entities

Suppose tax-exempt entities such as universities and municipalities face marginal tax rates of 0% on both taxable bonds and tax-exempt bonds. Absent restrictions, such taxpayers could profit by buying taxable bonds and selling tax-exempt bonds as long as a positive spread remained between the rates on the two securities. The equilibrium for tax-exempt investors requires that all assets bear zero implicit tax. But then arbitrage opportunities would arise for taxpayers facing positive marginal tax rates. Such taxpayers would buy tax-exempt municipal bonds and sell fully taxable bonds to create sufficient interest deductions to eliminate their taxable income. *As a result, no one would pay any taxes.* In addition to the tax-rule restrictions we have already discussed to prevent high-tax-bracket taxpayers from engaging in clientele-based arbitrage, additional restrictions prevent municipalities and other tax-exempt taxpayers from issuing arbitrarily large quantities of tax-exempt securities. Instead, they can issue tax-exempt securities only for certain qualified purposes.

One form of clientele-based arbitrage still seems to remain for municipalities. They can finance profit-making ventures that they own by issuing tax-exempt securities. That is, they can deduct the interest costs on tax-exempt securities from before-tax profits, and pay tax only on the remaining taxable income (so-called "unrelated business

---

[23]Note, however, while there is no restriction on borrowing and the deduction of interest to purchase stock, the dividends received deduction available to corporate investors can be reduced if the corporation borrows directly to purchase stock. Thus corporations need to be careful in undertaking this arbitrage activity to not run afoul of this restriction (see §246).

income") at corporate rates. Suppose that the profit-making business returns the risk-adjusted before-tax rate of return, R_b, and is financed at rate $R_b(1 - t_{Im})$, where t_{Im} is the implicit tax rate on municipal bonds. Then taxable income is $R_b - R_b(1 - t_{Im})$, or $R_b t_{Im}$, on a zero net investment. If the corporate tax rate is t_c, the municipality earns after-tax profits of $R_b t_{Im}(1 - t_c)$. For example, if R_b is equal to 10% and t_{Im} is equal to 30%, then the municipality earns 10%, financed by issuing municipal bonds at a 7% rate, or $10\%(1 - .30)$. The 3% profit, taxed at a 40% corporate tax rate, leaves a profit of 1.8% of the gross investment after tax on a zero net investment. Most municipalities do not run profit-making activities to profit from this arbitrage possibility. Perhaps market frictions, such as an inability to manage such activities efficiently or limits on the amount of tax-exempt debt they can issue, inhibit municipalities from undertaking this form of clientele-based arbitrage.

Summary of Key Points

1. Different economic activities are taxed differently, even if undertaken in the same organizational form. The unequal taxation of returns affects the demand for investment and thereby affects the before-tax rates of return. Specifically, if two assets yield identical pretax cash flows, but one is more heavily taxed than the other, then the price of the more lightly taxed asset will be bid up relative to the price of the more heavily taxed asset. Absent market frictions, asset prices adjust so that the after-tax rates of return are equalized across assets for all investors in the economy. Thus, differential tax treatment of asset returns gives rise to implicit taxes. For example, those investments that are tax-favored relative to fully taxable bonds earn lower before-tax rates of return than do fully taxable bonds. The difference in pretax rates of return between fully taxable bonds and the tax-favored asset is an implicit tax. That is, a tax is paid implicitly through the lower before-tax rates of return.

2. Investments that are tax-disfavored relative to fully taxable bonds earn *higher* before-tax rates of return than do fully taxable bonds, and, taking fully taxable bonds as the benchmark, the implicit tax on the relatively tax-disfavored asset is negative.

3. If the tax-deduction-equivalents of depreciation and tax credits on an investment have a present value equal to (greater than, less than) the present value of the period-by-period decline in the market value of the investment, the required before-tax rate of return on the investment will be equal to (less than, greater than) the before-tax rate of return on the fully taxable bond on a risk-adjusted basis.

4. Implicit taxes are typically not paid directly to the taxing authority. The taxpayer acts as a transfer agent of sorts for the government, with the taxpayer remitting a part of the tax to the beneficiary of a governmental subsidy or transfer payment. For example, municipal bond issuers receive the implicit tax as a subsidy. Customers of goods and services produced in capital-intensive industries with liberal depreciation allowances and tax credits pay lower prices. Renters face lower rental rates when depreciation allowances are very liberal.

5. In comparing the returns to different assets, it is important to distinguish between risk differences and taxation differences. Risky investments are priced to provide risk premiums. A risky investment that is lightly taxed (such as common stocks) can yield high before-tax rates of return and still bear substantial implicit tax relative to less risky assets that are fully taxed (such as taxable bonds).

6. If, in addition to differentially taxed assets, we have differentially taxed investors, the proper clientele for investments depends upon the mix of implicit and explicit taxes levied on the investments. The marginal investor setting prices in the market is the taxpayer who is indifferent between investing in the differentially taxed

assets. The proper clientele for high implicitly taxed investments are investors whose statutory tax rates exceed that of the marginal investor setting prices in the market. And the proper clientele for high explicitly taxed investments are investors whose statutory tax rates are less than that of the marginal investor.

7. Investors with statutory tax rates different from the marginal investor setting prices in the market are inframarginal investors. It is the inframarginal investors who form clearly identifiable clienteles as a function of the level of implicit tax rates across investments.

8. Many policymakers appear to ignore implicit taxes in their public statements. If we measure the progressiveness of our tax structure by focusing exclusively on explicit taxes, the U.S. tax structure does not appear very progressive. That is, the explicit tax as a percentage of the total income is about the same for wealthy and poor taxpayers. If, conversely, implicit taxes and subsidies are incorporated into the tax burden calculations, the tax schedule is much more progressive. The reason is that wealthy investors tend to own assets with high implicit taxes such as municipal bonds, common stock, and real estate.

9. In the absence of market frictions and tax-rule restrictions, if one savings vehicle or organizational form dominated another savings vehicle or organizational form, taxpayers could eliminate all their taxes through tax arbitrage. Tax arbitrage is the purchase of an asset (a long position) and the sale of another (a short position) to create a sure profit despite a zero level of net investment.

10. Organizational-form arbitrage arises when taxpayers take a long position in an asset through a tax-favored organizational form and a short position in the asset through an unfavorably taxed organizational form. Clientele-based arbitrage arises when taxpayers face different tax rates and when assets are taxed differentially, which gives rise to implicit taxes. Clientele-based arbitrage is a conversion of taxable income from an explicitly taxed to an implicitly taxed form, or vice versa.

11. Organizational-form arbitrage can reduce the tax on income to zero over investment horizons as short as for one tax year. This requires only that the returns on the long position held through the tax-favored organizational form are taxed at a lower rate than are the losses from the short position held through another tax-disfavored organizational form.

12. If the organizational-form arbitrage strategy involves a long position in an asset that gives rise to deferred taxable income and a short position that yields potential tax deductions, and the tax system does not provide tax rebates for negative taxable income, organizational-form arbitrage will not reduce the tax rate on income to zero.

13. Asset returns can be exempt from explicit taxation either through the nontaxability of future returns (as with municipal bonds in the United States) or through immediate deductibility of investment followed by full taxation of returns. Were it not for tax-rule restrictions relating to interest deductions, tax-exempt bonds would be more effective in clientele-based arbitrage strategies than would assets that achieve tax exemption due to the deductibility of investment cost.

14. Market frictions impede taxpayers' ability to undertake tax arbitrage. Most market frictions arise because information is costly and not all taxpayers have the same information. This is a point we will consider more thoroughly in the next chapter.

15. Many of the detailed provisions of the Tax Code represent restrictions on taxpayers' ability to effect tax arbitrage. As numerous as these restrictions might appear to be (and they are indeed numerous; we have mentioned only a few of the more important ones here), they are far fewer in number than if there were no market frictions (that is, if implementation of tax arbitrage strategies were costless).

Appendix 5.1

ADJUSTING FOR RISK USING THE CAPITAL ASSET PRICING MODEL

The capital asset pricing model can be written as

$$E(R_j) = R_f + \beta_j[E(R_m) - R_f]$$

where $E(R_j)$ denotes the expected return on security j, $E(R_m)$ denotes the expected return on the market over the same period, R_f denotes the risk-free rate of return, and β_j denotes the systematic risk of the security. Intuitively, β_j can be thought of as the quantity of risk that is priced by the market, and $[E(R_m) - R_f]$ can be thought of as the price per unit of risk. The product of the two terms is then quantity times price of risk or the risk premium R^{rp}, and this amount is incorporated in the expected return of the security. The risk-adjusted return R^{ra} for each security is then estimated as

$$R^{ra} = R^o - R^{rp} = R^o - \beta_j[E(R_m) - R_f]$$

where R^o is, as previously defined in the text, the required pretax total return. Thus to adjust for risk differences across securities we need an estimate of the β (beta) for each security and of $[E(R_m) - R_f]$. Historically, the difference between the realized return on the market and the risk-free rate has been approximately 8% per annum. Given an estimate of β—say 1.5—then the risk premium R^{rp} can be estimated as 1.5[.08] = .12, or 12%. We subtract this amount from the required (or expected)

pretax total return of the security to estimate the risk-adjusted return.

How do we obtain an estimate of a security's systematic risk? There are several commercial services that sell estimates of beta (for example, see the home page of BARRA, a provider of equity investment data including equity risk measures, http://www.barra.com/home/default.asp), and Value Line (http://www.valueline.com/) reports an estimate for each stock that it follows. In addition, there are several Web-based services that provide estimates. See, for example, http://www.stocksheet.com/ and enter the ticker symbol for your stock(s).

Finally, β can be estimated for each security of interest using the following procedure. β is defined as

$$\beta_j = \text{cov}(R_j, R_m)/\sigma^2(R_m)$$

where $\text{cov}(R_j, R_m)$ denotes the covariance between the return on the security and the market return, and $\sigma^2(R_m)$ is the variance of the market return. This term is the slope coefficient of a regression of R_j on R_m, and thus we can estimate β_j simply by regressing the return on the security on the market return (as represented by, for example, the S&P 500 index or the Dow Jones Industrial Average). Traditionally, the regression is estimated using 60 months of security returns.

Discussion Questions

1. True or False? Discuss.
   a. The implicit tax rate on an asset cannot be calculated without a benchmark asset against which to compare pretax returns.
   b. The implicit tax rate is always positive.

    c. The implicit tax rate is always less than the explicit tax rate.

    d. While explicit taxes are paid to taxing authorities, implicit taxes are subsidies paid to the issuers of securities, to consumers of goods and services, and to suppliers of factor inputs.

2. List five assets that bear positive implicit taxes. Carefully explain why each asset bears an implicit tax (that is, how is the asset tax-favored?).

3. Provide an example of an asset that bears a negative implicit tax and carefully explain why the asset bears a negative implicit tax.

4. Risk differences among assets mask the effects of differential taxation on returns. If we know the required after-tax risk premiums on assets, how can we determine the effects of differential taxation on their expected before-tax rates of return?

5. Capital investment in many countries is tax-favored. For example, in 1989, Singapore allowed a 100% tax depreciation write-off in the year of purchase for certain automated production equipment. Similar tax treatment was allowed on a variety of capital expenditures in the United Kingdom during the early 1980s. How do investment tax credits and liberal depreciation allowances affect the required before-tax rates of return on investment? Could the risk-adjusted before-tax rates of return on investment be lower than the tax-exempt riskless bond rate in equilibrium? Why? Could the risk-adjusted before-tax rate of return on investment be higher than the before-tax riskless bond rate?

6. Why do countries encourage investment by offering tax incentives such as investment tax credits or liberal depreciation allowances? What alternative methods exist to achieve the same goals? How would you judge whether tax incentives were superior to the alternatives?

7. What is an investment tax clientele? If the market sets implicit tax rates, why are we interested in determining the proper clientele for various investments? Why should a corporate strategist be interested in clienteles?

8. How does the concept of implicit taxes apply to investments undertaken in different tax jurisdictions?

9. What is organizational-form arbitrage? Give an example of organizational-form arbitrage that would create infinite wealth for a taxpayer. What conditions are necessary to prevent this from happening?

10. What is clientele-based arbitrage? Provide an example of such a strategy. Is clientele-based arbitrage restricted to high-tax-bracket taxpayers?

11. List some tax-rule restrictions that prevent organizational-form arbitrage. How do they succeed in preventing this arbitrage?

12. In the absence of tax-rule restrictions, how could pensions be used to effect organizational-form arbitrage? What restrictions are necessary to prevent pensions from being used in this manner?

13. Provide an example of organizational-form arbitrage using corporations and partnerships. What is an example of organizational-form arbitrage involving a long-term investment in common stocks? What restrictions are in place to limit taxpayers' abilities to avoid taxes from undertaking these strategies?

Exercises

1. a. A taxpayer is considering buying a fully taxable corporate bond. The bond has a remaining maturity of 5 years, promises to pay 6% interest annually (assume the coupon interest is payable annually), and has a face value of $1,000. The taxpayer faces a 31% tax rate on the interest income and requires a pretax rate of return of 6% to invest. What price is the taxpayer willing to pay for this bond?

   b. The same taxpayer is also considering buying a tax-exempt municipal bond. The municipal bond has a remaining maturity of 5 years, also promises to pay 6% interest annually (again the coupon interest is payable annually), and has a face value of $1,000. Assume the corporate and municipal bonds are equally risky. At what price is the taxpayer indifferent between the corporate and municipal bond? (Alternatively stated, what price is the taxpayer willing to pay for the municipal bond assuming he requires a pretax rate of return of 6% and faces a marginal tax rate of 31%?) How does this exercise tie to the discussion of implicit taxes in the text?

2. If the before-tax rate of return on a riskless fully taxable bond is 7% and the before-tax rate of return on a riskless tax-favored asset is 5%, what is the implicit tax rate on the tax-favored asset? If a tax-exempt riskless asset earns a before-tax rate of return of 4%, what is the explicit tax rate for the marginal investor on the riskless tax-favored asset that returns 5%?

3. Calculate the implicit and explicit tax rates for the following three assets. The required pretax total rate of return R^o for each asset is: 20% for both the fully taxable asset and the partially taxable asset and 8% for the tax-exempt asset. The required pretax risk premium R^{rp} for each asset is 7% for the fully taxable, 10% for the partially taxable, and 3% for the tax-exempt asset. Prepare a table similar to Table 5.2 (first ignoring risk differences and then adjusting for risk differences across assets). Discuss your results.

4. Calculate the implicit and explicit tax rates for the following three assets. The required pretax total rate of return R^o for each asset is: 15% for the fully taxable asset, 20% for the partially taxable asset, and 10% for the tax-exempt asset. The required pretax risk premium R^{rp} for each asset is 3% for the fully taxable, 9% for the partially taxable, and 0% for the tax-exempt asset. Prepare a table similar to Table 5.2 (first ignoring risk differences and then adjusting for risk differences across assets). Discuss your results. In particular, when ignoring risk differences:
   a. What is the top statutory tax rate?
   b. Is the partially taxable asset really partially taxable or is it tax-disfavored?
   c. After adjusting for risk differences, what is the top statutory tax rate? Which asset is most risky?

5. The investments below all bear the same *after-tax* risk premium, r^{rp}. Calculate the risk-adjusted pretax rates of return R^{ra} for assets II, III, and IV, as well as the expected pretax total return (*unadjusted* for risk, R^o) for assets III and IV. Explain your answer, and give examples of each of these assets observed in the marketplace.

Asset	Expected Pretax Total Return R^o	Tax Treatment of Risk Premium	Risk-Adjusted Pretax Return R^{ra}	Tax Treatment of Risk-Adjusted Return	Risk-Adjusted After-Tax Return R^{ra}
I	20%	Fully taxable	10%	Fully taxable	6%
II	12%	Tax-exempt	?	Tax-exempt	6%
III	?	Taxed at $t = 25\%$	?	Tax-exempt	6%
IV	?	Taxed at $t = 25\%$	?	Fully taxable	6%

6. Assume that the investor's tax rate is 40% and that in a competitive equilibrium all assets must earn the same after-tax after-risk adjusted returns of 7% ($= r^*$) for the investor to be indifferent between the assets. The investor is considering two assets: asset 1 and asset 2. The required pretax total rate of return R^o on asset 1 is 16% and on asset 2 is 14%. Analyze the following three cases.

Case 1. Suppose both assets are fully taxable—that is, $g = 1$. Because both assets are fully taxable, it is obvious that they must be of different risk for the required pretax total rates of return to differ. What is the pretax risk premium, R^{rp}, for each asset? From a purely tax standpoint, which asset will the marginal investor prefer?

Case 2. Suppose both assets are equally risky with a required after-tax risk premium of $r^{rp} = 3.5\%$. Because both assets are equally risky, it is obvious that they must be differentially taxed for the required pretax total rate of return to differ. Suppose $g_1 = .86$ and $g_2 = .625$ where g is the percentage of income from the asset included in taxable income and the subscript denotes asset 1 and 2, respectively.

- Show that the investor will be indifferent between the two assets (from a tax standpoint).
- Which asset would you choose if your marginal tax rate was 30%?
- Which asset would you choose if your marginal tax rate was 50%?

Case 3. Now suppose both assets are differentially taxed and differentially risky. For asset 1, $g_1 = .80$ and $r^{rp} = 3.88\%$. For asset 2, $g_2 = .20$ and $r^{rp} = 5.88\%$. (Because the after-tax risk premiums differ between the two assets, they are not equally risky.)

- Which asset is tax-favored?
- Which asset is more risky?
- Which asset will the investor (with a marginal tax rate of 40%) prefer?
- Which asset would you choose if your marginal tax rate was 30%?
- Which asset would you choose if your marginal tax rate was 50%?

7. If half the interest earned on the savings portion of an insurance policy were taxable, would it still be possible for taxpayers to eliminate their taxable income, in the absence of tax-rule restrictions and market frictions? Illustrate your answer to this question by assuming that the taxpayer's taxable income before arbitrage strategies is $100,000 and the before-tax interest rate is 10%.

8. Suppose that insurance policies were fully tax-exempt but (a) policies pay less than the fully taxable bond return to cover the costs of the insurance company and (b) loans can be secured only at a higher rate than the fully taxable bond rate to cover the lenders' costs. Can we use an insurance policy strategy to eliminate the tax on the $100,000 of taxable income? What is the implicit tax rate on this strategy? How does it arise and where does it go? Would every taxpayer want to use this strategy?

Tax Planning Problems

1. Assume you are a tax planner for a client with the following concerns.
   a. Suppose there exists three riskless assets. The first yields a fully taxable return of 7% before tax; the second yields a pretax return of 6%, only half of which is taxable; and the third yields a 5% fully tax-exempt return. Over what range of tax rates does each asset yield the highest after-tax return? How does this relate to tax clienteles?
   b. Suppose the tax rate schedule is as follows: 20% on the first $5,000 of investment income, 30% on the next $5,000 of investment income, and 40% on investment income exceeding $10,000. If you had $150,000 to invest and you had to invest in only one of the three assets, which one would maximize after-tax income?
   c. Can you beat the investment strategy in (b) by investing in a portfolio of assets? What is the optimal investment (the one that maximizes after-tax income) over the range of investment from $0 to $500,000?

2. Suppose that taxable bonds maturing in 5 years yield 10% per year before tax.
   a. What risk-adjusted appreciation rate on a non-dividend-paying common stock is required for the following taxpayers to be indifferent between investing in bonds and stock for 5 years:
      1. taxpayers paying a 30% tax rate on taxable bond interest and a 30% tax rate on capital gains when realized; and
      2. taxpayers paying a 30% tax rate on taxable bond interest and a 50-50 chance (the outcome being independent of the stock return) of a 20% and a 30% tax rate on capital gains when realized.
   b. If the taxpayer in (a.2.) were the marginal investor setting prices in the marketplace, what would be the implicit tax rate on the returns to stock?
   c. If the taxpayer in (a.2.) were the marginal investor setting prices in the marketplace, what arbitrage strategies would be available in a frictionless setting to the following investors:
      1. a tax-exempt entity;
      2. an individual taxpayer who can deduct interest expense on borrowing and who faces a 40% tax rate on ordinary income and a 30% tax rate on capital gains and losses;
      3. an individual taxpayer who can deduct interest expense on borrowing and who faces a 40% tax rate on both ordinary income and capital gains and a 30% tax rate on capital losses.
   d. Suppose we have an investor who faces a 30% tax rate on dividends and an expected tax rate of 20% on capital gains when they are realized 5 years from now. If a stock pays an annual dividend at the end of each year equal to 5% of the stock price at the beginning of the year, what appreciation rate on the stock is required to enable a 7% after-tax return per year over a 5-year period?
   e. What would be the implicit tax rate on the returns to the stock in (d)?
3. Following a substantial earthquake, a major West Coast university suffered $100 million in property damage. Suppose that this loss enabled the university to borrow an additional $100 million worth of tax-exempt bonds. The university issues 20-year zero-coupon bonds yielding 7% to maturity—that is, the university will pay bondholders $100 million $\times 1.07^{20}$, or $386.97 million, at maturity. Any gift money raised from friends of the university can be invested to earn 10% in riskless taxable bonds.
   a. How much must the university raise in gifts to pay off its bond obligation at maturity?
   b. How would your answer change if the bonds matured in 30 years rather than in 20 years?
4. Suppose you are a high-tax-bracket taxpayer. How could you take advantage of a situation in which the implicit tax rate on a tax-exempt asset is different from the marginal tax rate on income from a fully taxable asset? How would a low-tax-bracket taxpayer take advantage of this situation? What impediments (both frictions and restrictions) exist to limit your ability to take advantage of this arbitrage possibility?
5. Assume you face a progressive tax rate system. Show that it does not pay for you to reduce your explicit tax rate on fully taxable income to below the implicit tax rate on tax-exempt securities. Under what conditions would you choose not to engage in clientele-based arbitrage when your marginal tax rate exceeds the implicit tax rate on tax-exempt securities, even absent restrictions on the deductibility of interest on loans?
6. Assume you work for a local municipality. Further assume that there are no tax-rule restrictions preventing a municipality from buying taxable bonds financed by tax-exempt bonds yielding a lower before-tax rate of return. What arbitrage strategy should the municipality adopt? When does the opportunity disappear? Once

the municipality no longer has arbitrage opportunities, what arbitrage opportunities must exist for taxable investors? When do these opportunities disappear? When will neither tax-exempt nor taxable investors face arbitrage opportunities simultaneously? What tax-rule restrictions are necessary to prevent this form of clientele-based arbitrage?

7. Assume you work for a local municipality. Under what conditions is it tax advantageous for municipalities to undertake profit-making ventures? Why don't we see more municipality-operated activities? Can you think of some taxable business ventures currently operated by municipalities? Would the same arguments apply to other tax-exempt entities such as universities, hospitals, and charities?

8. The CFO of the ABC Corporation asks you to address the following three questions. ABC faces a top corporate marginal tax rate of 35% on both ordinary income and on capital gains.

   a. The firm is considering investing in some equipment costing $500,000. A 10% investment tax credit is available on the equipment. The equipment is depreciable using straight-line depreciation over 3 years with a zero salvage value. The firm uses an after-tax discount rate for this type of investment of 10%. The CFO asks you to estimate the present value of the tax savings from this investment. Assume the tax credit and first-year depreciation are taken immediately. How do the present value of the tax deductions compare with immediate expensing of the total outlay (with no investment tax credit)?

   b. The equipment above is expected (assumed here for simplicity) to generate a one-time pretax cash flows of approximately $805,255 at the end of year 5. The CFO asks you to estimate the expected annualized pretax and after-tax rates of return on this investment. Would you recommend undertaking this investment? Is this a tax-favored investment? Does it bear implicit taxes?

   c. The firm has $5 million in short-term investments. The money is to be used to expand facilities. However, due to regulatory delays in obtaining environmental approval, the expansion has been delayed 5 years. The firm now wishes to invest the funds in longer-term higher-yielding securities. The firm is considering three options.

      i. Invest in corporate bonds yielding 12% per annum pretax.

      ii. Invest in non-dividend-paying corporate equities, expected to earn 12% per annum pretax.

      iii. Invest in preferred stock of other corporations paying a 10% dividend per year. The corporation is eligible for a 70% dividends received deduction.
         Which option would you recommend and why? State any assumptions you need to make.

   d. The CFO asks you to prepare a proposal outlining any tax arbitrage strategies that the firm might be able to undertake to reduce its taxes. In preparing your proposal, make sure that the strategies do not run afoul of the tax-rule restrictions listed in this chapter. Provide a numerical example for each strategy to illustrate how it would work and how much in taxes it would save.

References and Additional Readings

Atwood, T. J., 2003. "Implicit Taxes: Evidence from Taxable, AMT, and Tax-Exempt State and Local Government Bond Yields," *Journal of the American Taxation Association* (Spring), pp. 1–20.

Ayers, B., B. Cloyd, and J. Robinson, 2002. "The Effect of Shareholder-Level Taxes on Stock Prices: Evidence from the Revenue Reconciliation Act of 1993," *The Accounting Review,* pp. 933–947.

Ayers, B., C. Lefanowicz, and J. Robinson, 2000. "The Effects of Goodwill Tax Deductions on the Market for Corporate Acquisitions," *Journal of the American Taxation Association* (Supplement), pp. 34–50.

Berger, P., 1993. "Explicit and Implicit Tax Effects of the R&D Tax Credit," *Journal of Accounting Research* (2), pp. 131–171.

Callihan, D., and R. White, 1999. "An Application of the Scholes and Wolfson Model to Examine the Relation Between Implicit and Explicit Taxes and Firm Market Structure*" Journal of the American Taxation Association* (Spring), pp. 1–19.

Desai, M., 2002. "The Corporate Profit Base, Tax Sheltering Activity, and the Changing Nature of Employee Compensation." Working paper 8866. Cambridge, MA: NBER.

Dhaliwal, D., M. Erickson, and R. Trezevant, 1999. "A Test of the Theory of Tax Clienteles for Dividend Policies," *National Tax Journal,* pp. 179–194.

Dhaliwal, D., M. Erickson, M. M. Frank, and M. Banyi, 2003. "Are Shareholder Dividend Taxes on Corporate Retained Earnings Impounded in Equity Prices?" *Journal of Accounting and Economics,* pp. 179–200.

Dhaliwal, D., O. Z. Li, and R. Trezevant, 2003. "Is a Dividend Tax Penalty Incorporated into the Return on a Firm's Common Stock?" *Journal of Accounting and Economics,* pp. 155–178.

Erickson, M., 1998. "The Effect of Taxes on the Structure of Corporate Acquisitions," *Journal of Accounting Research* (2), pp. 279–298.

Erickson, M., and E. Maydew, 1998. "Implicit Taxes in High Dividend Yield Stocks," *The Accounting Review* (October), pp. 435–458.

Erickson, M., and S. Wang, 1999. "The Effect of Transaction Structure on Price: Evidence from Subsidiary Sales," *Journal of Accounting and Economics* (April), pp. 149–176.

Fama, E., and K. French, 1998. "Taxes, Financing Decisions, and Firm Value," *Journal of Finance,* pp. 819–843.

Guenther, D., 1994. "The Relation Between Tax Rates and Pre-Tax Returns: Direct Evidence from the 1981 and 1986 Tax Rate Reductions," *Journal of Accounting and Economics* (November), pp. 379–393.

Hanlon, M., J. Myers, and T. Shevlin, 2003. "Dividend Taxes and Firm Valuation: A Re-Examination," *Journal of Accounting and Economics,* pp. 119–153.

Harris, T., and D. Kemsley, 1999. "Dividend Taxation in Firm Valuation: New Evidence," *Journal of Accounting Research,* pp. 275–291.

Hayn, C., 1989. "Tax Attributes as Determinants of Shareholder Gains in Corporate Acquisitions," *Journal of Financial Economics* (June), pp. 121–153.

Henning, S., and W. Shaw, 2000. "The Effect of the Tax Deductibility of Goodwill on Purchase Price Allocations," *Journal of the American Taxation Association* (Spring), pp. 18–37.

Henning, S., W. Shaw, and T. Stock, 2000. "The Effect of Taxes on Acquisition Prices and Transaction Structure," *Journal of the American Taxation Association* (Supplement), pp. 1–17.

Kern, B., and M. Morris, 1992. "Taxes and Firm Size: The Effect of Tax Legislation During the 1980s," *Journal of the American Taxation Association* (Spring), pp. 80–96.

Lang, M., and D. Shackelford, 2000. "Capitalization of Capital Gains Taxes: Evidence from Stock Price Reactions to the 1997 Rate Reduction,*" Journal of Public Economics,* pp. 69–85.

Manzon, G., and G. Plesko, 2002. "The Relation Between Financial and Tax Reporting Measures of Income," *Tax Law Review,* pp. 175–214.

Scholes, M., P. Wilson, and M. Wolfson, 1990. "Tax Planning, Regulatory Capital Planning, and Financial Reporting Strategy for Commercial Banks," *Review of Financial Studies,* pp. 625–650.

Shackelford, D., 1991. "The Market for Tax Benefits: Evidence from Leveraged ESOPs," *Journal of Accounting and Economics,* pp. 117–145.

Shackelford, D., 2000. "Stock Market Reaction to Capital Gains Tax Changes: Empirical Evidence from the 1997 and 1998 Tax Acts," In *Tax Policy and the Economy,* Vol. 14, ed. Poterba, J. Cambridge, MA: MIT Press.

Shackelford, D., and T. Shevlin, 2001. "Empirical Tax Research in Accounting," *Journal of Accounting and Economics* (September), pp. 321–387.

Shevlin, T., and S. Porter, 1992. "The Corporate Tax Comeback in 1987: Some Further Evidence," *Journal of the American Taxation Association* (Spring), pp. 59–79.

Weaver, C., 2000. "Divestiture Structure and Tax Attributes: Evidence from the Omnibus Budget Reconciliation Act of 1993," *Journal of the American Taxation Association* (Supplement), pp. 54–71.

Wilkie, P., 1992 "Empirical Evidence of Implicit Taxes in the Corporate Sector," *Journal of the American Taxation Association* (Spring), pp. 97–116.

Yin, G., 2000. "How Much of the Recent Evidence of a Corporate Tax Shelter Problem is Explained by Increased Stock Option Activity?" Working Paper. Charlottesville, VA University of Virginia School of Law.

Zodrow, G., 1991. "On the 'Traditional' and 'New' Views of Dividend Taxation," *National Tax Journal,* pp. 497–509.

CHAPTER

6

NONTAX COSTS OF TAX PLANNING

After completing this chapter, you should be able to:

1. Explain how a progressive tax rate system influences firms' risk-taking and hedging incentives.

2. Explain how a progressive tax rate system influences firms' organizational form choices.

3. Describe how transaction costs and hidden-action problems affect tax planning.

4. Describe how hidden-information problems affect tax planning.

5. Describe how financial reporting issues influence tax planning.

Although the world would be easier to understand if economic exchanges could be undertaken free of all transaction costs, such costs are pervasive. Moreover, different ways of organizing economic activity give rise to differences in transaction costs. But we also wish to emphasize that different ways of organizing economic activity give rise to differences in tax costs. Hence the efficient organizational choice is not necessarily the one that minimizes transaction costs, once taxes are considered as well. Similarly, it would be shortsighted to suggest that efficient organizational choice is determined by minimizing taxes, because different tax plans generally give rise to differences in transaction and other nontax costs.[1] We cannot emphasize too strongly the importance of these nontax costs in forging efficient tax plans.

Casual observation suggests that the effect of taxes pervades the way that production and exchange are organized. It is equally indisputable that organizational arrangements arise because information is asymmetrically distributed among economic agents. Workers must often be monitored or offered incentives to induce them

---

[1]If these nontax cost differences are viewed as implicit taxes (after all, this is a tax planning text), then the (deceptively) simple decision rule of seeking to minimize taxes is an efficient one. However, we will maintain the distinction between implicit taxes (as differences in pretax rates of return arising from differential explicit tax treatment) and other nontax costs.

to perform in the owners' best interests. Customers must often be offered warranties to induce them to buy products, and still a variety of consumer protection groups exist. Independent third parties are required to audit the financial statements of publicly owned corporations. And even absent any regulatory requirements, many firms voluntarily pay substantial sums to third parties to verify certain information disclosures designed to facilitate economic exchanges among parties who are not equally well-informed.

In many contracting problems, a desire to achieve tax minimization encourages precisely the same organizational arrangements as do solutions to incentive problems among differentially informed and opportunistic agents. When this occurs, outside observers (such as researchers, consultants, corporate raiders, investment bankers, and regulators) face a so-called **identification problem** in sorting out which economic force is responsible for the observed contractual relations.

However, tax considerations and information-related transaction cost considerations often have conflicting implications for efficient organizational design. Sometimes tax considerations dominate in importance, and sometimes information considerations dominate. But frequently, both factors are important and trade-offs must be made. Because of the need to make these trade-offs, efficient tax planning is often quite distinct from tax minimization. We develop this theme in this chapter and illustrate it in several later chapters.

So far, uncertainty has not been prominent in our discussion. We begin to remedy that here. In particular, we distinguish between two types of uncertainty:

- **Symmetric uncertainty,** where all contracting parties are equally well-informed, but still uncertain, about what the future cash flows from an investment might be.
- **Strategic uncertainty** (also known as information asymmetry), where the contracting parties are not equally well-informed about what the future investment cash flows might be.

We further distinguish between two types of information asymmetry regarding future cash flows. The first arises when one contracting party has control over an action choice that affects future cash flows, where the action choice is *unobservable* to other contracting parties (so-called **hidden-action** or **moral hazard** situations). The second type of information asymmetry arises when one contracting party has observed a characteristic of the production function she cannot control that affects future cash flows, and that characteristic is only imperfectly observable by the other contracting parties (so-called **hidden-information** or **adverse selection** situations).[2]

In this chapter, we illustrate how each form of uncertainty gives rise to efficient tax planning strategies that sacrifice tax minimization. We discuss the effects of symmetric uncertainty in the context of progressive tax rate schedules. Progressive tax rate schedules can influence a firm's risk-taking incentives (even if the firm is risk-neutral) with respect to investment choices and hedging activities and can influence organizational choice (for example, joint venturing with more profitable entities).

---

[2]For further elaboration, see Arrow (1985).

Hidden-action problems can inhibit tax arbitrage through capital market activities (by influencing borrowing and lending rates) and can influence contracting in labor markets. Hidden-information problems can impede asset sales that might minimize taxes.

Income shifting and organizational forms that minimize taxes often give rise to costs along other dimensions, leading to a trade-off between taxes and nontax costs. For example, income shifting within an organization might require more centralized organizational structures, but information asymmetries might require more decentralized organizational structures. Shifting income across time will often result in costs arising from financial reporting consequences of the income shifting. Using limited partnerships or joint ventures (including special purpose entities) can create serious conflicts of interest (agency costs) between parties. Many tax planning activities can result in unfavorable financial reporting effects, leading to a trade-off between tax benefits/savings and costs arising from reporting lower earnings or higher debt-equity (leverage) ratios. Thus efficient tax planning requires the tax planner to identify and weigh the nontax costs of any tax plan against the tax benefits.

6.1 SYMMETRIC UNCERTAINTY, PROGRESSIVE TAX RATES, AND RISK-TAKING

As we defined the term, symmetric uncertainty is where all contracting parties are equally well-informed (that is, there is no asymmetric information) but uncertain about what the future cash flows from an investment might be. Uncertainty about future cash flows means that the investment is risky. When uncertainty about future cash flows (or profitability) is linked with a **progressive income tax system,** some taxpayers may be less inclined to take on risky investments than they might otherwise be. Assume a tax rate schedule as follows:

- If income is positive, you pay a tax of 40%.
- If income is negative, the tax rate is 0%; that is, you get no tax refund.[3]

This tax rate schedule is progressive. In Figure 6.1, it is graphed (tax payable on the y-axis and taxable income on the x-axis) as the dark line kinked at the origin. When graphed it appears as a convex function and so is also called a convex tax function.

Suppose you have $100,000 to invest in one of two projects. One of the projects is riskless, yielding a certain profit of $20,000. The alternative project is risky, yielding a profit of $150,000 half the time and a loss of $100,000 half the time. Because each outcome for the risky project is equally likely, the expected pretax profit is $25,000 or .5($150,000) + .5(−$100,000). These pretax expected returns appear on the horizontal axis in Figure 6.1. For the moment, assume that you are indifferent between a particular payoff with certainty and a risky payoff with equal expected value. In other words, you are risk-neutral.

---

[3]Assume for the purposes of this example that tax losses can be carried neither back nor forward to offset income earned in other years. We discuss the effect of carrybacks and carryforwards later in the chapter and take a closer look at them in the next chapter.

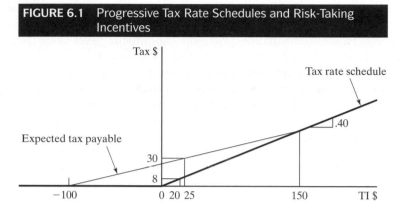

FIGURE 6.1 Progressive Tax Rate Schedules and Risk-Taking Incentives

In which project would you invest absent any taxes? Given your indifference toward risk, you would choose the project providing the higher expected pretax profit. That project is the risky project, by $5,000, or $25,000 − $20,000. Alternatively stated, the expected pretax rate of return for the risky project is 25%, or 25,000/100,000, compared with 20% for the riskless project.

How does the progressive tax rate schedule affect project choice? Quite dramatically, as the following after-tax profit numbers show:

Riskless project: $20,000(1 − .40) = $12,000 after tax
                                Expected after-tax rate of return = 12%
Risky project: .5[$150,000(1 − .40)] + .5(−$100,000) = −$5,000 after tax
                                Expected after-tax rate of return = −5%

The riskless project is now *preferred* over the risky one by $17,000 after tax, despite being the inferior choice (by $5,000) in the absence of taxes. (Note: For simplicity here we are assuming that the investment is not tax deductible.) Why is the riskless project now tax-preferred? Because the tax rate schedule is progressive, the expected tax is $22,000 higher for the risky project than for the riskless one ($30,000 compared with $8,000 as plotted in Figure 6.1). This example shows a general feature of a progressive (or convex) tax system: The average tax rate paid increases with the variability of taxable income levels.[4] So, even when taxpayers are risk-neutral and face a progressive tax rate schedule, they exhibit risk aversion toward assets with variable pretax returns.[5]

As discussed in Chapter 4, corporations can carry back losses to obtain refunds of taxes paid in the last 2 years or carry the losses forward for 20 years to offset future taxes payable. While these rules reduce the progressiveness of the tax rate schedule, if

---

[4]Readers with a mathematical background might recognize this as an application of Jensen's Inequality $E[f(X)] > f[E(X)]$, where $f(X)$ is the convex tax schedule.
[5]For further discussion, see Fellingham and Wolfson (1985).

losses have to be carried forward (such as for start-up companies), the tax rate schedule is still progressive (kinked) around zero taxable income. Thus start-ups face progressive tax rate schedules. In the extreme, if the risky investments do not prove successful (because of technology changes, lack of customer demand, failure of the research and development program to generate products), then the start-up effectively faces the tax rate schedule in our example (tax losses obtain no tax benefit). In these situations, the progressive tax rate schedule offers advantages to existing successful business (such as Microsoft Corporation, IBM, Intel, Merck) to undertake risky investments, because the losses can be immediately deducted against the business' other income, which reduces the after-tax cost of the investment. For start-ups with no income, however, there is a non-zero probability that the tax losses will not be used. Thus, a progressive tax rate schedule discriminates against start-ups resulting in several implications.

R&D and O&G Activities

Qualifying research and development (R&D) expenditures in the United States are immediately deductible as incurred under Section 174 of the IRC. Moreover, the sale of successfully developed technology generally gives rise to capital gains. Similarly, oil and gas (O&G) investments receive favorable tax treatment because drilling and exploration expenditures are immediately deductible. Further, O&G investments receive a percentage depletion allowance in which 15% of revenues from the well is explicitly tax exempt[6] and part of the income (sale of the well) may be subject to favorable capital gains treatment. Recall that immediate deductibility of an investment, followed by full taxation of the returns at the same tax rate, is equivalent to tax exemption. With favorable taxation on the payoffs, the after-tax rates of return can exceed the pretax rates of return (and can even turn a negative pretax return into a positive after-tax rate of return).

To illustrate the effects of Tax Code progressivity on firms' incentives to undertake R&D (and O&G), suppose a corporation makes an R&D investment of $1 (for realism, you can easily add 6 or 7 zeros). Initially suppose the firm's marginal tax rate is 40%. Any income generated from the investment will be taxed in the future, when the firm's tax rate is expected to be 30%. Suppose further that an R&D tax credit of 10% of the investment expenditure is immediately available. The research is very risky:

Probability	*Payoff*	*Tax Rate*
90%	$0 (worthless)	—
10%	$11 (successful)	30%

The expected pretax rate of return is 10%, or $(.90 \times \$0) + (.1 \times \$11) = \$1.10$, of expected cash return on a $1 investment. But the expected after-tax rate of return is

---

[6]The percentage depletion allowance is limited to the lessor of 65% of the firm's taxable income before the depletion allowance or 100% of the taxable income from the well (§613).

considerably higher, even if we assume that the $11 return in the event of a successful outcome is fully taxed at 30%:

$$\frac{\$1.10(1-.30)}{\$1.00-\$.40-\$.10} - 1 = \frac{\$.77}{\$.50} - 1 \quad \text{or} \quad 54\%$$

The denominator is the after-tax cost of the investment: $1 cash investment less the $.40 tax saved from the deduction and the $.10 tax credit. If the research is undertaken by a firm with accumulated tax losses (called net operating loss (NOL) carryforwards) or by a start-up company with no income against which to offset the R&D deductions or the R&D tax credits, the after-tax returns decline dramatically. For example, suppose the R&D expenditures are effectively deductible at a rate of 20%,[7] the present value of the R&D tax credit is only 5%, and any income is still taxed at 30%. Then the after-tax expected rate of return declines from 54% to only 2.7%, or [$.77/($1.00 − $.20 − $.05)] − 1.

One possible response to the unfavorable tax treatment that results in these situations is to undertake the investment anyway and suffer the tax cost. Another response is to abandon the investment. Either way, the tax rules discourage research expenditures by low-tax firms. However, low-tax firms can finance the activity in a way that sells the rights to favorable tax treatment to a party that is in a better position to take advantage of the tax write-offs.

The tax shelter industry in the 1970s and early 1980s was, in part, motivated by the progressiveness of the tax rate schedule for start-up high technology firms. Further, in the 1970s, the top individual statutory tax rate exceeded the top corporate statutory tax rate, so even profitable firms could benefit if they could place the tax deductions in the hands of higher taxed taxpayers. Firms created limited partnerships (LPs, see Chapter 4 for a discussion of these partnerships) in which limited partner interests were sold to outside parties (high-tax individuals) that could better use the immediate deductibility of the R&D and O&G (at tax rates up to 70%). Further, any payoffs were taxed at favorable capital gains to these parties. The company doing the research or exploration received a management fee and an interest in any revenue generated from licensing or selling the developed technology/oil. Shevlin (1987) provides empirical evidence consistent with the tax motivation for forming R&D LPs.[8] He found that firms sponsoring R&D LPs were younger and had more NOL carryforwards than firms conducting R&D in-house. Wolfson (1985) examines the effect of taxes on oil and gas partnerships.

Both these activities are tax-favored and so investors in limited partnerships likely bear implicit taxes by bidding up the prices of the limited partnership interest (or by accepting a lower pretax rate of return). Thus the R&D or O&G firm organizing the partnership is able to raise funds at a lower cost. Also because the investment bears implicit taxes, high-tax-rate investors are the natural clientele for these investments (and hence they were marketed to wealthy and high-income individuals).

As effective as these partnerships may be from a tax standpoint, they can create severe nontax costs. Such entities require considerable administrative costs to organize, including sales commissions and investment banking fees that can easily run to 10% or more of the total amount invested. Partnerships also may require disclosures

---

[7]A 20% tax rate arises here because the deduction has to be carried forward for 10 years, then deducted at a tax rate of 40%, and the present value at 7% per annum results in an effective tax rate of 20%: $.40/(1.07)^{10}$.
[8]See also Beatty, Berger, and Magliolo (1995).

to investors regarding the nature of the research that compromise the firm's competitive advantage. Further, as discussed in the next sections, these arrangements give rise to nontax costs arising from strategic uncertainty (both hidden-information and hidden-action problems). Thus, tax planners must weigh the tax benefits and nontax costs of these organizational forms.

The Tax Reform Act of 1986 (TRA 86) effectively put an end to limited partnerships as a way to sell the tax benefits to outside parties better able to use them, because **passive activity losses** cannot be deducted against other types of income (that is, nonpassive income) until the underlying investments are sold. Losses from limited partnership interests were classified in TRA 86 as passive activity losses for individual taxpayers. Since 1986, start-ups and low tax firms are likely to form joint ventures with older, more profitable corporations that can use the tax benefits (that is, these firms face a less progressive tax schedule). These joint ventures may suffer fewer agency (nontax) costs because both parties are likely more involved in the venture's activities. Further, joint ventures can also be motivated by nontax factors: outside parties may bring special research, marketing, or administrative expertise to the venture as well as risk-sharing benefits.

Progressive Tax Rates and Hedging

For corporations facing progressive tax schedules, **hedging** lowers expected tax liabilities. This decrease occurs through lowering the variance of the distribution of expected taxable income. Hedging can be undertaken via financial instruments such as options, swaps, and other derivatives. Thus taxes can offer motivation for firms to hedge their activities (in addition to hedging to reduce the expected costs of financial distress and to reduce agency costs between debt holders and shareholders).[9]

Graham and Smith (1999) provide some empirical estimates of firms' tax incentive to hedge. Graham and Smith analyze over 80,000 firm-year observations for corporations on Standard & Poor's Compustat database. This database contains financial statement information for a majority of publicly traded U.S. firms. The researchers find that in approximately 50% of firm-years, corporations face convex (progressive) tax rate schedules and thus have a tax-based incentive to hedge. In 25% of firm-years, firms face a linear tax rate function and thus have no tax incentive to hedge. In the remaining 25% of firm-years, the firms face a concave (regressive) tax rate function and thus face a tax-based disincentive to hedge.

For the 50% of firm-years facing a convex tax rate function, approximately 25% have potential tax savings from hedging that appear material. For the remaining 75% of the cases, the tax savings are small. Further, their results suggest that corporations are most likely to face a convex tax rate function when (1) their expected taxable incomes are near the kink in the statutory tax schedule (that is, taxable income is positive and near zero);[10] (2) their incomes are volatile; and (3) the corporation is likely to switch back and forth between profits and losses.

---

[9]For further discussion of firms' incentives to hedge, see Nance, Smith, and Smithson (1993).

[10]For firms with expected continuing losses and existing NOL carryforwards, the firm has an incentive to increase the variance of taxable incomes so as to increase the probability of a large positive outcome against which it can offset the losses. This very well could describe some Internet-based companies, such as Amazon.com.

6.2 TAX PLANNING IN THE PRESENCE OF RISK-SHARING AND HIDDEN-ACTION CONSIDERATIONS

In Chapter 5, we discussed in very general terms how market frictions drive a wedge between the buying and selling prices of assets, and this helps to prevent tax arbitrage opportunities from being used to eliminate income taxes. We illustrated the effects of the borrowing rate for funds exceeding the lending rate on the desirability of effecting organizational-form and clientele-based arbitrage. We now examine this issue more closely.

Contracting in Capital Markets

Suppose there were no restrictions on the deductibility of interest on loans that are fully secured by single premium deferred annuities (SPDAs). Would we expect the pretax rates of return on the annuity contract to be the same as the rate paid on the loan? The answer is no. The insurance company offering the deferred annuity contract must charge for its operating costs, as must the bank lending the funds.

What operating costs exist for the insurance company? The insurance company has a sales force that earns commissions for educating the public about deferred annuities. The company must also manufacture an information system to keep track of its assets and its policyholders, as well as invest in a system of internal controls to ensure that all funds received are invested and to assure all prospective policyholders that it is solvent. Moreover, the company must incur costs to create contracts that specify clearly its property rights and those of its policyholders in various contingencies. Annual operating expenses of companies offering deferred annuities have averaged 1.75% to 2% of funds invested.[11]

What costs are there for the lender? The lender must also develop and maintain an information system and a system of internal controls and incur costs to write contracts. The lender must also pay brokers (for example, loan officers) to identify appropriate borrowers. In addition, the lender must invest resources to investigate the insurance company whose deferred annuity secures the loan. The lender must be convinced that the insurance company assets backing the deferred annuity are adequate to pay market rates of return to annuity holders. Moreover, the lender must incur costs to ensure that the deferred annuity cannot be cashed out by the owner and put to alternative uses without the lender's knowledge. Otherwise, the loan would not really be secured. All of these costs add up. As a result, it is not unusual for the spread between the riskless borrowing rate and the secured lending rate to exceed 300 basis points or 3%.

For example, one simple way to engage in secured borrowing is to borrow from a brokerage house or bank, pledging your stocks as collateral. Such loans are essentially riskless to the lender because investors are initially permitted to borrow up to only 50% of the value of the stock. The broker can sell stocks if they decline in value to the point where they begin to jeopardize full repayment of the loan. Despite the apparent riskless nature of the loans, brokerage houses frequently charge interest rates well above the cost of borrowing (a 2% spread is common). In part, this spread pays for the

---

[11]*Fund Action* (February 11, 1991), p. 3.

costs that brokers might incur if forced to sell customers' shares in big market drops and customers sue because they allege they did not receive fair treatment.

Of course, one would expect that extremely large investors, including groups of individual investors, can arrange for lower spreads, perhaps as low as .5%. These low transaction costs result from economics of scale, because most of the transaction costs we have mentioned are fixed in nature. If this is a correct characterization, such large investors would indeed have less difficulty borrowing to invest in some tax-favored savings vehicle like deferred annuities, which is the kind of tax arbitrage that we discussed in Chapter 5. As a result, the tax system must impose restrictions on these activities. Perhaps the threat of these large, low-cost transactors has led to the specific restriction that secured borrowing to finance the purchase of single premium deferred annuities would render the interest expense nondeductible.

With secured borrowing to purchase deferred annuities ruled out by tax-rule restrictions, let's now consider whether things look much different with *unsecured* borrowing. The rates on unsecured borrowing can be dramatically higher than the rates on secured borrowing. Moreover, unlike the case of secured borrowing, the borrowing rates for unsecured loans tend to increase with the level of borrowing for a given individual. The reason for this is fairly straightforward and relates to strategic uncertainty—hidden actions. Borrowers cannot always be trusted to act in ways they promise to act. That is, they may take actions that imperil the cash flows that stand behind the contracts (because they do not bear all of the costs of reduced cash flow), and lenders typically cannot observe such actions.

Suppose your entire life savings of $100,000 is invested in riskless bonds, and you have no liabilities. You go to the bank and apply for a $50,000 loan. You tell the bank that the loan is to finance a vacation and an investment, and you prefer not to invade your $100,000 savings account for these purposes. With $100,000 in riskless assets, we might suppose that the bank need not charge much of a default premium.

But suppose the vacation and investment you had in mind entailed liquidating your savings account, going to Las Vegas, and betting $150,000 on the color red in a single spin of a fair roulette wheel. Would the bank be very happy? Not likely. If you win, you make a profit of $150,000 less a small fee for the use of the bank's $50,000 for the bet. If you lose, you lose only your $100,000 because you will default on the bank loan. Assuming that winning and losing are equally likely, your expected profit, ignoring the small fee for the "rent" on $50,000 for one day, is $25,000, or $.5(\$150,000) + .5(-\$100,000)$. Your expected winnings of $25,000 are precisely equal to the bank's expected loss.

But you can do even better by taking on more risk. Suppose your strategy were to bet everything on the number "7 red" with a 40-slot roulette wheel. Now the payoffs are $6,000,000 (or $40 \times \$150,000$) with probability 1/40, less $50,000 to repay the loan, for a net return of $5,950,000, and $0 with probability 39/40. For this bet, the expected terminal cash position is $148,750 (or $\$5,950,000 \times 1/40$), and the expected profit increases to $48,750 (or $\$148,750 - \$100,000$). The bank is repaid only 1 time in 40. As a result, its expected dollar payoff is $1,250 on a $50,000 investment. Of course, your expected profit (and the bank's expected loss) could be made arbitrarily close to $50,000 by increasing the actuarially fair risk further; for example, if your number comes up after the first spin, reinvest everything on another spin.

The limited personal liability provided by the bankruptcy laws encourages unsecured debtors to engage in riskier investments because they do not bear fully the cost of such risks. An unfortunate aspect of this incentive problem is that an unsecured borrower, who definitely intends not to buy risky assets, may have no cost-effective way of convincing the lender that this is the case.

One way to lessen the problem is for the borrower to establish a reputation for not taking strategic advantage of the lender (for example, by building up a good credit history with the lender). Tax shelter syndicators and investment advisors are very aware of the benefits of establishing a reputation, as we will discuss below. But the moral here is that information costs resulting from strategic uncertainty (hidden action) drive deeper the wedge between borrowing and lending rates.

No wonder lenders often write extensive loan covenants into loan agreements that restrict borrowers' behavior. But such covenants are costly to write because there are so many possible future contingencies, some of which cannot even be foreseen at the time of contracting. These covenants are also costly to monitor. As a result, they cannot completely prevent opportunistic behavior on the part of borrowers. Further, restrictive covenants can prove costly to borrowers, by hindering their activities in costly ways. As suggested in Chapter 5, these costs can reduce dramatically the number of capital market transactions that can be exploited to reduce taxes in a cost-effective way.

Contracting in Labor Markets

Let us now consider employee compensation contracting in simple settings. We begin with a single-period setting where there are no hidden-action (moral hazard) problems—that is, the employer need not worry about the employee's taking actions on the job that are unobservable to the employer and that may improve the employee's welfare at some expense to the employer. This will enable us to expose easily the nature of the identification problem that we discussed earlier.

Suppose that the employee is subject to a constant tax rate independent of compensation received. The employer, though, is subject to a progressive income tax rate function. If profits are high, so is the tax rate. While it might seem unusual that employees face constant tax rates and employers face progressive tax rates, this is not really so. Assume, for example, that the employees are highly paid executives, whose marginal tax rates are constant; and the employer is a start-up venture with expenses that currently generate net operating losses, but with profits expected in the future. In such a setting, the tax-minimizing contract is one that loads up on compensation to the employee when profits are high (in the future) and the tax deduction to the employer for compensation paid is worth the most. Similarly, compensation should be minimized when profits and tax rates for the employer are low (which they are at the present time).

In this compensation plan, the employee foregoes current income for future compensation that is tied to the firm's profits. Note how this contract looks like an incentive-based arrangement despite the absence of any incentive problems. This arrangement could arise due to tax motives or incentive motives or both. This collection of possibilities is what we mean by an identification problem. Such problems make it difficult to untangle the reasons we observe various contractual arrangements. Without a rich understanding of the situation, outside observers could easily misinterpret the economics of the contractual arrangements.

Suppose the firm assigns a manager to undertake a risky project. The project yields a pretax profit, before employee compensation expense, of $400,000 half the time and −$100,000 half the time. As in our earlier example, the tax rate is 40% when taxable income is positive and 0% otherwise. This tax schedule applies to both the firm and its employee. Assume that both the employee and the firm's owners are risk-neutral. The employee has job alternatives that pay the equivalent of $75,000 in salary. This means that the firm must offer a compensation contract that matches the after-tax salary of $45,000, or $75,000(1 − .40), available elsewhere.

What sort of compensation contract should the employee be offered? Note that a $75,000 salary contract would not be efficient from a tax planning standpoint. Why? Because half the time (when a loss is generated) the employer would obtain no tax benefit from the salary payment. It would be better to pay nothing when profits are negative and a bonus of $150,000 when profits are positive. Because each situation occurs half the time, the *expected* pay is $75,000, and this satisfies the compensation requirements of the employee.

The expected after-tax cost of this arrangement to the firm is $45,000, or .5($0) + .5[$150,000(1 − .40)]. This is $15,000 less than the expected after-tax cost of a $75,000 salary contract. The savings results from avoiding a compensation payment of $75,000 when the tax rate is 0% rather than paying it when the tax rate is 40% (a tax difference of $30,000), which occurs half the time.

Conflicts Between Risk-Sharing and Tax Minimization

Let us now suppose that the employee is risk-averse, while the employer is indifferent towards risk. Because the employee is willing to pay to avoid risk, whereas the employer does not mind bearing risk, it is desirable, from a risk-sharing standpoint, for the employee to be offered a pure wage contract, independent of the firm's profitability. This would result in the employer bearing all the risk of profit uncertainty.

But if the employee faces a constant tax rate and the employer an increasing tax rate, a pure wage contract results in an increase in joint tax payments relative to the tax-minimizing contract (a bonus contract that shifts all the risk to the *employee*). So, the two parties will find it desirable neither to minimize taxes nor to shield the risk-averse party from all risk. Instead, they will trade off the two forces.

Conflicts Between Incentive Contracting and Tax Minimization

Now let us expand our compensation contracting problem by introducing *hidden-action* concerns and contracts that extend over several time periods. Tax rates will be allowed to vary over time, and the employer will be concerned with aligning employee incentives with the employer's interests.

In particular, suppose the employer's tax rate today is greater than it will be in the future. Such a tax rate configuration favors immediate salary over deferred compensation: It is preferable to take tax deductions when the employer's tax rate is highest, which it is presently. Further suppose that the employee faces the opposite tax rate configuration, rates are low today and will be high in the future. This further reinforces the desirability of accelerating compensation payments: The employee recognizes taxable income when tax rates are low. Finally, suppose that the employee can earn at least as much on marginal investments after tax as can the employer. This also favors current compensation, because deferred compensation effectively results in the employer investing on the employee's behalf. So the tax-minimizing contract is clearly one that "loads up" on current compensation.

But now suppose that the employee works in a firm in which a durable good is manufactured where employer and employee interests conflict. In particular, assume that the employee can take one of two actions. Action 1 is working hard and leads to the product lasting W periods. Alternatively, the employee can take action 2, which is shirking, in which case the product lasts S periods, where S is less than W. The employee prefers action 2 to action 1, but the market value of increased product durability is assumed to exceed this personal cost difference. In other words, if the employer could observe the employee's actions, the employer would be willing to pay a bonus for hard work that more than compensates for the personal cost to the employee of the additional effort.

We also assume that bankruptcy constraints and labor laws prevent the employer from exacting a large penalty from the employee in the event that the product is observed to last only S periods, revealing that the employee has shirked. Finally, assume that the employee's objective is to maximize lifetime consumption, where consumption tomorrow is almost as good as consumption today. Consumption takes place as the employee receives compensation.

Then, ignoring tax considerations, the efficient incentive arrangement entails deferring compensation to the employee until after the manufactured product has been observed to last more than S periods, revealing that the employee performed the more costly (and more valuable) action. But this is in direct conflict with the tax-minimizing contract, which would accelerate compensation to take advantage of the tax rates changing over time. The production efficiency gains from deferring compensation may be insufficient to compensate for the resulting additional tax payments, and in general the two considerations must be traded off.

In our example, employer and the employee tax rates were such that immediate salary reduced taxes relative to deferred compensation. Suppose that the tax rates over time were reversed and that, for tax reasons alone, deferred compensation is the desired contract. To defer compensation with a deferred compensation contract the employee must be an unsecured creditor of the employer. When the employee is an unsecured creditor, she will want to ensure that the firm remains solvent. This may result in the employee passing up positive net present value projects if they also increase the risk of the firm defaulting on the deferred compensation contract. As with previous examples, tax minimization may have to be sacrificed to align incentives properly.

6.3 TAX PLANNING IN THE PRESENCE OF HIDDEN-INFORMATION CONSIDERATIONS

The examples considered so far have illustrated how the organizational arrangements encouraged by focusing narrowly on tax minimization may conflict with those encouraged by risk-sharing or hidden-action considerations. We turn next to an example in which tax minimization may not be achievable because of hidden-information problems. The classic setting in which this arises is in the sale of an asset (such as in the used car market). The seller is assumed to be better informed than the buyer about the quality or value of the asset being sold.

Suppose that a firm has generated large tax losses in past years and currently has NOL carryforwards that are about to expire unused or will not be used before tax rates drop. Suppose further that it is widely understood that, if a profitable firm merges with our NOL firm, some taxes can be saved. As noted, sellers of assets are often better informed about the value of the assets for sale than are prospective buyers. If the owners of the NOL firm know that the firm is worth more than the expected value assessed by prospective buyers given their limited information, there may not exist a mutually agreeable price at which to sell the firm. Stated a bit more formally, if high-value firms are unable to distinguish themselves in the marketplace from low-value firms, high-value firms may be forced to withdraw from the market unless the tax gains are large enough to offset the bargain sales price (for high-value firms) that clears the market.

Of course, the sale of a business does not represent the only means by which the owners of the NOL firm could cash in the wasting asset that NOL carryforwards represent. But as we will discuss in future chapters, all of the substitutes (including issuing stock, repurchasing debt, effecting a sale and leaseback of depreciable assets, among many other candidates) incur nontrivial transaction costs. And such costs may overwhelm the tax benefits of restructuring. So, in a friction-filled world, the common occurrence of NOL carryforwards, which clearly does not indicate a tax-minimizing state of affairs, need not imply inefficient tax planning.

A related situation in which the taxpayer may rationally forego tax benefits is the sale of a depreciable business asset to recognize an immediate tax loss at ordinary rates. In this case, the asset has declined in value by more than the accumulated tax depreciation to date. The alternative to selling the asset is to recognize the loss in the future through depreciation deductions, but in a present-value sense this is undesirable unless tax rates are expected to increase significantly in the future. Or it might be desirable to sell an asset that has appreciated in value if the gain is taxed at favorable rates and the new buyer is permitted to depreciate the asset at ordinary tax rates based on the stepped-up (to market value) tax basis. In both cases, buyers and sellers may agree that they could gain by trading the asset. Where the seller is better informed about the value of the asset than is the buyer, however, they may fail to reach mutually agreeable contractual terms.

6.4 TAX PLANNING AND ORGANIZATIONAL DESIGN

When a complex organization is composed of distinct legal entities, its left pocket is often taxed differently from its right pocket. This consideration applies not only to multinational enterprises but also to enterprises that operate exclusively within a single country. Sources of differences in taxation across legal entities include (1) multistate taxation, (2) industry-specific taxation, (3) size-specific taxation, and (4) special rules relating to net operating losses and tax credits. In the NOL and tax credit case, tax rules often prevent these attributes (NOLs and tax credits) from offsetting the tax liability of any other entity in the consolidated group following a merger. Shifting income from one pocket to the next may require considerable coordination, and tax rules often induce a greater degree of centralization of management than would otherwise be optimal. **Centralized management** is defined as top management making most of the decisions for the organization. Conversely, because centralization for tax planning purposes may undermine the efficiency of **decentralized management** for nontax reasons, it is often desirable to sacrifice tax benefits to achieve these other goals.[12] Tax rules are not unique in affecting organizational design. Similar issues arise with respect to myriad legal rules and regulatory policies such as trade laws and antitrust laws.

Related considerations arise in choosing between local and foreign suppliers of goods used in production. Suppose that local supply is more cost-effective, ignoring taxes, than is foreign supply (for example, because of lower monitoring costs, lower coordination costs, and lower transportation costs). But vertical integration with a foreign supplier may enable the corporation to recognize profits in a tax jurisdiction where the tax rate is lower, perhaps through judicious transfer pricing (subject to the scrutiny of the taxing authority, as we discuss in greater depth in the chapters on multinational tax planning). Conversely, judicious transfer pricing for tax planning purposes may pollute the planning and control features of a transfer pricing system in a decentralized firm where important information is widely dispersed.

Another example in a multinational organizational setting where tax and nontax considerations often conflict is in the choice between setting up a foreign subsidiary and a foreign branch. The laws and property rights that apply to foreign subsidiaries and foreign branches often differ in important ways, as do the tax treatments of these two organizational forms. Foreign operations are discussed in the later chapters on multinational tax planning.

As we discussed earlier, firms facing progressive tax schedules have tax-based incentives to form limited partnerships and joint ventures. When the outside investors do not play an active role in the management of the firm—a necessary condition for limited partners to obtain limited liability protection—hidden-action problems arise:[13]

1. The provision and pricing of goods and services by the R&D or O&G firm to the LP (resource allocation issues).
2. The R&D or O&G firm learning information relevant to other projects from the LP-funded activity (proving up).
3. All revenues or income arising from the R&D or O&G program not being fully measurable (payoff allocation and measurement).
4. The R&D or O&G firm continuing the LP activity when it is no longer economically justified from the LP investors' viewpoint, because the limited partners are funding the activity (overinvestment).
5. The R&D or O&G firm not exercising its option to exploit commercially the developed technology or O&G reserves (undercompletion).

We can illustrate the undercompletion problem as follows. If a limited partnership venture (or joint venture) is formed in response to the progressive tax schedules, then a

---

[12]If the lower-level (or on-site) managers have superior information than upper-level (or off-site) managers about conditions facing the lower level, then allowing the lower-level managers to make decision based on their superior information likely leads to better decisions. Allowing lower-level managers to make decisions is defined as decentralized management. See Phillips (2003) for an empirical analysis of how firms compensate business unit managers to motivate them to consider taxes in their decisions.

[13]See Wolfson (1985) for further discussion.

desire to maximize the tax benefits has the limited partners funding the up-front investment so that they can claim the up-front deductions at their high tax rates. This is called a functional allocation drilling program in the O&G area. The sponsoring firm acts as the general partner (GP) and is responsible for the completion costs that come after drilling takes place. After drilling, the well is either completed or abandoned. Moreover, the GP alone knows the status of the drilled hole. The GP often bears 100% of completion costs, but gets less than 100% of any resulting revenues, which creates the undercompletion problem. For example, suppose the GP takes LP dollars to drill a well. The GP looks down the hole and sees $2 worth of oil. Suppose it costs $1 to complete the well. If the GP were a sole proprietor, the well would be completed (regardless of the number of LP dollars spent in drilling because they are a sunk cost: it is profitable to spend $1 to recover $2). But suppose the GP in the partnership is entitled to receive only 40% of any revenue (a typical sharing percentage in these programs). The GP will spend $1 but only receive $.80 if the well is completed, so it is not in the GP's best interest to complete the well, and there is a $1 opportunity loss from abandonment.

This incentive problem can be minimized by drilling *exploratory* wells, which are wells having a low probability of being marginal. In an exploratory well, there is a high probability that no oil will be found at all and a low probability that a lot of oil will be found (in other words, the probability of a marginal well is relatively low). By contrast, developmental drilling results in a relatively high fraction of marginal wells.

Incentive problems may also be reduced when part of the return to the GP comes from establishing a reputation as a skillful or honest general partner. Wolfson (1985) provides empirical evidence consistent with functional allocation programs drilling a higher percentage of exploratory wells than other types of programs (such as balanced programs (50/50 exploratory/developmental wells) and developmental programs) and that reputation effects are priced in the marketplace: A good track record enables sponsors to charge a higher price for the right to buy into subsequent partnerships.

6.5 CONFLICTS BETWEEN FINANCIAL REPORTING AND TAX PLANNING

Another set of nontax costs arise when the results of tax planning bring about lower reported earnings to shareholders and other stakeholders in the firm. While corporate taxpayers typically wish to report low levels of taxable income to the taxing authority, they often wish to report high levels of income to investors. There are numerous reasons why managers might be concerned about the numbers in their financial statements:

1. Compensation contracts for top managers are often based on accounting earnings.
2. Bond covenants written by lenders to curb conflicts of interest between the lender and the borrower are often based on accounting numbers such as debt to equity ratios, restrictions on dividends as a percent of retained earnings, current assets to current liabilities, and interest coverage or earnings before interest/interest.
3. Analysts and investors use accounting numbers to price securities (both debt and equity), and managers might be concerned that reporting lower income could lead to lower stock prices and higher interest costs.

4. Regulators often use accounting numbers to monitor and regulate firms.
5. Lobbyists and other interested parties use accounting numbers to push for increased taxes and other penalties.
6. Large differences between book income and taxable income can lead to greater scrutiny and audit adjustments by the IRS.

Often in tax planning there will be a conflict between tax savings/benefits and **financial reporting costs.** However, there is not always a trade-off to be made between tax savings and negative financial reporting consequences. For example, in setting up R&D limited partnerships, the sponsor firm avoids having to issue debt or to expense the R&D, which would result in higher leverage ratios and lower reported earnings. That is, not only are these LPs tax motivated but they also have favorable accounting consequences. Thus if the researcher or outside observer fails to consider both motivations, false inferences and flawed policy recommendations might result. Further, tax rules often differ from financial reporting rules (for example, depreciation rules differ between tax and book), resulting in differences between taxable income and reported accounting income.[14] These differences must be kept in mind in determining whether there are any financial reporting implications of any tax plan.

Still, many transactions that reduce taxable income also reduce income reported to shareholders. For example, whenever a firm owns assets for which the market value is below book value for tax purposes, loss recognition is available if the assets are sold, but this move would also typically require recognizing a financial reporting loss (the amount of loss likely differs because the tax basis likely differs from the accounting book value because of differences in depreciation schedules for tax and book purposes). The many companies that purchased oil, silver, or gold mining properties in the early 1980s fall squarely into this category. Even if buyers and sellers agree completely on asset values, sellers might be concerned that the sale of such assets at a loss would increase their cost of capital by an amount exceeding the tax savings. Alternatively, managers whose compensation is tied to reported profitability might rationally forego tax savings due to an inherent conflict of interest. In this latter case, the sacrifice of tax savings is due to a hidden-action problem. Shareholders might prefer that the manager sell assets to reduce taxes in this circumstance, but as outsiders they may lack the requisite information to discipline the manager who chooses not to do so.

Income Shifting Across Time

As discussed in Chapter 4, firms have incentives to defer (accelerate) taxable income if statutory tax rates are expected to decline (increase). The corporate tax rate reductions in TRA 86 offered firms incentives to defer income and gave researchers an opportunity to examine firms' willingness to trade-off tax savings with financial reporting costs. However, in addition to financial reporting costs, it is important to note that

---

[14]It is important to understand why accounting numbers differ from tax numbers. As discussed in Appendix 2.2 in Chapter 2, Congress writes the tax rules to achieve various objectives: to raise revenue, to redistribute wealth, and to influence economic activities. Accounting rules focus on providing information about the firm's activities (operating performance, for example) useful to decision makers such as investors, lenders, suppliers, and other users of the information. Thus it is not surprising that taxable income differs from accounting income.

there are a variety of nontax costs associated with shifting income. There could be tax costs to the other party to whom or from whom income is shifted (an example of multilateral tax planning). Also, shifting income can change the timing of underlying economic activities, which may bring about large nontax costs such as reduced operating efficiencies, deterioration in customer relations, and additional inventory holding costs (arising from delaying shipping). The planning and coordination of income-shifting activities also entails administrative and implementation costs, and managerial compensation plans might be affected by shifting income across periods.

Guenther (1994) examines the effect on firms' income shifting around TRA 86 of three nontax factors that fall under the rubric of financial reporting costs: political costs (proxied by firm size), costs of violating debt covenant restrictions, and costs associated with management compensation plans. He predicts larger firms are more sensitive to political scrutiny and thus more likely to choose income-decreasing accruals. He predicts that firms closer to violating debt covenant agreements may be unwilling to reduce current reported income. Guenther uses a firm's leverage ratio as a proxy for how close the firm is to debt covenant violation. Finally, he argues that firms with higher managerial ownership levels will be more likely to shift financial statement income to reduce taxes. Guenther reports results indicating larger firms were more willing to shift income (reduce reported income) and firms with higher leverage ratios were less willing to report lower income. He found no relation between income shifting and the level of manager ownership. Thus his results suggest a trade-off in firms' willingness to shift income to save taxes at the expense of debt covenant violation costs.

Maydew (1997) examines whether firms with NOL carrybacks shifted income in the years following TRA 86. The reduction in corporate statutory tax rates in 1987 and 1988 offered firms with tax losses an incentive to increase their tax losses, enabling them to claim a refund at the higher tax rate of 46% rather than the new rate of 34%. In aggregate, Maydew estimates his sample firms shifted approximately $27.2 billion of income to increase their NOL carrybacks to obtain a net tax savings of $2.3 billion. He estimates that firms shifted approximately $2.6 billion less operating income because of costs associated with increasing leverage. Thus leverage appears as a relatively large nontax cost.

LIFO/FIFO Studies

An example of where tax planning and financial reporting considerations may conflict that has received considerable attention by tax accountants is the choice among alternative inventory valuation methods. LIFO (last-in, first-out) is an inventory accounting method that minimizes taxes (in those countries where it is an acceptable accounting method) when prices are rising, inventory levels are nondecreasing, and tax rates are not increasing over time. If LIFO is used for tax purposes in the United States, it must also be used for financial reporting purposes (the LIFO conformity rule). As such, taxable income can be reduced only by reducing profits reported to shareholders, lenders, and other interested parties, and this may discourage the tax-minimizing strategy.

LIFO Adoption

As we just noted, under certain conditions (increasing inventory prices and nondecreasing inventory levels), LIFO offers firms tax savings but, due to the LIFO conformity rule, also lowers reported profits. Over time LIFO firms have been allowed via footnote disclosures to report sufficient information for users to estimate FIFO-based (first-in, first-out) earnings. Thus users have access to both earnings numbers. However, because LIFO-based earnings are reported in the income statement, contracts (and even possibly capital market participants) that rely on audited reported numbers will use the lower LIFO-based earnings. Thus LIFO adoption offers tax savings but with financial reporting costs. Inventory holding costs are also higher because firms want to avoid LIFO liquidations (see below). These holding costs arise from storing, financing, and insuring the inventory and from incurring higher administrative record-keeping expenses. This trade-off has been examined both empirically (for example, among others by Dopuch and Pincus, 1988) and by survey methods (Cushing and LeClere, 1992). The evidence suggests that tax savings are a major determinant, with debt and earnings management concerns playing, at best, a minor role in the LIFO adoption choice.

LIFO Liquidation

LIFO offers firms the opportunity to report increased profits (and increased taxable income) if the sales quantity exceeds the purchase quantity for the period. This is known as a LIFO liquidation because the firm is dipping into old inventory cost layers. In addition, because LIFO includes the latest cost figures in the cost of goods sold, by purchasing additional inventory at year-end, firms can lower taxable income and reported earnings. Several studies have examined this issue and report evidence consistent with the idea that financial reporting concerns, such as smoothing reported earnings and increasing earnings when leverage ratios are high so as to reduce possible bond covenant violation costs, influence the firms' inventory management.[15]

LIFO Abandonment

Firms abandoning LIFO face two tax costs: the tax due on the LIFO reserve (which tax can be spread out over future periods) and the opportunity cost of foregone current and future tax benefits of using LIFO. LIFO abandonment, however, often has favorable financial statement effects: higher current and future earnings and higher inventory values. These effects can relax loan agreement restrictions lowering costs of (technical) default. Johnson and Dhaliwal (1988) examine the trade-off between taxes and financial statement effects in firms' decisions to abandon LIFO for inventory costing. They use three variables to measure firms' proximity to debt restrictions: leverage, slack in working capital constraints, and dividend payment constraints. They report that LIFO abandonment firms are, on average, both more highly levered and closer to violating minimum working capital requirements than are firms that continue to use LIFO, consistent with the conclusion that financial statement effects influence the decision. Abandonment firms also have larger NOL carryforwards, consistent with these firms facing lower tax costs to the abandonment.

---

[15]See, for example, Dhaliwal, Frankel, and Trezevant (1994) and Hunt, Moyer, and Shevlin (1996).

Regulatory Costs

Financial reporting concerns extend to regulators as well as investors. For example, U.S. banks must maintain a minimum level of "regulatory capital" to preserve operating independence from bank regulators. Moreover, the quantity of federally insured demand deposits that banks are permitted to issue is tied to regulatory capital. To the extent transactions that reduce taxable income also reduce regulatory capital (and most do), banks may rationally sacrifice tax savings. This is particularly true of banks that face a relatively high probability of failure and low levels of regulatory capital, because such institutions find it particularly attractive to borrow money at the riskless rate by issuing insured demand deposits. Scholes, Wilson, and Wolfson (1990) document that banks coordinate their tax planning with nontax considerations in managing their investment portfolios. That is, firms forgo tax savings by not selling marketable securities with unrealized losses and even incur tax costs by selling securities that have appreciated to boost regulatory capital. Beatty, Chamberlain, and Magliolo (1995) and Collins, Shackelford, and Wahlen (1995) extend the Scholes, Wilson, and Wolfson paper to examine the multiple ways, in addition to gains and losses from selling marketable securities, banks can manage their earnings, regulatory capital, and taxes and find that regulatory capital and financial reporting concerns dominate the tax concerns. However, Collins, Geisler, and Shackelford (1997) document that taxes as well as regulatory concerns and financial reporting effects are important in the insurance industry.

Beatty and Harris (1999) and Mikhail (1999) extend the above studies to examine the role of ownership structure in firm's choices with the prediction that privately owned firms are likely more aggressive tax planners than publicly owned firms. Beatty and Harris examine banks and Mikhail examines life insurance firms, and both report results consistent with private firms being more aggressive tax planners, implying the nontax costs are lower for private firms. Mikhail notes that private firms differ from public firms in two major respects. First, private firms do not have to worry about stock market reactions to their reported earnings and, second, private firms likely have fewer hidden information problems because the managers are also owners. Thus, private firms are less concerned with financial reporting and hidden-information problems in their tax planning. In addition to private and public insurance firms, Mikhail examines mutual life insurance firms that have diffuse ownership with a separation of owners from managers and, thus, hidden-information problems similar to public firms but do not face stock market pressures. Mikhail finds that mutual firms do not manage taxes similar to his public firms and concludes that public firms are likely less aggressive tax planners because of concerns with the incentive compensation contracts necessary to control the hidden information problems.

Asset Sales and Divestitures

Asset sales, individually or as a group (the latter are called divestitures), are closely related to LIFO liquidation and LIFO abandonment studies. Asset sales are also in the spirit of the sale of marketable securities to manage earnings as in the banking studies we just discussed. Bartov (1993) reports that both earnings motivations (earnings smoothing and debt covenants) and taxes influence the timing of asset sales. Maydew,

Schipper, and Vincent (1999) examine how firms trade off tax and nontax costs in the decision to divest assets via a taxable sale rather than a tax-free spin-off. With positive tax rates and zero nontax costs, assets with an unrealized taxable gain could be spun off tax-free and assets with unrealized tax deductible losses could be sold to provide tax benefits. They find that for a sample of 270 asset divestitures during 1987–1995, at least 30% of the taxable asset sales and 33% of the nontaxable spin-offs were tax-disadvantaged, suggesting either significant nontax costs or foregone tax benefits. They report evidence consistent with firms incurring tax costs in order to achieve favorable financial reporting outcomes and to raise cash.

Dollar Estimates of Firms' Willingness to Forego Tax Savings

The studies we just mentioned document that firm managers trade off tax savings with nontax costs, in particular costs arising from financial statement effects of any tax plans. This raises the question of how much firms are willing to "pay" (by foregone tax savings) for favorable financial statement outcomes. Alternatively stated, an estimate of the foregone tax savings provides an estimate of the lower bound of financial statement costs. Several studies provide evidence on this issue.

Engel, Erickson, and Maydew (1999) examine trust preferred stock (TRUPS) to develop lower and upper bounds estimates of what firms were willing to pay for favorable balance sheet treatment. Briefly, TRUPS are treated as debt-like for tax purposes in that the preferred dividends are tax deductible—similar to interest—while for financial accounting purposes, TRUPS are treated like traditional preferred stock (that is, nondebt) on the balance sheet. (TRUPS are discussed in greater detail in Chapter 12.) Issuers of TRUPS used the proceeds to retire outstanding traditional preferred stock, to retire outstanding debt, and for general corporate uses. For TRUPS issuers that retired debt, tax deductibility was retained while the debt-asset ratio declined on average by 12.8%.[16] Engel, Erickson, and Maydew then estimate the lower and upper bounds of the costs to the firm of reducing the debt-asset ratio. The lower bound is derived as the average actual issuance costs of the TRUPS across issuers estimated to be $10 million. The upper bound is estimated using the TRUPS issuers that retired debt rather than outstanding traditional preferred stock. By not retiring the traditional preferred stock, the issuers chose to forgo tax benefits of, on average, $43 million. Thus firms were willing to pay between $10 and $43 million to reduce their debt-asset ratio by 12.8%, improving their balance sheet.

As discussed in Chapter 8, Matsunaga, Shevlin, and Shores (1992) estimate the net tax benefits foregone by firms not disqualifying incentive stock options and thus also provide estimates of how much firms are willing to give up to avoid reporting lower earnings. In this case, by not disqualifying, the firms avoided on average a 2.3% reduction in reported earnings at an average net tax benefit foregone of $.551 million.

Political Cost Impediments to Tax Planning

We stated in Chapter 5 that politicians, the public at large, and lobbyists (seeking to secure tax favors for certain private parties) often scrutinize the level of taxes public

---

[16]Engel, Erickson, and Maydew (1999) list the potential benefits of reducing leverage (rating agency effects, relaxation of bond covenants, and possibly perceived reduction in the risk of the firm) but do not test whether these are significant explanatory variables explaining the choice.

corporations pay. And perhaps because the implicit tax concept is not well understood, corporations that pay substantial sums of implicit tax, but little explicit tax, are not always viewed as paying their fair share of the tax burden. When firms that are in the public eye succeed in reducing taxes in socially unacceptable ways, the public often has a way of "getting even." Effective tax planning for certain organizations requires a more subtle calculus in this case.

For example, the Citizens for Tax Justice (CTJ), in a series of widely reported studies in the early and mid 1980s, estimated and listed individual firm's effective tax rates and argued that many large and profitable corporations paid little or no federal taxes. Congress introduced the alternative minimum tax book income adjustment (the AMTBIA), which was motivated in large part by the perception that large firms were paying little in taxes while at the same time reporting high profits to shareholders. The AMTBIA directly linked the calculation of the alternative minimum tax to a firm's reported financial accounting earnings (or book income). Specifically, 50% of the excess of reported pretax book income over (pre-AMTBIA alternative) taxable income was included as a tax preference item (that is, added back) in estimating alternative taxable income. Academics and financial accountants believed this link would lead firms likely affected by this adjustment to reduce their reported book income to reduce their tax bills. A number of studies document that firms shifted income in response to the AMTBIA but find little evidence that financial reporting costs constrained this shifting.[17]

Other Book-Tax Conformity Costs

In addition to the AMTBIA adjustment, TRA 86 also required firms use the accrual basis in calculating taxable income. Prior to 1986, corporations could use either the cash basis (except for inventory) or the accrual basis to calculate taxable income.[18] Guenther, Maydew, and Nutter (1997) examine 66 cash method corporations before and after this change. Prior to the tax law change, as expected, the cash-basis corporations exhibited little trade-off in their tax planning and financial reporting. However, subsequent to the change, these same firms deferred income for financial statement purposes—book-tax conformity led these firms to change their book accounting so as to save taxes.

When filing their tax returns, corporations must provide a reconciliation between taxable income and book earnings. Mills (1998) examines whether the magnitude of the difference between taxable income and book income affects IRS audits. Using confidential tax return data, she finds that proposed IRS tax adjustments are positively associated with the magnitude of the difference that book income exceeds taxable income. These results imply that firms cannot costlessly reduce taxable income even in those cases where book income is not affected by the tax planning strategy.

---

[17]See, for example, Gramlich (1991); Manzon (1992); Boynton, Dobbins, and Plesko (1992); and Dhaliwal and Wang (1992).

[18]With cash basis accounting, the firm claims a deduction when the cash payment is made or recognizes income when cash is received. Under the accrual basis, income and deductions can be recognized at a different point in time than when cash is received or paid. For example, an accrual taxpayer includes a credit sale in income even though cash is not yet received.

Other Informational Cost Impediments to Tax Planning

Tax planning is a huge business.[19] Billions of dollars are spent each year in the United States alone to secure professional assistance in reducing tax obligations. In addition, billions of dollars are spent each year in maintaining records to support taxpayers' claims concerning their tax obligations. Finally, billions of dollars are spent each year in legal and administrative fees to write and to enforce contractual agreements that are designed, in part, to reduce the joint tax burdens among contracting parties. Effective tax planning must be viewed relative to the costs of implementing these strategies. Although complex contracts may succeed in reducing more conflicts of interest among contracting parties, simple contracts are often observed in practice. Similarly, simple tax planning strategies may be more efficient from an overall cost standpoint than more complicated strategies that would result in reduced tax payments.

Summary of Key Points

1. A progressive tax rate system encourages taxpayers to invest as though they were more risk-averse than they really are, that is, taxpayers will undertake less risky projects. This is because, with progressive taxes, average tax payments increase with the variability of taxable income. This increases the after-tax cost of investment or, alternately stated, lowers the after-tax expected rate of return. Such a tax system increases the after-tax cost of risky investments for start-up firms because they likely face a progressive tax system (due to, for example, the tax loss carryback and carryforward rules). These firms are likely to enter joint ventures to reduce the tax costs.

2. While limited partnerships and joint ventures offer a tax-advantageous way to structure risky investments between parties facing different tax structures, such arrangements are not without costs. All joint investments create conflicts of interest. The party responsible for making decisions for the venture has an incentive to act in ways that are in its own best interest, and this interest may not coincide with the actions that the co-investor(s) would prefer.

3. The presence of conflicts of interest creates demand for ways to reduce the costs of these conflicts. Monitoring, incentive contracts, performance bonds, warranties, reputation, and lawsuits are all responses to this demand.

4. A progressive tax rate system encourages some firms to undertake hedging activities and diversification to reduce the volatility of cash flows and taxable income and increase the after-tax expected rate of return.

5. Market frictions cause the borrowing rate for funds to exceed the lending rate. These costs are high in part because borrowers cannot always be trusted to act as they promise. In particular, they might have incentives to take actions that are unobservable to lenders and that have unfavorable implications for their cash flows, which in turn impairs borrowers' abilities to repay their debts.

6. In realistic market settings, where information differences among contracting parties are pervasive, efficient tax planning may deviate substantially from tax minimization.

---

[19]See Slemrod and Blumenthal (1993) and Slemrod (1997) for detailed estimates of compliance and other costs for the corporate sector. Mills, Erickson, and Maydew (1998) examine the determinants of firms' tax planning expenditures and the payoffs to tax planning. They estimate that, for every dollar spent on tax planning by large firms, the firms save $4 in explicit taxes.

7. Lenders seek to enhance the collectability of loans by writing extensive loan covenants that restrict borrowers' actions. But such covenants, which are costly to write and to monitor, are imperfect in preventing opportunistic behavior by borrowers. Moreover, restrictive covenants may restrain borrowers from taking actions that would benefit both the borrower and the lender.

8. In organizational contracting problems, it is often difficult for outside observers, such as consultants, corporate raiders, investment bankers, regulators, or researchers, to determine whether contracts tied to profits are motivated by incentive considerations, tax considerations, or both. This identification problem makes it difficult to know what economic problem gave rise to the contractual microstructure.

9. When an employer is risk-neutral and an employee is risk-averse, a pure wage contract allocates risk-bearing between the parties in an efficient manner, ignoring taxes. If a profits-based compensation contract is preferred for tax purposes, however, tax considerations and risk-sharing considerations will be in conflict, and the two forces must be traded off.

10. Under conditions of moral hazard (hidden-action problems), a deferred compensation contract might have attractive incentive features. If, under such circumstances, an immediate salary is preferred for tax reasons, a conflict arises between the two forces, and they must be traded off.

11. Tax-savings strategies might naturally be sacrificed where there are hidden-information problems. The seller of an asset is generally better informed than are prospective buyers about the quality or value of the asset being sold. Tax considerations might favor the sale of an asset to realize a loss that reduces taxable income. Prospective buyers, however, will have difficulty in distinguishing whether the motivation for selling the asset is to secure tax benefits or that the asset is no longer as productive as the seller asserts. As a result, the asset might not be sold because the buyer is rationally unwilling to pay full value for it, and tax benefits would be sacrificed.

12. Tax planning considerations often conflict with nontax considerations in such organizational design issues as hierarchical structure (the degree of centralization and vertical integration) and whether to organize certain operations as branches or subsidiaries.

13. Many tax planning strategies affect financial reporting to shareholders and other less direct "stakeholders" of the firm. Many tax-reducing strategies require transactions that reduce income reported to these other parties. To the extent financial accounting numbers are used in contracts (such as compensation, bond covenants, regulation) and by outside stakeholders (such as analysts and investors in valuing the firm's stocks and bonds), nontax costs of the business increase, and tax reduction may be discouraged.

14. Effective tax planning must be viewed relative to the costs of implementing the requisite strategies. In addition to certain organizational inefficiencies such strategies may introduce, these costs include securing professional advice, keeping records, and writing and enforcing contracts. Thus effective tax planning must be distinguished from tax minimization.

Discussion Questions

1. True or False? Discuss.
   a. In a progressive tax rate system, risk-neutral investors prefer volatile assets over riskless assets because they can average their tax rates.

   b. In a progressive tax rate system, risk-neutral investors will demand portfolio diversification and hedging.
   c. Hidden-information problems arise when symmetrically informed parties hide information from each other.
   d. Hidden-action problems arise because it is costly for principals to monitor the actions of agents.
   e. Symmetric uncertainty about future cash flows causes employees to prefer salary to deferred compensation contracts.

 2. What role do hidden-action problems play in causing the borrowing rate for funds to be greater than the lending rate? Can we eliminate hidden-action problems? Why or why not? How does the difference in borrowing and lending rates affect the taxpayer's ability to undertake clientele-based arbitrage?

 3. What is an "identification problem"? Illustrate conditions under which there might be an identification problem involving: employee-employer compensation contracting; sale of an asset; a merger. Why is it important for outsiders to recognize when an identification problem may be present?

 4. If employers are risk-neutral and employees are risk-averse, why is a salary contract optimal, ignoring tax and asymmetric information considerations? Under what conditions in employee compensation contracting are tax- and risk-sharing considerations in conflict? As a result of these conflicts, do employees bear more risk than if the goal were simply to allocate risks efficiently?

 5. In the presence of hidden-action problems, under what conditions will a deferred compensation contract both minimize taxes and provide desirable work incentives for employees?

 6. How do hidden-information problems affect the costs of corporate restructuring? Might the tax benefits of such restructurings be sacrificed by corporations because of these problems?

 7. What role do hidden-action problems play in limited partnerships and other joint ventures? How might the cost of these problems be reduced?

 8. What is the undercompletion problem? Provide an example in an R&D drug research setting. How might the costs of this problem be reduced?

 9. How might tax considerations conflict with financial reporting considerations? Provide an example from the banking industry.

10. How might bond covenants influence a firm's tax planning activity? Provide an example for firms that use LIFO for inventory costing.

11. Managers are often concerned about the impact on reported profits of any actions recommended by the tax planning department. Explain why.

12. If managers are compensated, in part, on the basis of a bonus based on accounting earnings, they are likely to object to any tax plans that reduce reported earnings. What actions could the firm take to mitigate this concern?

13. What are the tax benefits of deferring income recognition in advance of a decline in statutory tax rates? What, if any, are the nontax costs?

14. How might tax savings be sacrificed to achieve organizational design efficiencies or to mitigate political costs?

Exercises

 1. Suppose the tax rate is 30% if taxable income is positive and 0% if taxable income is negative. Calculate the expected tax payable for the following four projects. Note that for each project the expected taxable income is $50,000. For each

project, also calculate the expected average tax rate (expected total taxes divided by expected taxable income). Explain and discuss your results.
   a. Certain payoff $50,000.
   b. 50% chance of $100,000 and a 50% chance of $0.
   c. 50% chance of $200,000 and a 50% chance of a loss of $100,000.
   d. 50% chance of $500,000 and a 50% chance of loss of $400,000.
   This problem can be solved by preparing a graph similar to Figure 6.1.
   (1) Draw in the tax rate schedule for taxable income in the range −$500,000 to +$500,000 with taxable income on the horizontal axis and tax payable on the vertical axis.
   (2) Mark the two endpoints on the tax schedule for each project. (For project 2 the two endpoints are $0 and $50,000). Draw a straight line between the two outcomes.
   (3) Draw a vertical line upward from the horizontal axis at taxable income equal to $50,000.
   (4) Finally, read off the expected tax payable for each project where the expected tax payable is the intersection point of the lines in (2) and (3).

2. Suppose the tax rate is 0% for taxable income less than $0 (again no tax refunds for losses and no NOL carryback or carryforwards). For positive taxable income up to and including $25,000, the tax rate is 15%; for taxable income greater than $25,000 but less than $50,000, the tax rate is 25%; and for taxable income greater than $50,000, the tax rate is 34%. Calculate the expected tax payable for the following two projects. Explain and discuss your results.
   a. 50% chance of $100,000 and a 50% chance of loss of $50,000.
   b. 50% chance of $75,000 and a 50% chance of loss of $25,000.

3. Suppose the tax rate is 30% if taxable income is positive and 0% if taxable income is negative. Consider the before-tax payoffs to the following three projects:
   a. Riskless: 10% for sure
   b. Moderately risky: 30% half the time   −10% half the time
   c. Quite risky: 300% one time in 10   −20% nine times out of 10
   Required:
   (1) Calculate the before-tax and after-tax expected rates of return for each project.
   (2) How does the variability of returns affect the expected tax rate? Why?
   (3) Does this tax structure encourage or discourage high technology start-up ventures?

4. Assume the firm's after-tax cost of capital is 6% per annum. What is the benefit of deferring $1 of income for 1 year, for 2 years, for 5 years assuming the firm's marginal tax rate is 35%? Suppose the firm expects the top statutory tax rate to increase to 40% next year. Does it still pay to defer income for 1 year, for 2 years, for 5 years? Explain and discuss your results.

5. Suppose Sonics Inc. just started business this period. The firm purchased 400 units during the period at various prices as follows:

Date	Units	Unit Cost	Total
January	100	$10	$1,000
March	100	$12	$1,200
June	100	$14	$1,400
October	100	$15	$1,500
Total	400		$5,100

The firm sold 250 units at $30 each on the following dates:

Date	Units	Unit Price	Total Sales
February	75	$30	$2,250
May	90	$30	$2,700
August	75	$30	$2,250
December	10	$30	$300
Total	250	$30	$7,500

Assume the firm faces a marginal tax rate of 35%:
a. Calculate taxable income and taxes payable assuming the firm uses FIFO (first-in, first-out) for inventory costing purposes.
b. Calculate taxable income and taxes payable assuming the firm uses LIFO (last-in, first-out) for inventory costing purposes.
Discuss your results, including any nontax costs that might be associated with either inventory costing system.
6. Assume Sonics Inc., from the prior exercise, uses LIFO with the periodic inventory system. Thus the LIFO cost of ending inventory at year 1 of 150 units is $1,600 (100 @ $10 + 50 @ $12). Suppose in year 2, Sonics reports the following purchases and sales.

Date	Units	Unit Cost/Price	Total
Purchases			
June	100	$17	$1,700
Sales			
July	200	$30	$6,000

a. Calculate taxable income and taxes payable (again assuming Sonics faces a marginal tax rate of 35%) for year 2. How many more units did Sonics sell than purchase? What is the difference in the unit cost and latest purchase price for each of these units?
b. Instead of purchasing 100 units in June, Sonics purchased 110 units. Recalculate taxable income and taxes payable.
c. Instead of purchasing 100 units in June, Sonics purchased 90 units. Recalculate taxable income and taxes payable.
d. How many units should Sonics have purchased to avoid dipping into earlier layers of inventory?
e. Do you notice any opportunities for Sonics Inc. to smooth reported net income (by varying the amount purchased relative to sales)? Are there any costs associated with this strategy? Does FIFO offer the same opportunities?
f. Suppose the top managers of Sonics are compensated, in part, by a bonus linked to reported net income. What inventory costing method might you expect the managers to favor? What costs to the firm arise from this choice?

Tax Planning Problems

1. A tax planner for a start-up biotechnology company is advising her client about how to efficiently organize R&D activities. One suggestion the tax planner made is to form a joint venture with another biotech company. List and explain the tax benefits and nontax costs and benefits of such a plan. Does it matter if the other company is a start-up company or an established, profitable company?

2. An owner-manager of a firm is contemplating selling it to any one of a number of prospective buyers. The firm has net operating loss carryforwards (NOLs) known to be worth $50 million more to the buyers than to the seller. While the current owner knows the value of the firm, the prospective buyers are uncertain whether the firm is worth $500 million (including the extra $50 million value in NOLs) or $700 million. The poorly informed buyers consider both possibilities to be equally likely.
   Required:
   a. How much should buyers offer to acquire the firm?
   b. Will the seller always accept the highest rational offer made?
   c. How does the analysis change if the uncertain values of the firm are $500 million and $540 million rather than $500 million and $700 million?
3. Suppose you work for a business that runs a fleet of cars the sales personnel use. The fleet consists of 30 Toyota Camry sedans. All the expenses (insurance, registration, fuel, maintenance, and repairs) are paid by the firm. You have determined that it is cost-effective (from a tax and operations cost viewpoint) to "roll the fleet over" every 3 years. You plan to auction the cars.
   a. Are there any agency costs (incentive problems) with the arrangement that the firm pays all the costs of operating the cars?
   b. Are there any agency costs with selling the cars?
   c. How might you mitigate the problems in parts a and b? Outline any new problems your suggestions might create.
4. Suppose you are a high-tax-bracket taxpayer. How could you take advantage of a situation in which the implicit tax rate on a tax-exempt asset is different from the marginal tax rate on income from a fully taxable asset? What nontax costs exist to limit your ability to take advantage of this arbitrage possibility? Are there any ways to reduce these nontax costs?
5. You have been retained by a large Internet-based firm to advise the compensation committee on how best to compensate the chief executive officer (CEO). The CEO is risk-averse and his actions are not fully observable (hidden-action problems). The Internet firm is currently generating tax losses, but if some investments prove successful, it will begin paying taxes in 3 years. What issues must the firm consider and how might it structure a compensation contract that takes into account the manager's risk aversion and hidden actions and the tax positions of both the company and the CEO?
6. Suppose the top corporate statutory tax rate will decrease from 35% to 30% next year. The CFO of ABC Corporation wants to defer as much income as possible and asks you to prepare a detailed list of actions to shift income (that is, ways in which the firm can shift income). For each action, she wants you to outline any nontax costs associated with the action.

References and Additional Readings

Arrow, K., 1985. "The Economics of Agency" in *Principals and Agents: The Structure of Business,* edited by J. W. Pratt and R. J. Zeckhauser. Boston, MA: Harvard Business School Press. pp. 37–51.

Bartov, E., 1993. "The Timing of Asset Sales and Earnings Manipulation," *The Accounting Review* (October), pp. 840–855.

Beatty, A., P. Berger, and J. Magliolo, 1995. "Motives for Forming Research &

Development Financing Organizations," *Journal of Accounting and Economics* (March-May), pp. 411–442.

Beatty, A., S. Chamberlain, and J. Magliolo, 1995. "Managing Financial Reports of Commercial Banks: The Influence of Taxes," *Journal of Accounting Research* (2), pp. 231–261.

Beatty, A., and D. Harris, 1999. "The Effects of Taxes, Agency Costs and Information Asymmetry on Earnings Management: A

Comparison of Public and Private Firms," *Review of Accounting Studies* (December), pp. 299–326.

Boynton, C., P. Dobbins, and G. Plesko, 1992. "Earnings Management and the Corporate Alternative Minimum Tax," *Journal of Accounting Research* (Supplement), pp. 131–153.

Calegari, M., 2000. "The Effect of Tax Accounting Rules on Capital Structure and Discretionary Accruals," *Journal of Accounting and Economics,* pp. 1–31.

Choi, W., J. Gramlich, and J. Thomas, J., 2001. "Potential Errors in Detecting Earnings Management: Reexamining Studies Investigating the AMT of 1986," *Contemporary Accounting Research,* pp. 571–613.

Collins, J., G. Geisler, and D. Shackelford, 1997. "The Effects of Taxes, Regulation, Earnings, and Organizational Form on Life Insurers' Investment Portfolio Realizations," *Journal of Accounting and Economics* (1997), pp. 337–361.

Collins. J., D. Shackelford, and J. Wahlen, 1995. "Bank Differences in the Coordination of Regulatory Capital, Earnings, and Taxes," *Journal of Accounting Research* (2), pp. 263–291.

Cushing, B., and M. LeClere, 1992. "Evidence on the Determinants of Inventory Accounting Policy Choice," *The Accounting Review* (April), pp. 355–366.

Dhaliwal, D., M. Frankel, and R. Trezevant, 1994. "The Taxable and Book Income Motivations for a LIFO Layer Liquidation," *Journal of Accounting Research* (Autumn), pp. 278–289.

Dhaliwal, D., and S. Wang, 1992. "The Effect of Book Income Adjustment in the 1986 Alternative Minimum Tax on Corporate Financial Reporting," *Journal of Accounting and Economics* (1), pp. 7–26.

Dopuch, N., and M. Pincus, 1998. "Evidence on the Choice of Inventory Accounting Methods: LIFO Versus FIFO," *Journal of Accounting Research* (Spring), pp. 28–59.

Engel, E., M. Erickson, and E. Maydew, 1999. "Debt-Equity Hybrid Securities," *Journal of Accounting Research* (Autumn), pp. 1–26.

Fellingham, J., and M. Wolfson, 1985. "Taxes and Risk Sharing," *The Accounting Review* (January), pp. 10–17.

Graham, J., and D. Rogers, 2001. "Do Firms Hedge in Response to Tax Incentives?" *Journal of Finance,* pp. 815–839.

Graham, J., and C. Smith, 1999. "Tax Incentives to Hedge," *Journal of Finance* (December), pp. 2241–2262.

Gramlich, J., 1991. "The Effect of the Alternative Minimum Tax Book Income Adjustment on Accrual Decisions," *Journal of the American Taxation Association* (Spring), pp. 36–56.

Guenther, D., 1994. "Earnings Management in Response to Corporate Tax Rate Changes: Evidence from the 1986 Tax Reform Act," *The Accounting Review* (January), pp. 230–243.

Guenther, D., E. Maydew, and S. Nutter, 1997. "Financial Reporting, Tax Costs, and Book-Tax Conformity," *Journal of Accounting and Economics* (3), pp. 225–248.

Hunt, A., S. Moyer, and T. Shevlin, 1996. "Managing Interacting Accounting Measures to Meet Multiple Objectives: A Study of LIFO Firms," *Journal of Accounting and Economics* (June), pp. 339–374.

Johnson, W., and D. Dhaliwal, 1988, "LIFO Abandonment," *Journal of Accounting Research* (Autumn), pp. 236–272.

Klassen, K., 1997. "The Impact of Inside Ownership Concentration on the Trade-off Between Financial and Tax Reporting," *The Accounting Review* (3), pp. 455–474.

Manzon, G., 1992. "Earnings Management of Firms Subject to the Alternative Minimum Tax," *Journal of the American Taxation Association* (Fall), pp. 88–111.

Matsunaga, S., T. Shevlin, and D. Shores, 1992. "Disqualifying Dispositions of Incentive Stock Options: Tax Benefits versus Financial Reporting Costs," *Journal of Accounting Research* (Supplement), pp. 37–76.

Maydew, E., 1997. "Tax-Induced Earnings Management by Firms with Net Operating Losses," *Journal of Accounting Research* (Spring), pp. 83–96.

Maydew, E., K. Schipper, and L. Vincent, 1999. "The Impact of Taxes on the Choice of Divestiture Method," *Journal of Accounting and Economics* (December), pp. 117–150.

Mikhail, M., 1999. "Coordination of Earnings, Regulatory Capital and Taxes in Private and Public Companies." Working paper. Cambridge, MA: MIT.

Moyer, S., 1990. "Capital Adequacy Ratio Regulations and Accounting Choices in Commercial Banks," *Journal of Accounting and Economics* (July), pp. 123–154.

Mills, L., 1998. "Book-Tax Differences and Internal Revenue Service Adjustments," *Journal of Accounting Research* (2), pp. 343–356.

Mills, L., M. Erickson, and E. Maydew, 1998. "Investments in Tax Planning," *Journal of the American Taxation Association* (Spring), pp. 1–20.

Nance, D., C. Smith, and C. Smithson, 1993. "On the Determinants of Corporate Hedging," *Journal of Finance* (March), pp. 267–284.

Northcutt, W., and C. Vines, 1998. "Earnings Management in Response to Political Scrutiny of Effective Tax Rates," *Journal of the American Taxation Association* (Fall), pp. 22–36.

Petroni, K., and D. Shackelford, 1999. "Managing Annual Accounting Reports to Avoid State Taxes: An Analysis of Property-Casualty Insurers," *The Accounting Review* (3), pp. 371–393.

Phillips, J., 2003. "Corporate Tax Planning Effectiveness: The Role of Compensation-Based Incentives," *The Accounting Review* (July), pp. 847–874.

Scholes, M., P. Wilson, and M. Wolfson, 1990. "Tax Planning, Regulatory Capital Planning, and Financial Reporting Strategy for Commercial Banks," *Review of Financial Studies,* pp. 625–650.

Shackelford, D., and T. Shevlin, 2001. "Empirical Tax Research in Accounting," *Journal of Accounting and Economics,* pp. 321–387.

Shevlin, T., 1987. "Taxes and Off-Balance Sheet-Financing: Research and Development Limited Partnerships," *The Accounting Review* (July), pp. 480–509.

Slemrod, J., 1997. *Measuring Taxpayer Burden and Attitudes for Large Corporations: 1996 and 1992 Survey Results.* Office of Tax Policy Research Working Paper No. 97-1. Ann Arbor, MI: University of Michigan Press.

Slemrod, J., and M. Blumenthal, 1993. *The Compliance Costs of Big Business.* Washington, DC: The Tax Foundation.

Wolfson, M., 1985. "Empirical Evidence of Incentive Problems and their Mitigation in Oil and Gas Tax Shelter Programs" in *Principals and Agents: The Structure of Business* edited by J. W. Pratt and R. J. Zeckhauser. Boston, MA: Harvard Business School Press. pp. 101–125, 221–224.

7

THE IMPORTANCE OF MARGINAL TAX RATES AND DYNAMIC TAX PLANNING CONSIDERATIONS

After completing this chapter, you should be able to:

1. Define and distinguish among the concepts of marginal tax rate, average tax rate, and effective tax rate.

2. Explain and illustrate the difficulties of estimating corporate marginal tax rates.

3. Explain, given an uncertain future, the importance of the adaptability of a tax plan, the reversibility of a tax plan, and the ability to insure against adverse changes in tax status.

Where differences in tax rates exist across taxpayers, across time, across organizational forms, and across economic activities, taxpayers have incentives to contract with one another in ways that may alter their marginal tax rates. In Chapter 5, we demonstrated that with differentially taxed assets and the absence of frictions and restrictions, clientele-based arbitrage ensures that all taxpayers face the same total marginal tax rates.[1] We also showed that tax-rule restrictions and market frictions reduce the set of circumstances in which clientele-based arbitrage can be implemented effectively. In this chapter, we begin by defining the marginal tax rate and

---

[1]Recall that for a high-tax-rate taxpayer, clientele-based arbitrage means taking a long position in a relatively tax-favored asset (one that bears a relatively high degree of implicit tax) and a short position in a tax-disfavored asset (one that bears relatively more explicit tax). For the low-tax-rate taxpayer, clientele-based arbitrage means taking a long position in a tax-disfavored asset and a short position in a tax-favored asset. In contrast, organizational-form arbitrage means taking a long position in an asset or a productive activity through a *favorably* taxed organizational form and a short position in an asset or a productive activity through an *unfavorably* taxed organizational form.

distinguish it from average and effective tax rates. We argue that average and effective tax rates are inappropriate for tax planning, that is, for decision making. We also illustrate complications in determining the marginal tax rate for decision making, which further constrains tax arbitrage and tax planning activities.

We then consider strategies that an entity might undertake to alter its marginal tax rate via tax arbitrage techniques. The tax planner's problem is to minimize a broadly defined measure of tax (current and future) given the history of decisions and outcomes that brought the firm to where it is today. Most investment and financing decisions are undertaken in an uncertain environment. Once plans are implemented, events unfold; given the outcomes of the process, entities must decide how to alter their investment and financing decisions. And given these outcomes, many entities would prefer to undertake clientele-based arbitrage strategies to change their marginal tax rates if it were costless to do so. Restrictions and frictions curtail such strategies. We consider the tax planning strategies available to low-tax-bracket firms, such as those with net operating losses, investment tax credits, or alternative minimum tax credit carryforwards.

We follow this with a discussion with one centered on dynamic tax planning strategies—that is, how to plan for future contingencies. Recall that efficient tax planning requires identifying appropriate taxpayer-specific investment and financing clienteles. Identification is relatively straightforward in a static environment. But when decisions have uncertain consequences over many tax years, such clienteles depend on the reorganization costs of altering investment and financing policies in response to changes in taxpayers' circumstances. In the presence of uncertainty regarding future pretax cash flows and the tax rules themselves, a premium is placed on contracts that offer flexibility in tax planning to respond to unexpected changes in tax status. But building flexibility, however, into contracts does not come free. For example, it may require a degree of mutual trust among the contracting parties (as in discretionary employee bonus plans) that cannot be sustained. In addition, flexibility typically requires greater contracting costs.

Suppose a firm knows that because its tax rate is high in the current period, it should finance new projects with debt to take advantage of explicit tax deductions for interest payments. However, the firm is unsure of its future tax rate. It could issue equity instead of debt, but the implicit tax deduction provided by an equity issue is usually of less value than the explicit tax deduction of bond interest if the firm is fully taxable. A more flexible approach would be to borrow money for 1 year, and if the firm's tax rate in 1 year's time remains high, it can issue debt for an additional year. However, certain fixed costs associated with issuing debt make it more economical to issue longer term debt. Efficient tax planning here requires trading off the transaction cost savings from issuing less flexible debt (that is, long-term debt) against the restructuring cost or the cost of being in the wrong clientele if this is less than the restructuring cost in the event the firm's tax rate declines in the future and bonds become more expensive than equity.

Note that the problem cannot be solved simply by the firm issuing callable debt. Lenders also incur fixed costs each time they undertake an investment. They pay brokerage fees and incur costs to investigate the credit risk of the borrower. Still, callable debt does have interesting flexibility features that may make it tax efficient despite the costs it imposes on the investor.

Consider also the question of whether to buy or lease depreciable assets, such as office buildings or manufacturing equipment. As we have already discussed, depreciable assets are tax-favored under the present tax system of generous depreciation allowances. As a result, the efficient owners from a tax standpoint are those with the highest marginal tax rates because they benefit most from the generous depreciation allowances. Firms with lower marginal tax rates are better off leasing. Suppose a firm's tax rate is currently very high, but the rate is likely to decline in the future, at which point it would no longer be tax-efficient to own depreciable assets. Under what conditions should the firm purchase the depreciable assets? The answer depends on the probability that the firm's tax rate will decline as well as the resulting cost of being in the wrong clientele. If it leases the asset, it bears the cost of being in the wrong clientele now, when its rate is high. If it buys the asset, it may bear the cost of being in the wrong clientele later if its tax rates does, in fact, decrease. The cost of being in the wrong investment or financing clientele at some future date, if the firm's tax rate changes, depends on several factors. We explore three of them here:

1. The reversibility of the tax plan
2. The adaptability of the tax plan
3. The ability to insure against adverse changes in tax status

7.1 MARGINAL TAX RATE: DEFINITIONAL ISSUES

In Chapter 5 we showed that differentially taxed assets give rise to implicit taxes in that the before-tax rates of return on more heavily taxed assets exceed those on more lightly taxed assets. In Chapters 5 and 6 we showed that frictions give rise to transaction costs. The implicit tax is the same for all investors, but the frictions component (transaction costs) is more idiosyncratic. It depends not only on the individual or entity attempting to undertake clientele-based arbitrage, but also on the microstructure of a transaction. We have argued that high marginal-tax-rate taxpayers have an incentive to hold assets that are granted tax-favored treatment and that low-tax-rate investors prefer to hold tax-disfavored assets. And if the costs of buying and selling assets are not too high, taxpayers with relatively extreme (high or low) marginal tax rates have an incentive to engage in tax arbitrage. To engage in clientele-based arbitrage, or more generally in any tax planning activity, it is important that the taxpayer know his marginal tax rate. Thus we turn to a discussion of marginal tax rates.

We define the **marginal tax rate** as the present value of current plus deferred income taxes (both explicit plus implicit) to be paid per dollar of additional (or marginal) taxable income (where taxable income is grossed up to include implicit taxes paid). Notice here that we extend the definition of marginal tax rate to include the effect of a current dollar of taxable income on future period tax liabilities. And because total taxes are important to investment decisions, the marginal tax rate includes the implicit tax as well as the explicit tax. Sometimes we will focus only on the explicit tax component of the marginal tax rate, and sometimes we will focus only on the implicit tax component. When we do, we will refer to these as the **marginal explicit tax rate** and the **marginal implicit tax rate,** respectively.

To explain and illustrate the concept of the marginal explicit tax rate (*metr*) for a corporate taxpayer, it is useful to consider 4 scenarios—whether taxable income in the current period is positive or negative (TI_t) and whether the firm has a net operating loss carryforward at the beginning of the period (NOL_{t-1}):

	$TI_t < 0$	$TI_t > 0$
$NOL_{t-1} = 0$	1	3
$NOL_{t-1} > 0$	2	4

Scenario 1: $TI_t < 0, NOL_{t-1} = 0$ Suppose a corporate taxpayer calculates its current period taxable income as a loss of $10 million. The firm has been profitable in the recent past with a taxable income of $6 million in each of the past 5 years. The firm paid taxes at the top statutory tax rate of 35% in each of these years and because of its recent profitability has no NOL carryforward at the beginning of the year. What is its marginal tax rate in the current period given the tax loss? Does earning another dollar of income escape taxation, implying a zero *metr*? No. The firm can carryback the tax loss (currently up to 2 years)—the carryback is first applied to claim a refund of taxes paid in year −2 of $2,100,000 or $6 million × .35, using up the first $6 million of the loss leaving $4 million to be carried back to year −1 to claim a refund of $1,400,000 or $4 million × .35. If the firm had earned an extra dollar of income in the current period, the tax loss would have been $1 less or $9,999,999, implying $1 less carryback and 35 cents less refund. Thus earning an additional dollar of income in the current period results in 35 cents less refund, implying a *metr* of 35%. More formally, if the entire amount of the loss can be carried back, then the *metr* in the current period, $t = 0$, is given by

$$metr_t = str_{t-v} \qquad (7.1)$$

where *str* is the statutory tax rate in the period $t - v$ where v is the period in which the carryback loss is exhausted (and with a current limit of 2 years on carryback, $v = 1$ or 2).

If the firm has insufficient positive taxable income in the carryback period to exhaust the tax loss, the remaining tax loss must be carried forward, meaning the firm has an NOL carryforward at the end of the current period. We discuss this case in the following scenario.

Scenario 2: $TI_t < 0, NOL_{t-1} > 0$ Suppose a corporate taxpayer calculates its current period taxable income as a loss of $10 million. The firm has been unprofitable in the recent past such that it has a $5 million NOL carryforward at the beginning of the current period. Thus at the end of the current period, it has a $15 million NOL carryforward that it can deduct against future income.

With $15 million of NOLs, the firm faces no immediate tax liability on an extra dollar of income. Does this mean its marginal tax rate is 0%? Far from it. Suppose the firm expects to earn $6 million per year starting in year +1. The prospect of earning $6 million per year of taxable income means that the firm will begin to pay taxes in 3 years. So an extra dollar of taxable income today would trigger a tax payment of 35 cents in 3 years. The present value of this tax, assuming the firm's after-tax discount rate is 7%, is $.35/1.07³ = 28.57 cents, so the corporate marginal explicit tax rate in this case is 28.57%. More generally, for a firm with an NOL carryforward at the end of period t, the current period marginal explicit tax rate is calculated as

$$metr_t = \frac{(\$1 * str_s)}{(1 + r)^s} \qquad (7.2)$$

where, str_s denotes the expected statutory tax rate in period s, the future period in which the firm is eventually taxed on the extra dollar of income earned in the current period, and r is the firm's after-tax discount rate.

If the current statutory rate of 35% is scheduled to change in 1 year to 25%, then the current marginal explicit tax rate of our NOL firm would be 20.41% (or $.25/1.07^3$), although the rate for a firm without NOLs would remain 35%. Analogously, if the statutory rate is scheduled to increase to 50% in 1 year, the current marginal explicit tax rate of our NOL firm would be 40.81% (or $.50/1.07^3$). This illustrates that in the face of tax rate changes over time, the marginal tax rate of NOL firms can exceed that of firms paying taxes at the full statutory rate!

Scenario 3: $TI_t > 0, NOL_{t-1} = 0$ Suppose a corporate taxpayer calculates its current period taxable income as a positive $10 million. The firm has been profitable for many years such that it has no NOL carryforward at the beginning of the year and is expected to be profitable for many years to come. In this scenario, an extra dollar of income would trigger an immediate tax of 35 cents, assuming that the top statutory corporate tax rate is 35%, so the *metr* is 35%.

Suppose instead of forecasting positive taxable income into the foreseeable future, the firm forecasts a drop in demand for its products and expects to report a positive taxable income of $4 million in year +1 but a tax loss of $15 million in year +2 returning to positive profits thereafter. The tax loss in year +2 can be carried back to the current period to claim a refund of all taxes paid in the current period and leaving the firm with a $5 million NOL carryforward at the end of the current period (period t). If the firm had earned an extra dollar of income in the current period such that its taxable income would be $10,000,001, then the tax refund in period 2 would be 35 cents higher, leaving a $4,999,999 carryforward at the end of the period.[2] Even though this result might appear to be a wash, an opportunity cost arises due to the time value of money because the IRS does not pay interest on funds arising from an NOL carryback. Assuming an after-tax discount rate of 7%, the opportunity cost is $.35 - .35/(1.07)^2 = .0443$. However there is more: By earning the additional dollar of income in the current period, the NOL carryforward at the end of period 2 is reduced by $1, resulting in an increase in taxes on an additional dollar of income in the future. Suppose the NOL would have been used up in period +3 where the statutory tax rate is also 35%. Thus we have to add $.35/(1.07)^3 = .2857$ to the *metr* calculation meaning that the firm's *metr* is $.0443 + .2857 = .329$ or 32.9%, not 35%. More formally,

$$Metr_t = str_t - str_n/(1+r)^n + str_s/(1+r)^s \tag{7.3}$$

where n is the future period in which the refund is claimed ($n = 1$ or 2) and s is the future period in which the NOL carryforward at the end of period n is eventually used up. In words, the *metr* is the difference between the current period statutory tax rate and the present value of the refund in n years plus the additional taxes due in s years when the NOL is eventually used up.

Finally, given that the current tax rules limit the carryback period to 2 years, if a currently profitable firm does not expect to incur tax losses within the next 2 years,

---

[2]If the tax loss in year +2 can be completely carried back to the current period, then earning an additional dollar of income in the current period does not affect the amount of the refund so the *metr$_t$* equals the *str$_t$*.

then it is safe to assume its *metr* in the current period is the statutory tax rate it faces in the current period.

Scenario 4: TI$_t$ > 0, NOL$_{t-1}$ > 0   Suppose a corporate taxpayer calculates its current period taxable income as a positive $10 million. The firm has experienced losses in recent years resulting in an NOL carryforward of $6 million at the beginning of the period. If the firm had earned an additional dollar of income in the current period, it would have no effect on the use of the NOL carryforward and would result in an additional 35 cents of taxes in the current period.

    If the NOL carryforward at the beginning of the period had been $12 million, then the current period taxable income of $10 million would have escaped taxation, leaving $2 million NOL carryforward at the end of the current period. Earning an additional dollar of income in the current period, the NOL carryforward at the end of the period would have been reduced by $1 to $1,999,999 and the *metr* on this additional dollar of income is estimated as in scenario 2, equation (7.2).

Estimating Corporate Marginal Tax Rates

The above scenarios thus raise the question as to how does one estimate a firm's *metr*. For firms with NOL carryforwards, the tax planner needs to estimate the number of years before the NOL will be used up. This means forecasting future period taxable income. For a tax planner internal to the firm, access to the firm's budgets and plans can help these forecasts. For tax planners external to the firm (for example, accounting and economics researchers, policymakers, and parties dealing with the firm) forecasts can be made in a variety of ways, two of which are discussed here.

    Manzon (1994) suggests the following simple approach to estimating the number of periods, s, before the firm returns to tax paying status. He exploits a simple valuation model to derive an estimate of the expected future constant stream of taxable income as follows:

$$V = E/r \qquad\qquad (7.4)$$

where V is the market value of the firm's common equity, E is expected future earnings or taxable income, and r is the after-tax discount rate. Rearranging, we can estimate E:

$$E = V^* r \qquad\qquad (7.5)$$

Given an estimate of future annual earnings (taxable income), we can now solve for s, the number of periods before we use up the NOL carryforward, by dividing the NOL amount by our estimate of E:

$$s = NOL_t / E_t \qquad\qquad (7.6)$$

We then insert s into equation (7.2) or (7.3), depending on the firm's circumstances, and estimate the marginal explicit tax rate. For example, suppose a firm has an NOL carryforward of $2 million, a market value of equity of $6.250 million, and $r = .07$. These data imply an expected annual future taxable income of $437,500 from (7.5), further implying $s = 4.57$ years from (7.6). With an estimate of $s = 4.57$ years, and assuming the statutory tax rate is expected to remain at 35% over the foreseeable future and taxes are paid at the end of the year (implying $s = 5$), the marginal explicit tax rate equals 25%.[3]

A more complex procedure is to forecast future taxable income based on the firm's historical taxable income series. Shevlin (1990) and Graham (1996b) developed a simulation approach. Shevlin incorporates the NOL carryback and carryforward rules and Graham extends the approach to include tax credits and the corporate alternative minimum tax. The simulation approach is somewhat complex and requires several assumptions to implement, and the interested reader is referred to the original papers.[4] However, Graham's estimates for a large sample of publicly listed firms can be accessed at the following Web address: www.duke.edu/~jgraham under the "tax rates" option.

Plesko (2003) uses 1 year of actual corporate tax return data to evaluate the accuracy of the simulation approach to estimating *metrs*. He finds the simulation approach is reasonably accurate but notes that his analysis uses only 1 year of taxable income data, thus ignoring the important effects of the carryback and carryforward rules. Shevlin (1990) reports the following mean *metr* estimate across 100 firms in each of the four scenarios discussed above for the sample year 1974 in which the top corporate statutory tax rate was 48%.

	$TI_t < 0$	$TI_t > 0$
$NOL_{t-1} = 0$	1. 27.66%	3. 42.56%
$NOL_{t-1} > 0$	2. 21.50%	4. 26.62%

Consistent with what we might expect, firms in scenario 3 exhibit the highest estimated *metrs*, firms in scenarios 1 and 4 exhibit intermediate values of *metrs*, with firms in scenario 2 (current period losses with an NOL carryforward at the end of the year) exhibiting the lowest estimates. Shevlin suggested a trichotomous classification of firms: those firms in scenario 3 are assumed to face the highest rates, those in scenario 2 the lowest rates, and those in scenarios 1 and 4 intermediate rates. This classification scheme thus only requires an estimate of the current period taxable income and beginning of period NOL.[5] Plesko (2003) reports evidence that such a classification scheme works well.

Foreign, State, and Local Corporate Taxes

Corporations pay income tax in several jurisdictions in addition to the federal government. Multinational companies pay foreign taxes on their overseas operations. Foreign income is generally not taxed in the United States until repatriated to the United States and a credit for foreign taxes paid is provided against U.S. taxes. We discuss these issues more in later chapters. Firms located in California or Massachusetts pay

---

[3]Note that Manzon's approach cannot be implemented for private firms because they do not have publicly available market value data.

[4]An easy-to-read discussion of the procedure appears in Graham and Lemmon (1998).

[5]A warning is in order here. As we discuss in the next chapter, the use of employee stock options complicates the estimation of firm's taxable income from its financial statements. Hanlon and Shevlin (2002) discuss the issue and Graham, Lang, and Shackelford (2004) re-estimate simulated marginal tax rates after adjusting financial-statement-based estimates of taxable income for the ESO tax deduction, which for many companies is very large. We discuss Graham et al.'s results in the next chapter.

state income tax at 10%, while firms in Texas and Washington state pay zero state tax on income (they pay other taxes based on, for example, net worth or sales revenue). Some counties and cities also assess their own income taxes. To obtain a comprehensive or total marginal tax rate, the additional state and local taxes should be included along with federal taxes to determine the overall marginal tax rate. Note that state and local income taxes are deductible at the federal level,[6] so the state tax rate should not be simply added to the federal rate to obtain statutory tax rates for the *metr* calculation. Rather, the total statutory tax rate is calculated as

$$(t_{\text{fed}}) + (t_{\text{state}} + t_{\text{local}})(1 - t_{\text{fed}})$$

For example, assume the federal statutory tax rate is 35%, while the sum of state and local taxes is 10%. The total statutory tax rate is $.35 + (.10)(1 - .35) = 41.5\%$. Deductibility at the federal level reduces the state and local tax rate to 6.5% $[.10(1 - .35)]$.

Individual Taxpayers' Marginal Tax Rate

Individual taxpayers who conduct businesses requiring Schedule C on their tax return also face the carryforward and carryback rules for Schedule C business losses. Individuals also face carryforward rules on capital losses and passive losses. Individual taxpayers must carryforward capital losses to the extent they exceed capital gains plus $3,000. Passive losses can offset only passive income, and thus passive losses must be carried forward to offset future passive income. For individuals, the marginal tax rate is also affected by the presence of rules that tie certain tax deductions to the level of adjusted gross income. For example, under U.S. law, medical deductions, miscellaneous itemized deductions, and the deductibility of certain losses on passive investment activity are tied to the level of adjusted gross income. In the case of medical and miscellaneous deductions, higher income leads to a permanent loss of deductions, and in the case of passive loss deductions (for example, on real estate activity), higher income may lead to a postponement of the deduction.

To illustrate the effect of these factors on an individual taxpayer's marginal tax rate, suppose that an extra dollar of income reduces tax deductions permanently by $.10 and postpones the deductibility of $.50 of losses for 5 years. The current statutory tax rate is 40%, and it will be 45% in 5 years. If the after-tax discount rate of the taxpayer is 7%, the marginal tax rate on a dollar of current taxable income is calculated as follows:

$$
\begin{array}{rl}
\$1.00 & \text{of additional income} \\
+\ \$0.10 & \text{permanent loss of tax deduction} \\
+\ \underline{\$0.50} & \text{temporary loss of tax deduction} \\
=\ \$1.60 & \text{of additional taxable income currently.}
\end{array}
$$

This gives rise to $\$1.60 \times 40\% = \$.64$ of additional current tax.

An additional deduction of $.50 in 5 years at a tax rate of 45% reduces taxes, in present value, by $\$.50 \times 45\%/1.07^5$, or $.16. The overall increment to tax on the dollar of extra taxable income, then, is $\$.64 - \$.16 = \$.48$, so the marginal tax rate is 48%.

---

[6]Generally, federal income taxes are not deductible at the state level.

Average and Effective Tax Rates

We define the **average tax rate** as the present value of current plus deferred income taxes (both explicit plus implicit taxes) divided by the present value of taxable income (where taxable income is again grossed up to include implicit taxes paid). This measure captures a taxpayer's tax burden better than do conventional measures such as effective tax rates.

Two popular definitions of **effective tax rates** are as follows: (1) As discussed in Appendix 2.2 in Chapter 2, for financial reporting purposes it is the sum of currently payable and deferred tax expense divided by net income before tax. Both the numerator and the denominator exclude implicit taxes. Moreover, the tax expense figure is insensitive to the timing of tax payments. That is, a dollar of taxes paid currently is treated no differently than a dollar of taxes to be paid many years into the future. (2) For "tax reformer" (for example, Citizens for Tax Justice) purposes, the effective tax rate is defined as taxes paid currently divided by net income before tax. The numerator excludes not only implicit taxes but also tax deferrals, that is, timing differences in calculating income for tax purposes and for financial reporting purposes.

We argue that effective tax rates have little economic meaning. And while average tax rates, as defined here, may be used to gauge the extent to which taxpayers are paying their fair share of taxes, they are not especially useful for tax planning purposes. Note however that, because of the difficulty of estimating implicit taxes for both individuals and corporate taxpayers, most studies of corporate tax burdens do not include implicit taxes in their analyses. Thus these analyses are incomplete at best and, at worst, seriously flawed, leading to false policy recommendations. In making economic choices such as investment or financing decisions, it is the marginal tax rate that is important.

Problems with Effective Tax Rates

Let us now show why using effective tax rates can be very deceiving. Assume that the before-tax rate of return on fully taxable bonds is 10% and that the municipal bond rate is 7%. This implies that the implicit tax rate is 30%. We know that an investor prefers municipal bonds if her marginal tax rate on holding taxable bonds, all of which is explicit, exceeds that on holding municipal bonds, all of which is implicit. This preference is pretty straightforward. To set the stage for our analysis of the marginal tax rate, let us now complicate things a bit by assuming that it is possible to sell taxable bonds and to buy municipal bonds. Note that this transaction could be accomplished either by taking out a loan and using the proceeds to buy municipal bonds, in which case interest deductibility is restricted by the tax rules, or by selling some current holdings of taxable bonds and using the sale proceeds to buy municipal bonds, in which case tax-rule restrictions may not apply.

Let us suppose our taxpayer undertakes this transaction through an existing partnership whose operating decisions, such as selecting what products to make, have already been determined. These operating decisions will give rise to $600,000 in taxable income. Assume that the statutory ordinary tax rate for each of the partners, t_p, is 40%. For the moment we will ignore the restraints on the deductibility of interest on loans to finance the purchase of municipal bonds. Suppose that the partnership borrows $6,000,000 for 1 year at the beginning of the year. This financing decision gives rise to

$600,000 in deductible interest expense. If the proceeds of the loan are used to buy municipal bonds, the taxable income from the partnership would be zero. As a result, the so-called effective tax rate at the partnership level would be zero. The partnership income is taxed to the partners, however, at the 30% implicit tax rate on municipal bonds rather than at their 40% ordinary rate on taxable income. The partners are able to accomplish some tax reduction—though not 100%, as the effective tax rate implies—by using clientele-based arbitrage to switch from paying explicit taxes on ordinary taxable income to paying implicit taxes on tax-favored assets. The $6,000,000 invested in municipal bonds at 7% yields $420,000 in after-tax income, exactly 70% of the $600,000 in taxable income of the partners before the investment and financing decisions were undertaken.

Although the effective tax rate has been reduced to zero, suppose the partnership continued to borrow at a 10% before-tax rate and purchased municipal bonds with the proceeds at a 7% before-tax rate of return. This move creates negative taxable income at the partnership level, which is passed through to the partners.[7] The arbitrage remains profitable until the taxable income of the partners is reduced to such a level that their own personal tax rates on ordinary income become 30%.[8]

This illustration points to another difficulty with effective tax rate measures. The effective tax rate of the partners on their $600,000 of partnership income would be negative in this case. The negative effective tax rate arises because the calculation ignores the considerable sums of municipal bond interest, earned and taxed implicitly, while including fully the tax savings on the interest deductions. This rate is hardly a meaningful rate in the face of a 30% implicit tax on municipal bond income. Moreover, the effective tax rate measure provides no guidance in identifying desirable clientele-based arbitrage strategies; for example, it does not indicate when to stop borrowing and investing the loan proceeds in municipal bonds.

Note that this example could have also been developed for a corporate taxpayer issuing $6 million of corporate bonds to reduce its other taxable income to zero and investing the proceeds in the municipal bonds. In this case the corporate effective tax rate is also zero: $0/$420,000 (zero explicit taxes/earnings before taxes of $420,000 on the municipal bonds). This example can also be used to illustrate the calculation of the average tax rate:

$$\frac{\text{(Sum of explicit and implicit taxes)}}{\text{(Taxable income including a gross-up to include implicit taxes paid)}}$$

The sum of explicit and implicit taxes is $0 + $180,000, or 3% of $6 million. Taxable income including a gross-up to include implicit taxes paid is $0 + ($420,000 + $180,000), resulting in an average tax rate of 30%, or $180,000/$600,000, which in this simple case equals the implicit tax rate because there are no explicit taxes.

---

[7] We are assuming that the "passive loss limitations" on partnership activities do not prevent partners from taking current tax deductions for their share of partnership loss. And, for pedagogical reasons, we are once again assuming that it is possible to deduct interest on loans used for the purpose of buying or holding municipal bonds.

[8] Note that if each partner does not have identical marginal explicit tax rates, partners may disagree on how much borrowing is desirable. As long as the partners know the amount of borrowing at the partnership level, however, they could adjust the level of borrowing on personal account, if necessary.

7.2 TAX PLANNING FOR LOW MARGINAL-TAX-RATE FIRMS

A low marginal-tax-rate firm has a number of tax planning options available. For simplicity, assume that the firm has an NOL carryforward of $20 million and that, if no tax planning actions are taken, the NOL will be used up in year 12, because the firm expects to generate more tax losses before it generates positive taxable income. Assuming a statutory tax rate of 35% for the foreseeable future and an after-tax discount rate of 10% gives a marginal explicit tax rate of $.35/(1.10)^{12} = 11\%$.

As we discussed, because the firm faces a low marginal explicit tax rate, clientele-based arbitrage suggests that the firm buy highly taxed securities such as corporate bonds (assuming the marginal investor in corporate bonds faces a higher marginal explicit tax rate). This will give rise to income taxable (explicitly) at 11%, or an after-tax rate of return of $R_b(1 - metr)$. If the firm does not have cash available to invest, what type of securities, if any, should it issue? Issuing corporate bonds gains the firm nothing because the after-tax cost will equal $R_b(1 - metr)$ or worse, given that borrowing rates exceed lending rates because of the financial intermediation and frictions discussed in Chapters 5 and 6. The firm could issue preferred stock to other corporations because it will then obtain an implicit tax deduction arising from the dividends received deduction available to corporate investors. That is, the after-tax cost of issuing preferred stock will be lower than the after-tax cost of issuing corporate bonds because highly taxed corporations will bid up the price of the preferred stock to capture the dividends received deduction.

Issuing preferred stock to buy bonds is not necessarily the most effective way to exploit the firm's temporarily low tax rate. The firm also might consider a number of other strategies:

- Enter into deferred compensation contracts with employees.
- Sell some equipment to high marginal-tax-rate taxpayers who can better use accelerated depreciation deductions and lease back the equipment at a bargain rental rate, thereby realizing an implicit tax subsidy. This type of transaction is referred to as a sale-leaseback arrangement.
- Form an R&D partnership with high marginal-tax-rate taxpayers to allow them to obtain the tax benefits from writing off R&D expenditures in exchange for current income.
- Retire any current outstanding debt and issue preferred stock (or issue common stock if it bears high implicit taxes).
- Consider a merger with a company that faces a higher marginal tax rate. A highly taxed organization might be able to pay more for the right to use the firm's NOLs than they are worth internally to the firm. However, in a friction-filled world, it is not likely that NOL companies will be able to sell their losses for anywhere near $.35 on the dollar, which is the statutory tax rate in this example. One reason is that the cost to evaluate a prospective merger partner can be large, and buyers must charge for these costs. In addition, buyers must worry about hidden-information problems, as we discussed in Chapter 6. Another reason, as we will discuss in the later chapters on mergers and acquisitions, are the express limitations in the Tax Code on the ability of the acquirer to use the acquired firm's NOLs, foreign tax credits, R&D credits, and capital loss carryovers (called tax attributes of

the target firm). These limitations, in Code Sections 382 and 383, reduce the value of these attributes to the acquiring firm.

And note that if the firm's future tax rates are decreasing because of statutory decreases in rates and it cannot use up its NOLs internally before statutory tax rates decline, a merger with a high-tax-rate firm becomes more desirable than when tax rates are constant or increasing through time.

Of course, costs to implement a tax-motivated restructuring apply to all of these alternatives. A sale-and-leaseback involves contracting costs, monitoring costs, and possibly explicit tax costs like depreciation recapture, as we will discuss more fully in later chapters. R&D limited partnerships may be very expensive to organize and operate and may suffer from severe incentive problems, as we discussed in Chapter 6. Retiring debt is also not costless to the firm. As always, efficient tax planning requires that these frictions be considered very carefully.

This analysis can be quickly complicated by recognizing that the firm's future taxable income stream, before any tax planning activities, is uncertain. Suppose the firm stands a 70% chance of earning $25 million next period and a 30% chance of it incurring a tax loss of $10 million. In this case, if the firm earns $25 million next year its $metr = 32\%$, or $.35/1.10^1$. If the firm incurs a loss, then its *metr* will continue to be 11%. In this still somewhat simple scenario the firm's current period expected *metr* then is $.70(.32) + .30(.11) = .257$, or 25.7%. What should the firm do in this case? If municipal bonds are priced to bear an implicit tax of 30%, clientele-based arbitrage suggests that our firm facing a *metr* of 25.7% should buy fully taxable securities and issue preferred stock. However, if the firm issues preferred stock and buys corporate bonds and the $25 million gain occurs in the next period, the firm will find itself in the wrong clientele because its realized *metr* will be 32%. This outcome leads us into a discussion of the concepts and importance of the adaptability and reversibility of tax plans.

7.3 ADAPTABILITY OF THE TAX PLAN

Most tax plans cannot be reversed without excessive cost. **Adaptive tax planning** is designed to offset the cost of being in the wrong clientele following unexpected changes in tax status where reversibility is impossible or impractical. We discussed this concept in Chapter 4 in the context of corporations that find the partnership form of organization to be tax-advantageous following changes made by the 1986 Tax Reform Act in the United States. Many corporations would like to have reorganized as a partnership subsequent to the Act. However, for most of them, the tax and nontax costs of the reorganization exceeded the tax benefits. If these firms knew when they first organized that the law would change in the future to favor partnerships, many of them might have organized as a partnership from the start. We also discussed ways in which corporations could undertake transactions that would move them closer to *de facto* partnership tax treatment without undergoing changes in legal organizational form. In particular, the corporate tax burden is mitigated when the corporation distributes pretax profits to owners, employees, and other factor suppliers in forms that are tax deductible at the corporate level. For example, owner-employees could tie their compensation more closely to their firm's profitability.

If a firm purchases depreciable assets and its tax rate declines, the costs of selling the assets may far outweigh the benefits. In addition to the costs to broker the deal, the transaction might give rise to ordinary taxable income (arising from depreciation recapture) as well as taxable capital gains. Moreover, for tax purposes, the new owner may not be able to use as generous a depreciation schedule as the old owner. For example, an office building purchased during the period 1987–1993 in the United States was depreciable over a 31.5-year period on an accelerated basis. If the building were sold after 1993, however, its new owners would be entitled only to straight-line depreciation over 39 years, or 40 years for alternative minimum tax purposes.

However, if the firm's objective in selling the property is to transfer the rights to depreciation deductions to a higher bracket taxpayer, better alternatives might be available. In particular, it could cost less to restructure other assets and equities of the firm. For example, tax-favored assets like municipal bonds or common stocks might be sold and replaced with ordinary income-producing assets, such as high-yield bonds, at reduced transaction costs, or firms might issue stock and purchase bonds with the proceeds. If the firm can use these substitutes at sufficiently low cost, it would not be very costly for the firm to be in the wrong investment clientele if tax rates decline unexpectedly.

Transaction Costs and Tax Clienteles

Let us illustrate how the joint presence of transaction costs and uncertainty with respect to future tax status can influence tax clienteles. Suppose you are choosing between two investments, fully taxable bonds yielding 10% pretax per year and tax-exempt bonds yielding 7% per year. Both investments have 3-year maturities. At the time of investment, you are unsure, because of the uncertain profitability of your other investments already in place, as to whether your tax rate will be 40% over the 3 years or 0%. You assess a 70% chance of the former. This makes your expected marginal tax rate 28%, or .7(40%) + .3(0%).

If you are risk-neutral and if you must choose one investment or the other and hold it for the entire 3-year period, you would be better off choosing taxable bonds. At an expected tax rate of 28%, taxable bonds yield 7.2% after tax, while tax-exempt bonds yield only 7%.[9]

Now let us consider what your optimal strategy would be if you could sell your asset and purchase the other at the end of the first year at an annualized cost of 1% after tax. Suppose that at the end of the first year you discover whether your tax rate for the next 2 years, as well as for the year just ended, will be 40% or 0%.

If you purchased taxable bonds, you will wish you had purchased exempt bonds if your tax rate turns out to be 40%. At a tax rate of 40%, exempt bonds yield 7% and taxable bonds yield 6% after tax. However, if the annualized cost of switching from taxable to tax-exempt bonds is 1% after tax, no advantage could be gained from switching, and you would be stuck earning 6% after tax in years 2 and 3. Thus the

---

[9]If you are sufficiently risk-averse, you might prefer the tax-exempt bonds because they yield 7% for sure whereas taxable bonds yield 10% after tax 30% of the time and 6% after tax 70% of the time. Although taxable bonds generate a higher *expected* return, the return is also riskier due to tax rate uncertainty. Note that tax-exempt bonds are taxed at a known implicit tax rate.

expected return per year is 7.2%, calculated as follows:

$$\text{Expected after-tax accumulation per dollar invested}$$
$$= \$1[(.70 \times 1.06 \times 1.06^2) + (.30 \times 1.10^3)] = \$1.233$$

where the first term $(.70 \times 1.06 \times 1.06^2)$ denotes the 70% probability of the 40% tax rate outcome. Thus your first-year after-tax return from the fully taxable bonds is 6%. You then switch into the municipals yielding 6% (after the 1% switch costs) for 2 years. The second term $(.30 \times 1.10^3)$ denotes the 30% probability of the 0% tax rate outcome, and so you keep holding the fully taxables earning 10% per year for 3 years. The expected rate of return per year is $1.233^{1/3} - 1$, or 7.2%.

Conversely, if you purchased exempt bonds and your tax rate turns out to be 0%, you will wish you had purchased taxable bonds, since taxable bonds would yield 10% after tax or 3% more than tax-exempt bonds—but at least you could secure a 9% return in years 2 and 3 (10% less the 1% annualized transaction cost) by switching to taxable bonds. Thus investing in tax-exempt bonds and switching to taxables if tax rates turn out to be 0% yields 7.4% *per year,* calculated as follows:

$$\text{Expected after-tax accumulation per dollar invested}$$
$$\$1(.70 \times 1.07^3 + .30 \times 1.07 \times 1.09^2) = \$1.24$$

where the first term $(.70 \times 1.07^3)$ denotes the 70% probability of the 40% tax rate outcome. You would keep holding municipals at 7% to give you the 3-year return 1.07^3. The second term $(.30 \times 1.07 \times 1.09^2)$ denotes the 30% probability of the 0% tax rate outcome, and so you switch out at the end of the first year of the 7% municipals into the fully taxables, yielding 9% (after the 1% switch cost) for 2 years. The expected rate of return per year is $1.24^{1/3} - 1$ or 7.4%. In this case, tax-exempt bonds emerge as the investment of choice in the first period due to the greater value of the restructuring option.

We leave it as an exercise for the reader to verify that, in the absence of transaction costs, *taxable bonds* would be the investment of choice in the first period. Over the 3-year period, they would yield 7.7% per year after tax versus 7.6% for tax-exempt bonds. In the absence of transaction costs, optimal decisions can be made simply by knowing the expected tax rates. This is no longer true in the presence of transaction costs.

Adaptability in Investment and Financing Decisions

With tax rate uncertainty and transaction costs, it can pay to purchase or issue short-term securities at less favorable yields relative to longer-term securities. Short-term securities introduce an element of flexibility that is valuable in such circumstances. For similar reasons, it might pay to issue callable securities or to purchase puttable securities, even if such options are costly, or it might be desirable to issue (or purchase) securities that can be repurchased (resold) in the marketplace at low cost. This problem is related to the one of choosing the efficient duration of legal agreements where there is a trade-off between the fixed costs of writing contracts and the deteriorating efficiency of the agreements over time as circumstances change. In our tax planning problem, one source of the deteriorating efficiency of the agreements is the possibility of being in the wrong tax clientele due to unexpected changes in tax rates.[10]

---

[10]Another example, for individual taxpayers, is a traditional IRA which, as discussed in Chapter 3, offers the ability to be rolled over, or converted, into a Roth IRA. Hulse (2003) provides an analysis of the value of this option.

7.4 REVERSIBILITY OF TAX PLANS

In some contracts, if tax rates or tax rules change in ways that make existing agreements inefficient, the contracts can be voided. If the contract can be voided when specified tax-related contingencies occur, then the contract allows for the **reversibility of tax plans.** Consider the following examples.

1. Closely held U.S. corporations run the risk that the IRS will view a salary payment to an owner-manager as a disguised dividend. In such a case, the corporation loses its tax deduction for the payment. The corporate minutes of many closely held organizations provide that, if the IRS claims that owner-employees have received excessive compensation and treats these payments as disguised dividends, the recipients should return the payments to the corporation. In other words, the transaction is reversed due to the unfavorable tax treatment accorded the transaction, and the firm avoids the cost of being in the wrong clientele for paying a dividend.

2. Many municipal bonds used to fund private activities include standard clauses in the contract that provide for a refund to the investor in the event that the IRS deems the bonds to be taxable because they are not issued for an exempt purpose.

3. Many public utilities have issued preferred stock with mandatory redemption features; that is, the corporation is required to redeem the shares of investors over a period of, say, 5 to 10 years. This contractual feature could prompt the IRS to argue that the preferred stock should be classified as bonds, because preferred stock is supposed to have unlimited life.

   Now, why would the IRS wish to have the preferred stock treated as bonds for tax purposes? After all, preferred stock dividends are not tax deductible but bond interest is. The reason relates to the investor side of the contract. In particular, although U.S. corporations are exempted from paying tax on a substantial fraction of the preferred stock dividends paid by other U.S. corporations, they are fully taxable on bond interest. And what are the likely tax characteristics of the issuer of the preferred stock? As we described earlier, the issuer is likely to have relatively low marginal tax rates, so it cannot use interest deductions as effectively as can other more highly taxed entities.

   An interesting incentive problem may arise if the IRS, after auditing the tax returns of issuers of redeemable preferred stock, argues that the securities are really bonds rather than preferred stocks. If the issuer agrees to this interpretation, the dividend payment is treated as interest, and a valuable tax deduction results. This would result in a double deduction. The borrower already received an implicit deduction by issuing the preferred stock at a reduced dividend rate to reflect the tax-favored status of dividends to corporate investors. Classifying the securities as bonds at a later date gives rise to an explicit deduction as well. Of course, the preferred stockholders might sue the issuer or the issuer's lawyers in this case. Moreover, the firm's reputation in the capital market might be severely damaged, which could raise the cost of capital in the future. Finally, if investors were concerned about this incentive problem, they would demand a higher return to compensate them up front, which could prove costly to the issuer.

To mitigate this incentive problem, the indentures for securities issued by such firms as Public Service of New Mexico, which has issued several series of mandatory redeemable preferred stock, include an indemnity clause. If the holders of the preferred stock lose the dividend received deduction, Public Service of New Mexico promises to increase the yield. However, it also reserves the right to redeem the entire series immediately in this case. Note that Public Service does not *guarantee* to redeem the entire series, however, perhaps because it may be efficient for them to be issuing bonds at that time anyway.

4. An exception to the rule that dividend payments are nondeductible to the U.S. corporations that declare them deals with dividends paid on shares held by employee stock ownership plans (ESOPs). An ESOP is a type of pension plan that invests primarily in the stock of the employer on behalf of its employees.[11] The tax deductibility of such dividends has been controversial ever since it was first introduced into law. To guard against adverse changes in the law, some shares issued to ESOPs (typically convertible preferred stock) contain provisions making the shares callable at the issuer's discretion in the event the dividend deduction is eliminated.[12]

7.5 ABILITY TO INSURE AGAINST ADVERSE CHANGES IN TAX STATUS

Tax status can change unexpectedly for at least two reasons besides differences between projected and actual future profitability:

1. How the taxing authority and the courts will interpret the tax laws
2. Future legislative changes in the tax law

In a number of countries, including the United States and Canada, a taxpayer can reduce tax treatment uncertainty by requesting an advance ruling from the tax authority on how a proposed transaction will be treated for tax purposes. In the United States, such requests must include a comprehensive statement of facts describing the proposed transaction, along with a documentation of the relevant points of judicial, statutory, and secondary authority. The legal costs of such requests are typically in the $20,000 to $40,000 range, but some requests can be quite a bit more costly, especially those involving complicated multinational corporate reorganizations. Of course, the risk in seeking such clarification of the rules is that the IRS may rule unfavorably and is likely to audit the return unless the return is filed in a manner consistent with the ruling. As a result, the taxpayer might be better off undertaking the transaction without a ruling request, taking an aggressive position on the tax return, and hoping that the IRS either ignores the issue or that the examining agent rules favorably.

A second way that a taxpayer can secure insurance against unexpected tax treatment is to purchase professional legal opinions. Tax sheltered limited partnership and real estate investment trusts (REITS) are notorious for the many facets of the

---

[11]We discuss ESOPs in more detail in Chapter 9.
[12]See, for example, Morgan Stanley's "Leveraged ESOP Presentation for Unocal Corporation," (February 15, 1989), III-3.

investment for which tax treatment uncertainty exists. In fact, the Securities and Exchange Commission requires that all limited partnership prospectuses contain an extensive section on risk factors, including "Income Tax Aspects" of the investment which thoroughly discusses uncertainties regarding tax treatment. General comments and warnings such as the following are common:

> Qualifying as a real estate investment trust (a "REIT") under the Internal Revenue Code of 1986, as amended (the "Code") requires complying with highly technical and complex tax provisions that courts and administrative agencies have interpreted only to a limited degree. Due to the complexities of our ownership, structure, and operations, the Trust is more likely than are other REITs to face interpretive issues for which there are no clear answers. Also, facts and circumstances that we do not control may affect the Trust's ability to qualify as a REIT. The Trust believes that since the taxable year ended December 31, 1995, the Trust has qualified as a REIT. The Trust intends to continue to operate so as to qualify as a REIT. However, the Trust cannot assure you that the Trust will continue to qualify as a REIT. If the Trust failed to qualify as a REIT for any prior tax year, the Trust would be liable to pay a significant amount of taxes for those years. Similarly, if the Trust fails to qualify as a REIT in the future, our liability for taxes would increase. (Starwood Hotels and Resorts, Form S-3 Registration Statement, Filed 11/18/99, p. 12)

> As the General Partner has not requested a ruling from the IRS respecting any of the tax consequences of the Partnership, there is an inherent and substantial risk that such benefits claimed might be challenged in whole or in part by the IRS. Such risk is materially increased by reason that direct authority is lacking in several areas involved and that certain of the tax incidents discussed herein are under continuous IRS review. (Granada 4, Filed 9/23/85, p. 36)

It is also common to publish the professional opinion of legal counsel in the prospectus. For example:

> With respect to the material tax issues and tax advantages anticipated by an investment in the Partnership, Reynolds, Allen and Cook, Incorporated, counsel to the General Partner and the Partnership, is of the opinion that the significant tax benefits in the aggregate, as anticipated from an investment in the Partnership as discussed herein, probably will be realized by the Partners. (*Ibid.*)

Firms merging with or acquiring another firm often obtain legal opinion as to the tax treatment of the planned transaction structure. For example, the Boeing Company in its 1998 10-K filing with the SEC discussed its proposed acquisition of part of the Rockwell International Corporation as follows:

> Consummation of the Transaction is conditioned on the receipt of opinions of counsel that (i) the Contribution and the Distribution qualify as transactions described in Sections 351 and 355 of the Code and/or as a "reorganization" under Section 368(a)(1)(D) of the Code and (ii) the Merger qualifies as a "reorganization" under Section 368(a)(1)(B) of the Code. An opinion of

counsel is not binding on the Internal Revenue Service ("IRS") or the courts.[13]

In its 1996 acquisition of McDonnell Douglas Corporation, the Boeing Company in an online document entitled "Exchanging McDonnell Douglas Stock to Boeing Stock" states

> According to opinions received from attorneys for Boeing and McDonnell Douglas, the receipt of Boeing stock in exchange for McDonnell Douglas stock will be tax-free for U.S. Federal income tax purposes, except that shareholders will recognize gain or loss with respect to cash received in lieu of fractional shares of Boeing stock.

Given a legal tax opinion, investors can and typically do sue the lawyers in the event that significant expected tax benefits, on which legal counsel has expressed a favorable opinion, are disallowed by the IRS.

The two forms of insurance we just discussed both deal with uncertainty over existing tax rules. But some forms of insurance also exist regarding legislative changes. For example, in November 1984, the U.S. Treasury Department announced its proposal to overhaul the federal income tax system. Among many proposed changes was one to reduce maximum federal tax rates to 35% as of July 1, 1986. Because lower tax rates reduce the value of depreciation deductions, many limited partnerships that invested in real estate and other depreciable assets were having trouble raising funds in the face of this uncertainty. In response to investor concern, a number of partnership contracts provided that the limited partners' share of profits would be increased if the tax proposals were passed. An example is the Stanford Capital Realty Fund, Ltd.:

> The General Partner has agreed, in the event of reduction in the Maximum Tax Rate effective for any year prior to 1990, to reduce its interest in Net Sale or Refinancing Proceeds available for distribution after the Capital Return Date (that is, after limited partners have already received distributions from the partnership equal to 100% of their initial investment), to attempt to mitigate any adverse impact upon Limited Partners of such a reduction in the Maximum Tax Rate.

The prospectus then gives the tax-rate-contingent formula for sharing profits and works through an example based on tax-loss projections given in the prospectus. If the maximum federal tax rate on July 1, 1986, were to decline to 35% in the example, "[t]he percentage of Net Sale or Refinancing Proceeds to which the Limited Partners would be entitled would increase from the current 83.33% to 95.17% (and the General Partner interest would decline from 16.67% to 4.83%)."

Another uncertainty back in early 1986 hung on the fate of the Investment Tax Credit (ITC) in the pending tax bill. Although tax reform was discussed throughout 1986, there was considerable doubt as to whether a tax bill would be passed at all. Conditional on passage, it was uncertain whether the ITC would disappear and, if so, whether the elimination would be retroactive to January 1, 1986; July 1, 1986; January 1, 1987; or some other date. To insure against loss of ITC benefits for investors, PLM, a

---

[13]These Code sections are discussed in more detail in later chapters and the reader does not need to understand the structure of the Boeing transaction here.

major syndicator of equipment-leasing deals, wrote contracts in early 1986 guaranteeing that if investment tax credits were lost between January 1, 1986, and July 1, 1986 (and they were), PLM would guarantee a generous level of leasing income to investors.

These illustrations involving Stanford Capital Realty and PLM are examples of **tax indemnities.** The issuer of securities indemnifies the investor against less favorable tax treatment than that promised. Such indemnities may conserve costs in that investors need not research the tax rules as comprehensively, given the insurance. However, the contracting parties should also be sensitive to the allocation of risk if they are risk-averse. Tax indemnities typically allocate all of the tax risk to one party, which is not always efficient, but concentrating the risk in the hands of one party may provide efficient incentives for lobbying against unfavorable changes in tax rules. It may also induce the insuring party to effect adaptive tax planning—organizational restructuring—following changes in tax rules.

As another example of tax indemnities, $15 billion worth of tax-exempt industrial revenue bonds, issued between 1982 and 1985, contained indentures that would increase interest rates by as much as 300 basis points, or 3%, if statutory corporate tax rates were cut prior to the maturity of the bonds. The objective here was to compensate the bondholders in the event the value of the tax-exemption feature of the bonds diminished. As a result of the enactment of the 1986 Tax Act, along with lower tax rates, the interest on such bonds increased by $300 million.

Tax indemnities also arise in connection with employee stock ownership plans (ESOPs). Loans made to the ESOP by certain qualified lenders for the purpose of purchasing stock have been eligible, since 1984, for tax exemption of 50% of the related interest income. Lenders reduce the rate at which they are willing to make such loans because of the 50% interest exemption. It is typical for the firm sponsoring the ESOP to agree to compensate the lender for a variety of adverse changes in the tax law that affect the value of the 50% exemption.[14] In a document entitled "The Decision to Establish a Leveraged Employee Stock Ownership Plan," Merrill Lynch Capital Markets describes the typical tax indemnities as follows:

> Tax indemnities are meant to protect the investor from three risks: (a) a change in statutory tax rates, (b) a change in tax law affecting the investor's 50% interest exclusion, and (c) a disqualification of the employer's ESOP debt or plan. Risks (a) and (b) can be categorized as taxable events and mitigated by a provision which adjusts the ESOP rate up or down to the taxable equivalent rate of return to which the investor originally committed. Risk (c) is an event under the employer's control. Should the employer cause the ESOP debt or plan to become disqualified, the ESOP rate would be grossed-up to the taxable equivalent yield and the employer would reimburse the investor for any penalties and/or other costs or taxes incurred by the investor. (1989, pp. 20–21)

Still another example is the indemnity that Bankers Trust New York Corporation provided to its preferred stock shareholders in August 1989. The Prospectus Supplement for its "Fixed/Adjustable Rate Cumulative Preferred Stock, Series D," on

---

[14]See Lawrence N. Bader and Jenny A. Hourihan, *The Investor's Guide to ESOP Loans* (Salomon Brothers, Inc.), March 1989.

page S-9, contains a section entitled "Changes in the Dividends Received Percentage." Recall that U.S. corporations receiving dividend income from other U.S. corporations are exempted from taxation on a large fraction of the income (Internal Revenue Code Section 243). In the case of the Bankers Trust preferred stock issue, the relevant fraction (often called the "dividends received deduction percentage") is 70%. The Prospectus Supplement contains the following provision:

> If one or more amendments to the Internal Revenue Code of 1986, as amended (the "Code"), are enacted that change the percentage specified in Section 243 (a) (1) of the Code or any successor provision (the "Dividends Received Percentage"), then the (Dividend) Rate . . . for Dividend Periods commencing on or after the effective date of such change shall be adjusted by multiplying the Rate . . . by a factor, which will be the number determined in accordance with the following formula, and rounding the result to the nearest basis point:
>
> $$\frac{1 - .34(1 - .70)}{1 - .34(1 - \text{DRP})}$$
>
> For purposes of the above formula, "DRP" means the Dividends Received Percentage applicable to the dividend in question.

A final way to insure against unfavorable changes in tax laws is to purchase investments that will be affected favorably by the tax law changes or take short positions in securities that will decline in value if the tax laws are changed. For example, if you were concerned about unexpected declines in federal tax rates, you might wish to avoid the purchase of municipal bonds, the prices of which are likely to fall if tax rates are reduced as they become less tax-favored. Similarly, a syndicator of real estate deals might sensibly have taken short positions in the common stock of real estate investment companies prior to passage of the 1981 or 1986 tax acts in the United States. The 1981 Tax Act was extremely favorable to real estate and the 1986 Tax Act was rather unfavorable, so a loss on the short position would have occurred in 1981 and a gain would have arisen in 1986. These gains and losses would have offset the changes in profitability from the syndication business.

7.6 TAX PLANNING WHEN A TAXPAYER'S MARGINAL TAX RATE IS STRATEGY-DEPENDENT

In many tax planning situations, the firm's marginal tax rate is affected by the very decisions that the firm undertakes to alter its investment and financing activities. For example, if the firm buys bonds with the proceeds of a preferred stock issue, the additional taxable cash flows generated from the bond interest income can affect the computation of the marginal tax rate. If clientele-based arbitrage activities do alter a firm's marginal tax rate, it cannot rely on its initial calculation to make an optimal decision. It is what we mean when we say that the computation of the marginal tax rate is **strategy-dependent.** Strategy dependence increases the complexity of tax planning.

We have already illustrated the concept of strategy dependence in Chapter 5 where we showed that a taxpayer subject to a progressive tax would wish to engage in certain clientele-based arbitrage transactions only in limited volume. The reason is that as the transactions alter the investor's marginal tax rate, the attractiveness of further transactions decreases.

The strategy dependence of marginal tax rates also hampers researchers and others in their examination of the role of taxes in firms' investment and financing decisions. For example, theory predicts that high tax firms will use debt to lower their tax bills, or that high tax firms should exhibit higher debt levels. By increasing debt, however, firms increase their interest deduction and lower their marginal tax rate. Thus, in equilibrium, all firms may appear to face similar marginal tax rates. If so, tests can fail to detect a relation between ex post debt levels and ex post marginal tax rates when, in fact, high-tax firms increased their debt levels to garner the tax shield offered by debt. Two solutions address this problem. First, instead of examining debt levels, the researcher can examine the role of taxes in new debt issuances. Both Mackie-Mason (1990) and Graham (1996a) illustrate how a "debt changes" (rather than "debt levels") approach allows a more powerful test of the role of taxes in corporate capital structure decisions. Second, use marginal tax rates (and, where necessary, other variables) estimated on a but-for approach (also referred to as pre- or as-if measures). An example of this approach is Graham, Lemmon, and Schallheim (1998) in which they show that debt levels and the usual after-financing tax rates are negatively correlated but that debt levels and before-financing tax rates—but-for marginal tax rates—are positively associated as predicted by theory.

A second relevant problem plaguing the study of debt levels, as well as other firm choices, is that a firm's capital structure reflects past decisions that were based on expectations that may not have been fulfilled because of unexpected outcomes, such as a change in product markets, competition, the economy, or tax policy. Thus, even if decisions were tax-motivated when undertaken, in subsequent periods these decisions may appear contrary to predicted tax responses. Because it is costly to restructure capital, cross-section studies of debt levels may erroneously conclude that taxes do not affect capital structure decisions. In other words, firms may not immediately or quickly restructure their economic balance sheets because of recontracting costs when their tax status changes unexpectedly. Thus, cross-sectional tests of debt levels can fail to find a tax effect when it actually exists.

Unanticipated changes in tax rules and tax status should be viewed as the rule rather than the exception for most taxpayers. It is important to factor such uncertainty into the tax planning process and to be prepared to plan your way out of undesired clienteles as the uncertainty is resolved. Our objective is to provide you with tools necessary to approach this task in a systematic and rational fashion.

Summary of Key Points

1. To calculate the marginal tax cost of a dollar of fully taxable income requires that the effect on the value of future period tax liabilities be included. One must also include the effects of additional income on the availability of tax deductions and tax credits.
2. Effective tax rates are commonly used to determine the average rate of tax paid by taxpayers. Two popular definitions exist, both of which fail to include implicit taxes and a proper adjustment for the present value of future taxes to be paid.

3. Properly adjusted to include implicit taxes and the present value of deferred taxes, average tax rates allow comparisons across taxpayers of tax burdens per dollar of income. But such tax rates provide little guidance for identifying tax clienteles.

4. For a given configuration of risk-adjusted pretax rates of return on various assets, marginal tax rates sort taxpayers into investment and financing clienteles. Clientele-based arbitrage exploits differences in the total (explicit plus implicit) marginal tax rate that applies to income from different assets. The result of undertaking clientele-based arbitrage is typically to reduce the total marginal tax rate.

5. When statutory tax rates are constant over time, firms that experience net operating loss carryforwards (NOLs) typically face lower marginal tax rates than those that do not. In the presence of NOLs and other carryforwards, the current marginal tax rate is sensitive to future changes in statutory tax rates.

6. As marginal tax rates change over time, so do investment and financing clienteles. Because it is costly to change investment and financing clienteles as tax status changes, taxpayers place a premium on strategies that allow activities to be reorganized at low cost.

7. Contractual arrangements that can be voided when specified tax-related contingencies occur introduce an element of reversibility into tax plans.

8. Adaptive tax planning is designed to offset the cost of being in the wrong clientele following unexpected changes in tax status where reversibility is impossible or impractical.

9. In the presence of transaction costs to change investment and financing clienteles, taxpayers need to know more than simply the expected marginal tax rates to choose efficient tax planning strategies. For example, it is important to know the probability distribution of tax rates as well as the costs of changing investment and financing strategies in the event that changes in tax rates cause investors to be in the wrong clientele.

10. How the taxing authority and the courts will interpret the tax laws, future legislative changes in the tax laws, and what the exact amount of future income will turn out to be represent sources of possible change in tax status that may place taxpayers into undesirable investment and financing clienteles.

11. Tax treatment uncertainty can be mitigated by requiring an advance ruling from the taxing authority on how a proposed transaction will be treated for tax purposes.

12. Professional legal opinions can also reduce tax treatment uncertainty. Such opinions are often published for the benefit of third parties who rely on representations made regarding favorable tax treatment of particular contractual arrangements.

13. In many contracts, one party explicitly indemnifies other parties against tax treatment that turns out to be less favorable than that promised. Such provisions are designed to reduce the costs of contracting.

14. A taxpayer's marginal tax rate is often affected by the very investment and financing strategies implemented to take advantage of its initial tax status. This adds an element of "recursion" to tax planning. We refer to marginal tax rates in this case as being strategy-dependent. Thus in realistic settings it is rather challenging to calculate the marginal tax rate.

Appendix 7.1[15]

MEDICAL SAVINGS PLANS AND DYNAMIC TAX PLANNING

To close our discussion of dynamic tax planning and make a link to our first "applications" chapter, which is on compensation planning, we consider a tax planning problem relating to medical expense reimbursement plans. In the United States, medical expenses, including insurance premiums, are tax deductible only to the extent they exceed 7.5% of adjusted gross income. This, if your salary plus other income were equal to $100,000, you could not normally deduct the first $7,500 in health care costs. If your employer establishes a qualified plan, however, you can have part of your salary paid into a medical reimbursement plan. The salary you contribute into the plan will not be taxed to you. And the reimbursements you receive for medical expenses will not be taxable. The end result is that you obtain tax deductions for your medical expenses.

This plan has a hitch. You must decide at the beginning of the year how much to contribute to the plan. Any excess of contributions over reimbursements for the year is nonrefundable. Instead, the excess goes to cover administrative costs of the plan.

Suppose your tax rate is 30%. Let C denote your contributions into the plan, and let M denote your medical expenses for the year, which are uncertain at the beginning of the year. If you set C too low (below M), you sacrifice 30 cents worth of tax benefits for each dollar of unfunded medical expenses. Why? You lose a tax deduction of $M - C$ dollars. If you set C too high (above M), you will lose the excess at an after-tax cost of 70 cents for each dollar of excess funding. This is a "newsboy problem": If you underfund (you "stock out" of inventory), you lose 30 cents per dollar of underfunding; if you overfund (you have excess perishable inventory that must be scrapped), you lose 70 cents per dollar of overfunding. The optimal amount of funding is some amount *below* your best guess of medical costs because overfunding costs more than underfunding.

How does this problem tie to dynamic tax planning? On the adaptability dimension, if your demand for medical services falls below your funding level, you may be able to accelerate routine checkups or medical treatments that would normally be undertaken the following year; or you might try to arrange to prepay for next year's medical insurance. As for reversibility, if you plan taxes cooperatively with your employer, then your employer could agree to supplement your salary in the event your medical expenses fall well below funding levels. In this case, you might be inclined to fund substantially more than in the case in which all overfunded amounts are forfeited to the plan. Of course, the tax planning advantages of these arrangements must be balanced against the administrative costs of implementing them.

---

[15]This section was stimulated by a problem developed by Evan Porteus for a decision sciences course taught in the Stanford MBA program.

Discussion Questions

1. True or False? Explain.
   a. In undertaking tax planning strategies, the effective tax rate has no meaning.
   b. In calculating marginal tax rates for the purpose of determining investment and financing clienteles, it is appropriate to ignore deferred taxes.
   c. By borrowing, taxpayers can always reduce their personal tax rate on partnership income to the implicit tax rate on municipal bonds.
   d. The marginal tax rate of firms with net operating loss carryforwards (NOLs) is below that of firms currently paying tax by a discount factor reflecting the delay in when the NOL firm is expected to begin paying taxes.
2. How is the marginal tax rate affected by the presence of rules that reduce current tax deductions by a fraction of incremental income? How is the marginal tax rate affected by the presence of rules that postpone current tax deductions or tax credits by a fraction of incremental income?
3. What alternative investment and financing instruments can firms use to alter their marginal tax rate? Why might the firm prefer to repackage its capital structure (the mix of financial instruments it issues to finance operations) instead of changing its operating decisions to effect clientele-based arbitrage?
4. How difficult is it in reality to compute the corporation's marginal tax rate? Why? What are the factors that are really important? If we observe that a firm has net operating losses, does this mean that the firm has not hired a very smart tax planning strategist?
5. What does it mean for a tax plan to be reversible? Give some examples to illustrate this concept. What costs are associated with contractual provisions that make tax plans reversible?
6. What is the meaning of the term *adaptability of tax plans?* Give some examples to illustrate the concept. What are the costs of undertaking such plans?
7. Why might a firm offer insurance against adverse changes in tax status? Do you see a great deal of this form of insurance? Why or why not?
8. Why might the taxing authority agree to provide advance rulings on the tax treatment of proposed transactions? Why might it refuse to make rulings in some cases?
9. Why would a taxpayer be willing to pay a lawyer to provide a written opinion to a third party of the tax treatment to be accorded a particular set of transactions?
10. What is meant by the term *strategy dependence* as it relates to the computation of the marginal tax rate? How does strategy dependence affect the computation of the marginal tax rate? How does it affect decision-making strategies?

Exercises

1. Suppose a firm is equally likely to earn $2 million this year or lose $3 million. The firm faces a tax rate of 40% on each dollar of taxable income, and the firm pays no taxes on losses. In this simple one-period scenario, ignore the carryback and carryforward rules. The firm's expected taxable income is thus a loss of $500,000 calculated as .50(−$3) + .50($2). What is the firm's expected marginal tax rate?

   Suppose a second firm is equally likely to earn $3 million this year or lose $2 million. This firm also faces a tax rate of 40% on each dollar of taxable income (and the firm pays no taxes on losses). Again in this simple one-period scenario, ignore the carryback and carryforward rules. The firm's expected taxable income is thus a profit of $500,000 calculated as .50($3) + .50(−$2). What is the firm's expected marginal tax rate?

   Explain and discuss your results. Why is the first firm's marginal tax rate not 0%? Why is the second firm's marginal tax rate not 40%?

2. Suppose a firm has a tax loss of $5 million in the current period. The firm's after-tax discount rate is 10%. Over the preceding 5 years the firm has reported the following taxable income:

Year	−5	−4	−3	−2	−1	Current
Taxable income ($ millions)	$1	$1	$1.5	$3	$3	−$5
Statutory tax rate	40%	40%	35%	35%	30%	30%

a. If the carryback period is 3 years, what is the firm's marginal explicit tax rate in the current period?
b. If the carryback period is 2 years, what is the firm's marginal explicit tax rate in the current period?
c. Suppose the carryback period is 2 years and taxable income in period −1 was only $1 million. What is the firm's marginal explicit tax rate in the current period?

3. Suppose a firm has a tax loss in the current period of $10 million, which when added to prior tax losses gives it an NOL carryforward of $15 million. The top statutory tax rate for the foreseeable future is 35%. Assume an after-tax discount rate of 10% and future taxable income per annum of $2 million.
a. What is the firm's marginal explicit tax rate?
b. What is the firm's marginal explicit tax rate if the top statutory tax rate is expected to increase to 40% within the next 2 years?

4. Find the annual report for some publicly listed high technology company in your local area that has losses. Refer to the tax footnote in the report to extract the NOL carryforward. Assume an after-tax discount rate of 10%. Calculate the firm's marginal explicit tax rate using the Manzon (1994) market value approach. For those wishing to use Amazon.com data, Amazon reported an NOL carryforward as of December 31, 2002, of $2.5 billion. Discuss and explain your result.

5. Consider the illustration in Section 7.3 where you are choosing between two investments, fully taxable bonds yielding 10% pretax per year and tax-exempt bonds yielding 7% per year. Both investments have 3-year maturities. At the time of investment, you are unsure—because of the uncertain profitability of your other investments already in place—as to whether your tax rate will be 40% over the 3 years or 0%. You assess a 70% chance of the former. This makes your expected marginal tax rate 28% or .7 × 40% + .3 × 0%. If you are risk-neutral and if you must choose one investment or the other and hold it for the entire 3-year period, you would be better off choosing taxable bonds. At an expected tax rate of 28%, taxable bonds yield 7.2% after tax, while tax-exempt bonds yield only 7%.

   Now let us consider what your optimal strategy would be if you could sell your asset and purchase the other at the end of the first year. At the end of the first year you will find out whether your tax rate for the next 2 years (as well as for the year just ended) will be 40% or 0%. At the end of the subsection, it is stated, "We leave it as an exercise for the reader to verify that in the absence of transaction costs, *taxable bonds* would be the investment of choice in the first period. Over the 3-year period, they would yield 7.7% per year after tax, versus 7.6% for tax-exempt bonds."

   Show that this statement is correct.

6. Consider the illustration in Section 7.3 where an investment choice was being made between taxable and tax-exempt bonds in the presence of tax rate uncertainty and transaction costs.
a. Would you prefer to invest in 3-year taxable bonds or 3-year tax-exempt bonds yielding 10% and 7% pretax, respectively, if the annualized cost to switch from taxable to tax-exempt bonds, or vice versa, at the end of year 1 were 3% rather than 1%?

b. If instead of 3-year bonds that yield 10% per year (taxable) and 7% per year (tax-exempt), you could buy 1-year bonds at yields of 9.75% for taxables and 6.83% for tax-exempts, would you do so? Because they are 1-year bonds there are no switching costs.

Tax Planning Problems

1. Suppose a firm has a tax loss in the current period of $10 million, which when added to prior tax losses gives it an NOL carryforward of $15 million. The current top statutory tax rate is 35% but is expected to increase to 45% in 2 years. Assume an after-tax discount rate of 10% and future taxable income per annum of $2 million. The firm has a large NOL carryforward. Should the firm undertake clientele-based arbitrage by issuing preferred stock and buying corporate bonds?

2. Your colleague picks up the 2002 annual report of The Boeing Company and finds that Boeing reports an effective tax rate of 27.1% for fiscal year 2002. He argues that Boeing thus faces a low tax rate. It should not have much long-term debt in its capital structure, your colleague maintains, and it should have issued preferred stock, invested idle cash in taxable bonds, and should be leasing assets. Evaluate your colleague's argument.

3. A currently profitable bricks-and-mortar retail firm (for example, Barnes and Noble) is under attack from several Internet start-up firms. The top management has decided to join the Web competition and open up an Internet store. Given the strong competition and price-cutting by the up-start Internet firms, the future profitability of the firm is uncertain. Given this doubt, the firm's CFO is concerned about the firm being in the wrong investment and financing clientele. She has asked you to prepare a memo outlining possible actions, together with your recommendations, that the firm might take to reduce the expected costs of finding itself being in the wrong clientele. She has asked that any assumptions you make be made explicit.

4. An electric utility company recently issued $25 million of mandatory redeemable preferred stock that is redeemable in 10 years. In its audit, the IRS wishes to classify the preferred stock as debt. This reclassification would mean that the dividends on the preferred stock would be reclassified as interest expense and thus would be tax deductible. The CFO is ecstatic because this will reduce the firm's tax bill. However, he did not rise to the CFO position simply by luck and has asked you to prepare a memo explaining the pros and cons of such a reclassification. You should note that the top managers of the utility are paid a sizable bonus each year based on the firm's earnings, that the company is planning to raise additional capital to fund expensive plant construction, and that the firm's profitability is unchanged since it issued the preferred stock.

5. Suppose you operate a very profitable sole proprietorship (keep dreaming). Your current-year marginal tax rate is 40%, but you expect it to increase to 50% next year due to legislative changes.

    Your business includes exclusive rights to distribute microcomputer software packages in specified geographical areas. Your typical gross margin on software sales for the programs distributed is an impressive 50%.

    The end of the year is approaching, and you wonder whether a special price reduction to promote sales in the current tax year would be desirable. You assess that a 10% across-the-board price reduction for the remainder of the year will generate $400,000 of new sales, but $800,000 of normal sales for the rest of the year will be made at a 10% discount.

    Moreover, $1,000,000 of next year's sales will be cannibalized. That is, a 10% price cut will result in $1,000,000 of next year's product line being sold this year for

$900,000, and $800,000 of normal sales for the rest of this year will yield only $720,000 in revenues, but you will also pick up $400,000 in new sales this year.

    a. How much better or worse off would you be *before and after tax* if you employ the year-end sales strategy and it goes according to plan?

       Your customers fall roughly into three categories: corporations whose tax rates typically will not change from this year to next year; individuals who are not entitled to tax deductions for the purchase of your software; and small businesses, many of whom face tax rate increases similar to yours. Assume such businesses take tax deductions for the purchase of software in the year the software is acquired.

    b. How are these customers likely to respond differently to the temporary price-cut?

6. When evaluating new projects and investments, the ABC Corporation calculates after-tax cash flows and earnings assuming the firm's marginal tax rate equals the top federal statutory tax rate of 35%. The firm is a large multinational with operations in many foreign countries as well as many states in the United States.

    a. Under what future profitability conditions is it advisable for the ABC Corporation to use the statutory tax rate in its project evaluations?

    b. What problems might arise by ignoring foreign, state, and local taxes in these project evaluations?

    c. The firm's financial accountant calculates the company's effective tax rate is 25% and argues that the firm should be using this rate in its project evaluations. Do you agree?

       Suppose the ABC Corporation, due to the Asian economic crash and Internet-based competition, faces some uncertainty about its future profitability.

    d. What effect might this uncertainty have on the firm's marginal tax rate?

    e. Given this uncertainty, the firm's CFO, who is concerned about the firm being in the wrong investment and financing clientele, asks you to prepare a memo outlining possible actions, together with your recommendations, that the firm might take to reduce the expected costs of finding itself being in the wrong clientele. She asks that any assumptions you make be made explicit.

References and Additional Readings

Graham, J., 1996a. "Debt and the Marginal Tax Rate," *Journal of Financial Economics* (May), pp. 41–74.

Graham, J., 1996b. "Proxies for the Marginal Tax Rate," *Journal of Financial Economics* (October), pp. 187–221.

Graham, J., M. Lang, and D. Shackelford, 2004. "Employee Stock Options, Corporate Taxes and Debt Policy," *Journal of Finance,* forthcoming.

Graham, J., and M. Lemmon, 1998. "Measuring Corporate Tax Rates and Tax Rate Incentives: A New Approach," *Journal of Applied Corporate Finance* (Spring), pp. 54–65.

Graham, J., M. Lemmon, and J. Schallheim, 1998. "Debt, Leases, Taxes, and the Endogeneity of Corporate Tax Status," *Journal of Finance* (1), pp. 131–162.

Hanlon, M., and T. Shevlin, 2002. "Accounting for Tax Benefits of Employee Stock Options and Implications for Research," *Accounting Horizons* (March), pp. 1–16.

Hulse, D., 2003. "Embedded Options and Tax Decisions: A Reconsideration of the Traditional vs. Roth IRA Decision," *Journal of the American Taxation Association* (Spring), pp. 39–52.

Mackie-Mason, J., 1990. "Do Taxes Affect Corporate Financing Decisions," *Journal of Finance* (December), pp. 1471–1493.

Manzon, G., Jr., 1994. "The Role of Taxes in Early Debt Retirement," *Journal of the American Taxation Association* (Spring), pp. 87–100.

Plesko, G., 2003. "An Evaluation of Alternative Measures of Corporate Tax Rates," *Journal of Accounting and Economics,* pp. 201–226.

Shevlin, T., 1990. "Estimating Corporate Marginal Tax Rates," *Journal of the American Taxation Association* (Spring), pp. 51–67.

CHAPTER

8

COMPENSATION PLANNING

After completing this chapter, you should be able to:

1. Enumerate the factors relevant to determine whether current salary or deferred compensation is tax-preferred.

2. Determine when reimbursement of business meals and entertainment is tax-preferred to salary.

3. Outline when demand loans are useful tax planning tools.

4. Describe the taxation of restricted stock, incentive stock options (ISOs), and nonqualified stock options (NQOs).

5. Determine when ISOs are tax-preferred over NQOs.

6. Decide when restricted stock and employee stock options might be exercised early for tax reasons.

7. Discuss the implications of §162(m) for compensation design.

Up to this point in the book, we have been developing the basic framework of effective tax planning in a global environment. We now turn to applications of the framework in specific topics. In this chapter, we discuss the tax planning aspects of employee compensation planning. As in many of the applications chapters, the two themes that we stress are (1) the importance of considering all parties to a contract and (2) the nontax features of the tax planning alternatives. To begin, Table 8.1 lists some categories of compensation, along with their tax treatment to both the employee and the employer.

Many compensation experts (including those who contribute to the popular press and tax journals) have concluded that the compensation alternatives listed in Table 8.1 are ordered in terms of decreasing desirability. In fact, however, once a global contracting perspective is adopted—one that takes account of both tax and nontax considerations of both the employer and employee—none of the compensation alternatives listed in Table 8.1 can be ranked unambiguously. We illustrate the importance of the global contracting perspective by comparing some of the alternative compensation components listed in the table.

TABLE 8.1 Compensation Alternatives		
Category	*Employee Tax Effects*	*Employer Tax Effects*
Nontaxable fringe benefits	Never taxed	Immediately deductible
Pensions	Deferred tax with tax exemption on investment returns	Immediately deductible
Incentive stock options (ISOs)	Deferred tax at capital gains rates	Never deductible
Deferred compensation	Deferred tax at ordinary rates	Deferred deduction
Restricted stock	Deferred tax at ordinary rates	Deferred deduction
Nonqualified stock options (NQOs)	Deferred tax at ordinary rates	Deferred deduction
Stock appreciation rights (SARs)	Deferred tax at ordinary rates	Deferred deduction
Interest-free demand loans	Deferred tax at ordinary rates	Deferred deduction
Interest-free term loans	Immediately taxed at ordinary rates	Immediately deductible
Cash salary	Immediately taxed at ordinary rates	Immediately deductible*
Cash bonus	Immediately taxed at ordinary rates	Immediately deductible*

*Cash salary and bonus are deductible by the corporation provided that the §162(m) limitation is met.

8.1 SALARY VERSUS DEFERRED COMPENSATION

Let us start by considering a **deferred compensation contract** between an employer and an employee. An employee can arrange to save for future consumption by agreeing to defer the receipt of current compensation until some future date. As we will see, whether this deferment is desirable purely from a tax standpoint, ignoring incentive considerations for now, depends on both the employee's and the employer's current and future tax rates as well as on the opportunities each has to invest idle funds in the marketplace.

The specific question we now wish to consider is whether to offer an employee salary paid today or a deferred compensation contract that promises to pay a stipulated amount at time period n. To see whether current salary or deferred compensation is preferred, we must avoid comparing apples and oranges. A convenient way to proceed is to determine the deferred compensation amount or bonus that leaves either the employer or the employee indifferent between the two plans and then see which of the plans is preferred by the other party to the contract. This will identify the mutually preferred contract. Through negotiations, both parties can be made better off by sharing the gains from tax planning.

For example, how much can an employer afford to provide to an employee in n periods as a deferred compensation payment in exchange for not paying $100 of salary to the employee today? If compensation is deferred, so is the timing of the tax deduction to the employer and the timing of taxable income to the employee. Note that by not paying $100 of salary today, the employer saves only $100(1 - t_{c0})$ dollars after tax, where t_{c0} is the employer's marginal tax rate today.[1] In n years, the after-tax savings to the employer from salary deferral wold accumulate to $100(1 - t_{c0})(1 + r_{cn})^n$, where r_{cn}

---

[1]Although t_{c0} might be thought of as the current corporate tax rate, the employer need not be a corporation for the following analysis to apply.

is the employer's annualized after-tax rate of investment return on marginal investments made for a period of n years. It is the rate of return that the employer can achieve with the after-tax cash saved from deferring the salary payment to the employee.

When the deferred compensation payment is made at time n (in the amount of D_n), the employer receives a tax deduction, so the after-tax cost of the payment becomes $D_n(1 - t_{cn})$, where t_{cn} is the employer's marginal tax rate in year n. To be indifferent between current salary and a deferred payment, the employer must be able to set aside $100(1 - t_{c0})$ now to satisfy its future deferred compensation obligation: After-tax deferred compensation payment at time n is equal to what the $100(1 - t_{c0})$ after-tax dollars saved by not paying current salary would accumulate to if invested for n periods. That is:

$$D_n(1 - t_{cn}) = \$100(1 - t_{c0})(1 + r_{cn})^n$$

or

$$D_n = \$100(1 + r_{cn})^n \frac{(1 - t_{c0})}{(1 - t_{cn})} \tag{8.1}$$

If the employer's tax rate is constant over time ($t_{c0} = t_{cn}$), the employer can afford to pay its own after-tax rate of return on the $100 of salary as deferred compensation. If the tax rate is increasing, however, the employer can afford to pay an even larger amount of deferred compensation in the future because future deductions are more valuable. Conversely, if the tax rate is decreasing, the employer can afford to pay less than the after-tax rate of return on the savings.

Suppose that the after-tax corporate rate of return on investment is 6%, and tax rates are constant across time. The employer is contemplating a 5-year ($n = 5$) deferred compensation contract. That is, rather than paying $1 of salary currently, the employer is considering a deferred compensation payment to be made in 5 years. If the employer's tax rate were constant, the employer could afford to offer a deferred payment of

$$(1 + .06)^5 = \$1.34$$

How much more or less can the employer afford if its tax rate changes over time? The answer appears in Table 8.2. The differences can be significant. For example, if the employer's current tax rate is 50% and it will be 30% in 5 years, Table 8.2 indicates that the employer can afford a deferred compensation payment of only 96 cents in 5 years

TABLE 8.2	Deferred Compensation: Sensitivity to Changes in Tax Rates over Time		
t_{c0}	*30%*	*40%*	*50%*
t_{cn}			
30%	1.34	1.15	.96
40%	1.56	1.34	1.12
50%	1.87	1.61	1.34

Assumes 5-year deferral period and an after-tax investment return of 6% per year.
t_{c0}, t_{cn} = employer's current and future marginal tax rates, respectively.
Body of table reports deferred compensation amounts that have the same after-tax cost to the employer as a dollar of immediate salary.

for each dollar of current salary deferred. However, if the employer's tax rate increases from 30% to 40%, the employer can afford a deferred payment equal to $1.56 for each dollar of current salary postponed for 5 years.

Now that the employer is indifferent between a salary and a deferred compensation contract, let us turn to the employee. What contract does the employee prefer? The employee must compare salary today versus a deferred compensation payment *n* periods from today. That is,

$$\text{Salary} = \$100(1 - t_{p0})(1 + r_{pn})^n$$

$$\text{Deferred compensation} = D_n(1 - t_{pn})$$

and substituting for D_n from equation (8.1)

$$= \$100(1 + r_{cn})^n \frac{(1 - t_{c0})}{(1 - t_{cn})}(1 - t_{pn})$$

The employee will prefer whichever contract provides more after-tax dollars in *n* years. A little algebra shows that salary will be preferred to deferred compensation if and only if:

$$\frac{(1 - t_{p0})(1 + r_{pn})^n}{(1 - t_{pn})(1 + r_{cn})^n} > \frac{(1 - t_{c0})}{(1 - t_{cn})} \tag{8.2}$$

The left-hand side of the equation is the ratio of the after-tax accumulation to the employee of taking current salary to the after-tax accumulation to the employee of deferred compensation. The right-hand side is the ratio of the corporation's current and future tax rates.

In this relation, three key factors combine to determine precisely whether salary or deferred compensation is preferable.

1. The employee's tax rate today versus her tax rate *n* periods from today. If the employee's tax rate is declining, then deferred compensation tends to be preferable because the income is recognized when the employee's tax rate is low.
2. The employer's tax rate today versus its tax rate *n* periods from today. If the employer's tax rate is increasing, then deferred compensation tends to be preferable because the employer prefers to take the deduction when tax rates are high.
3. The after-tax rate of return on investment for the employer versus that of the employee. If the employer can save at a higher after-tax rate of return than can the employee, then deferred compensation tends to be preferable. In effect, a deferred compensation contract allows the employee to save at the employer's higher rate of return on investment.

Because deferred compensation is favored if the employee's tax rate is expected to *decrease* in the future, deferral may be especially appropriate for employees who expect to face a lower tax rate in retirement or for employees on temporary assignment in a high-tax-rate foreign country.[2] Deferred compensation arrangements may

---

[2] Some tax jurisdictions do not permit the deferral of taxable income through the adoption of deferred compensation arrangements. It is an example of a tax-rule restriction.

also be desirable when tax rates are expected to decrease due to statutory changes in tax rates voted by the legislature. Here, however, one must be careful not to adopt a unilateral tax planning perspective. A decline in tax rates for the employee need not favor deferred compensation if tax rates also decline for the employer. We will take a closer look at this common phenomenon.

Because deferred compensation is favored if the employer's tax rate is expected to increase in the future, deferral may be especially appropriate when a firm in a NOL carryforward position cannot effectively use current tax deductions. Deferring compensation increases current taxable income but reduces future taxable income. This smoothing of taxable income is tax-advantageous for firms experiencing NOL carryforwards.

For the employer with an opportunity to earn at a greater after-tax rate of return than its employees, saving through the corporation by way of a deferred compensation contract is tax-advantageous. To see this, assume that $r_{pn} = 6\%$ and $r_{cn} = 8\%$. Then, after tax, deferred compensation beats salary by a factor of

$$(1.08/1.06)^n - 1 = 1.9\% \quad \text{for } n = 1 \text{ year}$$
$$9.8\% \quad \text{for } n = 5 \text{ years}$$
$$20.1\% \quad \text{for } n = 10 \text{ years}$$

Even though this difference may not be as striking as changing tax brackets, it is still worth considering. However, we do not want to overemphasize the importance of differences in after-tax earnings opportunities that are available to the employer and the employee. If the difference was large, employers presumably would borrow money from employees and invest it until the difference largely disappears. In other words, deferred compensation arrangements do not represent a unique means of exploiting differences in after-tax investment opportunities of employers and employees. The same is true of changing tax brackets over time. As we will see, many substitutes for deferred compensation contracts allow the shifting of taxable income across time periods.

Employer and Employee Tax Rates Both Expected to Fall

We can use equation (8.2) to examine the case when both the employer and employee expect their tax rates to fall in the future. Salary can be tax-preferred to deferred compensation even when the employee's tax rate is decreasing over time. For example, the tax rate of many nonmanagement employees dropped from the 25% vicinity to 15% with the passage of the 1986 Tax Act. A deferral of compensation might seem quite desirable under such circumstances. After all, it enables employees to reduce tax payments by 40% per dollar of compensation received (from $.25 to only $.15). Yet in most businesses, salary was tax-preferred in such circumstances. Why? Because the employer's preference for an immediate tax deduction was even stronger than the employee's preference for deferred taxation.

Consider a corporate employer facing a 46% tax rate in 1986 and a 34% tax rate in 1988. For each $100 of salary deferred from 1986, the employer could afford to pay only $D_n = \$82$, or $\$100(1 - .46)/(1 - .34)$, in compensation in 1988, plus after-tax earnings on investment for 2 years. Each compensation alternative had a present cost to the employer of $54 after tax. To the employee taxed at a rate of 25%, the $100 salary was worth $75 after tax. Even at the 15% tax rate in 1988, however, the $82 in deferred compensation, plus interest for 2 years, had a present value of only $82(1 - .15) or $70 to the employee. So, despite the employee's drop in tax rate, salary was tax-preferred relative to deferred compensation. If the deferred compensation payment was set at the level that made the employer indifferent between salary and deferred compensation, salary would have provided the employee with 75/70, or in excess of 7%, more in after-tax compensation than would deferred compensation.

For more highly paid employees that faced a 50% marginal tax rate in 1986 and a 28% rate in 1988, deferred compensation was the superior arrangement from a tax standpoint: $100 of salary in 1986 was worth $50 after tax, and the $82 in compensation, deferred until 1988, was worth $59 after tax or $82(1 − .28). This amount is 18% more than current salary.

To go one step further, suppose the employer is a tax-exempt entity, like a university, a municipality, or a charitable foundation. Such entities could have afforded to pay $100 plus after-tax earnings for 2 years for each dollar of compensation deferred from 1986 to 1988. Even if the employee could earn the same after-tax return as the tax-exempt employer, a highly compensated employee in this circumstance would keep $100(1 − .28), or $72 after tax on the dollar received in 1988, which is 44% more than the $50 retained on salary received in 1986. Moreover, the employee is unlikely to be able to earn as high an after-tax return as can the tax-exempt employer, thereby providing an additional benefit of compensation deferral. Despite the substantial tax savings, most of these organizations failed to establish compensation deferral programs. Unless the nontax costs of entering into deferred compensation arrangements were extremely high, substantial tax savings were left "lying on the table."

In this section we have emphasized the effects of changes in tax rates and differences in investment opportunities on the preferences of employers and employees for current or deferred compensation contracts. Whether deferred compensation contracts are desirable also depends on incentive contracts between employees and employers as discussed in Chapter 6, as well as on uncertainty regarding the employee's and employer's future tax rates and income levels.

8.2 SALARY VERSUS FRINGE BENEFITS

Now that we have illustrated the importance of considering the tax implications of compensation plans to all of the contracting parties, let us consider some of the other compensation alternatives. Let us begin with **fringe benefits** such as employer-provided term life insurance or business meals. Whether fringe benefits are preferred to salary depends on two factors:

1. Whether employees can deduct, on their own tax returns, the cost of fringes they pay for themselves
2. The extent to which employees place personal value on employer-provided fringes relative to their cost to the employer

To illustrate the importance of these two factors, let us consider the following cases.

EXAMPLE 1:
Suppose the employer contemplates paying $1,400 for group term life insurance and group health insurance in lieu of $1,400 in additional salary.

Because the employer receives a $1,400 tax deduction whether the expenditure is for salary or insurance, the employer is indifferent between the two alternatives. Suppose the employee is in a 30% tax bracket. Although $1,400 in salary gives rise to $980 in cash after tax, the fringe benefits are nontaxable, so the employee keeps $1,400 worth of benefits after tax. If, however, the employee were to purchase the fringes directly and could not take a tax deduction for their cost, $2,000 of salary would be required to buy the same benefits:[3]

$$\$2,000(1 - .30) = \$1,400$$

One problem here is that if these benefits are to qualify for tax-favored treatment, they must be offered on a nondiscriminatory basis to essentially all employees. Unlike cash salary, fringe benefits such as life and health insurance cannot be traded for other commodities easily. To some employees, the personal value of the benefits could be less than $980, or $1,400(1 − .30), the after-tax value of the salary alternative. For example, although costly to the employer, some employees with absolutely no bequest motive find life insurance to be a worthless benefit. For such employees, salary is a more efficient compensation component despite the tax-favored treatment accorded these benefits. A related problem arises when a wife and husband receive redundant benefits from their respective employers, such as health insurance that covers the entire family.[4]

EXAMPLE 2:
Employer reimbursement of business meals and entertainment expense.
    Assume an employee incurs expenses of $5,000 for business meals and entertainment for the year. If the employee is reimbursed for these expenses, the reimbursement is nontaxable and no expense deduction is allowed to the employee. If, however, the employer provides a salary supplement, the payment is taxable but the employee is eligible for a tax deduction.

Under the current tax rules, an employee's business meals and entertainment

1. are deductible only as miscellaneous itemized deductions, and
2. are deductible only to 50% of the expenditure.
3. Moreover, miscellaneous itemized deductions are deductible from taxable income only to the extent they exceed 2% of adjusted gross

---

[3]Part or all of the health insurance premiums may be tax deductible for some employees. An itemized deduction for medical expenses, which includes insurance costs, is currently permitted in the United States to the extent they exceed 7.5% of adjusted gross income. In addition, part of the life insurance premium paid by the employer may be taxable to the employee.

    Recall from Chapter 1 that adjusted gross income is defined as follows: Total income less exempt income (for example, municipal bond interest income) equals gross income. Gross income less deductions for adjusted gross income (such as business expenses other than those incurred as an employee) equals adjusted gross income. Adjusted gross income less the greater of the standard deduction and itemized deductions (including limited amounts of medical expenses, state and local income and property taxes, interest, charitable contributions, and miscellaneous itemized deductions) and personal exemptions equals taxable income. The tax on taxable income is equal to the preliminary tax from the statutory tax rate schedule less tax credits.

[4]For some employees, a "cafeteria plan," wherein employees can pick and choose among several fringe benefits, may help mitigate this problem.

income, which is taxable income plus itemized deductions plus personal exemptions.[5]

4. If the employer reimburses the employee, the employee reports no income or deductions, but the employer can deduct only 50% of the reimbursement.

Analysis for Taxable Employer

Suppose the employee faces a 30% marginal tax rate, has adjusted gross income of $100,000, and has other miscellaneous itemized deductions of $2,500. Assume that the employer's marginal tax rate is 40%. Should the employee be reimbursed or should the employer simply offer the employee a "bonus" or "salary supplement"?

A $5,000 reimbursement costs the employer:

$$\$5,000 - 40\%(50\% \times \$5,000) = \$4,000$$

The employer is indifferent between this reimbursement and a salary supplement of $4,000/(1 - .40) = $6,667. Both cost the employer $4,000 after tax. For the employee, the reimbursement leaves $5,000 after tax because the reimbursement is not taxed. The salary supplement, however, leaves the employee better off:

$$\$6,667 - 30\%[\$6,667 - 50\%(\$5,000) + 2\%(\$6,667)] = \$5,377,$$
or $377 more after tax

The salary supplement is fully taxable and the expenses are 50% deductible, but the additional adjusted gross income of $6,667 reduces allowable itemized deductions by 2%.[6]

Analysis for Tax-Exempt Employer

If the employer were a tax-exempt entity, reimbursement would always be the desirable strategy. The employer is indifferent between $5,000 in reimbursement and $5,000 in salary supplement. A $5,000 salary supplement leaves only

$$\$5,000 - 30\%[\$5,000 - 50\%(\$5,000) + 2\%(\$5,000)] = \$4,220$$
or $780 less than reimbursement after tax

Going one step further, if the other miscellaneous deductions of the employee of the tax-exempt entity had been only $500 rather than $2,500, the difference would have been even more dramatic. A $5,000 salary supplement would leave:

$$\$5,000 - 30\%[\$5,000 - 50\%(\$5,000) + \$1,500 + 2\%(\$5,000)] = \$3,770$$
or $1,230 less after tax

---

[5]In 1990, Congress introduced a phase-out for itemized deductions to limit the amount of itemized deductions for higher-income taxpayers. Taxpayers whose adjusted AGI exceeds a threshold amount ($139,500 in 2003, or $69,700 for married filing separately) must reduce the amount of allowable itemized deductions by 3% of the excess of AGI over the threshold amount. However, the amount of the reduction is limited to 80% of allowable itemized deductions. Further, deductible medical expenses, investment interest expense, casualty and theft losses, and gambling losses are excluded from the 3% reduction rule. We ignore the phase-out in our text examples.

[6]Our analysis here ignores social security (6.2%) and Medicare taxes (1.45%) on any salary payments. Both the employee and employer pay these taxes. The 6.2% social security tax is paid on all earnings up to a threshold ($87,000 in 2003), but no limit is placed on earnings subject to the Medicare tax. The interested reader can incorporate these taxes into the algebra.

Of course, nontax factors must be considered here as well. They include the administrative costs as well as the incentive effects of reimbursement plans. Reimbursement plans may encourage overspending, although the absence of such an arrangement may lead to underspending.

8.3 COMPENSATORY LOANS

To help key employees buy a home when moving to a new area, businesses frequently offer interest-free loans as part of their compensation package. Interest-free loans also may help key employees exercise stock options. The tax treatment depends on the type of interest-free loans, which come in one of two broad categories:

1. **Demand loans** are repayable on employer demand and may be made for a specified term if repayment is required on termination of employment.
2. **Term loans** are repayable at a specified future date, whether employed by the firm at that time or not.

Because they are more common and more interesting for tax planning purposes, we will concentrate on demand loans.[7] The tax implications of demand loans are as follows:

1. The employer realizes no tax deduction and the employee realizes no taxable income when the loan is made.
2. As time passes, the employer imputes compensation expense and the employee imputes compensation income equal to the applicable federal rate times the loan amount; the employer (employee) also imputes interest income (expensc) of cqual amount. In other words, we pretend, for tax purposes, that a loan is made at the applicable federal rate of interest and that the employer pays the employee additional salary equal to the interest on the loan.[8]

At first blush, it might appear that neither the employer nor the employee has any net tax deduction or taxable income: Imputed compensation is exactly offset by imputed interest. However, the employee can invest and earn interest on the proceeds of the loan. For example, suppose the applicable federal interest rate is 10%. At the beginning of the year, the employer makes a $50,000 interest-free loan to an employee for 1 year and reduces year-end salary by $5,000. The employee invests the proceeds of the loan at 10%, which results in the following:

$$\$50,000 \times 10\% = \$5,000 \qquad \text{Imputed compensation income}$$
$$(\$50,000 \times 10\%) = (\$5,000) \qquad \text{Imputed interest expense}$$
$$\$50,000 \times 10\% = \$5,000 \qquad \text{Actual interest income (and cash)}$$
$$\text{Net: } \$5,000 \text{ pretax cash, taxed as salary}$$

So a 1-year interest-free loan at the beginning of the year in exchange for a reduction in year-end salary is the equivalent of cash salary.

---

[7]Term loans give rise to immediate income taxation in an amount equal to the present value of the forgiven interest under the loan.

[8]The applicable federal rate is the federal short-term rate in effect under §1274(d) for the period for which the interest is being imputed.

But now let us alter the circumstances. Suppose that, at the beginning of the year, the employer and employee anticipate that their tax rates will remain constant over the next 2 years. Consequently, salary and deferred compensation are equally desirable, and, as a result, a salary contract is selected.

Suppose that towards the end of the year, it becomes apparent that the employer's tax rate in the following year will be higher and/or the employee's rate will be lower. One possible tax planning response is to reduce salary toward year-end and defer payment until the start of the next period. Another tax planning response is to reduce current salary toward year-end and provide an interest-free demand loan. This response will defer the income until the interest on the loan is earned with the passage of time. If a deferral of more than 1 year is desired, the loan can be made for a longer period of time, but then it must be made contingent on the continued employment of the employee. This arrangement can work fine if mutual trust characterizes the employer and employee relationship, but otherwise problems could arise.[9]

This way of using interest-free loans to defer income recognition is intriguing for two reasons:

1. The employee need not be an unsecured creditor of the employer, as is required with deferred compensation arrangements.
2. The arrangement can be used to respond to unexpected changes in tax rates that take place during the period, in other words, interest-free loans score high on the adaptability dimension.

8.4 CASH BONUS PLANS

Another compensation arrangement that may satisfy the demand for flexibility when tax rates change unexpectedly over time is a bonus plan, where the bonus is paid at year-end and the amount of bonus is at the discretion of the compensation committee of the board of directors rather than being set by a prespecified formula. With mutual trust between the employer and the employee, the bonuses can be timed strategically to coincide with high tax rates for the firm and low tax rates for the employee. Although such plans are extremely common in practice, they are probably used more for incentive reasons than for tax planning reasons. However, the Omnibus Budget Reconciliation Act of 1993 introduced an impediment, Section 162(m) discussed below, to using discretionary bonuses to shift income for large corporations.

As an example, Chrysler Corporation accelerated the timing of its 1990 incentive compensation payouts to managers. Such payments were typically made in January, but they were moved up a month because the 1990 Tax Act generated an increase in tax rates for most Chrysler executives, beginning January 1, 1991. The president of Chrysler indicated that the change in timing was made because "tax rates are higher next year" (*The Wall Street Journal,* December 24, 1990).

General Motors Corporation, by contrast, considered but rejected a proposal to make executive incentive payments in December of 1990 rather than January of 1991. Although the switch "would have cut taxes for GM's top-ranking executives, [it would]

---

[9]One of the requirements to get deferred compensation treatment is that the employer and employee sign an agreement before the beginning of the compensation period.

have increased the tax bite for managers further down the ladder" (*The Wall Street Journal,* February 8, 1991).

8.5 STOCK-BASED COMPENSATION COMPONENTS

Management compensation packages typically include one or more types of equity-based compensation components. The most common are **employee stock options (ESOs), stock appreciation rights (SARs),** and **restricted stock.**

Restricted Stock

Restricted stock grants are awards of stock to employees. Most grants restrict the employee from selling the stock until some future date, referred to here as the vesting date. Section 83 of the Tax Code details the tax treatment of restricted stock. Employees do not recognize taxable income until the vesting date, and hence we classify restricted stock as a form of deferred compensation. The amount of taxable income is the value of the stock on the vesting date.[10] The granting corporation receives a compensation tax deduction equal to the amount of income recognized by the employee.

However, under Section 83(b), recipients of restricted stock can elect to be taxed on the value of the grant at the grant date, hereafter referred to as a Section 83(b) election. Under a **Section 83(b) election,** the value of the restricted stock at grant date is taxed as ordinary income, and any subsequent price appreciation (or depreciation) is treated as capital gains (losses) qualifying for favorable long-term capital gains tax rates, provided the stock is held more than 12 months. When might an employee elect this treatment? An intuitive answer might be when the employee expects the stock price to increase dramatically between the grant and vesting date and thus believes it is desirable to convert this future price appreciation from ordinary income to capital gains via the Section 83(b) election. However a Section 83(b) election is a risky strategy—if the stock price declines after the election is made, the employee has paid taxes on a phantom gain (although the subsequent stock price declines give rise to future capital loss deductions). But if the employee is very confident that the stock price will increase over the vesting period, an alternative strategy that does better than the Section 83(b) election, is to purchase additional stock with the funds that would have been used to pay the taxes on the early election.[11] This strategy however is even riskier because the employee now owns even more stock. This additional risk compared to the do-nothing strategy is a nontax cost of the Section 83(b) election and its alternative of purchasing additional stock.

To show that a Section 83(b) election is dominated, from a purely tax viewpoint ignoring risk issues, by the alternative strategy of purchasing additional stock, we

---

[10]In some instances, the employee pays some small amount for the stock. We assume this amount is zero in our discussion.

[11]McDonald (2003) also arrives at this conclusion and shows the result more formally and provides a somewhat expanded analysis relative to that here. In certain unusual circumstances, such as the employee not being able to buy or sell stock on his personal account, a Section 83(b) election may be optimal. McDonald also shows that the election is even less desirable for dividend-paying stocks. We show below that a Section 83(b) election might be tax-favored if the employee expects to face a higher tax rate on ordinary income at the vesting date.

introduce the following notation:

P_0 is the stock price on the grant date,

P_1 is the stock price on the vesting date, when the stock is assumed to be sold,

t_p as previously, is the employee's marginal tax rate on ordinary income,

t_{cg} as previously, is the employee's marginal tax rate on, capital gains and

r is the after-tax borrowing rate of the employee.

If the employee holds the restricted stock through the vesting period and then sells the stock, the after-tax accumulation per share of restricted stock is simply

$$P_1(1 - t_p) \tag{8.3}$$

If the employee makes a Section 83(b) election the question arises as to what funds are used to pay the taxes at the grant date. A simple assumption is to assume the employee borrows the necessary amount to pay the taxes, $P_0 \times t_p$, at after-tax rate r.[12] The borrowing plus interest is repaid when the stock is sold at the subsequent vesting date. The after-tax accumulation from this strategy is

$$P_1 - (P_1 - P_0)t_{cg} - P_0 t_p (1 + r)^n \tag{8.4}$$

where the first term is the gross proceeds from selling the stock, the second term is the capital gains taxes due on the gross proceeds, and the third term is the total amount of borrowing and interest to be repaid (at date 1, which is n periods from the grant date).

An alternative to the Section 83(b) election is to borrow the amount of taxes that would be due under the Section 83(b) election and buy additional stock in the corporation. The additional shares that can be purchased is simply $P_0 t_p / P_0 = t_p$. That is, for each share of restricted stock that is granted, this strategy involves the employee purchasing t_p extra shares. If t_p is .35, the employee purchases .35 of one share per share of restricted stock granted. The after-tax accumulation from this strategy is then

$$P_1(1 - t_p) + t_p P_1 - t_p (P_1 - P_0)t_{cg} - P_0 t_p (1 + r)^n \tag{8.5}$$

where the first term is the after-tax proceeds from the original grant of restricted stock, the second term is the gross proceeds from the extra shares purchased at the grant date, the third term is the capital gains taxes due on the extra shares purchased, and the fourth term is the repayment of the borrowing with interest when all the shares are sold at the vesting date.

A Section 83(b) election is not optimal when the after-tax accumulation from the second strategy exceeds the after-tax accumulation from the Section 83(b) election, that is, (8.5) > (8.4). Thus,

$$P_1(1 - t_p) + t_p P_1 - t_p (P_1 - P_0)t_{cg} - P_0 t_p (1 + r)^n > P_1 - (P_1 - P_0)t_{cg} - P_0 t_p (1 + r)^n$$

The $P_0 t_p (1 + r)^n$ term cancels out, and expanding the first term gives

$$P_1 - P_1 t_p + t_p P_1 - t_p (P_1 - P_0)t_{cg} > P_1 - (P_1 - P_0)t_{cg}$$

---

[12]The result is equivalent if we assume the employee purchases additional stock from liquidating other investments earning an after-tax rate of return r. That is, r simply represents the after-tax opportunity cost of funds to the employee.

leaving

$$(P_1 - P_0)t_{cg} - t_p(P_1 - P_0)t_{cg} > 0$$

which simplifies to the condition

$$(P_1 - P_0)t_{cg}(1 - t_p) > 0 \tag{8.6}$$

This expression is positive whenever $P_1 > P_0$, which is the condition that motivates the employee to consider a Section 83(b) election in the first place. Thus if the employee expects the stock price to increase over the period between the grant and vesting date, a Section 83(b) election is not optimal because it is dominated by the alternative strategy of borrowing the amount of taxes that would be payable under the Section 83(b) election and using these funds to buy additional stock. A simple numerical example illustrates the analysis.

EXAMPLE:
Suppose an employee is granted 1,000 shares of restricted stock with a current stock price of $25. The employee is restricted from selling the stock for 3 years until it vests. The employee faces a current tax rate of 35% on ordinary income and 15% on long-term capital gains. These rates are not expected to change over the vesting period. Finally, the employee faces a 10% after-tax borrowing rate. The employee expects the stock price to increase to $40 by the vesting date.

If the employee does nothing and simply waits until the vesting period and then sells the stock, the after-tax accumulation per share is given by equation (8.3)

$$P_1(1 - t_p) = \$40(1 - .35) = \$26$$

A Section 83(b) election with borrowing to pay the taxes results in an after-tax accumulation given by equation (8.4)

$$P_1 - (P_1 - P_0)t_{cg} - P_0t_p(1 + r)^n = \$40 - (\$40 - \$25).15 - \$25(.35)(1 + .10)^3$$
$$= \$26.104$$

Instead of a Section 83(b) election, the employee can borrow the amount of the taxes due under the election and purchase additional stock. The after-tax accumulation with this strategy is given by equation (8.5)

$$P_1(1 - t_p) + t_p P_1 - t_p(P_1 - P_0)t_{cg} - P_0t_p(1 + r)^n$$
$$= \$40(1 - .35) + .35(\$40) - .35(\$40 - \$25).15 - \$25(.35)(1 + .10)^3$$
$$= \$27.5665$$

Thus this strategy results in a greater after-tax accumulation of $27.5665 − $26.104 = $1.4625 per share or $1462.50 over the 1,000 shares of restricted stock. Alternatively, we can use equation (8.6) to directly determine whether a Section 83(b) election is preferable in this example.

$$(P_1 - P_0)t_{cg}(1 - t_p) = (\$40 - \$25).15(1 - .35) = \$1.4625 > 0$$

Thus, the election is not optimal.

			Difference
	Section 83(b)	**Borrow and Buy**	**Equation (8.5) −**
P_1	**Do Nothing**	**Election**	**Additional Stock**	**Equation (8.4)**

TABLE 8.3 Restricted Stock: Analysis of After-Tax Accumulations to Section 83(b) Election versus Borrowing and Purchasing Additional Stock

P_1	Do Nothing	Section 83(b) Election	Borrow and Buy Additional Stock	Difference Equation (8.5) − Equation (8.4)
	Equation (8.3)	Equation (8.4)	Equation (8.5)	Equation (8.6)
$20	$13.00	$ 9.10	$ 8.62	−$0.49
$25	$16.25	$13.35	$13.35	$0.00
$30	$19.50	$17.60	$18.09	$0.49
$35	$22.75	$21.85	$22.83	$0.98
$40	$26.00	$26.10	$27.57	$1.46
$45	$29.25	$30.35	$32.30	$1.95
$50	$32.50	$34.60	$37.04	$2.44
$60	$39.00	$43.10	$46.52	$3.41

Table values based on following: $P_0 = \$25$, $t_p = .35$, $t_{cg} = .15$, $n = 3$ years, $r = .10$.

Table 8.3 summarizes the outcomes given a range of stock prices on the vesting date. The table illustrates that if the stock price is expected to increase, a Section 83(b) election is dominated by the alternative strategy of borrowing and buying additional stock. If the stock price is not expected to increase or is expected to increase by only a small amount, then doing nothing and simply selling the stock at the vesting date dominates.[13]

Employee Tax Rates Expected to Rise

Might it be optimal to make a Section 83(b) election if the employee expects to face a higher tax rate on ordinary income at the vesting date? Let t_0 (t_1) be the tax rate on ordinary income at the grant date (vesting date). We can modify equations (8.4) and (8.5) as follows. The Section 83(b) election remains

$$P_1 - (P_1 - P_0)t_{cg} - P_0 t_0 (1 + r)^n \qquad (8.7)$$

And the alternative strategy of borrowing and buying additional stock becomes

$$P_1(1 - t_1) + t_0 P_1 - t_0 (P_1 - P_0)t_{cg} - P_0 t_0 (1 + r)^n \qquad (8.8)$$

where the second, third, and fourth terms all use the tax rate on ordinary income at the grant date because this reflects the amount of borrowing and additional shares purchased. The election is optimal if (8.7) > (8.8). The last term is common to both equations and drops out. We can expand the first term in equation (8.8) such that P_1 drops out leaving

$$P_1 t_1 - t_0 P_1 + t_0 (P_1 - P_0)t_{cg} - (P_1 - P_0)t_{cg} > 0$$
$$= P_1(t_1 - t_0) - (P_1 - P_0)t_{cg}(1 - t_0) > 0$$
$$= \frac{(t_1 - t_0)}{(1 - t_0)t_{cg}} > \frac{(P_1 - P_0)}{P_1} \qquad (8.9)$$

---

[13]Specifically, if the stock price is expected to appreciate by less than $r/(1 - t_p)$, then the do-nothing strategy dominates.

Thus, whether the election is optimal depends on the increase in ordinary-income tax rate relative to the expected increase in stock price.

EXAMPLE:

Assume the same facts as the above restricted stock example, except that the employee faces a current tax rate of 35% and expects to face a tax rate on ordinary income of 50% on the vesting date.

The do-nothing strategy results in $P_1(1 - t_1) = \$40(1 - .50) = \$20$. A Section 83(b) election results in an after-tax accumulation using equation (8.7) of

$$P_1 - (P_1 - P_0)t_{cg} - P_0t_0(1+r)^n$$

$$\$40 - (\$40 - \$25).15 - \$25(.35)(1 + .10)^3 = \$26.10$$

The alternative borrow-and-buy strategy results in an after-tax accumulation using equation (8.8) of

$$P_1(1 - t_1) + t_0P_1 - t_0(P_1 - P_0)t_{cg} - P_0t_0(1+r)^n$$

$$\$40(1 - .50) + .35(\$40) - .35(\$40 - \$25).15 - \$25(.35)(1 + .10)^3 = \$21.57$$

In this example, the election is optimal because the tax savings from being taxed at the lower rate exceed the earnings on the additional shares that can be purchased. Alternatively, we can directly use equation (8.9)

$$\frac{(t_1 \quad t_0)}{(1 - t_0)t_{cg}} > \frac{(P_1 - P_0)}{P_1}$$

$$\frac{(.50 - .35)}{(1 - .35).15} > \frac{(\$40 - \$25)}{\$40}$$

$$1.538 > .375$$

indicating that the election is optimal in this example.

Employee Stock Options and Stock Appreciation Rights

A stock option is a right to acquire stock at a specified price (exercise price) for a specified period of time (until the expiration date of the contract). Employee stock options arc typically granted with an expiration date of 5 to 10 years and at an exercise price equal to the price of the underlying stock at the date of grant. Although the options may be quite valuable in that the expected return to the employee from owning the options may be substantial, the granting of options typically is a nontaxable event.[14] Instead, taxation of the compensation is deferred until the option is exercised, unless the option is an "incentive stock option," as discussed later.

---

[14]If an option is granted at an exercise price below the price of the underlying stock at the date of grant (so-called "in-the-money" options), compensation expense (income) equal to the excess of the stock price over the exercise price of the option may have to be recognized by the employer (employee) at the date of grant. Of course, the value of the option may be significantly greater than simply the difference between the current value of the stock and the exercise price of the option. Moreover, some firms (for example, Digital Equipment Corporation) have imposed restrictions on the exercise of options that are granted at an exercise price below the stock price. Such restrictions postpone the recognition of taxable income until such time as the restrictions lapse.

Stock appreciation rights (SARs) provide employees with cash payments equal to the change in market value of the firm's stock over some specified period of time. Taxation occurs when the employee exercises the right to receive the appreciation on the stock that has occurred since the date of grant. As with stock options, the employee does not make a payment to the firm in the event that the stock price declines below its value at the grant date. As a consequence, the expected return to the employee on a SAR can far exceed the expected appreciation on the stock.

To illustrate, suppose the current stock price is $20 per share, and this is the price at which the stock option or the SAR is granted. The future stock price is uncertain. Assume that its value on the expiration date of the option or the SAR is uniformly distributed between $10 and $40. That is, its future price is certain not to be below $10 or above $40, but every point in between is equally likely.[15] This uncertainty can be represented as in Figure 8.1.

The expected value of the future stock price is $25, or ($40 + $10)/2. If the future stock price turned out to be equal to the expected value of $25, the employee would receive $25 − $20 or $5 in cash from the SAR. Similarly, the employee would pay $20 to exercise the option to purchase stock worth $25, thereby realizing a "bargain" of $5. The $5 bargain could be converted into cash by selling the underlying stock in the market for $25, but the expected cash value of the SAR and option exceeds $5. Why? Because if the terminal stock price is less than $20, the employee receives $0 rather than a negative sum, whereas the employee keeps 100% of the terminal stock price in excess of $20. Because the stock price finishes "in-the-money" (that is, above $20) two-thirds of the time, and when it finishes in-the-money, its expected value is $30, or ($40 + $20)/2, the expected amount to be received under the option or SAR is $6.67, or 2/3 × ($30 − $20). The expected option or SAR value, then, relative to holding stock is $1.67, or $6.67 − $5.00, to be paid at the expiration date of the option or SAR.

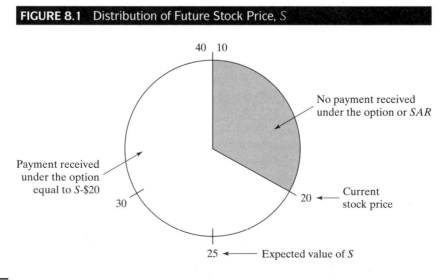

FIGURE 8.1   Distribution of Future Stock Price, *S*

[15]A uniform distribution for stock prices is not descriptively accurate for securities. The assumption is made here for pedagogical reasons.

Suppose that the present value of the $1.67 is $1.25; then a year-end grant of 20,000 SARs or stock options would be equivalent, ignoring taxes and other considerations (such as risk-sharing and incentives), to a bonus of $25,000. Unlike a bonus, however, the granting of a stock option or SAR does not give rise to immediate taxation. Instead, compensation deferral is achieved. Deferral may or may not be desirable from a tax planning standpoint depending on the current and future tax rates of the employee and the employer. If compensation deferral is desirable, however, it may be a useful alternative to a deferred salary or deferred bonus arrangement. Such deferrals require an agreement prior to the services being rendered by the employee, while deferrals through SARs and options do not.

Tax Issues Relating to Incentive Stock Options and Nonqualified Stock Options

As we mentioned earlier, not all employee stock options are taxed the same. For tax purposes, the two types of options are **nonqualified stock options (NQOs)** and **incentive stock options (ISOs).** The time line in Figure 8.2 should prove useful in comparing NQOs and ISOs.

On exercising an NQO, the employee recognizes a gain of $(P_e - X)$, where P_e is the stock price on the exercise date and X is the exercise price determined at the grant date. This gain is taxed as ordinary income, t_p. With an ISO, the gain at the exercise date is deferred until the stock is sold and is taxed at capital gains rates, t_{cg}.[16] Although it might seem as though ISOs dominate NQOs, to draw such a conclusion is to commit the error of unilateral tax planning. It is also important to consider the tax consequences to

FIGURE 8.2 Tax Treatment of NQO and ISO to Employee and Employer			
Date	*Option Granted*	*Option Exercised*	*Stock Sold*
Stock price:	X	P_e	P_s
Example:	$10	$15	$25
Tax consequences to the employee			
NQO	None	Ordinary income of $P_e - X = \$5$	Capital gain of $P_s - P_e = \$10$
ISO	None	None	Capital gain of $P_s - X = \$15$
Tax consequences to the employer			
NQO	None	Ordinary deduction of $P_e - X = \$5$	None
ISO	None	None	None

[16]ISOs are defined in §422 and must satisfy several criteria. For example, stock obtained under an ISO cannot be disposed of within 2 years of the grant date nor within 12 months after exercise. Otherwise the ISO is "disqualified." ISOs cannot be granted with an exercise price below the stock price at grant date, and the aggregate stock value covered by the ISOs (number of options times grant date stock price) is limited to $100,000 per year per employee.

the employer. The employer receives no tax deduction for the compensation paid to employees via ISOs. In contrast, NQOs give rise to an ordinary tax deduction for the employer at the same time and in the same amount as the ordinary income recognized by the employee.

We can derive conditions under which one type of option is jointly preferred by the employee and employer over the other. In multilateral tax planning, to derive conditions under which one type of option is tax-preferred over another we must consider both parties. A simple way to consider multilateral interests is to hold one party indifferent and then determine what choice the other party favors. We will hold the employee indifferent between the two option types by having the firm reimburse the employee for any difference in tax costs between the two options. We assume the stock obtained from either option type is sold on the same future date at price P_s.

For simplicity, assume the option is granted with an exercise price (denoted X) equal to the stock price at grant date (denoted P_g), thus $X = P_g$. The employee prefers the ISO when the taxes due on the ISO are less than those due on the NQO:[17]

$$\text{ISO taxes} < \text{NQO taxes}$$
$$(P_s - X)t_{cg} < [(P_e - X)t_p + (P_s - P_e)t_{cg}]$$

The taxes due on the ISO can be partitioned into two parts: the tax due on the gain between the grant date and exercise date, even though the tax is not paid until the stock sale date, and the tax due on the gain between the exercise date and stock sale date:

$$[(P_e - X)t_{cg} + (P_s - P_e)t_{cg}] < [(P_e - X)t_p + (P_s - P_e)t_{cg}]$$

which simplifies to

$$(P_e - X)t_{cg} < (P_e - X)t_p$$
$$(P_e - X)(t_{cg} - t_p) < 0 \tag{8.10}$$
$$(P_e - X)(t_p - t_{cg^*}) > 0$$

where t_{cg^*} is the present value of the capital gains tax rate, also referred to as the effective capital gains tax rate, reflecting the deferral for n periods of the capital gains tax for the ISO—that is, $t_{cg^*} = t_{cg}/(1 + r)^n$. Note that the deferral period is measured from the exercise date until the stock sale date. Because the employee would not exercise the option if it were not in-the-money ($P_e > X$), the ISO is preferred by the employee whenever the tax rate on ordinary income exceeds the present value of the tax rate on capital gains: $t_p > t_{cg^*}$. Thus, even if ordinary income and capital gains are taxed at the same rate, the employee will prefer an ISO because the ISO defers the tax on the gain at exercise until the stock is sold.

---

[17]To achieve capital gains treatment on the stock price appreciation after exercise of an NQO, the stock must be held for at least 12 months. If the stock price declines after exercise but before sale, the employee has a capital loss (short-term or long-term depending on the holding period). Finally, note that while the gain at the exercise date of the ISO may be deferred until the sale date, it is not always so. This gain, while not included in the calculation of regular taxable income, is included as a preference item in calculating the individual alternative minimum tax (AMT), which could trigger tax at the exercise date. Because the ISO gain is a preference item in the AMT calculation, the individual can then receive credit for the taxes paid at the exercise date against the regular taxes due on the final stock sale date. That is, exercise of an ISO might trigger the alternative minimum tax, which has the effect of accelerating the taxes otherwise payable at the final sale date. In effect, the deferral advantages of an ISO are lost. We ignore the alternative minimum tax here.

Thus to make the employee indifferent, the firm needs to reimburse the employee for the difference in taxes as in equation (8.10), and because the reimbursement is taxable to the employee, the reimbursement amount is

$$\frac{(P_e - X)(t_p - t_{cg^*})}{(1 - t_p)}$$

This payment is deductible to the employer.

The employer prefers the NQO when[18]

$$(P_e - X)t_c - \frac{(P_e - X)(t_p - t_{cg^*})}{(1 - t_p)}(1 - t_c) > 0 \qquad \textbf{(8.11)}$$

This equation can be simplified as follows:

$$\frac{(P_e - X)t_c(1 - t_p) - (P_e - X)(t_p - t_{cg^*})(1 - t_c)}{(1 - t_p)} > 0$$

$$\frac{(P_e - X)}{(1 - t_p)}[t_c(1 - t_p) - (t_p - t_{cg^*})(1 - t_c)] > 0$$

$$[t_c(1 - t_p) - (t_p - t_{cg^*})(1 - t_c)] > 0$$

$$t_c - t_p + t_{cg^*} - t_{cg^*}t_c > 0$$

$$t_c(1 - t_{cg^*}) - t_p + t_{cg^*} > 0$$

$$t_c > \frac{(t_p - t_{cg^*})}{(1 - t_{cg^*})} \qquad \textbf{(8.12)}$$

Equation (8.12) shows that NQOs are preferred if the corporation's marginal tax rate exceeds the difference in the employee's tax rate on ordinary income less the effective capital gains tax rate divided by one minus the employee's effective capital gains tax rate. Alternatively stated, the ISO is preferred if the incremental taxes to the employee of the NQO exceed the value of the deduction to the employer: $(t_p - t_{cg^*})/(1 - t_{cg^*}) > t_c$. In Table 8.4, we use equation (8.12) to calculate the required corporate marginal tax rate, presented in boldface, above which NQOs will be tax-preferred by both parties for various employee tax rates and holding periods.

As the employee's expected holding period of the stock obtained from exercising an ISO increases, the effective or present value of the capital gains rate declines. If the stock obtained from exercising an ISO is held until the employee's death, the gain at exercise escapes income taxation altogether and thus the effective capital gains tax rate is zero. As the effective capital gains tax rate declines, the required corporate tax rate above which NQOs are jointly preferred by both parties increases. Prior to TRA 86, NQOs were tax-preferred only if employees had short holding periods with high-tax corporate employers. For example, with a holding period of 5 years, corporations had to have tax rates above 41.7% before NQOs were jointly tax-favored. But with an employee expected holding period of 20 years or higher, the required corporate tax rate cutoff was 47.3% or higher before NQOs were tax-favored, and thus NQOs were not tax-favored by any corporations because the top corporate tax rate was 46%. In the 1988–1991 period, when employees faced the same tax rate of 28% on

---

[18]Note that the corporate tax rate here is the expected rate for the year in which the NQO is exercised.

TABLE 8.4 Values of Corporate Marginal Tax Rate, t_c, Above Which NQOs Are Jointly Preferred by Employer and Employee

Time Period			Holding Period in Years after Exercise of ISO and Implied t_{cg*} for Holding Period				
			1	5	10	20	Death
	t_p	t_{cg}			t_{cg*}		
Pre-TRA 86	.50	.20	.187	.143	.102	.052	0
		t_c	**.385**	**.417**	**.443**	**.473**	**.50**
1988–1991	.28	.28	.261	.200	.142	.072	0
		t_c	**.025**	**.10**	**.161**	**.224**	**.28**
1993–1997	.396	.28	.261	.200	.142	.072	0
		t_c	**.182**	**.245**	**.296**	**.349**	**.396**
1998–2002	.396	.20	.187	.143	.102	.052	0
		t_c	**.257**	**.296**	**.328**	**.363**	**.396**
2003–present	.35	.15	.140	.107	.076	.039	0
		t_c	**.244**	**.272**	**.296**	**.324**	**.35**

$t_{cg*} = t_{cg}/(1+r)^n$ where n is the expected holding period in years. Employees' after-tax discount rate is assumed to be 7%. t_c is solved using equation (8.12).
NQO preferred if $t_c > (t_p - t_{cg*})/(1 - t_{cg*})$.

ordinary income and capital gains, ISOs offered only deferral advantages and the required corporate tax rate cutoff declined, thus making NQOs more tax-favored for more corporations. As the tax rate on ordinary income increased to 39.6% and capital gains rates either held at 28% (1993–1997) and then declined to 20% (1998–2002), ISOs again offered both capital gains and deferral advantages to employees facing the top 39.6% rate, and thus the required corporate tax rate increased. With the reduction in both the top ordinary income tax rate (favoring NQOs) and capital gains rate (favoring ISOs) in 2003, the effects offset somewhat but the required corporate marginal tax rate above which NQOs are tax-favored declined slightly.

EXAMPLE 1:

If the employer and the employee always face the same tax rate on ordinary income ($t_p = t_c$), then NQOs are preferred to ISOs because the derivation of equation (8.12) can be rearranged as follows:

$$t_c - t_p + t_{cg*} - t_{cg*}t_c > 0$$

with $t_p = t_c$

$$t_p - t_p + t_{cg*} - t_{cg*}t_c > 0$$
$$t_{cg*}(1 - t_c) > 0$$

which is satisfied if

$$t_{cg*} > 0$$

In other words, with NQOs and $t_p = t_c$, no net tax is paid on the stock price appreciation between the grant date and the exercise date because the tax paid by the employee is equal to the tax reduction achieved by the employer. By contrast, tax *will* be paid with an ISO, although it will be delayed until the stock is sold and the tax will be at capital gains rates. Therefore, NQOs are preferred when $t_p = t_c$ due to the asymmetric tax treatment of the employer and the employee under ISOs.

EXAMPLE 2:

If the employer's tax rate exceeds the employee's, NQOs are even more preferred over ISOs because the net tax paid becomes negative with the NQO. However, if the employer's tax rate is below the employee's, the ISOs could be preferred. Specifically, as shown in Table 8.4, ISOs are preferred if $t_c < (t_p - t_{cg^*})/(1 - t_{cg^*})$. So for employees facing high tax rates, ISOs may have a place in the compensation programs of companies with low tax rates, such as start-up companies or other companies with net operating loss (NOL) or investment tax credit carryforwards.

Evidence on the Role of Taxes in the Choice of ISOs

On an aggregate level, the relative use of ISOs, also known as qualified options, and NQOs has changed over time consistent with changes in the tax laws favoring one or the other option type. For example, Hite and Long (1982) document that firms switched from ISOs to NQOs after the Tax Reform Act of 1969 lowered the top rates faced by individuals; t_p fell relative to t_c, making ISOs less tax-favored. Similarly, the Tax Reform Act of 1986 reduced the attractiveness of ISOs considerably because the top individual rate was set below the top corporate rate and the capital gains rate was set equal to the tax rate on ordinary income. Balsam, Halperin, and Mozes (1997) report that after 1986 NQO usage increased relative to ISOs.[19]

Disqualifying Dispositions of ISOs

One of the interesting tax-planning features of ISOs is that they allow the firm to receive NQO tax treatment if tax rates change such that NQO tax treatment is tax-favored relative to ISO tax treatment. This feature is another example of the adaptability of a tax plan as discussed in Chapter 7. Specifically, firms can receive NQO tax treatment by having the employee undertake a disqualifying disposition of the ISO. A **disqualifying disposition** of an ISO occurs when the option-holder disposes of the stock within 12 months of exercise. The disqualification means that the ISO is then taxed as an NQO. In a disqualifying disposition, the firm's gross tax benefit (GTB) is $(P_e - X)t_c$. However, the employee's tax costs are higher due to the difference in tax treatment of NQOs and ISOs, which is given in equation (8.10). A disqualifying disposition results in the employee facing an incremental tax cost because the gain on exercise $(P_e - X)$ is now taxed as ordinary income rather than at capital gains rates and the tax on the gain is no longer deferred until the stock sale date.

Whether a disqualifying disposition is tax-favored can be analyzed similarly to the initial grant. Suppose we hold the employee indifferent by having the firm reimburse the option-holder for incremental tax costs. Of course the payment, denoted R for reimbursement, is taxable to the option-holder and therefore needs to be grossed up by $(1 - t_p)$. At the same time, this payment is tax deductible to the firm. Thus a

---

[19]However, Madeo and Omer (1994) report that firms that switched from ISOs to NQOs following the 1969 Tax Act tended to be firms with low tax rates, when the tax model here predicts that it would be the high-tax firms switching. Austin, Gaver, and Gaver (1998) report evidence that the firm's marginal tax rate appears to have played little role in the choice of option type during the 1981–1984 period, with the choice appearing to be driven by minimizing the executives' tax burden. Thus the evidence is somewhat mixed on taxes driving the choice between ISOs and NQOs. See also Balsam, Halperin, and Mozes (1997) for further evidence.

disqualifying disposition is tax-favored if the net tax benefits (NTBs) are positive:

$$NTB = GTB - \frac{R}{(1 - t_p)}(1 - t_c) > 0$$

Substituting $(P_e - X)t_c$ for GTB and R from equation (8.10) we get[20]

$$NTB = (P_e - X)t_c - \frac{(P_e - X)(t_p - t_{cg^*})}{(1 - t_p)}(1 - t_c) > 0 \qquad \textbf{(8.13)}$$

EXAMPLE:

Suppose an employee holds 100 ISOs with an exercise price of $10 and a current stock price of $25. The employee faces a tax rate of 28% on both ordinary income and capital gains. The firm faces a tax rate of 34%. (These tax rates were in effect in the post-TRA-86 period). The employee plans to hold the options for another 5 years to maturity before exercising and has an after-tax discount rate of 10%. Should the firm and employee consider a disqualifying disposition of the ISOs?

We first need to calculate the present value of the capital gains tax rate $t_{cg^*} = t_{cg}/(1 + r)^n = .28/(1.10)^5 = .174$. If the options are disqualified, the firm stands to gain gross tax benefits (GTBs) of $15(.34) = $5.10 per option. The employee faces an increase in tax costs of $15(.28 − .174) = $1.59 per option from equation (8.10). If we solve holding the employee indifferent between disqualifying and not disqualifying, then the employee requires a pretax payment of $1.59/(1 − .28) = $2.21 per option. The after-tax cost of this payment to the firm is $2.21(1 − .34) = $1.46. Thus, as shown in equation (8.13), a disqualifying disposition would save the two parties $5.10 − $1.46 = $3.64 per option, or $364 in total.

Many firms that could have saved substantial sums in taxes by paying cash to employees to disqualify ISOs in the post-TRA-86 era failed to do so. Why? One possibility is that they were simply unaware of the advantages. At least one fly in the ointment is that the firm's payment to the option holder, $R/(1 - t_p)$, is recorded as an expense in calculating the firm's accounting earnings and thus reduces reported earnings. This reduction in accounting earnings represents a nontax cost of the transaction. Matsunaga, Shevlin, and Shores (1992) predict that firms with higher leverage (debt/total assets), lower interest coverage (earnings before interest/interest), and lower dividend coverage (earnings/dividends) face higher nontax costs and are thus less likely to undertake a disqualifying disposition of ISOs. They report results consistent with these predictions.[21]

---

[20]Equation (8.13) can be simplified to equation (8.12), but it is convenient to use (8.13) to analyze the disqualifying disposition.

[21]An alternative to a disqualifying disposition is the conversion or swapping of NQOs for ISOs. Matsunaga et al. (1992) find little evidence that many firms converted. Similar to a disqualifying disposition, with a conversion, accounting compensation expense to the firm may arise from reimbursing the employee. Also, if NQOs are issued in exchange for ISOs when the exercise price is *below* the current market price, accounting compensation expense must be recognized for the difference. Apparently this requirement discouraged many firms from converting. The interested reader is also referred to the Microsoft Corporation annual reports for 1988–1990, in which the firm reported gross tax benefits of $11.5, $14, and $20 million from disqualifying dispositions and ISO conversions for the 1988, 1989, and 1990 fiscal years. Microsoft paid 50% of its gross tax benefits to employees to induce them to undertake the disqualification and/or conversion.

The Role of Taxes in the NQO Exercise Decision

Most options have a contract life or term to maturity from the grant date of 10 years. However, many employees exercise their options well before their maturity date.[22] Early exercise can stem from a need for liquidity, consumption, diversification so as to reduce the amount of wealth at risk within the firm, and/or tax reasons.[23] Before turning to the tax reasons, early exercise motivated by consumption or the need for diversification requires the employee to exercise and shortly thereafter sell the stock. Because sale of stock within 12 months of exercise of an ISO leads to a disqualifying disposition and thus increased taxes, NQOs rather than ISOs are more likely to be exercised early for liquidity and/or diversification reasons.

Early exercise of an NQO for tax reasons might arise either from an incentive to start the "clock" rolling for capital gains treatment on any subsequent stock price appreciation or an expected future increase in tax rates on ordinary income. The analysis of the early exercise decision to start the clock rolling for capital gains treatment on any subsequent stock price appreciation is similar to the analysis of the Section 83(b) election for restricted stock. Recall, a Section 83(b) election is not optimal unless we expect tax rates on ordinary income to increase (and stock price to increase). We show this conclusion also applies to the early exercise of ESOs. To analyze the early exercise decision, we assume the employee borrows at an after-tax rate r, or equivalently liquidates other investments earning r, to pay the exercise price and taxes on the ESO, $X + (P_e - X)t_p$, where P_e is the stock price on the date at which we are considering early exercise. The borrowing and interest is repaid at the later stock sale date. The after-tax accumulation under this early exercise strategy is

$$P_s - (P_s - P_e)t_{cg} - [X + (P_e - X)t_p](1 + r)^n \qquad (8.14)$$

where the first term is the gross proceeds from the subsequent sale of the stock, the second term is the capital gains due on the sale, and the third term is the amount of borrowing and interest to be repaid.

An alternative strategy is to borrow the amount that would be paid for early exercise (the exercise price and taxes) and buy additional stock. The employee can buy $N_s = [X + (P_e - X)t_p]/P_e$ of additional shares. The after-tax accumulation from this strategy is

$$(P_s - X)(1 - t_p) + N_s P_s - N_s (P_s - P_e)t_{cg} - N_s P_e (1 + r)^n \qquad (8.15)$$

where the first term is the after-tax proceeds from the ESO exercise sale of the stock, the second term is the gross proceeds from the additional stock purchased by the employee, the third term is the tax due on these additional shares, and the fourth term is the amount of borrowing and interest to be repaid. Borrow-and-buy additional shares is tax-favored if its after-tax accumulation is greater than that of early exercise,

---

[22]Huddart and Lang (1996) document the early exercise behavior of over 50,000 employees from eight different corporations. Hemmer, Matsunaga, and Shevlin (1996) examine the exercise behavior of the top managers from 65 firms.

[23]Employees often have much of their wealth tied up in the value of the firm. This wealth includes the present value of their future earnings. Risk-averse employees would like to diversify their portfolio of wealth to reduce its risk. One method is to exercise their options and sell the stock with the proceeds invested in some other asset, reducing the overall risk of the employee's wealth. Huddart (1994) develops this intuition more formally.

equation (8.15) > (8.14). Note that $N_s P_e = [X + (P_e - X)t_p]$, the amount borrowed is the same under both alternatives, so that the last term is common to both alternatives and drops out of the comparison.

$$(P_s - X)(1 - t_p) + N_s P_s - N_s(P_s - P_e)t_{cg} - P_s + (P_s - P_e)t_{cg} > 0$$
$$P_s - X - (P_s - X)t_p + N_s P_s - N_s(P_s - P_e)t_{cg} - P_s + (P_s - P_e)t_{cg} > 0$$
$$N_s P_s - X - (P_s - X)t_p + (P_s - P_e)t_{cg}(1 - N_s) > 0 \qquad \textbf{(8.16)}$$

One can show that this expression is always positive and thus early exercise to start the clock rolling to obtain favorable capital gains treatment is not tax-favored.[24] Note however that both are very risky strategies—if the stock price declines, the early exercise-and-hold strategy results in paying taxes on phantom gains while the additional purchase strategy results in losses.[25] This additional risk compared with the do-nothing strategy is a nontax cost of the Section 83(b) election and its alternative of purchasing additional stock.

EXAMPLE:
Suppose an employee holds an option with an exercise price of $10. The current stock price is $15, and the employee fully expects the stock price to increase to $35 at the option maturity date in 3 years. The tax rate on ordinary income is 35% and on capital gains is 15%. These rates are not expected to change. The employee can borrow at an after-tax rate of 10%. The employee is considering two alternative strategies: borrowing and exercising the stock now and holding the stock 3 years before selling versus borrowing and buying additional shares and exercising and selling all shares after 3 years.

The after-tax accumulation from the early exercise strategy is given by equation (8.14)

$$P_s - (P_s - P_e)t_{cg} - [X + (P_e - X)t_p](1 + r)^n$$
$$= \$35 - (\$35 - \$15).15 - [\$10 + (\$15 - \$10).35](1 + .10)^3 = \$16.36$$

The after-tax accumulation to the borrow-and-purchase additional stock strategy is given by equation (8.15)

$$(P_s - X)(1 - t_p) + N_s P_s - N_s(P_s - P_e)t_{cg} - N_s P_e(1 + r)^n$$

where $N_s = [X + (P_e - X)t_p]/P_e = [\$10 + (\$15 - \$10).35]/\$15 = .7833$ shares. Thus,

$$(\$35 - \$10)(1 - .35) + .7833(\$35) - .7833(\$35 - \$15).15 - .7833(\$15)(1 + .10)^3$$
$$= \$25.676$$

---

[24]The proof is available at http://faculty.washington.edu/shevlin/swems/. Also see McDonald (2003) for an alternative approach with formal proofs.

[25]The future losses are deductible as capital losses offsetting other capital gains or carried forward and deducted at $3,000 a year: Taxes are paid on $(P_e - X)$ at t_p, while the subsequent losses are deducted at t_{cg^*}. Further note that if the employee expects the stock price to decline, the best strategy is to exercise and sell the stock immediately before the price decline. See Neil Weinberg "Out of Options" (*Forbes* April 29, 2002, pp. 50–54) for a discussion of losses suffered by employees exercising NQOs early and borrowing to buy additional shares.

TABLE 8.5   Analysis of the NQO Early Exercise Decision: Exercise Early or Borrow and Buy Additional Stock[a]

P_s	Early Exercise	Borrow and Buy Additional Stock	Difference
	Equation (8.14)	Equation (8.15)	Equation (8.16)
$15	−$0.64	−$0.64	$0.00
$20	$3.61	$5.94	$2.33
$25	$7.86	$12.52	$4.66
$30	$12.11	$19.10	$6.99
$35	$16.36	$25.68	$9.32
$40	$20.61	$32.26	$11.65
$45	$24.86	$38.84	$13.98
$50	$29.11	$45.41	$16.30
$60	$37.61	$58.57	$20.96

[a]Table values based on: $X = \$10$, $P_e = \$15$, $t_p = .35$, $t_{cg} = .15$, $n = 3$ years, $r = .10$

The after-tax accumulation of the borrow-and-buy additional stock strategy exceeds that of the early exercise strategy by $9.32 = $25.68 $16.36. Alternatively, we can use equation (8.16) to directly calculate the difference:

$$N_s P_s - X - (P_s - X)t_p + (P_s - P_e)t_{cg}(1 - N_s)$$
$$= .7833(\$35) - \$10 - (\$35 - \$10).35 + (\$35 - \$15).15(1 - .7833) = \$9.32$$

As illustrated in Table 8.5, the tax advantage to the borrow and buy additional shares (or the tax disadvantage of the early exercise alternative) increases with the expected increase in stock prices.

Tax Rates Are Expected to Increase

Now consider the case where the employee's ordinary tax rates are expected to increase from t_{p1} in the current period to t_{p2} in the next period. Under what conditions should an NQO-holder exercise in the current period? The employee will favor exercise before the tax rate change when the after-tax gain from early exercise is greater than the after-tax gain on later exercise after the tax rate has increased. But what is the expected after-tax gain arising from later exercise? The present value of the expected pretax gain from later exercise is given simply by the current value of the option W, which we can estimate using an option valuation model such as the Black–Scholes model. The expected after-tax gain is then $W(1 - t_{p2})$. Thus early exercise is tax-favored if

$$(P_e - X)(1 - t_{p1}) > W(1 - t_{p2})$$

or

$$\frac{(P_e - X)}{W} > \frac{(1 - t_{p2})}{(1 - t_{p1})} \tag{8.17}$$

The left-hand side is the ratio of the gain to date on the option, or the option's intrinsic value, to the present value of the option. The right-hand side is the ratio of tax rates. Because the value of an option always exceeds its intrinsic value, except in the instant before maturity, the left-hand side is always less than unity. The ratio approaches unity when the option is deep in-the-money—the stock price is far greater than the exercise price—or when the option has only a short time to maturity. An out-of-the-money or at-the-money option ($P \leq X$) or an option with a long maturity will have a low ratio. Let's interpret this relation: If tax rates are not expected to increase, the right-hand side equals unity. Because the left-hand side is always less than unity, the option will not be exercised early for tax reasons.[26] If tax rates are expected to increase $t_{p2} > t_{p1}$, the ratio $(1 - t_{p2})/(1 - t_{p1})$ is less than unity, and it is possible that the left-hand side will exceed this ratio. In particular, for deep in-the-money options with a short term to maturity, the ratio approaches unity, and early exercise before the tax rate increase captures a large fraction of the value of the option with the value taxed at the lower current rate.

> **EXAMPLE:**
> Suppose an employee expects the top statutory tax rate to increase from 30% to 40% and holds two sets of options. The current stock price is $50. The first set of options, with an exercise price of $10 and an option value of $41, is close to maturity. The second set of options, with an exercise price of $30 and an option value of $28, has 6 years to maturity. Should the employee exercise either series early, before the tax rate increase? The expected tax rate increase results in a ratio on the right-hand side of equation (8.17) of $(1 - .40)/(1 - .30) = .857$. Thus if the ratio on the left-hand side of (8.17) is greater than .857, the employee should exercise early.
>
> For series 1: $\frac{(P_e - X)}{W} = (\$50 - \$10)/\$41 = .9756 > .857$, so early exercise is tax-favored.
>
> For series 2: $\frac{(P_e - X)}{W} = (\$50 - \$30)/\$28 = .7143 < .857$, so early exercise is not tax-favored.

During the 1992 presidential elections, the widespread belief was that the top rates on ordinary income would increase. Proposals suggested an increase in the top rate from 31% for the tax year 1992 to 36% and 39.6% for tax years 1993 and thereafter. In fact, these rates became law. Thus during the last few months of 1992, high-tax-rate individuals faced the situation we covered in our last example. The financial press highlighted Disney's CEO Michael Eisner as exercising options with pretax gains of approximately $182 million to save approximately $15.6 million in taxes, or $182 (.396 − .31).[27] Huddart (1998) examines exercise behavior around this time period and reports evidence consistent with tax-motivated early exercise of deep in-the-money and shorter-term options.

---

[26]Recall that options can be exercised early for liquidity or diversification reasons. Finally, note that we have implicitly assumed the employer's tax rate is unchanged. Unless the employer also expects its tax rate to increase, the employer will prefer early exercise, because the employer company gets the tax deduction earlier, but at the cost of losing any incentives offered by the option to the employee.

[27]See, for example, "Disney Officials Get $187 Million from Stock Sale," *The Wall Street Journal* (December 2, 1992). See note 6 of Huddart (1998) for a list of other press articles.

Financial Accounting and Tax Comparison of Restricted Stock, Stock Appreciation Rights, and Stock Options

For a variety of reasons we discussed in Chapter 6, managers are not indifferent to the level of profits they report to shareholders and third parties for any given performance. Different methods of compensation have different tax and financial reporting implications. For example, a deferred cash compensation arrangement for work to be performed in one particular year typically gives rise to compensation expense for financial reporting purposes in the period in which the services are rendered. For accounting purposes, restricted stock is accounted for as compensation expense, reducing reported earnings. The value of the restricted stock grant at the grant date is amortized over the vesting period (usually using a straight-line approach). A stock appreciation right, which may have the same cost to the employer at the date of grant as restricted stock or a deferred cash compensation arrangement, does not give rise to compensation expense until the stock appreciates in value in the future. A stock option that is granted at an exercise price equal to the extant price of the underlying stock need not give rise to compensation expense at any time over the life of the option in the United States under current financial reporting rules.[28] SFAS 123 encourages but does not require firms to recognize the fair value of options granted as compensation expense in calculating net income reported in the income statement. Firms not recognizing compensation expense must however provide footnote disclosures in the financial statements showing the effects on net income and earnings per share as-if if the options were to be treated as compensation expense. Hence, firms that wish to avoid the recognition of compensation expense for financial reporting purposes, thereby increasing reported profits, have a natural preference for stock options over other forms of compensation. Until recently, close to 100% of firms elected footnote disclosure rather than recognition. However, in an apparent response to the recent corporate financial reporting scandals (e.g., Enron, Adelphia, Worldcom, Tyco, etc.), several hundred firms have announced they will begin recognizing compensation expense associated with ESOs.[29]

Suppose one share of restricted stock, a stock appreciation right, a nonqualified stock option, and an incentive stock option are issued with an exercise price equal to the current stock price of $10 at the end of period 0. The stock, which pays no dividends, increases in value by $1 each year for the next 4 years. The restricted stock and SAR each vest in 4 years, whereas, the options expire in 2 years when the stock price is $12, and the stock that is acquired on exercising the option is sold 2 years later at a price of $14. Table 8.6 indicates the tax consequences to the employee and the employer for the alternative stock-based compensation instruments.[30]

---

[28]The current accounting for employee stock options can be found in Statement of Financial Accounting Standard 123 "Accounting for Stock-Based Compensation" (SFAS 123) issued by the Financial Accounting Standards Board in October 1995 and effective for fiscal years beginning after December 15, 1995.

[29]The Financial Accounting Standards Board (FASB) and the International Accounting Standards Board (IASB) are both examining proposals to require firms to recognize compensation expense in the amount of the grant date fair value of ESOs. FASB also issued a standard dealing with the accounting issues for firms voluntarily changing from disclosure to recognition of ESO compensation expense. See "Accounting for Stock-Based Compensation—Transition and Disclosure—An Amendment of FASB Statement No. 123," Statement of Financial Accounting Standards No. 148, Financial Accounting Standards Board, 2002.

[30]We ignore the cash flow differences between the different equity instruments. Note also that different assumptions will alter the comparisons.

TABLE 8.6 Tax Consequences to Employees and Employers of Four Stock-Based Compensation Alternatives

Event	Options/RS Granted				Options Exercised				Stock Sold	
Time period	0		1		2		3		4	
Stock price	$10		$11		$12		$13		$14	
Tax consequences to	ee	er	ee	er	ee	er	ee	er	ee	er
RS	0	0	0	0	0	0	0	0	$-14t_p$	$+14t_c$
SAR	0	0	0	0	0	0	0	0	$-4t_p$	$+4t_c$
NQO	0	0	0	0	$-2t_p$	$+2t_c$	0	0	$-2t_{cg}$	0
ISO	0	0	0	0	0	0	0	0	$-4t_{cg}$	0

RS = Restricted Stock, SAR = Stock Appreciation Right, vest in 4 years.
NQO = Nonqualified Option, ISO = Incentive Stock Option, vest and expire in 2 years.
ee = employee, er = employer.
t_p = employees' tax rate on ordinary income, t_c = employers' tax rate on ordinary income,
t_{cg} = employees' tax rate on capital gains.

For the special case where the ordinary tax rate of the employee is equal to that of the employer, the total tax consequences to the two parties across the alternatives are shown in Table 8.6. These results suggest that among the alternatives, restricted stock and stock appreciation rights are the most attractive from a tax standpoint, followed by nonqualified options, with incentive stock options the least tax-favored. If the employee's tax rate on ordinary income is below that of the employer, the preference ordering among the four compensation alternatives is the same, with the magnitude of the tax differences increased. Recall that if the employee's tax rate is well above the employer's rate (for example, if the employer faces current or future tax loss carryforwards), the preference ordering could be reversed. Also note in this example that the NQO is exercised earlier than the SAR. If the NQO is exercised at the same time as the SAR, the tax consequences would be the same for the two instruments.

What about financial reporting consequences? Although nonqualified stock options and incentive stock options need never give rise to compensation expense in the income statement for financial reporting purposes, restricted stock and stock appreciation rights yield compensation expense each period, with SAR compensation expense varying as the stock price changes each period. Financial reporting expense for each instrument is summarized in panel B of Table 8.7. Rightly or wrongly, such financial reporting considerations often appear to swing the choice in favor of the more expensive compensation arrangements from a tax standpoint.[31]

Compensation in Venture-Capital-Backed Start-Ups

The ISO-NQO trade-off has a counterpart in start-up companies backed by venture capital firms. In many circumstances, management of the start-up ventures are given common stock and the venture capitalists are given convertible preferred stock. To provide incentives and rewards for managers, the price at which the preferred stock can be converted into common stock is often made contingent on the performance of

---

[31]Matsunaga (1995) provides evidence consistent with firms using employee stock options in lieu of cash compensation to avoid the reduction in reported financial accounting earnings.

TABLE 8.7 Total Tax Consequences of Four Stock-Based Compensation Alternatives When the Ordinary Tax Rates of Employees and Employers Coincide

Panel A	Tax Effects					
	Time period	0	1	2	3	4
	Instrument					
	RS	0	0	0	0	0
	SAR	0	0	0	0	0
	NQO	0	0	0	0	$-2t_{cg}$
	ISO	0	0	0	0	$-4t_{cg}$

Panel B	Financial Statement Expense					
	Time period	0	1	2	3	4
	Instrument					
	RS	0	$2.50	$2.50	$2.50	$2.50
	SAR	0	$1	$1	$1	$1
	NQO	0	0	0	0	0
	ISO	0	0	0	0	0

the company: If the company does well, say, in terms of accounting measures of performance, the conversion price to the venture capitalists increases.

The higher conversion price on the preferred stock is effectively a bonus to members of the management group who hold common shares. The higher the conversion price, the smaller the number of new shares issued to the venture capitalists and the more each remaining share is worth to management. This bonus is taxed to managers as deferred capital gains because they are taxed at a later date when they sell their shares. The bonus is not tax deductible to the company. Note that a cash bonus would result in immediate tax to managers at their personal tax rate. Even though this tax liability may appear worse than the stock-based bonus arrangement, the cash bonus would also yield an immediate corporate tax deduction. Therefore, the company could afford a larger tax-deductible cash bonus than a nondeductible stock-based bonus. As with NQOs, the cash bonus arrangement is typically more efficient for tax reasons.

Other Influences of Taxes on Compensation Structure

In response to the perception that executive salaries were excessive and unrelated to firm performance, Congress in the Omnibus Budget Reconciliation Act of 1993 added **Section 162(m)** to the Tax Code, which limits corporate tax deductions for compensation to $1 million per individual. Firms can avoid the limitation by qualifying their compensation plan as performance-based or by deferring the excess compensation to a time period in which it is deductible. To qualify for the performance-based exception, the following criteria must be met:

1. The compensation must be linked to the executives' attainment of objective performance goals such as stock price, market share, sales goals, and the like.
2. The performance goals must be established by the firm's compensation committee of two or more independent directors.
3. The shareholders must approve the compensation plan.
4. The compensation committee must certify that the performance goals have been met before payment is made.

Note that employee stock options generally satisfy the performance-related exception. Any portion of salary in excess of $1 million is not deductible. Discretionary bonuses that might be used to shift income between periods in anticipation of tax rate changes, as we discussed earlier in the chapter, run afoul of this limit to the extent the nonperformance-related total compensation exceeds $1 million.

Empirical evidence suggests while many firms did qualify their compensation plans so as to retain corporate tax deductions, many did not. In a sample of 297 publicly held U.S. firms, Johnson, Nabar, and Porter (1999) report that 46% of the firms did not preserve the deduction, 42% took actions to qualify their plans, and the remaining 12% deferred excess compensation. Balsam and Ryan (1996, note 1) provide the following information: Leucadia National Corporation stated in its proxy statement dated July 1, 1994, it was forgoing the deduction because "the Committee agreed that the lack of flexibility in determining executive compensation under (pre-established performance criteria) would not be in the best interest of the company." Both Johnson et al. (1999) and Balsam and Ryan (1996) predict that those firms not qualifying their plans faced larger recontracting costs and higher levels of executive risk aversion. Tying compensation more closely to performance imposes risk on executives because firm performance (for example, stock price and market share) is also influenced by factors outside the managers' control. Risk-averse executives require a risk premium to compensate them for the increased risk. Both studies provide evidence consistent with their predictions. Thus the tax planner must factor §162(m) into compensation design: Whether to qualify the compensation plan and if so, what performance goals to use.

Concluding Remarks

We have now discussed all the compensation components listed in Table 8.1 except for pensions, which is the topic of our next chapter. Furthermore, we have focused on the tax aspects of compensation. We do not want, however, to leave the impression that taxes are all that matter with respect to compensation. A number of nontax elements to compensation relate to motivating employees in order to mitigate the hidden-information and hidden-action problems discussed in Chapter 6 and the financial accounting differences between various compensation tools. These nontax elements are extremely important in compensation design.

Summary of Key Points

1. In determining the desirability of compensation alternatives, the tax consequences to both the employer *and* the employee must be considered.
2. Although employees prefer to receive taxable compensation at times and in ways that result in the income being taxed at lower rates, holding the compensation amounts fixed, employers prefer to pay tax-deductible compensation at times and in ways that result in the payments being deductible at high rates. By adjusting the level of compensation to reflect the tax costs and benefits of the compensation alternatives, the interests of employers and employees can be made to coincide.
3. In evaluating whether salary is tax-preferred over deferred compensation, both the current and future tax rates of both parties (the employee and employer) must be considered as well as the after-tax earnings rate available to both parties. For example, while falling employee tax rates over time favor deferred compensation arrangements, such contracts may be undesirable when employer tax rates are also falling over time.

4. Nontax factors, such as incentive and risk-sharing considerations between employees and employers, might tip the choice in favor of current compensation even though deferred compensation is tax-favored, or vice versa.

5. Even though certain fringe benefits yield tax deductions for employers and tax-exempt benefits for employees, such benefits are inferior to taxable cash compensation if employees place little personal value on the fringe benefits.

6. Reimbursement of business meal and entertainment expenses is tax-favored over salary supplements in the United States, where the employer faces low tax rates, but salary supplements can be preferred when employers face high tax rates.

7. Interest-free demand loans can yield tax treatment similar to deferred compensation arrangements. And although interest-free demand loans are more flexible than other deferred compensation arrangements in some respects, they require a great deal of mutual trust between the employer and the employee to be used effectively for tax planning purposes.

8. Discretionary cash bonus plans can be a very effective tax planning tool because bonuses can be timed strategically to coincide with high tax rates for the employer and with low tax rates for the employee. However, such plans may run afoul of IRC §162(m) restrictions on nonperformance-based total compensation, and they also require a great deal of mutual trust between the employer and the employee.

9. Restricted stock is similar to a deferred compensation arrangement—the employee recognizes taxable income at the vesting date at which time the employer obtains a tax deduction. Employees can make a Section 83(b) election recognizing taxable income at the grant date with future price appreciation (and depreciation) treated as capital gains (losses). A Section 83(b) election is generally not tax-favored unless the employee expects her tax rate on ordinary income to increase in the future.

10. The popularity in the United States of incentive stock options (ISOs) in the early and mid-1980s may have resulted from unilateral tax planning. Nonqualified stock options (NQOs) impose more tax on employees but yield significantly higher tax benefits for employers.

11. Many ISOs that could have been disqualified or converted into NQOs following passage of the 1986 Tax Act at very significant tax savings were not disqualified or converted. One possible explanation is the adverse financial reporting consequences of this tax-saving transaction: It would require the recognition of considerable sums of compensation expense in reports sent to shareholders and creditors.

12. In addition to liquidity or diversification motivations, employees might exercise employee stock options early for tax reasons—either to start the clock rolling to achieve capital gains treatment on subsequent stock price appreciation, or in advance of expected increases in tax rates. Similar to the analysis for restricted stock, the former is generally not tax-favored, while the latter can be tax-favored.

13. Managers in venture-capital-backed start-ups are often compensated in ways that yield deferred capital gains rather than immediate taxation at ordinary rates. Like ISOs, however, such compensation arrangements yield no tax deduction to the firm and therefore may be inferior to cash compensation alternatives. The more tax-efficient compensation arrangement often yields reduced income for financial reporting purposes. Some firms are apparently more interested in looking rich to investors than they are in looking poor to the tax collector.

14. In comparing compensation alternatives, such nontax factors as differences in administrative costs and in employee incentive effects may overwhelm the tax factors in importance.

Appendix 8.1

ACCOUNTING FOR THE TAX BENEFITS OF EMPLOYEE STOCK OPTIONS

As discussed in the chapter, the firm obtains a tax deduction equal to the amount of ordinary income recognized by the employee at the exercise date of a nonqualifed employee stock option. For financial accounting purposes, the vast majority of firms do not recognize compensation expense related to ESOs. However, these firms then must provide footnote disclosures as if earnings were calculated expensing ESOs.[32]

The different treatment implies a permanent difference as per Chapter 2—the item flows through one set of books (tax) but not the other books (accounting). But, alas, that is not how the difference is treated for accounting purposes. Instead of simply reducing current tax expense as a normal permanent difference (increasing accounting net income), the ESO tax benefit is credited directly to shareholders' equity and income taxes payable (the liability account) is reduced. The credit increases shareholders' equity and is based on the argument that the firm's equity increases because it receives both the exercise price from employees and the tax benefits from the Treasury when it issues the shares. The reduction in income taxes payable shows up in the Statement of Cash Flows as an add back to net income because, in calculating net income, current tax expense is overstated by the amount of the ESO tax benefit. This treatment has implications for how we interpret reported current tax expense and estimate taxable income.

A simple numerical example illustrates the issue. Suppose the following as facts:

Sales	$1000
Cost of goods sold	−400
R&D	−200
Depreciation − book	−120
Interest expense	−100
Municipal bond interest income	+50
Pretax book income (PTBI)	230

Other information:

Corporate statutory tax rate = 35% = str.
Depreciation for tax purposes = $200.
Municipal bond interest income is tax exempt (that is, excluded in the calculation of taxable income).
The firm also has an ESO tax deduction of $30 (giving the firm an ESO tax benefit of $30 × .35 = $10.50).

---

[32]As noted in the text, several hundred firms have announced that they will begin recognizing compensation expense associated with ESOs. Such recognition of compensation expense will give rise to a temporary difference because the expense is recognized in the grant year and over the vesting period, whereas the tax deduction is taken when the ESO is exercised which by definition is after the ESO is vested. This temporary difference gives rise to a deferred tax asset. Further, the grant date fair value that is the basis of the compensation expense will differ from the exercise date value, which is the deduction amount. If the deduction is greater than the grant date fair value (the compensation expense), the excess tax amount is credited to shareholders' equity rather than a reduction in current tax expense.

These facts imply the following

	Book	Tax
Sales	$1000	$1000
Cost of goods sold	−400	−400
R&D	−200	−200
Depreciation	−120	−200
Interest expense	−100	−100
Municipal bond interest income	+50	
ESO tax deduction		−30
Pretax book income (PTBI)	230	
Taxable income		70

Note that current tax payable then is taxable income × statutory tax rate = $70 × .35 = $24.50. But in calculating and reporting current tax expense, firms *do not* reduce current tax expense by the amount of the ESO tax benefit. That is, they estimate and report current tax expense as

$$= (\text{PTBI} - \text{temporary differences} \\ - \text{permanent differences}) \times .35$$
$$= (\$230 - \$80 - \$50) \times .35$$
$$= \$100 \times .35 = \$35$$

A financial statement reader unaware of this calculation would derive an incorrect estimated taxable income = reported current tax expense/.35 = $100 (see Chapter 2, appendix equation A2.4). Thus, because current tax expense is overstated by the amount of the ESO tax benefits, current tax expense overstates the amount of actual current taxes payable and thus an estimate based on equation (A2.4) overstates taxable income!

The fix (for most firms) is to adjust the reported current tax expense as

$$= (\text{Reported current tax expense} - \text{ESO} \\ \text{tax benefits})$$
$$= (\$35 - \$10.50)$$
$$= \$24.50 \qquad\qquad \textbf{(A8.1)}$$

And the estimated taxable income = adjusted current tax expense/statutory tax rate

$$= \$24.50/.35 = \$70$$

This adjustment can also be represented as estimated taxable income

$$= (\text{PTBI} - \text{temporary differences} \\ - \text{permanent differences}) \\ - \text{ESO tax deduction})$$
$$= (\$230 - \$80 - \$50 - \$30)$$
$$= \$70 \qquad\qquad \textbf{(A8.2)}$$

where the ESO tax deduction is estimated as the reported ESO tax benefit/.35.

Analysis of Corporate Disclosures

The following is extracted from Microsoft Corporation's 2002 Annual Report.

Microsoft Corporation's
STOCKHOLDERS' EQUITY STATEMENTS

In millions	Year Ended June 30		
	2000	**2001**	**2002**
Convertible preferred stock			
Balance, beginning of year	$980	$—	$—
Conversion of preferred to common stock	(980)	—	—
Balance, end of year	—	—	—
Common stock and paid-in capital			
Balance, beginning of year	13,844	23,195	**$28,390**
Common stock issued	3,554	5,154	**1,801**
Common stock repurchased	(210)	(394)	**(676)**

In millions			*Year Ended June 30*
	2000	*2001*	*2002*
Sales/(repurchases) of put warrants	472	(1,367)	—
Stock option income tax benefits	5,535	2,066	**1,596**
Other, net	—	(264)	**536**
Balance, end of year	23,195	28,390	**31,647**
Retained earnings			
Balance, beginning of year	13,614	18,173	**18,899**
Net income	9,421	7,346	**7,829**
Other comprehensive income:			
Cumulative effect of accounting change	—	(75)	—
Net gains/(losses) on derivative instruments	—	634	**(91)**
Net unrealized investment gains/(losses)	(283)	(1,460)	**5**
Translation adjustments and other	23	(39)	**82**
Comprehensive income	9,161	6,406	**7,825**
Preferred stock dividends	(13)	—	—
Immaterial pooling of interests	97	—	—
Common stock repurchased	(4,686)	(5,680)	**(6,191)**
Balance, end of year	18,173	18,899	**20,533**
Total stockholders' equity	$41,368	$47,289	**$52,180**

Microsoft does not explicitly discuss the ESO tax benefits in the tax note or ESO disclosures but includes the item in its Stockholders' Equity Statements and Statement of Cash Flows. Recall from the discussion in Chapter 2, equation (A2.4), we can estimate taxable income as current tax expense/top statutory tax rate. The estimates are tabled below in row B. From the amounts labeled ESO tax benefits in the Stockholders' Equity Statement and the current tax expense reported in the income tax note, we can derive a revised estimate of Microsoft Corporation's taxable income.

	Microsoft Corporation	*1998*	*1999*	*2000*	*2001*	*2002*	*Total*
A.	Reported U.S. current tax expense	$2,518	$4,067	$4,744	$3,243	$3,644	$18,216
B.	Estimated taxable income (A/.35)	7,194	11,506	13,554	9,266	10,411	51,931
C.	Reported ESO tax benefit	1,553	3,107	5,535	2,066	1,596	13,457
D.	Adjusted U.S. current tax expense (A − C)	965	920	−791	1,177	2,048	4,319
E.	Adjusted estimated taxable income (D/.35)	2,757	2,629	−2,260	3,363	5,851	12,340
F.	Reported U.S. pretax book income	5,072	10,649	11,860	9,189	8,920	45,690
G.	ESO tax deduction = (C/.35)	3,294	8,877	15,814	5,903	4,560	38,449

Row C presents the reported ESO tax benefits. For discussion, we focus here on the year 2000. The ESO tax benefit of $5,535 in fiscal year 2000 gives an adjusted current tax expense of −$791 (row D) resulting in a revised estimate of taxable income of −$2,260 (row E) compared with the unadjusted taxable income estimate of $13,554 (row B)! An alternative way to explain this outcome, is that the ESO tax benefit of $5,535 implies an ESO tax deduction of $5,535/.35 = $15,814 million (last row). The $15,814 million deduction wiped out Microsoft's U.S. taxable income! In fact, it appears as though Microsoft had a tax loss for U.S. tax purposes, which it probably carried back for a refund. Note also that the ESO tax deduction represents the taxable gain recognized by Microsoft's employees in 2000 for the exercise of their nonqualified ESOs. Over the 5-year period 1998 to 2002, Microsoft appears to have saved over $13 billion in federal taxes, reducing its taxable income from nearly $52 billion to $12 billion.

A Complication

If a firm has a net operating loss carryforward and it places a valuation allowance on the associated deferred tax asset (see discussion in Chapter 2 Appendix 2.2), then it is more difficult to ascertain the amount of any ESO tax deduction. Without a valuation allowance, the credit to shareholders' equity for ESO tax benefits is the amount of actual tax cash savings and/or expected future cash tax savings (if the deduction is part of an NOL carryforward which will be used in the future). However, in a year when a valuation allowance is placed against the NOL deferred tax asset, the amount of the ESO tax benefit offset by the valuation allowance is not recognized as a credit to shareholders' equity. In this case, the financial statement user will underestimate (or derive a zero estimate of) the amount of the ESO tax deduction. For these firms, a better estimate of the ESO tax deduction can be derived from the ESO footnote disclosures of the firm. The ESO deduction for a period can be estimated as the number of ESOs exercised times an estimate of the stock price at exercise less the weighted average exercise price of the exercised options. The unknown variable here is the stock price at the exercise date. A reasonable estimate is the weighted average exercise price on the new ESOs granted in the same period. The estimate of the ESO deduction is obviously sensitive to the stock price used and for stocks with more volatile stock prices, the ESO tax deduction is likely to be more noisy.

We illustrate the approach using an extract from Microsoft's 2002 Annual Report from the Employee Stock and Savings Plans note.

Microsoft Corporation
Notes to Financial Statements
NOTE 15   EMPLOYEE STOCK AND SAVINGS PLANS
STOCK OPTION PLANS

The Company has stock option plans for directors, officers, and employees, which provide for nonqualified and incentive stock options. Options granted prior to 1995 generally vest over four and one-half years and expire 10 years from the date of grant. Options granted between 1995 and 2001 generally vest over four and one-half years and expire seven years from the date of grant, while certain options vest either over four and one-half years or over seven and one-half years and expire after 10 years. Options granted during 2002 vest over four and one-half years and expire 10 years from the date of grant. At June 30, 2002, options for 371 million shares were vested and 543 million shares were available for future grants under the plans.

Stock options outstanding were as follows:

In millions, except per share amounts

Average	Shares	Price per Share Range	Weighted
Balance, June 30, 1999	766	$0.56–$83.28	$23.87
Granted	304	65.56–119.13	79.87
Exercised	(198)	0.56–82.94	9.54
Canceled	(40)	4.63–116.56	36.50
Balance, June 30, 2000	832	0.56–119.13	41.23
Granted	224	41.50–80.00	60.84
Exercised	(123)	0.59–85.81	11.13
Canceled	(35)	13.83–119.13	63.57
Balance, June 30, 2001	898	0.56–119.13	49.54
Granted	**41**	**48.62–72.57**	**62.50**
Exercised	**(99)**	**1.02–69.81**	**12.82**
Canceled	**(38)**	**1.15–116.56**	**68.67**
Balance, June 30, 2002	**802**	**0.79–119.13**	**53.75**

For various price ranges, weighted average characteristics of outstanding stock options at June 30, 2002 were as follows:

In millions, except per share amounts

| Range of Exercise Prices | Outstanding Options | | | Exercisable Options | |
	Shares	Remaining Life (Years)	Weighted Average Price	Shares	Weighted Average Price
$0.79–$5.97	36	1.6	$4.83	35	**$4.82**
5.98–13.62	44	0.5	11.19	42	**11.18**
13.63–29.80	90	2.0	15.02	84	**14.97**
29.81–43.62	73	2.7	32.19	66	**32.09**
43.63–60.00	191	6.9	55.81	41	**54.03**
60.01–69.50	146	6.4	66.24	35	**66.53**
69.51–83.28	80	5.1	71.17	21	**71.84**
83.29–119.13	142	4.2	89.87	47	**89.29**

For comparison purposes, we include the disclosed ESO tax benefit and the resulting grossed-up ESO tax deduction. For Microsoft, the estimates derived from the ESO footnote disclosures are within a reasonable range of the disclosed tax benefits.

		2000	2001	2002
A.	Number ESOs exercised	198	123	99
B.	Weighted average stock price on new grants	$79.87	$60.84	$62.50
C.	Weighted average exercise price of ESOs exercise	9.54	11.13	12.82
	Estimated ESO tax deduction (A × (B − C))	13,925	6,114	4,918
D.	Disclosed ESO tax benefit	5,535	2,066	1,596
	Estimated ESO tax deduction (D/.35)	15,814	5,903	4,560

The Microsoft note also provides some information about vesting periods and maturity life of the ESOs as well as details for the current and prior 2 years of the balance of ESOs outstanding, granted, exercised, and cancelled. Microsoft discloses that the number of ESOs granted decreased dramatically from 304 million in 2000, 224 million in 2001, to 41 million in 2002. This likely signals a shift in compensation policy at Microsoft, confirmed by Microsoft's announcement in July 2003 that they were shifting from using ESOs to restricted stock to compensate employees. Nevertheless, at the end of fiscal year 2002 (June 30 for Microsoft), the company reports 802 million ESOs outstanding with a weighted exercise price of $53.75 ranging from 79 cents to $119.13. More detailed disclosures of the exercise prices of the ESOs outstanding at the end of June 30, 2002, are also reported. The note (not presented here) also presents the pro forma income statement as required by SFAS 123 as if the firm recognized compensation expense arising from the ESOs.

Finally, to provide some idea of the magnitude of tax savings firms have obtained from ESOs, we list below the ten NASDAQ firms that received among the largest tax savings over the period 1999—2002. We also present these tax savings as a percentage of cash flow from operations because the tax savings are a direct reduction in cash outflows because of the lower tax payments. Over the 4-year period, Microsoft was the largest beneficiary, with over $12 billion saved in taxes representing 23.9% of the $51.5 billion cash from operations. Cisco Systems reduced taxes by $4.79 billion, which was 20.4% of cash flows from operations (CFO). Dell, Intel, and Sun Microsystems were the next biggest recipients of tax savings. Note that these tax benefits also approximate the taxes paid by employees on the exercise of ESOs so that the net effect on federal government tax revenues is approximately zero.

	ESO Tax Benefits 1999–2002	Cash Flow from Operations 1999–2002	%
Microsoft Corporation	$12,304	$51,503	23.89%
Cisco Systems	4,790	23,472	20.41%
Intel Corporation	2,098	42,879	4.89%
Oracle	1,742	10,152	17.16%
Dell Computer	2,716	15,456	17.57%
Sun Microsystems	1,844	9,237	19.96%
Yahoo! Inc.	267	1,123	23.78%
Siebel Systems	331	1,550	21.35%
Amgen	1,024	6,590	15.54%
Adobe Systems	251	1,527	16.44%

Finally, because NQOs give rise to a tax deduction, this deduction must be factored into estimations of corporate marginal tax rates. Graham, Lang, and Shackelford (2004) hand collect ESO tax benefit data for 200 firms, estimate an adjusted taxable income, and then estimate each corporations marginal tax rate via the simulation method discussed in Chapter 7. For the NASDAQ 100 firms, they find that the median estimated marginal tax rate decreased from 31% to 5%—a dramatic drop consistent with the median firm obtaining large tax benefits from ESOs. Note however these estimates are derived in a bull market where stock prices and hence ESO values increased dramatically. For the 100 S&P firms, the effect was much smaller, reflecting the fact that these firms issue fewer ESOs.

Discussion Questions

1. Why is the list of compensation alternatives in Table 8.1 not necessarily ordered from most desirable to least desirable for an employee?

2. Why might salary be preferred to deferred compensation even if the employee's tax rate is falling over time? Illustrate your answer using the changes in tax rates introduced in the TRA 86. Was salary preferred for both higher and lower compensated employees?

3. In determining the tax advantage of a current salary contract versus a deferred compensation contract, why is it useful to set the contractual terms so as to hold one party indifferent to the choice of the contract? Does it matter whether the employee or employer is made indifferent between the two choices?

4. With the change in marginal tax rates in the TRA 86, would it have been tax-disadvantageous for tax-exempt institutions such as Stanford University to establish deferred compensation arrangements in 1986 for their employees? Why might such institutions not have established these programs at that time?

5. What are the tax benefits of a fringe benefit such as employer-supplied life and health insurance? What are the nontax costs associated with such a program? Why would some employees prefer salary to the insurance program?

6. When is it efficient for the employer to reimburse the employee for business meals and entertainment expenditures? How does the 2% limitation on miscellaneous itemized deductions affect the decision? What nontax factors might influence the decision?

7. Illustrate how a demand loan can serve to defer compensation. Why does such a program require mutual trust between employees and their employers?

8. When are discretionary bonus plans attractive tax planning vehicles? What incentives might induce the employer to renege on the bonus? What prevents the employer from reneging?

9. Is each statement true or false?
   a. The expected return on stock appreciation rights always exceeds the expected return on the underlying stock.
   b. The financial reporting differences for compensating employees with stock appreciation rights and stock options lead small start-up companies to prefer granting stock appreciation rights to their employees.
   c. A nonqualified option is preferable to an incentive stock option for tax purposes.
   d. TRA 86 made incentive stock options less attractive.

10. In deriving equation (8.12) comparing ISOs and NQOs, how were any stock price changes after exercise of an ISO treated?

11. If an employee exercises an NQO early in advance of an expected tax rate increase, what costs or benefits might accrue to the employer?

12. Does an employee realize any benefits from exercising an ISO in advance of an expected tax rate increase?

13. General Motors Corporation, in its 1994 Proxy Statement to shareholders, stated the following: "Compensation Deductibility Policy— . . . the Committee believes the regulation to be discriminatory toward the stockholders of publicly held corporations . . ." Why might General Motors' compensation committee hold this belief?

14. General Motors Corporation, in its 1997 Proxy Statement to shareholders, stated the following: "To the extent it is practicable and consistent with the Corporation's executive compensation philosophy, the Committee intends to comply with Section 162(m) of the Internal Revenue Code (and any regulations promulgated thereunder) in order to preserve the deductibility of performance-based compensation in excess of $1 million per taxable year to each of the Named Executive

Officers. . . . If compliance with the Section 162(m) rules conflicts with the compensation philosophy or is deemed not to be in the best interests of shareholders, the Committee will abide by the compensation philosophy, regardless of the tax impact of such actions." Why might noncompliance with Section 162(m) be in the best interests of shareholders (because by receiving a tax deduction for compensation the firm saves taxes, which increases cash flows)?

15. Below are extracts from Cisco Systems 2000 and 2002 Annual Reports. In your own words, describe the effects of ESOs on Cisco's taxes from 2000 to 2002.

Extract from July 2002 Annual Report

At July 29, 2000, the Company provided a valuation allowance on certain of its deferred tax assets because of uncertainty regarding their realizability due to expectation of future employee stock option exercises. As of July 28, 2001, the Company had removed the valuation allowance because it believed it was more likely than not that all deferred tax assets would be realized in the foreseeable future and was reflected as a credit to shareholders' equity.

The Company's income taxes payable for federal, state, and foreign purposes have been reduced, and the deferred tax assets increased, by the tax benefits associated with dispositions of employee stock options. The Company receives an income tax benefit calculated as the difference between the fair market value of the stock issued at the time of exercise and the option price, tax effected. These benefits were credited directly to shareholders' equity and amounted to $61 million, $1.8 billion, and $3.1 billion in fiscal 2002, 2001, and 2000, respectively. Benefits reducing taxes payable amounted to $61 million, $1.4 billion, and $2.5 billion in fiscal 2002, 2001, and 2000, respectively. Benefits increasing gross deferred tax assets amounted to $358 million and $582 million in fiscal 2001 and 2000, respectively.

Extract from July 2000 Annual Report

The Company's income taxes payable for federal, state, and foreign purposes have been reduced, and the deferred tax assets increased, by the tax benefits associated with dispositions of employee stock options. The Company receives an income tax benefit calculated as the difference between the fair market value of the stock issued at the time of exercise and the option price, tax effected. These benefits were credited directly to shareholders' equity and amounted to $3.08 billion, $837 million, and $422 million for fiscal 2000, 1999, and 1998, respectively. Benefits reducing taxes payable amounted to $2.49 billion, $837 million, and $422 million for fiscal 2000, 1999, and 1998, respectively. Benefits increasing gross deferred tax assets amounted to $582 million in fiscal 2000.

The Company has provided a valuation allowance on certain of its deferred tax assets because of uncertainty regarding their realizability due to expectation of future employee stock option exercises. Deferred tax assets of approximately $963 million at July 29, 2000, pertain to certain tax credits and net operating loss carryforwards resulting from the exercise of employee stock options. When recognized, the tax benefit of these credits and losses will be accounted for as a credit to shareholders' equity rather than as a reduction of the income tax provision.

Exercises

1. Your employer is considering paying you deferred compensation in 5 years or a cash bonus of $1 million today. Here are the facts.
   - Your tax rate today is 50%.
   - Your tax rate in 5 years will be 35%.
   - Your employer's tax rate today is 30%.

- Your employer's tax rate in 5 years will be 40%.
- Both you and your employer have an after-tax discount rate of 7%.
    a. What is the highest deferred compensation payment (received 5 years from now) that your employer would be willing to pay?
    b. What is the lowest deferred compensation payment (received 5 years from now) that you would settle for?
    c. Can you and your employer get together and write a mutually beneficial deferred compensation contract? If so, describe the contract (amount).

2. Suppose you will retire in 9 years. Throughout your life you will face a tax rate of 31% and earn an after-tax rate of return of 8% on your investments. Your company's pension plan earns a 12% return, and the company itself earns a 10% after-tax return on its own projects. The company faces a current tax rate of 34% and will face a 40% rate in year 9.
    a. How much in deferred compensation (D*) would the company have to pay you in year 9 to make you indifferent between future compensation and a $100 bonus now?
    b. How much of a contribution to your pension plan (P*) would the company have to make to make you indifferent between pension benefits in 9 years and a $100 bonus now?
    c. What is the present value of the after-tax cost of each form of compensation (current bonus of $100, deferred compensation of D*, and pension plan contribution of P*) to the company, using a discount rate of 10%?
(Exercise written by Richard Sansing, Dartmouth College.)

3. Under current law, employer-paid health insurance premiums are deductible by the employer and not taxable to the employee. Suppose instead only the first $1,000 of such premiums were nontaxable. If an employee was in the 15% tax bracket, how much would his employer have to pay him in cash to make him indifferent between the cash and $3,000 of health insurance premiums? Assume the employee cannot deduct any health insurance premiums he pays himself because his medical expenses are far below 7.5% of adjusted gross income. What if his tax bracket were 31%?

4. Suppose you are an employee of Toys4u.com and incurred $8,000 of company-related meals and entertainment (M&E) during the year. The company is evaluating whether to reimburse you directly or to pay additional salary and have you claim your M&E expenditures on your personal tax return.
    a. Assuming Toys4u.com's marginal tax rate is 35%, what salary will make the firm indifferent between reimbursement to you of $8,000 and salary?
    b. Assuming Toys4u.com is willing to offer you $8,000 reimbursement and salary of $X, solved in (a), which will you choose if your marginal tax rate is 28%?
    c. Will your answer to (b) change if your marginal tax rate is 39.6%?

5. Suppose you are an employee of Pactruck who just received 10,000 shares of restricted stock which vest in 4 years. Your current and expected tax rate on ordinary income is 35% and on capital gains is 15%. The stock is currently trading at $15 and you expect it to appreciate at 20% per annum over the next 4 years. You face an after-tax borrowing rate of 7%. You plan on selling the stock as soon as it vests. Should you simply hold the restricted stock through vesting and sell at that time or make a Section 83(b) election? As an alternative to the Section 83(b) election, you consider borrowing and purchasing additional stock using the money you would have used to pay the taxes on the Section 83(b) election. Evaluate this alternative.

    Discuss any nontax costs associated with a Section 83(b) election and the alternative borrow-and-buy additional stock strategies. What is the ex post outcome if the stock price appreciates at 15% per annum? At 10% per annum? Fails to appreciate at all? Declines by 5% per annum?

6. Same facts as exercise 5. But now you expect your tax rate on ordinary income to decline to 20% in year 3. How do your answers in exercise 5 change? Would you make the Section 83(b) election? Evaluate the borrow-and-purchase additional stock strategy.

7. Same facts as exercise 5. But now you expect your tax rate on ordinary income to increase to 50% in year 4. How do your answers in exercise 5 change? Would you make the Section 83(b) election? Evaluate the borrow-and-purchase additional stock strategy.

8. Suppose you are employed by MS Corporation. In 1996, you received nonqualified employee stock options (NQOs) to acquire 10,000 shares of MS's stock at an exercise price of $40 share. On that date, the stock traded at $35 per share. In 1997, you exercised your options when the stock price was $48 per share. In 1998, you sold the stock for $50 per share.
   a. What is the amount and character (ordinary or capital gain) of your income in 1996, 1997, and 1998 because of these transactions?
   b. How much is MS's tax deduction and when is it deductible?
   c. How much will MS report as compensation expense each period?
   d. IIow will your answers to questions (a), (b), and (c) change if the options were incentive stock options?
   (Exercise written by Richard Sansing, Dartmouth College.)

9. Wahoo, Inc. is a high-tech Internet company. It is trying to decide whether to issue NQOs or ISOs to its employees. Each employee will get 10 options. For purposes of this problem, assume that the options are exercised in 3 years and that the underlying stock is sold in 5 years. Here are the facts.
   • Corporate tax rate = 35%
   • Personal (employee) ordinary income tax rate = 40%
   • Personal (employee) capital gains tax rate = 28%
   • Personal (employee) after tax discount rate = 5%
   • Exercise price of the options = $5
   • Market price of Wahoo stock at date of grant = $4
   • Market price of Wahoo stock at date of exercise = $30
   • Market price of Wahoo at date of sale = $40
   a. Considering these facts, which type of option plan does Wahoo, Inc. prefer?
   b. Which type of option plan do Wahoo's employees prefer?
   c. Which type of plan should be used? Why?
   d. Assuming that you knew that the personal capital gains tax rate was going to be cut to 20% in 4 years from the current 28%, which type of plan should be used? Why?

10. In December 1992, Michael Eisner and the late Frank Wells of Walt Disney exercised a large number of stock options. The facts are summarized here.

	Options Granted	Previously Exercised	Exercised 11/30/92***	Grant Date	Expiration Date	Exercise Price
Eisner	8.16 m	3.16 m	5.00 m*	1984	1994	$3.59
	6.00 m			1989	1999	$17.14
	2.00 m			1989	1999	$19.64
Wells	7.36 m	5.72 m	1.64 m**	1984	1994	$3.59
	2.25 m			1989	1999	$17.14
	0.75 m			1989	1999	$19.64

*Of the shares acquired, 3.45 million were sold immediately.
**All of the shares acquired were sold immediately.
***Goldman Sachs executed these sales at $40 per share.

- In 1984, Michael Eisner became chairman of Walt Disney and Frank Wells became president. In late 1992, the options originally granted in 1984 were exercised when the stock price was $40 per share. Both Eisner and Wells were subject to the top marginal tax rate in 1992, which was 31%. Assume that both had salaries in excess of $1 million.
- In late 1992 there was a high probability that Clinton's tax act would be passed, effective for 1993, and that the top tax rate for individuals would increase to 39.6%, the corporate rate would increase to 35%, and deductions for executive compensation in excess of $1 million would be disallowed.
  a. Ignoring present value considerations, how much did Eisner and Wells together personally save in taxes by exercising their options in 1992 instead of waiting until 1993 or 1994?
  b. Michael Eisner exercised 5 million options and immediately sold 3,450,000 of the shares. What were the cash flow consequences to Eisner of these two transactions, including taxes?
  c. Eisner told *The Wall Street Journal* he had to exercise the options in 1992 to avoid Disney incurring a substantial additional tax liability. Consider the claim that the early exercise saved Disney shareholders roughly $90 million in corporate income taxes. Assume that the corporation could not deduct any compensation paid in 1993 over $1 million.
  d. Recompute your answer to (c) using the actual law as enacted, which has two provisions relevant for this problem. The first is that the $1 million disallowance did not take effect until 1994. The second is that transitional rules would have grandfathered these options and made the expenses fully deductible.
  e. If early exercise was such a good deal for Disney, why did not Eisner and Well exercise all their options instead of just the options granted in 1984?
  (Exercise written by Richard Sansing, Dartmouth College.)
11. The following is extracted from notes and Consolidated Statements of Shareholders' Equity in Cisco System's 2000 and 2002 Annual Reports. Estimate Cisco's taxable income ignoring the effects of the ESO tax deduction and then taking into account the ESO tax deduction. Discuss your results.

	1998	*1999*	*2000*	*2001*	*2002*
Reported US pretax book income	$1,950	$2,092	$2,544	–$1,727	$1,550
US current tax expense	855	1,164	1,843	581	929
ESO tax benefits	422	837	3,077	1,755	61

Tax Planning Problems

1. It is late 1999 and you are a successful oil executive currently working in Alaska for a major oil company. Tomorrow morning you will have the opportunity to negotiate with your employer to receive some amount of deferred salary in 5 years in exchange for $75,000 of your year 2000 compensation. If this compensation is not deferred, it will be paid to you on December 31, 1999, as a year-end bonus. Both you and your employer can earn a before-tax rate of return of 12%. Your employer's combined federal and state income tax rate is 40% and is expected to remain constant throughout the 5-year period.

   Because Alaska does not have an individual income tax, you will pay only a federal tax of 39.6% on income earned in 1999. However, you are being transferred to New York at the beginning of next year, where you will be groomed for a top-level position in the firm. You expect your combined federal, state, and city income tax rate to be 50% in the year 2000 and to remain at this level throughout the 5-year period.

a. What is the highest deferred compensation payment that your employer would be willing to pay?

b. What is the lowest deferred compensation payment that you would settle for?

c. Can you and your employer get together and write a mutually beneficial deferred compensation contract?

    Now suppose you are married to a psychic. As you are making your computations in preparation for tomorrow's meeting, your spouse informs you that she is getting a clear image of you drinking beer at a bar on the Gulf Coast of Florida while reading a copy of *Deep Sea Fishing Weekly* dated 5 years from today and demanding that the bartender give you the AARP discount for retirees (which you will not get because you are not old enough).

d. Your spouse interprets this image as indicating that you will snap mentally from the stress 5 years from now (2004), quit your job, move to Florida, where you become the captain of a small charter boat, and pay federal income taxes at a 31% rate when your deferred compensation is received in the year 2004. Note: Your spouse has never been wrong before. Under these conditions, what is the lowest deferred compensation payment that you would settle for?

e. Under these new conditions, can you and your employer get together and write a mutually beneficial deferred compensation contract?

2. Suppose Congress is expected to increase the corporate tax rate from 35% to 45% next year. RealNet.Com is scheduled to pay its CEO a salary of $1 million in the current period. The CEO's tax rate is 40%. The CEO is also entitled to a bonus that is up to the discretion of the compensation committee. As an adviser to the compensation committee, compare and contrast the following tax planning strategies.

a. Do nothing.

b. Defer a large part of the salary ($300,000) from the current period to the next period.

c. Defer the bonus from the current period to the next period.

d. Issue an interest-free demand loan of $3 million to the CEO, assuming the applicable federal rate of interest is 10%.

3. Suppose you are an employee of HP Corporation. You face a personal marginal tax rate on ordinary income of 50%, and on capital gains the tax rate is 20%. Your after-tax opportunity cost of capital is 7% per year. You hold 100 employee stock options that have an exercise price of $20 per option, and the current stock price is $35.

a. Assume the options you hold are incentive stock options (ISOs). What is the present value of any tax due given that you intend to hold the stock for 10 years after exercise? What is the present value of any tax deduction that HP might get, assuming HP's marginal tax rate is 10%?

b. Repeat part (a) but now assume the options are nonqualified stock options. Compare and summarize your results.

Now change the facts as follows. Suppose the tax law changed such that HP's marginal tax rate is 34% and your tax rate is 28% on both ordinary income and capital gains.

c. Repeat (a) assuming the 100 options are incentive stock options.

d. Repeat (c) assuming the 100 options are nonqualified stock options. Summarize and compare the results of (c) and (d). Do you notice any tax planning opportunities available to the employee and HP?

4. Suppose you are a high-level employee of Drugstore.Com. You currently hold 50,000 NQOs, each with an exercise price of $20. The options vest—that is, you are no longer restricted from exercising them—in 1 month. Your current and expected future tax rate on ordinary income is 39.6% and on capital gains is 20%. The stock is currently trading at $35, and you expect the stock to appreciate at 20% per year over the remaining 7 years of the options life. You have an after-tax discount rate of 10%. Should you exercise the NQOs immediately on vesting and hold the stock or hold the options through to maturity before exercising? Would your answer change if you held ISOs instead of NQOs?

5. Suppose you hold two series of options, both NQOs. Because of a big promotion you expect your tax rate to increase from a current 31% to 39.6%. The current stock price is $70. The first set of options, close to maturity, has an exercise price of $25 and an estimated Black–Scholes option value of $48. The second set of options, with 5 years to maturity, has an exercise price of $50 and an estimated option value of $30. Should you exercise either series of options in advance of your big promotion?

References and Additional Readings

Austin, J., J. Gaver, and K. Gaver, 1998. "The Choice of Incentive Stock Options vs. Nonqualified Options: A Marginal Tax Rate Perspective," *Journal of the American Taxation Association* (Fall), pp. 1–21.

Balsam, S., and D. Ryan, 1996. "Response to Tax Law Changes Involving the Deductibility of Executive Compensation: A Model Explaining Corporate Behavior," *Journal of the American Taxation Association* (Supplement), pp. 1–12.

Balsam, S., R. Halperin, and H. Mozes, 1997. "Tax Costs and Nontax Benefits: The Case of Incentive Stock Options," *Journal of the American Taxation Association* (Fall), pp. 19–37.

Desai, M., 2002. "The Corporate Profit Base, Tax Sheltering Activity, and the Changing Nature of Employee Compensation." Working paper 8866. Cambridge, MA: NBER.

Graham, J., M. Lang, and D. Shackelford, 2004. "Employee Stock Options, Corporate Taxes and Debt Policy," *Journal of Finance,* forthcoming.

Hanlon, M., and T. Shevlin, 2002. "Accounting for Tax Benefits of Employee Stock Options and Implications for Research," *Accounting Horizons* (March), pp. 1–16.

Hemmer, T., S. Matsunaga, and T. Shevlin, 1996. "The Influence of Risk Diversification on the

Early Exercise of Employee Stock Options by Executive Officers," *Journal of Accounting and Economics* (February), pp. 45–68.

Hite, G., and M. Long, 1982. "Taxes and Executive Stock Options," *Journal of Accounting and Economics* (4), pp. 3–14.

Huddart, S., 1994. "Employee Stock Options," *Journal of Accounting and Economics* (September), pp. 207–231.

Huddart, S., 1998. "Tax Planning and the Exercise of Employee Stock Options," *Contemporary Accounting Research* (Summer), pp. 203–216.

Huddart, S., and M. Lang, 1996. "Employee Stock Option Exercises: An Empirical Analysis," *Journal of Accounting and Economics* (July), pp. 157–172.

Johnson, M., S. Nabar, and S. Porter, 1999. "Determinants of Corporate Response to Section 162(m)." Working paper. Ann Arbor, MI: University of Michigan.

Madeo, S., and T. Omer, 1994. "The Effect of Taxes on Switching Stock Option Plans: Evidence from the Tax Reform Act of 1969," *Journal of the American Taxation Association* (Fall), pp. 24–42.

Manzon, G., and G. Plesko, 2002. "The Relation Between Financial and Tax Reporting Measures of Income," *Tax Law Review* (55), pp. 175–214.

Matsunaga, S., 1995. "The Effects of Financial Reporting Costs on the Use of Employee Stock Options," *The Accounting Review* (January), pp. 1–26.

Matsunaga, S., T. Shevlin, and D. Shores, 1992. "Disqualifying Dispositions of Incentive Stock Options: Tax Benefits versus Financial Reporting Costs," *Journal of Accounting Research* (Supplement), pp. 37–76.

McDonald, R. 2003. "Are There Tax Reasons to Exercise a Compensation Option?" Working paper. Evanston, IL: Northwestern University.

McGill, G., and E. Outslay, 2002. "Did Enron Pay Taxes? Using Accounting Information to Decipher Tax Status," *Tax Notes* (August 19).

9

PENSION AND RETIREMENT PLANNING

After completing this chapter, you should be able to:

1. Explain the differences between a defined contribution pension plan and a defined benefit pension plan.

2. Analyze and compare the after-tax returns to current salary, pension plan, and deferred compensation.

3. Explain and illustrate the Black–Tepper tax arbitrage pension strategy.

4. Explain why it might pay to overfund a defined benefit pension plan.

5. Compare alternative strategies of funding retiree health care costs.

6. List the benefits of employee stock ownership plans.

To encourage saving for retirement, many countries give favorable tax treatment to pension compensation, and pension plans have become extremely important components of the compensation package for both employers and employees. We stressed in Chapter 3 the following points concerning alternative savings vehicles:

1. Contributions into the plan are tax deductible up to prescribed limits.
2. Earnings on pension investments are tax exempt.
3. Employees defer payment of tax until they receive payments from the plan.[1]

In this chapter, we discuss the tax advantages of corporate pension funds and highlight their nontax costs and benefits. We first discuss different types of pension plans and then compare them to salary and deferred compensation plans. We then discuss pension plan investment strategy (for example, stocks versus bonds) and funding strategy (how much to put into the plan). In the last two sections of this

---

[1]These three conditions apply to all pension savings accounts except for Roth IRAs, where, as discussed in Chapter 3, contributions are not tax deductible, that is, after-tax dollars are contributed to the plan, and payments from the plan are tax-free.

chapter, we discuss postretirement health care plans and employee stock ownership plans.

9.1 TYPES OF PENSION PLANS

The two major categories of corporate pension plans are defined contribution plans and defined benefit plans. In a **defined contribution corporate pension plan** the employer and, in some cases, the employee makes contributions into an account that will accumulate pension benefits on behalf of the employee. As its name implies, a defined contribution plan specifies contributions into the plan. Employees might be required to contribute 5% of their compensation to receive a matching 10% contribution by their employer. The employees' ultimate pension benefit depends on the amounts contributed into the plan and on investment performance. The employer does not guarantee the amount of its employees' pension benefit. In this regard, corporate defined contribution plans are similar to individual retirement accounts (IRAs) although contribution limits for corporate pension plans are far more generous than for IRAs.[2] Examples of corporate defined contribution plans include profit-sharing plans, money-purchase plans, 401(k) plans, employee stock ownership plans, and thrift plans. For example, a profit-sharing plan might require the employer to contribute a fixed fraction of the salary of the employee if profits exceed designated levels and a lesser fixed fraction if profits fall below these levels.

In a defined contribution pension plan, the employer deposits the contribution into an employee account. Because employees bear the risk of investment performance, they are often given a choice among different investment alternatives in which to invest the money in their pension account, such as a bond fund, a stock fund, and a guaranteed annuity from an insurance company, which promises to pay the employee a specified annual amount in retirement.[3] The contributions are tax deductible,[4] and the earnings on the assets in the account are tax-deferred until withdrawn by the employee. An employee's withdrawals from the account in retirement are taxed as ordinary income. Tax rules require that employees, if retired, begin withdrawing by April 1 following the year in which the employee reaches age 70.5. The withdrawal amount must be at least what would be available from a fixed life annuity at that time although the withdrawal amount can be based on a joint annuity payable over the lives of the employee and a beneficiary. Except in the case of death or disability, the employee typically must pay a 10% excise tax in addition to the regular tax on withdrawals prior to age 59.5 (prior to age 55 for early retirees).

---

[2]Individuals may contribute up to $3,000 per year of pretax dollars into an IRA compared with a maximum contribution of the lesser of (1) 100% of the employee's eligible pay or (2) $40,000 to a defined contribution plan. Defined benefit plans face contribution limits if they are overfunded, that is, when plan assets exceed plan liabilities discussed later in the chapter.

[3]Some companies contribute their own stock into 401(k) plans. This imposes risk on the employee because much of their wealth is then concentrated in the firm. If the firm fails, not only is the employee out of work but his or her 401(k) investment in the company stock loses much of its value. See "When 401(k)s are KO'd," *Fortune* (January 7, 2002), p. 104 discussing Enron employees' pension fund losses.

[4]The employer deducts its contribution in calculating corporate taxable income, and the employee contributions, if any, reduce salary that is subject to taxation; that is, contributions are made from pretax salary.

A **defined benefit corporate pension plan** promises the employee a stated benefit at retirement, often based on salary and/or years of service, usually in the form of an annuity. Defined benefit plans are either flat benefit plans or salary-related plans.[5] A flat benefit plan, usually provided to union employees, stipulates that the employee will receive a fixed dollar amount per year based on years of service—for example, $20 per month per year of service not to exceed 25 years. A salary-related plan typically provides a benefit that is a percentage of an employee's salary. For example, a salary-related plan might provide the employee with an annual annuity of 2% of her average salary over her last 5 years of employment for each year she worked for the firm. If the employee's salary averaged $120,000 in the last 5 years of her 15 years of employment before leaving the firm at age 50, she could receive a pension at age 65, the firm's normal retirement age, of $36,000 per year, or 15 × .02 × $120,000. To fund these promises, employers contribute to a pension trust. Unlike defined contribution plans, employees need not worry about the investment performance of the assets in the pension fund as long as the fund contains sufficient assets to support these promised benefits.

It is more difficult to value the promises to employees in a defined benefit plan than in a defined contribution plan. Each year, actuaries determine the required contributions to fund the target retirement annuity for defined benefit plans. They estimate the discount rate to value the retirement liability, the terminal salary to forecast the amount of the annuity, the life expectancy of employees and their survivors, the earnings rate on assets in the pension fund, the expected employee turnover rates, and the possibility of the employees' disability and death. All these assumptions make it difficult to define precisely the corporation's pension liability and its funding requirements. As a result, by changing the assumptions, actuaries have considerable latitude in determining the tax-deductible funding requirements of pension plan sponsors.

Some descriptive data on private—that is, nongovernment—pension plans in the United States appear in Table 9.1. Assets held by private pension plans totaled $4 trillion in 1998, the latest year for which data are available.[6] Defined contribution (DC) plans held $2.085 trillion of assets, with $1.936 trillion held in defined benefit (DB) plans. There are 673,626 DC plans covering 50.3 million active employees compared with 56,405 DB plans covering 23 million active employees. DC plans are smaller on average, covering 74 employees compared with 365 employees for DB plans. DB plans

---

[5]A third type of defined benefit plan is a cash balance plan. In a typical cash balance plan, the benefits are defined in terms of an account balance. However, the employer is responsible for ensuring that the account has the promised balance. A participant's account is credited each year with a "pay credit," such as 5% of compensation, and an "interest credit," which is either a fixed rate or a variable rate linked to some interest index. Fluctuations in the value of the plan's investments do not directly affect the benefit amounts promised to participants. Thus, the investment risk on plan assets is borne by the employer. For further discussion of these plans, see A. Arcady and F. Mellors, "Cash Balance Conversions: Assessing the Accounting and Business Implications," *Journal of Accountancy* (February 2000), pp. 22–28, and E. McCarthy, "Staying Off the Cover of Time," *Journal of Accountancy* (February 2000), pp. 31–34. McCarthy discusses IBM's conversion from a traditional defined benefit plan to a cash balance plan. See also "Not Your Father's Pension," *The Wall Street Journal* (August 25, 2003), p. A10. The U.S. Department of Labor also has a frequently asked questions section on its Web site: *http://www.dol.gov/ebsa/FAQs/faq_compliance_cashbalanceplans.html.*
[6]The numbers are compiled by the federal government from Form 5500 reports filed with the Department of Labor by pension plan sponsors for 1996 plan years. The Department of Labor Web site, *www.dol.gov*, contains summary tables and other information on pension plans. See also "Retirement Prospects in a Defined Contribution World," edited by Dallas Salisbury, published by the Employee Benefit Research Institute (EBRI), 1997. The EBRI Web site, *www.ebri.org*, contains a wealth of information.

TABLE 9.1 Descriptive Data on Private U.S. Pension Plans for 1998

	Defined Contribution	Defined Benefit	Total
Assets	$2,085,250,000	$1,936,600,000	$4,026,841,000
Number of plans	632,626	56,405	730,031
Number of total participants (active, retired, separated)	57,903,000	55,200,000	99,455,000
Number of active employees covered	50,335,000	22,994,000	73,328,000
Average number of active employees per plan	74	408	
Asset Allocation			
Bonds	15.2%	37.9%	
Equity	40.9%	43.4%	
Other	43.9%	18.7%	

are most common among large firms while DC plans are popular among firms of all sizes. Both DC and DB plans allocate approximately the same percentage of total assets to equities, but DB plans hold a much larger percentage of bonds. We discuss this difference later in this chapter.

Among employees covered by either pension plan, in 1998, approximately 56% were covered by DC plan(s) only, approximately 30% by both DC and DB plans, and about 14% only by a DB plan. These percentages mark a significant change from 20 years prior, when only 32% of pension-covered employees were in DC plans compared with 87% in DB plans. The growth in DC plans has mostly occurred via 401(k) plans introduced in The Revenue Act of 1978. In 1998, 401(k) plans topped the 300,000 mark and make up 41% of all pension plans, cover 51% of all active participants, and hold 38% of all pension plan assets. Further, in 1998, 47% of all contributions to pension plans were made by employees, compared with only 11% in 1978. A number of factors explain this change in coverage or increased popularity of DC plans. DC plans are easier to administer, the risk of investment is borne by the employee, which possibly requires a risk premium for the employee, and financial accounting is simpler.[7] In addition, Congress has made it more difficult to extract excess assets from DB plans via pension terminations, and the sustained stock market increase over the last 15 years (at least until 2001) has resulted in many DB plans being fully funded, reducing the tax advantages.

9.2 A COMPARISON OF SALARY AND PENSION COMPENSATION

Because of the tax exemption on the returns to the assets in the pension account, it might appear that a contribution to a pension dominates an equal dollar amount of salary. But even ignoring nontax factors, this is not so in all cases. Suppose an employer

---

[7]The accounting for pension plans is laid out in Statement of Financial Accounting Standards 87 "Employers' Accounting For Pensions," Financial Accounting Standards Board (1985).

contemplates depositing \$100 into a defined contribution pension fund for its employee. If t_{c0} is the corporate tax rate today, the after-tax cost to the corporation of the contribution would be $\$100(1 - t_{c0})$, the same as the after-tax cost of \$100 of salary. As a result, the employer is indifferent between paying \$100 of salary and making a \$100 pension contribution.

For the employee, \$100 invested in the pension fund grows in value to $\$100(1 + R_{pen})^n$ in n periods, where R_{pen} is the before-tax rate of return on assets invested in the pension account.[8] Just what this before-tax return might be depends on the assets held in the pension account. Recall from Chapter 4 that the tax-favored treatment of the returns on stock, compared with the tax treatment of corporate bonds, implies that the before-tax risk-adjusted returns on shares would be well below the before-tax returns on bonds.[9]

If employees compare the after-tax accumulation in a pension with that of taking a current salary and investing the after-tax amount on their own for n periods, their after-tax accumulations would be

$$\text{Pension:} \quad \$100(1 + R_{pen})^n (1 - t_{pn}) \tag{9.1}$$

$$\text{Salary:} \quad \$100(1 - t_{p0})(1 + r_{pn})^n \tag{9.2}$$

where r_{pn} is the annualized after-tax rate of return per year available on personal non-pension investments, t_{p0} is the current marginal tax rate of the employee, and t_{pn} is the marginal tax rate on ordinary income of the employee at time n. Pensions will be preferred to salary when equation $(9.1) > (9.2)$

$$\$100(1 + R_{pen})^n (1 - t_{pn}) > \$100(1 - t_{p0})(1 + r_{pn})^n$$

which can be rearranged to

$$\frac{(1 + R_{pen})^n}{(1 + r_{pn})^n} > \frac{(1 - t_{p0})}{(1 - t_{pn})} \tag{9.3}$$

When personal tax rates are constant over time ($t_{p0} = t_{pn}$), the right-hand side of (9.3) equals 1, and pensions provide higher after-tax accumulations than salary as long as the before-tax return on pension investments exceeds the after-tax return on non-pension investments ($R_{pen} > r_{pn}$). But suppose that the employee could earn after-tax at the same rate as the pension fund could earn before tax. A possible example here is the savings component of a "cash value" (whole life or universal life) insurance policy. In this case, ignoring nontax considerations, the only motivation for a pension plan would be declining marginal tax rates for the employee. Of course, cash-value life insurance policies do bear transaction cost-related implicit taxes, as we discussed in Chapter 5, so pension investments would normally be expected to provide an investment return advantage.

---

[8] R_{pen} might be different for investments in the pension fund than outside the pension fund. For example, pension funds are not permitted to invest in certain kinds of assets. Pension funds also cannot invest as general partners in partnerships without attracting corporate taxation on their share of the income. Pension funds face some corporate taxation on the income they earn as limited partners in partnerships that engage in borrowing.

[9] The tax-favored treatment on stock includes favorable capital gains treatment provided the stock is held for longer than 12 months; the tax on gains can be deferred until the stock is sold; and the capital gains taxes can be avoided altogether by holding the stock until death or by donating appreciated stock to charity.

An important nontax cost of pension plans for some employees is that a pension investment is illiquid. Particularly for younger employees, pension investment may entail greater postponement of consumption than they desire. And while the opportunity to borrow to finance consumption can mitigate this disadvantage, the mitigation may be very slight, if at all, when significant transaction costs are associated with borrowing and where interest expense on personal borrowing is not fully tax deductible. In such circumstances, employees may require a rate of return far greater than R_{cn} per period after-tax for them to prefer pension compensation over salary.

Because pension compensation yields future taxable income to the employee, whereas salary yields current taxable income, pensions become more desirable as future tax rates decline relative to current tax rates. In this regard, the 1981 and 1986 Tax Acts in the United States, both of which reduced tax rates, provided particularly strong incentives to undertake pension investments prior to the reduction in rates. These acts provided huge windfalls to older employees, many of whom had been expecting to face nearly twice as high a marginal tax rate in retirement as they may end up facing.

Perhaps in recognition of this windfall, TRA 86 introduced a number of new rules that limit the advantages of pension plans for high-income taxpayers, including a substantial reduction in the maximum potential tax-deductible pension plan contribution. As a result, numerous firms were led to provide supplemental pension benefits for their employees that are essentially deferred compensation plans; that is, the employer loses an immediate deduction for the compensation and is taxable on the income earned on invested funds.

Rates of Return on Investments In and Out of Pension Accounts

We have assumed implicitly that investors earn a higher rate of return in the pension account than they could investing on their own. Although it may seem unlikely that the employee can earn at a higher after-tax rate of return outside the pension account than inside the account, it is certainly possible. Let us consider the following examples:

1. Employees may be forced to invest in common stock in the pension plan, which is a common feature of employee stock ownership plans, and such assets may bear high implicit taxes yielding low pretax rates of return.
2. Family tax planning strategies may also permit investment deductions to be taken at high tax rates and income to be taxed at low rates (at the household level). That is, high income parents might take tax deductions for part of the cost of investments early in the life of a tax sheltered project and, later in its life, gift their interest in the shelter to lower-tax-bracket family members if the project starts producing income. As a result, the after-tax rates of return at the household level could exceed the before-tax rates of return in pension accounts.
3. Alternative savings vehicles such as investing in life insurance policies or single premium deferred annuities may provide before-tax rates of return that are close to those available to employees in pension plans.

Antidiscrimination Rules

A major nontax disadvantage of both defined benefit as well as defined contribution pension plans is that highly compensated employees and a certain percentage of the firm's moderately compensated employees must be included in the firm's pension plan to qualify for tax-favored treatment. Highly compensated employees and, generally, older employees might want pension accounts. Moderately compensated employees, particularly the younger ones, typically prefer to consume now, to save later in their life, and to fund their pension plans when their tax rates are higher in the future.

As a result, if lower-income employees prefer salary to pension, they will not be willing to give up $100 of before-tax salary for $100 of pension contribution. For example, they might value the $100 pension contribution at only $80 and thus, to be indifferent, they might require $125 of pension contribution for each $100 of salary, but the corporation only is indifferent between paying $100 of salary and depositing $100 into a defined contribution pension plan. In many cases, the more highly compensated employees must end up covering the $20 shortfall. They do so indirectly by trading off more than a dollar of salary reduction for each dollar they receive in pension contributions.[10]

Empirically, pension benefits, particularly in defined benefit plans, have been heavily skewed to older employees in the economy, which is efficient for tax planning purposes for reasons we have already presented. The actuarial rules that determine whether the plan is "top heavy" with too many highly compensated employee dollars going into the plan make it easier to skew benefits to the older and more highly compensated employees than would be possible with a defined contribution plan. That is, the "rules" say that the plans cannot be top heavy, but it is relatively easier to get around them with a defined benefit plan than with a defined contribution plan.

9.3 DEFERRED COMPENSATION VERSUS PENSION

From earlier discussion in this chapter and in Chapter 8, we know an employer is indifferent, from a tax standpoint, between a dollar of current pension contribution or salary and

$$D_n \equiv [(1 - t_{c0})/(1 - t_{cn})](1 + r_{cn})^n$$

dollars of deferred compensation in n periods, where t_{c0} and t_{cn} represent the employer's current and future tax rates and r_{cn} represents the annual after-tax rate the employer can earn on marginal investments. That is, the employer can afford to pay deferred compensation of $1, plus its after-tax earnings on the dollar in salary or pension contribution postponed for n years, adjusted for changes in its tax rate over time.

For the employee, the deferred compensation payment provides an after-tax accumulation, for each dollar of salary or pension contribution sacrificed, of

$$D_n(1 - t_{pn}) = \frac{(1 - t_{c0})(1 + r_{cn})^n}{(1 - t_{cn})}(1 - t_{pn}) \tag{9.4}$$

In comparison, each dollar contributed to a pension plan would yield, in n periods,

$$(1 + R_{pen})^n(1 - t_{pn}) \tag{9.5}$$

---

[10]TRA 86 tightened up the antidiscrimination requirements. To qualify for tax-favored treatment, the ratio of contributions of highly compensated employees to total contributions became more limited. Forcing more employees who prefer salary to pension into the plan reduces the benefit of maintaining corporate pension plans for those who want such plans.

Deferred compensation is preferred to pension if equation (9.4) > (9.5)

$$\frac{(1 - t_{c0})(1 + r_{cn})^n}{(1 - t_{cn})}(1 - t_{pn}) > (1 + R_{pen})^n(1 - t_{pn}) \qquad **$$

which can be rearranged to

$$\frac{(1 - t_{c0})}{(1 - t_{cn})} > \frac{(1 + R_{pen})^n}{(1 + r_{cn})^n} \qquad \textbf{(9.6)}$$

Note that the employee's tax rates are irrelevant to this comparison, because both compensation arrangements give rise to taxation in the future. In other words, $(1 - t_{pn})$ is on both sides of the ** equation so the term cancels out.[11] If the corporate tax rate is expected to be higher in the future, that is, $t_{cn} > t_{c0}$, and $R_{pen} = r_{cn}$, then deferred compensation is preferred to pension. For example, if t_{c0} is 20% and t_{cn} is 35%, then $(1 - .20)/(1 - .35)$ is 1.23, which implies that deferred compensation is preferred to pension by 23%. If the employer has a defined benefit pension plan in place under such circumstances, it may pay a corporation to underfund, not overfund, the pension plan.

Conversely, suppose that $r_{cn} = 7.5\%$ and $R_{pen} = 10\%$. Then, deferred compensation is preferred to pension as long as

$$1.23 > (1.10)^n/(1.075)^n$$

which will occur if $n < 10$ years.

More tax rules restrict funding a defined benefit pension plan than restrict deferred compensation plans. With pension plans (1) minimum funding requirements may force a corporation to take a tax deduction for funding earlier than would be necessary under a deferred compensation plan; (2) administration and legal costs are higher than for deferred compensation plans; and (3) many more antidiscrimination rules apply than for deferred compensation programs.

The objective of the Congress in providing tax-favored treatment to pension plans was to encourage broad-based retirement savings, which to the introduction of contribution limits and nondiscrimination rules. Deferred compensation arrangements are free from these limits. They can also be used advantageously in special tax planning situations. For example, an executive on assignment for 2 or 3 years in a Scandinavian branch office where local tax rates are high would prefer a deferred compensation program to salary. Income could be received at substantially reduced home-country tax rates when returning to the home country. The employer cannot target such an individual with a pension plan.

The biggest nontax problem with deferred compensation programs is that, to avoid constructive receipt in which the employee is taxed as if she received the income in the current period, the employee must be an unsecured creditor of the firm.[12] A pension trust, by contrast, does provide security to the extent it is funded and/or insured. The beneficiary has a claim against the trust and the insurance agency.

---

[11]If the dates of future taxation differ, however, then employee tax rates become relevant to the comparison.
[12]This problem can be mitigated by setting aside funds in a trust on behalf of employees, a so-called "rabbi trust," but to avoid constructive receipt of income, secured creditors of the firm must have legal priority over the trust beneficiaries to the assets in the trust in the event of bankruptcy.

9.4 THE STOCKS-VERSUS-BONDS PUZZLE

Because the earnings on assets in pension funds are tax exempt, pension funds form a natural clientele to invest in fully taxable assets, such as corporate and government bonds, and tax disfavored assets. Recall, common stocks are tax-favored investments because they offer deferral and taxation at capital gains rates to the extent that current earnings are not distributed as dividends each period, thus we expect them to bear implicit taxes. High-tax rate taxpayers form the natural clientele for corporate stocks, not tax-exempt pension plans. Thus it is somewhat surprising that 35% to 45% of pension dollars in both defined contribution and defined benefit plans have been invested in common stocks over the years. For example, as reported in Table 9.1, approximately 40% of pension assets in both DC and DB plans are invested in equities. During the decade from 1985 to 1995, this percentage has fluctuated between 33% and 44% for DB plans and 31% to 41% for DC plans.

Some have argued that corporate pension fund managers are willing to abandon investment in tax-disfavored assets for which pension funds are the natural clientele to garner the higher total rates of return available in stock. Until high-yield bonds came into vogue, it was not possible to earn risk premiums without investing in stock, but Fischer Black (1980) and Irwin Tepper (1981), in two separate articles, had a good counter to this line of attack. They argued that the corporation could secure the risk premiums without sacrificing the tax benefits of investing in bonds.

The **Black–Tepper tax arbitrage strategy** is to effect organizational-form arbitrage as outlined in Table 9.2. Suppose, as in plan A in Table 9.2, that a firm has $1 in its pension fund invested in stock that earns a risky return of r_c.[13] Alternatively, consider plan B. Suppose the firm has $1 in its pension plan invested in bonds earning R_b. If the corporation now borrows $1 on corporate account when its marginal tax rate is t_c and buys common stock with the proceeds of the loan, its net after-tax rate of return on

TABLE 9.2 Stock Investment in the Pension Fund (Plan A) Compared with Bonds in the Pension Fund Along with Debt-Financed Stock on Corporate Account (Plan B)

	Investment	*Return*	*Example*
Plan A:			
Pension:			
Purchase stock	$1	r_c	15%
Plan B:			
Pension:			
Purchase bonds	$1	R_b	10%
Corporation:			
Issue bonds	−$1	$-R_b(1-t_c)$	−6.5%*
Purchase stock	$1	r_c	15%
Net position (pension plus corporation)	$1	$r_c + R_b t_c$	18.5%
Plan B − Plan A	$0	$R_b t_c$	3.5%

*For $t_c = 35\%$

---

[13]Recall, r_c is the after corporate-level tax rate of return of the issuing firm but before the shareholder-level tax of the holder.

corporate account is $r_c - R_b(1 - t_c)$ with this strategy. The total return on the pension fund investment in bonds and the corporate investment in stock, financed by issuing bonds, is $r_c + R_b t_c$ which exceeds the return from investing in stocks (plan A) by $R_b t_c$.

Note that the risk of the two strategies is exactly the same. The return from plan B exceeds that from plan A by a sure $R_b t_c$, irrespective of what happens to stock prices. The advantage of undertaking this organizational-form arbitrage arises from the corporation's ability to borrow on corporate account to secure the interest deduction and to invest the proceeds in the pension fund through the strategy illustrated in Table 9.2.

A few holes appear in the preceding argument, however. First, we have assumed that the corporation pays no tax on the return to investing in shares on corporate account. In fact, taxes must be paid, although the annualized corporate tax rate on shares, denoted t_{cs}, may be well below t_c. For a corporation, returns on stock investments are tax-favored because of the dividend received deduction and deferral of taxation on share appreciation until the stock is sold. If the firm were to hold its own shares on corporate account, the return would be tax exempt.

If the effective annualized tax rate on shares held on corporate account is t_{cs}, then a slight change in arbitrage strategy displayed in Table 9.2 is required. In particular, the corporation will now need to issue $1/(1 - t_{cs})$ dollars of bonds and invest the proceeds in stock to maintain the same level of risk in plan B and plan A. As Table 9.3 shows, as long as the effective annualized corporate tax rate on shares held on corporate account, t_{cs}, is below the ordinary corporate tax rate, t_c, there remains an arbitrage opportunity, although it is not as large as when we assumed t_{cs} to be equal to zero as we did in Table 9.2.

Table 9.3 indicates that the annual tax advantage of funding the pension plan with bonds rather than stock is equal to the pretax interest rate on bonds times $(t_c - t_{cs})/(1 - t_{cs})$. The advantage increases as the corporate tax rate, t_c, increases and decreases as the corporate tax rate on shares, t_{cs}, decreases. Because TRA 86 both decreased t_c and increased t_{cs},[14] the tax advantage of investing the pension fund assets in bonds has diminished over the last 15 years.

The second hole in the argument is that the analysis in Tables 9.2 and 9.3 ignores the nontax costs associated with implementing the arbitrage strategy. Bondholders cannot be sure that the corporation will maintain the position in bonds in the pension fund. After all, the pension fund has its own trustees, who could decide to revert to a strategy of investing in stocks in the pension fund after the loan was in place. This uncertainty increases the risk for bondholders. As a result, they might charge a higher rate of interest on the loan to cover their monitoring costs. Moreover, the firm could go bankrupt, and in bankruptcy it is not possible for the bondholders to claim the accumulated value of the $1 of bonds in the pension plan. Pension beneficiaries have first claim against the pension plan assets. As a result, the bondholders must look to the risky stock portfolio on corporate account as security for their loan, which most likely would cause the borrowing costs to increase further. For example, if the before-tax borrowing rate were 12.3% instead of 10%, the after-tax cost of the debt would be 8%,

---

[14]Specifically, TRA 86 decreased the corporate tax rate on ordinary income, t_c, from 46% to 34% and changed the tax treatment of corporate capital gains. Before 1986, corporate capital gains were taxed at a lower rate than ordinary income, 28% compared with 46%. After the act, capital gains were taxed at the same rate as ordinary corporate income, 34%. Thus increasing the corporate capital gains tax rate increases t_{cs}.

TABLE 9.3 Stock Investment in the Pension Fund (Plan A) Compared with Bonds in the Pension Fund Along with Debt-Financed Stock on Corporate Account (Plan B) with Positive Effective Annualized Tax Rate on Shares Held (versus Zero in Table 9.2)

	Investment	*Return*	*Example*
Plan A:			
Pension:			
Purchase stock	$1	r_c	15%
Plan B:			
Pension:			
Purchase bonds	$1	R_b	10%
Corporation:			
Issue bonds	$-\$1/(1 - t_{cs})$	$\dfrac{-R_b(1 - t_c)}{(1 - t_{cs})}$	-8.125%*
Purchase stock	$\$1/(1 - t_{cs})$	$\dfrac{r_c(1 - t_{cs})}{(1 - t_{cs})}$	15%
Net position (pension plus corporation)	$1	$r_c + \dfrac{R_b(t_c - t_{cs})}{(1 - t_{cs})}$	16.875%
Plan B – Plan A	$0	$\dfrac{R_b(t_c - t_{cs})}{(1 - t_{cs})}$	1.875%

*For $t_c = 35\%$ and $t_{cs} = 20\%$ [15]

or $.123(1 - .35)$. At this rate, the arbitrage opportunity in Tables 9.2 would just disappear: The return to plan B would be 15%, composed of +10% in the pension account, plus 15% from stock less 10% after-tax cost of borrowing on corporate account. The return to plan B is the same as the return to plan A with no arbitrage.

It is worth noting that the arbitrage argument does not work as well for defined contribution plans as for defined benefit plans. Whereas the assets in defined benefit plans can be viewed as being owned by the employers that promise beneficiaries a certain level of benefits and thus the employer captures the benefit of the tax arbitrage, the assets in defined contribution plans are owned by the beneficiaries. If beneficiaries in defined contribution plans wish to earn the risk premium on stock, they must effect the organizational-form arbitrage on personal account by borrowing to purchase stock. With limited interest deductibility for individuals, and with a large spread between the rate at which individuals borrow and the rate at which they can earn on bonds held in the pension plan, such organizational-form arbitrage strategies become too expensive to be profitable. Consequently, nontax factors, especially the desire to earn risk premiums on stock relative to bonds, may lead pension fund beneficiaries to

[15]Given t_c of 35%, a holding period n of approximately 13 years—a reasonable holding period for pension asset investments—implies an effective annualized corporate tax rate t_{cs} on non-dividend-paying corporate stock of 20%. The effective annualized corporate tax rate is solved by noting $r_c(1 - t_{cs}) = r_{cs}$, where r_c is the return on shares after the issuing company's taxes but before the shareholder-level taxes (denoted t_{cs}) and r_{cs} is the return on shares after both the issuing company's taxes and the shareholder-level taxes (in this case another corporation). Given $r_c = .15$, then $r_{cs} = .12$. Thus we need to solve for n that satisfies the following relation: $[(1 + r_c)^n(1 - t_c) + t_c]^{1/n} - 1 = .12$.

prefer nontrivial amounts of stock to be invested in their pension funds, despite the implicit tax such tax-favored investments bear. This argument is consistent with the lower allocation of DC plan assets to bonds as reported in Table 9.1—5% for DC plans compared with 38% for DB plans.

Prior to Frank (2002), researchers had failed to find any association between a firm's tax benefits and the allocation of pension assets to bonds (see, for example, Bodie, Light, Morck, and Taggert, 1987; and Peterson, 1996). Among other differences to prior studies, Frank uses an expanded sample over an extended time period to examine the issue. She estimates a regression of the percentage of defined benefit plan assets invested in bonds on the tax benefit from the arbitrage strategy.[16] She finds a significant positive relation between the two variables. And as predicted, she finds no such association for defined contribution plans. These results are consistent with firms undertaking the Black–Tepper tax arbitrage strategy.

9.5 DOES IT PAY TO MAINTAIN AN OVERFUNDED PENSION PLAN?

Until the market decline of 2001, many U.S. corporate pension funds were **overfunded** by wide margins, because the stock market boomed during the past 15 years.[17] An overfunded plan is one where the market value of the plan assets exceeds the present value of the firm's expected liability to its employees.

Advantages and Disadvantages

Several advantages and disadvantages accompany the overfunding of a pension plan, which we now discuss.

Expectations of Changing Tax Rates

In 1986, U.S. corporations facing a marginal tax rate of 46% knew that in 1987 their marginal tax rate would fall to 40%, and they could anticipate that their marginal tax rates would fall further to 34% in 1988. This expectation encouraged overfunding in 1986. Moreover, each dollar invested in the pension plan in 1986 grows at the before-tax rate R_{pen} until it is withdrawn from the fund. By reducing its future funding, when its marginal tax rate is 34%, the corporation realizes a return bonus of 22%, or $(1 - .34)/(1 - .46) - 1$. This opportunity did not go unnoticed by General Motors Corp. GM made a "special, unrequired contribution ... of $1.04 billion (in 1986) ... to its U.S. pension plans to take advantage of tax deductions."[18] As another example of strategic timing of pension plan contributions and **pension plan reversions,** Exxon terminated several of its overfunded pension plans in 1986, when it was experiencing "tax-free" status due to net operating losses for tax purposes.

---

[16]Frank (2002) partitions the tax benefits from the tax arbitrage into two components: the benefit of issuing bonds on corporate account to finance equity investments and the benefit of investing the DB assets in bonds. Her results suggest that most of the tax benefit arises from the financing with corporate bonds.

[17]The Pension Benefit Guaranty Corporation estimates that in 2003 the corporate DB plans are now underfunded in aggregate by as much as $400 billion. See, for example, "House Backs Cut in Pension Outlays Over Two Years," *The Wall Street Journal* (October 9, 2003, online).

[18]*The Wall Street Journal* (September 16, 1987), p. 16.

The Internal Revenue Service is well aware of the benefits of generous levels of pension funding when tax rates are high. During 1990, the Service announced its intention to conduct 18,000 audits of defined benefit pension plans for the 1986 tax year, expecting to raise hundreds of millions of dollars in additional tax revenues. In particular, it targeted plans that assumed unrealistically low interest rates on investments and unrealistically early retirement dates for plan participants.[19] Such assumptions imply larger current funding requirements to meet promised retirement benefits.

Investing in Stocks, Overfunding, and Flexibility

Why have corporations invested so much of their pension assets in tax-favored assets, especially stock? As we have already noted, this was particularly mysterious prior to TRA 86 because one important reason the corporation has for overfunding its pension fund is that it can earn at a higher rate after-tax in the pension account than on corporate account. Holding stocks reduces this advantage.

The answer to this question is also the answer to the following question: How can a firm overfund its pension plan? Actuaries, in setting pension contribution levels, are likely to assume conservative (low) earnings rates on pension assets to ensure that pension promises to beneficiaries can be fulfilled. The lower the assumed rate of return on investment, the greater is the current funding requirement if the pension fund is to have sufficient assets to meet promised payments. If the assets in the pension fund are invested only in riskless bonds, the actuary is forced to select a rate of return that is close to the rate earned on the bonds. If actuaries set the earning rate at this level, it would not be possible to overfund the pension plan.

But if the fund invests in stocks, the actuary might choose a lower earning rate on the assets to cushion the fund against adverse changes in the market value of its common stocks. For example, the actuary might wish to prevent the fund's market value from falling below a prescribed level more than 5% of the time. The greater the possible variation in the returns on the pension assets, the greater is the chance that the initial market value of the fund's assets will fall to this level at some future date. However, the greater the initial market value of the fund, the less likely it is to fall to this prescribed value given the variation in the returns on the underlying fund. By setting a low earning rate—or, equivalently, a low discount rate to be used in calculating the present value of the promised future pension payments—the actuaries can "authorize" an increase in funding to the desired level. The firm then can build up its excess assets by investing, in part, in common stock. At a later time, when it switches into bonds, the actuary will typically increase the assumed earnings rate on pension assets, thereby indicating an overfunded pension plan. Tax rules require that the excess assets in the pension fund be amortized over a number of years by reducing contributions each year. Thus, for this period of time, the firm can achieve the advantage of investing at the before-tax rate in bonds. It can also realize the tax rate advantage from advance funding if tax rates should fall in the future.

In summary, investing some of the pension assets in stocks allows flexibility in defining the funding level and thus in defining the tax-deductible annual contribution.

---

[19]*New York Times* (June 2, 1990), p. 22.

This flexibility allows the firm to time contributions in periods when the firm faces high tax rates (increased contributions) and low tax rates (reduced contributions).

Investment Alternatives with Overfunded Assets

Being able to earn at the before-tax rate of return in the pension fund, as compared with the after-tax rate of return on corporate account, is one of the advantages of overfunding the plan. Generally, the risk-adjusted rate of return on assets in the pension fund will exceed the rate of return on marginal investments undertaken on corporate account. This generalization is true even if the firm can generate superior profits at the corporate level. After all, the Black–Tepper strategy suggests the firm can borrow to fund the pension plan while still undertaking the superior corporate investments. This approach dominates not funding the pension plan. Interest on the debt used to fund the pension contributions is tax deductible at the corporate level, while investment returns on assets in the pension account are tax exempt. Of course, we must not forget that nontax costs associated with convincing lenders that the firm has superior investments could increase borrowing costs to such an extent that the firm should forgo funding the pension plan.

Because the corporation "owns" the excess assets in the pension plan, its best investment strategy is to hold high explicitly taxed assets such as high-yielding risky bonds in the pension account.[20] If the firm commits to a policy of holding bonds in its pension plan, the borrowing rate on the bonds used to finance the contributions would be less than if the corporation undertook more risky investment strategies in the plan. As discussed earlier, however, it is difficult to commit to such an investment policy in advance. Once again, the deadweight costs associated with issuing risky debt would reduce the advantage of overfunding the plan.

Moreover, prior to TRA 86, corporations held 50% of their pension fund assets in stock and 50% in bonds. The rate of return advantage of investing the excess assets at the before-tax rate would be reduced by 50% of the implicit tax on shares. For example, if bonds returned 10% before tax and common stocks generated a risk-adjusted return of only 7% before shareholder-level tax, r_c, the combined pension fund portfolio would have returned 8.5%, or $.5(10\%) + .5(7\%)$, for an implicit tax rate of 15%, or $(10\% - 8.5\%)/10\%$. Moreover, the corporation could invest in other tax-advantaged assets, such as cash-value life insurance policies. So the tax advantages of overfunding the pension fund may have been small.

Following TRA 86, however, the tax disadvantage of investing pension plan assets in stocks became considerably less. Recall from Chapter 4, Table 4.3, that the annualized effective explicit tax rate on shares, t_s, increased after 1986, implying that the implicit tax on shares should have become relatively low. As a result, U.S. and foreign pension funds became excellent candidates for increased investment in U.S. stocks.

The 1987 Tax Act restricted the level of overfunding in a defined benefit pension plan. Corporations cannot deduct further contributions if the assets in the plan exceed 150% of the termination liability. To reduce the probability of hitting this funding

---

[20]To the extent that ambiguity is involved regarding who owns the excess assets in a pension fund—the employer or employees—an additional nontax cost comes into play in overfunding the pension plan.

limit, many corporations are moving their asset mix toward bonds. However, as already noted, the desirability of stocks relative to bonds as a pension fund investment can be affected greatly by the flexibility in contributions offered by stocks.

Possibility of an Excise Tax

If the corporation were to surrender its pension plan and capture the excess pension assets, which is labeled a plan termination or asset reversion, it may face an excise tax in addition to the regular corporate tax on these assets. For example, TRA 86 imposed a 10% excise tax on excess assets withdrawn from a terminated pension plan in most circumstances, and the excise tax was raised to 15% in 1988 and 20% in 1989.[21] Did the imposition of excise taxes affect the number of terminations? Apparently so. While $6.6 billion of pension plan assets reverted to their corporate sponsors upon termination of their pension plans in 1985, and another $4.3 billion in reversions took place in 1986, only $1.9 billion and $1.1 billion worth of reversions occurred in 1987 and 1988, respectively (Peterson, 1989). Also, a pension plan termination results in all unvested benefits vesting on termination. In addition, many employees express displeasure when a defined benefit plan is replaced with a defined contribution plan. This displeasure arises because the risk of having sufficient assets on retirement is shifted from the firm to the employee and because often the expected total pension benefits are reduced for many employees who have been shifted to defined contribution plans.

The firm does not have to surrender its pension fund, however, to recapture its excess assets. It can (1) reduce future funding levels by changing plan assumptions, and (2) increase promised pension benefits for its employees in lieu of salary increases or bonuses. Reducing salary to employees or contributions to the plan will increase the corporation's current taxable income and reduce the level of overfunding in the plan.

Nontax considerations affect these choices. Employees might not give up a dollar of salary or bonus for an extra dollar of pension benefit. For them, the cost of borrowing to meet current consumption needs might exceed the returns that they can earn on this form of deferred compensation, as we discussed earlier. To compensate such employees, the employer might have to sweeten pension benefits so substantially that it might not be advantageous to take this path to reduce overfunding in the plan.

Incentive to Underfund Because Pension Represents a Put Option

Before the passage of the Employee Retirement Income Security Act (ERISA) in 1974, firms with defined benefit pension plans had a valuable put option because they could put the assets of the pension plan to the beneficiaries to satisfy the legal claims of the plan beneficiaries. After the passage of ERISA, firms now can put the pension plan assets plus 30% of the market value of the firm to the Pension Benefit Guarantee Corporation (PBGC) to satisfy the pension claims. This change reduced but did not eliminate the value of the pension put.

The pension put option offers incentives to underfund the pension, and the value of the put option varies with increases in the variance of the returns on the pension assets,

---

[21]The 1990 Tax Act raises the excise tax rate to 50% in certain circumstances.

favoring stock investments in the pension plan, and variance of the firm's net assets, encouraging more risky investments by the firm if there is some chance of putting the option to the PBGC.

Empirical Evidence on Determinants of Defined Benefit Plan Pension Funding

Several researchers have empirically examined the determinants of pension funding. Francis and Reiter (1987) report the overfunding of defined benefit pension plans being positively associated with firms' estimated tax benefits. They also examine a number of other motivations for firms' funding levels. They find larger firms follow a funding strategy that both reduces reported income (contributions to the pension plan are reported as pension expense during their sample time period) and increases the reported funding ratio in order to reduce potential political costs. They also report evidence that the closer firms are to violating bond covenants, the greater the underfunding. Further, underfunding is more common among firms with unionized employees, which the researchers interpret to mean underfunding is a mechanism to bond these employees to the firm. Thus the research results indicate that not only tax motivations but also nontax motivations such as financial statement and employee incentive effects influence the level of funding.

Thomas (1988) finds that firms' tax status as proxied by the existence of a net operating loss carryforward

- Is negatively associated with funding levels: NOL firms fund at a lower level.
- Influences the choice of actuarial variables: NOL firms choose less conservative assumptions, implying lower funding levels.
- Influences the use of defined benefit plans: NOL firms are less likely to choose defined benefit plans.

These results suggest that taxes are an important determinant of pension choices and funding.

Other researchers have examined the **pension plan termination** decision. Examples include Thomas (1989), Mittelstaedt (1989) and Clinch and Shibano (1996). Thomas concludes that terminations seem to be motivated by cash needs rather than tax, accounting, or transfer of wealth considerations. Mittelstaedt's results generally echo those of Thomas. Clinch and Shibano, however, using a different approach to estimating tax effects, find that tax considerations significantly influence whether and when a firm withdraws excess pension assets via a termination.

9.6 FUNDING POST-EMPLOYMENT HEALTH CARE BENEFITS

Retiree health benefits were first offered in the late 1940s, when the postwar economy was booming, businesses were profitable, and the number of retirees relative to the number of workers was small. Retiree health benefits arose as part of collective bargaining agreements, and employers were willing to provide the benefits because the cost was small relative to total compensation. With the enactment of Medicare in 1965, employer obligations and costs were lowered because employers were able to integrate their benefits with Medicare benefits. Both funding and accounting for these benefits were not of great concern and most employers were on a pay-as-you-go basis. However, over the last 20 years, the workforce has aged, the ratio of retirees to active workers has increased, expected life spans have risen, and health care costs have increased dramatically. These changes have caused the cost of the benefits to increase.

Partially in response to the increase in the unfunded promises, the Financial Accounting Standards Board in 1990 changed the accounting for retiree health care benefits.[22] Prior to this change, most firms did not recognize a liability for the unfunded promises and delayed recognition of an expense until the period in which the cost was paid. Statement 106 now requires firms to estimate the present value of the promised benefits and to accrue both a liability and recognize an expense each year of the employee's working life. Consequently, because many firms do not prefund retiree health care costs, large liabilities appeared on firms' balance sheets. This result led many firms to reevaluate their promises and many employers have attempted to modify or drop retiree health care benefits over the objections of both current workers and retirees. In 1996, 40% of employers provided health care coverage to their retirees under age 65 compared with 46% of employers in 1993. The numbers for retirees over age 65 were 33% in 1996 compared with 40% in 1993. Larger firms are more likely to provide coverage.

The U.S. General Accounting Office (GAO) in a 1997 report concluded (1) the available data on employer-based retiree health benefits paints a limited but consistent picture of eroding coverage with a steady decline in number of retirees covered, and (2) a key characteristic of the United States's voluntary, employer-based system of health insurance is an employer's freedom to modify the conditions of coverage or to terminate benefits.[23] In an earlier report, the GAO estimated that the accrued liability of U.S. corporations for retiree medical benefit promises made to employees exceeds $400 billion. Even though this amount is less than half the accrued liability for pension promises, retiree medical benefits, unlike pension benefits, are largely unfunded. A 1999 survey by Watson Wyatt Consulting Firm (see *www.watsonwyatt.com*) indicated that, of 612 Fortune 1000 companies responding, 20% of the companies prefund their retiree medical plans. The vast majority of firms operate on a pay-as-you-go basis.

What is the best way for a firm to fund retiree medical benefits? In most cases, advance funding of such benefits cannot be done in as tax-advantaged a way as the advance funding of pension benefits. Except in 401(h) plans and collectively bargained Voluntary Employee Benefit Association programs (VEBAs), current tax deductions cannot be taken for advance funding. Deductions are available for advance funding through a 401(h) plan but such plans are expensive to administer. Moreover, the annual contribution to such plans cannot exceed 25% of the contributions made to the employer's pension plans. So when a firm's pension plan is overfunded, contributions to the pension and to a 401(h) plan are not permitted at all.

---

[22]See Statement of Financial Accounting Standard 106 "Employers' Accounting for Postretirement Benefits Other Than Pensions," Financial Accounting Standards Board (1990).
[23]See "Retiree Health Insurance: Erosion in Employer-Based Health Benefits of Early Retirees" (July 11, 1997), HEHS-97-150, U.S. Government Accounting Office. See also the GAO's Web site *www.gao.gov*.

Firms have at least two alternative ways in which they might fund retiree medical benefits:

1. Inform employees that pension benefits will be sweetened and that employees will be made responsible for paying their own medical benefits.
2. Employ a pay-as-you-go plan, whereby the firm pays for employees' expenses as they are incurred in retirement.

The Sweetened Pension Benefit Approach

Suppose the firm wishes to cover the cost of a $1 future medical benefit n years from today for its employee. If pension benefits are supplemented, the employee will receive taxable pension income at time n. After paying tax on this income at personal tax rate t_{pn}, the employee will require a full $1 to pay for the medical benefits, because the expenditure will not be tax deductible.[24] So the amount of taxable pension benefits required at time n is

$$\$1/(1 - t_{pn})$$

The current cost to the employer of providing this benefit is the amount that must be deposited into the pension plan today less the value of the tax deduction, at a tax rate of t_{c0}, that the employer obtains for the pension contribution. Because the pension fund is tax exempt, its assets grow at the before-tax rate, R_{pen}. So, to accumulate $1/(1 - t_{pn})$ dollars in n periods, when the funds in the retirement plan earn income at rate R_{pen} per period, the employer must deposit the following amount into the pension fund:

$$\frac{1}{(1 - t_{pn})} \times \frac{1}{(1 + R_{pen})^n}$$

Because of the tax deductibility of the contribution to the pension account, this calculation would result in an after-tax current cost, C, to the employer of [25]

$$C \equiv \frac{1}{(1 - t_{pn})} \times \frac{1}{(1 + R_{pen})^n}(1 - t_{c0}) \tag{9.7}$$

For example, suppose the employer wishes to provide the employee with $1 to pay for medical benefits when the employee retires in 30 years. The retiree's expected tax rate in retirement is 28%, the employer's current tax rate is 35%, and the pension fund earns 10% per year on its investments. How much will the employer need to contribute to the pension plan today to provide the $1 after-tax to the retiree in 30 years? Substituting the parameter values into equation (9.7) gives an after-tax current period contribution of 5.17 cents. That is, 5.17 cents after-tax—7.95 cents pretax—contributed by the corporation will grow at 10% for 30 years to $1.39 which is reduced to $1 after the retiree pays tax at 28% on withdrawing the $1.39.

---

[24] As discussed in Chapter 8, medical costs are deductible in the United States as itemized deductions only to the extent they exceed 7.5% of the taxpayer's adjusted gross income and then only to the extent itemized deductions exceed the standard deduction that is available as an alternative.

[25] An alternate way to derive equation (9.7) is to solve for the current cost, C, of providing $1 to the employee in retirement in the following equation: $\frac{C}{(1 - t_{c0})}(1 + R_{pen})^n(1 - t_{pn}) = \$1$. A current contribution of C to the pension plan is tax deductible to the firm, the contribution grows at R_{pen} for n periods, and is then taxed to the employee on withdrawal. Rearranging we get (9.7).

The Pay-As-You-Go Approach

In the absence of advance funding of the benefits through a tax-qualified trust, the employer usually receives no current tax deduction. Instead, the employer secures a tax deduction in the future at time n when the benefit payment is made. If the benefit is provided to the employee as a fringe benefit through a group health benefit plan, as is typical, the employee is not taxed on the receipt of the benefit. Therefore, the employer need pay only $1 at time n to satisfy the obligation. If the employer can invest funds on corporate account in the interim at an after-tax rate of r_c per year, then the current cost or present value to the employer is

$$\frac{(1 - t_{cn})}{(1 + r_c)^n} \tag{9.8}$$

Advance funding through the pension account is the superior choice if the current cost of the pension contribution is less than the current cost of the pay-as-you-go approach

$$\text{Equation (9.7)} < \text{Equation (9.8)}$$

$$\frac{1}{(1 - t_{pn})} \times \frac{1}{(1 + R_{pen})^n}(1 - t_{c0}) < \frac{(1 - t_{cn})}{(1 + r_c)^n}$$

which can be rearranged to

$$\frac{(1 - t_{c0})}{(1 - t_{pn})(1 - t_{cn})} \times \frac{(1 + r_c)^n}{(1 + R_{pen})^n} < 1 \tag{9.9}$$

Note that in the special case in which the employer's tax rates are constant over time, the pension funding route is cheaper if

$$\frac{(1 + r_c)^n}{(1 + R_{pen})^n} < (1 - t_{pn}) \tag{9.10}$$

If r_c were equal to R_{pen}, the unfunded alternative would dominate, because it would allow employees to receive the benefits tax-free, whereas the pension benefits would be taxable.

When might r_c be equal to R_{pen}? When the employer is tax exempt, such as a university or a not-for-profit hospital, or when the taxpaying employer invests idle funds in cash-value life insurance policies without incurring any implicit taxes. Another case in which r_c may be close to R_{pen} is where the corporation funds its health care program by investing in its own common stock. Because a U.S. corporation pays no tax on the dividend or capital gain income it earns from holding its own common stock, the risk-adjusted after-tax return on the stock will be below the pretax bond rate only to the extent the stock bears implicit tax.

However, suppose that r_c is less than R_{pen}. Then a trade-off must be made between earning at a higher after-tax rate by advance funding through a pension and providing a tax-exempt benefit to employees by not funding the plan. For example, suppose r_c is equal to 7%, R_b is 10%, and the employer's tax rate is constant over time. In Table 9.4, we show the employee's tax rates at time n, t_{pn}, below which pension funding beats the unfunded alternative. At higher values of t_{pn}, it is too costly to forego the advantage of tax exemption for medical benefits, at retirement, available through the unfunded

TABLE 9.4	Employee's Tax Rate, t_{pn}, Below Which Pension Funding Dominates Corporate Pay-As-You-Go Funding of Retiree Health Benefits	
n	$\dfrac{(1+r_c)^n}{(1+R_{pen})^n}$	t_{pn}
5	.8709	.13
10	.7585	.24
20	.5752	.42

n = time horizon in years

R_{pen} = 10% = Pension fund investment rate of return

r_c = 7% = After-tax rate of return on corporate investments, assuming employer's tax rates are constant through time ($t_{c0} = t_{cn}$)

alternative. Note that longer horizons favor advance funding through the pension account because the advantage of tax-free investment becomes more important.

Other Factors Relevant to the Funding Decision

1. Future medical costs are uncertain. Employees must bear this risk if a supplemental pension plan is used, but not in an unfunded plan or a 401(h) plan.
2. In an unfunded plan, the employee bears the risk of default on the promise. For example, a leveraged buyout of the corporate employer can expose employees to a substantial risk of default on such unfunded obligations.
3. Increasing employer tax rates favor unfunded plans: Tax deductions are secured at higher tax rates.
4. Unfunded plans are more desirable for employees with high tax rates. So they may be more advantageous where the work force is predominantly white-collar rather than blue-collar.
5. There are administrative costs associated with operating 401(h) plans. These costs can make unfunded plans more desirable than 401(h) plans even when the latter are available. For example, tax-exempt entities will typically find unfunded plans preferable to 401(h) plans.

9.7 EMPLOYEE STOCK OWNERSHIP PROGRAMS

An **employee stock ownership plan** (ESOP) is a special type of defined contribution plan, similar to an individual retirement account, a Keogh account, or a Code Section 401(k) plan. ESOPs were popular in the late 1980s, but their popularity has declined since that time due to some tax-rule changes. We discuss ESOPs here, although briefly, because ESOPs established in the late 1980s still exist today. In 1998, there were 8,956 ESOP plans covering 7.748 million employees with total plan assets of $411 billion. We will also see how difficult it is to identify tax and nontax motivations for using ESOPs.

Just like other defined contribution plans, the corporation makes tax-deductible annual contributions to the ESOP, which are generally used to buy company stock or to pay down a loan that was used to acquire company stock when the program was initiated. Each year, employees are allocated, tax-free, company shares, and any investment income accumulates tax-free within the ESOP. Employees pay tax when they receive dividend distributions on ESOP shares during their working lives, when they receive other distributions from the ESOP during retirement, or when they otherwise leave the firm and "cash out" of the plan. (However, when employees leave the firm they can roll their ESOP shares into an individual retirement account to continue to defer payment of any tax.) Unlike most defined contribution plans, the ESOP is required to invest primarily in the stock of the company establishing the plan, and this is commonly taken to mean that the ESOP must hold at least 50% of its assets in the sponsoring company's stock. Investment in the company stock concentrates the employee's wealth in the firm, increasing the risk borne by the employee—a nontax cost of ESOPs and 401(k) plans.

Also unlike other defined contribution plans, the ESOP can borrow to buy company stock to prefund the required number of shares that the firm expects to credit to its employees over the term of the loan. Such plans are called "leveraged ESOPs." As the firm contributes to the ESOP and debt is paid down, shares are credited to employees' accounts. Moreover, qualified lenders can exclude 50% of the interest that they receive on the ESOP loan. If lending markets are competitive and if there are no special costs associated with ESOP loans, the risk-adjusted before-tax rate of return on the **ESOP Loan**, R_{EL}, will be given by the following relation:

$$R_{EL}(1 - .5t_c) = R_b(1 - t_c)$$

or

$$R_{EL} = R_b(1 - t_c)/(1 - .5t_c) \tag{9.11}$$

where R_b is the fully taxable rate on an equivalent loan. So if corporate marginal tax rates are 34%, it implies that the rate of interest on the loan will be 79.5% of the fully taxable rate. Shackelford (1991) compares the actual rates offered on ESOP loans, R_{ELA}, to the theoretical rate, R_{EL}, to calculate a discount ratio as follows:

$$\text{Discount ratio} = (R_b - R_{ELA})/(R_b - R_{EL}) \tag{9.12}$$

Shackelford estimates R_b as the interest rate stated in the ESOP loan agreement if for some reason the lender is not entitled to the 50% exclusion—that is, the rate on the ESOP loan if interest on it were fully taxable to the lender. The discount rate represents the percentage of the tax benefits enjoyed by the borrower. He finds that the discount rate averages between 67% to 79%. Alternatively stated, lenders retain between 33% and 21% of the tax benefits. Shackelford notes that the perception by Congress that lenders were retaining too much of the tax benefits of the loan subsidy led Congress, in the 1989 Tax Act, to restrict the 50% exclusion to loans in which the ESOP was the majority shareholder in the sponsoring company, which curtailed their popularity somewhat. Shackelford also presents evidence, consistent with the existence of tax clienteles, that the lenders are high marginal tax rate firms.

A final tax benefit to ESOPs, introduced in the 1986 Tax Act, is that the corporation can deduct any dividends that are used to pay down the ESOP loan or are paid directly to employees on their ESOP shares. Under Code Section 404(k), the corporation can deduct dividends to an ESOP if (1) the dividends are paid in cash directly to

ESOP participants, (2) the dividends are paid to the ESOP and it distributes them to participants within 90 days of the close of the plan year, or (3) the dividends on ESOP stock are used to make payments on an ESOP loan. Scholes and Wolfson (1990) provide a critical examination of the tax benefits claimed by proponents of ESOPs, including the dividend deduction, and make a good case that the tax benefits can be obtained via other organizational arrangements. They conclude that it is likely that nontax reasons contribute to the popularity of ESOPs.

One nontax reason why ESOPs became popular—and perhaps the most important one—is that they have been used effectively to thwart hostile takeover attempts, particularly in the state of Delaware.[26] In early 1989, Polaroid won an important decision in the Delaware Chancery Court, which upheld Polaroid's issuance of 14% of its stock to an ESOP prior to the initiation of a hostile tender offer by Shamrock Holdings. The ESOP helped Polaroid's management defeat Shamrocks' bid for its stock because employees voted their Polaroid shares with management. Delaware law requires that a firm wait 3 years after it acquires a 15% interest in a target before it can merge with the target, unless it can secure an 85% vote of the target shareholders. The waiting period can impose substantial costs on the acquiring firm if it had plans to use the target firm's assets as collateral for interim or longer-term loans. Firm managers might establish an ESOP because they believe that employee-shareholders are more likely to vote with them than outside shareholders. Polaroid's use of an ESOP as a successful takeover defense mechanism stimulated considerable interest in ESOPs.

ESOPs have been used by firms to sell company divisions to employees, to defer the capital gains tax incurred by owners of private companies on the sale of their shares to the ESOP, to allocate interest payments domestically to free up foreign tax credit limitations,[27] to replace existing defined benefit pension plans, to replace other types of defined contribution plans, and to replace postretirement health care programs. In replacing postretirement health care programs with an ESOP plan, employees are required to fund their own postretirement health care costs from their accumulation in the ESOP—a form of prefunding by the employing firm but at the cost to the employee of increased risks associated with health care costs. As discussed in the earlier section, prefunding is not always tax-advantageous.

Beatty (1995) examines the stock market reaction to corporate announcements of ESOP formations. She finds (1) stock returns were positively associated with the estimated tax benefits of ESOP debt; (2) negative stock returns for companies subject to a takeover attempt at the time of the ESOP announcement, suggesting that the corporate control effects of ESOPs are important; and (3) some evidence that ESOPs are related to increases in firm productivity.

---

[26]Approximately half the firms listed on the New York Stock Exchange are incorporated in Delaware.

[27]As we will see in Chapters 10 and 11, TRA 86 made foreign tax credit limitations a significantly greater concern than it had been previously. The United States restricts foreign tax credits to an amount equal to foreign taxable income divided by worldwide income times the U.S. tax rate on worldwide income. One way to increase the allowed limit is to increase foreign source income as a percentage of worldwide income. Under Code Section 861, interest generated on domestic debt must typically be allocated partially to foreign activities, thereby reducing foreign source income in the preceding calculation. It is possible to allocate 100% of the interest on certain ESOP debt to domestic income, increasing foreign source income and thereby increasing the allowable foreign tax credits.

In summary, an ESOP provides a pension savings alternative to more conventional tax-qualified retirement plans, one that provides employees with an ownership interest in the firm. Employee ownership might improve the firm's productivity as employee interests become better aligned with the firm's other shareholders. But such compensation arrangements may come at the expense of other more efficient forms (ignoring taxes), both for risk-sharing and incentive reasons. Moreover, severe nontax costs can be a factor if an ESOP must refinance to repurchase shares from departing employees. Shares that are initially contributed to the trust must eventually be cashed out, and high transaction costs might be incurred to accomplish this task, particularly in smaller businesses.

Summary of Key Points

1. To encourage saving for retirement, many countries give favorable tax treatment to pension compensation. In the United States, employers receive an immediate tax deduction for pension contributions, while employees are taxed only when they receive payments in retirement. Moreover, qualified pension trusts are tax exempt, so earnings in the trust accumulate tax-free.

2. The two broad categories of pension plans are defined benefit plans and defined contribution plans. In defined benefit plans, the employees' retirement benefits are fixed by a contractually specified formula and may be subject to considerable uncertainty regarding how much and when the employer will fund the promised benefits. In defined contribution plans, the employer's pension plan contributions are fixed by a contractually specified formula and, depending on how well the pension fund investments perform, subject to considerable uncertainty regarding how much the employees will receive in retirement benefits.

3. Even when nontax factors are ignored, pensions do not always dominate salaries as a compensation alternative. In particular, if employees' tax rates are expected to increase over time, current compensation may be preferable.

4. When nontax factors are considered, current compensation is sometimes preferred to pensions because pension plans may force some employees to postpone consumption to a greater extent than they would like.

5. Nonqualified deferred compensation arrangements are typically less tax-favored than qualified arrangements, such as pension plans. Not only must the employer defer the timing of the tax deduction in nonqualified arrangements, but the income earned on assets set aside to fund nonqualified deferred compensation is taxed to the employer. Nevertheless, deferred compensation plans face far fewer tax-rule restrictions than do pension plans, making them attractive in a broader set of circumstances. In particular, they are commonly used for highly paid employees who face binding constraints on contributions to qualified retirement plans.

6. Even though it is tax-advantageous to invest pension plan contributions in assets that bear little implicit tax, such as bonds and other interest-bearing securities, a substantial fraction of plan contributions are invested in tax-favored assets, such as stocks and real estate because many of these tax-favored assets are also risky. Such an investment strategy is sensible only in the presence of substantial transaction costs of undertaking alternative strategies/investments and a desire to invest in risky assets in the hopes of earning risk premiums. In the absence of transaction costs, such risk premiums could typically be earned in a more tax-favored way by borrowing funds to invest in risky assets outside the pension plan and holding interest-bearing securities in the pension plan.

7. An advantage of defined benefit over defined contribution pension plans is a firm's ability to "overfund" the former. This advantage is greatest when employer tax

rates are falling over time and when the difference between the after-tax rate of return on pension plan assets and the after-tax rate of return on marginal invest-ments by the employer outside the pension plan is highest.

8. Retiree health benefits can be funded in several ways in the United States. The most tax-advantaged are 401(h) plans or collectively bargained plans, but the avail-ability of these arrangements is restricted. These plans allow a current tax deduc-tion for advance funding, tax-free compounding of investment returns on plan assets, and tax exemption of benefits to employee recipients in retirement.

9. Alternative ways in which to fund retiree medical benefits include sweetening pen-sion benefits in exchange for making retirees responsible for their own medical expenses and pay-as-you-go plans, where the employer pays for employees' expenses as they are incurred in retirement. The benefit of the pension plan alter-native is that the employer receives an earlier tax deduction and funds accumulate free from tax in a pension trust. The benefit of an unfunded plan is that employees can receive retiree benefits free from tax because retiree health benefit payments can be structured as part of a tax-free medical benefit program. The unfunded alternative is more attractive the higher the employees' tax rates in retirement, the higher the employer's future tax rate relative to its current tax rate, and the lower the benefit of tax-free compounding of investment returns in a pension plan.

10. An employee stock ownership plan (ESOP) is a defined contribution plan that invests primarily in employer securities on behalf of employees.

11. Special tax provisions apply to ESOPs. For example, dividends paid on employer stock held by the ESOP, and distributed to employees, are tax deductible to the corporation. In addition, half the interest on certain ESOP loans used to purchase employer stock is tax exempt to qualified lenders although, following the 1989 Tax Act, this benefit is available only to new ESOP financings that own a majority of the employer stock.

12. ESOPs are often adopted by companies that are rumored to be takeover candi-dates. By locking up shares in presumably friendly hands, ESOPs add to manage-ment's arsenal of takeover defense weapons. In fact, given that ESOPs do not appear to offer unique tax or incentive benefits relative to alternative organiza-tional arrangements, their popularity in the late 1980s may well have been driven by their antitakeover characteristics.

Appendix 9.1

EXCISE TAX COMPLICATIONS

An interesting investment planning problem confronted U.S. taxpayers with ample accumulations in their qualified retirement programs during the period 1986 to 1996. We discuss it here because it provides another illustration of how taxes can affect risk-taking incentives. TRA 86 introduced a new 15% excise tax that applies when benefits to a participant from all qualified plans including IRA accounts, 401(k) plans, and defined benefit plans exceeded the maximum of $150,000 and $120,000 indexed for inflation after 1986. The excise tax clearly reduced the benefit of accumulating funds in a pension plan. With a 15% excise tax in addition to the regular tax on pension plan distributions in excess of $150,000, a pension beneficiary facing a 30% tax rate pays tax at the rate of 45% on the excess pension fund distribution. The excise tax was repealed in the Taxpayer Relief Act of 1997, effective for distributions after December 31, 1996.

When the tax rate on pension fund distributions exceeds the current tax rate on salary income, taxpayers must trade off the advantages of investing at a before-tax rate of return in the pension account against the higher tax rate on pension income. For example, suppose a taxpayer currently faces a 30% tax rate and expects to face a 40% tax rate in retirement. Pension investments earn 10% per year and personal investments yield 7% after-tax.

If the investment horizon is 10 years, a dollar of current salary reinvested at 7% after-tax yields

$$\$1(1 - .30) \times 1.07^{10} = \$1.38$$

A dollar of current pension contribution invested at 10% yields

$$\$1 \times 1.10^{10} \times (1 - .40) = \$1.56$$

This figure is 13% more than current salary despite the high tax rate in retirement, but if a 15% tax were added to the 40% regular tax rate, the after-tax pension accumulation would drop to $1.17, which falls short of the salary accumulation by $.21.

Note, however, that an increase in the investment horizon may enable the tax-free compounding of the pension to overcome the disadvantage, even of the 15% excise tax. Over a 20-year horizon, for example, the salary would accumulate to $2.71 after-tax, or $1(1 - .30) \times 1.07^{20}$, while the pension would accumulate to $3.03, $1 \times 1.10^{20} \times (1 - .40 - .15)$. So the pension now does better by 12%.[28] A 20-year horizon is not as long as might appear at first blush. After all, most pensions are removed periodically over the retiree's life rather than in a lump sum at the time of retirement.[29]

The 15% excise tax on excess distributions may have discouraged investment in risky assets. For example, consider the case of a taxpayer who would have accumulated an amount that fell just short of the level that triggers the 15% excise tax if the pension was invested in riskless bonds. If, instead, the taxpayer invested the pension fund in stocks and realized a high rate of return, the gains

---

[28]Note, however, that a single premium deferred annuity accumulates to $3.11, that is, $1(1 - .30)[1.10^{20} \times (1 - .40) + .40]$. This result is 3% more than the pension accumulation. A pretax return on the SPDA of only 9.5% per year would yield only $2.86.

[29]Special tax rules apply to lump-sum distributions from certain retirement plans in the United States, and because favorable tax treatment can result, some retirees elect lump-sum distributions.

above the riskless rate on bonds would have been subject to the excise tax. However, if the stock performed poorly, the taxpayer would have escaped the excise tax. This asymmetric tax treatment could have caused taxpayers to invest more conservatively in their pension accounts. As discussed in Chapter 6, progressive tax rates can induce risk aversion by the taxpayer in deciding on the investment policies of the fund.

Discussion Questions

1. What are the major differences between a defined contribution pension plan and a defined benefit pension plan?
2. When is it tax-advantageous for a firm to pay salary instead of an equivalent pension contribution?
3. What are the nontax costs associated with providing pension benefits for employees?
4. Under what conditions will the returns on investing outside the pension fund be greater than the returns on investing inside the pension fund?
5. How does the length of time that the pension contribution will remain in the pension account affect whether pension is preferred to salary? Under what conditions is the duration of the pension investment irrelevant?
6. How does the Black–Tepper stocks-versus-bonds puzzle pertain to pension planning? Is it still tax-advantageous for corporations to hold bonds in their pension accounts subsequent to the 1986 Tax Act?
7. What is the meaning of the term *overfunded* in terms of a pension plan? What are the advantages and disadvantages to the corporation and its employees of an overfunded pension plan?
8. What role does the actuary play in deciding on whether the fund is overfunded or underfunded? How does this role affect dynamic tax planning strategies for the pension fund?
9. What are the tax and nontax factors in choosing between compensating employees by way of a pension plan versus a deferred compensation program?
10. What factors are relevant to determining whether retiree medical benefits should be funded in advance?
11. What is an ESOP? Why has Congress encouraged their use over the years?
12. Three purported tax advantages of an ESOP are that the corporation can make tax-deductible contributions to fund the ESOP or pay down the principal on an ESOP loan, that qualified lenders can exclude from taxation 50% of the interest that they receive on the ESOP loan, and that the dividend paid on the shares held in the ESOP are tax deductible under certain circumstances. Do you agree with these claims?

Exercises

1. Suppose a firm faces a current tax rate of 35% but expects this rate to fall to 20% in the future. Employees on average face a current marginal tax rate of 31% but expect this rate to fall to 20% when they retire in 15 years. The firm can earn 12% pretax on its pension investments and 10% after-tax on corporate account. Employees on average can earn 10% after-tax on their investments. Which among salary, pension, and deferred compensation is tax-preferred? Explain your results.
2. Suppose a firm has a defined benefit pension plan and faces a marginal tax rate on ordinary income of 35%. The firm can earn or issue fully taxable bonds that yield 12% and can purchase stock yielding 18%. Describe and illustrate the tax benefits to the Black–Tepper arbitrage strategy for this firm assuming the firm pays no tax on the stock investment yielding 18%. Explain your results.
3. Suppose a firm has a defined benefit pension plan and faces a marginal tax rate on ordinary income of 35%. The firm can earn or issue fully taxable bonds that yield

12% and can purchase stock yielding 18%. The firm faces an annualized corporate tax rate, t_{cs}, of 25% on stock investments. Describe and illustrate the tax benefits to the Black–Tepper arbitrage strategy for this firm.

4. Suppose an employer wishes to provide an employee with $1,000 to pay for medical benefits when the employee retires in 25 years through a sweetened pension plan payment. The retiree's expected tax rate in retirement is 20%, the employer's current tax rate is 35%, and the pension fund earns 12% per year on its investments. How much will the employer need to contribute to the pension plan today to provide the $1,000 after-tax to the retiree in 25 years?

5. An employer wishes to provide health care benefits to its workers when they retire. The firm faces a current marginal tax rate of 35% and expects to face this rate in the future. On average, employees face a current tax rate of 31%, which is expected to fall to 20% in retirement. The firm earns 12% pretax in its pension account and 15% pretax from its own operations. The average years until retirement for employees is 20 years. The firm is considering funding the promised retiree health care costs through either a sweetened pension benefit or on a pay-as-you-go approach. Under the pay-as-you-go approach, the benefit to employees will be provided as part of a fringe benefit package that is tax deductible to the employer while the employees are not taxed on the receipt of the benefit. Which alternative—the sweetened pension benefit or pay-as-you-go approach—is tax-preferred?

Tax Planning Problems

1. Suppose taxpayers were given a new option under the tax law for retirement funding. The new option requires that they forego a current tax deduction for pension plan contributions. Any contribution would accumulate in the pension fund free of tax, and distributions from the plan to beneficiaries would also be tax-free.

   The usual rules provide for current tax deductibility of pension plan contributions and full taxation of pension plan distributions at ordinary tax rates. The tax rates at which contributions reduce taxes and the tax rates at which distributions increase taxes may differ because they occur at different points in time.
   a. Who would prefer the new option?
   b. What would likely happen to taxes collected by the government in the short run? In the long run?
   c. What would likely happen to the aggregate amount of savings undertaken through pension accounts?
   d. How would the new option compare to one in which pension plan contributions give rise to current tax deductions and pension plan distributions are taxed at the same rate at which deductions were taken?
   e. How would the new option compare to a plan with the following?
      • Pension plan contributions give rise to current tax deductions.
      • Pension plan distributions are taxed at the ordinary tax rates that apply at the time the distributions are made.
      • Distributions are taxed at a rate above (below) the rate at which contributions are deductible and taxpayers receive a tax credit or pay additional tax equal to the difference in tax rates multiplied by the pension plan contributions?

2. The chief financial officer of a profitable firm asks you to explain the advantages, if any, to his firm of overfunding the firm's defined benefit pension plan. Do these advantages accrue to a firm with a defined contribution pension plan?

3. A firm currently has an overfunded defined benefit pension plan and is short of cash. The chief financial officer is considering terminating the defined benefit plan to recapture the "excess assets." The firm will replace the defined benefit plan with a defined contribution plan to continue to provide pension benefits to its employees.

What are the tax and nontax costs and benefits of the CFO's planned action? What alternatives to the termination are available to the firm? Briefly compare these alternatives to a termination.

4. A newly established firm wants to establish a pension plan for its employees. The firm hires you to prepare a report comparing a defined benefit pension plan with a defined contribution pension plan. The firm also requires a recommendation from you as to which plan better suits them. On questioning management, you learn that the firm's future profitability is likely to be highly variable—sometimes large profits, at other times possible losses. You also learn that the firm is an aggressive tax planner. What type of pension plan would you recommend? Explain your reasoning.

5. The accompanying table can be used to make paired comparisons of the desirability of salary, deferred compensation, and pensions as a function of

a = current and future employer marginal tax rates
b = current and future employee marginal tax rates
c = the earnings rates on investment that the employer and employee can achieve
n = the number of periods of compensation deferral.

Use the table to answer the following questions and explain how the table enables you to determine the answers.

Salary vs. Deferred Compensation vs. Pensions

b	c	a n	0.80 5	0.80 10	0.80 20	1.00 5	1.00 10	1.00 20	1.20 5	1.20 10	1.20 20
						Values for $a/(bc^n)$					
0.70	0.98		1.26	1.40	1.71	1.58	1.75	2.14	1.90	2.10	2.57
0.70	1.00		1.14	1.14	1.14	1.43	1.43	1.43	1.71	1.71	1.71
0.70	1.02		1.04	0.94	0.77	1.29	1.17	0.96	1.55	1.41	1.15
0.80	0.98		1.11	1.22	1.50	1.38	1.53	1.87	1.66	1.84	2.25
0.80	1.00		1.00	1.00	1.00	1.25	1.25	1.25	1.50	1.50	1.50
0.80	1.02		0.91	0.82	0.67	1.13	1.03	0.84	1.36	1.23	1.01
0.90	0.98		0.98	1.09	1.33	1.23	1.36	1.66	1.48	1.63	2.00
0.90	1.00		0.89	0.89	0.89	1.11	1.11	1.11	1.33	1.33	1.33
0.90	1.02		0.81	0.73	0.60	1.01	0.91	0.75	1.21	1.09	0.90
1.00	0.98		0.89	0.98	1.20	1.11	1.22	1.50	1.33	1.47	1.80
1.00	1.00		0.80	0.80	0.80	1.00	1.00	1.00	1.20	1.20	1.20
1.00	1.02		0.72	0.66	0.54	0.91	0.82	0.67	1.09	0.98	0.81
1.10	0.98		0.80	0.89	1.09	1.01	1.11	1.36	1.21	1.34	1.63
1.10	1.00		0.73	0.73	0.73	0.91	0.91	0.91	1.09	1.09	1.09
1.10	1.02		0.66	0.60	0.49	0.82	0.75	0.61	0.99	0.89	0.73
1.20	0.98		0.74	0.82	1.00	0.92	1.02	1.25	1.11	1.22	1.50
1.20	1.00		0.67	0.67	0.67	0.83	0.83	0.83	1.00	1.00	1.00
1.20	1.02		0.60	0.55	0.45	0.75	0.68	0.56	0.91	0.82	0.67
1.30	0.98		0.68	0.75	0.92	0.85	0.94	1.15	1.02	1.13	1.38
1.30	1.00		0.62	0.62	0.62	0.77	0.77	0.77	0.92	0.92	0.92
1.30	1.02		0.56	0.50	0.41	0.70	0.63	0.52	0.84	0.76	0.62

$$a = (1 - t_{c0})/(1 - t_{cn})$$
$$b = (1 - t_{p0})/(1 - t_{pn})$$
$$c = (1 + r_1)/(1 + r_2)$$

where

- t_{c0} and t_{cn} are employer current and future marginal tax rates, thus $a > 1$ $(a < 1)$ implies employer tax rates are expected to increase (decrease).
- t_{p0} and t_{pn} are employee current and future marginal tax rates, respectively, thus $b > 1$ $(b < 1)$ implies employee tax rates are expected to increase (decrease).
- n denotes the number of time periods (i.e., length of the employment contract).
- r_1 and r_2 denote interest rates; the precise definitions vary depending on the compensation comparison for which the table is used.

To get you started, recall from Chapter 8 that salary will be preferred to deferred compensation if:

$$\frac{(1 - t_{p0})(1 + r_{pn})^n}{(1 - t_{pn})(1 + r_{cn})^n} > \frac{(1 - t_{c0})}{(1 - t_{cn})} \tag{8.2}$$

Given the definitions of a, b, and c, in the table, (8.2) can be rewritten as

$$bc^n > a$$
$$= a/bc^n < 1$$

and, in defining c, $r_1 = r_{pn}$ and $r_2 = r_{cn}$.

a. If $r_1 = r_{pn}$ and $r_2 = r_{cn}$, what do table values greater than 1.00 tell you about the desirability of salary relative to deferred compensation?

b. What portion of the table—that is, which rows and columns—is relevant to a comparison of salary and pensions? What are the appropriate definitions of r_1 and r_2 in this case? And what do table values greater than 1.00 tell you?

c. What portion of the table is relevant to a comparison of pensions and deferred compensation? What are the appropriate definitions of r_1 and r_2 in this case? And what do table values greater than 1.00 tell you?

You have been asked to provide tax planning assistance in formulating compensation policy for several of your corporate clients. You have three types of clients, each with seven types of employees.

Employer clients	t_{c0}	t_{cn}
(1) Tax exempt	0%	0%
(2) Net operating loss carryforward firm	22%	35%
(3) Currently profitable corporation but expects future losses	35%	19%

Employees	t_{p0}	t_{pn}
(1) Maintenance workers	15%	15%
(2) Young employees anticipating some career advancement	28%	40%
(3) Senior executive nearing retirement who has saved little for retirement	40%	15%
(4) Moderately high-income employee near retirement	31%	15%
(5) Mid-career nonmanagement employee expecting moderate career advancement	34%	40%
(6) Highly compensated junior management employee expecting demotion	40%	33%
(7) MBA student working October to December in the first year of employment and 12 months per year in all future years of employment	20%	40%

d. For the case of $r_p = r_c = R_{pen}$, for which employee/employer/length-of-the-employment-contract (EEL) combinations would you recommend that marginal compensation dollars be allocated to?
(1) Salary
(2) Deferred compensation
(3) Pension

e. Consider only employer client 3 and employees 1, 3, and 7. For the case of $r_p = r_c$ and R_{pen} exceeding r_c by approximately 2%, for which of the relevant EEL combinations would you recommend that marginal compensation dollars be allocated to?
(1) Salary
(2) Deferred compensation
(3) Pension

References and Additional Readings

Beatty, A., 1995. "The Cash Flow and Informational Effects of Employee Stock Ownership Plans," *Journal of Financial Economics,* pp. 211–240.

Black, F., 1980. "The Tax Consequences of Long-Run Pension Policy," *Financial Analysts Journal* (July–August), pp. 1–28.

Bodie, Z., J. Light, R. Morck, and R. Taggert, 1987. "Funding and Asset Allocation in Corporate Pension Plans: An Empirical Investigation," edited by Z. Bodie, J. Shoven, and D. Wise. *Issues in Pension Economics,* Chicago IL: University of Chicago Press, pp. 15–44.

Chang, S., and D. Mayers, 1992. "Managerial Vote Ownership and Shareholder Wealth: Evidence from Employee Stock Ownership Plans," *Journal of Financial Economics,* pp. 103–131.

Clinch, G., and T. Shibano, 1996. "Differential Tax Benefits and the Pension Reversion Decision," *Journal of Accounting and Economics* (1), pp. 69–106.

Francis, J., and S. Reiter, 1987. "Determinants of Corporate Pension Funding Strategy," *Journal of Accounting and Research* (1), pp. 35–59.

Frank, M., 2002. "The Impact of Taxes on Corporate Defined Benefit Plan Asset Allocation," *Journal of Accounting Research* (4), pp. 1163–1190.

Gordon, L., and J. Pound, 1990. "ESOPs and Corporate Control," *Journal of Financial Economics,* pp. 525–556.

Mittelstaedt, F., 1989. "An Empirical Analysis of Factors Underlying the Decision to Remove Excess Assets from Overfunded Pension Plans," *Journal of Accounting and Economics* (4), pp. 369–418.

Peterson, M., 1996. "Allocating Assets and Discounting Cash Flows: Pension Plan Finance" in *Pension, Savings, and Capital Markets,* edited by P. Fernandez, J. Turner, and R. Hinz. Washington, DC: U.S. Department of Labor, Pension and Welfare Benefits Administration. pp. 1–26.

Peterson, M., 1989. "Pension Terminations and Worker-Stockholder Wealth Transfers." Working paper. Boston, MA: Department of Economics, MIT.

Scholes, M., Wolfson, M., 1990. "Employee Stock Ownership Plans and Corporate Restructuring: Myths and Realities," *Financial Management Journal,* pp. 48–58.

Shackelford, D., 1991. "The Market for Tax Benefits: Evidence from Leveraged ESOPs," *Journal of Accounting and Economics* (2), pp. 117–145.

Tepper, I., 1981. "Taxation and Corporate Pension Policy," *Journal of Finance* (March), pp. 1–14.

Thomas, J., 1988. "Corporate Taxes and Defined Benefit Pension Plans," *Journal of Accounting and Economics* (3), pp. 199–237.

Thomas, J., 1989. "Why Do Firms Terminate Their Overfunded Pension Plans?" *Journal of Accounting and Economics* 11 (4), 361–398.

CHAPTER

10

MULTINATIONAL TAX PLANNING: INTRODUCTION AND INVESTMENT DECISIONS

After studying this chapter, you should be able to:

1. Describe the differences between territorial and worldwide taxation.

2. Distinguish between the tax treatment of foreign branches and foreign subsidiaries.

3. Perform basic foreign tax credit calculations.

4. Understand the implications of the rules for Subpart F income.

5. Analyze how taxes affect the location of investment.

6. Evaluate the key factors in the decision to repatriate or reinvest excess profits.

The study of international taxation needs almost no motivation. International trade and investment continue to grow at a faster pace than domestic trade and investment. Many prototypical "American" firms earn more abroad and pay more taxes abroad than they do in the United States. Cross-border mergers and acquisitions occur almost daily as entire industries consolidate and firms vie for global dominance, or at least survival. As cross-border transactions and ownership become more important, so does the need to understand how the income from such transactions is taxed. Moreover, the traditional principles of taxation become murky as commerce becomes based less on physical items and more on intangibles such as services, communications, and intellectual property. Such shifts pose problems to taxing authorities and offer opportunities for smart tax planners.

The basic issue in international taxation is that when firms invest abroad or engage in international trade, they become subject to the tax laws of at least two countries.

Each country, of course, applies its own set of tax laws to the firm to determine how much of the firm's income is subject to taxation. For example, what country or countries tax a telecommunications firm's income from a long-distance call from the United States to Germany that was routed through a satellite miles above the earth's surface? Does your answer change if the satellite is owned by a Cayman Islands subsidiary that leases the satellite back to the U.S. parent?

Although tax systems around the world have a great deal in common, they also differ from one another along a variety of dimensions. Marginal tax rates can vary from essentially 0% in certain tax-haven countries to as much as 60% in certain high-tax countries; the definition of income can vary dramatically from country to country; the use of nonincome taxes vary considerably; taxpayers may be taxed on only domestic income or on worldwide income. The patchwork of tax laws that multinationals are subject to can lead to the same dollar of income being taxed by a single jurisdiction, by more than one jurisdiction, or, in some cases, taxed by no jurisdiction.

But with variation in tax laws also lies opportunities. The variation in tax laws across countries provides fertile ground for creative tax strategies, many of which involve shifting income from high-tax jurisdictions to low-tax jurisdictions. In some cases shifting requires changing the physical structure of transactions, for example, where a factory is located; but in many cases the tax treatment can be improved by simply altering the financial structure of a transaction, for example, by routing investments through holding companies located in tax-favorable countries.

Why so much variation in tax laws across countries? Much of it arises from policy objectives. Several U.S. policy objectives address foreign taxation issues. The first is to relieve taxpayers from double (or more) taxation of the same income. The foreign tax credit (FTC) is an example of a provision designed to mitigate double taxation. The second objective is to aid in the U.S. balance-of-payments position by encouraging exports. Whether this objective is desirable is a matter of some debate among economists. Often, taxes are used as a strategic weapon by governments to attract certain kinds of business to their borders and to achieve certain economic goals.[1]

This and the next chapter will draw on many of the fundamental concepts outlined earlier in the book. The principle of shifting income from high- to low-tax jurisdictions is, of course, a vital concept in international taxation. Implicit taxes will be important when deciding where to locate investment. Although it may sound odd at first, sometimes it does not make sense to locate investments in tax havens. Finally, as with all tax strategies, we will emphasize the importance of taking into account the nontax costs of the strategy.

Before you can understand and appreciate international tax planning, you must have some foundation in the tax laws applicable to international commerce. Section 10.1 of this chapter lays such a foundation. The elements of the foundation include the ways that countries can approach international taxation, the ways that firms can

---

[1]The same tax competition exists within the United States at the state level. See Anand and Sansing (2000) and Goolsbee and Maydew (2000).

structure foreign operations, and foreign tax credits. Sections 10.2 and 10.3 examine the decision of where to invest and when to repatriate, respectively.

10.1 OVERVIEW OF MULTINATIONAL TAXATION

At the most basic level, the two approaches to taxation of foreign income are the worldwide system and the territorial system. Most industrialized countries, such as the United States and Japan, employ the **worldwide system,** while a small number of countries employ the territorial system. In the **territorial tax system,** the country taxes only income that was earned within its borders. Even though that statement sounds logical, determining where income was earned can be an elusive issue in practice, as we will see in Chapter 11. Under the worldwide tax system, a country generally will tax the worldwide income of its permanent residents and domestic corporations and will rely on foreign tax credits to mitigate double taxation of foreign income.

To begin our exploration, we must distinguish between those taxpayers subject to worldwide taxation and those subject to taxation on U.S.-source income only. The United States taxes U.S. citizens, whether they are U.S. residents or not, and U.S. corporations on their worldwide income. The same is true of resident aliens, including anyone holding a green card, which confers permanent resident status.[2] In contrast, foreign corporations and nonresident aliens are taxed by the United States only on income derived *within* the United States or income that is deemed to be "effectively connected with a U.S. trade or business."[3] So while the United States has a worldwide tax system, only U.S. corporations, citizens, and resident aliens are subject to worldwide taxation. Foreign corporations and nonresident aliens are essentially subject to territorial taxation by the United States. An element of practicality is at work here. Even if the United States foolishly tried to subject foreign corporations and nonresident aliens to worldwide taxation, it would be impossible to enforce such a tax, and the diplomatic uproar would almost certainly lead to retaliatory taxes against U.S. corporations and citizens. Most other countries with worldwide tax systems operate in the same manner, taxing only their residents and domestic corporations on their worldwide income and taxing the rest only on their domestic-source income.

At this point, the system of worldwide taxation may sound unfair. You might ask, does the United States really tax the income that GE earns in Brazil, when Brazil has already taxed the same income? GE's Brazilian income would be taxed twice and would seem to leave it at a competitive disadvantage relative to local Brazilian firms. The answer is the **foreign tax credit (FTC).** To avoid having more than one jurisdiction tax the same income, countries with worldwide tax systems give foreign tax credits for

---

[2]People can also be classified as resident aliens, and hence subject to worldwide taxation, by having a "substantial presence" in the United States. A substantial presence occurs if the person is in the United States for at least 31 days in the current year and 183 days during the current year and the last 2 years, with each day in year −1 counting at 1/3 and each day in year −2 counting at 1/6. Special rules exempt many students and diplomats from the substantial presence test. Bilateral tax treaties can have an impact as well.

[3]Nonresident aliens are people who are not permanent residents of the United States and do not meet the substantial presence test. For example, a German citizen living in Germany would be a nonresident alien for U.S. purposes, while a German citizen living year-round in the United States would not be.

taxes paid to other countries. As we shall see in this chapter and the next, however, the system of foreign tax credits does not always prevent double taxation. Indeed, foreign tax credit planning presents some of the biggest problems and opportunities in international taxation.

Avoiding Worldwide Taxation

A popular misconception is that a U.S. citizen can, after making her millions on Wall Street or in the Bay Area, set up residence in a Caribbean tax haven and live out the rest of her life on the beach, tax-free. Such dreams are as old as income taxation itself. As stated earlier, the United States subjects its citizens to taxation on their worldwide income, even those citizens who have permanently moved out of the country. Neither the foreign earned income exclusion, which exempts moderate amounts of foreign earned income from U.S. taxation, nor the foreign tax credit will help a U.S. citizen shelter passive income abroad. Other tax-reduction tactics include setting up offshore corporations or banks, but anti-abuse rules render most of those techniques ineffective.

A few generally wealthy U.S. citizens have dislodged themselves from worldwide taxation by renouncing their citizenship and moving to tax havens.[4] Such a move comes with substantial tax and nontax costs, however. Even as a noncitizen, spending too much time in the United States risks triggering what is called the "substantial presence test" and being taxed on worldwide income. Moreover, the income from a U.S. business is still subject to U.S. taxation. The main advantage of giving up U.S. citizenship is the possibility of avoiding U.S. income taxes on capital gains and dividends. In response to public outrage from press accounts of such activity, Congress continues to strengthen what are known as the expatriation rules, which subject capital gains from sales of U.S. corporations to U.S. taxation for up to 10 years following the expatriation and make it difficult for those who renounce their U.S. citizenship from obtaining visas to reenter the United States.[5]

In addition to attracting persons interested in legal tax avoidance, tax havens also attract shady elements. Tax havens tend to have strict bank secrecy laws and do not have tax information-sharing agreements with the United States. Such privacy laws increase the attractiveness of tax havens to those laundering illegal income and those interested in evading taxes on their legal income. Tax havens compete with one another for business, and many even advertise on the Internet.[6]

Operating as a Branch versus a Foreign Subsidiary

We have learned that U.S. corporations are subject to taxation on their worldwide income, but what about the fact that most multinationals are collections of subsidiaries, many of which may be incorporated in foreign countries?[7] What counts as a U.S. corporation? The answer is any corporation incorporated under the laws of any

---

[4]See E. Lesly, "The Darts: Fear, Loathing, and Foam Cups," *Business Week* (July 10, 1995); R. Lenzner and P. Mao, "The New Refugees," *Forbes* (November 21, 1994); and "Leaving Indicator," *The Wall Street Journal* (April 18, 1994).
[5]See A. Fragomen and P. Hejinian, "Immigration Consequences of Abandoning U.S. Citizenship for Tax Reasons," *Tax Notes International* (November 2, 1998).
[6]See D. Hilzenrath, "Russians Use Tiny Island to Launder Billions," *Washington Post* (October 28, 1999).
[7]The word subsidiary refers to a corporation that is owned by another corporation.

state of the United States or the District of Columbia. All other corporations are foreign corporations. U.S. shareholders are generally not taxed on the income of a foreign corporation until it pays a dividend. Consider a U.S. parent corporation that has a number of U.S. subsidiaries and a wholly owned Italian subsidiary. The income of the U.S. parent and its U.S. subsidiaries will be subject to worldwide taxation, and these entities most likely will file a consolidated U.S. tax return. However, the Italian subsidiary's income generally will not be subject to U.S. taxation until it pays a dividend up to its parent, which is called repatriation. At the time of repatriation the income is reported on the parent firm's tax return.

These rules highlight an important difference between financial reporting and tax reporting. For financial reporting purposes, generally accepted accounting principles (GAAP) require firms to consolidate all subsidiaries, both domestic and foreign, in which they have 50% or more ownership. Consequently, the annual reports of multinationals represent their worldwide income and operations. In contrast, the U.S. tax returns of multinationals include the income and operations of the U.S. parent, U.S. subsidiaries, and repatriated income of foreign subsidiaries.[8] Income of foreign subsidiaries that is reinvested abroad is not generally reported on the U.S. tax return, except in certain cases, which we discuss later in the chapter.[9]

Most of the foreign income of U.S. multinationals is earned in **foreign subsidiaries.** An alternative, the **foreign branch,** can be extremely useful in certain cases. For U.S. purposes, a branch is essentially an entity not classified as a corporation. The so-called check-the-box regulations give firms considerable flexibility in selecting branch versus subsidiary treatment.[10] The idea behind these regulations is to let firms elect whether to treat their wholly owned foreign entities as corporations for U.S. tax purposes or as branches. The election is made by actually checking a box on a special form filed with the IRS. A different election can be made for each foreign entity. Certain foreign entities, known as "per se corporations," are not eligible for this election and must be classified as corporations for U.S. purposes. Per se corporations are generally foreign entities that are publicly tradable and have limited liability. Any foreign entity not a per se corporation can elect to be taxed as a branch or a corporation for U.S. tax purposes. Moreover, the regulations allow firms to change their election every 5 years. The election to be taxed as a subsidiary or a branch for U.S. purposes has no effect on the foreign taxation. For example, a foreign entity could be classified as a branch for U.S. purposes but still be taxed as a corporation by the foreign country. This flexibility to be taxed as a subsidiary or a branch has led to the development of a large number of tax-planning techniques.

The U.S. tax law offers both advantages and disadvantages to operating as a foreign branch rather than as a foreign subsidiary. Advantages of branch classification

---

[8]U.S. subsidiaries that are 80% or more owned by the parent, either directly or indirectly through other subsidiaries, can be included in the parent's consolidated tax return. U.S. subsidiaries that are 50% or more owned by the parent but less than 80% owned will be consolidated for financial reporting purposes but not for tax purposes.

[9]Foreign corporations will file U.S. returns, of course, if they have income "effectively connected with a U.S. trade or business," but they cannot generally file consolidated returns with U.S. corporations. Because consolidated tax returns allow for offsetting income and losses in different entities, it is generally best to structure operations so that foreign subsidiaries have only foreign income.

[10]Section 301.7701.

include the following:

1. Losses from foreign operations are immediately deductible against U.S. domestic income, which is especially important for start-up operations that can reasonably be expected to generate losses. Moreover, it is possible to change the branch into a corporation when operations turn profitable, that is, make a different check-the-box election to defer future income from U.S. taxation. The cost, however, is that the firm must recapture, as income, previously deducted losses.
2. Property can be transferred to a branch without fear of current taxation on appreciation. Some transfers of property to foreign subsidiaries, however, are taxable.

Disadvantages of operating as a branch include the following:

1. U.S. tax on the earnings of the branch cannot be deferred. In many cases, this factor is the most important, especially when the host country's tax rate is below that of the United States.
2. Some countries may require disclosure of data on worldwide operations to tax authorities. Not only may these reporting requirements be administratively burdensome, but they may also require disclosing sensitive competitive information.
3. Foreign corporate subsidiaries can more easily participate in nontaxable reorganizations than foreign branches.

Both advantages and disadvantages come along with operating as a branch under the local country's laws as well. The U.S. classification of a foreign entity as a branch or as a subsidiary has no bearing on the classification by the local tax authorities. As a result, four potential combinations of classification of wholly owned entities under U.S. and foreign law are (1) U.S. branch and foreign branch, (2) U.S. branch and foreign corporation, (3) U.S. corporation and foreign branch, or (4) U.S. corporation and foreign corporation.

Most foreign nations tax branches differently from the way they tax subsidiaries. For example, the way loss carryforwards are treated across foreign tax jurisdictions varies considerably. Although carryforwards are typically available to foreign subsidiaries, it is not the case in all countries. Moreover, some countries allow short carryforward periods, other countries allow some combination of carrybacks and carryforwards, and some countries allow carryforwards only. Some countries allow branches established in their country to carry losses forward, but this treatment is less common than for foreign subsidiaries.

Nontax considerations also play an important role in the choice of branch versus subsidiary. For example, in contrast to foreign subsidiaries, the liability of most branch operations is not limited to assets employed abroad. For this reason, domestic subsidiaries are often used to set up foreign branches to limit the parent corporation's legal liability on foreign operations.

Foreign Tax Credits

To understand the advantages of U.S. tax deferral for foreign subsidiaries, it is necessary to understand how foreign tax credits are calculated, as well as how the Subpart F rules work. In this section we introduce the basics; Chapter 11 takes a deeper look at the foreign tax credit rules and the problems and opportunities they give rise to.

To begin with, note that there are two types of foreign tax credits: direct foreign tax credits (Section 901) for taxes that are imposed *directly* on the U.S. taxpayer and indirect foreign tax credits (or deemed paid credits, Section 902). **Direct foreign tax credits** result when a tax is paid on the earnings of a foreign branch of a U.S. company or when withholding taxes are deducted from dividends or other forms of passive income paid to U.S. investors or U.S. parent corporations. **Indirect foreign tax credits** arise when dividends are received or deemed to be received from foreign corporations. The potential credit is equal to the taxes paid on the underlying "earnings and profits" that produced the dividend. Loosely defined, **earnings and profits (E&P)** is the tax version of retained earnings.[11] Indirect credits are available only to U.S. shareholders owning 10% or more of a foreign corporation. The foreign dividend included in U.S. income is the dividend received grossed-up to include both the withholding tax and any deemed paid taxes.

Not all foreign taxes are eligible for the foreign tax credit. In general, the United States allows foreign tax credits only for foreign taxes levied on income and withholding taxes on the repatriation of income. Thus, foreign property taxes, value-added taxes, and excise taxes are not eligible for the foreign tax credit unless an exception is made under a tax treaty. Foreign taxes not eligible for the foreign tax credit can be taken as a deduction for U.S. tax purposes, just like any other business expense. Credits are generally preferred to deductions, however, as a dollar of tax credit reduces the tax liability by $1, while a dollar of deduction reduces taxes by only $1 \times t_d$, where t_d is the domestic (U.S.) tax rate. The classification of a foreign tax as based on income for U.S. FTC purposes is sometimes a gray area. For example, the IRS and large oil companies have been involved in multibillion-dollar litigation over whether taxes levied on the extraction of oil, which are common taxes in Middle Eastern countries, qualify as taxes based on income for U.S. FTC purposes.[12]

Even if a foreign tax is classified as an income tax for U.S. purposes, that does not automatically mean that the U.S. corporation will get an immediate foreign tax credit equal to the foreign tax. In many countries the income tax rate exceeds the U.S. tax rate, and in such cases the United States will not give credit for more in taxes than would have been paid had the income been earned in the United States. The rules that prevent U.S. taxpayers from getting too much tax relief in the eyes of the tax authorities from foreign tax credits are known as the **foreign tax credit limitation** rules. Planning for foreign tax credits is among the most important tax considerations in the multinational arena.

We illustrate how the foreign tax credit mechanism works in Table 10.1. We assume that a U.S. multinational has established a subsidiary in Australia and one in

---

[11]Like the financial accounting concept of retained earnings, accumulated E&P increase with current earnings and decrease as dividends arc paid. The main difference between accumulated E&P and retained earnings is that the current earnings for E&P purposes is based on taxable income (with modifications) rather than GAAP-based earnings. The modifications to taxable income to arrive at current E&P include subtracting taxes paid and adding back exempt income such as municipal bond income. In general, the modifications tend to move E&P toward GAAP earnings.

[12]See, for example, *Exxon Corp. v. Commissioner,* 113 T.C. No. 24 (1999); *Phillips Petroleum Company v. Commissioner,* 104 T.C. 256 (1995).

TABLE 10.1 Example of the Indirect Foreign Tax Credit

	Subsidiary		
	A **Australia Alone**	**B** **Ireland Alone**	**Together**
Local taxable income	$100	$100	$200
Local tax (at 30% and 20%)	$30	$20	$50
Withholding tax on dividends (at 10%)	$7	$8	$15
Dividend net of foreign taxes	$63	$72	$135
U.S. taxable income from foreign dividends	$100	$100	$200
U.S. tax at 35%	$35	$35	$70
Foreign tax credit	$35	$28	$65*
Net U.S. tax on foreign dividends	$0	$7	$5
Dividend net of all taxes	$63	$65	$130
Foreign tax credit carryforward	$2	$0	$0

*Notice that the rows do not sum across. The reason has to do with the way the foreign tax limitation is calculated.

Ireland. Both subsidiaries earn $100. Assume for pedagogical purposes that the local tax rates on income earned in Australia and Ireland are 30% and 20%, respectively. The withholding tax rate on dividends remitted to the U.S. parent is 10% in both Australia and Ireland. That is, each subsidiary must pay to the host government 10% of the (prewithholding tax) dividend it paid to its parent. The remaining 90% of the dividend is remitted to its parent.

First consider column A, which assumes for the moment that the subsidiary in Ireland paid no dividend. The foreign subsidiary earns $100 of taxable income in Australia. The Australian tax rate is 30%, and $30 in Australian taxes are paid. This leaves $70 of local income to reinvest abroad or to pay as a dividend. Suppose that the $70 is paid as a dividend to the U.S. parent. By treaty with the United States, Australia assesses a 10% withholding tax on the dividend. As a result, $7 of the $70 dividend is withheld, and $63 is paid to the U.S. parent. If t_f is the foreign tax rate on income, and t_w is the withholding tax rate on dividends, the parent receives dividends of $(1 - t_f)(1 - t_w)$ per $1 of pretax income; for example, $100(1 - .3)(1 - .1) = \$63$. However, if the U.S. parent wants to take a foreign tax credit for the foreign taxes paid by its subsidiary, that is, a "deemed paid" or indirect foreign tax credit, then it must gross up the dividend to its pretax amount. The computation is as follows:

Dividend received	$63	
+ Withholding taxes	7	(Direct tax paid)
+ Indirect foreign taxes	30	(Deemed paid credit)
= Grossed-up dividend	$100	
U.S. tax at 35%	35	
− Foreign tax credit allowed	35	
= Additional U.S. tax due	$0	

The $30 deemed paid credit represents the local income taxes paid by the Australian subsidiary on the earnings from which the $70 dividend was paid.

$$\text{Deemed paid credit} = \frac{\text{dividend}}{\text{after-tax earnings and profits}} \times \text{foreign income taxes paid}^{13}$$

$$\text{(10.1)}$$

Because 100% of the after-tax earnings has been paid out as a dividend, the deemed paid credit is 100% of the foreign tax paid, or $30 in this case. As a result of the deemed paid credit of $30 and $7 of withholding tax, the $63 dividend results in $100 of taxable income. Equation (10.1) is more meaningful when the foreign subsidiary accumulates earnings over several years at different local tax rates and then pays a portion of those earnings to the parent as a dividend. In that case, which is quite common, equation (10.1) essentially says that the parent's indirect foreign tax credit is based on the average local tax rate that applied to the foreign subsidiary's income.

Notice that only $35 of the $37 of total foreign taxes paid can be used currently as a tax credit. The remaining $2 can be carried back up to 2 years and carried forward up to 5 years. To prevent a host of abuses, the United States imposes limitations on foreign tax credits. In general the foreign tax credit limitation is equal to the U.S. tax rate times the foreign source income. The FTC after limitation is equal to the minimum of the direct plus indirect foreign taxes paid and the FTC limitation, or min($7 + $30, $35) = $35.

Now consider column B. Suppose the Irish subsidiary declares a dividend equal to its income after paying local income taxes, but the Australian subsidiary declares no dividend. Given an Irish income tax rate of 20% plus an additional 10% withholding tax rate on dividends, we have the following results:

Dividend received	$72
+ Withholding taxes	8
+ Indirect foreign taxes	20
= Total U.S. taxable income (same as column A)	$100
U.S. tax at 35%	35
− Foreign tax credit allowed	28
= Additional U.S. tax due	$7

A dividend of $72 is paid to the parent. It results from the $80 of after-tax profits earned in Ireland, less a withholding tax of $8. As before, the total U.S. taxable income is $100 (or $72 + $8 + $20). The U.S. tax liability on the $100 of taxable income is $35. The foreign tax credit available is the minimum of the U.S. tax on the foreign income ($35) and the direct plus indirect foreign taxes paid ($8 of direct tax plus the $20 of deemed paid credit or $28). Therefore, the additional tax owed in the United States is $7 (or $35 − $28). Because the U.S. parent has $72 in hand before payment of additional U.S. taxes, it is left with $65 after payment of the additional U.S. taxes.

---

[13]Actually, the earnings and profits in (10.1) are the post-1986 accumulated earnings and profits. Similarly, the foreign income tax paid are the post-1986 foreign income taxes paid.

In the last column of Table 10.1, we assume that both subsidiaries declare dividends equal to their income after local income tax. Although not all countries do so, the United States and Japan allow the foreign tax credit limitation to be calculated based on worldwide income, rather than imposing a separate limitation on a country-by-country basis as Canada and many other countries do.[14] Given the ability to average the foreign tax rates paid on worldwide income, all of the $65 in foreign taxes paid can be used as a credit against the U.S. tax on foreign income. Why? Because the $70 foreign tax credit limitation is greater than the $65 foreign taxes paid. Essentially, the low-tax Irish operations provide $7 of excess foreign tax credit limitation that is used to soak up the $2 of excess foreign tax credits generated by the high-tax Australian operations.

Subpart F Income and Controlled Foreign Corporations (CFCs)[15]

Consider the following tax strategy. A highly profitable U.S. corporation sets up a wholly owned subsidiary in a tax haven through which it invests its excess funds in passive investments. Recall the general rule that income of foreign subsidiaries is not taxable to the U.S. parent until it is repatriated. Is it then possible for the U.S. parent to essentially earn tax-free returns indefinitely by investing through subsidiaries domiciled in tax havens? Perhaps, but the tax authorities have known about such strategies for a long time and have built up formidable anti-abuse rules, namely the **Subpart F** and **controlled foreign corporation (CFC)** rules. The Subpart F and CFC provisions are designed to prevent firms from forming paper foreign corporations in tax havens to record income from passive investments, sales, services, shipping operations, or oil-related activities. In general, these rules work by subjecting Subpart F income to U.S. taxation as if the income was repatriated to the U.S. parent when the income is earned, rather than when the subsidiary distributes cash to the parent.

Most foreign subsidiaries of U.S. corporations are classified as CFCs under Section 951 of the Internal Revenue Code. A CFC is a foreign corporation owned more than 50% in terms of voting power or market value by U.S. shareholders. A U.S. shareholder is any U.S. person, including a U.S. corporation, owning at least 10% of the foreign corporation's voting stock.

Classification as a CFC triggers several tax disadvantages:

1. Loss of the deferral on Subpart F income, which we will describe in a bit more detail later in this chapter.
2. Loss of tax deferral on earnings and profits reinvested by the CFC in U.S. property—that is, reinvestment in U.S. property is deemed to be equivalent to repatriation of profits to the parent. Reinvestment in U.S. property need not give rise to withholding tax by the country from which the funds are transferred.
3. Gain on the sale or redemption of CFC stock or gain on liquidation of a CFC results in ordinary income rather than in capital gain up to the CFC's earnings and profits not previously taxed as a deemed dividend.

---

[14]The United States does, however, require foreign tax credits to be computed separately on different "baskets" of income, as explained in Chapter 11.
[15]As this chapter was written Congress was considering changes to the Subpart F rules.

Note that CFC status can be avoided as long as shareholders are willing to share control with other owners. For example, a foreign corporation that is owned 50% by a U.S. corporation and 50% by an unrelated foreign investor would avoid CFC status. Similarly, a foreign corporation can be owned entirely by U.S. taxpayers and still avoid CFC status as long as a sufficient number of owners hold less than 10% of the voting stock; 11 equal shareholders will do the trick, for example.

A foreign corporation that is not a CFC can invest in assets that yield passive income, like interest-bearing securities, without triggering current U.S. taxation.[16] An investment in interest-bearing securities that is made through a foreign corporation in a tax-haven country where the income tax rate is low can offer a high rate of return after-tax to shareholders.

What exactly is Subpart F income? In general it is passive income that can be easily moved across jurisdictions and is therefore at risk from the perspective of the tax authorities of being shifted into tax havens. Subpart F has two main components: (1) income from the insurance of risks outside the country in which the CFC is organized and (2) income called "foreign base company income."

The insurance component of Subpart F income includes income derived from the insurance of risks outside the country in which the CFC is organized. This provision is designed to stop captive insurance companies controlled by U.S. corporations from shifting income from the United States to tax havens.

Foreign base company income, in turn, has five components:

1. Foreign personal holding company income or FPHCI (dividends, interest, rents, royalties, and so on)
2. Foreign base company sales income
3. Foreign base company service income
4. Foreign base company shipping income
5. Foreign base company oil-and-gas-related income

While the details of foreign base company income are beyond the scope of this book, we discuss two of its components to give you a flavor for the kinds of activities that are subject to the Subpart F provisions. FPHCI includes interest and interest equivalents received by a bank in its banking business; net gains from the sale or exchange of property that generates passive income, such as patents and land; and gains on commodities futures and foreign currency transactions. Note that passive income earned in foreign subsidiaries where the local tax rate is at least 90% of the U.S. tax rate is *not* treated as Subpart F income; it is the so-called "high-tax kickout." Foreign base company sales income is derived from the purchase or sale of personal property such as goods manufactured outside the country of incorporation as well as goods sold to a user outside the country of incorporation.

For the administrative convenience of both taxpayers and the IRS, Subpart F income is modified by the so-called 5-70 Rules. If foreign base company income of the CFC is less than the lesser of $1 million or 5% of the CFC's gross income, then the firm can treat the income as active income and ignore the Subpart F rules. If more than

---

[16]Other provisions that can come into play are the foreign personal holding company rules and the passive foreign investment company (PFIC) rules, which are beyond the scope of this text.

70% of the gross income of the CFC is foreign base company income, then 100% of the gross income of the CFC is treated as Subpart F income. These rules provide a potential trap of moderate consequences for taxpayers who are not careful and a tax-planning opportunity for those who are careful. For example, a CFC might find it beneficial to maintain passive investments that generate just less than 5% of its foreign base company income.

Inversion Transactions

The CFC rules apply only to U.S. shareholders of foreign subsidiaries. Many foreign countries, however, do not have CFC rules in their tax laws. In this respect, U.S.-based multinationals are disadvantaged compared with similarly positioned multinational corporations based abroad. This disparity has caused the management of some U.S. multinationals to consider structuring their corporate group so that the parent company would be incorporated abroad. A common form of this restructuring, known as an inversion transaction, involves placing the former U.S. parent corporation under a newly created foreign parent corporation formed in a low tax jurisdiction that does not have CFC rules, for example, Bermuda or the Cayman Islands. In certain respects, an inversion is a corporate equivalent of tax-motivated expatriations by individuals. The two main tax benefits to an inversion are removing foreign income from the U.S. corporate tax system and the ability to locate intercompany debt in the tax haven to achieve "interest stripping" of income out of the United States and into the tax haven. A similar principle holds for royalties on intangible assets. There are interest stripping provisions in Section 163(j) designed to mitigate such activities.[17]

In the 1980s and early 1990s, several U.S.-based multinational corporations engaged in tax-free inversion transactions. One particular transaction involved Helen of Troy, which makes personal care products. The public shareholders of Helen of Troy transferred their stock to a newly formed Bermuda corporation. The exchange qualified as a nontaxable exchange under Sections 351 and 368(a)(1)(B).[18] The transaction effectively moved a large portion of the corporation's income out of the U.S. tax base and into a country that has no corporate income tax (see Figure 10.1). The IRS and Treasury became concerned that the Helen of Troy transaction could be the first of many U.S. multinational departures. To prevent an exodus, the IRS ultimately issued a set of regulations under Section 367 known as the "anti-inversion regulations."[19] These regulations generally prevent outbound mergers and stock transfers from qualifying for tax-free treatment unless the shareholders of the transferred U.S. corporation receive less than 50% of the shares of the foreign acquiring corporation in the transaction. In other words, an outbound merger may still be accomplished tax-free if the foreign acquirer is larger than the U.S. target corporation. However, the transaction generally will be taxable to the corporate shareholders if the foreign acquirer is the smaller corporation or is merely a new holding company, as in the Helen of Troy inversion.

The anti-inversion regulations have not completely stopped corporations from migrating out of the United States. In some cases, U.S. corporations have simply

---

[17]See Cloyd, Mills, and Weaver (2003); Seida and Wempe (2002); and Desai and Hines (2002).
[18]Helen of Troy Limited, Prospectus/Proxy Statement, dated January 5, 1994. Acquisitions governed by Sections 368 and 351 are discussed in the chapters on mergers and acquisitions.
[19]Treasury Regulation Sec. 1.367(a)–3(c).

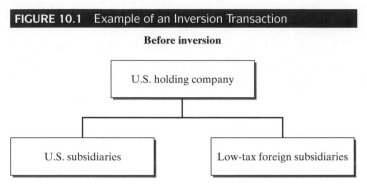

FIGURE 10.1 Example of an Inversion Transaction

Before inversion

U.S. holding company

U.S. subsidiaries

Low-tax foreign subsidiaries

Income of low-tax foreign subsidiaries eventually taxed at U.S. rates when income is repatriated or deemed repatriated (i.e., Subpart F) to U.S. parent.

After inversion

Tax-haven holding company

U.S. holding company

Low-tax foreign subsidiaries

U.S. subsidiaries

Income of low-tax foreign subsidiaries never taxed at U.S. rates because parent is now located in a tax-haven country. U.S. subsidiaries pay U.S. tax as before.

moved to foreign jurisdictions in taxable transactions, creating a higher up-front tax cost to their shareholders that is presumably offset by lower corporate-level taxes for the indefinite future.[20] Another consequence of the anti-inversion regulations is to complicate cross-border "mega mergers" involving U.S. corporations. Despite anti-inversion complications, transactions that effected a corporate migration and avoided the anti-inversion regulations include the mergers of Chrysler Corporation and Daimler Benz AG, Amoco Corporation and British Petroleum, and AirTouch Communications Inc. and Vodafone Group PLC.[21]

---

[20]See, for example, ADT Ltd. Joint Proxy Statement/Prospectus, dated January 3, 1997, describing the Tyco International Ltd. merger with Bermuda-based ADT; Fruit-of-the-Loom Ltd. Join Proxy Statement/ Prospectus, dated October 15, 1998, describing merger into new Cayman Islands holding company.
[21]Given the magnitude of these mergers, the corporate taxpayers asked for and received private letter rulings from the IRS concluding that the anti-inversion regulations would not apply. See, for example, PLR 9849014 (Chrysler/Daimler-Benz) and PLR 199929039 (AirTouch/Vodafone).

10.2 HOW TAXES AFFECT THE LOCATION AND STRUCTURE OF INVESTMENTS

You might be tempted to suppose that when a foreign country's tax rates are lower than domestic tax rates, the after-tax rates of return on investments should be higher in the foreign country. However, this assumption ignores the real possibility that pretax rates of return in the foreign country may be lower than those available domestically. In countries where the tax rate on income is relatively low, one would expect competition to bid up the price of investing in that country and force down pretax profitability. In other words, the foreign investments may bear *implicit taxes.* In addition, a number of nontax market imperfections may cause pretax returns to vary across countries, including restrictions on the free flow of capital across borders.[22]

For physical investments—factories and the like—firms must consider a variety of nontax costs in their location decisions. For example, despite an attractive Tax Code, auto companies are not rushing to build large factories in the Cayman Islands. Possible reasons include a lack of large pools of skilled labor and a lack of infrastructure. Other nontax factors include legal differences across countries (for example, some countries may have lax property rights and inefficient bureaucracies); access to markets (for example, it may help to sell goods in China if you manufacture there); and proximity to customers or suppliers (for example, bottling facilities are typically located near population centers because of the costs of transporting bottled liquids across long distances). With physical investments, taxes often matter on the margin when two or more possible locations are roughly equal on nontax dimensions. Empirical research using large samples of firms has found evidence that cross-country variation in tax rates does affect the location of investment.[23]

To illustrate the role of implicit taxes in investment decisions, suppose that your company has $100 million to invest in one of two mutually exclusive projects, one at home and the other, of equal risk, located in a lower-tax-rate foreign country. The tax rates and the rates of return available on the two projects appear in Table 10.2.

Note from Table 10.2 the $20\% - 18\% = 2\%$ implicit tax on investing abroad. Marginal dollars invested in the home country earn 20% pretax and 13% after a 35% tax. Marginal dollars invested in the foreign subsidiary earn 18% pretax and 15.3% after a 15% local tax. In this case the implicit tax disadvantage of foreign investment is not large enough to overcome its explicit tax advantage, and so foreign investment is

TABLE 10.2 Tax Rates and Rates of Return to Investing at Home and Abroad			
	Tax Rate	*Pretax Return*	*After (Local) Tax Return*
Home	35%	20%	13%, or 20%(1 − 35%)
Abroad	15%	18%	15.3%, or 18%(1 − 15%)

---

[22]In a nontax world with perfect, frictionless markets, one would expect capital to move freely across borders and prices bid up or down to the point where risk-adjusted expected returns were the same across all assets. Once market imperfections are allowed for, risk-adjusted expected returns could vary across assets and countries, even in the absence of taxation.

[23]See the Additional Readings at the end of the chapter.

TABLE 10.3 Investing $100 Million Abroad for 1 Year at 18% Pretax versus at Home at 20% Pretax (in $millions)

Invest Abroad

Before-tax accumulation	$118.0	($100 investment × 1.18)
Local tax (at 15% tax rate)	−2.7	(15% of 18)
After-local-tax liquidating distribution	115.3	($100 represents a nontaxable return of capital originally invested)
Additional tax at home	−3.6	[18 × (35% − FTC of 15%)]
Net liquidating distribution after all taxes	111.7	
After-tax rate of return	11.7%	[11.7/100, or 18%(1 − 35%)]
Invest at Home	13.0%	[20%(1 − 35%)]

favored. Rather, foreign investment is favored as long as the profits can be reinvested indefinitely, as we shall see shortly.

Why might an implicit tax arise in investing abroad? As we have said, implicit taxes can arise because the foreign country encourages investment by offering generous tax benefits, and competition for the right to garner these benefits results in lower before-tax rates of return. Nontax factors can also account for some of the observed implicit tax. Low tax rates are typically offered to lure business that would not otherwise be undertaken in the low-tax jurisdiction.

Given the investment opportunities described in Table 10.2, in which country should you invest? You might be tempted to go for the foreign investment, given its higher after-tax return, but it turns out the answer depends on the length of the investment horizon. Suppose that you invest abroad for only 1 year. At the end of the year, the foreign subsidiary repatriates all profits to the home country.

Despite the low local tax rate abroad, Table 10.3 shows that with a 1-year investment horizon you are better off investing at home. Investing abroad produces an after-tax return of only 11.7%, which compares poorly with the 13% after-tax return from investing at home. More generally, when the tax rate abroad is less than or equal to the tax rate at home, a 1-year investment yields an after-tax return of $R_f(1 - t_d)$ abroad and $R_d(1 - t_d)$ at home, where R_f is the pretax return abroad, R_d is the pretax domestic return, and t_d is the domestic tax rate. Notice that the domestic tax rate, t_d, applies to *both* investments. The reason is that each dollar of pretax income from the foreign investment triggers taxes of t_f by the local jurisdiction and t_d when the income is repatriated, less a foreign tax credit of t_f, so the net tax is $t_f + (t_d - t_f) = t_d$. The notation, which we use throughout the rest of the chapter, is summarized in Table 10.4. The bottom line is that, with a 1-year investment horizon and foreign tax rates lower than domestic tax rates, simply comparing the before-tax rates of return on the investments will suffice, because both investments will effectively be taxed at the domestic rate.

What happens if, instead of repatriating profits each year as earned, you can reinvest profits abroad at 15.3% after-local-tax instead of at 13% after-tax at home? If you could leave the investment abroad forever, you would earn 15.3% after-tax abroad compared with only 13% at home. Let us see what happens if you leave the investment abroad over intermediate-term horizons, say, for 5 years. At the end of 5 years you accumulate $100 million × 1.153^5 = $203.8 million abroad after local tax. At the end of 5 years, a $203.8 million liquidating distribution can be paid to the parent company

TABLE 10.4 Notation

R_d = Pretax (domestic) rate of return in the home country

R_f = Pretax (foreign) rate of return abroad

t_d = Domestic tax rate

t_f = Foreign tax rate

$r_f = R_f(1 - t_f)$, the after-local-tax rate of return abroad

$r_d = R_d(1 - t_d)$, the after-tax domestic rate of return

n = Length of the investment horizon

I = Amount invested

at home. This amount includes after-tax foreign profits of $103.8 million ($203.8 million less $100 million initially invested) on which home country tax must be paid. We must also compute the foreign taxes paid to determine the amount of pretax profits earned abroad.

If the foreign tax rate is constant over time, the taxable home country dividend is equal to the after-local-tax profits earned abroad, that is, $103.8 million, divided by 1 minus the foreign tax rate, t_f. Home country taxable income is equal to

$$\frac{I[(1 + r_f)^n - 1]}{(1 - t_f)} \tag{10.2}$$

where I denotes the amount invested, r_f denotes the after-local-tax rate of return abroad, and n denotes the length of time the investment is made abroad. The numerator of equation (10.2) simply states that the after-local-tax profit is equal to the after-local-tax accumulation less the original amount invested, or $(1 + r_f)^n - 1$ for each dollar invested. The denominator grosses up the after-local-tax profits to be pretax profits.

In our example, this calculation is equal to

$$\$103.8 \text{ million}/(1 - .15) = \$122.1 \text{ million}$$

To understand why grossing up the after-tax profits repatriated by a factor of $(1 - t_f)$ yields the pretax profit, note that

$$\text{Pretax profit} \times (1 - \text{tax rate}) = \text{After-tax profit}$$

so

$$\text{Pretax profit} = \text{After-tax profit}/(1 - \text{tax rate})$$

Our calculations reveal that, on liquidation in 5 years, the foreign investment yields home-country taxable income of $122.1 million. This income is subject to an additional home country tax at a rate of 20% (or 35% − 15%) because all taxable income will be taxed at rate t_d less a foreign tax credit at rate t_f, resulting in additional tax of $24.4 million. As a result, the net liquidating distribution retained by the parent company, after both foreign and home-country taxes, is $179.4 million (or $203.8 million − $24.4 million). The 5-year annualized after-tax rate of return from investing abroad is

$$(179.4/100)^{1/5} - 1 = 12.4\%$$

Because this amount is less than 13%, the home country after-tax rate of return, investing at home is still the better decision. More generally, each dollar of foreign investment, over an n-year investment horizon, yields an accumulation (after paying the home-country tax on repatriation of profits) of

$$(1 + r_f)^n - \frac{(1 + r_f)^n - 1}{(1 - t_f)}(t_d - t_f) \tag{10.3}$$

Equation (10.3) is best understood by dissecting its parts. The first term, $(1 + r_f)^n$, represents the after-local-tax accumulation abroad. In our example, r_f is 15.3%, or 18%(1 − 15%), and, when $n = 5$, $(1 + r_f)^n = 2.038$. Because equation (10.3) will be multiplied by our $100 million investment, 2.038 equals the $203.8 million accumulation we computed earlier. Next examine the ratio in the middle. The numerator, $(1 + r_f)^n - 1$, represents the after-local-tax earnings that are repatriated, which are grossed up to pretax levels by dividing by $1 - t_f$. In our example the ratio is 1.221. Finally, the term $(t_d - t_f)$ represents the home country tax due on repatriation in year n at rate t_d less the foreign tax credit, t_f, or 35% − 15% = 20% in our example. Combining the terms gives an after-all-taxes accumulation of 1.794 for each dollar invested, equaling the $179.4 million we computed earlier.

Consider now a home-country investment for n years, which accumulates to

$$[1 + R_d(1 - t_d)]^n \tag{10.4}$$

For 1-period investments ($n = 1$), we see from (10.3), and recalling that $r_f = R_f(1 - t_f)$, that foreign investment yields

$$1 + R_f(1 - t_d)$$

and domestic investment, from (10.4), yields

$$1 + R_d(1 - t_d)$$

It implies that, for short investment horizons, the *pretax* foreign return (R_f) must exceed the pretax domestic return (R_d) for foreign investment to dominate domestic investment.

Will foreign investment ever be more attractive than domestic investment if R_f is less than R_d? Yes, it will. As the investment horizon increases, the annualized after-tax return from investing abroad will approach the 15.3% after-local-tax return in our example. For example, in 5 years, foreign investment yields 12.4% per year after all taxes, and in 15 years it yields 13.5%. Investing abroad compares quite favorably with investing at home with longer investment horizons. A 15-year horizon, for example, yields an after-tax accumulation of an additional $40 million with a foreign investment than with a domestic investment.

Large Implicit Taxes and Foreign Investment Incentives

Suppose now that tax rates abroad are much more generous and cause implicit tax rates abroad to increase. For example, assume that the foreign country provides generous investment tax credits for investment in that country and that these credits are not available in the home country. To illustrate the effects of increasing the rate of implicit tax on the decision to invest abroad, we now expand our example to allow investment in three foreign countries. The investment opportunities are summarized in Table 10.5.

With this example we illustrate two ways in which implicit taxes and the foreign tax credit rules interact to affect the after-all-tax returns of foreign investments. Both effects are examples of the all taxes principle: that effective tax planning considers both taxes paid today and taxes paid in the future, as well as taxes paid explicitly and taxes paid implicitly. First, notice that investments in each of the foreign countries

TABLE 10.5 Returns on Investment in Three Countries with Differing Tax Rates			
	Explicit Tax Rate	*Pretax Return*	*After (Local) Tax Return*
Home	35%	20%	13%
Abroad (country 1)	15%	18%	15.3%
Abroad (country 2)	10%	17%	15.3%
Abroad (country 3)	0%	15.3%	15.3%

TABLE 10.6 After-Tax Accumulations from $100 Million Investment for Different Investment Horizons (in $millions)				
Horizon (years)	*1*	*5*	*15*	*30*
Home	$113.0	$184.2	$625.4	$3,911.6
Abroad$_1$ (implicit tax rate = 10%)	111.7	179.4	**670.6**	**5,498.4**
Abroad$_2$ (implicit tax rate = 15%)	111.1	175.0	**638.9**	**5,198.5**
Abroad$_3$ (implicit tax rate = 23.5%)	110.0	167.5	585.0	**4,688.6**

TABLE 10.7 After-Repatriation-Tax Returns for Different Investment Horizons				
Horizon (years)	*1*	*5*	*15*	*30*
Home	13%	13%	13%	13%
Abroad$_1$ (implicit tax rate = 10%)	11.7%*	12.4%	**13.5%**	**14.3%**
Abroad$_2$ (implicit tax rate = 15%)	11.1%	11.8%	**13.2%**	**14.1%**
Abroad$_3$ (implicit tax rate = 23.5%)	9.9%	10.9%	12.5%	**13.7%**

*These returns are computed by taking the after-tax accumulation, as given by equation (10.3), to the $1/n$ power and subtracting one.

face a lower explicit tax rate than domestic investments, lower pretax returns than domestic investments (the implicit tax effect) and larger after-local tax returns than domestic investment. Despite the larger after-local tax returns available for foreign investment, we will show that foreign investment dominates domestic investment only for long investment horizons.

The second effect is more subtle. Notice that we have held the after-local tax returns constant across the foreign countries. However, we will show that investments in country 1 dominate investments in countries 2 and 3 for every investment horizon. As we will show, foreign investors represent a special tax clientele because they tend to be attracted to investments with large explicit taxes and to avoid investments with large implicit taxes.

Although the after-local-tax return is the same in each foreign tax regime, the implicit tax rate varies among the countries. Even though the implicit tax rate in country 1, relative to investment at home, is 10%, or (20% − 18%)/20%, the implicit tax rate in country 2 is 15%, or (20% − 17%)/20%. And, for country 3, because of extremely generous tax benefits, the implicit tax rate is 23.5%. So what do these implicit tax rates imply for our decision of where to invest? It turns out the answer depends on our investment horizon—how many years before we repatriate our foreign earnings. Tables 10.6 and 10.7 offer several answers. Bolded figures indicate foreign investments that produce larger after-tax returns than domestic investment.

Notice that for all investment horizons, the lower the implicit tax abroad, the higher are the after-tax returns from investing abroad. While investing abroad in country 1 dominates investing at home by $45 million (for an original $100 million investment) for a 15-year horizon, investing in country 3 falls short of investing at home by $40 million for the same horizon. This difference exists even though the after-local-tax rate of return is the same in each foreign country.

What explains the variation in after-tax returns? Unlike direct foreign taxes and deemed paid foreign taxes, implicit taxes paid in the foreign country are not eligible for the foreign tax credit. Instead, they are deductible, in a sense, in calculating home-country taxable income. But a deduction reduces home-country taxes by only the domestic tax rate, or $0.35 on the dollar in our example. So whether investment is sensible in the foreign country depends on the implicit tax on investments in the foreign country, as well as on the length of time before the foreign earnings are to be repatriated to the home country, thereby terminating the deferral period.

To see this scenario another way, suppose that tax-exempt securities, such as municipal bonds in the United States, are available for investment in foreign country 1, where the explicit tax rate is 15%. Assume that the before-tax rate of return on fully taxable bonds is 10% and the tax-exempt bond rate is 8.5%, so that both bonds have an 8.5% return after foreign taxes have been paid. Assuming that the home country treats the interest on the tax-exempt bonds as taxable income on repatriation (remember, the bonds are only tax exempt in the foreign country), home-country investors face an additional repatriation tax in the home country of 2.975% of the amount invested abroad, or 8.5%(.35), for an after-tax return of only 5.525%.

Fully taxable bonds are more attractive to home-country investors investing in country 1 than are tax-exempt bonds. As with tax-exempt bonds, fully taxable bonds yield 8.5% after payment of local taxes. On repatriation, however, 6.5% is earned after tax, or 10%(1 − .35). This amount is 0.975% more than the return from investing in the foreign tax-exempt bonds. Even though the foreign tax credit system effectively allows a 100% refund of the explicit tax, the implicit tax is only refunded at a rate of 35% by the domestic tax reduction on the reduced pretax return. It reconciles to the 0.975% difference in after-all-tax returns as follows: (100% − 35%) × 1.5% implicit tax = 0.975%. As a result, foreign investors tend to be attracted to high explicitly taxed assets and therefore represent a special tax clientele.

10.3 THE DECISION TO REPATRIATE OR REINVEST

After a firm has invested abroad, it faces a subsequent decision with respect to the earnings accumulated abroad. Should the earnings generated by foreign subsidiaries be repatriated—distributed to the parent—or should they be reinvested abroad? Your first reaction might be that earnings and profits in subsidiaries in low-tax countries, or "low tax earnings," should be reinvested abroad as long as possible, because repatriation may trigger additional U.S. tax.

The correct answer, as usual, is more complex. The following formal analysis builds on the formulae from Chapter 3 that we used to evaluate different investment alternatives. Relevant factors for the analysis include (1) the length of the reinvestment horizon; (2) the proportion of investment that is represented by earnings and profits; and (3) whether marginal investments in the foreign country earn more, after local tax, than marginal investments in the United States. For sufficiently long investment horizons, a higher after-local-tax rate of return abroad is sufficient to conclude that reinvestment abroad is desirable. In many cases, as we will show, after-tax wealth is maximized by repatriating foreign earnings even though doing so might result in paying additional U.S. taxes. This analysis will illustrate two aspects of the all taxes principle that runs throughout the book. Specifically, maximizing after-tax wealth requires that you consider not only the taxes paid today but also taxes paid in the future and implicit taxes paid when tax-favored investments have low pretax rates of return. Finally, financial reporting consequences accompany the decision to reinvest versus repatriate—an example of the all costs principle. Specifically, firms do not have to record deferred tax liabilities for the repatriation taxes on earnings deemed to be indefinitely reinvested abroad (APB 23).

To answer the question of whether to repatriate or reinvest abroad, we will compare the after-all-tax accumulations from the two alternatives. Let us assume, as we did in Table 10.2, that the home-country and foreign-country tax rates are 35% and 15%, respectively. The pretax and after-tax rates of return available at home are 20% and 13%, and those available abroad are 18% and 15.3%, respectively.

Let us assume that the firm has $100 million in accumulated earnings and profits in the foreign country. Should the $100 million continue to be reinvested locally or repatriated and invested at home? If the $100 million is repatriated, the parent will report $117.65 million of taxable income on its home-country return:

$$\$100 \text{ million}/(1 - 15\%) = \$117.65$$

After taking a foreign tax credit, the parent will pay home-country tax of

$$\$117.65(35\% - 15\%) = \$23.53 \text{ million}$$

after taking advantage of the 15% foreign tax credit allowance.[24] These calculations leave $76.47 million (or $100 million − $23.53 million) to invest at home at a rate of 13% after tax.

More generally, if *EP* represents the amount of earnings and profits that are repatriated, the amount remaining after paying the home-country tax is[25]

$$EP - \frac{EP}{1 - t_f}(t_d - t_f) = \frac{EP(1 - t_d)}{1 - t_f} \tag{10.5}$$

---

[24]This computation is a compact version of the indirect foreign tax credit computation illustrated in Table 10.2. Dividing the $100 million retained earnings by 1 minus the foreign tax rate grosses up the earnings and profits to pretax levels. This pretax earnings and profits of $117.65 is taxable income to the parent when repatriated, attracting $117.65 million(35%) = $41.18 million of tax before taking into account the foreign tax credit. The foreign tax credit equals the foreign taxes paid of $117.65 million(15%) = $17.65 million. As a check on the computations, note that the $117.65 pretax earnings and profits less the $17.65 foreign taxes paid equals the $100 million earnings and profits that are repatriated.

[25]This example assumes the home country has a worldwide tax system with foreign tax credits, rather than a territorial system. It also assumes that the home-country tax rate, t_d, exceeds the foreign-country tax rate, t_f. Otherwise, no home-country tax would be due upon repatriation.

If the company reinvests this amount at home for n periods at an after-tax rate of return of r_d, the accumulation in n periods is

$$\frac{EP(1 - t_d)}{(1 - t_f)}(1 + r_d)^n \qquad \textbf{(10.6)}$$

Conversely, if the firm reinvests the \$100 million of earnings and profits abroad, it can earn a return of 15.3% after local tax and repatriate the accumulated amount at the end of n periods. After repatriation in n periods and payment of the home-country repatriation tax, the parent company is left with

$$\text{\$100 million}(1.153)^n - (35\% - 15\%)\frac{\text{\$100 million}(1.153)^n}{1 - 15\%}$$

More generally, reinvesting an amount EP abroad for n periods leaves, after repatriation tax,

$$EP(1 + r_f)^n - \frac{EP(1 + r_f)^n}{1 - t_f}(t_d - t_f) = \frac{EP(1 - t_d)}{1 - t_f}(1 + r_f)^n \qquad \textbf{(10.7)}$$

or \$76.47 million $\times (1.153)^n$ in our example versus \$76.47 million $\times (1.13)^n$ if funds are repatriated and invested at home. For our example, it means that reinvesting abroad is superior to repatriation for any length investment horizon.

Comparing expressions (10.6) and (10.7), we see that the only difference is whether the last term is $(1 + r_d)^n$ or $(1 + r_f)^n$. Therefore, reinvesting abroad dominates repatriation whenever the after-local-tax rate of return on foreign investment, r_f, exceeds the after-tax rate of return on home country investment, r_d. And the preference for reinvestment in this situation is true for any length investment horizon. The intuition for this result is difficult for many students to understand. But the key is that although reinvesting abroad does defer the tax on repatriation, this benefit is offset by the fact that reinvesting causes the deferred taxes to grow in direct proportion to the growth of the investment. To ignore investment horizon in repatriation decisions is a special case, however, as we will now demonstrate.

Subpart F Income and Controlled Foreign Corporations

In the situation we just described, home-country taxation of foreign subsidiary income was postponed merely by reinvesting the foreign subsidiary income locally in active investments. If reinvestment opportunities in active investments are poor, it could be preferable to invest in passive investments abroad, such as Eurobonds, which might provide similar before-tax rates of return as those available by investing in passive assets such as domestic bonds in the home country. In many countries, however, passive income earned abroad is taxed by the home country as it is earned rather than when it is repatriated. In the United States, such tax treatment is required under Subpart F of the Tax Code.

How do these regulations change the firm's decision of whether to invest earnings and profits abroad in passive investments? If the pretax rate of return on passive investments is the same abroad as it is at home, then it pays to reinvest abroad whenever foreign earnings and profits would attract a home-country tax on repatriation. The reason is that reinvestment abroad postpones the repatriation tax on the foreign earnings and profits. In contrast to the example in equations (10.5) and (10.6), in the case of Subpart F income-producing investments, this tax is a fixed nominal amount based on the accumulated earnings and profits to date. Using our example, if the firm repatriates all of its foreign earnings and profits and invests at home for n periods at pretax rate R_d, it accumulates

$$\left[\$100 \text{ million} - \frac{\$100 \text{ million}}{1 - .15}(.35 - .15)\right][1 + R_d(1 - t_d)]^n$$

$$= \$76.47 \text{ million}[1 + R_d(1 - t_d)]^n$$

More generally, repatriating EP_0 immediately and investing at home at pretax rate R_d for n periods yields

$$\left[EP_0 - \frac{EP_0}{1 - t_f}(t_d - t_f)\right][1 + R_d(1 - t_d)]^n \qquad (10.8)$$

Suppose instead that the firm leaves the earnings and profits abroad and invests in passive assets that yield a pretax return of R_f. The annual return from such assets after paying the home-country tax will be

$$R_f(1 - t_f) - \frac{R_f(1 - t_f)}{1 - t_f}(t_d - t_f) = R_f(1 - t_d) \qquad (10.9)$$

After repatriation in n years and after paying a repatriation tax on the original earnings and profits that have not yet attracted a repatriation tax, the net accumulation is

$$EP_0[1 + R_f(1 - t_d)]^n - \frac{EP_0}{1 - t_f}(t_d - t_f) \qquad (10.10)$$

where EP_0 represents the accumulated earnings and profits at the time the firm begins reinvesting earnings and profits in passive foreign assets. EP_0 therefore represents the non-Subpart F earnings and profits that will not face domestic taxation until repatriated in year n. Using our example and assuming $R_f = R_d$, if the firm reinvests its earnings and profits abroad in passive assets, the net accumulation after n years will be

$$\$100 \text{ million}(1 + r_d)^n - \frac{\$100 \text{ million}}{1 - .15}(.35 - .15)$$

The first term in this expression represents the net-of-tax accumulation from the earnings and profits reinvested in passive foreign assets. The second term represents a *fixed* amount of tax due only on repatriation. It turns out that if the home country imposed an interest charge on the repatriation tax at rate r_d per period, it would be a matter of indifference whether the foreign earnings were reinvested abroad or repatriated, but such a charge is not levied. As a result, the longer the earnings are reinvested abroad, the lower is the present value of the tax. So reinvesting abroad remains superior to repatriating.

In fact, reinvesting abroad in passive assets can beat repatriation even when the pretax return available on foreign passive assets is below that available at home. In most cases, however, firms can invest in the same passive assets, such as stocks and bonds, abroad as they can domestically, so the pretax return on passive investments abroad will often equal the pretax return on passive domestic investments.

Investment and Repatriation Policy When the Foreign Tax Rate Exceeds the Domestic Tax Rate

In our analysis, comparisons of foreign and domestic investment accumulations were complicated because repatriation of foreign earnings gave rise to an additional tax. When the foreign tax rate exceeds the domestic rate, repatriation triggers no additional tax, assuming there is no foreign withholding tax. With these assumptions, it is straightforward to show that foreign investment is preferred to domestic investment, for *any* length investment horizon, if and only if the after-local-tax rate of return abroad exceeds the after-tax rate of return at home, $r_f > r_d$. The *same* condition determines whether reinvestment abroad is preferred to repatriation of foreign earnings and profits.

Summary of Key Points

1. Generally, two different tax regimes apply to the income earned by multinational businesses. Some countries, such as the United States and Japan, tax worldwide income of resident companies. A small number of countries employ a territorial tax system, where only the income earned domestically, at least for active businesses, is taxed.

2. Companies can structure their foreign operations as either branches or subsidiaries. Income from foreign branches is taxable in the home (parent) country as it is earned. In contrast, income from foreign subsidiaries is generally deferred from home-country taxation until it is repatriated. The principal exception is that passive income—so-called Subpart F income in the United States—is typically ineligible for tax deferral and is taxed in the home country as it is earned.

3. Foreign tax credit systems attempt to mitigate multiple taxation of foreign income by allowing credits for income taxes paid to foreign governments. The credits are subject to limitations. The most important limitation for U.S. taxpayers is that the foreign tax credit cannot exceed the U.S. tax on the foreign-source income.

4. The advantages of investing abroad for a multinational firm facing a worldwide tax system depend on tax and nontax factors. Pretax returns abroad can differ from those available domestically because of differences in implicit taxes. These implicit taxes might arise because of nontax costs unique to operating in certain foreign countries.

5. For multinational firms with high home-country tax rates that are subject to taxation on worldwide income by the home country, investment should be undertaken in the country with the highest after-local-tax rate of return. With a 1-year investment horizon and foreign tax rates lower than domestic tax rates, simply comparing the before-tax rates of return on the investments will suffice, because both investments would eventually be taxed at the domestic rate.

   For multiyear investment horizons, the choice depends on the level of the implicit tax. The greater the implicit tax, the longer the deferral period must be before investing in the lower-tax-rate country produces a greater after-tax accumulation than does investing at home. In effect, the firm can defer the higher home-country tax on foreign profits reinvested abroad, but this strategy often comes at the expense of earning a lower pretax rate of return on investment abroad than on domestic investment.

6. Once profits have been earned in a low-tax foreign country, firms face the repatriate versus reinvest decision—that is, whether the accumulated profits should be reinvested abroad or repatriated to the parent. If the reinvestment will be made in investments that do not produce Subpart F income, the decision depends on whether the after-local-tax rate of return is higher abroad than domestically. If foreign after-tax rates of return exceed domestic after-tax rates of return, it is better to reinvest

abroad. This preference is true whether the investment horizon is short or long. Different results occur if the reinvested profits would produce Subpart F income or if the foreign country has a greater tax rate than the home country.

Discussion Questions

1. Why do countries with worldwide tax systems give foreign tax credits?
2. In principle, countries can band together to create uniform tax laws to ensure that each dollar of income is taxed once and only once. What are the costs and benefits of such uniformity from the perspective of lawmakers?
3. Can U.S. citizens avoid paying taxes to the United States by living and working abroad?
4. Consider a wealthy U.S. citizen who earns $1.3 million per year in dividends and capital gains from her portfolio of U.S. stocks. Can she legally avoid having this income subject to U.S. tax by forming an offshore holding company and having the holding company own the stock? She has her holding company reinvest the dividends and capital gains, so she personally receives no cash from her investments.
5. What are the tax differences between operating as a foreign branch and a foreign subsidiary of a U.S. corporation? What are the advantages and disadvantages of each form?
6. Why do U.S. multinationals generally like the "check-the-box" regulations?
7. What is the difference between a direct foreign tax credit and an indirect (deemed paid) foreign tax credit?
8. What are the foreign tax credit limitations and why do they exist?
9. Under what conditions will foreign tax credits result in a U.S. corporation paying exactly the same tax on foreign income as it would if this income were earned directly in the United States?
10. What is Subpart F income? How does the taxation of Subpart F income affect the ability of U.S. corporations to defer U.S. taxation on income earned by controlled foreign corporate subsidiaries?
11. Do low tax rates in a foreign country imply that expected after-tax rates of return on marginal investments should be higher than on domestic investments? Explain.
12. Is your answer to the prior question dependent on whether the investment funds come from earnings and profits or from new investment dollars? Explain.

Exercises

Unless otherwise stated, for all problems and exercises assume that foreign operations are corporations and are treated as such for U.S. purposes under the check-the-box regulations.

1. California Graphics is a U.S. corporation with $200 million of U.S.-source income and $10 million of foreign-source income. In addition, California Graphics has three-quarters ownership of a Canadian partnership that has total pretax earnings of $30 million, all Canadian source and subject to a 40% Canadian tax rate. The Canadian partnership repatriated $5 million of earnings back to California Graphics in the current year. For U.S. purposes, California Graphics treats the Canadian partnership as a branch under the check-the-box regulations.
   a. How much taxable income will California Graphics report on its U.S. tax return?
   b. Suppose that, instead of electing to treat the Canadian partnership as a branch, California Graphics elects to treat it as a subsidiary for U.S. purposes. How much taxable income will California Graphics report on its U.S. tax return?
2. Michigan Motors is a U.S. corporation with $1 billion of U.S.-source income. In addition, Michigan Motors owns 60% of Detroit Parts, a U.S. corporation with a

total of $200 million of U.S.-source income, and 100% of Air Paris, a French corporation that has $500 million of French-source income. Neither Detroit Parts nor Air Paris repatriated any earnings in the current year. Assume no book tax differences except those caused by differences in consolidation requirements.

   a. How much GAAP income will Michigan Motors report on its consolidated income statement?

   b. How much taxable income will Michigan Motors report on its U.S. tax return?

3. Manhattan Pictures is a U.S. corporation that owns 100% of Alpha, a Greek corporation. Manhattan Pictures receives a dividend of $42,000 from Alpha. Alpha has $320,000 of accumulated earnings and profits and has paid foreign taxes that total $60,000. Manhattan Pictures' taxable income before consideration of the dividend is $30,000. Manhattan Pictures is subject to a flat 35% U.S. tax rate.

   a. What is Manhattan Pictures' deemed paid foreign taxes with respect to the Alpha dividend?

   b. What is Manhattan Pictures' FTC?

   c. How much U.S. tax after FTC will be paid on the dividend?

   d. How much dividend does Manhattan Pictures get after all taxes are paid?

4. Hawkeye Networks is a U.S. corporation with no foreign-source income of its own, but it does have wholly owned subsidiaries in Korea and Singapore. The Korean subsidiary has $43 million of pretax Korean-source income, faces a 40% Korean tax rate, and pays a $10 million dividend to Hawkeye Networks. The Singapore subsidiary has $7 million of pretax Singapore-source income, faces a 25% Singapore tax rate, and pays a $2 million dividend to Hawkeye.

   a. How much foreign-source income will Hawkeye Networks report on its U.S. tax return?

   b. Now suppose the Singapore subsidiary's income is Subpart F income. How much foreign-source income will Hawkeye Networks report on its U.S. tax return?

   c. Make the same assumptions as in part (b), but also assume that Hawkeye Networks owns only 38% of the Singapore corporation. Assume Hawkeye Networks' share of the Singapore corporation's pretax income remains $7 million and its share of the dividend remains $2 million. The remaining 62% of the Singapore corporation is owned by a Chinese firm. How much foreign-source income will Hawkeye Networks report on its U.S. tax return?

5. Illinois Steel is a specialty steel manufacturer that does business in the United States, Canada, and Brazil. Illinois Steel is organized as follows. The parent, Illinois Steel, is incorporated in Illinois and had pretax income from its U.S. operations of $5 million in 1999. Illinois Steel owns 100% of the stock of ISB, its Brazilian subsidiary, which reported pretax income of $3 million in 1999. Illinois Steel directly owns its Canadian operations (that is, the Canadian group is a branch), which recorded pretax income of $10 million in 1999. Assume all earnings are reinvested in the country where they were earned. Assume the tax rates in the countries are: United States, 35%; Canada, 30%; Brazil, 25%. What is Illinois Steel's 1999 U.S. tax liability after foreign tax credits?

Tax Planning Problems

Unless otherwise stated, for all problems and exercises assume that foreign operations are corporations and are treated as such for U.S. purposes under the check-the-box regulations.

1. Bloomington Pharmaceuticals is a U.S. corporation considering where to locate a new manufacturing facility. The facility will require an investment of $50 million, and any profits during the n-year investment horizon will be reinvested in the facility

and will earn the same pretax return as the original investment. After n years the facility will be sold for an amount equal to the cumulative investment in the facility, that is, the original investment and all of the reinvested earnings and profits. All the proceeds are repatriated to Bloomington Pharmaceuticals. Bloomington Pharmaceuticals has the possibilities narrowed down to three locations: Tucson, Arizona; Ireland; and Mexico. The pretax returns and local tax rates follow:

	Tax Rate	Pretax Return
Tucson	35%	20%
Ireland	10%	16%
Mexico	20%	18%

a. Suppose that the investment horizon is 5 years ($n = 5$). After paying any home-country tax due on repatriation, how much after-tax accumulation will Bloomington Pharmaceuticals have under each of the three location scenarios?
b. Suppose instead that the investment horizon is 15 years ($n = 15$). After paying any home-country tax due on repatriation, how much after-tax accumulation will Bloomington Pharmaceuticals have under each of the three location scenarios?
c. Make the same assumptions as in part (b), but also assume that the location decision is being made following a recession in the United States. Catering to protectionism sentiment among the electorate, Congress passes an anti-multinational tax law that greatly expands the scope of Subpart F to include, among other things, income from pharmaceutical facilities. How do your answers to part (b) change? Specifically, after paying any home-country tax due on repatriation, how much after-tax accumulation will Bloomington Pharmaceuticals have under each of the three location scenarios?

2. Ithaca Snowboards Corporation is a large U.S. producer of in-style winter recreational equipment and apparel. Ithaca Snowboards currently has its primary facilities in the United States as well as distribution and marketing operations in a wholly owned Liechtenstein subsidiary. To expand into Asia, Ithaca Snowboards is considering setting up distribution and marketing operations in Japan. Currently, Ithaca Snowboards has $150 million of U.S. taxable income per year while its Liechtenstein subsidiary generates $100 million of Liechtenstein-source income, none of which is repatriated to Ithaca Snowboards. For simplicity assume that, if Ithaca Snowboards makes no changes, its income streams will continue in perpetuity. Ithaca Snowboards faces a 35% U.S. tax rate and a 15% Liechtenstein tax rate.
a. What is Ithaca Snowboards' U.S. tax liability, and what is its worldwide tax liability?
b. Now suppose that, to meet payments on its debt and to pay dividends to its shareholders, it is necessary for Ithaca Snowboards to make its Liechtenstein subsidiary repatriate all of its earnings to Ithaca Snowboards each year. What will be Ithaca Snowboards' U.S. tax liability and its worldwide tax liability?
c. Continuing from part (b), now suppose that Ithaca Snowboards also sets up operations in a Japanese subsidiary. Assume that such operations will pay tax at a 45% Japanese tax rate and will generate an additional $80 million of income, all Japanese source. Assume that unlike the Liechtenstein subsidiary, the Japanese subsidiary repatriates none of its income. What will be Ithaca Snowboards' U.S. tax liability and its worldwide tax liability?
d. Continuing from part (c), now assume that the Japanese subsidiary does repatriate all of its earnings each year. What will be Ithaca Snowboards' U.S. tax liability and worldwide tax liability?

3. Carolina Industries is a U.S. corporation with a wholly owned Argentinean subsidiary that has $400 million of accumulated earnings and profits. Carolina Industries has in the past reinvested foreign income in the country where it was earned but is reassessing this policy. Assume Carolina Industries can obtain a 20% pretax return in the United States, where the tax rate is 35%, or it can obtain a 15% pretax return by investing in a 10-year project in Argentina, where the tax rate is 25%, and then repatriating any earnings and profits to the United States.

   a. Should Carolina Industries have its Argentinean subsidiary repatriate its earnings and profits or reinvest them in Argentina? Specifically, what is the after-tax (including taxes on repatriation) accumulation to Carolina Industries under the two choices after the 10 years?

   b. Continue from part (a), except assume the investment horizon is 20 years. Does the longer investment horizon affect your decision of whether to repatriate now or reinvest in Argentina? Would any investment horizon affect your decision?

   c. Continue from part (a), except assume that the firm has no decent active investment opportunities. Instead the firm can invest in passive assets that will generate a pretax return of 12% whether they are in held in the United States or in Argentina. The income from any such passive investments in Argentina will produce Subpart F income, although the original $400 million of accumulated earnings and profits were not Subpart F income. Does the Subpart F income affect your decision of whether to repatriate now or reinvest in Argentina? What is the after-tax accumulation (including taxes on repatriation) to Carolina Industries under the two choices after the 10 years?

   d. Continue from part (a), except assume that, instead of an Argentinean subsidiary, Carolina Industries owns a Danish subsidiary that faces a 45% Danish tax rate and has access to an investment that will generate a 24% pretax return. Should Carolina Industries have its Danish subsidiary repatriate its earnings and profits or reinvest them in Denmark? What is the after-tax accumulation (including taxes on repatriation) to Carolina Industries after the 10 years?

   e. Continue from part (a), except assume that, at the beginning of year 10, Congress reduces the U.S. corporate tax rate from 35% to 22%. Does this change affect your decision to reinvest versus repatriate? What is the after-tax (including taxes on repatriation) accumulation to Carolina Industries under the two choices after the 10 years?

4. You are advising a U.S. corporation called Biometrics that has operations in the United States, Ireland, and Canada. Assume that Ireland taxes Biometrics at 10%, Canada at 45%, and the United States at 35%. Biometrics has $50 million of taxable income from its U.S. operations, $30 million from its Irish operations, and $20 million from its Canadian operations. Biometrics conducts its Canadian and Irish operations in the foreign equivalents of a partnership. Biometrics repatriates one-half of the after-local-tax profits of its Irish operations back to the United States each year but reinvests all of the Canadian profits in Canada. All of Biometrics' Irish and Canadian income falls into the same "basket" for purposes of the foreign tax credit.

   a. Assume that, under the check-the-box regulations, Biometrics elects to have its Canadian and Irish operations taxed as branches for U.S. purposes. How much tax will Biometrics pay in each of the three countries?

   b. In the situation from part (a) and without regard to the FTC limit, how much foreign tax credit would Biometrics get for its Canadian and Irish taxes?

   c. Based on parts (a) and (b), what is Biometrics' FTC limit?

   d. Now suppose Biometrics elects to have its Canadian branch be taxed as a corporation for U.S. income tax purposes, without affecting the Canadian tax treatment as a partnership, creating a so-called "reverse hybrid." Because Biometrics (U.S.) is legally liable for the Canadian taxes, Biometrics is counted as having currently paid the $9 million in Canadian taxes for U.S. FTC purposes under the technical taxpayer rule, even though none of Biometrics' Canadian income is currently subject to U.S. taxation. (Despite the fact that the technical taxpayer rule is well supported by authority, some consider it an aggressive strategy and the IRS has issued Notice 98-5 indicating it is considering rules to prevent mismatch between the time the foreign taxes are treated as paid and the time the foreign income is recognized as earned by the United States.) How much tax will Biometrics pay in each of the three countries in which it operates?

   e. In the situation from part (d) and without regard to the FTC limit, how much foreign tax credit would Biometrics get for its Canadian and Irish taxes?

   f. Based on parts (d) and (e), what is Biometrics' FTC limit?

5. Prove that, when the foreign tax rate exceeds the domestic rate, foreign investment is preferred to domestic investment, for any investment horizon, if and only if the after-local tax rate of return abroad exceeds the after-tax rate of return at home, $r_f > r_d$. Also prove that the same condition determines whether reinvestment abroad is preferred to repatriation of foreign earnings and profits.

Warning: The problems below are extremely challenging.

6. A U.S. multinational company owns 100% of two foreign subsidiaries, one each in countries A and B, both of which are controlled by foreign corporations or CFCs.

Country	Pretax Investment Returns Tax Rate	Passive	Active	Withholding Rate on Dividends
United States	40.0%	10.0%	10.0%	0.0%
A	30.0	10.0	9.0	0.0
B	60.0	10.0	14.5	0.0

Rules: Each foreign subsidiary pays tax on all local income, that is, income earned in the respective host country, at local tax rates as given in the preceding table. Local pretax rates of return on passive and active investments are also given. The United States taxes foreign-source income in one of two ways:

- Deemed income when income is repatriated, such as when dividends are paid by the CFCs to the parent.
- Deemed distributions of Subpart F (passive) income:
  - *De minimus provision:* If passive income or, more precisely, so-called foreign base company income is less than the lesser of $1 million or 5% of total pretax income for the subsidiary, then no income is deemed to have been distributed to the parent.
  - *De maximus provision:* If passive income exceeds 70% of total pretax income for the subsidiary, then 100% of the income is deemed to have been distributed to the parent in the year earned.
  - Otherwise, 100% of only the passive income is deemed to have been distributed to the parent in the year earned, with active income being taxed in the United States only as dividends are paid to the parent.

In this problem we focus primarily on the reinvestment and repatriation problem. We will ignore issues of financing, and we will consider issues of new investment only indirectly.

Each of our two foreign subsidiaries has assets in place that give rise to $100 in locally taxed income at the end of each of the next 5 years, at which point these assets will disappear. The $100 in locally taxed income comes in the form of cash, which is to be repatriated or reinvested. Each company also has $1,000 in cash either to invest in some combination of active and passive investments in the local economy or to repatriate to the parent.

Any repatriation is treated as a dividend to the extent of previously untaxed earnings and profits; note, however, that Subpart F income is treated as previously taxed income for this purpose. Assume that the $1,000 cash in each of countries A and B represents capital investment, not previously untaxed profits. Therefore, this capital can be repatriated to the United States immediately without incurring any U.S. income tax or foreign withholding tax. Once profits are generated, however, distributions come first out of earnings and profits. Further assume that no additional capital can be transferred from the United States to the foreign countries, from country A to country B, or from country B to country A.

Required: For parts (a) through (f), determine an optimal investment and repatriation policy as well as how to allocate income that is reinvested in the local economy between active and passive investments over a 5-year horizon. Any cash available in either subsidiary at the end of year 5 must be repatriated to the parent at that time.

This problem is surprisingly difficult, despite the simple structure we have imposed on it. Make any assumptions you feel are necessary to proceed. If you do not get a satisfying solution in a reasonable amount of time (say, 8 hours), you should describe the trade-offs you considered in attempting to solve the problem. You may provide qualitative answers where you feel it is appropriate.

You should ignore the parts of our rules that deal with the 5% de minimus and 70% de maximus provisions in answering parts (a) through (e).

a. Assume that passive income from country A, passive income from country B, active income from country A, and active income from country B fall into four different "income baskets" for foreign tax credit purposes. Note that the implication of this assumption is equivalent to what would occur in the case of a country-by-country foreign tax credit limitation.

b. Assume that active income from the two subsidiaries falls into the *same* overall income basket for foreign tax credit purposes. Similarly, passive income from the two subsidiaries falls into the same passive income basket. In other words, the foreign tax credit limitation is applied separately to passive and active income, but foreign tax on passive (active) income from country A can be "averaged" with the tax paid on passive (active) income from country B.

c. Qualitatively, how does the analysis change if the initial endowment of $1,000 in countries A and B will be taxed on repatriation as an ordinary dividend and treated as neither previously taxed Subpart F income nor repatriation of capital? (You may assume that the nature of this dividend income is such as to place it in the overall income basket for foreign tax credit purposes.)

d. How are your answers to parts (a) and (b) affected if repatriation is not required at the end of year 5 but instead income can be reinvested locally for many years before repatriation?

e. Qualitatively, how would your previous answers be affected if withholding taxes on dividends were imposed by country A? By country B?

f. Qualitatively, how do the 5-70 Subpart F rules affect your previous answers?

7. A U.S. multinational firm facing a 40% tax rate at home has a wholly owned foreign subsidiary in a jurisdiction where the tax rate is only 25%. The subsidiary was

initially capitalized by a loan that has since been repaid. All that remains in the foreign subsidiary is $150 million of equity. The $150 million represents earnings and profits that have already been taxed at a rate of 25% in the host country. Any repatriation of these profits to the U.S. parent would trigger taxable income in the United States. The host country imposes no withholding tax on dividends repatriated from the foreign subsidiary to the United States.

 a. How much U.S. taxable income would result if a dividend of $150 million were paid by the foreign subsidiary to the U.S. parent?

 b. How much additional U.S. tax would be due?

 c. How would the net repatriation, or dividend less additional taxes, be affected if a 10% withholding tax were levied by the foreign government on the dividend?

 d. Suppose the $150 million could be reinvested in active business projects at an annual rate of 13% before tax and 9.75% after local tax in the host country. Alternatively, funds invested in the United States earn 15% before tax and 9% after tax. Would you prefer to repatriate or to reinvest abroad if your investment horizon is 1 year? 5 years? 10 years? 20 years?

 e. How would your answers to (d) change if the host country imposed a 10% withholding tax on dividends?

 f. Suppose the U.S. tax rate was scheduled to increase to 45% in the next year. That is, any taxable income triggered from current repatriations is taxed at 40%, but any future repatriation will be taxed at 45%. Moreover, the rate earned on funds invested in the United States now declines from 15%(1 − 40%), or 9%, to 15%(1 − 45%), or 8.25%. How would your answers to (d) change?

 g. Suppose, once again, that the U.S. tax rate is 40%. But now suppose that active investment opportunities in the foreign country are poor. The 13% pretax investment return applies only to passive investments such as bonds. And the returns on these passive investments trigger immediate taxation in the United States as Subpart F income. Funds invested in the United States continue to earn 15% before tax. How would this scenario affect the desirability of reinvesting abroad?

8. This question builds off the fact pattern in the prior problem. Specifically, how would your answers to the prior problem be affected if the $150 million of equity in the foreign subsidiary were earnings and profits that had been taxed previously in the host country at a rate of 35% rather than 25%?

References and Additional Readings

A good survey of the economics and accounting research on international taxation.

Hines, J., 1997. "Tax policy and the activities of multinational corporations," in *Fiscal Policy: Lessons from Economic Research,* edited by A. Auerbach. Cambridge, MA: MIT Press, pp. 401–445.

Other economics and accounting research on multi-jurisdictional taxation:

Altshuler, R., and S. Newlon, 1993. "The Effects of U.S. Tax Policy on the Income Repatriation Patterns of U.S. Multinational Corporations," in *Studies in International Taxation,* edited by A. Giovannini, R. G. Hubbard, and J. Slemrod. Chicago: University of Chicago Press, pp. 77–115.

Altshuler, R., S. Newlon, and Randolph, W., 1995. "Do Repatriation Taxes Matter? Evidence from the Tax Returns of U.S. Multinationals," in *The Effects of Taxation on Multinational Corporations,* edited by M. Feldstein, J. Hines, and G. Hubbard. Chicago: University of Chicago Press, pp. 253–276.

Anand, B., and R. Sansing, 2000. "The Weighting Game: Formula Apportionment as an Instrument of Public Policy," *National Tax Journal,* pp. 183–199.

Collins, J., D. Kemsley, and D. Shackelford, 1995. "Tax Reform and Foreign Acquisitions: A Microanalysis," *National Tax Journal,* pp. 1–21.

Collins, J., and D. Shackelford, 1995. "Corporate Domicile and Average Effective Tax Rates: The Cases of Canada, Japan, the United Kingdom, and the United States," *International Tax and Public Finance.*

Collins, J., and D. Shackelford, 1997. "Global Organization and Taxes: An Analysis of the Dividend, Interest, Royalty, and Management Fee Payments Between U.S. Multinationals' Foreign Operations," *Journal of Accounting and Economics,* pp. 151–173.

Cloyd, C., L. Mills, and C. Weaver, 2003. "Firm Valuation Effects of the Expatriation of U.S. Corporations to Tax Haven Countries," *The Journal of the American Taxation.*

Desai, M., and J. Hines, 2002. "Expectations and Expatriations: Tracing the Causes and Consequences of Corporate Inversions," *National Tax Journal.*

Goolsbee, A., and E. Maydew, 2000. "Coveting Thy Neighbors' Manufacturing: The Dilemma of State Income Apportionment," *Journal of Public Economics.*

Grubert, H., 1995. "Taxes and the Division of Foreign Operating Income Among Royalties, Interest, Dividends and Retained Earnings." Working paper. U.S. Treasury Department.

Hines, J., 1995. "Taxes, Technology Transfer, and the R&D Activities of Multinational Firms," in *The Effects of Taxation on Multinational Corporations,* edited by M. Feldstein, J. Hines, and R. G. Hubbard. Chicago: University of Chicago Press.

Hines, J., 1996a. "Altered States: Taxes and the Location of Foreign Direct Investment in America," *American Economic Review.*

Hines, J., 1996b. "Dividends and Profits: Some Unsubtle Foreign Influences," *Journal of Finance.*

Hines, J., and R. G. Hubbard, 1990. "Coming Home to America: Dividend Repatriations by U.S. Multinationals," in *Taxation in a Global Economy,* edited by A. Razin and J. Slemrod. Chicago: University of Chicago Press.

Hines, J., and E. Rice, 1994. "Fiscal Paradise: Foreign Tax Havens and American Business," *Quarterly Journal of Economics,* pp. 149–182.

Kemsley, D., 1998. "The Effect of Taxes on Production Location," *Journal of Accounting Research,* pp. 921–941.

Seida, J., and W. Wempe, 2002. "Market Reaction to Corporate Inversion Transactions," *Tax Notes* (Nov. 25, 1998).

Slemrod, J., 1990. "Tax Effects of Foreign Direct Investment in the U.S.: Evidence from a Cross-Country Comparison," in *Taxation in the Global Economy,* edited by A. Razin and J. Slemrod. Chicago: University of Chicago Press.

Wilson, P., 1993. "The Role of Taxes in Location and Sourcing Decisions," Studies in International Taxation, edited by A. Giovannini, G. Hubbard, and J. Slemrod. Chicago: University of Chicago Press, 195–231.

11

MULTINATIONAL TAX PLANNING: FOREIGN TAX CREDIT LIMITATIONS AND INCOME SHIFTING

After studying this chapter, you should be able to:

1. Understand the foreign tax credit limitations and the incentives they create.

2. Appreciate the implications of type-of-income and country-by-country foreign tax credit limitations.

3. Describe some methods of shifting income across jurisdictions.

4. Explain the tax planning opportunities of foreign investors.

In the previous chapter we examined how taxes affect the decision to invest domestically or abroad and how taxes affect the repatriation decisions of firms whose foreign investments are generating profits. In most of the previous chapter, we considered firms that were in **excess limitation** positions with regard to their foreign tax credits (FTCs). That is, we generally assumed that firms received full credit on their U.S. tax returns for their foreign taxes paid. In this chapter, we take a closer look at FTCs and tax planning issues that arise when FTC limitations are binding. Firms subject to binding FTC limitations do not receive full credit on the U.S. tax returns for their foreign taxes paid and are said to be in **excess credit** positions. We discuss the incentives to shift income across jurisdictions for firms in excess credit positions and the corresponding rules for determining the source of income and the allocation of expenses. We also discuss incentives for foreign investors to shift the character of their income for withholding tax purposes, as well as some recent tax planning techniques broadly referred to as "loss importation transactions."

11.1 FOREIGN TAX CREDIT LIMITATIONS AND INCENTIVES

Countries generally limit the extent to which FTCs can reduce firms' tax liabilities. The United States computes the **FTC limitation** on a worldwide basis each year as follows:

$$\frac{\text{Foreign-source income}}{\text{Worldwide income}} \times \text{U.S. tax on worldwide income} \qquad \textbf{(11.1)}$$

Foreign-source income includes foreign income earned through foreign branches, foreign income repatriated from foreign subsidiaries, and foreign income deemed to be repatriated from foreign subsidiaries, or Subpart F income. For U.S. purposes, foreign-source income is determined under U.S. tax rules, which may differ from the tax rules of the foreign countries to which the firm is also paying taxes.

Worldwide income is the firm's taxable income in the United States and is the sum of foreign-source income and domestic-source income. The **U.S. tax on worldwide income** is the U.S. tax liability before allowing for FTCs and is equal to:

$$\text{U.S. tax on worldwide income} = t_{US} \times \text{Worldwide income} \qquad \textbf{(11.2)}$$

As a result, the FTC limitation generally simplifies to:[1]

$$\text{FTC limitation} = \text{Foreign-source income} \times t_{US} \qquad \textbf{(11.3)}$$

Example of Excess FTC Limitation

Suppose a U.S. parent corporation has one wholly owned subsidiary located in Brazil, as shown in Figure 11.1. Assume the U.S. tax rate is 35% and the Brazilian tax rate is 25%. After paying Brazilian taxes, the Brazilian subsidiary repatriates all of its after-tax earnings to the U.S. parent. For simplicity, assume the Brazilian withholding tax rate

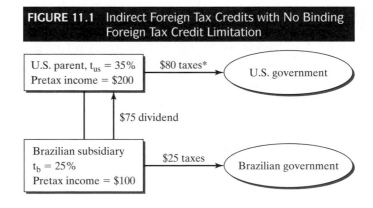

FIGURE 11.1 Indirect Foreign Tax Credits with No Binding Foreign Tax Credit Limitation

*U.S. taxes = ($200 + $75 + $25) .35 − min ($25, $100 × .35) = $80.

---

[1]In calculating the FTC limitation, if foreign-source income exceeds worldwide income (that is, the organization experienced domestic losses), the United States requires that a value of 100% be substituted for the ratio of foreign-source income to worldwide income. Thus, U.S. multinationals facing domestic losses may face more significant FTC limitations than do firms that are profitable domestically. In other words, firms with domestic losses may have more difficulty obtaining refunds of foreign taxes paid.

assessed on repatriations to the United States is 0%.[2] Assume the Brazilian subsidiary has income of $100 and the U.S. parent has domestic-source income of $200 before counting the repatriation of the Brazilian income. What is the firm's U.S. tax liability?

U.S.-source income	$200	
Foreign-source income	$100	($75 dividend + $25 deemed paid taxes)
U.S. tax rate	35%	
Foreign tax rate	25%	
Foreign taxes paid = $100 × .25	$25	
FTC limitation = $100 × .35	$35	
FTC = min($25, $35)	$25	
U.S. tax before FTC = $300 × .35	$105	
FTC	$25	
U.S. tax after FTC	$80	

The total worldwide taxes paid by the firm are $80 + $25 = $105. The firm's worldwide effective tax rate is $105/$300 = 35%. This firm is said to be in an excess limitation FTC position because its FTC limit ($35) exceeds the foreign taxes paid ($25). The firm is getting a full dollar of credit for every dollar of foreign taxes paid.

It is interesting to consider whether the firm has an incentive to engage in tax planning to reduce its Brazilian taxes. Suppose for the moment that, through tax planning, the firm could reduce its Brazilian taxes by $3 without affecting the level of its foreign-source income—at least not the U.S. tax-law computation of foreign-source income. Although the foreign taxes paid would decrease from $25 to $22, the FTC would also decrease from $25 to $22, causing the U.S. tax liability to increase by $3. The net tax savings is zero. Essentially, every dollar of foreign taxes saved simply increases the firm's U.S. tax liability by a dollar. Paradoxically, firms in excess limitation FTC positions sometimes have little or no incentive to engage in tax planning to reduce their foreign taxes, at least not when they expect to always be in an excess limitation position and their foreign income is currently taxable in the United States, which is an important assumption in the analysis. In fact, firms with nonbinding foreign tax credit limitations can have an incentive to negotiate with foreign governments to increase their foreign taxes in return for enhanced government services such as employee training programs.

From the U.S. government's perspective this result is not a desirable feature of the FTC rules. Suppose the United States could agree to a partial reduction of the firm's FTCs, say 60 cents on the dollar, for every dollar of foreign tax the multinational firm saves through tax planning. Both the U.S. government and the multinational would come out ahead, but at the expense of the foreign country. In this example the firm would reduce its Brazilian tax liability by $3 but would lose only $1.80 of FTCs. The firm is therefore ahead by $1.20 and the U.S. government is ahead by $1.80. Such an

---

[2]In most countries, withholding taxes are assessed on repatriations at rates of up to 30% of the gross repatriation in addition to the income tax assessed on the earned income. The actual withholding tax rate depends on the form of the repatriation (for example, the rate on dividends may differ from the rate on interest) as well as on the tax treaty that may exist between the two countries in question.

arrangement would be an unusual example of multilateral tax planning that pits a firm and one government against another government. Such arrangements would be difficult to implement because they likely would lead to diplomatic tension and possible retaliatory taxes by the foreign country.

Now consider the tax burden on the foreign income. The total taxes on the Brazilian income are equal to (1) the Brazilian tax liability plus (2) the portion of the U.S. tax before FTC attributable to the $100 of Brazilian income minus (3) the FTC, or $25 + $35 − $25 = $35. The total effective tax rate on the Brazilian income is therefore $35/$100 = 35%. It turns out that, under the FTC limitation rules, the effective worldwide tax rate a U.S. firm pays on its foreign income is the *greater* of the U.S. tax rate (35%) or the foreign rate (25%). In this example the U.S. rate exceeded the foreign tax rate and thus the effective worldwide tax rate on the foreign income was the U.S. rate. The next example will consider the case where foreign tax rates exceed the U.S. rate.

Example of Excess FTC Credit

Now suppose that, instead of a Brazilian subsidiary facing a 25% Brazilian tax rate, the U.S. parent owns a Portuguese subsidiary facing a 40% Portuguese tax rate, as shown in Figure 11.2. How does this scenario change the analysis, given some additional facts regarding U.S.- and foreign-source income?

U.S.-source income	$200	
Foreign-source income	$100	($60 dividend + $40 deemed paid taxes)
U.S. tax rate	35%	
Foreign tax rate	40%	
Foreign taxes paid = $100 × .40	$40	
FTC limitation = $100 × .35	$35	
FTC = min($40, $35)	$35	
U.S. tax before FTC = $300 × .35	$105	
FTC	$35	
U.S. tax after FTC	$70	

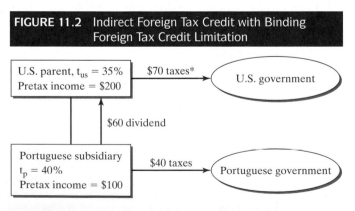

FIGURE 11.2 Indirect Foreign Tax Credit with Binding Foreign Tax Credit Limitation

*U.S. taxes = ($200 + $60 + $40) .35 − min ($40, $100 × .35) = $70.

In contrast to the prior example, the increased foreign tax rates increase the foreign taxes paid by $15. However, the FTC limitation rules allow the FTC to increase by only $10. As a result, the firm's worldwide taxes paid increase by $5 (from $105 to $110). The firm is said to be in an excess credit position because it is not receiving current credit for all of its foreign taxes paid. The $5 of foreign taxes that the firm was not able to take as a credit on the U.S. return are eligible for a 2-year carryback and a 5-year carryforward. The firm could take a *deduction* for all $40 of foreign taxes paid rather than a credit of $35. Although a credit is preferred to a deduction, all else equal, a deduction may be desirable in some circumstances where large amounts of credits would otherwise expire unused. Deducting foreign taxes paid is also useful when those foreign taxes are not eligible for the foreign tax credit.[3]

What is the effective worldwide tax rate on the foreign income? The total taxes on the foreign income are equal to (1) the foreign tax liability plus (2) the portion of the U.S. tax before FTC attributable to the $100 of foreign income minus (3) the FTC, or $40 + $35 − $35 = $40. The total effective tax rate on the foreign income is therefore $40/$100 = 40%. As with the prior example, the effective worldwide tax rate on the firm's foreign income is the greater of the U.S. tax rate (35%) or the foreign rate (40%).

Because U.S. corporate tax rates are lower than those of many foreign countries, it is common for U.S. multinationals to be in excess credit positions. Recall that firms in excess *limitation* positions can sometimes have no incentive to reduce their foreign tax liabilities. Do firms in excess *credit* positions have an incentive to engage in tax planning that reduces their foreign tax liabilities? The answer is yes. Suppose that, through tax planning, the firm could reduce its Portuguese tax liability by $3 without affecting its foreign-source income. The foreign taxes paid would decrease from $40 to $37, but the firm's FTC would remain at $35, and therefore the U.S. tax liability would remain the same. The net tax savings is $3. For firms in excess credit positions, every dollar of foreign taxes saved will, in many cases, reduce the firm's worldwide tax burden by $1.

Firms in excess credit positions also have an incentive for another major type of tax planning—shifting income across jurisdictions. Specifically, firms have an incentive to shift income from being domestic source to being foreign source for U.S. tax purposes, while not changing the classification for foreign tax purposes. This strategy may at first sound nonsensical, but recall that U.S. tax rules govern the classification of income as U.S. source or foreign source for U.S. FTC purposes. Foreign countries have their own tax laws, however, which often produce different classifications of foreign-source and domestic-source income. In the realm of international tax, the same transactions are typically subject to different sets of tax laws that need not be in sync with one another.

In the example of the Portuguese subsidiary, suppose the firm was able to shift $30 from U.S.-source to Portuguese-source income for U.S. tax purposes only, as illustrated in Figure 11.3. For the moment do not concern yourself with how such a shift is done; later in the chapter we examine the rules that determine source of income,

---

[3]Only foreign income and withholding taxes are eligible for the FTC. Foreign taxes not based on income, such as value-added taxes (VAT), are not eligible unless an exception is made under a tax treaty. See, for example, F. Cinotti, "Creditability of Italian IRAP Tax Under Sections 901 and 903 of U.S. Internal Revenue Code," *Tax Notes International* (November 22, 1999).

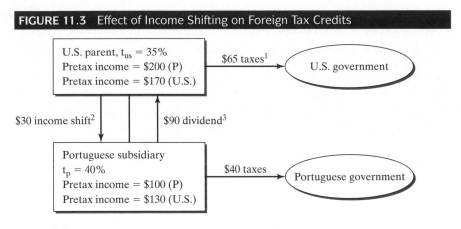

FIGURE 11.3 Effect of Income Shifting on Foreign Tax Credits

[1]U.S. taxes = ($170 + $90 + $40) .35 − min ($40, $130 × .35) = $65.

[2]The strategy is to shift $30 of income from the U.S. parent to the Portuguese subsidiary for U.S. purposes only, i.e., without affecting the actual Portuguese taxes paid.

[3]To keep the example comparable with the prior examples, the subsidiary must distribute all of its *U.S.-defined* earnings and profits, which is now $90. The subsidiary may borrow or take a capital contribution from the parent to finance the dividend.

apportionment of expenses, and transfer pricing. To keep the example comparable with the prior examples, we again assume that the subsidiary distributes all of its earnings and profits to the U.S. parent. The income shifting then will require a $90, or $130 − $40, dividend to the parent.

	U.S.-Defined	*Portuguese-Defined*
U.S.-source income	$170	$200
Foreign-source income	$130	$100
Foreign taxes paid = $100 × .40	$40	
FTC limitation = $130 × .35	$45.5	
FTC = min($40, $45.5)	$40	
U.S. tax before FTC = 300 × .35	$105	
FTC	$40	
U.S. tax after FTC	$65	

The increase in foreign-source income increases the FTC limit from $35 to $45.5, which allows the firm to take credits for the full $40 in foreign tax paid, rather than the $35 credit had no income been shifted. In turn, the firm's U.S. tax liability decreases by $5, from $70 to $65. Note that no change occurs in the firm's Portuguese tax liability because the income shifting was for U.S. purposes only. A great deal of the tax planning for U.S. multinationals centers around maximizing U.S.-defined foreign-source income through income shifting. Multinationals in other countries with foreign tax credit systems act in a similar way. Much shifting takes place via transfer price manipulation and other low-cost accounting changes rather than changing the physical operations of the firm.

Example of FTC with Multiple Subsidiaries

Now let us change the prior example so that the U.S. parent has both a Brazilian subsidiary and a Portuguese subsidiary, as illustrated in Figure 11.4. How do the foreign tax credit rules work in this case?

	United States	*Brazil*	*Portugal*	*TOTAL*
Taxable income	$200	$100	$100	$400
Foreign taxes		$25	$40	$65
FTC limitation = $200 × .35				= $70
FTC = min($65, $70)				= $65
U.S. tax before FTC = 400 × .35				= $140
FTC				= $65
U.S. tax after FTC				= $75

Because actual foreign taxes paid are less than the FTC limitation, all $65 in foreign taxes paid can be taken as a credit against the U.S. income tax liability, which leaves a $75 U.S. income tax liability. Even with the income from the Portuguese subsidiary that was taxed at a rate higher than the U.S. rate, the firm does not have an FTC limitation problem because the low-tax Brazilian income increases the FTC limit more than it increases the foreign taxes paid. In other words, allowing the mixing of high-tax and low-tax foreign incomes helps to make the FTC limitation less restrictive. Firms often time the repatriation of income from high- and low-tax-rate subsidiaries with this in mind, and sophisticated software assists companies in computing the tax effects of different repatriation scenarios.

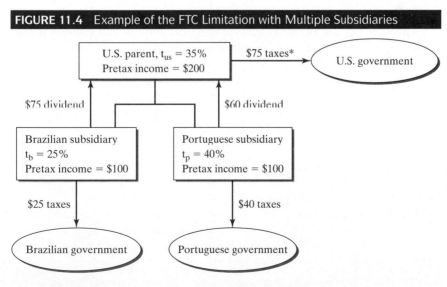

FIGURE 11.4 Example of the FTC Limitation with Multiple Subsidiaries

*U.S. taxes = ($200 + $100 + $100) .35 − min ($40 + 25, ($100 + 100) × .35) = $75.

Country-by-Country FTC Limitations

Most countries, however, do not allow indiscriminate mixing of high- and low-tax-rate foreign income in their FTC limitation calculations. The United States, for example, makes firms calculate a separate FTC limitation on various baskets of income—a subject we will examine in more detail in the next section. Other countries, such as Canada, employ a **country-by-country limitation.**[4]

Suppose that instead of being a U.S. corporation, the parent corporation in our example was resident in a country that imposed its FTC limitation on a country-by-country basis. In that case the FTC limitation for the Brazilian subsidiary would be $100 \times .35 = \$35$, and so all of the $25 of Brazilian taxes paid would be creditable on the parent's tax return. The FTC limitation on the Portuguese subsidiary would also be $100 \times .35 = \$35$, so only $35 of the $40 of Portuguese taxes paid would be creditable on the parent's tax return. Making firms compute their FTC limits on a country-by-country basis reduces the ability to mix high- and low-tax-rate income together to maximize foreign tax credits.

Separate Basket Limitations

As we stated earlier, the United States requires its multinationals to compute the foreign tax credit limitation separately for each separate **basket of income.** The motivation for the separate basket approach to FTC limitations is to prevent corporations from undermining the limitations. For example, if a firm faced a severe FTC limitation, it would have incentive to "stuff" income-earning assets into subsidiaries located in tax-haven countries where tax rates are low. Avoiding the implicit taxes that often result from investing in active businesses in low-tax countries would be a particularly strong incentive to invest in securities, which have pretax returns that are the same no matter where they are held (i.e., an Irish investor holding a U.S. T-bill receives the same *pretax* return as a U.S. investor would holding the same T-bill). This move would reduce the average tax rate on foreign-source income and give rise to larger credits for the foreign tax paid in high-tax countries.

The U.S. tax law permits the averaging of high-tax and low-tax foreign manufacturing income for FTC limitation purposes, but it does *not* permit the averaging of low-taxed passive investment income with high-taxed manufacturing income. Like the country-by-country FTC limitations used by some countries, the U.S. baskets of income computations prevents firms from getting full credit for their foreign taxes paid. Currently, U.S. multinationals must perform separate FTC calculations on the following baskets of income:

- Passive income
- Financial services income
- Shipping income
- High withholding tax income
- Foreign trade income

---

[4]More accurately, Canada's direct FTC system employs a country-by-country FTC limitation, while its indirect FTC system allows averaging across countries. See I. Gamble, "Canada's Foreign Tax Credit System for Multinationals," *Tax Notes International* (November 22, 1999).

- Certain foreign sales corporation (FSC) income
- Dividend income from noncontrolled foreign corporations owned 10% or more by the taxpayer

Any income not in a specific basket goes into the general limitation basket.

To appreciate the significance of the separate basket approach to foreign tax credit limitations, let us reconsider an earlier example. Suppose the subsidiary in Brazil generates $80 of passive (Subpart F) income and $20 of manufacturing-related income. It pays a tax of $25 to Brazil. The subsidiary in Portugal generates $100 of manufacturing-related income, pays a tax of $40 to Portugal, and pays a $60 dividend to the U.S. parent. Because more than 70% of the Brazilian subsidiary's income is Subpart F income, 100% of it is deemed to have been distributed to the U.S. parent whether an actual distribution has been made or not. Hence, $200 of foreign income is taxable in the United States, and the resulting U.S. tax is $70 (or 35% × $200), before the foreign tax credit.

What foreign tax credit amounts are permitted? On the $80 of passive income, it is the minimum of actual foreign taxes paid and the U.S. tax on the income

$$= \min\left(\frac{80}{100} \times \$25, 35\% \times \$80\right) = \min(\$20, \$28) = \$20$$

On the $20 + $100 of general basket income:

$$= \min\left[\left(\frac{20}{100} \times \$25\right) + \$40, 35\% \times \$120\right] = \min(\$45, \$42) = \$42$$

So only $42 of the $45 of foreign tax paid on the $120 of foreign income that falls into the general overall income basket is available as a foreign tax credit. The $3 excess can be carried back 2 years and forward 5. Note that, if the $200 of foreign-source income could be lumped into a single basket as we did in our earlier examples, all $65 of foreign tax paid would be available as a foreign tax credit for U.S. tax purposes.

FTC Limitations and the Capital Structure of Foreign Subsidiaries

As we have demonstrated, firms in excess credit positions have incentives to reduce their taxes paid in foreign countries. In the context of repatriation, where FTC limitations are binding and firms therefore have excess FTCs, it becomes desirable to distribute profits from foreign subsidiaries in ways that are tax deductible abroad. Therefore, it becomes more attractive to repatriate profits by way of

- Interest on debt owed to the U.S. parent or U.S. subsidiaries
- Rent on leases with the U.S. parent or U.S. subsidiaries
- Royalties on licenses
- Transfer pricing for goods and services to shift income from high-tax jurisdictions to lower-tax jurisdictions

Equity financing also has its advantages, however. Consider the flexibility in timing repatriation by way of dividends to coincide with a period of low tax rates in the United States. By contrast, the timing of repatriation by way of interest, rent, and royalties is much less controllable. Debt contracts and rental contracts, for example, require a certain amount of foreign profits to be repatriated each period.

An additional consideration here that is absent in the purely domestic context is that the different forms of repatriation (dividends, interest, rent, and royalties) may be subject to different levels of withholding tax, which makes the repatriation alternatives even less perfect substitutes for one another. The repatriation of foreign profits through transfer-pricing manipulation, for example, typically avoids withholding taxes entirely. Because withholding tax rates on different forms of repatriation also vary from country to country because tax treaties are bilateral rather than multilateral, it is sometimes important to consider alternative routes from a foreign corporation in one tax jurisdiction to another corporation in a different tax jurisdiction through which repatriations can travel to maximize after-tax repatriations. Finally, some firms have devised methods of structuring and financing their foreign operations to "double-dip." For example, some debt structures may allow for the same interest payments to be deductible in more than one country and some leases may be structured to generate deductions in more than one country, that is, double-dip leases. Such planning techniques make use of inconsistencies between the way different countries treat the same transactions for tax purposes.

11.2 SHIFTING INCOME ACROSS JURISDICTIONS

Transfer Pricing

When income is taxed at different rates in different countries, it is typically not a matter of indifference how worldwide income is allocated to the various countries, especially in the face of potential limitations on foreign tax credits. In multinational corporations, many goods and services are routinely transferred among related entities in different tax jurisdictions. **Transfer prices**—the prices at which goods and services are transferred between related entities—can have an important impact on worldwide taxes. The relationship of the entities would appear to provide great tax planning opportunities by setting transfer prices judiciously. For example, if a U.S. automaker wanted to shift income from a U.S. source to a foreign source it could reduce the price it charges its foreign subsidiaries for parts. In contrast, in high-tax-rate foreign jurisdictions, transfer pricing represents not only a way to repatriate profits in a tax-deductible fashion, but also a way to avoid the imposition of withholding tax. Congress and the IRS recognize these tax planning opportunities, and **Section 482** of the Code has been made available to the IRS as an important weapon to deal with overzealous tax planning.

The regulations for Section 482 indicate that transactions between related parties must be priced as if they involved unrelated parties: **Arm's length pricing** is the rule. The basic problem here, however, is that the circumstances under which the related parties find it desirable to integrate vertically are systematically different from those in which transactions take place at arm's length in the market. Information differences are smaller with related parties than with outsiders. Hence, the notion of an arm's length price in a related-party transaction is rather ill-defined. A second problem is that the good or service being transferred frequently has no ready market outside the special relationship between the related parties. Transfer pricing for income from intangible assets such as patents and trademarks can be particularly contentious.

The guidelines in the transfer-pricing regulations can be unclear. To mitigate some of the uncertainty, the IRS allows firms to enter into **advance pricing agreements.** Under such agreements, the firm submits its proposed transfer-pricing methodology to the IRS for review. If the IRS agrees, then in principle the firm's transfer pricing should not be challenged as long as the firm adheres to the agreement.

Source of Income Rules

Related to the transfer-pricing tax rules are the rules governing the **sourcing of income.** Sections 861–864 deal with the allocation of worldwide income to U.S. source versus foreign source. As we have demonstrated earlier in the chapter, whether income is deemed to be U.S. source or foreign source has several important implications. For U.S. taxpayers, it primarily affects the FTC limitations. It is also important to nonresident aliens and foreign corporations, however, because they are taxed in the United States only on income derived from within the United States, from business "effectively connected with" the conduct of U.S. trade or business, and from the disposition of investments in U.S. real property.

Many of the rules for sourcing income seem like common sense, at least until one examines the details. For example, income from the sale of real estate is sourced according to the location of the property. For example, if the property is located in the United States, it is domestic-source income. Income from services is sourced according to where the services are performed. Rents and royalties are sourced according to where the property producing the income is located. Special rules apply to income from international communications and transportation. Many of these rules are beyond the scope of this book, but we will examine the controversial rules for apportionment of domestic interest expense. Over the years, Congress has also passed provisions designed to encourage exports, such as the **Foreign Sales Corporation (FSC)** rules. The European Union challenged the legality of the FSC rules before the World Trade Organization (WTO) and since that time Congress has been grappling to design a tax relief package for exporters that does not violate trade agreements. This controversy is ongoing as this chapter is written.

Interest

Interest expense incurred in the United States is allocated between U.S. and foreign income on the basis of the value of the taxpayer's assets (book or market) that generate U.S.-source and foreign-source income. Interest expense allocated to foreign-source income reduces the FTC limitation by reducing the amount of foreign-source income for foreign tax credit purposes. Firms have used several strategies to mitigate the allocation of domestic interest to foreign operations.

First, where allocation of U.S. interest deductions is costly due to binding FTC limitations, it is possible to substitute preferred stock for debt as a means of financing. Preferred stock dividends are not subject to the interest allocation rules. Empirical research has found that the introduction of the interest allocation rules in 1986 did cause a small but significant increase in multinational firms' use of preferred stock financing.[5]

---

[5]See J. Collins and D. Shackelford (1992).

Second, firms can undertake U.S. borrowing through a U.S. subsidiary that is less than 80% owned by the majority shareholder. In such a case, the subsidiary could not be consolidated for U.S. tax purposes, so the interest would not be allocated to the parent's foreign-source income. Ford Motor Co. used exactly this strategy to avoid having to allocate interest expense abroad on the debt created in its $3.35 billion acquisition of Associates Corp.[6] This strategy enabled Ford to preserve significant sums of foreign tax credits that would otherwise have become unavailable. To accomplish this tax-saving feat, Ford sold off 25% of Associates by issuing money market preferred stock with voting rights. This tax deconsolidation arrangement is not without cost, however. Preferred stock dividends are not explicitly tax deductible to the issuer, although preferred stock does have a lower pretax cost of capital than debt (an implicit tax effect), because 70% of the dividends received are excluded from the taxable income of U.S. corporate shareholders.[7]

A third strategy is to move the borrowing to high-tax foreign subsidiaries. Because only U.S. interest is allocated to foreign-source income, many U.S. multinationals are substituting foreign borrowing for U.S. borrowing as a source of capital for their foreign subsidiaries. They are reducing the equity in their foreign subsidiaries, particularly in high-tax jurisdictions, where debt financing is especially desirable. This move not only reduces foreign taxes paid in the high-tax foreign jurisdiction, it also reduces Section 861 interest allocation costs. The costs of borrowing abroad, however, might be quite high for many foreign subsidiaries: They might not have sufficient capital abroad to leverage themselves to meet their desired financing requirements. Moreover, they can run afoul of the "thin capitalization" rules of such countries as Germany, France, and Switzerland. Thin capitalization rules place limits on deductibility of interest when firms' debt to equity ratios become large.[8]

11.3 U.S. TAX TREATMENT OF FOREIGN INVESTORS

Investments by foreigners in securities of the U.S. government or securities of U.S. corporations are generally not subject to U.S. income tax. Instead, the United States subjects such investments to **withholding taxes** at rates varying from 0% to 30%. Withholding taxes are generally levied on payments of dividends, interest, rents, and royalties, and the rates are often reduced through **bilateral tax treaties** with other nations. Most countries have withholding taxes. Firms often attempt to route dividends and the like through countries that have favorable tax treaties, a practice known as **treaty shopping.**

U.S. subsidiaries of foreign corporations are subject to U.S. taxation like any other U.S. corporation. When a U.S. subsidiary repatriates its income to its foreign parent, however, it also faces a withholding tax on the dividend payment. Sometimes foreign corporations do business in the United States without setting up a U.S. corporation— that is, they conduct business through a branch operation. In that case, the foreign corporation is subject to U.S. taxation on its "income effectively connected with a U.S.

---

[6]*The Wall Street Journal* (October 12, 1989).
[7]See M. Erickson and E. Maydew, "Implicit Taxes in High Dividend Yield Stocks," *Accounting Review* (October 1998).
[8]See Richardson, Hanlon, and Nethercott, "Thin Capitalization Rules: An Anglo-American Comparison," *The International Tax Journal* (Spring 1998).

trade or business." To tax U.S. subsidiaries and U.S. branches of foreign corporations on an equal basis, the United States also levies a **branch profits tax** of up to 30% on the "dividend equivalent amount" of U.S. branches of foreign corporations. Branch profits taxes are common in other countries as well and, as with withholding taxes, may be reduced through tax treaties.

To encourage foreigners to make deposits in U.S. banks and to invest in U.S. Treasury bills, notes, and bonds, most interest income received by foreign investors is subject to a 0% withholding tax. Capital gains on the sale or exchange of U.S. capital assets are typically not subject to U.S. taxation. An exception is gains on the sale of ownership interests in U.S. real property.

Many countries with wealthy foreign investors (such as Kuwait) have no tax treaty with the United States. Consider a wealthy foreign investor from a nontreaty country who wants to invest in the U.S. equity markets but is not enamored with the prospects of a 30% withholding tax on dividends and does not want to restrict his investing to non-dividend-paying stocks. What can the investor do? Although the specific methods are beyond the scope of this text and are likely to evolve over time in response to IRS scrutiny, investors have used a variety of options involving derivative securities. For example, one option has been to invest in U.S. equities indirectly through the use of synthetic securities, such as buying U.S. Treasury bonds and entering into a cash-settlement forward contract to purchase the desired equity security from an investment bank.[9] Others have entered into total return swaps with investors in the country in which the client wants to invest.[10] Which method, if any, foreign investors use to avoid withholding taxes depends on the nontax costs of each strategy, in particular the transactions costs and the tax risks of the various strategies. However, as transactions costs continue to fall over time with decreasing costs of computing and communications, repackaging cash flows for tax purposes becomes more and more feasible. The proliferation of financial innovation continues to pose great challenges for the taxing authorities, particularly in taxes on income from financial assets, which can be easily repackaged using derivatives.

Summary of Key Points

1. The FTC limitation is found by taking the ratio of foreign-source income to worldwide income and multiplying this ratio by the U.S. tax on worldwide income. If the U.S. tax rate is a constant fraction of worldwide income, the FTC limitation simplifies to foreign-source income multiplied by the U.S. tax rate.
2. Firms that have nonbinding FTC limitations and current taxation of foreign income can have little or no incentive to reduce foreign taxes paid, because each dollar of reduction in foreign tax paid results in an additional dollar of U.S. tax from the corresponding reduction in the FTC.
3. A binding FTC limitation means that the United States will refund less than 100% of foreign taxes paid. Under such conditions, U.S. multinationals are wise to reduce their foreign taxes paid. Firms also have an incentive to shift U.S.-defined

---

[9]See G. May, "Flying on Instruments: Synthetic Investment and the Avoidance of Withholding Tax," *Tax Notes International* (November 11, 1996); and R. Avi-Yonah and L. Swartz, "U.S. International Tax Treatment of Financial Derivatives," *Tax Notes* (March 31, 1997).

[10]For example, an investor might swap the return on a basket of foreign stocks for the return on the S&P 500.

income to be foreign source, if such shifting does not affect the foreign-defined source of the income.

4. Foreign tax credits in excess of the FTC limitation can be carried back up to 2 years and carried forward up to 5 years. Firms may also elect to take a deduction for foreign taxes paid instead of a credit, but such an election is not generally desirable unless the firm has large FTCs about to expire unused or has paid foreign taxes not eligible for the FTC.

5. FTC limitations in the United States are calculated separately for a variety of categories of income or so-called separate basket limitations. This categorization is to prevent firms from stuffing investments into tax-haven countries to increase foreign-source income and reduce the average foreign tax rate to below the U.S. rate.

6. With binding FTC limitations it becomes desirable for U.S. multinationals to distribute profits from foreign subsidiaries in ways that are tax deductible abroad. Otherwise taxes would be paid on foreign profits at a foreign tax rate that is above the domestic rate. Examples of ways to distribute profits in a tax-deductible manner include (a) interest on debt issued by a foreign subsidiary, (b) rent on leases to a foreign subsidiary, (c) royalties on licenses granted to a foreign subsidiary, and (d) the judicious use of transfer prices for goods and services exchanged among entities in the same affiliated group.

7. Transfer pricing procedures may result in the repatriation of foreign profits in a way that escapes withholding tax entirely. The IRS uses Section 482 as a weapon against overzealous tax planning and requires that transactions among related parties be priced as if they involved unrelated parties. This arm's length pricing is difficult to achieve and administer, and it is the source of many disputes between the IRS and taxpayers.

8. Foreign investors are subject to withholding taxes on income from passive investments such as dividends and interest. Withholding taxes are often reduced under tax treaties. Foreign investors can avoid withholding taxes by constructing synthetic investments from derivatives. These synthetic investments have the same pretax cash flow as the real investment would, but they would be exempt from withholding taxes. Such synthetic investments are particularly attractive to foreign investors from countries with which the United States does not have a tax treaty.

Discussion Questions

1. Do all U.S. corporations have an incentive to reduce their foreign taxes paid? Why or why not?
2. Consider a U.S. corporation with a single foreign branch in Greece. Suppose the firm's foreign taxes paid are less than the foreign tax credit limitation and the firm expects to remain in this position indefinitely. Would the firm be for or against a Greek tax increase that would go to fund special employee training programs from which it would benefit?
3. Under what circumstances will a U.S. corporation have an incentive to shift U.S.-source income to be foreign-source income?
4. How is the foreign tax credit limitation determined? How does worldwide averaging work? If the firm had no plans to repatriate income from a low-tax country, would it be advisable to do so if foreign tax credit carryforwards from the repatriation of income from high-tax countries were about to expire?
5. Why might a firm wish to repatriate income from a subsidiary in a low-tax country? If it does so, is it advisable to repatriate income from a high-tax country at the same time? Why?
6. Why does the United States require that repatriated foreign income be separated into baskets by type of income, with separate foreign tax credit limitations applied

to each basket? Does the presence of separate baskets increase the U.S. tax on foreign income?

7. What are the advantages of using equity to capitalize the operations of foreign subsidiaries? What are the advantages of using debt, or debt-like substitutes such as royalty arrangements, to finance foreign operations?

8. What is the import of Section 482 for firms forming subsidiaries in foreign tax jurisdictions? Do taxpayers have much freedom in setting prices of goods and services that they transfer to and from their own subsidiaries?

9. How does the definition of foreign-source income affect the computation of the foreign tax credit limitation?

10. What financing alternatives can the U.S. firm employ to reduce the effect of Section 861's allocation of U.S. interest to foreign source? What are the benefits and costs of these alternatives?

11. How are foreign investors taxed when they invest in the U.S. securities markets?

12. What can foreign investors from nontreaty countries do to avoid withholding taxes on their U.S. investments?

Exercises

1. California Cars is a U.S. manufacturer of electric cars. California Cars has $5 billion of U.S. taxable income—$4 billion of which is U.S.-source income and $1 billion of which is foreign-source income. California Cars faces a U.S. tax rate of 35% and paid foreign taxes of $280 million. The firm's foreign-source income falls in the general limitation basket. It is the first year of California Cars foreign operations, so don't worry about foreign tax credit carryforwards or carrybacks.

   a. What is California Cars' foreign tax credit, and what is its worldwide tax paid for the year?

   b. Now suppose that California Cars engaged in tax-reduction strategies abroad, reducing its foreign taxes to $200 million but holding all else constant. What is California Cars' foreign tax credit, and what is its worldwide tax paid for the year?

   c. What possible benefit might California Cars receive from reducing its foreign taxes paid in part (b)? In particular, suppose that the foreign country in which California Cars operates is likely to enact a dramatic increase in its tax rate next year.

2. Georgia Peaches, Inc., is a large U.S. peach grower. Georgia Peaches has U.S.-source income of $1.5 billion, faces a U.S. tax rate of 35%, and paid foreign taxes of $200 million. The firm also reports $500 million of foreign-source income on its U.S. return, all in the general limitation basket. It is the first year of Georgia Peaches' foreign operations, so don't worry about foreign tax credit carryforwards or carrybacks.

   a. What is Georgia Peaches' foreign tax credit, and what is its worldwide tax paid for the year?

   b. Now suppose that Georgia Peaches engaged in tax-reduction strategies abroad, reducing its foreign taxes to $150 million but holding all else constant. What is Georgia Peaches' foreign tax credit, and what is its worldwide tax paid for the year?

3. Wisconsin Cheese Corp. is a large producer of gourmet cheese and has recently expanded overseas. In its first year of international operations (year 1), Wisconsin Cheese had $1 billion of U.S. taxable income, faced a 35% U.S. tax rate, and paid $100 million of foreign taxes. The $1 billion of taxable income includes $200 million of foreign-source income and $800 million of U.S.-source income.

   a. What is Wisconsin Cheese Corp.'s year 1 foreign tax credit, foreign tax credit carryover, and U.S. tax liability?

   b. Now assume that, in year 2, Wisconsin Cheese again has $1 billion of U.S.-source income, again faces a 35% U.S. tax rate, and paid $120 million of foreign taxes. In year 2, the firm reported $500 million of foreign-source income on its U.S. return. What is Wisconsin Cheese Corp.'s year 2 foreign tax credit, foreign tax credit carryover, and U.S. tax liability?

4. Triangle Health is a pharmaceutical firm located in North Carolina's Research Triangle. Triangle Health this year acquired extensive foreign operations, so it is not concerned with foreign tax credit carryforwards or carrybacks. In the current year, Triangle Health has $500 million of U.S.-source income and faces a 35% U.S. tax rate. Triangle Health's U.S. tax return also includes $600 million of foreign-source income from Germany, on which Triangle Health has paid $300 million in German taxes. All of the German-source income falls in the general limitation basket. Triangle Health also has $200 million in income from its Irish operations, on which Triangle Health has paid $20 million in Irish taxes. The total U.S. taxable income is therefore $1.3 billion ($500m + $600m + $200m). All of the Irish-source income falls in the general limitation basket.

   a. What is Triangle Health's foreign tax credit and U.S. tax liability?

   b. Now assume that, instead of all falling in the general limitation basket, the Irish income falls in a passive basket, with the German income in the general limitation basket. What is Triangle Health's foreign tax credit and U.S. tax liability?

Tax Planning Problems

1. Hoosier Industries is a U.S. multinational corporation with two wholly owned subsidiaries, one in Malaysia and one in Japan. The local tax rates are 35% in the United States, 20% in Malaysia, and 45% in Japan. Each of the three corporations generates $100 million of locally taxed income. No withholding taxes are applicable here. All the foreign income falls in the general limitation basket.

   a. After paying taxes, the Malaysian subsidiary repatriates its after-tax earnings. Suppose that none of the Japanese earnings are repatriated. What is Hoosier's current U.S. tax liability after foreign tax credits?

   b. Instead, suppose that both subsidiaries repatriate their after-tax earnings. How would this change your answer to part (a)?

   c. Return to the original fact pattern. Suppose that the Malaysian-source income fell in a passive income basket, while the Japanese-source income fell in the general limitation basket. How would this change your answer to part (a)?

   d. Building on part (c), suppose that both subsidiaries repatriate their after-tax earnings. How would this change your answer to part (c)?

2. American Pie Corporation is a large U.S. manufacturer of frozen pies. In year 1, American Pie has $100 million of Canadian-source income, taxed at a 40% Canadian rate. American Pie's U.S.-source income is negative $30 million due to a casualty loss arising from a fire in its primary warehouse, giving American Pie $70 million of U.S. taxable income. The U.S. tax rate is 35%. American Pie has $5 million of foreign tax credit carryforwards from the prior year. In year 2, American Pie projects that it will again have $100 million of Canadian-source income, taxed at a 40% Canadian rate. However, American Pie's U.S.-source income will increase to $150 million.

   a. What is American Pie's foreign tax credit and U.S. tax in year 1?

   b. What is American Pie's foreign tax credit and U.S. tax in year 2?

   c. Suppose that American Pie could accelerate $30 million of U.S. source income from year 2 into year 1. How does this option change your answers to parts (a) and (b)?

3. Caribbean Tours is a U.S. corporation that operates several cruise ships. Caribbean Tours has U.S.-source income of $300 million and foreign-source income of $200 million. Caribbean Tours paid $40 million in foreign taxes. The U.S. tax rate is 35%.
   a. How much U.S. tax and total worldwide tax will Caribbean Tours pay after taking into account any foreign tax credits to which it is entitled?
   b. Now suppose that Caribbean Tours' foreign taxes were instead $70 million. How much U.S. tax and total worldwide tax will Caribbean Tours pay after taking into account any foreign tax credits to which it is entitled?
   c. Now suppose that Caribbean Tours' foreign taxes were instead $100 million. How much U.S. tax and total worldwide tax will Caribbean Tours pay after taking into account any foreign tax credits to which they are entitled?
   d. Continuing with part (c) with $100 million of foreign taxes, suppose that Caribbean Tours was able to undertake a tax planning strategy that would reclassify $60 million of U.S.-source income to foreign-source income. The reclassification would, however, affect *both* the U.S. classification of income and the foreign classification of income. In other words, U.S.-source income would decrease by $60 million under both the U.S. rules and under the foreign rules, while foreign-source income would increase by $60 under both the U.S. rules and the foreign rules. At the average foreign tax rate of 50%, the tax planning strategy will increase the amount of foreign taxes paid by $30 million, to $130 million. With this strategy, how much U.S. tax and total worldwide tax will Caribbean Tours pay after taking into account any foreign tax credits to which it is entitled?
   e. Again continuing with part (c) with $100 million of foreign taxes, suppose Caribbean Tours was able to undertake a tax planning strategy that would reclassify $60 million of U.S.-source income to foreign-source income. The reclassification would, however, affect *only* the definition of U.S.-source and foreign-source income for U.S. purposes. The reclassification does *not* affect the taxes Caribbean Tours pays to any foreign jurisdiction. With this strategy, how much U.S. tax and total worldwide tax will Caribbean Tours pay after taking into account any foreign tax credits to which they are entitled?

4. A U.S. company is planning to form a foreign subsidiary to undertake a profitable project in a country where the tax rate is 25%. The company's tax rate in the United States is 35%.
   a. If the withholding tax rate on dividends paid from the foreign country to the United States is 20%, how much U.S. taxable income will be recognized for each dollar of dividends *received* by the U.S. parent?
   b. Assuming this income is the only foreign-source income for the U.S. company, what will be the additional U.S. tax liability after foreign tax credit for each dollar of dividend received?
   c. Suppose all foreign profits could be repatriated to the U.S. parent by way of interest payments on debt rather than by way of dividend payments. This move would reduce foreign taxable income to zero. How much more or less worldwide profit after tax would result for a 1-year investment horizon per dollar of foreign income before interest and foreign taxes if withholding tax rates on interest were 0%? If withholding tax rates on interest were 30%?
   d. Suppose that profits earned in the foreign country can be reinvested at a rate of 10% before interest and taxes, the same as in the United States. How does the desirability of debt versus equity financing change as the investment horizon increases?

5. Suppose dividend payments were made tax deductible in calculating corporate taxable income in the United States. Assume that, if dividends are received from foreign subsidiaries and the U.S. parent in turn distributes the dividends to its shareholders, the shareholders are permitted to take foreign tax credits for the foreign taxes they have paid indirectly. Foreign tax credits are limited, however, to an amount equal to shareholders' U.S. tax rate multiplied by the foreign-source income they have received.

For example, suppose a wholly owned subsidiary in a foreign country earns $1 of pretax income, pays local tax of $.20, and declares a dividend of $.80 to its U.S. parent. The U.S. parent in turn declares an $.80 dividend to its shareholders, thereby avoiding taxable income on the receipt of the dividend. Shareholders must recognize $1.00 of taxable income ($.80 in dividends plus $.20 of indirect foreign taxes paid) and are eligible for a foreign tax credit of up to $.20. The tax credit is equal to exactly $.20 if their U.S. tax rate is 20% or more.

How might the preceding set of rules, relative to current U.S. taxation, affect the propensity of tax-exempt investors to invest in purely domestic versus multinational businesses?

References and Additional Readings

Collins, J., D. Kemsley, and M. Lang, 1997. "Cross-Jurisdictional Income Shifting and Earnings Valuation," *Journal of Accounting Research*.

Collins, J., D. Kemsley, and D. Shackelford, 1997. "Transfer Pricing and the Persistent Zero Taxable Income of Foreign-Controlled U.S. Corporations," *Journal of the American Taxation Association* (Supplement), pp. 68–83.

Collins, J., and D. Shackelford, 1992. "Foreign Tax Credit Limitations and Preferred Stock Issuances," *Journal of Accounting Research* (Supplement), pp. 103–124.

Grubert, H., T. Goodspeed, and D. Swenson, 1993. "Explaining the Low Taxable Income of Foreign-Controlled Companies in the U.S.," in *Studies in International Taxation,* edited by A. Giovannini, R. G. Hubbard, and J. Slemrod. Chicago: University of Chicago Press.

Harris, D., 1993. "The Impact of U.S. Tax Law Revision on Multinational Corporations' Capital Location and Income Shifting Decisions," *Journal of Accounting Research* (Supplement), pp. 111–140.

Harris, D., R. Morck, J. Slemrod, and B. Yeung, 1993. "Income Shifting in U.S. Multinational Corporations," in *Studies in International Taxation,* edited by A. Giovannini,

R. G. Hubbard, and J. Slemrod. Chicago: University of Chicago Press.

Jacob, J., 1996. "Taxes and Transfer Pricing: Income Shifting and the Volume of Intra-Firm Transfers," *Journal of Accounting Research,* pp. 301–312.

Klassen, K., M. Lang, and M. Wolfson, 1993. "Geographic Income Shifting by Multinational Corporations in Response to Tax Rate Changes," *Journal of Accounting Research* (Supplement), pp. 141–173.

Mills, L., and K. Newberry, 2003. "Cross-Jurisdictional Income Shifting by Foreign-Controlled U.S. Corporations." Working paper. Tucson, AZ: University of Arizona.

Newberry, K., 1998. "Foreign Tax Credit Limitations and Capital Structure Decisions," *Journal of Accounting Research,* pp. 157–166.

Olhoft, S., 2002. "The Tax Avoidance Activities of U.S. Multinational Corporations." Working paper. Iowa City, IA: University of Iowa.

Seida, J., and R. Yetman, 2003. "Business Purpose/Profit Motive: Compaq's Purchase and Sale of Shell Common Stock," in *Cases in Tax Strategy,* third edition, edited by M. Erickson. Boston, MA: Pearson Custom Publishing.

12

CORPORATIONS: FORMATION, OPERATION, CAPITAL STRUCTURE, AND LIQUIDATION

After studying this chapter, you should be able to:

1. Explain the tax consequences of forming a corporation.

2. Explain some of the special tax rules that apply to corporations.

3. Understand the possible tax benefits of leverage in firms' capital structures.

4. Appreciate the role of debt-equity hybrids in firms' capital structures.

5. Describe the possible tax treatments of corporate distributions and share repurchases.

6. Understand how corporations and their shareholders are taxed in liquidation.

P artnerships and sole proprietorships are more numerous than corporations in the United States. However, corporations are the dominant form of U.S. business in terms of aggregate revenues, profits, or just about any measure of the magnitude of economic activity. Most large business entities in the United States are corporations.[1] A solid understanding of business tax strategy, therefore, must include some familiarity with the tax rules that are specific to corporations and the effects and incentives provided by such corporation-specific rules. This chapter provides the fundamentals of corporate taxation. It also prepares the reader for the mergers and acquisitions chapters, because much of mergers and acquisitions taxation is an extension of the fundamental rules of corporate taxation.

---

[1]Notable exceptions are the large accounting and professional services firms such as KPMG and PricewaterhouseCoopers that operate as limited liability partnerships (LLPs) because of regulatory restrictions on the use of the corporate form by accounting firms.

When we speak of corporations in this chapter, we are actually referring to corporations taxed under Subchapter C of the Internal Revenue Code. Some corporations are taxed under Subchapter S and are known as "S corporations," but they are taxed for the most part like partnerships and are discussed in Chapters 4 and 15.[2] C corporations are the dominant form of business in the United States. All publicly traded corporations are C corporations, as are many privately held and closely held corporations. Again, unless we say otherwise, "corporation" means "C corporation" in this text.

The hallmark of corporate taxation is **double taxation** of corporate profits. Corporations are said to be subject to double taxation because the earnings of a corporation are taxed once at the corporate level and again at the shareholder level when the corporation pays out dividends. Dividend payments are not tax deductible to the corporation. Most of the special tax rules for corporations, as well as the mergers and acquisitions rules discussed in Chapters 13–17, are designed to enforce double taxation of corporate profits. As you read this chapter, keep in mind the tax authorities' overarching goal of double taxation, and the tax rules will make more sense to you. In many cases, simply remembering the concept of double taxation will allow you to predict how the tax law treats a given situation.

Double taxation of corporate profits has been controversial because it likely discourages corporate formation and distorts economic behavior. Reducing this distortion became a priority with policymakers and in 2003 Congress acted to reduce double taxation by lowering the tax on dividends received by individuals. Specifically, prior to 2003 dividends received by individuals counted as "ordinary" income and were therefore subject to taxation at potentially high rates just like salary income. The exact rate depended on the year and the tax bracket, but was as high as 39.6% in some years. That all changed in 2003. As part of a broad package of tax rate reductions, Congress changed the law to provide for a maximum tax rate of 15% on dividend income to individuals. At the same time Congress reduced the maximum tax rate on long-term capital gains from 20% to 15%. While corporate tax rates were unchanged in 2003, reducing shareholder-level taxes had the effect of reducing the double taxation of corporate profits.

The chapter is organized in terms of the life cycle of the corporation: corporate formation, operations, distributions, and liquidation. The chapter begins with a discussion of corporate formations under Section 351—the basic concepts applying to the taxation of corporate formations also apply to nontaxable acquisitions. In Section 12.2 we discuss some of the special tax rules governing corporate operations, specifically those tax rules that differ from GAAP. Sections 12.3 and 12.4 examine taxes and capital structure, covering the classic finance theory on the tax benefits of leverage as well as recent empirical evidence, and also a discussion of debt-equity hybrid securities, such as trust preferred stock. Section 12.5 presents the tax rules applicable to getting cash out of the corporation and into the hands of shareholders by either declaring dividends or repurchasing shares. Section 12.6 discusses a case of

---

[2]We do not mean to imply that S corporations are taxed *exactly* like partnerships; S corporations are subject to many tax rules that are different from partnerships. Partnerships are taxed under Subchapter K of the Internal Revenue Code.

tax planning for distributions—the nearly $2 billion in taxes saved by Seagram and DuPont in a single transaction. Section 12.7 concludes with a brief discussion of corporate liquidations, completing the life cycle of the corporation. Some of the material overlaps with earlier chapters, e.g., double taxation of corporations is a big part of Chapter 4 and book-tax differences are discussed in an appendix to Chapter 2.

12.1 CORPORATE FORMATION

When a corporation is formed, one or more investors—individuals, other corporations, etc.—contribute property to the newly formed corporation in exchange for the newly issued stock of the corporation. Absent any special rules, such an exchange would be a taxable event and the investors would be taxed on the difference between their basis in the property contributed and its fair market value. However, if forming corporations routinely triggered taxation that would inhibit entrepreneurial activity and investment. To better allow capital to flow to its highest and best use, the Tax Code has long allowed most corporate formations to be nontaxable, or more precisely, tax-deferred. The idea is to leave the parties in approximately the same tax position as they were before the corporate formation.

Section 351 is the key Tax Code section for corporate formation. It is an important section of the Tax Code and will help you understand nontaxable acquisitions in later chapters. Section 351 applies when three conditions are met: (1) the investors contribute property to the corporation, (2) the investors receive stock in the corporation, and (3) the investors collectively control 80% or more of the corporation after the transaction. Each of these requirements has additional nuances that are beyond the scope of this text (for example, when does intellectual property count as property for the purposes of Section 351 and when does it count as services?).

Most corporate formations satisfy all three requirements. Some secondary offerings can also meet these requirements, provided the investors taking part in the secondary offering collectively own 80% or more of the corporation after the offering.[3]

If Section 351 governs the transaction, then the investors are taxed on the lesser of their realized gain and the **boot** they receive in the transaction.[4] Think of boot as cash or other property received, including most anything except the firm's stock, e.g., T-bills. The corporation to which the property is contributed is not taxed (Section 1032).

For example, Art, Ira, and Marty each contribute property to form AIM Corporation. Art contributes oil wells with a fair market value of $470,000 and a basis

---

[3]A secondary offering occurs when an existing corporation issues additional stock.

[4]Section 351 treatment is mandatory if its requirements are met. In the rare case that Section 351 would not apply to a corporate formation, the entire transaction would be taxable, and, in rare cases, not qualifying under Section 351 can be desirable. Therefore, the shareholders contributing property to the corporation would recognize gain to the extent the fair market value of the stock they receive exceeded the basis of the property they contribute to the corporation. Shareholders contributing services in exchange for stock would recognize ordinary income to the extent of the fair market value of the stock received. The shareholders' basis in the corporation's stock would equal its fair market value, as would the corporation's basis in property received. An example of a corporate formation not covered by Section 351 would be if Smith and Dean together formed DS Corporation, with Smith contributing cash for half of the stock of DS and Dean contributing services for the other half of DS. Because the shareholder(s) contributing property (Smith) controlled less than 80% of the corporation, Section 351 would not apply.

of $100,000, and receives 47% of the stock of AIM. **Tax basis** (or simply "basis") is generally equal to the amount paid for an asset. Ira contributes $100,000 cash and networking equipment with a fair market value and tax basis of $370,000, also receiving 47% of the stock of AIM. Marty contributes a sports memorabilia collection with a fair market value of $150,000 and tax basis of $70,000, in exchange for the remaining 6% of the stock of AIM and $90,000 cash.

How will each party be treated for tax purposes? Art will take a basis in his AIM stock equal to the basis of the property he contributed, $100,000, which is called a **substituted basis.** Presumably the fair market value of the AIM stock is approximately equal to the $470,000 fair market value of the oil wells contributed, so if Art later sells the stock he will be taxed on his $370,000 unrealized gain. In that sense, Section 351 just defers taxation but does not eliminate it. Art's holding period in the AIM stock will include the time he held the contributed property; for example, if he had owned the oil wells for 14 months then he is treated as if he had held the AIM stock for 14 months. AIM will take a $100,000 basis in the oil wells, which is called a **carryover basis.** If AIM sold the oil wells it would recognize a $370,000 gain, so Art's original $370,000 unrealized gain now exists at both his level and the corporation's level. AIM's holding period in the oil wells will include the 14 months that Art had owned them. So even if AIM sold the oil wells immediately after receiving them in the corporate formation, the gain would be a long-term capital gain because the holding period exceeds the 12-month cutoff for determining whether a capital gain is long-term or short-term.

Ira will take a basis in his AIM stock equal to the basis of the property that he contributed, or $470,000 ($100,000 plus $370,000). The holding period of 37/47ths of his AIM stock will include the holding period of his networking equipment contributed, while 10/47ths of his AIM stock will start fresh because it was acquired through a cash contribution. AIM will take a $370,000 carryover basis in the networking equipment and obviously a $100,000 basis in the cash received (the basis of $1 cash is $1).

Marty's case is the tricky one. Because Marty received cash (boot) he will be taxed on the transaction. Specifically, he will recognize a gain (but never a loss) equal to the lesser of the boot received or the realized gain. The boot received is $90,000. The realized gain is the difference between the fair market value and the basis of the property contributed, or $150,000 − $70,000 = $80,000. Thus the taxable (or recognized) gain is equal to min ($90,000; $80,000) = $80,000. Marty will take a basis in the AIM stock received equal to the basis of what he contributed, plus any gain recognized, less any boot received. In this case $70,000 + $80,000 − $90,000 = $60,000.

Does the tax treatment for Marty make sense? The fair market value of the AIM stock received by Marty must be equal to the fair market value of what he gave, or $150,000 less the $90,000 cash received equals $60,000. Because the fair market value and tax basis of the AIM stock are both $60,000, after the transaction Marty has no unrealized gains. Before the transaction Marty had an unrealized gain of $80,000. He recognized $80,000 of gain in the transaction, so he should not (and does not) have any more unrealized gain.

AIM will take a basis in Marty's contributed assets equal to Marty's old basis plus any gain Marty recognized, or $70,000 + $80,000 = $150,000.

Here is an interesting side note: Was this transaction fair? Art contributed property that essentially came with a hidden tax liability equal to the unrealized gain on his property ($370,000) times the corporate tax rate. Art's GAAP financial statements will not necessarily reveal the deferred tax liability before the corporate formation, because deferred tax liabilities arise from differences between GAAP book value and tax basis, not between fair market value and tax basis. If the fair market values we quoted do not reflect the hidden tax liability in Art's contribution, then Art got the best of Ira and Marty by transferring his unrecorded tax liability to the corporation that they jointly own. Corporate formation can be a trap for the unwary.

12.2 TAXATION OF CORPORATE OPERATIONS

Most of the tax rules to which corporations are subject are the same tax rules applicable to individuals. For example, the schedules used to calculate depreciation deductions are the same across taxpayers. Corporations are, however, subject to a number of special tax rules. This section provides a brief overview of the special tax rules applicable to corporations and how these rules differ from the generally accepted accounting principles (GAAP) that firms follow in their financial reporting.

Book-Tax Differences: Taxable Income versus GAAP Income

Like all taxpayers, firms pay income taxes based on their taxable income. You can think of taxable income as being similar to GAAP income in the sense that both represent some measure of revenues less some measure of expenses. However, differences between GAAP and the tax law arise because of differences in objectives. The objectives of GAAP are to provide information that is useful in investment and credit decisions; in assessing cash flow prospects; and in assessing the firm's resources, claims to those resources, and changes in them.[5] In contrast, Congress has many objectives when making the tax law, including raising revenue, stimulating the economy, and encouraging or discouraging certain behaviors. These differences in objectives lead to a number of differences between GAAP income and taxable income.

The differences that separate book income from tax income are collectively referred to as **book-tax differences** and include items such as municipal bond interest, which is tax exempt at the federal level but counts as income for GAAP purposes. Different methods are also used for computing depreciation expense for GAAP and tax purposes. Amortization of goodwill recorded for purchase accounting acquisitions is usually not tax deductible. Book-tax differences are reflected in financial statements in two places: temporary differences such as depreciation are reflected in the deferred tax liability or asset, while permanent differences such as tax exempt interest are reflected in the effective tax rate reconciliation, which is part of the tax footnote to the financial statements.[6]

The good news is that, despite these differences, if you have a basic knowledge of financial accounting, you already know a lot about corporate taxation. For example, like their GAAP-based financial statements, corporations must use the accrual

---

[5]See Kieso, Weygandt, and Warfield (2004) and "Objectives of Financial Reporting by Business Enterprises," *Statement of Financial Accounting Concepts No. 1* (Stamford, CT: FASB, November 1978).
[6]Interested readers can learn the details of accounting for book-tax differences by reading Statement of Financial Accounting Standards (SFAS) 109.

method when computing their taxable income.[7] That is, income is recognized as it is earned rather than when the cash is collected, and expenses are recognized as they are incurred rather than when they are paid. Further, when corporations prepare their income tax returns, they start with their audited GAAP numbers and make adjustments for differences between GAAP and the tax law. Unless a specific reason indicates an adjustment, the GAAP number winds up being the tax number.[8]

As previously stated, most corporations must use the accrual basis. Some corporations are allowed to use the cash method to compute their noninventory-related taxable income, but generally this exception is limited to corporations with less than $5 million in revenue per year. Individuals can use the cash method, and usually do, except to the extent they have inventory.

Net Operating Losses

When a firm has negative taxable income for the year, it is called a **net operating loss,** or NOL. Under current laws, firms are allowed to carry back NOLs up to 2 years and carry them forward up to 20 years to offset taxable income in those years. Some readers may recall that prior to tax law changes in 1997 the NOL carryback period was 3 years and the NOL carryforward period was 15 years (a temporary provision also existed in 2001 and 2002 allowing for a 5-year carryback period). NOLs are discussed in detail in Chapters 4 and 7.

Gains and Losses and Tax Basis

Tax gains and losses generally are computed in the same manner as in financial accounting. For example, if a firm purchased a building for $100,000, depreciated it by $40,000 over some period, and later sold it for $70,000, then the firm would report a $10,000 gain on the sale. The gain would be computed as the difference between the proceeds ($70,000) and the asset's book value of $100,000 − $40,000.

In tax the idea is the same, except that the amount the asset was purchased for is referred to as its *tax basis,* and the tax basis less any accumulated depreciation is referred to as the asset's **adjusted basis.** Often we will just use *basis* as shorthand for *adjusted basis.* Also recall that the accumulated depreciation for tax and GAAP purposes can be different, leading to differences between the gain or loss for tax and financial accounting.

Capital Gains and Losses

Most taxable income is so-called **ordinary income.** Examples include income from wages, services rendered, income from the sale of inventory, and interest income. Gains and losses from the sale of **capital assets,** however, are capital gains and losses and are treated somewhat differently.

What is a capital asset? Most assets not used in a trade or business are considered capital assets, including stocks, bonds, puts, calls, etc. Inventory is not a capital asset.

---

[7]Some small corporations can use the cash method.
[8]For a discussion of implicit pressure to conform tax and book income, see Guenther, Nutter, and Maydew (1997) and Mills (1998).

Contrary to conventional wisdom, equipment and buildings used in a trade or business are *not* capital assets. They are Section 1231 assets, and will be discussed in upcoming text. If a capital asset has been held for more than 1 year, the capital gain or loss from its sale is considered a long-term gain or loss.

Taxpayers are required to keep track of capital gains and losses separately from ordinary income. A complex netting procedure surrounds capital gains and losses, but we will not go into it here. If an individual has net long-term capital gains for the year those gains are taxable at a maximum rate of 15% under current law. This rate compares favorably with the maximum individual tax rate of 35% under current law. No special capital gains rate is granted for corporations, however. Corporations pay the same rate on capital gains and ordinary income, generally 35%. Many people who are not tax savvy erroneously believe that corporations also have a special low long-term capital gains rate, but corporations have not had a special capital gains rate since the mid-1980s.

Net capital losses occur when the taxpayer has more capital losses than capital gains. Net capital losses cannot be used to offset ordinary income. Corporations are allowed to carry back net capital losses up to 3 years and carry them forward up to 5 years, and such carrybacks and carryforwards can be used to offset capital gains in those years. In contrast, individuals can use up to $3,000 of net capital losses per year to offset ordinary income. Individuals cannot carry back net capital losses, but can carry them forward indefinitely.

Section 1231 Assets

Section 1231 assets are assets that are used in a trade or business and have been held for more than 1 year, other than inventory. Examples include most buildings, machines, equipment, and land. If the taxpayer has net 1231 gains for the year, then such gains count as long-term capital gains. If the taxpayer has net 1231 losses for the year, then such losses count as ordinary losses and can hence offset ordinary income. Thus, 1231 gains and losses represent the best of both worlds—gains taxable at potentially low long-term capital gains rates and losses deductible at high ordinary rates. Because, under current law, corporations pay tax on capital gains and ordinary income at the same rates, Section 1231 does not have as much importance as it once did. It is still useful, however, because net 1231 losses can be used to offset the corporation's ordinary income, whereas net capital losses cannot offset ordinary income. Also, to the extent individuals have 1231 gains from a sole proprietorship or flowing from a partnership, those gains can be taxed at the low 15% capital gains rate.

Dividends Received Deduction

Recall that the overarching principle of corporation taxation is the double taxation of corporate profits. Even though Congress likes double taxation, it tries to avoid imposing more than two layers of taxation on corporate earnings. The **dividends received deduction** is designed to prevent triple or more taxation when corporations receive dividends from other corporations. The amount of the dividends received deduction depends on how much the dividend-receiving corporation owns of the dividend-paying corporation. With less than 20% ownership, the dividends received deduction is 70%, from 20% to 79.9% ownership the dividends received deduction is 80%, and with 80% or more ownership comes a 100% dividends received deduction, or complete exclusion.

For example, if Exxon owned 10% of GE and received $100 million of dividends from GE, then Exxon would only be taxable on $100 million × (1 − .7) = $30 million of those dividends. With a corporate tax rate of 35%, this deduction translates to a 10.5% tax rate on dividend income (assuming less than 20% ownership). How many layers of tax will be paid on GE's earnings? One layer paid by GE as it earns its profits, a partial layer paid by Exxon when it receives a dividend from GE, and another layer paid by Exxon's shareholders when Exxon pays a dividend or when they sell their Exxon stock and pay capital gains tax.

Consolidated Tax Returns

Most of what we think of as corporations are actually collections of corporations—the parent corporation and its subsidiaries and their subsidiaries and so on. GAAP mandates consolidation of subsidiaries when the parent owns 50% or more of a subsidiary. It does not matter whether the subsidiary is domestic or foreign; all that matters is control. Thus, when you examine GM's financial statements you are examining GM's worldwide operations.

The tax rules for consolidations are somewhat different. First, only domestic subsidiaries can be part of the U.S. consolidated tax return. Foreign subsidiaries are not consolidated. Second, the ownership level for tax consolidation is 80%. Thus, a subsidiary that was 70% owned by the parent would be consolidated for GAAP purposes but not for tax.

Corporations are not forced to file consolidated returns but generally find it in their best interests to do so. The benefit of a consolidated return is that taxable income of one subsidiary can be offset by losses of another subsidiary. This benefit is major, especially to the extent that income in the various subsidiaries is not highly correlated. Without a consolidated return the profitable subsidiaries would pay taxes and the unprofitable subsidiaries would have to rely on carrying back or forward their losses to offset their own income. Special rules inhibit the ability of a profitable company to purchase corporations with NOLs and use the purchased NOLs to offset the profitable company's income. These rules are discussed in Chapter 16.

12.3 POSSIBLE TAX BENEFITS OF LEVERAGE IN FIRMS' CAPITAL STRUCTURES

One of the most critical issues in forming and operating a corporation is determining the proper mix of debt and equity in the firm's capital structure. Whether a tax benefit can come from leverage is one of the oldest questions in corporate finance, dating back at least as far as Modigliani and Miller's (M&M) seminal work in 1958. Many readers will have already have a working knowledge of capital structure theory from their corporate finance classes, so we will provide only a brief overview in this book.[9] We begin with the origins of modern thought on capital structure (M&M, 1958) and work our way up to contemporary thinking and state-of-the-art empirical research on the subject. The discussion builds on concepts introduced earlier in the text, in particular

---

[9]Most good corporate finance textbooks discuss the theory of the tax benefits of leverage; see R. Brealey and S. Myers, *Principles of Corporate Finance,* 7th edition (McGraw-Hill).

the concept of implicit taxes, the concept of tax clienteles, and the effects of nontax costs.

Theory of the Tax Benefits of Leverage

Like a physicist who explains the laws of nature by first considering movement in a frictionless world, M&M (1958) explain capital structure by first examining leverage in perfect capital markets. A **perfect capital market** has no transactions costs, no information asymmetries, no bankruptcy costs, and no taxes. M&M (1958) prove that, with perfect capital markets, no gain comes from leverage. The intuition is straightforward. Imagine the value of the corporation's cash flows as represented by an extra-large pizza. The slices of pizza represent claims on the corporation's cash flows. Whether the slices are labeled equity or debt does not affect the size of the entire pizza. If the capital markets are perfect, no pizza is lost or gained by slicing it in different ways or by labeling the slices as debt or equity. The conclusion of the M&M (1958) paper is that, absent some market imperfection, capital structure will not affect the value of the firm and is therefore irrelevant. M&M recognize, of course, that in reality markets are not perfect and that those market imperfections may cause the value of the firm to depend on its capital structure. But M&M represent a major innovation in thinking by focusing the debate on the effects of the various market imperfections on optimal capital structure.

For the most part, we will focus on the role of taxes in capital structure. M&M relax the assumption of perfect capital markets to include corporate taxation toward the end of their 1958 paper and then give the matter of corporate taxes a fuller examination in their 1963 paper. They show that, if markets are perfect except for the existence of corporate taxes, the value of the firm is increasing in its leverage. Why? Because dividend payments on equity are not tax deductible to the corporation, whereas interest payments on debt are. Therefore, the label put on the pizza slices does matter with corporate taxation. The three types of pizza slices are debt, equity, and taxes (the government's claim on the firm's cash flows). Pizza slices labeled as debt reduce the size of the government's tax slice, whereas slices labeled as equity do not. The value of the levered firm, V_L, is equal to the value of an unlevered all-equity firm, V_U, plus the tax benefit of the leverage. M&M (1963) show that the present value of the tax benefit to leverage is equal to τD, where τ is the corporate tax rate and D is the amount of debt.

$$V_L = V_U + \tau D \qquad \textbf{(12.1)}$$

Because the value of the firm is increasing in the amount of leverage, in the M&M (1963) world all firms would want to be at a "corner solution" in which they pay out all of their cash flows in the form of interest on debt. Again, M&M realized that most firms are not so extremely levered, and their analysis was meant to further our understanding of the forces involved in the capital structure decision and the magnitude of those forces.

Quickly the debate turned to what other market imperfections or nontax costs keep firms from being fully levered. Bankruptcy costs were an obvious candidate; as firms increase their leverage, they increase the chances that in some states of the world they will not have sufficient cash flows to cover their interest payments. Bankruptcy or more general financial distress can be a cumbersome and costly process, and the increased likelihood of incurring financial distress costs may serve as a counterbalance to the tax benefits of leverage. However, with every dollar of debt increasing the value of the firm by τ—35 cents per dollar of debt at current tax rates—it was hard to imagine bankruptcy costs being much of a counterbalance; the tax gain from leverage is massive in the M&M 1963 world.

But the drama continued, albeit at the slow pace of academic research. In the 1970s, the pendulum swung back to no tax gains from leverage with Miller's (1977) paper. Miller (the second "M" of "M&M") examined a world of perfect capital markets, except that he now allowed for personal- as well as corporate-level taxation. Miller considered the case where the investor-level taxes on equity were less than the investor-level taxes on debt. For example, the return on a growth stock may be taxed at long-term capital gains rates, currently 15%, or may be taxed at a 0% tax rate if they are held until death.[10] Interest on debt, however, is taxed at ordinary tax rates, which are currently as high as 35% at the federal level.

Miller reasons that investors who should be concerned with after-tax rates of return will bid up the price of equity until its risk-adjusted after-tax return is the same as that on debt. In other words, equity will bear an implicit tax, or lower pretax rate of return, relative to debt, because equity returns are tax-favored at the investor level. Said another way, the pretax, risk-adjusted cost of debt financing must be greater than equity financing in order to compensate investors for the higher tax rates they pay on interest income. Miller shows that, under certain conditions, the increased pretax return that must be paid on debt financing exactly offsets the tax benefits from the corporate-level interest deductions. Assuming all firms face the same marginal tax rate, any given corporation then faces no net tax benefit from debt financing.[11] Miller's reasoning is extremely important because it shows that, even in the absence of bankruptcy costs, costs to debt financing (high investor-level taxes) can offset the corporate-level tax advantage of interest deductibility.

Unfortunately, no one knows for sure whether implicit tax effects are present in debt and equity, let alone how big the implicit taxes might be. Why the uncertainty? The most direct way to measure the effects of taxes on pretax returns would be to observe the pretax returns on a stock and a bond that had exactly the same risk. Unfortunately, such experiments are hard to find. Further, because equity is usually more risky than debt, the expected return on equity is typically larger than the return on debt. Without precise estimates of how risk affects expected returns, it is difficult to isolate the effects of taxes on returns.[12] How risk is priced remains a matter of some controversy in economics and finance. Thus, the pretax returns to assets are likely some function of their risk and their tax treatment, but it is extremely difficult to disentangle the size of the two effects in practice.

DeAngelo and Masulis (1980) extend Miller's (1977) analysis to allow for "non-debt tax shields" such as depreciation expense. As we have seen in earlier chapters,

---

[10]At death, the tax basis of a decedent's assets are stepped-up to fair market value, and the potential income taxation on the unrealized gains on the assets are exempt from income tax.

[11]Although no individual firm prefers debt over equity, an optimal amount of debt at the economywide level can be calculated in Miller's (1977) world. The reasoning is subtle, and curious readers are referred to the source.

[12]Chapter 5 analyzes the differences in pretax returns that should hold in theory for securities that differ in terms of both tax treatment and risk.

firms with a greater likelihood of net operating losses have smaller expected marginal tax rates than other firms. The greater a firm's nondebt tax shields, the lower is its expected tax benefit from interest tax deductions, giving rise to an optimal amount of leverage for each firm. DeAngelo and Masulis (1980) represent an important step in the theory of capital structure because for the first time tax effects alone are shown to cause each firm to have an optimal amount of debt. No longer does theory predict extremes of no tax benefits to leverage (Miller, 1977) or massive tax benefits from leverage (M&M, 1963). DeAngelo and Masulis (1980) lead to an important testable prediction. Firms with large amounts of nondebt tax shields should borrow less than firms with small amounts of nondebt tax shields, an example of a tax clientele effect.

Empirical Work on the Tax Benefits of Leverage[13]

Shevlin (1990) and Graham (1996) extend DeAngelo and Masulis (1980) by providing empirical estimates of firms' expected marginal tax rates, taking into account firms' current and past taxability, as well as the probably of future net operating losses. Graham (1996) applies the marginal tax rate estimates to the role of taxes in capital structure and finds that firms' leverage is increasing in their marginal tax rates. Graham (1996) recognizes that, as a firm borrows more, the increased interest deductions increase the firm's probability of future net operating losses, reducing the marginal tax benefit of leverage. As the firm borrows more and more, eventually the marginal benefit of leverage equals the marginal cost and the firm stops borrowing. Graham's (1996) results strongly suggest, but do not prove, that a tax gain from leverage exists.

Graham (2000) takes this argument one step further, using his marginal tax rate estimates to produce firm-specific estimates of the actual tax benefits of leverage that firms obtain at their current debt levels, as well as the maximum tax benefits of leverage they could obtain if they were more fully levered. Graham (2000) estimates that roughly 7% to 10% of the value of the average firm is accounted for by the tax benefits of leverage. The big unresolved issue, however, is whether investor-level taxes affect the pretax cost of debt capital relative to equity. In a subsequent review of the literature, Graham (2003) sums it up as "The truth is we know little about the identity or tax status of the marginal investor(s) between any two sets of securities and deducing this information is difficult. It would be useful if future research could quantify the relative importance of personal taxes on security prices, with an eye towards feedback into capital structure decisions."

12.4 DEBT-EQUITY HYBRIDS

Provisions in the Tax Code keep firms from being too thinly capitalized. Many countries, such as Germany, set maximum ratios of debt to equity that firms can have in their capital structure for tax purposes. The United States, however, has more subjective rules. In Section 385, Congress granted the Treasury authority to write regulations

---

[13]See the references for additional research on taxes and capital structure.

governing which securities will be treated as debt and which ones will be treated as equity for tax purposes. At least in theory, highly levered firms risk having their debt reclassified as equity for tax purposes and therefore losing their interest deductions. Despite the broad authority given to it by Congress more than 20 years ago, Treasury has yet to issue final regulations on Section 385. The question of what is debt and what is equity remains an area for considerable tax planning in the United States.[14]

Traditional Preferred Stock

Most tax and corporate finance books treat capital structure as a black-and-white choice between issuing common stock or issuing debt. In reality, firms have many hybrids between straight debt and common stock to choose from when raising capital. Traditional preferred stock has many characteristics of debt, such as fixed yields, no or limited voting rights, and preference over common stock in payment of dividends and in liquidation. A newer type of preferred stock called "trust preferred stock" has many of the same nontax features as traditional preferred stock but has markedly different tax consequences. We first discuss the taxation of traditional preferred stock and in the next section discuss taxation of trust preferred stock. For each type of preferred stock we compare the tax treatment to that of debt.

Traditional preferred stock is taxed as equity. At the issuer level, traditional preferred stock dividends are not tax deductible, whereas interest payments on debt are typically tax deductible. How dividends on preferred stock are taxed at the investor level depends on whether the investor is an individual or another corporation. If the investor is an individual, then in most circumstances the dividends will be taxed at a maximum tax rate of 15%. If the investor is another corporation then the dividend is only partially taxable due to the dividends received deduction that was described earlier in this chapter. Compared with debt, traditional preferred stock is tax-disadvantaged at the issuer level but is tax-advantaged to both individual investors and corporate investors. For example, a corporate investor choosing between investing in a bond that has a 9% yield and investing in a share of preferred stock that has an 8% yield will typically choose the preferred stock, assuming they have the same risk. The reason is that the after-tax yield on the bond will be 5.85%, or 9%(1 − .35), to the corporate investor, whereas the after-tax yield on the preferred stock will be 7.16%, or 8%[1 − .35(1 − .7)]. Because of the dividend-received deduction, preferred stock has, in the past, been thought to be largely held by other corporations. With the tax rate on dividend income received by individuals reduced to 15%, more individuals could wind up holding traditional preferred stock. Academia has not paid much attention to preferred stock, however, compared with common stock and debt. In one of the few studies of preferred stock, Erickson and Maydew (1998) document that preferred stock does bear implicit taxes because of the dividends received deduction received by corporate holders of preferred stock. Collins and Shackelford (1992) show that preferred stock issuance can have advantages for firms facing binding foreign tax credit limitations.

---

[14]The United States also has the so-called CERT rules (corporate equity reduction transactions) that basically limit the ability to carry back NOLs following a leveraged buyout. Other rules limit the deductibility of interest on high yield debt obligations (HYDO).

Trust Preferred Stock[15]

Starting in the mid-1990s, traditional preferred stock began to fall from favor because of a new and improved financial innovation often called **trust preferred stock.** The basic idea behind trust preferred stock was to create a security that would be treated as debt for tax purposes but would not be treated as a liability for financial reporting and regulatory purposes.

The first trust preferred issue by a U.S. firm was a $350 million issue by Texaco on October 27, 1993. Figure 12.1 illustrates the structure of the Texaco trust preferred offering. Because most trust preferred offerings follow the same basic structure, we will use the Texaco offering to describe the structure of trust preferred stock.[16]

Texaco first creates Texaco Capital LLC, which is essentially a "shell" corporation that is wholly owned by Texaco. Next, Texaco Capital issues trust preferred stock to investors for $350 million in cash. Simultaneously, Texaco issues $350 million of subordinated debentures to Texaco Capital in exchange for the $350 million proceeds of the trust preferred issue. The Texaco debentures have terms and yield that are

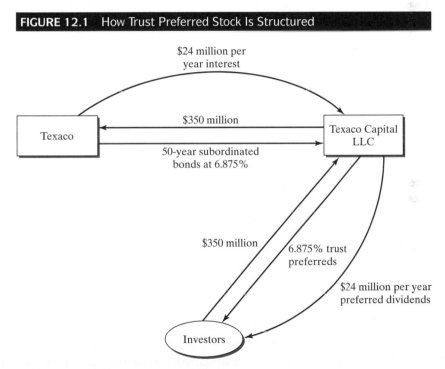

FIGURE 12.1 How Trust Preferred Stock Is Structured

$24 million per year interest

$350 million

Texaco

Texaco Capital LLC

50-year subordinated bonds at 6.875%

$350 million

6.875% trust preferreds

$24 million per year preferred dividends

Investors

Objective: Equity-like characterization on balance sheet, but debt characterization for tax purposes.

---

[15]This discussion is based on Engel, Erickson, and Maydew (1999).

[16]Actually Texaco issued monthly income preferred securities (MIPS), which are essentially the same thing as trust preferred stock. Most investment banks offer their clients a similar product but each generally gives their product a different name. Some acronyms include quarterly income preferred securities (QUIPS) and trust originated preferred securities (TOPRS) and trust preferred stock (TRUPS).

identical to those of the trust preferred stock and the debentures provide the cash flow source of the recurring dividend payments to trust preferred holders. For example, Texaco Capital's trust preferred stock pays dividends at 6.875%, identical to the yield on the subordinated Texaco debt held by Texaco Capital. Subsequent to the trust preferred issue, Texaco Capital simply acts as a conduit between Texaco and the trust preferred investors, with interest payments from Texaco on the debentures equaling the dividends paid to the trust preferred investors.

Contractually, trust preferred stocks are quite similar to traditional preferred stock. Texaco's trust preferred stocks have maturities of 50 years with a 50-year renewal option, so like traditional preferred stock, trust preferred stocks derive their market value almost entirely from the present value of their dividend payments. Most trust preferred stocks have maturities of between 20 and 50 years, with similar renewal options. Also like preferred stock, Texaco's trust preferred stocks generally are subordinated to all other debt. Texaco also has the right to defer payment of trust preferred dividends for up to 5 years at a time. However, as with traditional preferred stock, trust preferred stock issuers cannot pay dividends on their common stock while they are deferring trust preferred dividends. In the unlikely event of dividend deferral exceeding 5 years, trust preferred stock investors could appoint an outside trustee to Texaco Capital, which could then sue Texaco for defaulting on its debt obligation to Texaco Capital.

Tax Treatment of Trust Preferred Stock

The tax treatment of traditional preferred stock differs from that of trust preferred stock for both issuers and investors. Firms issuing traditional preferred stock receive no tax deductions for dividends paid on traditional preferred stock. Traditional preferred stock is, however, tax-advantaged to both corporate and individual investors. Corporations receiving dividend income are eligible for the dividends received deduction, which exempts 70% of the dividend income from taxation. Individual investors are taxed on dividend income from traditional preferred stock at a maximum rate of 15%. In contrast, trust preferred stock is treated as debt and thus its "dividends" are treated as interest under the tax law. Therefore, corporate holders of trust preferred stock are not eligible for the dividends received deduction because the trust preferred securities are allowed debt treatment through fully deductible annual dividend payments. Individual holders of trust preferred stock are taxed at ordinary tax rates to the extent they receive trust preferred dividends; there is no special 15% tax rate for trust preferred dividends.

Because trust preferred stock is not tax-advantaged to investors relative to traditional preferred stock, it is likely that issuers have to pay a higher pretax yield on trust preferred stock than they would on comparable traditional preferred stock. Whether a firm can reduce its cost of capital by replacing traditional preferred stock with trust preferred stock depends on the size of the additional yield that must be paid on trust preferred stock compared with traditional preferred stock as well as the level of the firm's marginal tax rates. For example, suppose the firm had a marginal tax rate of 35% and could issue traditional preferred stock at a 6.5% yield. If it could issue comparable trust preferred stock at anything less than a 10% yield, the firm would reduce its after tax cost of capital by replacing the 6.5% traditional preferred stock with trust preferred stock. However, with the 2003 tax changes reducing the tax rate on traditional preferred stock dividends to 15% for individual shareholders, the spread between the yield required by trust preferred investors and that required by traditional preferred stock investors could widen, decreasing the attractiveness of trust preferred stock relative to traditional preferred stock.

Financial Reporting Treatment of Trust Preferred Stock

Until recently, trust preferred obligations were typically presented on the balance sheet as a separate line item between the liabilities and shareholders' equity section, often described as "obligations under mandatorily redeemable preferred securities of affiliate" or "minority interest in subsidiary companies." By being classified outside of the liability section of the balance sheet trust preferred stock had an advantage over otherwise similar subordinated debt. The favorable balance sheet treatment that trust preferred stock provided was likely instrumental to its popularity among many issuers. However, this popularity could be short-lived. The FASB issued a new standard in 2003 requiring most trust preferred stocks to be classified as liabilities on the issuer's balance sheet.[17]

Regulatory Treatment of Trust Preferred Stock

Many trust preferred issuers are regulated firms such as commercial banks, insurance companies, and utilities. How trust preferred stock is treated for regulatory purposes adds another consideration beyond its tax and GAAP treatment. For example, commercial banks are required to maintain certain minimum levels of capital as a percentage of total assets and risk-weighted assets, which take into account the varying levels of risk of different assets (e.g., cash is less risky than mortgage receivables). When trust preferreds were first developed, it was unclear whether the Federal Reserve would approve them as regulatory capital. On October 21, 1996, the Federal Reserve ruled that trust preferred stocks may be included in equity capital for regulatory purposes. This regulatory treatment appears to have been a de facto prerequisite for commercial banks to issue trust preferred stock, because no bank had issued trust preferred stock before the Federal Reserve's announcement, but within a couple weeks of the announcement banks issued billions of dollars of trust preferred stock. Most large money-center banks have a billion or more dollars of trust preferred stock outstanding. For some time now, the industry practice of banks has been to report trust preferred stock as a liability for financial accounting, so the FASB's recent pronouncement requiring liability treatment should not affect the attractiveness of trust preferred stock to banks. Banks may continue to find trust preferred stock attractive as long as it continues to receive favorable treatment from regulators.

Zero-Coupon Bonds

We could also consider zero-coupon bonds to be a hybrid security. Zero-coupon bonds get their name from the fact that they pay no periodic interest. Rather, they are issued at a deep discount to their maturity value and the discount represents the interest that essentially accrues to the investor over time. Zero-coupon bonds are senior to equity in cases of financial distress, like a conventional bond. Further, zero-coupon bonds generally have a fixed rate of return determined by the issue price, the maturity value,

---

[17]See "Accounting for Certain Financial Instruments with Characteristics of Both Liabilities and Equity" *Statement of Financial Accounting Standards No. 150* (Stamford, CT: FASB, May 2003).

and the years to maturity. Like stockholders, however, holders of zero-coupon bonds generally have no right to cash flows from the corporation until some time in the future: at maturity in the case of a zero-coupon bond and at liquidation in the case of common stock. Regardless of whether we consider them to be debt or a debt-equity hybrid, zero-coupon bonds are quite common in firms' capital structures and a great deal of misconception surrounds the taxation of zero-coupon bonds. The following discussion captures the essentials of how zero-coupon bonds are taxed. We then illustrate the taxation of zero-coupon bonds with a numerical example.

The taxation of zero-coupon bonds—and most bonds, really—closely mirrors their financial accounting treatment. The main question is what to do when the bond is issued at a price other than face value. When a bond is issued below face value, the difference between the face value and the issue price is called the **discount.** Conversely, when a bond is issued above face value, the difference between face value and issue price is called the **premium.** In financial accounting, discounts and premiums are amortized over the life of the bond using the constant-yield-to-maturity method. Because a discount represents deferred interest the firm will pay on the bond, as it is amortized it increases the firm's interest expense. Amortization of premiums reduce the firm's interest expense.

In taxation, when a bond is issued for less than its face value, the difference is called **original issue discount (OID).** Zero-coupon bonds are issued at a deep discount and nearly always have OID. Holders of bonds with OID must accrue interest income over the life of the bond using the constant-yield-to-maturity method, as they do under GAAP. Thus, an investor in a zero-coupon bond must recognize interest income and pay tax on that income, each year as the income accrues, even though she has received no cash. Similarly, the corporation issuing a zero-coupon bond takes interest deductions for the amortized OID each year even though it makes no cash payments until the bond matures.[18]

Another more subtle set of rules in taxation applies to what are called "market discounts." A **market discount** occurs if the price of the bond falls after issuance, meaning that interest rates increased after issuance, and the bond is sold to a new investor. Like OID, market discounts must be amortized over the remaining life of the bond. Unlike OID, holders of market discount bonds do not have to recognize amortized market discount as interest income. Rather, any capital gain realized upon maturity or disposition of the bond is reduced by the amortized market discount.

Example of Taxation of Zero-Coupon Bonds

Suppose a corporation issues a zero-coupon bond with a face value of $10,000 and a 10-year life when the market rate on such bonds is 10%. The bond will have an issue price of $3,855, which is simply the present value of $10,000 in 10 years at 10%.

The bond has $10,000 − $3,855.43 = $6,144.57 of original issue discount (OID).[19] The OID represents deferred interest. Over the life of the bond the issuing corporation

---

[18]The Tax Code allows, but does not require, investors to amortize bond premiums over the life of the bond. In most cases, investors would elect to amortize the premium because doing so will reduce their currently taxable income.

[19]OID can also occur in interest-bearing bonds if they are issued at less than face value. Some de minimus rules exclude small discounts from the OID rules.

will report $6,144.57 of interest deductions using the constant-yield-to-maturity method.

The investor has an original basis in the bond of $3,855.43. The investor will recognize a corresponding $6,144.57 of interest income over the life of the bond, assuming the investor holds the bond until maturity, using the same yield-to-maturity method. Even a cash basis investor must recognize interest income during the life of the bond. The investor's basis in the bond increases by the amount of interest income recognized. By the bond's maturity, the investor will have a $10,000 basis in the bond, so the maturity will produce no gain or loss.

The following bond amortization schedule as shown in Table 12.1 will help illustrate the taxation of zero-coupon bonds.

The amortization table works this way: The interest expense is simply the bond's carrying value at end of the prior period multiplied by the effective yield of 10%, or $3,855.43(10%). The bond's carrying value at the end of the period is the carrying value from the end of the prior period plus the accrued interest expense from the current period, for example, $3,855.43 + $385.54 = $4,240.97.

Suppose that, at the end of year 1, the original investor sold the bond to a new investor and suppose that market interest rates had not changed. The bond would sell for the carrying value in Table 12.1 of $4,240.97, which is equivalent to the present value of the $10,000 maturity for 9 years at 10%. The OID transfers with the bond so the new investor will recognize $10,000 − $4,240.97 = $5,759.03 of interest income over the remaining 9-year life of the bond.

But what would happen if the new investor purchased the bond for a price different than $4,240.97? Suppose that, at the end of year 1, market interest rates on comparable bonds had decreased to 8%. In this case, the bond would sell for $5,002.49, which is the present value of $10,000 in 9 years at 8%. The old investor will recognize a gain of $5,002.49 − $4,240.97 = $761.52. The new investor will take the bond with only $4,997.51 of OID to be amortized over the life of the bond ($10,000 − $5,002.49).

Instead suppose that, at the end of year 1, interest rates on comparable bonds had increased to 12%. In this case, the bond would sell for $3,606.10. The bond has a discount of $6,393.90, which is broken down into two parts. The first part is the $5,759.03

TABLE 12.1	Example of a Bond Amortization Table for a Zero-Coupon Bond	
Year	*Interest Expense/Revenue*	*Bond Carrying Value*
Issue		**3,855.43**
1	385.54	4,240.97
2	424.10	4,665.07
3	466.51	5,131.58
4	513.16	5,644.74
5	564.47	6,209.21
6	620.92	6,830.13
7	683.01	7,513.14
8	751.31	8,264.46
9	826.45	9,090.90
10	909.09	10,000.00

of OID the original investor had at the end of year 1 ($10,000 − $4,240.97). The new investor will have to recognize the OID as interest income over the remaining 9-year life of the bond per Table 12.1. The second part of the discount is $634.87 of "market discount" ($4,240.97 − $3,606.10).[20] The market discount is also amortized over the remaining 9-year life of the bond but is not recognized as interest income. Rather, the accumulated market discount amortization will recharacterize as ordinary income what would otherwise be capital gain when the new investor later sells the bond or redeems the bond at maturity.

For example, if the investor held the bond to maturity, his basis in the bond would equal his $3,606.10 purchase price plus the $5,759.03 from OID interest income recognized in years 2–10, for a basis of $9,365.13. Without the market discount rules, the investor would recognize a $634.87 capital gain at maturity. The market discount rules will recharacterize the $634.87 gain as ordinary income.

12.5 TAXATION OF DISTRIBUTIONS AND SHARE REPURCHASES

A **distribution** occurs when a corporation pays cash or property to its shareholders without requiring something in return. In contrast, a share repurchase or **redemption** occurs when a corporation pays cash or property to its shareholders and gets some of its outstanding stock back in return. We begin by explaining the taxation of distributions and note that most redemptions are taxed under sale or exchange treatment, meaning that the selling shareholders recognize a capital gain or loss on their sale of stock back to the corporation. However, some redemptions are treated as distributions for tax purposes in which each shareholder sells a fixed proportion of their stock back to the corporation, such that after the redemption each shareholder owns the same proportion of the corporation as before the redemption.

Distributions can be taxed in three ways:

1. As a **dividend,** in which case the distribution is taxable as ordinary income to the shareholder receiving it.
2. As a **return of capital,** in which case the distribution is nontaxable but does reduce the shareholder's basis in the corporation's stock by the amount of the distribution.
3. As a **capital gain.** If the distribution is large enough to reduce the shareholder's basis in the stock to zero, any remaining distribution is taxed as a capital gain to the shareholder.

EXAMPLE 1:
Rachel receives a $10,000 distribution on the 5,000 shares of Berkeley Corporation that she owns. Her basis in the Berkeley stock is $25,000. If the distribution is taxed as a dividend, Rachel will report $10,000 of ordinary income on her return and her basis in Berkeley is unchanged.

---

[20]Two side notes: First, the old (selling) investor will recognize a $634.87 capital loss when he sells the bond at the end of year 1. Second, market discount can also occur in interest-bearing bonds if they sell for less than face value in the secondary market.

EXAMPLE 2:
With the same facts as Example 1, now assume that the distribution is not treated as a dividend. The distribution is treated as a nontaxable return of capital, and Rachel's basis in her Berkeley stock is reduced to $15,000.

EXAMPLE 3:
With the same facts as Example 2, now assume that Rachel's basis in Berkeley was only $7,000 at the time of the distribution. In this case, the first $7,000 of the distribution is treated as a return of capital, bringing Rachel's basis in her Berkeley stock to zero. The remaining $3,000 of the distribution is treated as a capital gain.

Most, but certainly not all, distributions are taxed as dividends. Distributions to shareholders are not deductible by the corporation. In contrast, interest paid to debt holders generally is deductible to the corporation.

The Concept of Earnings and Profits

When are distributions taxed as dividends? When they are paid out of something called *earnings and profits,* or **E&P.** The two kinds of earnings and profits are current earnings and profits and accumulated earnings and profits. **Current earnings and profits** is the tax analog to net income, while **accumulated earnings and profits** is the tax analog to retained earnings.

While E&P and retained earnings are similar concepts, they are calculated somewhat differently. In particular, E&P is calculated using procedures specified in the tax law, while retained earnings is calculated using generally accepted accounting principles (GAAP).

Current E&P is computed by starting with taxable income and making a series of adjustments. Most of the adjustments are intuitive if one recognizes that the earnings and profits concept tends to lie somewhere in the middle of taxable income and GAAP-based income. Some of the common additions to taxable income include the following:

1. Municipal bond interest, which is tax exempt but does increase the firm's E&P as it does the firm's GAAP income.
2. Federal income tax refunds, from NOL carrybacks for example. These refunds are not taxable but do increase the firm's E&P as they do the firm's GAAP income.
3. The dividends received deduction, which reduces the firm's taxable income but does not affect the firm's E&P nor does it affect the firm's GAAP income.
4. A deduction from an NOL carryforward from a prior year. Such NOLs reduce the firm's taxable income but do not affect the firm's E&P (nor do they affect the firm's GAAP income).

Some of the common subtractions from taxable income include the following:

1. Federal income taxes paid, which do not reduce taxable income, but do reduce E&P as they do GAAP income.
2. Nondeductible fines and penalties. Although subtractions, these do not reduce taxable income; they do reduce E&P, as they do GAAP income.

Finally, some adjustments can be either positive or negative. For example, the depreciation methods allowable for E&P purposes are less generous than those used to compute taxable income. Therefore, in the early years of an asset's life, firms will typically have to add back a portion of the depreciation they recognized for regular tax purposes when computing E&P. In the latter years of an asset's life, E&P depreciation will exceed regular tax depreciation, resulting in a negative adjustment to E&P.

Each year the firm computes its current E&P as described. Accumulated E&P is the sum of all prior years' current earnings and profits reduced by distributions from E&P.

Distributions are taxable as dividends if the corporation has sufficient accumulated or current E&P to cover the distribution. If the distributing corporation does not have sufficient E&P, then the distribution is treated as a return of capital and as a capital gain once the shareholder's basis in the stock is reduced to zero.

EXAMPLE 1:
Weiss Inc. pays a $50,000 dividend during 2001. Weiss began 2001 with $5 million of accumulated E&P and generated $200,000 of current E&P during 2001. The $50,000 is taxed as a dividend.

EXAMPLE 2:
With the same facts as example 1, now assume Weiss began 2001 with a $1 million negative E&P. The $50,000 is still taxed as a dividend because Weiss has positive current E&P of sufficient size to cover the distribution.

EXAMPLE 3:
With the same facts as example 2, now assume Weiss has negative current E&P of $1,000. In this case, the $50,000 distribution is treated as a return of capital, not a dividend, since Weiss had negative current and accumulated E&P.

Most distributions are taxed as dividends. Complicated rules govern the allocation of E&P to dividends made during a year that does not have sufficient E&P to have all the distributions taxable as dividends, and such rules are beyond the scope of this text.

As a practical matter, corporations are often lax about keeping the calculations of their E&P account up-to-date when they know they have positive E&P, in the same manner that individuals are often lax about balancing their checkbooks when they know they have enough money in their account to cover their expenses. Sometimes a corporation finds itself making a distribution that it suspects is not covered by E&P, such as distributions made after several years of losses. In such cases, corporations will often hire an accounting firm to do an "E&P study," reconstructing the corporation's E&P from the time the last E&P calculation was made, which may date back to the formation of the corporation to the present. Such studies, while profitable for the accounting firms, can be tedious, because they require the accountants to learn tax laws that may have been repealed decades earlier but are still relevant for computing the E&P arising from those years.

Special Kinds of Distributions

Occasionally, firms pay distributions in the form of property instead of cash. **Property distributions** are taxed the same way as cash distributions, except that the corporation must recognize a gain but cannot recognize a loss on the property as it leaves the corporation. If property distributions were not taxed, it would be easy for corporations to avoid double taxation of their earnings. Losses on property distributions are not deductible because, if they were, problems could arise with corporations and their shareholders setting unreasonably low valuations on the property to generate tax losses at the corporate level. The gain is the difference between the property's fair market value and the property's basis, and the gain may be capital or ordinary depending on property. The shareholder takes a basis in the property received equal to the fair market value of the property.

EXAMPLE:
Mills Corp. distributes property with a basis of $10,000 and a fair market value of $30,000 to a shareholder in lieu of a cash dividend. Mills Corp. will recognize a $20,000 gain. The shareholder will recognize $30,000 of dividend income and will take a $30,000 basis in the property received.

Constructive dividends occur when shareholders receive some benefit without the firm declaring a formal dividend. Most common in closely held firms, constructive dividends include, among other things, unreasonably large compensation to a shareholder-employee, shareholder use of corporate property such as a corporate jet, and below-market loans to shareholders. Constructive dividends are taxed the same as dividends if the firm has sufficient current or accumulated E&P.

EXAMPLE:
John owns all of the stock of Scott Corp. During the year, Scott Corp. pays John a $150,000 salary for managerial duties. John reports $150,000 of wage income on his return and Scott Corp. reports $150,000 of deductions for wages paid on its corporate tax return. Following an IRS audit, it is determined that John's reasonable compensation would have been $40,000. John will be treated as having received $40,000 of wage income and $110,000 of dividend income. (In most cases this distribution will give John the same tax outcome as $150,000 of wage income.) Scott Corp. will only be able to deduct $40,000 of wages paid, because dividends are not deductible to corporations. Dividends are deductible from E&P, so Scott Corp. will reduce its E&P account by $150,000, or $40,000 + $110,000.

Stock dividends occur when the corporation distributes additional stock to its existing shareholders. For example, a shareholder with 10 shares will receive 1 additional share if the firm issues a 10% stock dividend.[21] Notice that the shareholder's proportionate interest in the firm is not affected by the stock dividend. The corporate "pie" simply is sliced into thinner pieces, but the corporation has no more or less cash or resources after the stock dividend than before the stock dividend. Realizing that a stock dividend is essentially a nonevent, the Tax Code treats most stock dividends as

---

[21]Stock splits rely on essentially the same idea. For example, in a two-for-one stock split, a shareholder with 10 shares of stock will be given an additional 10 shares, for a total of 20 shares.

nonevents.[22] Returning to our example, assume the shareholder had a $5.50 basis in each of his 10 shares of stock. Following the 10% stock dividend, he will allocate his $55 of basis across 11 shares, for $5 of basis per share.

Distributions of **stock rights,** also known as warrants, are also generally nontaxable. If the fair market value of the rights is less than 15% of the value of the stock, then the rights have a zero basis unless the shareholder elects to allocate her stock basis across her stock and rights. If the fair market value of the rights is 15% or more of the value of the stock, then the shareholder must allocate her stock basis across her stock and rights. Such an allocation would be done based on the relative fair market value of the stock and the rights.

Taxation of Share Repurchases

A redemption occurs when the corporation repurchases some of its outstanding stock from its shareholders. In many cases, redemptions are accorded "sale or exchange" treatment for tax purposes. If so, the shareholders selling their stock have a capital gain or loss, calculated in the same manner as if they had sold their stock to a third party.

> **EXAMPLE 1:**
> Jo owns 1,000 shares of Hawkeye Inc., each share with a $2 basis for a total basis of $2,000. Hawkeye repurchases 200 of Jo's shares for $500. Jo recognizes a $100 capital gain ($500 − $400), which will be long-term or short-term depending on whether Jo's holding period in the stock is greater than or less than 12 months.

In some cases, however, redemptions are treated as dividends under the tax law.

> **EXAMPLE 2:**
> Building on example 1, if Jo was the sole owner of Hawkeye, then Jo would own 100% of Hawkeye before and after the redemption. A redemption and a dividend would have essentially the same economic effect—$500 of cash going from Jo's corporation (Hawkeye) to Jo, with Jo controlling 100% of Hawkeye the entire time—so the Tax Code would treat such a redemption as a dividend. Accordingly, Jo would recognize $500 of dividend (ordinary) income, assuming Hawkeye had sufficient E&P. Jo's original $2,000 basis would be spread across the remaining 800 Hawkeye shares for a new basis of $2.50 per share.

For a redemption to qualify for sale or exchange treatment it must fall under one of the following categories (Sections 302 and 303):

1. Distributions not essentially equivalent to a dividend
2. Substantially disproportionate distributions
3. Distributions in termination of a shareholder's interest
4. Certain distributions in partial liquidation
5. Distributions to pay a shareholder's death taxes

---

[22]In rare cases, stock dividends are taxable to their recipients. Generally this adverse treatment occurs if the stock dividend is designed to alter the shareholders' proportionate interests in the firm, such as having preferred shareholders receive common stock, or vice versa.

Redemptions that do not qualify under one of these categories are treated as dividends (assuming sufficient E&P).

Perhaps the most common provision giving rise to sale or exchange treatment is the disproportionate distribution provision in Section 302(b)(2). To be substantially disproportionate, the shareholder's ownership in the corporation after the redemption must be less than 80% of his interest before the redemption, and the shareholder must own less than 50% of the combined voting power in the corporation. Attribution rules apply, however, in determining the change in ownership and voting power. The specifics of such rules are beyond the scope of this text, but they generally require a shareholder's interest to include those of his spouse, children and grandchildren, parents, and in certain cases shares held by partnerships, corporations, and estates or trusts related to him.

EXAMPLE:

Suppose a husband and wife each owned 50% of a corporation and one-half of the husband's shares were redeemed by the corporation. For the purposes of determining whether the redemption will get sale or exchange treatment, the husband would be treated as having owned 100% of the corporation before and after the redemption, because all of his wife's shares are treated as his and vice versa.

When a redemption qualifies for sale or exchange treatment, the corporation generally reduces its E&P in proportion to the amount of stock redeemed. For example, if 10% of a corporation's stock is redeemed, generally the corporation will reduce its E&P account by 10%.

12.6 TAX PLANNING USING THE TAX RULES FOR DISTRIBUTIONS AND SHARE REPURCHASES

Individual shareholders tend to prefer sale or exchange treatment to dividend treatment because they have the opportunity to have their gain taxed at capital gains rates rather than ordinary rates. Further, only the portion of the proceeds from the redemption in excess of the basis is taxed under sale or exchange treatment, while the entire proceeds are taxed under dividend treatment. Corporate shareholders, however, may prefer dividend treatment for a redemption because corporations are only taxable on a portion of dividend income due to the dividends received deduction. The rules governing the taxation of share repurchases are designed to make it difficult to get sale or exchange treatment to prevent abuse by disguising dividends as share repurchases for the benefit of individual shareholders. Consequently, corporations who want to divest ownership in another firm have opportunities to use the Tax Code against itself by purposely failing the preceding rules and having a redemption be taxed as a dividend. Seagram did this on a massive scale in 1995, saving about $1.5 billion in taxes on the sale of its stake in DuPont. Congress was not pleased. The $1.5 billion tax loss to the government from this *single* transaction represented about 1% of the total corporate taxes collected that year. Without getting into the particulars of the legislative "fix" since enacted by Congress, the Seagram–DuPont strategy will not work under current law, at least not using the same structure as Seagram and DuPont used.[23]

12.7 TAXATION OF LIQUIDATIONS

A corporation liquidates by paying off its liabilities and then distributing all of its assets to its shareholders in exchange for their stock. The corporation then goes out of existence. In keeping with the principle of double taxation of corporations, two layers of tax are levied. First, Section 336 provides that the corporation will recognize all unrealized gains and losses on property distributed in liquidation. For example, if the corporation distributed a piece of land to a shareholder in liquidation and the land had a basis and fair market value of $100 and $150, respectively, then the corporation would recognize a $50 gain. It is common in liquidation for the firm to sell its assets for cash and then to distribute the after-tax proceeds to the shareholders. In that case the corporate layer of taxation occurs naturally as with any other sale of assets.

The second layer of taxation occurs at the shareholder level. The shareholders will recognize a capital gain or loss (long-term if they held their stock more than 1 year) on the difference between the fair market value of the cash and property they get from the corporation and the basis of the stock in the corporation that they surrender, as based on Section 331. For example, if Joe received $20 cash and $90 of property from the corporation and gave up stock that had a basis of $70, then Joe would recognize a $20 + $90 − $70 = $40 gain. Joe would take a $90 basis in the property received. Note that the corporation's E&P does not affect the taxation of the liquidating distribution.

Parent-Subsidiary Liquidations

The Tax Code contains several provisions that recognize that parents and subsidiaries are essentially a single economic entity. For example, the consolidated return rules generally allow a parent's losses to offset the income of its subsidiary, and vice versa. A similar set of provisions is found in Section 332, which allows parents to liquidate their subsidiaries without recognizing gain or loss.

To qualify under Section 332, the parent must own at least 80% of the total voting power of the subsidiary and at least 80% of the value of the subsidiary's stock. If the liquidation qualifies under Section 332, the rules are designed to put the parent into the shoes of the subsidiary. Specifically, the subsidiary recognizes no gain or loss upon liquidation under Section 332, while the parent takes a carryover basis in the assets of the subsidiary it receives. Similarly, the subsidiary's net operating loss carryovers, capital loss carryovers, and E&P transfer to the parent.

Summary of Key Points

1. The hallmark of corporate taxation is double taxation of corporate profits. Earnings of a corporation are taxed once at the corporate level and again at the shareholder level when the corporation pays dividends.
2. Corporate formations are usually nontaxable events under Section 351.

---

[23]For a detailed analysis of the Seagram–DuPont deal, see Erickson and Wang (1999) and Willens (1994, 1995).

3. Many similarities can be noted between GAAP and taxable income, but many book-tax differences also separate items such as depreciation and municipal bond income.
4. Corporations pay the same tax rate on capital gains as they do on ordinary income.
5. The dividends received deduction causes corporations to be only partially taxable on dividends that they receive from other corporations.
6. Whether leverage provides a tax benefit and, if so, how large the tax benefit is, has been a topic of controversy in finance for decades. The most recent research is consistent with a tax gain from leverage existing, but more research is needed to understand how large the gain from leverage is.
7. Many capital structure alternatives are available in addition to common stock and debt. Traditional preferred stock is like debt in that it has a fixed payment. It is treated as equity for tax purposes, so that the issuer cannot deduct dividends on straight preferred stock. Dividends on traditional preferred stock are taxed at low rates to both individual and corporate shareholders.
8. Trust preferred stock is treated as debt for tax purposes. Payments on trust preferred stock are tax deductible to the issuer as is interest expense and are taxable to the investor. Corporate investors are not eligible for the dividends received deduction on trust preferred stock. Trust preferred stock counts as Tier 1 equity capital for banks. In the past trust preferred stock has been presented between the liability and equity section for financial reporting purposes. In 2003 the FASB issued new rules requiring most trust preferred stock to be classified as a liability on the balance sheet.
9. Zero-coupon bonds are treated much the same for tax purposes as they are for GAAP purposes. The difference between the issue price and the maturity value is called original issue discount (OID). OID represents the interest component that accrues over the life of the bond. Issuers deduct OID interest expense over the life of the bond under the constant-yield-to-maturity method, while investors are taxable on OID interest income using the same method.
10. A distribution occurs when a corporation pays cash or property to its shareholders without requiring anything in return. Distributions can result in dividend, return of capital, or capital gains treatment, but dividend treatment is the most common.
11. A redemption occurs when a corporation repurchases some of its outstanding stock from its shareholders. Most redemptions are taxed under sale or exchange treatment, meaning that the selling shareholder reports a capital gain or loss for the difference between the selling price and the stock basis.
12. Liquidations occur when the corporation distributes all of its property to its shareholders in exchange for all of its outstanding stock. Liquidations are taxable to both the corporation and the shareholders. Liquidations of subsidiaries are an exception and are generally nontaxable to both the parent and subsidiary.

Discussion Questions

1. From an economic policy perspective, do you think the provisions in Section 351 that allow nontaxable corporate formation are desirable? Why or why not?
2. What is the dividends received deduction? Why did Congress allow such a deduction?
3. Do parent corporations generally prefer to file consolidated tax returns with their subsidiaries as opposed to filing separate returns? Why or why not?
4. According to Miller's (1977) paper, leverage does not increase firm value, even though interest expense on debt is tax deductible by corporations. Why?
5. Taking the perspective of a corporation that is raising capital, why would the pre-tax cost of equity and debt capital differ, other than because of differences in risk?

6. Why is it so difficult to measure the effects (if any) that taxes have on the pretax returns of assets?

7. What is trust preferred stock? What advantages does it have over plain vanilla preferred stock?

8. Many large banks have issued billions of dollars of trust preferred stock. Why do banks more so than, say, manufacturing firms appear to like trust preferred stock as a source of capital?

9. When a corporation repurchases shares of its stock from investors, do individual shareholders generally prefer the repurchase to be treated as a dividend for tax purposes or do they prefer it to be treated as a sale? What do corporate shareholders prefer? Why?

10. What are constructive dividends? Do you think constructive dividends are more likely to occur in large publicly traded corporations or small privately held corporations? Why?

Exercises

1. Which of the following scenarios will qualify under Section 351 as a nontaxable corporate formation? For those that do not qualify, what requirement of Section 351 do they violate?
   a. Ginger, Mary Ann, and Mrs. Howell form GMH Corp. Ginger contributes memorabilia in exchange for 40% of GMH's stock, Mary Ann contributes farmland in exchange for 30% of GMH, and Mrs. Howell contributes cash in exchange for the remaining 30%.
   b. Clyde founded ABC Corp. in 1998 and owns all of ABC's 1,000 shares of outstanding stock. In 2000, ABC issues 300 shares of new stock to Bonnie in exchange for land that Bonnie owned. Will Bonnie's contribution qualify under Section 351?
   c. With the same facts as part (b), now ABC issues 4,500 shares of new stock to Bonnie in exchange for Bonnie's land.
   d. Bert and Ernie form Duckie Corp. in late 1999. Bert contributes $10,000 cash in exchange for 60% of Duckie's stock, while Ernie contributes services in exchange for the remaining 40% of Duckie.

2. Conan and Andy decide to form a new corporation, LN Corp. Conan contributes property with a basis of $10,000 and a fair market value of $18,000 in exchange for 5 shares of LN stock and $13,000 in cash, which LN borrows from a bank to finance. Andy contributes property with a basis of $35,000 and a fair market value of $80,000 in exchange for 80 shares of LN stock.
   a. How much taxable gain or loss will Conan recognize as a result of the transaction?
   b. What basis will Conan take in the LN stock he receives?

3. Tar Heel Inc. pays $100,000 of dividends in 2000, with $25,000 going to your client, Mr. Big. Tar Heel began 2000 with $120,000 in accumulated earnings and profits and had $10,000 of current earnings and profits in 2000. Mr. Big has a $40,000 basis in his Tar Heel stock.
   a. How much dividend income will Mr. Big report from Tar Heel in 2000? What will Mr. Big's basis in Tar Heel be after the dividend?
   b. Assume instead that Tar Heel began 2000 with a $2,000 deficit balance in its earnings and profits account, but did have $10,000 of current earnings and profits for 2000. How much dividend income will Mr. Big report from Tar Heel in 2000?

4. At the beginning of year 1 GE issues a 10-year zero-coupon bond to Larry with a face value of $10,000 when the market rate on such bonds is 10%. The bond has an

issue price of $3,855, which is simply the present value of $10,000 in 10 years at 10%. Suppose that at the end of year 1 interest rates on comparable bonds had increased to 12%. Larry sells the bond to Joe for $3,606.10, which is simply the present value of the bond's remaining cash flows discounted at 12%.

   a. How much income, if any, will Joe have to report on his tax return for year 2 assuming he holds the bond the entire year?

   b. How much market discount will the GE bond have at the beginning of year 2 in the hands of Joe?

5. DMM Corporation is a diversified U.S. firm that has ownership stakes in two other U.S. corporations. Specifically, DMM Corporation owns 60% of the outstanding stock of TaxShelter.com and 10% of the outstanding stock of Litigation.com. During the year 2000, DMM Corporation itself had $10 million of taxable income, while TaxShelter.com and Litigation.com had $2 million and $3 million net operating losses, respectively. Neither TaxShelter.com nor Litigation.com have ever reported positive taxable income and neither pays any dividends. How much taxable income will DMM Corporation report on its 2000 consolidated tax return?

6. Which of the following are typical features of trust preferred stock, also known as monthly income preferred stock (MIPS)?

   a. Treated as debt on the issuer's GAAP balance sheet.

   b. Corporate recipients of trust preferred dividends are eligible for the dividends received deduction.

   c. Trust preferred stock is thought to have a greater pretax yield than traditional preferred stock of similar risk.

   d. Trust preferred stock dividends are deductible to the issuer.

   e. Trust preferred stock counts as Tier 1 capital for banks.

7. In late 2000, George, Al, and Ralph each contribute property to form GAJ Corporation. George contributes oil wells with a fair market value of $450,000 and a basis of $100,000 and receives 45% of the stock of GAJ. Al contributes $100,000 cash and networking equipment with a fair market value and tax basis of $350,000, receiving 45% of the stock of GAJ. Ralph contributes a collection of vintage automobiles with a fair market value of $150,000 and tax basis of $130,000 in exchange for 10% of the stock of GAJ and $50,000 cash. What tax basis will each take in their respective GAJ stock?

References and Additional Readings

A discussion of book-tax differences.

Guenther, D., S. Nutter, and E. Maydew, 1997. "Financial Reporting, Tax Costs, and Book-Tax Conformity," *Journal of Accounting and Economics,* pp. 225–248.

Hanlon, M., 2003a. "What Can We Infer About a Firm's Taxable Income From Its Financial Statements?" *National Tax Journal,* pp. 831–864.

Hanlon, M., 2003b. "The Persistence and Pricing of Earnings, Accruals, and Cash Flows When Firms Have Large Book-Tax Differences." Working paper. University of Michigan, Ann Arbor, MI.

Hanlon, M., S. Kelly, and T. Shevlin, 2003. "Evidence on the Possible Information Loss of Conforming Book Income and Taxable Income." Working paper. University of Washington, Seattle, WA and University of Michigan, Ann Arbor, MI.

Kieso, D., J. Weygandt, and T. Warfield, 2004. *Intermediate Accounting,* 11th edition. New York: Wiley.

Mills, L., 1998. "Book-Tax Differences and Internal Revenue Service Adjustments," *Journal of Accounting Research,* pp. 343–356.

Mills, L., and G. Plesko, 2003. "Bridging the Reporting Gap: A Proposal for More

Informative Reconciling of Book and Tax Income," *National Tax Journal,* pp. 865–893.

Shevlin, T., 2002. "Corporate Tax Shelters and Book-Tax Differences," *Tax Law Review,* pp. 427–443.

The theory and evidence of the tax benefits of leverage.

Brealey, R., and S. Myers, 2003. *Principles of Corporate Finance,* 7th edition. New York: McGraw-Hill.

Collins, J., and D. Shackelford, 1992. "Foreign Tax Credit Limitations and Preferred Stock Issuances," *Journal of Accounting Research,* pp. 103–124.

DeAngelo, H., and R. Masulis, 1980. "Optimal Capital Structure under Corporate Taxation," *Journal of Financial Economics* (March), pp. 5–29.

Dhaliwal, D., R. Trezevant, and S. Wang, 1992. "Taxes, Investment-Related Tax Shields, and Capital Structure," *Journal of the American Taxation Association,* pp. 1–21.

Engel, E., M. Erickson, and E. Maydew, 1999. "Debt-Equity Hybrid Securities," *Journal of Accounting Research,* pp. 249–274.

Fama, E., and K. French, 1998. "Taxes, Financing Decisions, and Firm Value," *Journal of Finance* 53 (June), 819–843.

Graham, J., 1996. "Debt and the Marginal Tax Rate," *Journal of Financial Economics,* 41–74.

Graham, J., 2000. "How Big Are the Tax Benefits of Debt?" *Journal of Finance,* pp. 1901–1941.

Graham, J., 2003. "Taxes and Corporate Finance: A Review," *Review of Financial Studies,* pp. 1074–1128.

Graham, J., M. Lang, and D. Shackelford, 2004. "Employee Stock Options, Corporate Taxes and Debt Policy," *Journal of Finance,* forthcoming.

Mackie-Mason, J., 1990. "Do Taxes Affect Corporate Financing Decisions?" *Journal of Finance* (December), pp. 1471–1493.

Miller, M., 1977. "Debt and Taxes," *Journal of Finance* (May), pp. 261–276.

Miller, M., and F. Modigliani, 1966. "Some Estimates of the Cost of Capital in the Electric Utility Industry, 1954–57," *American Economic Review* (June), pp. 333–391.

Modigliani, F., and M. Miller, 1958. "The Cost of Capital, Corporation Finance and the Theory of Investment," *American Economic Review* (June), pp. 261–297.

Modigliani, F., and M. Miller, 1963. "Corporate Income Taxes and the Cost of Capital: A Correction," *American Economic Review* (June), pp. 433–443.

Myers, S., 1984. "The Capital Structure Puzzle," *Journal of Finance,* pp. 575–592.

Scholes, M., M. Wolfson, and P. Wilson, 1990. "Tax Planning, Regulatory Capital Planning, and Financial Reporting Strategy for Commercial Banks," *Review of Financial Studies,* pp. 625–650.

Shevlin, T., 1987. "Taxes and Off-Balance Sheet Financing: Research and Development Limited Partnerships," *The Accounting Review,* pp. 480–509.

Shevlin, T., 1990. "Estimating Corporate Marginal Tax Rates with Asymmetric Tax Treatment of Gains and Losses," *Journal of the American Taxation Association,* pp. 51–67. (Not a capital structure paper, it does provide the basis for Graham's marginal tax rate estimates.)

A paper addressing the effects of taxation on the pricing of preferred stocks.

Erickson, M., and E. Maydew, 1998. "Implicit Taxes in High Dividend Yield Stocks," *The Accounting Review,* pp. 435–458.

A discussion of the Seagram–DuPont transaction.

Erickson, M., and S. Wang, 1999. "Exploiting and Sharing Tax Benefits: Seagram and DuPont," *Journal of the American Taxation Association,* pp. 35–54.

Willens, R., 1994. "Strategies for Divesting Equity Stakes in a Hostile Tax Environment," *Journal of Taxation* (August), pp. 88–93.

Willens, R., 1995. "DuPont/Seagram: Every Action Has an Equal and Opposite Overreaction," *Tax Notes* (June 5), pp. 1367–1371.

13 INTRODUCTION TO MERGERS, ACQUISITIONS, AND DIVESTITURES

After completing this chapter, you should be able to:

1. Understand the basic types of taxable acquisitions of freestanding C corporations.

2. Understand the basic types of tax-free acquisitions of freestanding C corporations.

3. Describe the basic options available to divest a portion of a corporation.

4. Explain the major tax implications of various acquisition and divestiture methods.

5. Describe major nontax issues associated with acquisition and divestiture methods.

6. Realize when goodwill is tax deductible and when it is not tax deductible.

This chapter* is the first in a series on mergers, acquisitions, and divestitures. We begin here with an overview of the economics of corporate reorganizations from the tax planner's vantage point. The next chapter concentrates on taxable acquisitions, where a freestanding C corporation's stock or assets are purchased by another corporation. Included in Chapter 15 is an analysis of taxable acquisitions of S corporations, a conduit-type entity. The fourth chapter in the series concentrates on tax-free acquisitions of freestanding C corporations. Such mergers and acquisitions may be effected without either a change in the basis of assets inside the corporation *or* a tax on target shareholders. Chapter 16 also considers the effects of an acquisition on a corporation's tax attributes, such as net operating loss carryforwards (NOLs). Chapter 17 analyzes various divestiture techniques including spin-offs, equity carve-outs and subsidiary sales.[1] Throughout the latter three chapters in this series, we focus

---

*Some of the material in this chapter and the next four is influenced by the writings of Martin Ginsburg and Jack Levin, notably their *Mergers, Acquisitions and Buyouts* texts (Little, Brown and Co. 1995; Aspen Publishers, Inc. 1999, 2001).

[1]In a spin-off, the divesting firm is separated into two entities tax-free. An equity carve-out is the sale of the stock of a subsidiary by a parent corporation. Equity carve-outs are also referred to as subsidiary IPOs. In a subsidiary sale, the divesting firm sells the stock or assets of a subsidiary to an acquirer, typically for cash.

on the tax and nontax costs and benefits of various acquisition and divestiture structures. We also provide a rigorous introduction to the most salient tax rules and regulations associated with mergers, acquisitions, and divestitures in each chapter. We do so because, in our opinion, readers without such knowledge will be unable to take full advantage of the tax planning framework we have used to build this text.

13.1 OVERVIEW OF ISSUES

What drives mergers, acquisitions, and divestitures? What are the major types of mergers, acquisitions, and divestitures? In this section, we provide answers to both questions.

Reasons for Mergers, Acquisitions, and Divestitures

At least three broad reasons can be given for acquisitions: (1) to improve economic efficiency, (2) to extend the power base of management, and (3) to effect transfers of wealth from one class of stakeholders to another. In the camp that stresses the improvement of economic efficiency, the arguments typically refer to the advantages of integration to achieve economies of scale and/or scope and gains that result from removing inefficient management.

The second camp stresses that many acquisitions stem from managerial demand for power, larger salaries, and job security, or more broadly, management self-interest triumphs over the interest of society. This argument arises particularly often in explaining conglomerate mergers, which proliferated in the second half of the 1960s. Because of this alleged self-interest, management wastes corporate resources acquiring other firms.

The third camp emphasizes how a change in corporate control can cause a transfer of some of the wealth of target corporation bondholders, employees, and other stakeholders to target shareholders. One way to accomplish such a wealth transfer is to increase leverage, thereby increasing the risk of default to creditors, such as bondholders, bank lenders, and employees who have been promised certain unfunded benefits such as postretirement health care, without increasing the level of promised payments. The wealth transfer may be also accomplished by canceling unwritten promises to employees, suppliers, customers, or the community to provide certain future benefits for which the firm has already received economic consideration.[2]

In a variation on this theme, some in the academic research community and in the financial press have argued that mergers and acquisitions are motivated by a desire to transfer wealth from stockholders, creditors, and employees to the investment banking community. Investment banking fees in a large deal can easily run into the tens of millions of dollars. These fees, however, remain a small fraction of the value of the assets restructured, and are small relative to the typical merger premium that target shareholders enjoy when a purchaser buys them out.

---

[2]For example, canceling a labor contract that is favorable to employees results in a wealth transfer to the owners of the company. Selling a factory that received special tax benefits at the time it was built transfers those benefits to the seller (target shareholders). These topics are covered in detail in many corporate finance textbooks.

Firms are motivated to divest for several reasons. The financial press typically argues that divestitures allow management to focus on core competencies. For this reason, the market typically views such divestitures as wealth-increasing for divesting parent shareholders. Others in academia and the financial press argue that a divestiture, particularly a spin-off, frees managers of the divested business to focus on the divested firm. Divesting parent managers occasionally motivate these divestitures with claims of market mispricing. Specifically, management or investment bankers claim that a particular segment of a firm's business is adversely affecting the pricing of the entire concern. Some financial analysts believe that divestitures solve this mispricing. Finally, management and financial analysts argue that greater access to capital markets motivates some corporate restructuring transactions.

Prior to the Tax Reform Act of 1986 (TRA 86), legislators, academics, and members of the financial press claimed that taxes motivated mergers and acquisitions. TRA 86 eliminated many of the potential tax benefits available in a merger or acquisition, particularly if the acquisition involved a **freestanding C corporation,** which is a regular corporation that is not 80% or more owned by another corporation.[3] Specifically, prior to 1987, in some acquisitions of freestanding C corporations, the tax benefits from a step-up in the tax basis of a target's assets exceeded the tax costs of obtaining the benefits.[4] A **step-up** occurs when the tax basis of a target's assets are written up in value to the purchase price. Since 1986, however, the tax cost of obtaining a step-up in the acquisition of a freestanding C corporation is nearly always greater than the tax benefits from the step-up. Tax benefits from a step-up in the target's assets are still available in acquisitions of subsidiaries of C corporations and in acquisitions of conduit entities such as S corporations. We mention these facts here because readers have probably heard about the importance of a step-up in an acquisition. However, in our experience, most students are unfamiliar with the intertemporal and interorganizational differences in the taxation of acquisitions along this dimension, or the viability of a step-up structure. Prior to 1987, the transfer of target firm NOLs to an acquiring firm could provide tax benefits. With TRA 86, postacquisition limitations on target firm NOLs have drastically reduced any potential tax benefits from the acquisition of these tax attributes.

Types of Mergers, Acquisitions, and Divestitures[5]

Acquisitions of freestanding companies can be structured to be taxable or tax-free. The status of a transaction (taxable or tax-free) defines the tax treatment of the transaction for the target's shareholders. Generally, the tax status of an acquisition is

---

[3]C corporations are so-called regular corporations and include but are not limited to the types that are traded on the NYSE and the NASDAQ, such as IBM, General Motors, Intel, Microsoft, and the like. Many privately held corporations are also C corporations. Recall, C corporations are taxed at the entity level on earnings, and their owners are also taxed on distributions from the corporation.

[4]The tax benefits from a step-up are derived from the increased depreciation available from the higher (stepped-up) basis of the target's assets in the acquirer's hands. Increased depreciation deductions reduce tax liabilities and therefore increase cash flow.

[5]The terms *merger* and *acquisition* are used synonymously. Some types of divestitures are also accurately referred to as acquisitions by the acquiring firm. For example, the sale of a subsidiary is a divestiture to the divesting parent firm at the same time that it is an acquisition by the acquiring firm. We do not distinguish between mergers and acquisitions in this text. We do however distinguish between the tax treatments used in various types of transactions. Readers should focus on the tax structures we discuss and not the common names applied to the transactions.

determined by whether the acquirer uses cash or stock to acquire the target. When the acquirer uses mostly stock, the transaction is usually tax-free. Tax-free is a misnomer; these transactions merely provide tax deferral until the stock received is sold for cash. Conversely, when cash is used to acquire the target firm, the deal is taxable.

A freestanding company can acquire other freestanding companies such as happened in the WorldCom/MCI merger, or it can acquire a subsidiary of another company, for example, Triarc's acquisition of Snapple from Quaker Oats. The tax status of an acquisition of another company's subsidiary can also be either taxable or tax-free. Unlike acquisitions of freestanding companies where the seller could be an individual or a tax-exempt entity, the selling shareholder in a subsidiary sale is a corporation. Several other significant factors differentiate the tax treatment of subsidiary sales and sales of freestanding corporations, which we discuss in Chapters 14 and 16. Recognizing the tax differences in acquisitions of subsidiaries and freestanding corporations is critical.

A corporation that wishes to divest a subsidiary, but does not wish to sell the entire subsidiary to another company, has several options. Most commonly the corporation can divest the subsidiary in a tax-free spin-off. A spin-off results in the division of the parent corporation into two or more distinct corporations, tax-free. Shareholders of the combined entity receive new shares in the spun-off subsidiary and after the transaction is completed, they own the stock of the newly spun-off business and the former combined entity, less the divested subsidiary. Another type of divestiture involves the sale of a portion of the equity of a subsidiary. In this type of divestiture, known as an equity carve-out, a divesting parent typically sells a noncontrolling equity stake of the subsidiary for cash to investors.

13.2 MAJOR TAX ISSUES ASSOCIATED WITH MERGERS, ACQUISITIONS, AND DIVESTITURES

Five major tax issues are associated with a merger, acquisition, or divestiture.

1. Will the restructuring transaction result in a tax on the selling firm's shareholders? In the case of a divestiture, will the transaction result in an immediate tax on the shareholders of the divesting corporation?
2. How will the acquisition or divestiture affect the tax attributes (for example, NOLs, tax credits) of the target firm or the divested business?
3. Will the restructuring transaction result in a taxable gain or loss at the selling or divesting corporation level?
4. Will the restructuring transaction result in a change in the tax basis of the assets of the target or the divested subsidiary?
5. Will the use of leverage in an acquisition generate tax savings?

Shareholder Tax Liabilities

In any type of acquisition or divestiture, selling shareholder tax consequences often influence the structure of the transaction and perhaps the pretax value of the deal. We briefly discuss the tax implications for selling shareholders in various types of mergers, acquisitions, and divestitures here.

Mergers and Acquisitions

A merger or acquisition can be taxable or tax-free. In a taxable transaction, target shareholders receive cash from the acquirer in exchange for the stock of the target firm.[6] Target shareholders recognize a taxable gain on the transaction equal to the difference between the purchase price and their basis in the stock of the target. If shareholders are individuals—not corporations or tax-exempt entities—and they have owned the stock for more than 12 months, the gain on the sale is a long-term capital gain and is taxed at 15% under current law.[7]

For an acquisition to be tax-free, it must meet several statutory requirements. Most notably, target shareholders must maintain a **continuity of interest** in the combined entity. For practical purposes, the continuity of interest test is met if 50% of the total consideration paid for the target company's equity is acquiring firm stock. If the transaction qualifies as tax-free, target shareholders do not recognize a gain or loss on the exchange of target shares for acquirer shares. However, if target shareholders receive cash from the acquirer, that cash triggers a taxable gain. It is important to note that transactions that are tax-free overall can nonetheless result in a taxable gain for target shareholders to the extent they receive cash.

Divestitures

If the divesting parent sells a division or subsidiary to another corporation for cash, the transaction will be taxable to the divesting corporation. But, unless the divesting corporation distributes the proceeds of the subsidiary sale to its shareholders, no taxable gain or loss is recognized by the divesting corporation's shareholders.[8] If the divesting corporation separates into two or more entities and distributes stock in the new entities to its shareholders in a spin-off, no gain or loss is recognized by shareholders receiving the distribution.[9] If the divesting corporation sells some of the stock of a subsidiary in an initial public offering—a so-called equity carve-out—usually no taxable gain is recognized by the divesting corporation and no taxable gain or loss is recognized by shareholders of the divesting corporation.

Effect on Tax Attributes

Corporations have a large array of tax attributes—net operating losses, various types of tax credits, bases in the stock and assets of subsidiaries, to name a few. In a merger or acquisition these attributes may either be eliminated or survive. Whether the attributes survive is determined by the **tax structure** of an acquisition. In a divestiture, the tax attributes of the divested corporation always survive. These surviving tax attributes

---

[6]It is unusual for an acquirer to purchase the assets of a freestanding target firm rather than its stock, particularly since TRA 86. Taxable asset acquisitions after 1986 result in two levels of tax, corporate and shareholder, and these tax costs generally overwhelm the tax benefits derived from stepping-up the tax basis of the target's assets in a taxable asset acquisition.

[7]For ease of exposition, we assume that the marginal capital gains tax rate is the current top capital gains tax rate (15%). From 1997 to 2003, the top capital gains rate was 20%. Between 1987 and 1997, the top capital gains tax rate for individual shareholders was 28%. Before 1987, the top capital gains tax rate was 20%.

[8]If the divesting corporation distributes the after-tax proceeds of the subsidiary sale to its shareholders in return for some of their stock, the distribution will be taxed as a sale and not a dividend under Section 302(b)(4).

[9]Although taxable spin-offs are unusual, they do occur. In such a case, the distribution is taxable to shareholders.

may remain in the hands of the seller or they may be transferred to the acquirer, and where these attributes reside post-transaction is again defined by the tax structure of the deal.

In most taxable acquisitions of freestanding C corporations, the tax attributes of the target survive, as does the target corporation itself, and are transferred to the acquirer.[10] However, net operating losses and credits are limited, reducing their value to acquirers. In a tax-free merger, the tax attributes of the target always survive and carry over to the acquirer. The use of net operating losses by acquirers is also limited in tax-free acquisitions.

In a subsidiary sale, the tax attributes of the sold subsidiary always survive. Whether the divesting firm retains the tax attributes or the acquirer obtains them is determined by the structure of the subsidiary sale. In a spin-off or equity carve-out, the tax attributes of the divested subsidiary survive, but may be limited.[11]

Target Corporate-Level Tax Effect of the Merger, Acquisition, or Divestiture

In a merger or acquisition, the acquirer can purchase the stock or assets of the target. If the acquirer purchases the target's assets in a taxable transaction, a taxable gain or loss will be recognized by the target corporation. If the acquirer purchases the stock of the target from the target's shareholders in either a taxable or tax-free transaction, no taxable gain or loss accrues at the target *corporation level.* As noted previously, there is a taxable gain or loss at the target shareholder level if the transaction is taxable.

In a subsidiary sale, the divesting corporation recognizes a taxable gain or loss if the transaction is taxable, and subsidiary sales are usually taxable transactions. Subsidiary sales can be structured as **stock sales** or as **asset sales.** The gain or loss recognized by the seller is computed as the difference between the purchase price and the seller's basis in the stock or assets of the subsidiary, whichever was sold.

In a spin-off, the divesting corporation does not recognize a taxable gain if the spin-off qualifies for tax-free treatment. If the spin-off is taxable, which is relatively unusual, a taxable gain or loss will be recognized by the distributing corporation as the difference between the fair market value of the divested subsidiary and the distributing corporation's tax basis in the divested subsidiary's **net assets.** Shareholders receiving stock of the spun-off entity also recognize a taxable gain on the transaction. Equity carve-outs generally do not result in a taxable gain or loss for the divesting corporation.

Change in the Tax Basis of the Target or Divested Subsidiary Assets

The tax basis of the assets of an acquired business can be stepped-up to the purchase price in certain taxable transactions. An increase in the tax basis of the assets, or a step-up in basis, of the target company creates increased future depreciation deductions, which provide valuable tax savings. But a change in the tax basis of the assets of

---

[10]In some types of taxable acquisitions of freestanding corporations, the tax attributes of the target firm are eliminated. These transaction structures are rare after TRA 86.

[11]The total value of the target's NOLs survive, however, their use postacquisition is limited. The limitation that applies to a target's NOLs constrains the annual use of the NOLs to a specified amount.

a freestanding C corporation rarely occurs under current tax laws in the United States. Prior to 1986, a step-up in the tax basis of the target's assets was much more common.[12] As illustrated in the following chapter, under current law the tax costs of obtaining this step-up typically are greater than the tax benefits from future additional depreciation deductions in acquisitions of freestanding C corporations. Conversely, acquisitions of S corporations and other conduit entities frequently result in a step-up in the tax basis of the target's assets. The incremental tax cost of a step-up structure when the target is an S corporation is much lower than the incremental tax cost of a step-up structure when the target is a C corporation.

Even though it is unusual for the sale of a freestanding C corporation to result in a step-up in the tax basis of the target's assets, a step-up is common in subsidiary sales. When a divesting corporation sells a subsidiary in a taxable transaction, the transaction is often structured so that a step-up in the tax basis of the assets of the sold subsidiary occurs.[13] Consequently, the acquiring firm may obtain substantial tax benefits in certain subsidiary sales.[14] Because a step-up is common in the acquisition of a subsidiary, but not in the acquisition of a freestanding corporation, the structuring and pricing of each type of transaction is different. In Chapter 17, we discuss the types of subsidiary sales that are likely to result in a step-up in the tax basis of the divested subsidiary.

Effect of Leverage on Mergers and Acquisitions

Debt-financed acquisitions are taxable transactions in which the acquirer purchases the target, whether a freestanding corporation or a subsidiary of another corporation, for cash. Various special interest groups and politicians claim that the tax deductibility of interest payments encourages debt-financed acquisitions. If managers of the target maintain low debt to equity ratios, and thereby fail to exploit the tax advantages of debt financing, the interest deduction on new debt financing allows purchasers to acquire such targets at bargain prices. If debt financing has become increasingly tax-advantageous since the early 1980s, however, it begs the question of why the target corporation cannot borrow or recapitalize *without* resorting to a debt-financed acquisition. The answer to such a question is that other nontax costs make one method of recapitalization more efficient than another tax-equivalent method.

13.3 NONTAX ISSUES IN MERGERS, ACQUISITIONS, AND DIVESTITURES

The tax effects of a merger, acquisition, or divestiture are important, but often the nontax effects of a restructuring are at least as, if not more, important. Sometimes nontax factors will have a greater influence on whether a transaction is completed than tax

---

[12]Even before 1986, step-up transactions were not as frequent as is commonly believed. For example, *Mergers & Acquisitions* ("The Threat of a Merger Tax," July–August 1986, p. 19) reported that only 17% of the largest acquisitions pre-1986 resulted in a step-up in the target's assets.

[13]These transactions either are structured as asset sales or are stock sales followed by a **Section 338(h)(10) election.**

[14]Cox Communications acquisition of Gannett's cable television business was structured in a manner that resulted in a step-up in the tax basis of Gannett's cable television assets. Cox reported that it estimated that the tax benefits associated from the step-up were worth approximately $350 million. (*Source:* Cox Communications, July 27, 1999, 8-K).

factors do. Also, nontax factors may determine the structure for an acquisition or divestiture despite significant foregone tax benefits or increased tax costs. Several types of nontax costs frequently influence corporate restructuring transactions:

1. Transactions costs
2. Contingent or unrecorded liabilities
3. Managerial and/or control issues

Prior to June 2001, acquisitions of freestanding companies could be accounted for using the purchase method of accounting or the pooling of interests method.[15] The **purchase method of accounting** requires the acquirer to write up the **financial accounting basis** of the target's assets to the purchase price, while the **pooling of interests method of accounting** allowed the acquirer to carry over the financial accounting basis of the target. Under prior rules, the amount of the write-up in the target's assets, under purchase accounting, ascribed to goodwill and other intangibles, would be amortized over a period of not more than 40 years. As a result, the purchase method of accounting typically resulted in lower acquirer financial accounting earnings in future periods, and it was asserted that acquiring firms often sought to structure an acquisition to qualify for pooling of interests accounting treatment to avoid the resulting earnings decreasing amortization charges.[16] The FASB eliminated the pooling of interests method of accounting for mergers and acquisitions as of June 2001 with FAS 141 and 142. Under these new financial accounting standards, the purchase method of accounting must be used for all acquisitions. However, goodwill is not amortized under the new rules, but rather goodwill values are written down if and when the acquirer determines that the recorded goodwill has been impaired. As we discuss at length later, just because an acquirer records goodwill for financial accounting purposes does not necessarily mean that goodwill is also recorded and recognized for tax purposes.

Transactions costs can include fees paid to professionals, information costs, and financing costs among others. In some cases, these costs become large enough to render an acquisition or divestiture too expensive to pursue. Contingent liabilities may influence the structure selected for an acquisition or divestiture or may hinder the completion of a transaction that would otherwise generate wealth for both the acquirer and the target. For example, an acquirer may forego the acquisition of a conglomerate with numerous valuable nontobacco subsidiaries because of potential litigation costs associated with a tobacco company subsidiary. Similarly, costs associated with managerial control may affect the completion of a transaction or the form in which the transaction is ultimately executed. For example, acquiring firms with a significant amount of managerial ownership may cancel the acquisition of a target company that demands acquiring firm stock as the primary consideration in the acquisition. Managers of the acquirer in such a situation would dilute their ownership through the exchange of acquirer stock for the target corporation.

---

[15]In the acquisition of a subsidiary, the purchase method of accounting could be used.
[16]In WorldCom's acquisition of MCI, analysts estimated that the use of purchase accounting would decrease the combined entities' future accounting earnings by $475 million per year ("WorldCom wants 'Pooling' for MCI Deal," *The Wall Street Journal,* October 8, 1997, p. B6).

13.4 FIVE BASIC METHODS TO ACQUIRE A FREESTANDING C CORPORATION

The five main methods for an acquirer (A) to purchase a freestanding target C corporation (T) are:

1. A's taxable purchase of T's assets
2. A's taxable purchase of T's stock followed by a Section 338 election, which results in a step-up/down in the tax basis of the target's assets
3. A's taxable purchase of T's stock *not* followed by a Section 338 election
4. A's acquisition of T's stock in a tax-free exchange
5. A's acquisition of T's assets in a tax-free exchange

To understand the tax implications of an acquisition, it is crucial to keep in mind which of the five methods is being used to effect the transaction. We refer to them repeatedly over the next several chapters.

In a taxable purchase of T's assets, the target corporation receives cash and/or notes for its assets, and it must pay taxes on the recognized asset sale gain. The gain can be ordinary or capital in nature depending on the assets sold. For example, the sale of inventory gives rise to ordinary income. The acquirer takes a basis in T's assets equal to the price paid, typically a stepped-up basis. If T's shareholders retain their shares, they do not realize capital gains or losses until T liquidates or they otherwise dispose of their shares.

In a taxable purchase of T's stock, T's shareholders receive cash or notes for their shares. A's basis in T's stock is generally the purchase price. Under Section 338, A can elect to treat the purchase of T's stock as if it purchased T's assets. As a result of the Section 338 election, the tax basis of T's assets are stepped-up to fair market value, which is the purchase price plus tax liabilities associated with the step-up. Then, T's tax attributes, other than an ability to use T's NOL carryforwards to reduce T's recapture and capital gains taxes on the asset sale, are eliminated. If A does not elect to treat its purchase of T's stock as an asset purchase under Section 338, however, the tax basis in T's assets carries over instead of being stepped-up, and T's tax attributes are preserved. Significant restrictions hinder A's ability to use these surviving tax attributes in both taxable and tax-free acquisitions.

If A acquires T's stock in a tax-free exchange under **Section 368,** T's shareholders will not, in general, recognize gains on the exchange of their T stock for A stock. In this case, A is not permitted to step-up the tax basis of T's assets. Moreover, A generally retains T's tax attributes. But as in a taxable purchase of T's stock when A does not elect under Section 338 to treat the transaction as an asset purchase, A has only limited use of T's net operating losses, capital losses, and tax credit carryforwards.

If A acquires T's assets in a tax-free exchange under Section 368 in exchange for A stock, and T's stockholders exchange their T stock for A stock, the T shareholders do not pay tax on the exchange. A takes a **carryover basis** in T's assets, that is, the tax basis to A is the same as it was in the hands of T, and A will generally acquire T's tax attributes. But, once again, the use of these attributes is limited. Table 13.1 summarizes the basic tax effects of the structures discussed in this section.

TABLE 13.1 Basic Structures Employed in the Acquisition of Freestanding C Corporations and Major Tax Implications of Each Structure

| Structural and Tax Factors | Taxable Acquisitions | | | Tax-free Acquisitions | |
	Asset Acquisition	Stock Acquisition with a §338 Election[1]	Stock Acquisition without a §338 Election	Asset Acquisition	Stock Acquisition
Typical form of consideration	Cash	Cash	Cash	Stock	Stock
Taxable to target shareholders[2]	Yes[3]	Yes	Yes	No	No
Target corporation-level taxable gain	Yes	Yes	No	No	No
Step-up in the tax basis of the target's assets	Yes	Yes	No	No	No
Target's tax attributes survive[4]	No[3]	No	Yes	Yes	Yes

[1]The §338 election results in the transaction being taxed like an asset sale.

[2]Tax-free acquisitions provide gain deferral and are not really tax-free, but rather tax-deferred.

[3]Only if the target corporation liquidates after the asset sale.

[4]Target tax attributes include net operating loss carryforwards (NOLs) capital loss carryforwards, and various types of tax credits.

13.5 FOUR METHODS TO DIVEST A SUBSIDIARY OR LINE OF BUSINESS

Four basic methods can be used in divesting a line of business:

1. A subsidiary stock sale
2. A subsidiary asset sale
3. A spin-off[17]
4. An equity carve-out

A subsidiary sale occurs when the divesting corporation sells the stock or assets of a subsidiary to another company. If the acquirer purchases the stock of the subsidiary, the acquirer and seller can jointly elect under **Section 338(h)(10)** to treat the stock sale as an asset sale. If the subsidiary sale is structured as an asset sale or as a stock sale accompanied by a Section 338(h)(10) election, the acquirer will obtain a stepped-up basis in the sold subsidiary's assets. If the subsidiary sale is structured as a stock sale without a Section 338(h)(10) election, then the acquirer will take a carryover basis in the assets of the acquired subsidiary.

In a nontaxable spin-off, the divesting firm distributes the stock in a subsidiary in which it owns at least 80% of the stock. The stock of the subsidiary is distributed to shareholders of the divesting parent pro rata. After the spin-off, shareholders own the stock of two independent companies. Spin-offs are almost always tax-free to the distributing corporation and its shareholders, and the tax basis of the assets of the divested (spun-off) firm carry over, meaning that no step-up is involved.

When a divesting firm sells the stock of a subsidiary to the public for cash in a so-called equity carve-out, the selling corporation is not taxed on the sale if the shares sold are held by the subsidiary. The tax basis of the subsidiary's assets is not changed in an equity carve-out. Table 13.2 presents an overview of the tax implications of various divestiture methods.

TABLE 13.2 Divestiture Methods and Major Tax Implications of Each Method

Tax Issue or Structural Factor	Subsidiary Stock Sale	Subsidiary Asset Sale[1]	Spin-off	Equity Carve-out
Cash received by divesting parent?	Yes	Yes	No	Yes
Taxable gain to divesting parent	Yes	Yes	No	Not usually
Taxable gain to divesting parent's shareholders	Not usually[2]	Not usually[2]	Not usually[3]	Not usually[2]
Step-up in the *tax basis* of the divested subsidiary's assets	No	Yes	No	No[4]

[1]A divesting parent can either sell the assets of the subsidiary or it can sell the stock of the subsidiary and make a §338(h)(10) election, which will result in the transaction being taxed as an asset sale.

[2]There is no tax at the divesting parent shareholder level unless the divesting parent distributes the after-tax proceeds of the stock or asset sale to shareholders.

[3]Spin-offs are typically structured to be tax-free and it is unusual for a spin-off to be taxable to the shareholders of the divesting parent.

[4]In certain circumstances, an equity carve-out can be structured so that the tax basis of the carved-out subsidiary's assets are stepped-up. The step-up is facillitated through a §338(h)(10) election.

---

[17]The two variations of a spin-off include a split-off and a split-up. They are discussed briefly in Chapter 17.

13.6 TAX DEDUCTIBILITY OF GOODWILL AND OTHER INTANGIBLE ASSETS UNDER SECTION 197

A tax issue associated with mergers, acquisitions, and divestitures often mentioned in the financial press is the tax deductibility of goodwill. In 1993, as part of the OBRA 1993, Congress enacted **Section 197,** which makes goodwill and nearly all other purchased intangible assets tax deductible. Prior to 1993, goodwill and many other types of intangible assets acquired in an acquisition were not amortizable or depreciable for tax purposes. Since 1993, most tax-based intangible assets are amortizable over a 15-year period.

However, a great deal of confusion surrounds the tax deductibility of goodwill. The financial press and even financial analysts often assume that goodwill that is recorded on a firm's financial statements is deductible for tax purposes, but in most cases, it is not. Tax-deductible goodwill arises only in acquisitions in which the tax basis of the target's assets are stepped-up. As we noted earlier in this chapter, it is rare for the target's assets to be stepped-up for tax purposes in acquisitions of freestanding C corporations; in other words, tax-deductible goodwill is rare. In contrast, with the purchase method of accounting, large amounts of financial accounting goodwill typically arise. This accounting goodwill does not necessarily appear on the tax-basis balance sheets; that is, it is not tax-deductible goodwill.

When then is goodwill tax deductible? Goodwill is tax deductible when the tax basis of the acquired firm's assets are stepped-up. A step-up in the acquired firm's assets occurs frequently in acquisitions of conduits, such as S corporations or partnerships, and in subsidiary sales, but not in acquisitions of freestanding C corporations.

It is often useful to know whether the goodwill on a firm's balance sheet is tax deductible. Under the recently enacted purchase accounting rules, firms are required to report the amount of tax-deductible goodwill recorded in an acquisition. However, firms are not required to report the amount of tax-deductible goodwill associated with pre-June 2001 acquisitions. For that reason, it is important in some cases to estimate the amount of tax-deductible goodwill on a firm's balance sheet. Figure 13.1 and Table 13.3 illustrate one technique for determining the amount of tax-deductible goodwill on a firm's balance sheet. Figure 13.1 contains a simplified balance sheet and income statement for a publicly traded firm called Pisces Foods. Table 13.3 presents the computations we soon describe.

Although the disclosures provided in tax footnotes are not always complete, it is often possible to make a good first approximation of the amount of financial accounting goodwill amortization expense that is not tax deductible. In the reconciliation of a corporation's actual tax liability to its tax liability at the statutory federal tax rate, it is common to see a separate line item relating to goodwill amortization expense that was not deductible for tax purposes, a so-called **permanent difference.** The goodwill amortization expense adjustment amount reported in the tax rate reconciliation is the amount by which the firm's actual tax expense differs from its tax expense at the statutory rate—taxable income on the income statement multiplied by the tax rate—due to nondeductible amortization expense. To determine the amount of nondeductible amortization expense, the amount reported in the reconciliation is divided by the statutory tax rate. In Figure 13.1, the reconciling amount for "Amortization of goodwill"

FIGURE 13.1   Excerpts from Pisces Foods 1996 Financial Statements

Pisces Foods
CONSOLIDATED STATEMENT OF INCOME *(in $ millions)*   *Year Ended December 31*

	1996	1995
Sales of services and products	8,605	5,548
Costs of services and products sold	(5,868)	(3,846)
Restructuring, litigation, and other matters	(979)	(319)
Marketing, administration, and general expenses	(2,406)	(1,323)
Operating profit (loss)	(648)	60
Other income and expenses, net	(86)	137
Interest expense	(456)	(236)
Loss from continuing operations	(1,190)	(39)
Income tax benefit	423	6
Other items (net)	862	23
Net income (loss)	95	(10)

Pisces Foods
CONSOLIDATED BALANCE SHEET *(in millions)*   *Year Ended December 31*

ASSETS:	1996	1995
Cash and cash equivalents	$220	$196
Customer receivables	1,561	1,431
Inventories	783	730
Uncompleted contracts costs over related billings	686	542
Program rights	431	301
Prepaid and other current assets	1,106	844
Total current assets	4,787	4,044
Plant and equipment, net	1,866	1,908
FCC licenses, net	1,240	1,586
Goodwill, net (note 2)	8,776	5,244
Other assets	3,220	3,758
Total assets	19,889	16,540
LIABILITIES AND SHAREHOLDERS' EQUITY:		
Short-term debt	$497	$306
Current maturities of long-term debt	4	330
Accounts payable	887	796
Uncompleted contracts billings over related costs	334	318
Other current liabilities	2,578	2,112
Total current liabilities	4,300	3,862
Long-term debt	4,991	7,031
Deferred taxes	1,227	1,621
Other noncurrent liabilities	3,619	2,573
Total liabilities	14,137	15,087

FIGURE 13.1 *(cont.)*

Pisces Foods
CONSOLIDATED BALANCE SHEET (in millions)   *Year Ended December 31*

ASSETS:	1996	1995
Shareholders' equity:		
Preferred stock	14	15
Common stock	609	426
Capital in excess of par value	5,376	1,847
Common stock held in treasury	(546)	(720)
Minimum pension liability adjustment	(796)	(1,220)
Cumulative foreign currency translation adjustments	11	(11)
Retained earnings	1,084	1,116
Total shareholders' equity	$5,752	$1,453
Total liabilities and shareholders' equity	$19,889	$16,540

Pisces Foods
NOTES TO THE FINANCIAL STATEMENTS

NOTE 2: AMORTIZATION OF GOODWILL

Goodwill is assigned a useful life of between 20 and 40 years and amortized using the straight-line method. Total goodwill amortization was $150 in 1995 and $270 in 1996.

NOTE 6: INCOME TAXES

RECONCILIATION OF INCOME TAX EXPENSE (BENEFIT) TO THE
TAX EXPENSE (BENEFIT) BASED ON THE STATUTORY RATE

	1996	1995
Federal income tax benefit at statutory rate	($417)	($14)
Increase (decrease) in tax resulting from:		
Amortization of goodwill	85	21
State income tax, net of federal effect	(69)	(2)
Lower tax rate on income of foreign sales corporations	(9)	(3)
Lower tax rate on net income of Puerto Rican operations	(17)	(29)
Gain on sale of stock of subsidiary and affiliate	—	12
Loss of foreign tax credit	3	3
Foreign rate differential	(26)	(12)
Nondeductible expenses	8	6
Dividends from foreign investments	8	2
Other differences, net	11	(1)
Income tax benefit from continuing operations	($423)	($6)

is $85. Dividing this reconciling amount by the top federal corporate income tax rate of 35% provides an estimate of the amount of financial accounting goodwill amortization expense that is not deductible for tax purposes. In our example, this amount is $85/35% = $242.86.

TABLE 13.3   Computation of Tax Deductible Goodwill for Pisces Foods

Panel A: Estimation of the Percentage of Goodwill Amortization Expense That Is Not Tax Deductible in 1996

	1996
Financial accounting goodwill amortization expense[1]	$270.00
Adjustment for nondeductible goodwill amortization expense in tax footnote[2]	85.00
Implied amount of goodwill that was not tax deductible[3]	242.86
Proportion of amortization expense that was not tax deductible[4]	89.95%

Panel B: Estimated Goodwill on the Balance Sheet That Is Not Tax Deductible

Total goodwill on the balance sheet	$8,776.00
Proportion of goodwill that is not tax deductible[5]	89.95%
Balance sheet goodwill that is not tax deductible[6]	$7,893.76
Balance sheet goodwill that is tax deductible[7]	$882.24

[1] Per footnote #2 of Pisces Foods footnotes in Figure 13.1

[2] Adjustment in the reconciliation of Pisces reported income tax expense (benefit) to the income tax expense (benefit) at the statutory federal tax rate for goodwill amortization that was not tax deductible. Source is footnote #6 in Figure 13.1

[3] The amount of financial accounting goodwill amortization that was not tax deductible can be estimated by dividing (2) by the statutory federal tax rate (35%). The amount reported in footnote #6 of Figure 13.1 ($85) was computed by multiplying the amount of goodwill amortization expense that was not tax deductible by the statutory tax rate.

[4] Dividing (3) by (1) provides an estimate of the amount of financial accounting goodwill amortization expense that was not tax deductible.

[5] The estimate computed in (4) is assumed to apply to all goodwill on the balance sheet. This assumption may significantly influence estimates if the useful lives of the goodwill that is tax deductible varies dramatically from those of the goodwill that is not tax deductible. Further, this assumption can be influenced by other idiosyncrasies associated with the period (and therefore the remaining useful life) in which various components of goodwill were recorded for book and tax purposes.

[6] Computed as (5) multiplied by goodwill on the balance sheet.

[7] Total goodwill on the balance sheet less (6).

The amount of goodwill amortization expense that is not tax deductible is divided by total financial accounting amortization expense to derive the percentage of goodwill amortization expense that is not tax deductible. This estimate provides a crude approximation of the amount of all goodwill on the balance sheet that is and is not tax deductible. In our example, the amount of nondeductible goodwill amortization expense is $242.86/$270 = 89.95%. An estimate of the amount of goodwill on the balance sheet that will generate tax deductions in future periods is computed by multiplying one minus the percentage of nondeductible amortization, or 1 − .8995, by the total amount of goodwill on the balance sheet. In this case, nondeductible goodwill is $7,893.76, and tax-deductible goodwill is $882.24. This estimate is crude and readers should be aware of the technique's limitations. However, a more refined estimate can be generated with this approach using several years' financial statements.

Summary of Key Points

1. The tax motivations for mergers include a desire to enhance depreciation deductions, to transfer valuable tax attributes such as net operating loss carryforwards to a company that values them more highly, and to create debt to secure interest deductions and thereby reduce corporate taxes.
2. None of the motivations listed in point 1 are unique to mergers and acquisitions. Indeed, some transactional alternatives can achieve the same gross tax benefits at a lower cost.
3. The five basic methods for a purchaser to acquire a freestanding target (T) include a taxable purchase of T's stock without a Section 338 election; a taxable purchase of T's stock with a Section 338 election; a taxable purchase of T's assets; a tax-free purchase of T's stock; and a tax-free purchase of T's assets. The term *tax-free* refers to the tax consequences of the transaction to the seller. The methods have different effects on the tax basis of the target's assets (Is it stepped-up or stepped-down to market value or does the basis carry over?) and the target's tax attributes (for example, NOLs and tax credit carryforwards).
4. The four basic methods to divest a subsidiary or a line of business include a spin-off; a subsidiary stock sale; a subsidiary asset sale; and an equity carve-out.
5. Section 197 made goodwill tax deductible. As an empirical fact, most goodwill recorded on U.S. firms' financial statements is not tax deductible. Tax-deductible goodwill is created only in transactions in which the tax basis of the acquired business's assets is stepped up. A step-up occurs almost exclusively in subsidiary sales and acquisitions of conduits, and not in acquisitions of freestanding C corporations.

Discussion Questions

1. What factors motivate acquisition transactions? Which do you think are most important?
2. What key tax factors are most influential in mergers and acquisitions? Are mergers and acquisitions unique in their tax consequences?
3. What are the tax benefits and costs of a transaction that changes the depreciable basis of an asset?
4. What are the tax advantages of transferring T's tax attributes to A? What transactional substitutes might T use to secure these advantages?
5. What are the five basic acquisition methods used to acquire freestanding companies?
6. What are four common divestiture techniques?
7. What is a step-up in the tax basis of a firm's assets? How does a step-up generate cash flow for an acquirer?
8. How often do step-up acquisition structures occur when the target is a freestanding C corporation?
9. With what organizational form or entity type are step-up acquisition structures common?
10. What are some of a firm's tax attributes? Why is an acquirer concerned with the affect of an acquisition on a target firm's tax attributes?
11. What does a carryover basis transaction imply about the basis of the assets of the target firm? Does a carryover basis transaction generate incremental cash flow for the acquirer? What type of acquisition does generate incremental cash flow for an acquirer? What is the source of this incremental cash flow?
12. What is the difference between a firm's financial accounting asset basis and its tax asset basis? How would you quantify such a difference? Be sure to mention specific accounts in the financial statements and techniques.

References and Additional Readings

Ginsburg, M., and J. Levin, 1995. *Mergers, Acquisitions, and Buyouts: A Transactional Analysis of the Governing Tax, Legal, and Accounting Considerations.* Boston, MA: Little, Brown and Company.

Ginsburg, M., and J. Levin, 2001. *Mergers, Acquisitions, and Buyouts.* Frederick, MD: Aspen Publishers, Inc.

Other academic research on the taxation of mergers, acquisitions, and divestitures.

Alford, A., and P. Berger, 1998. "The Role of Taxes, Financial Reporting, and Other Market Imperfections in Structuring Divisive Reorganizations." Working paper. Philadelphia, PA: University of Pennsylvania.

Amihud, Y., B. Lev, and N. Travlos, 1990. "Corporate Control and the Choice of Investment Financing: The Case of Corporate Acquisitions," *Journal of Finance* (June), pp. 603–616.

Asquith, P., R. Bruner, and D. Mullins, 1983. "The Gains to Bidding Firms from Merger," *Journal of Financial Economics,* pp. 121–140.

Auerbach, A., and D. Reishus, 1988. "The Impact of Taxation on Mergers and Acquisitions," in *Mergers and Acquisitions,* edited by A. J. Auerbach. Chicago: University of Chicago Press.

Ayers, B., C. Lefanowicz, and J. Robinson, 2000. "The Effects of Goodwill Tax Deductions on the Market for Corporation Acquisitions," *Journal of the American Taxation Association* (Supplement).

Brown, D., and M. Ryngaert, 1991. "The Mode of Acquisition in Takeovers: Taxes and Asymmetric Information," *Journal of Finance* (June), pp. 653–669.

Dhaliwal, D., and M. Erickson, 1998. "Wealth Effects of Tax-Related Court Rulings," *Journal of the American Taxation Association,* pp. 21–48.

Erickson, M., 1998. "The Effect of Taxes on the Structure of Corporate Acquisitions," *Journal of Accounting Research,* pp. 279–298.

Erickson, M., 2003a. "Comparing the Proposed Acquisitions of MCI by British Telecom,

GTE and WorldCom," in *Cases In Tax Strategy,* edited by M. Erickson. Upper Saddle River, NJ: Pearson Prentice Hall.

Erickson, M., 2003b. "Analyzing Quaker Oats' Sale of Snapple to Triarc," in *Cases In Tax Strategy,* edited by M. Erickson. Upper Saddle River, NJ: Pearson Prentice Hall.

Erickson, M., 2003c. "Tax Benefits in Triarc's Sale of Snapple to Cadbury Schwepps," in *Cases In Tax Strategy,* edited by M. Erickson. Upper Saddle River, NJ: Pearson Prentice Hall.

Erickson, M., 2003d. "The Effect of Entity Organizational Form on the Structure of, and Price Paid in, the Hi-Stat Acquisition," in *Cases In Tax Strategy,* edited by M. Erickson. Upper Saddle River, NJ: Pearson Prentice Hall.

Erickson, M., and S. Wang, 1999. "Exploiting and Sharing Tax Benefits: Seagram and DuPont," *Journal of the American Taxation Association* (Fall).

Erickson, M., and S. Wang, 2000. "The Effect of Transaction Structure on Price: Evidence from Subsidiary Sales," *Journal of Accounting and Economics.*

Erickson, M., and S. Wang, 2003. "Tax Benefits as a Source of Merger Premiums in Acquisitions of Privately Held Corporations." Working paper. Chicago: University of Chicago.

Franks, J., R. Harris, and C. Mayer, 1988. "Means of Payment in Takeovers: Results for the United Kingdom and the United States," in *Corporate Takeovers,* edited by A. J. Auerbach. Chicago: University of Chicago Press.

Hand, J., and T. Skantz, 1999. "Tax Planning in Initial Public Offerings: The Case of Equity Carve-outs." Working paper. Chapel Hill, NC: University of North Carolina.

Kaplan, S., 1989. "Management Buyouts: Evidence on Taxes as a Source of Value," *Journal of Finance* (July), pp. 611–632.

Landsman, W., and D. Shackelford, 1995. "The Lock-In Effect of Capital Gains Taxes: Evidence from the RJR Nabisco Leveraged Buyout," *National Tax Journal* (June), pp. 245–259.

Lehn K., J. Netter, and A. Poulsen, 1990. "Consolidating Corporate Control, Dual Class Recapitalizations versus Leveraged Buyouts," *Journal of Financial Economics,* pp. 557–580.

Martin, K., 1996. "The Method of Payment in Corporate Acquisitions, Investment Opportunities, and Management Ownership," *Journal of Finance* (September), pp. 1227–1246.

Maydew, E., K. Schipper, and L. Vincent, 1999. "The Effect of Taxes on Divestiture Method," *Journal of Accounting and Economics,* pp. 117–150.

Mitchell, M., and J. Netter, 1989. "Triggering the 1987 Stock Market Crash: Antitakeover Provisions in the Proposed House Ways and Means Tax Bill?" *Journal of Financial Economics,* pp. 37–68.

Robinson, J., 1981. "The Influence of Selected Tax Variables on Premiums Paid Upon Corporate Combination." PhD dissertation. Ann Arbor, MI: University of Michigan.

Schipper, K., and A. Smith, 1991. "Effects of Management Buyouts on Corporate Interest and Depreciation Tax Deductions," *Journal of Law and Economics* (October), pp. 295–341.

Stulz, R., R. Walkling, and M. Song, 1990. "The Distribution of Target Ownership and the Division of Gains in Successful Takeovers," *Journal of Finance,* pp. 817–883.

Travlos, N., 1987. "Corporate Takeover Bids, Method of Payment, and Bidding Firms' Stock Returns," *Journal of Finance* (September), pp. 943–963.

Weaver, C., 2000. "Divestiture Structure and Tax Attributes: Evidence from the Omnibus Budget Reconciliation Act of 1993," *Journal of the American Taxation Association* (Supplement).

14 | TAXABLE ACQUISITIONS OF FREESTANDING C CORPORATIONS

After completing this chapter, you should be able to:

1. Understand the types of acquisitions that result in a step-up in the tax basis of the target's assets and those types that do not.

2. Compute the prices at which a seller (target shareholders) and an acquirer are indifferent between various taxable acquisition structures.

3. Estimate the acquirer's tax basis in the target's stock and assets.

4. Understand the effect of acquisition structure on the target firm's tax attributes.

In Chapter 13 we introduced the major tax issues associated with corporate combinations and divestitures. In this chapter we focus on taxable acquisitions of freestanding C corporations. We consider the taxable acquisitions of an S corporation in the following chapter and the taxable acquisition of a division or a subsidiary of a corporation in Chapter 17.

In a **taxable acquisition,** the purchaser may buy either the assets or the stock of a target company. In the latter case, it is possible via election to treat a stock purchase, for tax purposes, as if the acquirer had purchased the target's assets. If the assets are purchased or if a step-up election is made in a taxable stock acquisition, a stepped-up (or stepped-down) tax basis in the target's assets is achieved. As a result, the acquired inventory will be charged off and the acquired fixed assets will be depreciated from a base equal to their fair market value at the time of acquisition. Tax-deductible goodwill will often result from the step-up in the tax basis of the target's assets.

The step-up in basis is not obtained without a cost, however. A tax must be paid on the ordinary income resulting from the sale of inventory and on any depreciation and other ordinary income recapture, as well as on any taxable capital gains. Prior to 1987, any capital gains associated with stepping up the tax basis of a target's assets were not subject to taxation. The Tax Reform Act of 1986 (TRA 86) made capital gains associated with asset sales taxable, a legislative change that altered dramatically the tax consequences of taxable mergers and acquisitions.[1]

In an acquisition, the overriding considerations are the following:

1. What are the tax consequences of the transaction for target shareholders?[2]
2. What are the incremental tax costs and tax benefits if the buyer changes the basis in the target's assets?
3. What happens to the target company's tax attributes, including its NOLs?

We begin the chapter with an overview of four cases that cover the broad spectrum of taxable acquisitions of freestanding C corporations, along with the major tax consequences associated with each structure. We defer discussion of tax-free acquisitions until Chapter 16. As part of our analyses, we discuss the structures that are most common and the reasons for the observed empirical regularities. We also discuss nontax aspects of each of these acquisition structures.

14.1 TAX CONSEQUENCES OF ALTERNATIVE FORMS OF CORPORATE ACQUISITIONS

Table 14.1 lays out the major tax consequences—for the **target company, acquiring company,** and shareholders of the target company—of the various taxable corporate acquisition structures. We consider four basic acquisition methods:

1. A taxable asset acquisition without liquidating the target corporation
2. A taxable asset acquisition followed by a complete liquidation of the target
3. A taxable stock acquisition followed by a Section 338 election
4. A taxable stock acquisition that is not followed by a Section 338 election

As indicated in Table 14.1, the target company recognizes a gain or loss on the sale if it sells assets, regardless of whether the asset sale is followed by a liquidation, *or* if it sells its stock and the acquirer elects under Section 338 to treat the transaction for tax purposes as a sale of assets. By contrast, neither a sale of stock that is *not* accompanied by a Section 338 election nor a tax-free reorganization generates a taxable gain for the target corporation.

Table 14.1 also shows that the target corporation's recognition of a taxable gain is linked to a change in the tax basis of the assets acquired (to market value) for the purchaser. Moreover, with the exception of a sale of assets by a target company that is not liquidated (Case 1), a change in the tax basis of acquired assets by the purchaser leads to a loss of the **target's tax attributes,** such as net operating loss and tax credit carryforwards.

As for tax consequences to the shareholders of the target company, the general rule is that when shareholders exchange their stock for consideration other than stock of the acquirer, they are taxed on the excess of the value received over their tax basis in the shares. Alternatively, target shareholders recognize a loss equal to the excess of their basis above the purchase price.

Having outlined the basic tax consequences of taxable acquisitions, we next analyze the factors relevant to choosing among the transactional alternatives. After briefly

---

[1] This change is commonly known as the repeal of the **General Utilities doctrine.**
[2] In general, there are no tax consequences for the shareholders of the acquiring firm.

TABLE 14.1 Significant Tax Consequences of Various Taxable Acquisition Structures: Acquisitions of Freestanding C Corporations

Structural or Tax Issue	Asset Acquisition		Stock Acquisition	
	Without Liquidation[1]	*With Liquidation*[2]	*With a §338 Election*[3]	*Without a §338 Election*[4]
Consideration/method of payment	Cash	Cash	Cash	Cash
Taxable gain at target *corporation* level	Yes	Yes	Yes	No
Taxable gain recognized by target shareholders	No	Yes	Yes	Yes
Step-up in the *tax basis* of the target's assets	Yes	Yes	Yes	No
Target's tax attributes survive	Yes	No	No	Yes
Tax deductible goodwill[5]	Yes	Yes	Yes	No

[1]Transaction in which the target corporation sells its assets to the acquirer for cash. The target corporation pays any resulting tax (or receives a tax refund) on the gain (loss) recognized but the target corporation does not distribute the proceeds of the asset sale to its shareholders.

[2]Same as (1), but in this case, the target corporation distributes the after-tax proceeds of the asset sale to its shareholders in redemption of all of their target stock. The target's stock is then cancelled and the target corporation vanishes.

[3]Target corporation shareholders receive cash from the acquiring firm in return for their target corporation shares. The acquiring corporation then makes a §338 election, post-stock acquisition, which results in a deemed sale of the target's assets to a phantom new company. This deemed sale results in a step-up in the tax basis in the target's assets.

[4]Target corporation shareholders sell their stock to the acquirer, but the acquirer does not make the step-up election (§338 election). There is no step-up in the tax basis of the target's assets; the acquirer takes a carryover basis in the target's assets.

[5]Financial accounting goodwill is typically recorded with the purchase method of accounting (required for all transactions post-June 2001). Tax-basis goodwill is only created if the tax basis of the target's assets are stepped-up.

discussing the tax and nontax implications of the four tax structures in Table 14.1, we quantify the differences between them.

Case 1: Taxable Asset Acquisition without a Complete Liquidation of the Target

This is our benchmark case. In this transaction, the identity of the target's shareholders does not change, and they retain control of the target firm.

The target's shareholders do not pay a direct tax on the asset sale unless they receive a dividend or sell their shares, because they retain their shares in the target company and do not receive any cash in the transaction.

Tax Consequences

If a firm sells its assets for a price that exceeds the tax basis in the assets—usually the original acquisition price less accumulated depreciation or amortization since acquisition—it realizes a gain. The way the gain is taxed depends on the nature of the assets sold. For example, gains from the sale of inventories and accounts and notes receivable acquired in the normal course of business for services rendered or inventory sold give rise to ordinary income. Gains from the sale of depreciable property used in a trade or business (so-called Section 1231 property) yield capital gains, except to the extent that past depreciation must be **recaptured** as ordinary income. Sales of **Section 1231 property** at a loss give rise to an **ordinary loss.** Other assets that might be sold, such as stock held for investment, are capital assets, and their sale triggers capital gains or losses. If a corporation suffers a capital loss, the loss can be used only to offset other current or future realized corporate capital gains. Ordinary losses can offset ordinary income or net capital gains.

For a comparison of taxable acquisitions of freestanding C corporations, assume the following facts:

- The target corporation (T) has assets with a basis of $100. **Historical cost** and current basis equals $100, accumulated depreciation is $0.
- T's shareholders have a basis in the stock of T of $100, and they have held the stock for more than 1 year.[3]
- T's shareholders are individual investors, not corporations or tax-exempt entities.
- The acquirer (A) wants to purchase the assets of T for $1,000.
- T does not have any NOLs, tax credit carryforwards, or loss carryforwards.
- T corporation does not have any liabilities.

Figure 14.1 illustrates the structure of the transaction. In a taxable asset sale without a liquidation of T corporation, T would recognize a gain on the sale of its assets of $900 ($1,000 less $100). This gain would be capital in nature, because the historical cost of T's assets is the same as its current basis. That is, no accumulated depreciation is recaptured and, for this reason, no ordinary income results from the sale. If T's asset

---

[3]It is extremely unusual for a C corporation's shareholders to have the same basis in their stock as the corporation has in its net assets, because shareholder stock basis does not change with the profits and losses of the company, while the corporation's net asset basis does. Similarly, when shareholders buy and sell shares, the basis of the new shareholders changes independent of changes in the basis in the corporation's net assets. For most publicly traded corporations, shareholder stock basis exceeds the corporation's net asset basis by a substantial margin. Consider, for example, an Internet company with a market capitalization of $10 billion and net assets of less than $100 million.

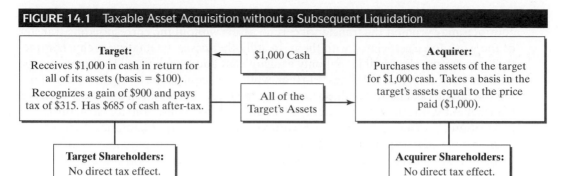

FIGURE 14.1 Taxable Asset Acquisition without a Subsequent Liquidation

basis was less than the historical cost due to depreciation, then the **recaptured depreciation** would be ordinary income.[4] For ease of illustration, we assume that no depreciation has been taken on T's assets. The $900 capital gain would be taxed, under current law, at T's top marginal tax rate. Ignoring state and local taxes and assuming that T's marginal federal tax rate is the top statutory tax rate (35%), we find that T would face a capital gains tax of $315 on the asset sale. Because T corporation does not liquidate under this scenario, it would retain all of its tax attributes. After taxes, T corporation therefore would have $685 ($1,000 less $315 of taxes) from the asset sale. T's shareholders do not face any tax on the asset sale as long as T does not liquidate.

In this first of our four cases, the acquirer, A, directly obtains the assets of T. Assuming that T's only asset was a building, A would take a basis in that building equal to the purchase price paid—in this case, a basis of $1,000. When T corporation is a business comprising many assets—tangible and intangible—the purchase price of the assets is allocated to the tangible and intangible assets based on an appraisal. Specifically, the **residual valuation approach** under **Section 1060** specifies the manner in which the purchase price is allocated to the assets of T.[5] Any portion of the purchase price allocated to goodwill will be amortizable over 15 years under **Section 197.** Returning to our simple numerical example, the acquirer corporation would obtain a step-up of $900 in the tax basis of T's assets ($1,000 new basis of T's assets in A's hands less $100 basis preacquisition). This $900 step-up gives rise to valuable increased depreciation deductions in future periods. We quantify the value of these additional tax deductions later in this chapter.

Nontax Consequences

With a taxable asset sale and no liquidation, the acquiring firm purchases the tangible assets of the target and may not acquire certain of its unrecorded liabilities. For example, the contingent liabilities of T corporation generally remain with T corporation. It may also be possible to leave other types of liabilities, such as environmental or

---

[4]Much of the depreciation recapture may cover various classes of Section 1231 property, and therefore the nature of the gain may be capital rather than ordinary income.

[5]With the residual method, the sale price is first allocated to cash and to cash equivalents. Then the fair market value of marketable securities, certificates of deposit, government securities, foreign currency, and so on, is allocated. This valuation is followed by an allocation of the fair market value to receivables, inventory, fixed assets, and then intangibles such as customer lists, plans, and formulas. The remainder of the purchase price that has not been allocated to specific tangible and intangible assets is allocated to goodwill.

labor-related, with the target corporation when purchasing its assets.[6] However, labor contracts may prohibit the transfer of certain assets without the corresponding transfer of the work force associated with them. In still other cases, facilitating such a contractual transfer may be feasible, but only at significant additional costs. The same may be true for environmental liabilities. Further, while the acquirer may benefit from obtaining the target's assets free of these liabilities, the target corporation may bear the cost. Consequently, the target may demand additional compensation for structuring an acquisition in a manner that leaves it with contingent and other liabilities. In most taxable and tax-free acquisitions, acquirers typically execute the purchase of the target through a subsidiary. Because the target is held in a separate corporate entity (subsidiary of the acquirer), the acquirer obtains some liability protection from the target's liabilities. Readers should note that acquisition of assets does not always protect the acquirer from the liabilities, recorded and unrecorded, of the target firm. As Ginsburg and Levin note, in *Mergers, Acquisitions, and Buyouts,* courts increasingly have held that the contingent liabilities of the target remain with the operating assets of the target's business. Thus, acquirers may be unable to "walk away" from the liabilities of the target, even in an asset purchase. This is a complex issue and deal makers are encouraged to seek the assistance of counsel when dealing with this issue.

When a target sells its assets, the costs of transferring title in each of those assets may be high. Title transfer is required with this structure because the acquirer is actually acquiring not the stock but the assets of the target. When stock is purchased, the acquirer obtains title to the target's assets indirectly through its ownership of the target's stock. Some types of assets are difficult to transfer. For example, certain contracts such as licenses and government permits are unassignable, or unassignable without a third party's consent.

Case 2: Sale of the Target Firm's Assets Followed by a Liquidation

Figure 14.2 illustrates the sale of a target's assets followed by liquidation. This transaction is similar to the transaction described in Case 1, but here the target distributes the after-tax proceeds of the asset sale to its shareholders in return for their T corporation shares in liquidation.

Tax Consequences

Unlike the situation in Case 1, T corporation's tax attributes vanish when it liquidates. However, if T has NOLs, it can offset both capital gain and ordinary income on the asset sale with its NOLs. We analyze the use of a target's NOLs to offset the gain on a step-up relative to preserving the target's NOLs in Chapter 16.

Returning to our facts from Case 1, we see that the tax consequences of the liquidation to the target corporation would be the same as in that case. The target would recognize a capital gain of $900 and pay a capital gains tax of $315. After corporate taxes, the target corporation, T, would have $685, which it would distribute to its

---

[6]Acquirers cannot, however, fully avoid the liabilities of the target by acquiring its assets instead of its stock. Ginsburg and Levin (1995), p. 1528, note that ". . . courts have increasingly held P (the acquirer) responsible for some or all of T's (the target) debts and contingent liabilities (especially tort liabilities for defective products) under the common law doctrines of '*de facto* merger' and 'successor liability.' This can occur when T's business has been transferred to P as a going concern and T goes out of existence (especially, but not exclusively, when T's shareholders receive an equity interest in P)."

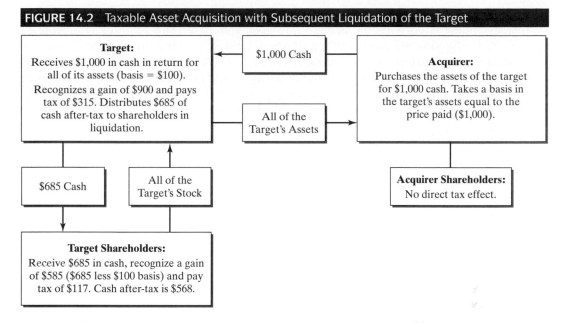

FIGURE 14.2 Taxable Asset Acquisition with Subsequent Liquidation of the Target

shareholders in return for all their T stock. T's shareholders would therefore recognize a gain on the stock repurchase of $585 ($685 less their basis of $100).[7] Because we are assuming that T's shareholders have held the T stock for more than 12 months, their capital gain on the stock redemption is long-term. Assume that investors' combined federal and state capital gains income tax rate is 20%, so T's shareholders would face a tax liability of $117, or 20% of $585.[8] After-tax, they would therefore have $568, or the $685 distribution minus $117 of capital gains taxes. The acquiring corporation would once again have a basis in T corporation's assets of $1,000—a $900 step-up.

Nontax Consequences

Because the basic structure of the acquisition remains an asset purchase, the nontax consequences are the same as in Case 1.

Case 3: Purchase of the Target's Stock Followed by a Section 338 Election

As we suggested in Case 1, the nontax costs of acquiring the assets of a target firm with far-flung operations and numerous tangible and intangible assets such as contracts and licenses may make a taxable asset sale structure prohibitive. Most taxable acquisitions of freestanding C corporations are structured as stock acquisitions, in part due to the nontax costs of an asset acquisition. Acquirers may, however, prefer to obtain the step-up in the tax basis of the target's assets associated with a taxable asset acquisition. The Tax Code provides an acquirer with the ability to obtain taxable asset sale treatment in a taxable stock acquisition, thereby avoiding the potentially onerous nontax costs associated with title transfers and nontransferable assets.

---

[7]Note that if shareholders had purchased T stock at different prices, some may have gains on the liquidation while others would have losses.
[8]In 2003, the top individual investor federal capital gains tax rate was reduced to 15%.

Under Tax Code Section 338, an acquirer can elect to treat a stock purchase of a freestanding C corporation as a taxable asset purchase. The acquirer is eligible to make the Section 338 election if it acquires at least 80% of the stock of the target firm within a 12-month period in a taxable manner, a so-called **qualified stock purchase.** The Section 338 election is made by the acquirer and does not require the consent of the target's shareholders.[9] Figure 14.3 illustrates a taxable stock acquisition of a freestanding target followed by a Section 338 election.

Tax Consequences

In a taxable stock acquisition followed by a Section 338 election, the target corporation is treated, for tax purposes, as if it sold its **gross assets**[10] to the new target for what is known as the **aggregate deemed sale price (ADSP).** *ADSP* is computed as:[11]

$$ADSP = P + L + t(ADSP - \text{Basis})$$

where

$P =$ the price paid for the stock of the target
$L =$ is the liabilities of the target (now assumed by the acquirer)
$t =$ the corporate tax rate
Basis $=$ the adjusted tax basis of the target's gross assets

ADSP is the gross tax basis of the assets of the target in the hands of the acquirer after the Section 338 election. Notice that the *ADSP* formula is self-referential; that is, *ADSP* is on both sides of the equation. The reason will become clear as we solve for *ADSP* using the numerical facts established in our example.

One fact is different: Here the acquirer is willing to pay $685 for the stock of the target corporation. We also assume that the acquirer makes a Section 338 election after acquiring the stock of the target. T's shareholders would therefore recognize a gain on the sale of their T stock of $585 ($685 less $100 basis). As before, this gain is capital in nature and under our assumptions, target shareholders would be subject to a capital gains tax of $117, leaving them with $568 after-tax. Because the transaction is structured as a stock acquisition, there is no taxable gain at the T corporation level. After the stock sale, T corporation becomes a subsidiary of the acquirer.

The acquiring firm, after obtaining 80% of the stock of the target, makes the Section 338 election. As a result of this election, T corporation (now a subsidiary of A) is deemed to have sold its assets to a hypothetical new target for *ADSP*. *ADSP* equals $1,000 under our scenario, computed as follows:

$$ADSP = \$685 + \$0 + 35\%(ADSP - \$100)$$
$$ADSP = \$685 + .35\,ADSP - \$35$$
$$.65\,ADSP = \$650$$
$$ADSP = \$1,000$$

The deemed sale of the target's assets for $1,000 results in a taxable gain of $900 ($1,000 *ADSP* less basis of $100) at the target corporation level. Assuming the top

---

[9]The election must be made within 8.5 months of the acquisition.
[10]Gross assets are total assets, while net assets are gross assets less liabilities. Net assets are typically synonymous with owner's equity.
[11]When the target has NOLs, the general form of the *ADSP* computation becomes $ADSP = P + L + t(ADSP - \text{Basis} - \text{NOL})$.

FIGURE 14.3 Taxable Stock Acquisition of the Target with a §338 Election

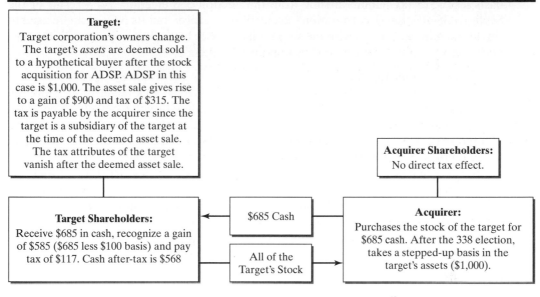

Target:
Target corporation's owners change. The target's *assets* are deemed sold to a hypothetical buyer after the stock acquisition for ADSP. ADSP in this case is $1,000. The asset sale gives rise to a gain of $900 and tax of $315. The tax is payable by the acquirer since the target is a subsidiary of the target at the time of the deemed asset sale.
The tax attributes of the target vanish after the deemed asset sale.

Acquirer Shareholders:
No direct tax effect.

Target Shareholders:
Receive $685 in cash, recognize a gain of $585 ($685 less $100 basis) and pay tax of $117. Cash after-tax is $568

$685 Cash

All of the Target's Stock

Acquirer:
Purchases the stock of the target for $685 cash. After the 338 election, takes a stepped-up basis in the target's assets ($1,000).

Postacquisition:

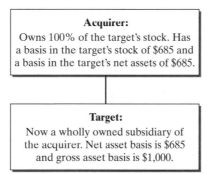

Acquirer:
Owns 100% of the target's stock. Has a basis in the target's stock of $685 and a basis in the target's net assets of $685.

Target:
Now a wholly owned subsidiary of the acquirer. Net asset basis is $685 and gross asset basis is $1,000.

marginal federal tax rate applies, a tax liability of $315 results. This tax liability is payable by the target corporation, which is a subsidiary of the acquirer after the stock purchase. In total, the acquirer has paid $1,000 for the target corporation: $685 for the target's stock and $315 for the tax liability associated with the Section 338 election. The *ADSP* computation is self-referential because the acquirer, through the target, contractually pays the tax associated with the Section 338 election. Hence, the deemed price paid for the target's assets (*ADSP*) includes the price paid for the stock *plus* the tax on the deemed asset sale, or $t(ADSP - \text{Basis})$. As a result of the election, the acquirer obtains a step-up in the target's assets of $900 ($1,000 *ADSP* less $100 preacquisition basis) and has a gross basis in these assets of $1,000. Any portion of the purchase price allocated to goodwill will be amortizable over 15 years under **Section 197.**

Unlike the case in a taxable asset acquisition, in a taxable stock acquisition, the acquirer has a tax basis in the stock and the assets of the target. Under the current scenario, the acquirer would have a basis in T's stock of $685 and a basis in T's gross assets of $1,000. The **net asset basis** of the target's assets would be $685, or $1,000 gross basis less $315 tax liability arising from the Section 338 election. As a result of the Section 338 election, T corporation's tax attributes vanish, but its NOLs can be used to shield the gain associated with the step-up in its asset basis. The *acquirer's* NOLs cannot be used to offset the gain on the step-up, however.

Nontax Consequences

Several nontax benefits are associated with a taxable stock acquisition. First, the transaction costs of obtaining the stock of a freestanding target are likely to be much smaller than the title transfer costs associated with an asset sale. Second, the problem of nontransferable assets is largely avoided with a stock acquisition, thereby providing the potential for significant nontax benefits in certain circumstances.

Several significant nontax costs are also associated with this structure. Unlike the case in an asset sale, the target corporation in a stock acquisition survives as a legal entity including its contingent liabilities. However, because the target becomes a *corporate* subsidiary of the acquirer, it enjoys some protection from legal liabilities through the properties of corporate ownership. That is, the acquirer's losses associated with the acquired firm should, in most cases, be limited to the amount paid for the target.

Case 4: Purchase of the Target's Stock without a Section 338 Election

Case 4 is the same as Case 3 except that the acquirer does not make the Section 338 election. The numerical facts remain the same, and the structure employed is nearly the same as Figure 14.4 illustrates.

Tax Consequences

With a taxable stock acquisition, the target's shareholders recognize a taxable gain equal to the purchase price less their basis in T's stock. Given the numbers in this case, target shareholders recognize a capital gain of $585 ($685 less $100 basis) on the stock sale to the acquirer and have $568 after tax. The target corporation's tax attributes survive, but are limited by **Section 382.**

The acquiring firm obtains the stock of the target firm and takes a basis in this stock equal to the purchase price paid, which is $685. The target becomes a subsidiary of the acquirer and because the acquirer did not make the Section 338 election, the asset basis of the target is not stepped-up for tax purposes. Therefore, the target's asset basis carries over and is $100 postacquisition. Notice that the acquirer's tax basis in the stock and assets of the target are $685 and $100, respectively.

Nontax Consequences

The nontax consequences of this transaction structure are essentially the same as those described for Case 3. One notable difference between Cases 3 and 4 occurs in the tax and financial accounting basis of the assets of the target. In Case 3, the gross financial accounting basis in the assets of the target would be approximately $1,000[12] as would the gross tax basis of the target's assets.

However, in Case 4, the acquirer's gross financial accounting basis in the target would be $685 while the gross tax basis of the target's assets postacquisition is $100. This

---

[12]This estimate ignores the effects of merger costs, such as investment banking fees, as well as other such items. The net asset tax basis is $685 as is the net financial accounting basis.

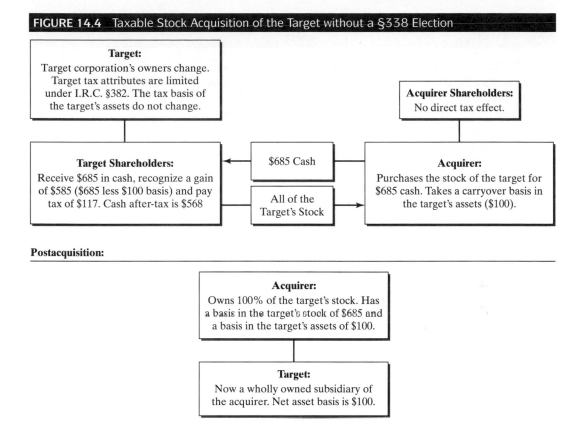

FIGURE 14.4   Taxable Stock Acquisition of the Target without a §338 Election

Target:
Target corporation's owners change. Target tax attributes are limited under I.R.C. §382. The tax basis of the target's assets do not change.

Acquirer Shareholders:
No direct tax effect.

Target Shareholders:
Receive $685 in cash, recognize a gain of $585 ($685 less $100 basis) and pay tax of $117. Cash after-tax is $568

$685 Cash

All of the Target's Stock

Acquirer:
Purchases the stock of the target for $685 cash. Takes a carryover basis in the target's assets ($100).

Postacquisition:

Acquirer:
Owns 100% of the target's stock. Has a basis in the target's stock of $685 and a basis in the target's assets of $100.

Target:
Now a wholly owned subsidiary of the acquirer. Net asset basis is $100.

difference in financial accounting and tax basis is often manifested to a large degree in the goodwill account on the acquirer's financial statements. That is, the acquirer will have a large amount of recorded goodwill that is *not* tax deductible under Case 4.[13] Under Case 3, any goodwill recorded in the acquisition will be tax deductible.

14.2 COMPARISON OF TAXABLE ACQUISITION STRUCTURES

The four preceding examples present the tax implications of the various taxable acquisition structures used when purchasing a freestanding C corporation. Even though that information is valuable, our objective is applying that knowledge to a tax planning problem. Which of these structures is best given the specific fact pattern presented? When does each of these structures become preferential?

Based on the preceding facts, which structure is optimal, from a tax perspective only? As demonstrated in prior chapters, we can solve for the optimal contract by setting one party indifferent and determining which contract the other prefers. Table 14.2 lays out the tax implications of the four structures discussed in section 14.1. Essentially what

---

[13]This disparity in the book and tax basis of the target's assets generate a significant deferred tax liability. There are reasons that firms should not record such a deferred tax liability. Those reasons are beyond the scope of this text.

TABLE 14.2 Comparison of the Tax Effects of Various Taxable Acquisition Structures: Acquisitions of Freestanding C Corporations

Fact Pattern:

Asset purchase price	$1,000.00
Stock purchase price	$685.00
$ADSP^{(1)} =$	$1,000.00
Target's net asset basis	$100.00
Target shareholder's stock basis	$100.00
$t_c =$	35%
$t_{cg} =$	20%
$r =$	10%
Amortization/depreciation period (n) =	10

	Transaction Structure			
	Asset Acquisition		**Stock Acquisition**	
	No Liquidation	**Liquidation**	**With a §338 Election**	**Without a §338 Election**
Purchase Price	$1,000.00	$1,000.00	$685.00	$685.00
Tax Costs:				
Tax paid by T corporation[2]	(315.00)	(315.00)	0.00	0.00
Tax paid by A from the §338 election[3]	0.00	0.00	(315.00)	0.00
Tax paid by T's shareholders[4]	0.00	(117.00)	(117.00)	(117.00)
Total Tax Paid	($315.00)	($432.00)	($432.00)	($117.00)
Target Shareholder Consequences:				
Gross cash received	n/a	685.00	685.00	685.00
Less: shareholder taxes[4]	n/a	(117.00)	(117.00)	(117.00)
After-tax cash to target's shareholders	n/a	$568.00	$568.00	$568.00
Acquirer Net After-Tax Cost:				
Gross cost	$1,000.00	$1,000.00	$1,000.00	$685.00
Less: present value of tax benefits[5]	(193.55)	(193.55)	(193.55)	0.00
Net after tax-cost of the acquisition	$806.45	$806.45	$806.45	$685.00
Acquirer's Tax Basis in the Target's:				
Stock	n/a	n/a	$685.00	$685.00
Assets	$1,000.00	$1,000.00	$1,000.00	$100.00

[1]$ADSP$ is the aggregated deemed sale price of the target's assets in a taxable stock transaction in which a §338 election is made. $ADSP$ is computed as: $ADSP = G + L + t_c(ADSP - BASIS)$; where G is the price paid for the target's stock, L are the target's liabilities, t_c is the corporate tax rate, and $BASIS$ is the gross tax basis of the target's assets preacquisition.

[2]Tax liability at the target corporation level from the sale of the target's assets preacquisition.

[3]Tax liability at the target corporation level on the deemed sale of its assets after the stock acquisition. The liability is ultimately the contractual responsibility, indirectly, of the acquiring firm because when the liability is triggered, the target is a subsidiary of the acquirer.

[4]Capital gains taxes resulting from the redemption of target shares by the target corporation in the liquidation following an asset sale and from the direct sale of the shares to the acquirer in the stock acquisitions.

[5]The present value of the tax savings resulting from stepping up the target's assets assuming that the step-up is amortized/depreciated straight-line over a 10-year period, the applicable tax rate is 35% and the after-tax discount rate is 10%.

we have done is set the seller (target shareholders) indifferent between the structures. That is, we computed the acquisition price required under each of the four structures to leave the target's shareholders with the same amount of cash after tax. Notice that the target's shareholders receive $568 after tax in the three right-hand scenarios in Table 14.2; and were the target to liquidate in Case 1, target shareholders would have $568 after tax in that scenario also.

To answer the question which structure is optimal (ignoring nontax costs), below we develop algebraic expressions that allow us to determine acquirer and seller indifference prices across various acquisition structures.[14] We use algebra only as a tool.[15]

Target shareholder's after-tax cash under Case 2 (asset sale followed by a liquidation) can be represented by equation (14.1) below. We first define the target shareholder's after-tax wealth as the liquidation proceeds, which is cash distributed by the target corporation after paying the corporate level tax, less the shareholder tax liability associated with the liquidation. We then specify the amount of cash distributed to shareholders in the liquidation algebraically, as a function of purchase price in equation (14.2).

$$
\begin{aligned}
ATAX_{asset} &= \text{Liquidation} - \text{Tax on liquidation} \\
&= \text{Liquidation} - (\text{Liquidation} - \text{Stock})t_{cg} \\
&= \text{Liquidation}(1 - t_{cg}) + \text{Stock} \times t_{cg}
\end{aligned}
\tag{14.1}
$$

$$
\begin{aligned}
\text{Liquidation} &= \text{Price}_{asset} - \text{Tax on asset sale} \\
&= \text{Price}_{asset} - (\text{Price}_{asset} - \text{Asset})t_c \\
&= \text{Price}_{asset}(1 - t_c) + \text{Asset} \times t_c
\end{aligned}
\tag{14.2}[16]
$$

where

$ATAX_{asset}$ = target shareholder's after-tax cash in a taxable asset sale
Liquidation = after-corporate-tax liquidation proceeds paid to target shareholders
Stock = target shareholder's stock basis
t_{cg} = the individual investor capital gains tax rate[17]
t_c = the corporate tax rate (ordinary and capital gain)
Price_{asset} = the price paid to the target corporation for its net assets
Asset = the net tax basis of the target's assets

Substituting the definition of Liquidation in equation (14.2) into equation (14.1) and simplifying we obtain:

$$
ATAX_{asset} = [\text{Price}_{asset}(1 - t_c) + \text{Asset} \times t_c](1 - t_{cg}) + \text{Stock} \times t_{cg}
\tag{14.3}
$$

---

[14]It is important to note that the analysis used ignores target shareholder tax attributes such as capital loss carryforwards, target corporation tax attributes such as NOLs and capital loss carryforwards, and that we assume all involved parties face the maximum individual or corporate tax rate. After working through the logic, readers should be convinced that such complications could be added quite easily. We omit them here for ease of illustration.
[15]Readers who prefer electronic spreadsheet models for such tasks may want to compare the algorithm used in their models to those presented here. The algebraic equations presented here should be logically identical to those in the spreadsheet models.
[16]We ignore the effect of target net operating losses on liquidation proceeds here for ease of illustration. As noted previously, target NOLs can be used to offset the gain associated with stepping up the target's assets.
[17]This rate includes both federal and state income taxes. The top federal capital gains tax rate for individuals is 15%, as of 2003.

We can represent target shareholder's after-tax cash under Case 3 and Case 4 by the following expression

$$ATAX_{stock} = Price_{stock} - TAX$$
$$= Price_{stock} - (Price_{stock} - Stock)t_{cg}$$
$$= Price_{stock}(1 - t_{cg}) + Stock \times t_{cg} \qquad \textbf{(14.4)}$$

where

$ATAX_{stock}$ = target shareholder's after-tax cash in a taxable stock sale

$Price_{stock}$ = the pretax price paid to target shareholders in a taxable stock acquisition, (other variables are as previously defined)

If we set equations (14.3) and (14.4) equal to each other, we find the price demanded by target shareholders in a taxable asset acquisition ($Price_{assct}$) given the price demanded in a taxable stock acquisition ($Price_{stock}$).

$$Price_{stock}(1 - t_{cg}) + Stock \times t_{cg}$$
$$= [Price_{asset}(1 - t_c) + Asset \times t_c](1 - t_{cg}) + Stock \times t_{cg} \qquad \textbf{(14.5)}$$

Substituting, rearranging, and simplifying yields the following expression:

$$Price_{asset} = (Price_{stock} - Asset \times t_c)/(1 - t_c) \qquad \textbf{(14.6)}$$

With the facts in Case 4 and given $Price_{stock} = \$685$, $Price_{asset}$ is equal to $1,000, which is computed as ($685 − $100 × 35\%$)/($1 − 35\%$) using equation (14.6). Table 14.2 indicates that the numerical solution provided by equation (14.6) does in fact leave target shareholders indifferent between a taxable stock sale at a price of $685 and a taxable asset sale at $1,000. That is, target shareholder's after-tax wealth is $568 in both cases.

Given target shareholder indifference, we then need to determine which of the transaction structures is the least costly to the acquirer after tax. To estimate the after-tax cost of each structure, we need an estimate of the value of the tax benefits associated with stepping up the tax basis of the target's assets. For ease of computation, we assume that the average depreciable/amortizable life of the target's assets is 10 years. Further we assume **straight-line depreciation/amortization,** an after-tax discount rate of 10%, and an appropriate corporate tax rate of 35%.[18] Under those assumptions, the step-up in the target's assets generates $90 per year ($900/10-year life) in additional depreciation deductions and $31.50 in tax savings each year for 10 years, or $90 multiplied by 35%. At a discount rate of 10%, the present value of the additional tax savings from the depreciation deductions is $193.55. Table 14.3 presents these computations.

From the acquirer's perspective, in Case 1, the net after-tax cost of acquiring the target is $806.45, or $1,000 acquisition cost less $193.55 in *incremental* tax savings from the step-up. The after-tax cost of acquiring the target under Case 2 is also $806.45 for the same reason. Under Case 3, the after-tax cost of acquiring the target is the sum of the $685 paid for the target's stock plus the $315 tax associated with the Section 338 election less the present value of tax savings from the step-up ($193.55), which is again

---

[18]These assumptions are overly general and do not represent the true complexity and economic effects associated with allocating the purchase price to the target's assets. We make these simplifying assumptions here for ease of illustration. It should be noted, however, that the allocation of the purchase price to various target asset classes (e.g., land vs. goodwill) can have a dramatic impact on the cash flows of the combined firm postacquisition.

TABLE 14.3 Estimation of Tax Benefits from Stepping up the Tax Basis of a Target's Assets

Fact Pattern:

Purchase price	$1,000.00
Target's net asset basis	100.00
Step-up[1]	900.00
Amortization/depreciation period	10
Depreciation method	straight-line
Annual incremental amortization/depreciation[2]	$90.00
t_c =	35.00%
r =	10.00%

Period	Incremental Depreciation[2]	Tax Savings[3]	Present Value of Tax Savings[4]
1	$90.00	$31.50	$28.64
2	90.00	31.50	26.03
3	90.00	31.50	23.67
4	90.00	31.50	21.51
5	90.00	31.50	19.56
6	90.00	31.50	17.78
7	90.00	31.50	16.16
8	90.00	31.50	14.69
9	90.00	31.50	13.36
10	90.00	31.50	12.14
Total	$900.00	$315.00	$193.55

[1]Step-up is the increase in the tax basis of the target's assets computed as the purchase price less the net asset basis preacquisition.

[2]Incremental amortization/depreciation deductions is the step-up divided by the amortization period.

[3]Tax savings are incremental amortization/depreciation deductions multiplied by the corporate tax rate (t_c).

[4]Present value of tax savings discounted at the after-tax rate discount rate (r).

$806.45. Under Case 4, the pretax cost of acquiring the target is $685, but no incremental tax benefits come from stepping up the tax basis of the target's assets. So after any tax benefits, the acquirer's net cost in Case 4 is $685.[19] Therefore, the acquirer prefers Case 4 to the other three options. Why? The acquirer's net after-tax cost is lowest under Case 4.

Does this conclusion seem reasonable? The optimal structure in our example is the one in which the tax basis of the target's assets is not stepped up. For each of the first three cases, we can see that the incremental tax cost of stepping up the target's assets is $315. Under Cases 1 and 2, the target corporation pays this incremental tax,

---

[19]Each of these four computations ignores the tax benefits attributable to the existing tax basis of the target's assets. The computations do so because those tax benefits are constant across transaction structure. Thus, those tax benefits have no incremental affect on the determination of the optimal tax structure.

while in Case 3 the acquiring firm pays it. In Case 4, no incremental tax cost is associated with stepping up the tax basis of the target's assets.

We also know that the present value of the tax benefits from stepping up the tax basis of the target's assets in Cases 1, 2, and 3 is $193.55. Therefore, the net *cost* of a step-up is $121.45, or $315 less $193.55. This answer is quite reasonable when we realize that the taxable gain associated with a step-up ($900) is equivalent to the amount of the step-up. Furthermore, the immediate associated tax liability is equal to the gross amount of tax savings derived from additional depreciation deductions; $900 step-up multiplied by 35% = $315 of additional deductions (see Table 14.3) that will be realized in future periods, assuming constant tax rates. With any discount rate greater than 0%, the present value of the tax savings from the step-up will be less than the tax liability due today from the step-up.

As we noted in Chapter 13, acquisitions of freestanding C corporations are rarely structured to result in a step-up in the tax basis of the target's assets. The reason is that it does not make sense to pay $1 in taxes today to generate $1 of tax savings over the next 10 or *n* years. In our numerical example in Table 14.2, it doesn't make sense to pay $315 in tax today to generate $193.55 in present value tax savings.

Analysis of Acquiring Firm Indifference Price

In equations (14.1) through (14.6) we expressed target shareholder's indifference between taxable acquisition structures algebraically. We can do the same for acquiring firms. Doing so will provide a relatively complete framework for you to analyze the tax consequences of a taxable acquisition of a freestanding C corporation. An acquiring firm's net after-tax cost in a taxable stock acquisition in which a Section 338 election is not made (Case 4) can be expressed as:

$$ATAXCOST_{stock} = Acqprice_{stock} - \text{Incremental tax benefits}$$
$$= Acqprice_{stock} - \$0$$
$$= Acqprice_{stock} \qquad \textbf{(14.7)}$$

where

$ATAXCOST_{stock}$ = the acquirer's net after-tax cost of the acquisition in a taxable stock transaction in which the target's assets are not stepped up

$Acqprice_{stock}$ = the price the acquirer pays for the target's stock in a taxable stock acquisition in which the target's assets are not stepped up

An acquirer's net after-tax cost in a step-up transaction can be expressed as follows. We use a taxable asset acquisition because algebraically, it is less complex than a Section 338 transaction. The results are identical if we use a taxable stock acquisition followed by a Section 338 election.

$$ATAXCOST_{asset} = Acqprice_{asset} - \text{Incremental tax benefits}$$
$$ATAXCOST_{asset} = Acqprice_{asset} - [(Acqprice_{asset} - Asset)/n] \times PVANN \times t_c \qquad \textbf{(14.8)}$$

where

$ATAXCOST_{asset}$ = the acquirer's net after-tax cost of the acquisition in a taxable asset acquisition

Acqprice$_{asset}$ = the pretax price paid by the acquirer for the target's net assets in a taxable asset acquisition

Asset = the target's net tax asset basis preacquisition

$PVANN$ = the present value of an annuity for n periods

t_c = the corporate tax rate

n = the period over which the step-up will be depreciated/amortized on a straight-line basis[20]

If we set equations (14.7) and (14.8) equal to each other, we can solve for the maximum price the acquirer will pay in a taxable asset sale, given the price in a taxable stock sale. Also, assume that the price an acquirer will pay in a taxable stock sale (Acqprice$_{stock}$) is the same as the price the target will demand (Price$_{stock}$) in equations (14.4) through (14.6).

$$\text{Price}_{stock} = \text{Acqprice}_{asset} - [(\text{Acqprice}_{asset} - \text{Asset})/n] \times PVANN \times t_c \quad \textbf{(14.9)}$$

After rearranging, we can express equation (14.9) as

$$\text{Acqprice}_{asset} = (\text{Price}_{stock} - \text{Asset} \times \text{Factor} \times t_c)/(1 - \text{Factor} \times t_c)$$

where Factor is equal to $PVANN/n$.

Using the facts in Table 14.2, we find that Acqprice$_{asset}$ is equal to

$$\text{Acqprice}_{asset} = (\$685 - \$100 \times .61445 \times 35\%)/(1 - .61445 \times 35\%)$$
$$= \$847.28$$

That is, the acquirer is indifferent between paying $685 in a taxable stock acquisition without a step-up election and paying $847.28 in a taxable asset sale. If we insert the maximum price the acquirer will pay in a taxable asset sale into equation (14.3), we find that target shareholder's after-tax wealth is $488.58,[21] which is less than the shareholder receives in a taxable stock sale at a price of $685. Hence, the taxable stock sale is the optimal structure.[22]

When then would a tax planner want to structure an acquisition of a freestanding company to result in a step-up in the tax basis of the target's assets? As a general rule, this structure makes sense only when the target has large NOLs that can be used to offset the gain on the step-up.[23] Due to limitations on the transfer of target NOLs in acquisitions, which we discuss in Chapter 16, offsetting the gain on a step-up can be an efficient use of the target's NOLs. However, even when the target has NOLs, a step-up structure may be suboptimal.

---

[20]A formula that reflects the complexities of accelerated depreciation methods and various asset classes (e.g., buildings and equipment) would be more realistic but unwieldy for our purposes. Readers can use the intuition derived from these equations to develop financial models that capture reality more precisely.

[21] $ATAX_{asset} = [\text{Price}_{asset}(1 + t_c) + \text{Asset} \times t_c](1 - t_{cg}) + \text{Stock} \times t_{cg}$

$ATAX_{asset} = [\$847.28(1 - .35) + \$100 \times .35] \times (1 - .20) + \$100 \times .20$

$ATAX_{asset} = \$488.58$ **(14.3)**

[22]That is, we reach the same conclusion regarding the structuring of the deal regardless of which party's (acquirer or target shareholders) after-tax wealth is held constant.

[23]A step-up structure also often makes sense in the acquisition of a foreign entity due to the tax treatment of dividend repatriation and the low incremental cost of a step-up structure in such an acquisition.

14.3 TAX DEFERRAL THROUGH INSTALLMENT SALE TAX TREATMENT

Prior to the late 1980s, substantial tax benefits were available from **installment sale** tax treatment. Such tax benefits are still available but at potentially significant nontax costs. Installment sale treatment allows a seller to defer gain recognition until the receipt of cash. In an installment sale transaction, sellers receive a debt instrument of the acquirer with taxable income recognized upon the receipt of periodic interest and principal payments on the security. Interest income is taxed as ordinary income and principal amounts trigger capital gain recognition for target shareholders. Because shareholders receive principal amounts over the life of the debt security, installment sale tax treatment can provide substantial tax savings via deferral.

Under current law, installment sale treatment is only available if the debt instrument received by target shareholders is not publicly traded. The fact that the acquirer's debt cannot trade publicly imposes a significant nontax cost on target shareholders. As a result, installment sale tax treatment has been much less common during the 1990s than it was in the 1980s. Although, installment sale tax treatment is oftentimes a pivotal tax issue in the sale/acquisition of small privately held corporations.

14.4 PRACTICAL ISSUES ASSOCIATED WITH STRUCTURING AND PRICING AN ACQUISITION

In the illustrations and discussion in Section 14.2 we assumed that all target shareholders were of the same type, faced the same tax rate, and had the same tax basis in the target's shares. In reality, of course, a target's shareholders will probably include individual investors from within and outside the United States, corporations, tax-exempt entities such as universities, and partially tax-exempt entities such as pension funds. Those target shareholders that are taxable investors have different tax attributes, including different tax rates and/or the presence of capital loss carryforwards, and tax bases in the stock of the target, both of which could affect the price at which they are willing to sell their target stock. Tax-exempt entities may be willing to sell shares at a lower pretax cost than taxable shareholders, all other things being equal.

The precise effects of the various tax statuses of a target's shareholders on acquisitions prices are not well understood. It seems prudent, however, to consider these issues as part of an overall acquisition strategy.

A tax planner can obtain information about the shareholders of a target firm from several sources. Information about institutional owners of various types can be obtained from CDA/Spectrum. Spectrum produces a quarterly report for publicly traded target firms with information about current institutional ownership and any changes therein.[24] Time-series analysis of these data therefore can provide a potential acquirer with a reasonable estimate of the proportion of a target's stock that is held by institutions and their tax bases in the target's stock.

Analysis of target firm's financial disclosures, such as 10-Ks, can provide information about other large block holders of the target's stock. Various financial databases

---

[24]Institutions covered by the report include mutual funds, corporations, and pension funds among several other types.

contain daily stock price and volume information for publicly traded firms. From these databases and assumptions about holding periods, potential acquirers can estimate an average shareholder tax basis in the stock of the target. The combination of these data sources provides tax planners with a reasonable first approximation of the tax liabilities or benefits (taxable losses) faced by target shareholders in a taxable acquisition.[25]

Estimating the Net Tax Basis of a Target's Assets

Throughout our discussions we have assumed a value for the net tax basis of a target's assets. As you undoubtedly realize, however, this figure is a key variable in the acquisition structuring decision. How do we estimate the net tax basis of a target's assets?

A first approximation can be derived from the target's financial statements. As you know, we can use two significant differences between the tax-basis and financial accounting basis balance sheet to estimate the net tax basis of a target's assets. The deferred tax account represents differences in a target's book and tax asset basis that are caused by **temporary differences,** such as accelerated depreciation for tax and straight-line depreciation for book. The second major difference between the book and tax basis of a firm's assets is any so-called permanent differences. The most obvious example of a permanent difference is goodwill that is not tax deductible; that is, goodwill that is reported in the financial statements but does not appear on the tax-basis balance sheet.[26] It is also necessary to control for financial accounting assets, such as deferred tax assets, which are not recorded for tax purposes.

The net tax basis of a target's assets then can be computed as the financial accounting basis in the net assets adjusted for deferred tax items and permanent differences such as goodwill. The difference between the book and tax basis of a firm's assets associated with temporary differences is multiplied by the tax rate to arrive at the deferred tax amount presented in the financial accounting balance sheet. Therefore, the book/tax-basis difference arising from temporary differences can be computed by *dividing* financial accounting deferred taxes by the tax rate. Estimating the amount of goodwill that is not tax deductible is also not difficult if the firm's disclosures are relatively complete (see Section 13.6 of Chapter 13).

An estimate of the gross tax basis of a firm's assets is the gross financial accounting assets (total assets on the balance sheet) plus/minus timing differences and minus permanent differences. When actually estimating the net tax basis (gross assets less liabilities) of a firm's assets, we must also control for financial accounting liabilities that are not recorded for tax purposes. For example, a deferred tax liability on a firm's balance sheet is not a liability on the tax-basis balance sheet. Hence, when subtracting the firm's liabilities from gross tax assets, we should not include the deferred tax liability in the tax-based liability figure.

Figure 14.5 contains the 1999 and 2000 income statement, balance sheet, and tax footnote disclosures for Loreto, Inc. We have combined several balance sheet items

---

[25]These estimates can also provide tax planners with an estimate of the potential tax savings associated with tax deferral. Chapter 16 addresses this issue in detail.

[26]Recall that, in taxable stock acquisitions in which a Section 338 election is not made, the tax basis of the assets of the target carryover. Purchase accounting would result in financial accounting goodwill from a write-up in the assets for financial accounting while there is no step-up in the target's assets for tax purposes. Many freestanding companies previously acquired other companies and have goodwill that is not tax deductible on their balance sheets from these prior acquisitions.

FIGURE 14.5 Financial Statements of Loreto, Inc.

Loreto
CONSOLIDATED STATEMENT OF INCOME *(in $ millions)*

	Year Ended December 31	
	2000	*1999*
Service sales	$5,204	$2,398
Product sales	3,401	3,150
Sales of services and products	8,605	5,548
Cost of services sold	(3,015)	(1,412)
Cost of products sold	(2,853)	(2,434)
Costs of services and products sold	(5,868)	(3,846)
Restructuring, litigation, and other matters (notes 1, 17 and 20)	(979)	(319)
Marketing, administration, and general expenses	(2,406)	(1,323)
Operating profit (loss)	(648)	60
Other income and expenses, net (note 19)	(86)	137
Interest expense	(456)	(236)
Loss from Continuing Operations before income taxes and minority interest in income of consolidated subsidiaries	(1,190)	(39)
Income tax benefit (note 6)	423	6
Minority interest in income of consolidated subsidiaries	(6)	(11)
Loss from Continuing Operations	(773)	(44)
Discontinued Operations, net of income taxes	(57)	110
Estimated gain (loss) on disposal of Discontinued Operations	1,018	(76)
Income from Discontinued Operations	961	34
Extraordinary item: Loss on early extinguishment of debt	(93)	—
Net income (loss)	$95	($10)

Loreto
CONSOLIDATED BALANCE SHEET *(in millions)*

	Year Ended December 31	
	2000	*1999*
ASSETS:		
Cash and cash equivalents (note 1)	$220	$196
Customer receivables (note 7)	1,561	1,431
Inventories (note 8)	783	730
Uncompleted contracts costs over related billings (note 8)	686	542
Program rights	431	301
Prepaid and other current assets	1,106	844
Total current assets	4,787	4,044
Plant and equipment, net (note 9)	1,866	1,908
FCC licenses, net (note 10)	1,240	1,586
Goodwill, net (note 2)	8,776	5,244
Deferred taxes (note 6)	3,220	3,758
Total assets	19,889	16,540
LIABILITIES AND SHAREHOLDERS' EQUITY:		
Short-term debt (note 11)	$497	$306
Current maturities of long-term debt (note 13)	4	330
Accounts payable	887	796
Uncompleted contracts billings over related costs (note 8)	334	318
Other current liabilities (note 12)	2,578	2,112
Total current liabilities	4,300	3,862

FIGURE 14.5   *(contd.)*

Long-term debt (note 13)	4,409	7,125
Deferred taxes (note 6)	1,809	1,527
Other noncurrent liabilities (note 14)	3,619	2,573
Total liabilities	14,137	15,087
Shareholders' Equity (note 15):		
Preferred stock	14	15
Common stock	609	426
Capital in excess of par value	5,376	1,847
Common stock held in treasury	(546)	(720)
Minimum pension liability adjustment (note 4)	(796)	(1,220)
Cumulative foreign currency translation adjustments	11	(11)
Retained earnings	1,084	1,116
Total shareholders' equity	$5,752	$1,453
Total liabilities and shareholders' equity	$19,889	$16,540

Loreto
NOTES TO THE FINANCIAL STATEMENTS
NOTE 2: AMORTIZATION OF GOODWILL
Goodwill is assigned a useful life of between 20 and 40 years and amortized using the straight-line method. Total goodwill amoritization was $150 in 1999 and $270 in 2000.

NOTE 6: INCOME TAXES
INCOME TAX EXPENSE (BENEFIT) FROM CONTINUING OPERATIONS (in millions)

	2000	*1999*
Current:		
Federal	($653)	$2
State	(116)	1
Foreign	32	22
Total current income tax expense (benefit)	(737)	25
Deferred:		
Federal	304	(43)
State	10	(4)
Foreign	—	16
Total deferred income tax expense (benefit)	314	(31)
Income tax benefit	($423)	($6)

Deferred income taxes result from temporary differences in the financial bases and tax bases of assets and liabilities. The types of differences that give rise to significant portions of deferred income tax liabilities or assets are shown in the following table:

CONSOLIDATED DEFERRED INCOME TAXES BY SOURCE (in millions)

	2000	*1999*
Deferred tax assets:		
Restructuring charges	$1,352	$1,133
Charges related to post-retirement benefits	1,868	2,625
Total deferred tax assets	3,220	3,758
Deferred tax liabilities:		
Accelerated depreciation and amortization	(1,809)	(1,527)
Total deferred tax liabilities	(1,809)	(1,527)
Deferred income taxes, net asset	$1,411	$2,231

FIGURE 14.5 *(contd.)*

RECONCILIATION OF INCOME TAX EXPENSE (BENEFIT)
TO THE TAX EXPENSE (BENEFIT) BASED ON THE STATUTORY RATE

	2000	*1999*
Federal income tax benefit at statutory rate	($417)	($14)
Increase (decrease) in tax resulting from:		
Amortization of goodwill	46	21
State income tax, net of federal effect	(69)	(2)
Lower tax rate on income of foreign sales corporations	(9)	(3)
Lower tax rate on net income of Puerto Rican operations	(17)	(29)
Gain on sale of stock of subsidiary and affiliate	—	12
Loss of foreign tax credit	3	3
Foreign rate differential	(26)	(12)
Nondeductible expenses	8	6
Dividends from foreign investments	8	2
Other differences, net	50	(1)
Income tax benefit from Continuing Operations	**($423)**	**($6)**

from a large publicly traded firm's financial statements to create the data for Loreto, Inc. in order to simplify our estimate of net asset tax basis.

We can estimate the net tax basis of this firm's assets at year-end 2000 as illustrated in Table 14.4. We start with the gross financial accounting basis of this firm's assets ($19,889) and subtract deferred tax assets of $3,220. We subtract deferred tax assets because this balance sheet account is not recorded for tax purposes.

We next make two adjustments for differences in the tax and book basis of Loreto's assets arising from temporary differences. Deferred tax assets reflect deductions taken for book purposes that have not yet been taken for tax purposes, such as restructuring charges. Dividing the deferred tax asset amount on the balance sheet by the tax rate produces the difference in book and tax basis due to the deferred tax item. In this case, tax-basis assets are higher than book-basis assets by $9,200.[27] A similar adjustment is made for deferred tax liabilities, although deferred tax liabilities reflect situations in which the tax asset basis is less than the financial accounting asset basis, as in accelerated depreciation. For this reason, we subtract the grossed-up deferred tax liability from financial accounting assets. In our example, the adjustment is $5,169 for deferred tax liabilities.

Goodwill that is not tax deductible appears on the financial accounting balance sheet but not the tax-based balance sheet. As a result, we need to estimate the amount of goodwill that is not tax deductible. We explained the mechanics of this computation in Chapter 13. Table 14.4 illustrates once again how this computation is performed.[28]

---

[27]Loreto likely took a large restructuring charge in a prior period. This charge reduces financial accounting asset basis. Such a charge is not tax deductible and therefore did not reduce the tax basis of Loreto's assets.
[28]Under FAS 142, for acquisitions after June, 2001, acquirers must disclose the amount of goodwill created in the acquisition.

TABLE 14.4 Estimating the Tax Basis of a Firm's Assets

		Year End 2000
Gross financial accounting asset basis		$19,889
Less:		
Deferred tax assets[1]		($3,220)
Plus Deferred Tax Asset Adjustment:		
Deferred tax assets	$3,220	
Implied difference in book and tax basis due to deferred tax assets[2]		9,200
Less Deferred Tax Liability Adjustment:		
Deferred tax liabilities	(1,809)	
Implied difference in book and tax basis due to deferred tax liabilities[3]		(5,169)
Less Goodwill That Is Not Tax Based:		
Goodwill on the balance sheet	$8,776	
Financial accounting goodwill amortization expense[4]	270	
Nondeductible amortization expense adjustment in the tax footnote[5]	46	
Estimated goodwill amortization expense that is not tax deductible[6]	131	
Percentage of goodwill that is not tax deductible[7]	48.68%	
Estimated balance sheet goodwill that is not tax deductible[8]		($4,272)
Estimated gross tax basis of the target's assets[9]		$16,429
Less Tax-Based Liabilities:		
Financial accounting liabilities on the balance sheet	$14,137	
Less: deferred tax liabilities[10]	(1,809)	
Tax liabilities		(12,328)
Net tax basis of the target's assets[11]		$4,101

[1]Deferred tax assets are recorded for financial accounting purposes but not for tax purposes. Hence they are not tax-based assets.
[2]Deferred tax assets divided by the corporate tax rate. This estimate reflects the difference in the book and tax basis of the firm's assets arising from deferred tax assets (e.g., restructuring charges).
[3]Deferred tax liabilities divided by the corporate tax rate. This estimate reflects the difference in the book and tax basis of the firm's assets arising from deferred tax liabilities (e.g., accelerated depreciation).
[4]Per footnote #2 (see Figure 14.8).
[5]Per footnote #6 (see Figure 14.8).
[6][5]divided by the corporate tax rate. Amount reported in[5] is the increase in tax expense due to non-deductible goodwill amortization expense. Dividing by the tax rate produces the amount of expense claimed for book purposes that was not tax deductible.
[7][6]divided by[4].
[8][7]multiplied by amount of goodwill on the balance sheet.
[9]Financial accounting total assets adjusted for deferred taxes, differences in book and tax basis arising from timing differences as manifested in deferred tax accounts and goodwill that is not tax deductible (not recorded on the tax-basis balance sheet).
[10]Deferred tax liabilities are not recorded on the tax-basis balance sheet and must be removed from financial accounting liabilities in order to estimate tax-based liabilities.
[11][9]less tax liabilities.

Using this approach, we estimate that nondeductible goodwill is $4,272. Our estimate of the gross tax basis of Loreto's assets then is $16,428.

Net tax basis can be estimated by subtracting tax-basis liabilities from the gross asset tax basis. Tax-basis liabilities are financial accounting liabilities less liabilities recorded for financial accounting purposes that are not recorded for tax purposes, as with deferred tax liabilities. We therefore subtract deferred tax liabilities from financial accounting liabilities to arrive at our estimate of tax-based liabilities of $12,328. An estimate of Loreto, Inc.'s net asset tax basis, as of year-end 2000, shown in Table 14.4, is $4,101—gross asset–basis less tax-basis liabilities.

Note that this technique provides a good first approximation, but that financial disclosures or lack thereof may result in substantial imprecision in estimates. Further, such approximations are difficult in multinational corporations.

Summary of Key Points

1. Mergers and acquisitions occur across a number of transactional forms. These alternative forms yield varying tax consequences to the target company, to the purchasing company, and to the shareholders of the target company.
2. Mergers and acquisitions that allow the buyer to step up the basis of assets acquired typically result in a loss of the target's tax loss and tax credit carryforwards, as well as other tax attributes of the target company. Such transactions also subject the target company to ordinary and capital gains tax. An example of such a transaction is a sale of the target's assets followed by a liquidation of the target company.
3. When the stock of a freestanding C corporation is acquired, the buyer may elect under Section 338 to treat the transaction *as if* the target's assets had been acquired, followed by a liquidation of the target company.
4. Prior to TRA 86, a tax advantage resulted from effecting a step-up. Under the so-called General Utilities doctrine, the corporate-level capital gain associated with the step-up in the target's assets was nontaxable. After 1986, the capital gain on the asset sale is fully taxable.
5. In the sale of a freestanding C corporation, a structure that results in a step-up in the target's assets is usually suboptimal from a tax perspective because the incremental tax cost associated with the step-up usually exceeds the incremental tax benefits. The notable exception to this general rule occurs when the target has substantial NOLs, which can be used to reduce the incremental cost of the step-up.
6. Although a step-up in a target's assets doesn't occur frequently in sales of entire freestanding C corporations, in two types of transactions a step-up structure is common. In sales of subsidiaries of companies, transactions are often structured in a manner that results in a step-up in the tax basis of the target's assets. It is also common to structure the sale of a conduit entity such as an S corporation in a similar manner.
7. Substantial differences in terms of nontax implications separate selling a target's assets from selling a target's stock. In the former case, title transfer costs may be excessive, although nontax benefits from liability avoidance can accrue to acquirers. In the latter case, acquisition transaction costs are likely lower, and with this structure the acquirer may be able to obtain certain assets such as licenses that will not transfer in an asset sale. With a stock acquisition, the acquirer obtains all the assets and liabilities, including contingent liabilities, a potentially significant cost associated with a stock acquisition.

Discussion Questions

1. What are the main tax considerations in the sale of a target's stock to a purchaser?
2. What are the disadvantages of effecting a change in the basis of all the firm's assets either by their sale, followed by a complete liquidation, or by a stock purchase, along with an election to treat the stock purchase as a purchase of all the firm's assets followed by a liquidation?
3. Because a purchaser can use a target's NOL carryforwards to offset the ordinary and capital gain and recapture tax on the sale of the target's assets, it has been argued that this reduces the cost of achieving a stepped-up basis in assets and makes it advantageous for the purchaser to acquire the target. Do you agree with this argument?
4. What types of transactions generate tax-deductible goodwill? How many acquisitions of freestanding C corporations, as a general rule, give rise to tax-deductible goodwill?
5. As a financial analyst or tax planner, how would you determine whether a potential target firm's goodwill was tax-based goodwill (deductible)?
6. What are the nontax benefits, if any, of an asset acquisition? What are the nontax costs, if any, of an asset acquisition?
7. What are the nontax benefits, if any, of a stock acquisition? What are the nontax costs, if any, of a stock acquisition?

Tax Planning Problems

1. Consider the following facts in order to quantify the tax costs of various taxable acquisition structures when the target is a freestanding C corporation. Wolverine, Inc., wants to purchase Reel Deal, Inc., in a taxable acquisition. Reel Deal is a freestanding C corporation with a net asset tax basis of $250. Reel Deal has no NOLs and is currently owned by five shareholders that have a basis in their Reel Deal stock of $5. Wolverine is planning to offer $10,000 for all of the assets of Reel Deal. The corporate tax rate is 40%, the after-tax discount rate is 15%, and the shareholder-level capital gains tax rate is 20%.
   a. How much cash after tax will the shareholders of Reel Deal have in a taxable asset sale at a price of $10,000?
   b. What is Wolverine's net after-tax cost of this transaction assuming that any step-up in Reel Deal's assets are amortized/depreciated over 15 years straight-line, the appropriate corporate tax rate is 40%, and the after-tax discount rate is 15%?
   c. What price could Wolverine pay for Reel Deal in a taxable stock acquisition without a Section 338 election? What would Wolverine's net after-tax cost of this structure be?
   d. Given the price computed in part (c), what would *ADSP* be if Wolverine decided to make the Section 338 election? What would Wolverine's net after-tax cost be with this structure of a taxable stock sale with a Section 338 election?
   e. Which structure should be used in this acquisition? Why?
2. Abaco is planning to acquire Cozumel Airlines, a freestanding C corporation, in expectation that new management can be brought in to achieve substantial operating efficiencies. You have been retained to advise Abaco on how to structure the acquisition.
   Two graduate school friends, Monique and Denise, own Cozumel Airlines. Together, they have a $1 million basis in their Cozumel Airlines stock. Both Monique and Denise have held their Cozumel Airlines stock for several years but must sell their stock for nontax reasons. Cozumel Airlines' tax-basis balance sheet contains $14 million of assets, no liabilities, and no net operating loss carryovers. All parties

agree that Cozumel Airlines would be worth $20 million to Abaco with no step-up in Cozumel's inside (asset) basis, but $21.25 million if its inside (asset) basis was stepped up to fair market value. Monique and Denise each face a 40% tax rate on ordinary income and a 20% tax rate on capital gains. The corporate tax rate is 35%.

Option 1: Abaco buys outright all Cozumel Airlines' assets for $18 million—a taxable asset acquisition. Cozumel Airlines pays resulting taxes on the sale, if any, and distributes the proceeds to Monique and Denise in a complete liquidation.

Option 2: Abaco pays Monique and Denise $ ___ million in cash for their stock in Cozumel and ***does not*** make a Section 338 election.

a. How much after-tax cash will Monique and Denise get in aggregate if Option 1 is chosen?

b. In Option 2, how much cash would Abaco have to pay to make Monique and Denise indifferent between Option 1 and Option 2?

c. What is Abaco's net present value if Option 1 is chosen?

d. What is Abaco's net present value if Option 2 is chosen—based on your answer to part (b)?

3. Walkers is planning to acquire Cayman Bank, a freestanding C corporation, in expectation that new management can be brought in to achieve substantial operating efficiencies. You have been retained to advise Walkers on how to structure the acquisition.

Two grad school friends, Joe and Jim, own Cayman Bank. Together, Joe and Jim have a $6 million basis in their Cayman Bank stock. Both Joe and Jim have held their Cayman Bank stock long enough to get long-term capital gain treatment but must sell their stock for nontax reasons. Cayman Bank's tax-basis balance sheet contains $3.5 million of assets, no liabilities, and $2.5 million of net operating loss carryovers. All parties agree that Cayman Bank would be worth $8 million to Walkers with no step-up in Cayman's inside (asset) basis, but would be worth $8.75 million if its inside (asset) basis was stepped up to fair market value. Joe and Jim each face a 40% tax rate on ordinary income and a 20% tax rate on capital gains. The corporate tax rate is 35%.

Option 1: Walkers buys outright all of Cayman Bank's assets for $7 million in a taxable asset acquisition. Cayman Bank pays resulting taxes on the sale, if any, and distributes the proceeds to Joe and Jim in a complete liquidation.

Option 2: Walkers pays Joe and Jim $___ million in cash for their stock in Cayman and ***does not*** make a Section 338 election.

a. How much after-tax cash will Joe and Jim get in aggregate if Option 1 is chosen?

b. In Option 2, how much cash would Walkers have to pay to make Joe and Jim indifferent between Option 1 and Option 2?

c. What is Walkers' net present value if Option 1 is chosen?

d. What is Walkers' net present value if Option 2 is chosen, based on your answer to part (b)?

e. Which structure is optimal? Why?

References and Additional Readings

See list at the end of Chapter 13.

15 | TAXABLE ACQUISITIONS OF S CORPORATIONS

After completing this chapter, you should be able to:

1. Explain the tax implications of various taxable acquisition structures of S corporations.

2. Understand when a structure that steps up the tax basis of the acquired S corporation is optimal and when it is not.

3. Compute the prices at which a seller (target shareholders) and an acquirer are indifferent between various taxable acquisition structures.

4. Understand the major tax differences between the taxable sale of an S corporation and the taxable sale of a C corporation.

A s illustrated in Chapter 10, the various organizational forms exhibit a number of tax and nontax differences. In this chapter, we analyze the tax treatment of taxable acquisitions of S corporations, which are conduit entities. We concentrate on S corporations but the same basic principles apply to acquisitions of other types of pass-through or conduit entities. As you will see, taxable acquisitions of S corporations and of conduits in general are quite different from taxable acquisitions of C corporations, which we discussed in the prior chapter. We do not discuss tax-free acquisitions of S corporations, although those structures are an option, because tax-free acquisitions of conduits are similar to tax-free acquisitions of C corporations. Moreover, a taxable structure typically dominates a tax-free structure when the target is a conduit such as an S corporation.

Because acquisitions of S corporations, partnerships, and other conduits such as LLCs are quite common, it is important to understand the basic tax issues associated with buying and selling a conduit. In fact, there are more S corporations than C corporations in the United States. Moreover, for medium and large businesses, as defined by the IRS, there are three S corporations or partnerships for every two C corporations.[1]

---

[1]For example, most joint ventures are conduit-type entities, and these enterprises are frequently sold to one of the partners or a third party. The issues covered in this section are therefore likely relevant in joint venture transactions, among others.

Thus, acquisitions of conduit entities are prevalent. As you will see, there are significant tax benefits available in acquisitions of conduit entities that are not typically available in the purchase of a C corporation. In our analysis of acquisitions of S corporations we do not discuss the nontax implications of various acquisition structures because they are similar to or the same as the nontax implications associated with acquisitions of C corporations.

Although an S corporation could be acquired in a tax-free acquisition, we restrict our analysis to taxable acquisitions of S corporations. Recall that S corporations are conduits whose earnings at the corporate level pass through to shareholders where they are taxed. Generally no tax is due at the S corporation level. We analyze the tax implications of acquiring the assets of an S corporation in a taxable transaction and the tax implications of a taxable stock acquisition of an S corporation. A taxable stock acquisition of an S corporation can be taxed as if the assets of the S corporation were sold if both the buyer and seller make a **Section 338(h)(10) election.**

In the taxable acquisition of an S corporation, the overriding considerations are (1) What are the tax consequences of the transaction for target shareholders?[2] and (2) What are the incremental tax costs and tax benefits if the buyer changes the basis in the target's assets?

15.1 TAX CONSEQUENCES OF TAXABLE S CORPORATION ACQUISITION STRUCTURES[3]

Table 15.1 lays out the major tax consequences—for the target company, the acquiring company, and the shareholders of the target company—of the three basic taxable methods used to acquire S corporations, which are:

1. A taxable asset acquisition followed by a complete liquidation of the target
2. A taxable stock acquisition followed by a Section 338(h)(10) election
3. A taxable stock acquisition that is not followed by a Section 338(h)(10) election

As indicated in Table 15.1, the target company recognizes a gain or loss on the sale if it sells assets *or* if it sells its stock and the acquirer and seller elect under Section 338(h)(10) to treat the transaction for tax purposes as a sale of assets. By contrast, a sale of stock that is *not* accompanied by a Section 338(h)(10) election does not generate a taxable gain at the target level. Rather, a tax is assessed at only the shareholder level on the stock sale. Table 15.1 also shows that the target corporation's recognition of a taxable gain is linked to a change in the tax basis of the assets acquired (to market value) for the purchaser.

Shareholders of the target company recognize a taxable gain in each of the three scenarios. In the first two scenarios, the taxable gain at the target corporation level

---

[2]In general, the shareholders of the acquiring firm experience no tax consequences.
[3]The remainder of the chapter is based in large part on "Tax Benefits as a Source of Merger Premiums in Acquisitions of Privately Held Corporations" by M. Erickson and S. Wang, 2003, University of Chicago and University of Southern California working paper.

TABLE 15.1 Significant Tax Consequences of Various Taxable Acquisition Structures: Acquisitions of S Corporations

Structural or Tax Issue	Asset Acquisition[1]	Stock Acquisition with a §338(h)(10) Election[2]	Stock Acquisition without a §338(h)(10) Election[3]
Consideration/method of payment	Cash	Cash	Cash
Taxable gain at target *corporation* level	Yes	Yes	No
Taxable gain recognized by target shareholders	Yes	Yes	Yes
Nature of target shareholder gain	Ordinary income and capital gain	Ordinary income and capital gain	Capital gain
Step-up in the *tax basis* of the target's assets	Yes	Yes	No
Tax-based goodwill[4]	Yes	Yes	No

[1]Transaction in which the target corporation sells its assets to the acquirer for cash. The target corporation does not pay any resulting tax (or receive a tax refund) on the gain (loss) recognized. Any gain or loss recognized passes through to target shareholders.

[2]Target corporation shareholders receive cash from the acquiring firm in return for their target corporation shares. The acquiring corporation and the target's shareholders then makes a §338(h)(10) election, which results in a deemed sale of the target's assets. The acquirer takes a stepped-up tax basis in the target's assets.

[3]Target corporation shareholders sell their stock to the acquirer, and the §338(h)(10) election is not made. There is no step-up in the tax basis of the target's assets; the acquirer takes a carryover basis in the target's assets.

[4]Financial accounting goodwill is typically generated in purchase accounting type acquisitions. Tax-basis goodwill is only created if the tax basis of the target's assets are stepped-up.

flows directly through to shareholders. No tax is levied at the S corporation level because the S corporation is a pass-through or conduit entity. The nature of the gain, whether ordinary or capital, at the S corporation level also passes through to shareholders. In the third scenario, the transaction is taxed as a stock sale, so no direct tax effect occurs at the S corporation level. Shareholders recognize taxable gain or loss on the sale of the S corporation stock.

Having outlined the basic tax consequences of the three basic types of taxable acquisitions of S corporations, we next analyze the factors relevant to choosing among the transactional alternatives. After briefly discussing the tax implications of the three tax structures, we quantify the differences between them.

Case 1: Taxable Asset Acquisition

The mechanics of a taxable acquisition of an S corporation's assets are essentially identical to those associated with a taxable asset acquisition of a C corporation.[4] Figure 15.1 provides a diagram of the structure of an asset acquisition followed by a liquidation when the target is an S corporation. As in any taxable asset acquisition, the seller recognizes a gain and the acquirer obtains a basis in the assets equal to the purchase price, plus various adjustments in certain circumstances. A major difference in this case, however, is that the S corporation does not pay a tax on the asset sale gain. Rather, that gain passes through to shareholders of the S corporation, who are responsible for any tax associated with the gain.

For illustrative purposes, we will use the same set of facts used in Chapter 14 to compare and contrast the tax implications of various acquisition structures. Table 15.2 provides an overview of the computations that follow. We make the following assumptions about the hypothetical S corporation sale:

- The target (T) S corporation has assets with a historical cost of $100 and accumulated depreciation of $0.
- T corporation shareholders have a tax basis in their T stock of $100, which they have held for more than 12 months.
- T corporation has no liabilities.
- The acquirer (A) pays T corporation $1,000 for the assets of T.

The asset sale will give rise to a gain of $900 ($1,000 price less $100 basis in the assets) at the T corporation level. This gain is capital in nature because no accumulated depreciation was associated with T's assets. Any recaptured depreciation on the sale would be ordinary income.[5] No tax will be due on the $900 capital gain at the T corporation level. The acquirer (A) will take a basis in the assets of T equal to the

---

[4]If the S corporation target was converted to S corporation status from C corporation status, additional taxes are levied on the sale of the S corporation's assets under Tax Code Section 1374.
[5]The type of property sold determines the tax treatment of recaptured depreciation. For purposes of this text, we assume that all recaptured depreciation is taxed as ordinary income. It is important for readers to be aware here, as elsewhere, that numerous additional technical complications must be considered. For example, recaptured depreciation on certain types of property (Section 1250 property) is taxed at 25% under current law, while other recaptured depreciation can be taxed at rates as high as 35%. Similarly, if some of the target's assets were inventory, the gain arising from the sale of those assets would be ordinary income.

FIGURE 15.1 Taxable Asset Acquisition with Subsequent Liquidation of the Target: Target Is an S Corporation

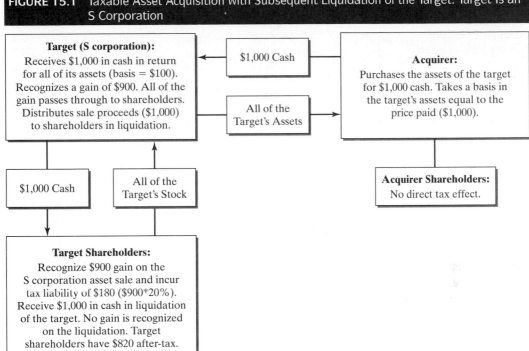

purchase price ($1,000). Therefore, A corporation obtains a step-up in tax basis of $900, as shown in Table 15.3. The purchase price will be allocated to the tangible and intangible assets of T in accordance with the residual method described in Chapter 14. Any portion of the purchase price allocated to goodwill will be amortizable over 15 years under **Section 197.**

The shareholders of T corporation will recognize a capital gain of $900 on the sale of T's assets. The nature of the gain (ordinary or capital) at the S corporation level passes through to the shareholders of T, hence the gain at the shareholder level is capital given our facts. Assuming the shareholders of T are individual investors—corporations cannot hold stock of S corporations—who are subject to the maximum statutory federal capital gains tax rate under current law, the shareholder tax on the asset sale is $180, or $900 multiplied by a 20% capital gains tax rate. Notice that T's shareholders must pay this tax whether or not they receive any cash from T corporation.

We are assuming here that T corporation liquidates after the asset sale. What is the tax on its shareholders on the liquidation? When T corporation recognizes the $900 gain on the asset sale, the gain is passed through to shareholders. Consequently, shareholders increase their basis in the stock of T corporation by the amount of the gain. The increase in shareholder basis occurs anytime that the S corporation recognizes gains, and provides the mechanism to ensure that only a single level of tax is levied on S corporation shareholders. Therefore, prior to the liquidation of T, the

Fact Pattern:

Stock purchase price	$1,000.00	$t_c =$	35%
Asset purchase price	$1,000.00	$t_{oi} =$	40%
Net tax basis in assets	100.00	$t_{cg} =$	20%
Historical cost	100.00	$r =$	10%
Accumulated depreciation	0.00	Amortization/depreciation	
Shareholder's tax basis in target's stock	100.00	period $(n) =$	10
Liabilities of target	0.00		

		S Corporation Acquisition Structure		
	Taxable Asset Acquisition	*Taxable Stock Acquisition with a §338(h)(10) Election*[1]	*Taxable Stock Acquisition without a §338(h)(10) Election*	*Taxable Stock Acquisition with a §338(h)(10) Election*[1]
Purchase price	$1,000.00	$1,000.00	$1,000.00	
Acquirer indifference price[2]				$1,246.58
Target Corporation:				
Taxable gain[3]	$900.00	$900.00	$0.00	$1,146.58
Taxable liability[4]	0.00	0.00	0.00	0.00
Shareholder Effect:				
Taxable gain[5]	$900.00	$900.00	$900.00	$1,146.58
Cash to shareholders	$1,000.00	$1,000.00	$1,000.00	$1,246.58
Tax liability[6]	180.00	180.00	180.00	229.32
After-tax cash	$820.00	$820.00	$820.00	$1,017.27
Acquirer Cost:				
Gross cost	$1,000.00	$1,000.00	$1,000.00	$1,246.58
Less: tax benefits[7]	193.55	193.55	0.00	246.58
Net after-tax cost	$806.45	$806.45	$1,000.00	$1,000.00
Acquirer Basis in:				
Target's stock	n/a	$1,000.00	$1,000.00	$1,246.58
Target's net assets	$1,000.00	$1,000.00	$100.00	$1,246.58

[1]A §338(h)(10) election causes the stock sale to be taxed as if the target's shareholders sold the assets of the target corporation instead of the target's stock.

[2]The purchase price at which the acquirer is indifferent between a transaction that is taxed as an asset sale (stock sale with a §338(h)(10) election) relative to a transaction that is taxed like a stock sale at a purchase price of $1,000 (column 3).

[3]Taxable gain at the target corporation level from the sale of the target's assets or the deemed sale of the target's assets under a §338(h)(10).

[4]Tax liability at the target corporation level on the taxable gain from the asset sale, stock sale or the deemed asset sale under §338(h)(10) election.

[5]Taxable gain at the target shareholder level. This gain is equivalent to the gain at the target corporation level as the gain passes through to target shareholders. The gain retains its character (ordinary or capital) as it passes through to target shareholders.

[6]Target shareholder tax liability is the taxable gain from the asset sale at the target corporation level multiplied by the appropriate tax rate [the value defined by footnote (3) multiplied by the shareholder tax rate on ordinary income or capital gains] or the taxable gain on a stock sale multiplied by the capital gains tax rate.

[7]The present value of the tax savings resulting from stepping-up the tax basis of the target's assets assuming that the step-up is amortized/depreciated straight-line over a 10-year period, the applicable tax rate is 35% and the after-tax discount rate is 10%.

TABLE 15.3 Estimation of Tax Benefits from Stepping up the Tax Basis of a Target's Assets

Fact Pattern:

Purchase price	$1,000.00
Target's net asset basis	100.00
Step-up[(1)]	900.00
Amortization/depreciation period	10
Depreciation method	straight-line
Annual incremental amortization/depreciation[(2)]	$90.00
$t_c =$	35.00%
$r =$	10.00%

Period	Incremental Depreciation[(2)]	Tax Savings[(3)]	Present Value of Tax Savings[(4)]
1	$90.00	$31.50	$28.64
2	90.00	31.50	26.03
3	90.00	31.50	23.67
4	90.00	31.50	21.51
5	90.00	31.50	19.56
6	90.00	31.50	17.78
7	90.00	31.50	16.16
8	90.00	31.50	14.69
9	90.00	31.50	13.36
10	90.00	31.50	12.14
Total	$900.00	$315.00	$193.55

[(1)]Step-up is the increase in the tax basis of the target's assets computed as the purchase price less the net asset basis pre-acquisition.

[(2)]Incremental amortization/depreciation deductions are the step-up divided by the amortization period.

[(3)]Tax savings are incremental amortization/depreciation deductions multiplied by the corporate tax rate (t_c).

[(4)]Present value of tax savings discounted at the after-tax rate discount rate (r).

shareholders of T have a basis in their T stock of $1,000 ($100 original basis plus the $900 gain on the asset sale). Consequently, when T liquidates and distributes the proceeds of the asset sale ($1,000) to its shareholders in return for their T stock, no gain is recorded on the liquidation because the shareholders of T have a basis in their T stock of $1,000.[6] After the liquidation then, T's shareholders have $820 after tax ($1,000 received in the liquidation less $180 tax on the capital gain).

---

[6]The taxation of conduit entities causes the entity owner to increase its basis in the stock of the entity for any gain recognized. In our example, the shareholders of the target would increase their basis in the stock of the target by the amount of the gain recognized on the asset sale ($900). Shareholder basis after the asset sale but before the liquidating distribution would therefore be $1,000 or the $100 presale basis plus the $900 corporate-level gain on the asset sale. Consequently, the target shareholder's basis in the stock of the S corporation is $1,000 before the corporate liquidation. This required basis adjustment prevents double taxation of the S corporation's income. Notice here that there is no gain or loss because the shareholder's stock basis is equivalent to the amount of the distribution.

Case 2: Taxable Stock Acquisition with a Section 338(h)(10) Election

Rather than acquire the assets of the S corporation, an acquirer can purchase the stock of the corporation. The transaction costs of acquiring the stock of an S corporation might be much lower than the costs of acquiring its assets because S corporations are by definition closely held, and an acquirer is likely dealing with a small group of shareholders. Therefore, the transaction costs associated with acquiring their shares would probably be relatively small.

However, a stock acquisition does not produce a step-up in the tax basis of the target's assets. An acquirer may prefer the tax consequences of a taxable asset purchase, while seeking to avoid the associated transaction costs. Under Section 338(h)(10), a taxable stock acquisition of an S corporation can be taxed as if the acquirer purchased the target's assets instead of its stock. A Section 338(h)(10) election is made jointly by the buyer and the seller.[7] In order to qualify for a Section 338(h)(10) election, the acquirer must obtain at least 80% of the target's stock during a 12-month period. In addition, the acquirer must obtain the explicit cooperation of the target's shareholders in the making of the election. Without the seller's consent, the acquirer cannot make a valid Section 338(h)(10) election.

It is important to note that, when a Section 338(h)(10) election is made, no tax is due on the stock sale, only a tax on the asset sale. Using the facts outlined in Case 1 and assuming a taxable stock acquisition followed by the Section 338(h)(10) election, we find that the shareholders of T would have $820 after tax ($1,000 purchase price less $180 tax liability), and the acquirer would obtain a $1,000 tax basis in the stock and assets of T. Table 15.2 illustrates the tax consequences of a taxable stock acquisition with a Section 338(h)(10) election, and Figure 15.2 illustrates the structure of the transaction. One difference between a taxable asset acquisition and a taxable stock acquisition is that T corporation would survive as a subsidiary of the acquirer in a taxable stock acquisition. T would lose its S corporation status however because one of its shareholders (A) would now be a corporation.

Case 3: Taxable Stock Acquisition without a Section 338(h)(10) Election

An acquirer can also purchase an S corporation in a taxable stock acquisition in which a Section 338(h)(10) election is not made. If the election is not made, the transaction is taxed as a stock sale, and the tax basis of the target corporation carries over, meaning that there is no step-up in the tax basis of the target's assets. Figure 15.3 illustrates the structure of a taxable stock sale of an S corporation without a Section 338(h)(10) election.

Returning to our facts from Case 1, assume that the acquirer is willing to pay $1,000 for the stock of T and that no Section 338(h)(10) election will be made. Under this structure, T corporation would become a subsidiary of the acquirer, and T corporation would lose its S corporation status because it would be owned by a corporation. A will take a

---

[7]Recall that a regular Section 338 election is made unilaterally by the acquirer.

FIGURE 15.2 Taxable Stock Acquisition of the Target with an I.R.C. §338(h)(10) Election: Target Is an S Corporation

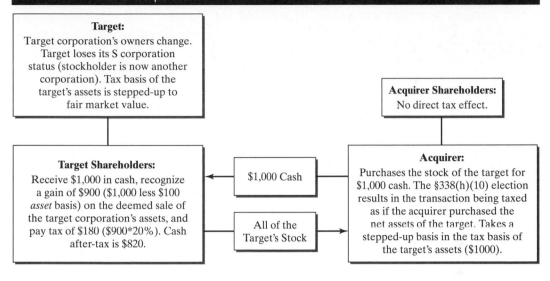

Target:
Target corporation's owners change. Target loses its S corporation status (stockholder is now another corporation). Tax basis of the target's assets is stepped-up to fair market value.

Acquirer Shareholders:
No direct tax effect.

Target Shareholders:
Receive $1,000 in cash, recognize a gain of $900 ($1,000 less $100 *asset* basis) on the deemed sale of the target corporation's assets, and pay tax of $180 ($900*20%). Cash after-tax is $820.

$1,000 Cash

All of the Target's Stock

Acquirer:
Purchases the stock of the target for $1,000 cash. The §338(h)(10) election results in the transaction being taxed as if the acquirer purchased the net assets of the target. Takes a stepped-up basis in the tax basis of the target's assets ($1000).

Postacquisition:

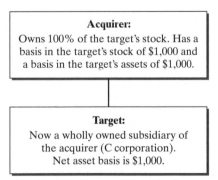

Acquirer:
Owns 100% of the target's stock. Has a basis in the target's stock of $1,000 and a basis in the target's assets of $1,000.

Target:
Now a wholly owned subsidiary of the acquirer (C corporation). Net asset basis is $1,000.

basis in the *stock* of T corporation equal to the price paid, or $1,000. The tax basis of T's assets will carry over and be $100. Hence, A does not obtain a step-up in the tax basis of T's assets and the corresponding tax benefits associated with the step-up. The shareholders of T corporation will recognize a capital gain of $900 on the sale of their *shares* to A for $1,000. Stock is a capital asset, and therefore the sale of stock gives rise to a capital gain. Assuming the appropriate capital gains tax rate is 20%, T's shareholders will face a capital gains tax liability of $180 and have $820 after tax.

Which Structure Is Optimal in the Sale of an S Corporation?

Which of the three taxable acquisition structures discussed is optimal in the sale of an S corporation, and what are the pivotal issues influencing the structure of an

FIGURE 15.3 Taxable Stock Acquisition of the Target without an I.R.C. §338(h)(10) Election: Target is an S Corporation

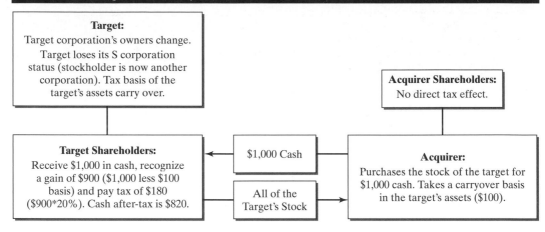

Postacquisition:

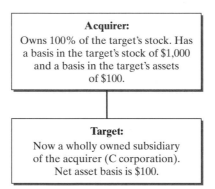

S corporation acquisition? Because the tax consequences of Cases 1 and 2 are identical, we compare Case 2 and Case 3, which also avoid nontax cost differences between stock and asset sales because Case 2 and Case 3 are both stock sales.

Which structure then is optimal between Case 2 and Case 3? We can algebraically express the relationship between the two structures in terms of target shareholder after-tax *wealth* and acquiring firm after-tax *cost*. In Case 2, a Section 338(h)(10) transaction, target shareholders after-tax wealth can be expressed as:

$$
\begin{aligned}
ATAX_{338h10} &= \text{Price}_{338h10} - \text{TAX} \\
&= \text{Price}_{338h10} - (\text{Price}_{338h10} - \text{Basis})t \\
&= \text{Price}_{338h10} - [(\text{Price}_{338h10} - \text{HCasset})t_{\text{cg}} + (\text{Accum} \times t_{\text{oi}})] \\
&= \text{Price}_{338h10}(1 - t_{\text{cg}}) + \text{HCasset} \times t_{\text{cg}} - \text{Accum} \times t_{\text{oi}}
\end{aligned}
\tag{15.1}
$$

where

$Price_{338h10}$ = the purchase price in a Section 338(h)(10) transaction[8]

Basis = the net asset basis of the target's assets, which is equal to the historical cost basis of the target's assets (HCasset) less the accumulated depreciation and amortization associated with the target's assets (Accum)[9]

t = the tax rate

t_{cg} = the appropriate capital gains tax rate for individual shareholders

t_{oi} = the ordinary income rate for individual shareholders

In Case 3, target shareholder's after-tax wealth can be expressed as

$$ATAX_{no338h10} = Price_{no338h10} - TAX$$
$$= Price_{no338h10} - (Price_{no338h10} - Stock)t_{cg}$$
$$= Price_{no338h10}(1 - t_{cg}) + Stock \times t_{cg} \qquad \textbf{(15.2)}$$

where

$Price_{no338h10}$ = the purchase price if the Section 338(h)(10) is not made

Stock = the target shareholder's basis in the stock of the target firm

The other variables are as defined previously.

We can find the purchase price with the election (Case 2) that leaves target shareholders indifferent between Case 2 and Case 3 at a given purchase price in Case 3, the no Section 338(h)(10) election scenario. We can do so by setting equation (15.1) and (15.2) equal to each other and then simplifying.

$$Price_{338h10} = Price_{no338h10} + [Stock^*t_{cg} - HCasset^*t_{cg} + Accum^*t_{oi}]/(1 - t_{cg}) \qquad \textbf{(15.3)}$$

Using equation (15.3), we see that target shareholders are indifferent between receiving $1,000 in Case 3 or $1,000 in Case 2 where the Section 338(h)(10) election is made.[10] Under Case 2 or Case 3, T's shareholders ultimately have $820 after tax when they receive $1,000 pretax. They are therefore indifferent between Case 2 and Case 3 at any price, given our simple fact pattern.

The acquiring firm's pretax cost of acquiring T corporation is $1,000 in each case. Under Case 2, A takes a tax basis in T's assets of $1,000; while under Case 3, A takes a basis in T's assets of $100. The $900 step-up in tax basis under Case 2 generates gross

---

[8]We assume that $Price_{338h10}$ exceeds HCasset. The algebraic relationship is slightly different if $Price_{338h10}$ is less than HCasset. As readers grasp the logic presented in equations (15.1) through (15.6), they can develop financial models that deal with various fact patterns and contingencies.

[9]Recall that recaptured depreciation can be taxed as ordinary income. Under the assumption that all recaptured depreciation gives rise to ordinary income, equation (15.1) estimates tax liabilities on recaptured depreciation at ordinary rates. The excess of the purchase price over the historical cost of the assets (HCasset) is capital gain. As a practical matter, in many circumstances some or all of what we are defining as recaptured depreciation will be taxed at capital gains rates. The algebraic expressions herein, and the corresponding financial models, can be modified to reflect these additional complexities. Alternatively, we could alter the fact pattern such that a portion of the target's assets are inventory. The deemed sale of inventory at a price in excess of cost would typically generate ordinary income.

[10]The second term on the right-hand side of equation (15.3) is equal to zero because (stock) basis equals asset basis (HCasset − Accum), and there is no accumulated depreciation on the assets of the target.

undiscounted tax savings of $315 ($900 multiplied by a 35% tax rate) for A. Assuming that these incremental depreciation deductions occur evenly over 10 years and an appropriate after-tax discount rate is 10%, the present value of the tax benefits from the step-up is $193.55 (see Table 15.3). The acquirer's *net* after-tax cost under Case 2 is therefore $806.45 ($1,000 less $193.55), while net after-tax cost is $1,000 under Case 3. Therefore Case 2 dominates Case 3.

It is apparent that, given our example numbers, the acquirer is willing to pay a higher pretax price in order to obtain the target shareholders' consent in making the Section 338(h)(10) election, because the acquirer's after-tax cost is lower, other things equal, when the Section 338(h)(10) election is made. How much more, then, is the acquirer willing to pay the seller to induce the seller to make the Section 338(h)(10) election, assuming that the acquirer believes $1,000 is a reasonable price to pay to acquire the target if the basis of the target's assets does not change (Case 3)? With Case 2, the net after-tax cost of the acquisition to the acquirer can be expressed as:

$$ATAXCOST_{338h10} = Acqprice_{338h10} - \text{Incremental tax benefits}$$
$$= Acqprice_{338h10} - t_c(PVANN)[(Acqprice_{338h10} - Asset)/n] \quad \textbf{(15.4)}$$

where

$Acqprice_{338h10}$ = the price that the acquirer will pay in a Section 338(h)(10) transaction

$PVANN$ = the present value of an annuity

t_c = the corporate tax rate

$Asset$ = the net tax basis of the target's assets

n = the useful life of the target's assets postacquisition

Under Case 3, the acquirer's net after-tax cost can be expressed as

$$ATAXCOST_{no338h10} = Acqprice_{no338h10} - \text{Incremental tax benefits}$$
$$= Acqprice_{no338h10} - \$0 \quad \textbf{(15.5)}$$

where

$Acqprice_{no338h10}$ = the price the acquirer will pay if the Section 338(h)(10) election is not made

The acquirer gains no incremental tax benefits in Case 3, because the tax basis of the target's assets is not stepped-up. The acquirer is indifferent between Case 2 and Case 3 when equation (15.4) equals equation (15.5). We assume for ease of exposition that $Acqprice_{no338h10}$ and $Price_{no338h10}$ are equivalent. That is, we assume that the acquirer and the target agree on the value of the target corporation if the Section 338(h)(10) election is not made and the tax basis of the target's assets does not change. Simplifying, we find

$$Acqprice_{338h10} = (Price_{no338h10} - t_c \times \text{Factor} \times Asset)/(1 - t_c \times \text{Factor}) \quad \textbf{(15.6)}$$

where Factor is equal to $PVANN/n$ and all other variables are as defined previously.

Given $Price_{no338h10}$ equals $1,000, the acquirer is indifferent between Case 3 at $1,000 and Case 2 at a price of $1,246.58 computed as[11]

$$Acqprice_{338h10} = (\$1,000 - .21506 \times \$100)/(1 - .21506)$$

---

[11]Factor equals .61445 when $n = 10$ and $r = 10\%$, so Factor $\times t_c = .21506$.

At that price, the acquirer would take a basis in the assets of T of $1,246.58. Stated another way, the acquirer would obtain a step-up in basis of $1,146.58. Under the same assumptions (10-year straight-line amortization, $t_c = 35\%$, $r = 10\%$), the present value of the $1,146.58 step-up is $246.58. Therefore, A's net after-tax cost under Case 2 at a price of $1,246.58 is $1,000.

Note that, even at a 24% pretax *premium,* or ($1,246.58 − $1000)/$1,000, in Case 2 A is equally well off after tax under Case 2 as it is in Case 3. At a purchase price of $1,246.58, T's shareholders would recognize a capital gain on the sale of T's assets of $1,146.58 ($1,246.58 less $100 basis in T's stock), pay capital gains taxes of $229.32 ($1,146.58 × 20%) and have $1,017.27 after tax. It amounts to $197.27 ($1,017.27 minus $820) more after tax than under the original Case 3. The last column of Table 15.2 illustrates these computations.

Advanced Analysis: S Corporation Acquisition

In Section 14.2 of Chapter 14, we illustrated why sales of freestanding C corporations are rarely structured in a manner that results in a step-up in the tax basis of the target's assets. In this section, we illustrated that, in S corporation acquisitions, structuring the transaction to achieve a step-up in the tax basis of the target's assets can leave both the acquirer and the target's shareholders better off after tax.

How do we explain why different acquisition structures are preferred with different target organizational forms? As with any tax planning strategy, the fundamental issue is a comparison of incremental tax costs with incremental tax benefits, holding nontax factors constant. In the case of an acquisition of a C corporation, the incremental cost of obtaining a step-up is usually the tax rate multiplied by the amount of the step-up (in Section 14.2 of Chapter 14, this amount was $315). The incremental tax savings from the step-up is the present value of the tax savings from the step-up (in Section 14.2, we estimated this amount as $193.55), which is always less than the incremental tax cost if tax rates are constant and discount rates are greater than 0%.

In the case of an S corporation acquisition, the incremental cost of the step-up is not the tax rate multiplied by the step-up amount. It is usually something less.[12] This is true because there is only one level of tax on an "asset sale" in an S corporation, while there are two levels of tax on an "asset sale" of a C corporation.[13] The example that we used for an S corporation acquisition is oversimplified, but it illustrates these fundamental principles. We next work through a more realistic example in which the incremental cost of asset sale tax treatment for the S corporation's shareholders is not $0.

The facts for our more realistic example are the following:

- T corporation, the target, is an S corporation that has assets with a net tax basis of $200. The historical cost of these assets is $400, and the assets have accumulated depreciation of $200.

---

[12]In our simple example, the incremental cost of the step-up was $0 because, under either Case 2 or Case 3, target shareholders faced a tax liability of $180.

[13]These two levels are the oft-repeated "double tax" on C corporations that was a centerpiece of the Bush Administration's refrain for reduction in individual investor dividend and capital gains tax rates in 2002 and 2003.

- T corporation has no liabilities, and it is owned by individual shareholders that have held their shares for more than 12 months and are subject to federal income taxes at the top statutory rates (20% for capital gains and 40% for ordinary income). T's shareholders have a basis in their T stock of $200.
- All recaptured depreciation is taxable at the ordinary income rate.
- The acquiring firm is willing to pay $1,000 to acquire the stock of T corporation when a Section 338(h)(10) election will not be made.

Should the acquirer and seller make the Section 338(h)(10) election? Table 15.4 illustrates the following computations. Starting with our base facts (column 1 of Table 15.4), T shareholders would have $840 after tax in a taxable stock sale without the election. The acquiring firm's net after-tax cost of this acquisition structure would be $1,000, with no incremental tax benefits from a step-up. To determine what structure is optimal, we must set one party to the transaction indifferent and find which structure is preferable to the other party, under the terms defined by the first party's indifference. At what pretax price, assuming that a Section 338(h)(10) election is made, would the target's shareholders be indifferent relative to the $1,000 purchase price and no election? We can solve for the pretax price by finding the price that leaves target shareholders with $840 after tax from equation (15.3).

$$\text{Price}_{338h10} = \text{Price}_{no338h10} + (\text{Stock}^* t_{cg} - \text{HCasset}^* t_{cg} + \text{Accum}^* t_{oi})(1 - t_{cg})$$
$$= \$1,000 + [\$200(t_{cg}) - \$400(t_{cg}) + \$200(t_{oi})]/(1 - t_{cg})$$
$$= \$1,050$$

At a purchase price of $1,050, the stock sale accompanied by a Section 338(h)(10) election would give rise to a $850 taxable gain at the T corporation level. Of this gain, $200 would be ordinary income (recaptured depreciation) and $650 would be capital gain ($1,050 less historical cost of $400). The $850 gain and the character of the gain passes through to T's shareholders. T's shareholders would therefore have a tax liability of $210 computed as 40% multiplied by $200 of ordinary income and 20% multiplied by $650 of capital gain. They would have $840 after tax ($1,050 price less $210 of taxes) and would be indifferent between receiving $1,000 pretax in a stock sale with no election and $1,050 in a stock sale with a Section 338(h)(10) election (see column 2 of Table 15.4).

Which structure then does A prefer: no election at a price of $1,000 or a deal priced at $1,050 with the election? The net after-tax cost of a taxable stock acquisition without a Section 338(h)(10) election is $1,000 ($1,000 purchase price and zero incremental tax benefits). If the election is made, and the purchase price is $1,050, A's net after-tax cost is $867.20.[14] The size of the step-up, if the election is made, is $850 ($1,050 purchase price less $200 net basis in T's assets), and the present value of the tax savings from the step-up is $182.80, using the same assumptions about depreciable lives, tax, and discount rates as previously. Clearly then, A prefers to pay the higher pretax price to get the step-up in T's assets.

---

[14]Notice that the acquirer's net after-tax cost is about 13% lower than when the election was not made.

Fact Pattern:

Stock purchase price	$1,000.00	$t_c =$	35%
Net tax basis in assets	200.00	$t_o =$	40%
Historical cost	400.00	$t_{cg} =$	20%
Accumulated depreciation	200.00	$r =$	10%
Shareholder's tax basis in target's stock	200.00	Amortization/depreciation	
Liabilities of target	0.00	period $(n) =$	10

	S Corporation Acquisition Structure			*Tax Benefit Split*[1]	
	Taxable Stock Acquisition without a §338(h)(10) Election	*Taxable Stock Acquisition with a §338(h)(10) Election*[2]	*Taxable Stock Acquisition with a §338(h)(10) Election*[2]	*Taxable Stock Acquisition with a §338(h)(10) Election*[2]	*Estimated Incremental After-Tax Benefit*
Purchase price—Base case	$1,000.00				
Seller's indifference price[3]		$1,050.00			
Acquirer's indifference price[4]			$1,219.19		
Tax benefit split[1]				$1,134.60	
Target Corporation:					
Taxable gain[5]	$0.00	$850.00	$1,019.19	$934.60	
Taxable liability[6]	0.00	0.00	0.00	0.00	
Shareholder Effect:					
Taxable gain[7]	$800.00	$850.00	$1,019.19	$934.60	
Cash to shareholders	$1,000.00	$1,050.00	$1,219.19	$1,134.60	
Tax liability[8]	160.00	210.00	243.84	226.92	
After-tax cash	$840.00	$840.00	$975.35	$907.68	$67.68
Acquirer After-Tax Cost:					
Gross cost	$1,000.00	$1,050.00	$1,219.19	$1,134.60	
Less: tax benefits[9]	0.00	182.80	219.19	200.99	
Net after-tax cost	$1,000.00	$867.20	$1,000.00	$933.61	$66.39
Acquirer Basis in:					
Target's stock	$1,000.00	$1,050.00	$1,219.19	$1,134.60	
Target's net assets	$200.00	$1,050.00	$1,219.19	$1,134.60	

[1]Purchase price that splits, approximately evenly, the net tax benefits from stepping-up the tax basis of the target's assets.

[2]A §338(h)(10) election causes the stock sale to be taxed as if the target's shareholders sold the assets of the target instead of the target's stock.

[3]The purchase price at which the seller is indifferent between making the §338(h)(10) election and not making the election when the purchase price is $1,000 (column 1).

[4]The purchase price at which the acquirer is indifferent between making the §338(h)(10) election and not making the election when the purchase price is $1,000 (column 1).

[5]Taxable gain at the target corporation level from the sale of the target's assets or the deemed asset sale associated with the §338(h)(10) election.

[6]Tax liability at the target corporation level on the taxable gain from the sale of the target's assets or the deemed sale of its assets with the §338(h)(10) election.

[7]Taxable gain at the target shareholder level. This gain is equivalent to the gain at the target corporation level in an asset sale or a stock sale with the §338(h)(10) election as the gain passes through to target shareholders. The gain retains its character (ordinary or capital) as it passes through to target shareholders. In a stock sale without the §338(h)(10) election, the gain is computed as the difference between the purchase price and target shareholder's stock basis. In the latter case, the gain is capital in nature.

[8]Target shareholder tax liability is the taxable gain from the stock or asset sale multiplied by the appropriate tax rate [the value defined by footnote (7) multiplied by the shareholder tax rate on ordinary income or capital gains].

[9]The present value of the tax savings resulting from stepping-up the tax basis of the target's assets assuming that the step-up is amortized/depreciated straight-line over a 10-year period, the applicable tax rate is 35% and the after-tax discount rate is 10%.

From A's perspective, the incremental cost of obtaining a step-up is $50 ($1,050 purchase price less $1,000 price without the election), and the incremental tax benefit is $182.80. Thus, A is better off by $132.80 after tax when the transaction is structured in a manner that results in a step-up in T's assets.[15] The $132.80 can be thought of as the net tax benefits from stepping up the tax basis of the target's assets. Incidentally, these tax benefits can be split between the acquirer and the target, as we will illustrate in a moment.

Under our new facts, we see the purchase price at which the acquirer is indifferent or the maximum price the acquirer will pay when T's assets are stepped-up is given by equation (15.6).

$$\text{Acqprice}_{338h10} = (\$1,000 - .21506 \times \$200)/(1 - .21506)$$
$$\text{Acqprice}_{338h10} = \$1,219.19 \tag{15.6}$$

The acquirer will therefore be indifferent between a stock acquisition without the Section 338(h)(10) election at a price of $1,000 and a stock acquisition with the election at a price of $1,219.19, because the acquirer's net after-tax cost under either scenario is $1,000, as illustrated in the first and third columns of Table 15.4.

For an advisor to target shareholders, the ability to estimate this price is obviously quite useful because the shareholders benefit from knowing the maximum price the acquirer will pay under varying acquisition tax structures. Notice that, at a price of $1,219.19, with the election, target shareholders have $975.35 after tax, which is about 16% more than if the election is not made and the purchase price is $1,000.

At any price between $1,050 and $1,219.19, with the Section 338(h)(10) election, both the acquirer and target shareholders are better off after tax than if the deal is priced at $1,000 and the election is not made jointly by the buyer and seller. As the purchase price approaches $1,050 ($1,219.19), the acquirer (target shareholders) is (are) relatively better off. Essentially, the difference between $1,050 and $1,219.19 is the incremental tax benefits from stepping up the tax basis of the target's assets that can be shared between the buyer and seller. For example, consider a price exactly halfway between these amounts ($1,134.60). At this price, target shareholder's after-tax wealth is $907.68, which is $67.38 more after tax than they receive if the transaction is priced at $1,000 and the *joint* election is not made. Similarly, the acquirer's net after tax cost is $66.39 less than if the deal is priced at $1,000 and the election is not made. The last two columns of Table 15.4 contain these computations. Notice that even at a pretax *premium* of 13.46% [($1,134.60 − $1,000)/$1,000] the acquirer is better off after tax by about 7% if the tax basis of the target's assets is stepped up.

Is this conclusion reasonable, or is it an ivory tower fantasy? What is the source of this value that increases both the buyer's and the seller's wealth?

The preceding equations formally explain this phenomenon but, stated simply, in an S corporation acquisition a step-up in the tax basis of the target's assets incrementally costs much less than the incremental benefits of such a step-up. That is, in the absence of a step-up election, S corporation shareholders face almost the same amount of tax they do if the step-up election is made. Therefore, the incremental cost of the election is often relatively low. The incremental tax benefit of the election, however, can be

---

[15]The difference in A's net after-tax cost is $132.80 as illustrated in the first two columns of Table 15.4.

large. The same is generally true in acquisitions of other types of conduits. The net benefit is the source of wealth gains that can be shared between the buyer and seller. Of course, informed parties should make the most of these net benefits when structuring and pricing an acquisition.

15.2 COMPARISON OF THE SALE OF SIMILAR S AND C CORPORATIONS

Important differences mark the way in which acquisitions of conduits (S corporations) and C corporations are taxed. Notably, two levels of tax characterize the acquisition of a C corporation and only one in the acquisition of an S corporation. Another difference relates to the tax rates that apply to the asset sale. In the case of a C corporation, the tax rate on the "asset sale" is 35% while, in an S corporation, the tax rate on the asset sale can be as low as 15%.[16] Here, via numerical illustration, we want to highlight these differences. The computations discussed in this section are illustrated in Table 15.5. The facts for this example include the following:

- The two identical corporations are T1 and T2: T1 is a C corporation and T2 is an S corporation.
- The net tax basis of each firm's assets is $200 ($400 historical cost, $200 accumulated depreciation).
- Neither firm has any liabilities.
- Shareholders of both T1 and T2 are individuals facing the maximum ordinary and capital gains tax rates (40% and 20%) under current U.S. law and have a tax basis in the stock of each corporation of $200.
- All parties agree that the present value of the after-tax future cash flows of T1 and T2 is $900 each.
- T1's ordinary income tax rate is 35% as is its capital gains tax rate.
- All recaptured depreciation is taxed at the ordinary income rate.
- An acquirer wishes to purchase both T1 and T2 and is willing to pay $900 for each company in a taxable stock acquisition in which the tax basis of the target's assets carries over.

What price will an acquirer (A) pay to purchase the *assets* of T1 and T2 in a taxable acquisition? Will shareholders accept this price? We first consider the tax consequences of a taxable stock sale.

Tax Consequences for T1 and T2 Shareholders in a Taxable Stock Sale

In each case, shareholders will have a capital gain of $700 ($900 purchase price less $200 stock basis) and will pay tax of $140 ($700 × 20%). After tax, the shareholders of both T1 and T2 will have $760.

---

[16]Notice that the tax rate on incremental tax deductions arising from a step-up in the tax basis of the target's assets (asset sale tax treatment) can be 35% or higher if the acquirer is a C corporation.

TABLE 15.5 Comparison of Acquisition Prices of S Corporations and C Corporations with Identical Tax Attributes and Cash Flows

Fact Pattern:

Stock purchase price	$900.00	$t_c =$	35%
Net tax basis in assets	200.00	$t_o =$	40%
Historical cost	400.00	$t_{cg} =$	20%
Accumulated depreciation	200.00	$r =$	10%
Shareholder's tax basis in target's stock	200.00	$N =$	10
Liabilities of target	0.00		

	S Corporation Acquisition Structure			C Corporation Acquisition Structure		
	Taxable Stock Acquisition without a §338(h)(10) Election	*Taxable Stock Acquisition with a §338(h)(10) Election*	*Taxable Stock Acquisition with a §338(h)(10) Election*	*Taxable Stock Acquisition without a §338 Election*	*Taxable Asset Acquisition*	*Taxable Asset Acquisition*
Purchase price	$900.00			$900.00		
Seller's indifference price[(1)]		$950.00			$1,276.92	
Acquirer's indifference price[(2)]			$1,091.79			$1,091.79
Target Corporation:						
Taxable gain[(3)]	$700.00	$750.00	$891.79	$0.00	$1,076.92	$891.79
Tax liability[(4)]	0.00	0.00	0.00	0.00	376.92	312.13
Shareholder Effects:						
Taxable gain[(5)]	$700.00	$750.00	$891.79	700.00	700.00	579.66
Cash received	$900.00	$950.00	$1,091.79	$900.00	$900.00	$779.66
Tax liability[(6)]	140.00	190.00	218.36	140.00	140.00	115.93
After-tax cash	$760.00	$760.00	$873.43	$760.00	$760.00	$663.73
Acquirer After-Tax Cost:						
Gross cost	$900.00	$950.00	$1,091.79	$900.00	$1,276.92	$1,091.79
Less: tax benefits[(7)]	0.00	161.29	191.79	0.00	231.60	191.79
Net after-tax cost	$900.00	$788.71	$900.00	$900.00	$1,045.32	$900.00
Acquirer Tax Basis in the:						
Target's stock	$900.00	$950.00	$1,091.79	$900.00	n/a	n/a
Target's net assets	$200.00	$950.00	$1,091.79	$200.00	$1,276.92	$1,091.79

[(1)]The purchase price at which the seller is indifferent between making the §338(h)(10) election and not making the election when the purchase price is $900 (column 1) when the target is an S corporation. When the target is a C corporation, the purchase price at which the seller is indifferent between an asset sale and a taxable stock sale without a §338 election at a price of $900 (column 4).

[(2)]The purchase price at which the acquirer is indifferent between making the §338(h)(10) election and not making the election when the purchase price is $900 (column 1) when the target is an S corporation. When the target is a C corporation, the purchase price at which the acquirer is indifferent between an asset sale and a taxable stock sale without a §338 election at a price of $900 (column 4).

[(3)]Taxable gain at the target corporation level from the stock sale or the deemed sale of the target's assets (S corporation) or the sale of the target's assets (C corporation).

[(4)]Tax liability at the target corporation level on the taxable gain from the stock sale, the deemed asset sale (S corporation) or the asset sale (C corporation).

[(5)]Taxable gain at the target shareholder level. This gain is equivalent to the gain at the target corporation level if the target is an S corporation as the gain passes through to target shareholders. The gain retains its character as it passes through to target shareholders. If the target was a C corporation, this is the gain on the liquidation (redemption of target shares by the target) of the C corporation after the asset sale.

[(6)]Target shareholder tax liabilities are computed based on[(5)] and the nature of the gain to the target's shareholders if the target was an S corporation. If the target was a C corporation, the tax liability is the gain[(5)] multiplied by the capital gains tax rate.

[(7)]The present value of the tax savings resulting from stepping-up the tax basis of the target's assets assuming that the step-up is amortized/depreciated straight-line over a 10-year period, the applicable tax rate is 35% and the after-tax discount rate is 10%.

Tax Consequences for A Corporation

A will take a basis in the stock of T1 equal to $900. T1 will become a subsidiary of the acquirer and the net tax basis of T1's assets will be $200. A will have the same basis in the stock and assets of T2. T2 will also become a subsidiary of A.

Indifference Point for T1's Shareholders (C Corporation) with an Asset Sale Structure

T1's shareholders will be indifferent between a stock sale at $900 and an asset sale when they have $760 after-tax from the asset sale. We can compute the purchase price they will demand as follows using Equation (14.6) from Chapter 14.[17]

$$\text{Price}_{\text{asset}} = (\text{Price}_{\text{stock}} - \text{Asset} \times t_c)/(1 - t_c)$$
$$\text{Price}_{\text{asset}} = (\$900 - 200 \times t_c)/(1 - t_c)$$
$$\text{Price}_{\text{asset}} = \$1{,}276.92 \tag{14.6}$$

Indifference Price for T2's Shareholders (S Corporation) with an Asset Sale Structure

T2's shareholders will be indifferent between a stock sale at $900 and an asset sale (stock sale with a Section 338(h)(10) election) when they have $760 after tax under the asset sale structure. We can compute the purchase price they will demand as follows using equation (15.3).[18] The second column of Table 15.5 presents this computation.

$$\text{Price}_{338h10} = \text{Price}_{no338h10} + [\text{Stock}(t_{cg}) - \text{HCasset}(t_{cg}) + \text{Accum}(t_{oi})]/(1 - t_{cg})$$
$$= \$900 + [200(t_{cg}) - 400(t_{cg}) + 200(t_{oi})]/(1 - t_{cg})$$
$$= \$950$$

---

[17]Alternatively, we can use a more general approach such as:

$$ATAX_{\text{shareholder}} = \text{Liquidation proceeds} - \text{Tax basis}$$
$$\$760 = \text{Liquidation proceeds} - [(\text{Liquidation proceeds} - \$200)20\%]$$
$$\$760 = \text{Liquidation proceeds} - 20\% \text{ Liquidation proceeds} + \$40$$
$$\$720 = 80\% \text{ Liquidation proceeds}$$
$$\text{Liquidation proceeds} = \$900$$
$$\text{Liquidation proceeds} = \text{Price} - \text{Tax}$$
$$\$900 = \text{Price} - [(\text{Price} - \$400) \times 35\% + (\$200 \times 35\%)]$$
$$\$900 = .65 \text{ Price} + \$70$$
$$\text{Price} = \$1{,}276.92$$

[18]Alternatively, we can use a more general approach such as:

$$ATAX = \text{Price} - \text{Tax}$$
$$ATAX = \text{Price} - (\text{Price} - \text{Basis}) \times \text{Tax rate}$$
$$ATAX = \text{Price} - [(\text{Price} - \text{Historical cost}) \times \text{Capital gains tax rate} + (\text{Accumulated depreciation}) \times \text{Ordinary income tax rate}]$$
$$\$760 = \text{Price} - [(\text{Price} - \$400) \times 20\% + (200 \times 40\%)]$$
$$\$760 = \text{Price} - 20\% \text{ Price} + \$80 - \$80$$
$$\$760 = 80\% \text{ Price}$$
$$\text{Price} = \$950$$

Will the Acquirer Pay T1's (C Corporation) Indifference Price in a Taxable Asset Sale?

In a taxable asset sale, A will obtain a step-up in the basis of the target's assets. We already computed that T1's shareholders will not agree to a taxable asset sale structure unless A pays them at least $1,276.93. Is A willing to pay that price to obtain a step-up in T1's assets?

If A pays $1,276.93 in a taxable asset acquisition, it will take a basis in T1's assets of $1,276.93. This step-up in basis is equal to $1,076.93 ($1,276.93 less $200 net tax basis in T1's assets preacquisition). Assuming that the step-up in basis is amortized straight-line over 10 years, that the appropriate tax rate is 35%, and that the after-tax discount rate is 10%, the present value of tax savings from the step-up is $231.60. A's net after-tax cost is therefore $1,045.43, which is more than A's net after-tax cost in a taxable stock acquisition ($900).

Alternatively, as the sixth column of Table 15.5 indicates, the maximum price that the acquirer will pay in a taxable asset sale is $1,091.79, which is computed using Equation (14.9) from Chapter 14. At that price, T1's shareholders receive $663.73 after tax, which is less than they receive in the taxable stock acquisition case at a price of $900. T1's shareholders would therefore not accept a taxable asset sale at $1,091.79. Therefore, a step-up in T1's assets is not optimal. This result is the same as obtained in Section 14.2 of Chapter 14. Notice here that the incremental cost of the step-up to A is $376.93 ($1,276.93 less $900 price with no step-up) and the incremental tax benefits from the step-up are $231.60.

Will the Acquirer Pay T2's (S Corporation) Indifference Price in a Taxable Asset Sale (Stock Sale with a Section 338(h)(10) Election)?

We already computed that T2's shareholders will not agree to a taxable asset sale structure—a stock sale with a Section 338(h)(10) election—unless A pays them at least $950. Is A willing to pay that price to obtain a step-up in T2's assets?

If A pays $950 in a taxable asset acquisition, it will take a basis in T2's assets of $950. This step-up in basis is equal to $750 ($950 less $200 net tax basis in T2's assets preacquisition). Assuming that the step-up in basis is amortized straight-line over 10 years, that the appropriate tax rate is 35%, and that the after-tax discount rate is 10%, the present value of tax savings from the step-up is $161.29. A's net after-tax cost is therefore $788.71 (see the second column of Table 15.5), which is less than A's net after-tax cost in a taxable stock acquisition ($900). So A will (gladly) pay $950 in a taxable stock acquisition followed by a Section 338(h)(10) election.

Continuing with the example, A will pay T2 more than $950 in a taxable asset acquisition. A will pay a pretax price that leaves its after-tax cost equal to $900. Specifically as illustrated in the third column of Table 15.5, A will pay *up* to $1,091.79 pretax in a transaction that is taxed as an asset acquisition and still be as well off as when it pays $900 in a taxable stock sale.[19] At a price of $1,091.79, and a taxable asset sale structure, T2's shareholders would have $873.43 after tax, which is $113.43 more after tax than in a taxable stock sale at $900. It is important to notice that S corporation

---

[19]We can compute this amount using equation (15.5).

shareholders are able to obtain $113.43 (about 15%) more after tax than their counterparts who sold the C corporation (T1).[20] Again, any price between $950 and $1,091.79 with a taxable asset sale type structure in an S corporation acquisition leaves both the acquirer and seller better off, and any price within that range provides a split of the tax benefits from the asset sale structure.

The point of these numerical exercises is simple but important. An S corporation can often be sold for a higher price pretax than a similar C corporation because the sale of an S corporation can be structured in a manner that results in a step-up in the tax basis of the target's assets in a cost-effective manner. That is, acquirers are willing to pay S corporation target shareholders for the tax benefits associated with the step-up. The same is not true of sales of C corporations. Acquirers of C corporations are not willing to incur the incremental costs of stepping up the tax basis of the target's assets. For tax planners who are selecting an organizational form for a new or reorganized business entity, conduits such as S corporations provide significant tax benefits relative to C corporations if and when the entire entity is sold to an acquirer, as illustrated in this section and in Table 15.5.[21]

Valuation Consequences and Issues

As we have seen in Section 15.1, the price at which a conduit entity (S corporation) is sold is a function of the tax structure of the transaction (e.g., taxable stock sale with and without a Section 338(h)(10) election). In Section 15.2, we demonstrated that comparable S and C corporations could sell for different prices due to tax differences that spring from organizational form. Specifically, the sale of an S corporation often includes a premium that is associated with incremental tax benefits from stepping up the S corporation's assets.

When evaluating a potential target corporation, or when contemplating the sale of a business, we often derive an estimate of the value of the subject company from comparable acquisitions. Similarly, the reasonableness of a purchase or sale price is often evaluated relative to comparable transactions. It is common to use various valuation benchmarks including multiples such as acquisition price to earnings or cash flows. Readers performing a so-called comparables analysis should be aware of the effect of organizational form and acquisition tax structure on acquisition prices as illustrated in Sections 15.1 and 15.2.

Installment Sale Tax Treatment

In many instances, buyers of privately held S corporations want to pay with installment debt, and S corporation shareholders are willing to accept installment debt because installment sale tax treatment can provide significant benefits to selling shareholders. As shown in this chapter, a taxable asset acquisition structure or a taxable stock sale with a Section 338(h)(10) election is usually the optimal tax structure in the purchase of an S corporation. Because installment sale tax treatment is possible in asset sale transactions or in a stock sale followed by a Section 338(h)(10) election, selling S corporation shareholders may defer reporting gain from the transaction until future installment payments are received.

---

[20]Compare the third and fourth columns of Table 15.5.
[21]The same basic principles apply to the sale of other types of conduit entities such as partnerships and LLCs with, of course, additional complicating factors.

Summary of Key Points

1. Acquisitions occur across a number of transactional forms. These alternative forms yield varying tax consequences to the target company, to the purchasing company, and to the shareholders of the target company.
2. In the sale of a freestanding C corporation, a structure that results in a step-up in the target's assets is usually suboptimal from a tax perspective because the incremental tax cost associated with the step-up usually exceeds the incremental tax benefits. The notable exception to this general rule occurs when the target has substantial NOLs, which can be used to reduce the incremental cost of the step-up.
3. In the sale of a conduit entity, such as an S corporation, it often makes sense to structure the acquisition in a manner that steps up the tax basis of the target's assets because the incremental cost of stepping up the basis of the target S corporation's assets is usually less than the tax savings associated with the step-up. Sales of conduits (S corporations) are quite different from acquisitions of C corporations in this respect.
4. A taxable stock sale of an S corporation can be taxed as an asset sale if the buyer and seller (target corporation shareholders) agree to make a Section 338(h)(10) election.
5. Tax planners who are considering organizational forms for a new entity should consider the differences in the taxation of acquisitions of conduits relative to the taxation of C corporations. Specifically, if planners anticipate a sale of the entire entity rather than an IPO, for example, a conduit can be sold for a higher pretax price than a C corporation, everything else being equal. As a result, the conduit entity may be the wealth-maximizing organization form, holding other factors constant.

Discussion Questions

1. What are the main tax considerations to a purchaser in the sale of a target's stock when the target is an S corporation?
2. What are the disadvantages of effecting a change in the basis of all the target's assets either by their sale or by a stock purchase along with a Section 338(h)(10) election to treat the stock purchase as a purchase of all the firm's assets?
3. What types of acquisitions of S corporations generate tax-deductible goodwill? How many acquisitions of S corporations, as a general rule, give rise to tax-deductible goodwill?
4. Why does the taxable acquisition of an S corporation give rise to incremental tax benefits from stepping up the target's assets while the acquisition of a freestanding C corporation does not?
5. If you were advising the founders of a new Internet-based business, what would you tell them about the benefits of using a conduit organizational form to operate their business?

Tax Planning Problems

1. Hurricane, Inc., is an S corporation. Orleans, Inc., wants to acquire Hurricane for cash. Hurricane's shareholders have a tax basis in their stock of $3,000 and Hurricane has assets with a net tax basis of $3,000 (cost = $4,500, accumulated depreciation = $1,500). Hurricane has no liabilities. Assume that the transaction can be structured one of two ways:

    Option 1: As a taxable stock acquisition without a Section 338(h)(10) election
    Option 2: As a taxable stock acquisition with a Section 338(h)(10) election

Further assume that Orleans is willing to pay $5,000 to acquire Hurricane under either structure, and that all depreciation claimed to date must be recaptured to the extent of the purchase price. Assume that all recaptured depreciation is taxed at the highest ordinary income rate and that no additional taxes will apply in an asset sale due to Tax Code restrictions relating to S corporations.

a. How much cash after tax will Hurricane's shareholders have under Option 1? Assume the tax rate appropriate for capital gains is 20% and for ordinary income is 40%.

b. How much cash after tax will Hurricane's shareholders have under Option 2? Assume the tax rate appropriate for capital gains is 20% and for ordinary income is 40%.

c. Assume that Orleans is willing to pay $5,000 using Option 1. At what purchase price when employing Option 2 are Hurricane's shareholders indifferent between the two transaction structures?

d. What is the maximum price that Orleans will pay under Option 2 assuming that Orleans will pay $5,000 under Option 1? Assume that any step-up amount is depreciated/amortized over 10 years using the straight-line method, that the marginal tax rate for Orleans is 35%, and that the after-tax discount rate is 10%.

e. Should the Section 338(h)(10) election be made? Why or why not?

f. If the answer to part (e) was yes, how much better off are Orleans and Hurricane at the midpoint price between the amounts you computed in parts (c) and (d), if the election is made, relative to no election at a price of $5,000?

2. Cambridge, Inc., is an S corporation. Courtesan, Inc., wants to acquire Cambridge for cash. Cambridge's shareholders have a tax basis in their stock of $5,000 (they have held the stock for 5 years), and Cambridge has assets with a net tax basis of $5,000 (cost = $7,500, accumulated depreciation = $2,500). Cambridge has no liabilities. Assume that the transaction can be structured one of two ways:

Option 1: As a taxable stock acquisition without a Section 338(h)(10) election, or

Option 2: As a taxable stock acquisition with a Section 338(h)(10) election

(Recall that this election results in the transaction being taxed as an asset sale.)

Further assume that Courtesan is willing to pay $12,500 to acquire Cambridge under either structure, and that all depreciation claimed to date must be recaptured to the extent of the purchase price. Assume that no additional taxes will apply in an asset sale due to Tax Code restrictions relating to S corporations.

a. How much cash after tax will Cambridge's shareholders have under Option 1? Assume the tax rate appropriate for capital gains is 20% and for ordinary income is 40%.

b. How much cash after tax will Cambridge's shareholders have under Option 2? Assume the tax rate appropriate for capital gains is 20% and for ordinary income is 40%.

c. Assume that Courtesan is willing to pay $12,500 using Option 1. At what purchase price P when employing Option 2 are Cambridge's shareholders indifferent between the two transaction options?

d. Given the purchase price you computed in part (c), which structure is optimal from Courtesan's perspective [Option 1 at a purchase price of $12,500, or Option 2 at a price P computed in part (c)]? Assume that any step-up amount is depreciated/amortized over 10 years using the straight-line method, the marginal tax rate for Courtesan is 35%, and the after-tax discount rate is 12%.

e. What is the maximum price that Courtesan will pay under Option 2 assuming that Courtesan will pay $12,500 under Option 1? Assume that any step-up amount is depreciated/amortized over 10 years using the straight-line method, the marginal tax rate for Orleans is 35%, and the after-tax discount rate is 12%.

    f. Should the Section 338(h)(10) election be made? Why or why not?

    g. Assume that you are an advisor to Cambridge's shareholders and that they agreed to pay you 30% of any after-tax increase in their wealth associated with your advice on this transaction. Could you increase their after-tax wealth beyond what they receive under Option 1? If yes, explain briefly how (20 words will do). If yes, how much could you increase their wealth after tax approximately (before your 30% fee) if Cambridge persuaded Courtesan to pay the maximum price computed in part (e)? How much would you stand to make if they listened to you? Use the assumptions in part (e) if necessary.

3. The following facts relate to the purchase of an S corporation and a C corporation. These two corporations have identical tax bases and are similar in every respect except for their organizational form. The acquirer is willing to pay $10,000 to purchase the stock of each corporation.

Fact Pattern:	
Stock purchase price	$10,000.00
Net tax basis in assets	500.00
Historical cost of assets	2,000.00
Accumulated depreciation	1,500.00
Shareholder's tax basis in target's stock	500.00
Liabilities of target	0.00
$t_c =$	35%
$t_o =$	40%
$t_{cg} =$	20%
$r =$	10%
$n =$	10

    a. What is the maximum price that an acquirer will pay to acquire the target C corporation in taxable asset sale given that it will pay $10,000 in a taxable stock acquisition?

    b. What is the maximum price that an acquirer will pay to acquire the target S corporation in taxable stock sale followed by a Section 338(h)(10) election given that it will pay $10,000 in a taxable stock acquisition without the election?

    c. What is the minimum price that the target's shareholders will accept under part (a)?

    d. What is the minimum price that the target's shareholders will accept under part (b)?

    e. Given your answer to parts (a) and (c), should a taxable asset sale structure be employed in the sale of the C corporation?

    f. Given your answers to parts (b) and (d), should the Section 338(h)(10) election be made in the sale of the S corporation?

    g. How much more cash after tax can shareholders of the S corporations get, relative to shareholders of the C corporation, assuming the acquirer pays the maximum price that it will pay in a Section 338(h)(10) transaction? Note that the C corporation is sold in a taxable stock sale at $10,000 and the S corporation is sold for the price you computed in part (b).

4. Assume that you are performing a comparable company analysis for a pending acquisition. You are advising the target company and the target company is a privately held S corporation. The comparable company acquisitions, for which you have data, are exclusively taxable acquisitions of freestanding C corporations.

Your assistant has computed the following common valuation benchmarks for the comparable company acquisitions.

	Mean	*Median*
Price to revenues	.82	.76
Price to book value	2.21	2.07
Price to earnings	23.4	18.6
Price to EBITDA	9.58	7.13

Further assume that the target company is considered similar to the comparable companies in terms of revenue and profitability prospects—that is, the target company is about the same as the comparables in terms of operations.

Would you recommend any adjustments to the comparable company analyses or would you tell your client to accept an acquirer's offer that is equal to the average price to EBITDA of the comparable company acquisitions?

References and Additional Readings

Cases:

Erickson, M., 2003. "The Effect of Entity Organizational Form on the Structure of, and Price Paid in, the Hi-Stat Acquisition," in *Cases In Tax Strategy 3rd edition* edited by M. Erickson. Upper Saddle River, NJ: Pearson Prentice Hall.

See list at the end of Chapter 13.

After completing this chapter, you should be able to:

1. Describe the four basic types of tax-free acquisitions of freestanding C corporations and the requirements for tax-free treatment.

2. Identify the tax consequences for the acquirer, the target, and the target's shareholders of various tax-free acquisition structures.

3. Compare the tax and nontax costs and benefits of taxable and tax-free acquisitions of freestanding C corporations.

4. Quantify the differential tax effects of taxable and tax-free acquisitions of freestanding C corporations.

5. Compute the prices at which a seller and an acquirer are indifferent between various taxable and tax-free acquisition structures holding nontax factors constant.

In the last two chapters we concentrated on taxable acquisitions of freestanding C corporations and taxable acquisitions of S corporations, respectively. Under all taxable structuring alternatives, the target's shareholders will face an immediate tax liability.[1] If the parties can agree to combine in a tax-free transaction under Tax Code Section 368 or Section 351, the target's shareholders avoid recognizing a current capital gain on the transaction. The buyer will also have access to the target's tax attributes, with some limitations, in a tax-free reorganization. However, in a tax-free acquisition, it is not possible to step up the tax basis of the target's assets.

In this chapter, we discuss various types of tax-free reorganizations under Section 368 and Section 351. We focus exclusively on tax-free acquisitions of freestanding C corporations in this chapter. The term *tax-free* is actually a misnomer because these

---

[1] As noted in Chapter 14, in some cases installment sale treatment may provide tax deferral.

transactions provide target shareholders with tax deferral of the gain on the acquisition, not tax-free treatment. In this chapter we discuss and analyze tax-free acquisitions using several numerical examples similar in nature to those in the prior two chapters. We also analyze the limitations imposed on a target's tax attributes by Section 382 in carryover basis transactions. Finally, we develop a formal algebraic model that quantifies the tax consequences of taxable and tax-free acquisition structures for the acquirer, the target corporation, and the target's shareholders. We use the model to compare the costs and benefits of various tax-free acquisition structures, relative to taxable transactions. We defer our discussion of tax-free acquisitions of corporate subsidiaries until Chapter 17.

16.1 BASIC TYPES OF TAX-FREE REORGANIZATIONS

Of the four basic tax-free methods to acquire a freestanding C corporation, three are defined under **Section 368(a)(1).** These three types are commonly known as **"A," "B," and "C" reorganizations.** The name is drawn from the subsection of Code Section 368(a)(1) under which each is defined; for example, Section 368(a)(1)(A) is the "A" form. The major differences between these reorganization structures relate to whether assets or stock is acquired and to the quantity and type of consideration required for tax-free treatment, such as at least 50% acquirer stock. Two variants of the Section 368 reorganization, known generally as **triangular mergers,** use a subsidiary of the acquiring firm to facilitate the acquisition. The fourth type of acquisition is defined by Section 351, which specifies the conditions under which a **corporate formation** will qualify for tax-free treatment.[2] Under any of these tax-free reorganization structures, target shareholders must recognize a taxable gain to the extent they receive cash or other forms of boot. Boot is broadly defined as cash and debt-type securities.

As we describe and contrast the various tax-free reorganization structures in this chapter, we will focus on the tax consequences of the structure to the acquirer, the target firm, and the target's shareholders. We pay particular attention to the resulting tax basis in the property transferred and received among these three parties.

First, we describe the general requirements for tax-free treatment in a merger. We then provide a detailed explanation of various types of tax-free reorganizations. Table 16.1 provides an overview of the tax consequences of the tax-free acquisition structures discussed in those sections.

General Requirements for Tax-Free Treatment under Section 368

In order to qualify as tax-free under Section 368, an acquisition has to meet several general requirements. First, target shareholders must maintain a continuity of interest in the assets of the target. For practical purposes, continuity of interest simply means that target shareholders must receive stock of the acquirer in return for their target shares.[3] Historically, the minimum amount of acquirer stock necessary to qualify for

---

[2]A merger can be structured as a corporate formation transaction.
[3]By obtaining acquiring firm stock, target shareholders maintain an interest in the target's assets—a so-called continuity of interest.

TABLE 16.1 Overview of Tax-Free Acquisition Structures of Freestanding C Corporations

	I.R.C. §368 "A"[1]	Triangular I.R.C. §368 "A"[2]	I.R.C. §368 "B"[3]	I.R.C. §368 "C"[4]	I.R.C. §351[5]
Consideration/ method of payment required for tax-free treatment	At least 50% acquiring firm stock. Stock can be voting, nonvoting, preferred, or common.	At least 80% acquiring firm stock, must be voting stock.	100% acquiring firm voting stock, stock can be preferred or common.	At least 80% acquiring firm voting stock.	Mixed consideration including stock, debt and cash. Transferors must receive stock of Newco and control Newco to qualify for tax-free treatment.
What is acquired? Primary benefits	Assets (1) flexibility of consideration (2) tax-free treatment for some target shareholders while providing cash to up to 50% of shareholders	Assets (1) some liability shield provided by subsidiary (2) avoids acquirer shareholder vote (3) assets of target that would not transfer can be acquired (reverse triangular merger)	Stock (1) simplicity and low transaction costs (2) target becomes a subsidiary of the acquirer providing some liability protection from target's liabilities (3) all assets of the target are acquired (e.g., licenses)	Assets (1) less restrictive consideration requirements (2) allows some avoidance of target's liabilities	Stock or Assets (1) very flexible in terms of providing target shareholders with desired form of consideration (e.g., cash or stock)
Primary costs	(1) assumption of all of the target's liabilities (2) some assets do not transfer (3) must qualify as a merger under state law	(1) restriction on type and quantity of stock consideration (2) must qualify as a merger under state law	(1) very restrictive rules with respect to consideration (2) all of the target's liabilities survive (3) dilution of the acquiring firm's shareholder control	(1) if boot used, all of target's liabilities count toward 20% nonstock limitation (2) some assets may not transfer	(1) can be complex structure that generates numerous tax and nontax issues that are not present in other structures

[1]Statutory merger in which the acquirer exchanges stock and boot with the target corporation in return for the target's assets and liabilities. The target liquidates and distributes the acquirer stock and boot to its shareholders in return for their target stock. [2]In a triangular statutory merger, the acquirer establishes a wholly owned subsidiary which exchanges acquirer stock and possibly some boot for the target's assets and liabilities. In this manner, the assets and liabilities of the target are held in a corporate subsidiary of the acquirer. [3]Stock for stock merger in which the acquirer directly exchanges its stock with target shareholders in return for their target stock. [4]A stock for asset merger that is similar to a statutory merger in form. [5]A corporate formation transaction in which the target corporation contributes stock or assets to a newly formed entity in return for stock and boot. Simultaneously, the acquirer contributes stock or assets to the new company in exchange for stock of the new company. The transaction is tax-free, to the extent of stock received, if it qualifies under §351.

tax-free treatment was 50% of the total acquisition consideration.[4] As we will discuss, certain types of transactions under Section 368 impose additional restrictions on the form and percentage of total consideration required for tax-free treatment.

Second, an acquirer cannot purchase a target company in a tax-free transaction and then liquidate the target's assets. This principle of **continuity of business interest** means that the acquirer must continue to use the assets of the target in a productive capacity postacquisition. The acquirer can, however, dispose of some of the target's assets after the transaction is completed. In fact, in some cases, for regulatory reasons, acquirers must sell off portions of the target's business. It is also important to note that the acquirer need not use the target's assets in the same business in which the target operated. The acquirer must simply use those assets in a productive capacity. Finally, the acquisition must have a valid business purpose and cannot be motivated purely as a mechanism to avoid tax. We next discuss specific types of tax-free acquisitions, requirements for tax-free treatment under each structure, and the tax implications of each structure.

16.2 SECTION 368 "A" REORGANIZATION: STATUTORY MERGER

Under a **Section 368 "A" reorganization,** which is depicted in Figure 16.1, the acquirer exchanges its stock and possibly some boot (e.g., cash) for the assets and liabilities of the target. The target corporation must distribute the consideration received from the acquirer to its shareholders in return for their target stock in liquidation. The **liquidating distribution** is tax-free as long as target shareholders receive stock of the acquirer. If they receive cash, the cash is taxable even if the transaction is tax-free. Specifically, target shareholders recognize a taxable gain that is the lesser of the gain realized or the boot received. Gain realized is computed as the difference between the purchase price (value of consideration received) and the selling shareholder's tax basis in the stock. Losses realized are not recognized, however. After the transaction, shareholders of the target become shareholders of the acquirer, which postmerger owns the assets of the target.

Requirements to Qualify for Tax-Free Treatment under Section 368(a)(1)(A)

"A" reorganizations must qualify as **statutory mergers** under applicable state law. As a result, the merger must be approved by both the acquirer's and the target's shareholders. For tax purposes, an "A" reorganization generally requires that at least 50% of the total consideration received by target shareholders in the acquisition is acquirer stock. Acquirers can use either voting or nonvoting stock to meet the continuity of interest test and they may also use either common or preferred stock.

---

[4]Several transactions in which only 40% of the consideration was acquirer stock have, however, qualified for tax-free treatment. See R. Willens, "Heller's Acquisition Validates Consensus View on 'Continuity of Interest,'" Lehman Brothers, (April 23, 1999).

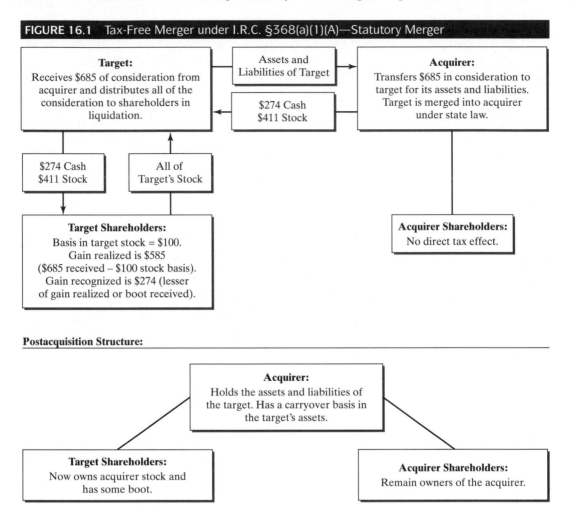

FIGURE 16.1 Tax-Free Merger under I.R.C. §368(a)(1)(A)—Statutory Merger

Target:
Receives $685 of consideration from acquirer and distributes all of the consideration to shareholders in liquidation.

Assets and Liabilities of Target

Acquirer:
Transfers $685 in consideration to target for its assets and liabilities. Target is merged into acquirer under state law.

$274 Cash
$411 Stock

$274 Cash
$411 Stock

All of Target's Stock

Target Shareholders:
Basis in target stock = $100.
Gain realized is $585
($685 received – $100 stock basis).
Gain recognized is $274 (lesser of gain realized or boot received).

Acquirer Shareholders:
No direct tax effect.

Postacquisition Structure:

Acquirer:
Holds the assets and liabilities of the target. Has a carryover basis in the target's assets.

Target Shareholders:
Now owns acquirer stock and has some boot.

Acquirer Shareholders:
Remain owners of the acquirer.

Of course, target shareholders will price the attributes of the type of security they receive from the acquirer. For example, target shareholders may demand additional compensation if they receive nonvoting stock of the acquirer. A benefit of this structure is that the acquirer can purchase the target partially for cash while at the same time providing tax-deferred consideration (acquirer stock) to those target shareholders seeking to avoid an immediate taxable gain.

Tax Consequences of a Section 368 "A"

In order to illustrate the tax consequences of the various tax-free acquisition structures, we again use a common set of facts. Table 16.2 contains the quantitative tax effects of various tax-free acquisition structures when applying these facts. Table 16.2 also includes, for reference, the tax effects of a taxable stock acquisition without a Section 338 election using the same input factors.

TABLE 16.2 Comparison of Tax Implications of Tax-Free Acquisitions of Freestanding C Corporations

Fact Pattern:

Purchase price	$685.00
Target shareholder stock basis	100.00
Net tax basis of target's assets	100.00
$t_c =$	35%
$t_{cg} =$	20%
$r =$	10%

	Tax-Free Acquisitions				Taxable Acquisitions
	$368 "A"[1]	$368 "B"[2]	$368 "C"[3]	$351[4]	Stock Sale without a $338 Election
Purchase Price:	$685.00	$685.00	$685.00	$685.00	$685.00
Cash	274.00	0.00	137.00	411.00	685.00
Stock	411.00	685.00	548.00	274.00	0.00
Target corporation tax liability[5]	0.00	0.00	0.00	0.00	0.00
Target shareholder gain recognized[6]	274.00	0.00	137.00	411.00	585.00
Target shareholder tax liability[7]	54.80	0.00	27.40	82.20	117.00
Target Shareholder After-Tax Wealth:					
Cash[8]	$219.20	$0.00	$109.60	$328.80	$568.00
Stock	411.00	685.00	548.00	274.00	0.00
Total	$630.20	$685.00	$657.60	$602.80	$568.00
Acquirer Net After-Tax Cost:					
Pretax cost	$685.00	$685.00	$685.00	$685.00	$685.00
Less: incremental tax savings[9]	0.00	0.00	0.00	0.00	0.00
Net after-tax cost	$685.00	$685.00	$685.00	$685.00	$685.00

[1]Assumes that the mix of consideration is 60% stock and 40% cash.

[2]The acquirer purchases the target for 100% stock as required by this structure.

[3]Assumes that the mix of consideration is 80% stock and 20% cash.

[4]Assumes that the mix of consideration is 40% stock and 60% cash.

[5]Tax liability at the target corporation level.

[6]Gain recognized by target shareholders is equal to the lesser of boot received or gain realized.

[7]Tax liability at the target shareholder level. Computed as the lesser of the gain realized or boot received multiplied by the capital gains tax rate.

[8]Cash received in the transaction less tax liability associated with any recognized gains (6).

[9]There are no incremental tax savings because there is no step-up in the tax basis of the target's assets.

The facts in our hypothetical Section 368 "A" transaction are as follows.

- The target, T, has assets with a net tax basis of $100 (historical cost equals $100 and no accumulated depreciation).
- T's shareholders have a basis in the stock of T corporation equal to $100, and they are individuals facing a capital gains tax rate (t_{cg}) equal to 20% (federal and state combined).

- Any acquirer stock received by T's shareholders in the transaction is held until death.[5]
- The acquirer, A, is willing to purchase the target for $685. The acquirer will use $274 in cash (40% of the total) and $411 of acquirer stock (60% of the total).

The shareholders of T will *realize* a gain of $585 on the acquisition. The realized gain is the difference between the value of consideration received ($685) and T's shareholder's basis in their T stock ($100). T's shareholders will recognize a gain of $274, which is computed as the lesser of the gain realized ($585) or boot received ($274). A recognized gain is the taxable gain while a realized gain is not subject to tax until it is subsequently recognized. As a result of the taxable gain of $274, T's shareholders incur a tax liability of $54.80 ($274 × 20%) and have $219.20 in cash after-tax and stock worth $411.

T's shareholders will take a **substituted basis** in the acquiring firm stock received in the transaction. A substituted basis means that the shareholders have the same basis in the A stock as they had in the T stock, plus any gain recognized and minus boot received. In this case, T's shareholders will take a basis in the A stock equal to $100 plus the gain recognized of $274 less the boot received of $274 for a basis of $100. If T shareholders were to sell this A stock for its fair market value ($411), they would recognize a capital gain of $311.[6] This gain brings the total gain eventually *recognized* on the transaction up to $585 ($274 + $311), which is equal to the gain *realized* on the transaction. The substituted basis computation we demonstrated previously ensures that the realized gain is ultimately recognized in total.

The acquirer will take a carryover basis in the assets of the target. In this case, A will also have a tax basis in the net assets of the target of $100. The acquirer will not have a basis in the stock of the target because the target was liquidated; that is, the stock of the target was cancelled. The tax attributes of the target will carry over to the acquirer, but they will be limited by **Section 382.** (We present the mechanics of the Section 382 limitations in Section 16.6.) The first column of Table 16.2 presents the particulars of the computations in this section.

Nontax Issues Associated with the Section 368 "A" Structure

Under this structure, the acquirer obtains all the liabilities of the target. As noted in Chapter 14, it is generally preferable for the acquirer to avoid target contingent liabilities if possible. This structure therefore subjects the acquirer to potentially significant nontax costs. In addition, because it is an asset acquisition, some of the target's assets (e.g., licenses, royalty agreements, and governmental permits) may not transfer to the

---

[5]Throughout these examples, we implicitly assume that all shareholders receive an equal proportion of stock and boot. As a practical matter, target shareholders often have a choice as to whether they want stock or cash in an acquisition but only if the tax structure permits the use of cash. The taxable gain from the acquisition is determined by each shareholder as a function of the consideration received and their basis in the target shares surrendered.

[6]T shareholders' holding period for the A stock is the same as it was for the T stock. That is, the holding period is also substituted.

target. These assets may be nontransferable based on the law or based on the contractual arrangement that created the asset.

An important consideration, from the target shareholders' perspective, relates to the consideration received. When target shareholders receive acquiring firm stock, they are subject to more risk than if they had received cash and used it to purchase a diversified basket of assets. This factor is true of all tax-free structures to the extent target shareholders receive stock of the acquiring firm. In the mid-1990s, in several notable examples, acquiring firms purchased numerous companies with their stock, only to see a subsequent collapse in the price of that stock.[7] Finally, in some cases, qualifying as a statutory merger can involve significant nontax costs that acquirers and targets may prefer to avoid.

Triangular Mergers

Figure 16.2 illustrates a **forward triangular merger.** Here the acquirer establishes a subsidiary through which it acquires the target. In a forward triangular "A" merger, the acquirer's subsidiary acquires the assets and liabilities of the target in exchange for stock of the acquiring firm. The surviving entity in the merger is the subsidiary of A. As you can see, this structure is similar to the basic A structure, except that A uses a subsidiary to facilitate the acquisition. Another notable difference is that A must acquire substantially all of T's assets, which is defined as 90% of the net fair market value of T's assets and 70% of the gross fair market value of those assets.

This type of structure provides a significant nontax benefit to the acquirer because the target's assets and liabilities, including contingent liabilities, are held in a subsidiary of A. As a result, the acquirer has some protection against contingent and unrecorded liabilities of T through the limited liability accorded to corporate ownership because T's assets and liabilities are held in a subsidiary of A. In addition, because the acquirer uses a subsidiary to complete the merger, acquiring firm shareholders do not have to formally approve a triangular merger. However, if the merger involves the exchange of a substantial amount of acquirer stock, the corporate charter of the acquiring firm may require formal shareholder approval of the deal.

In a **reverse triangular merger,** the surviving entity is the target corporation instead of the acquirer's subsidiary, which is a subsidiary of A after the transaction. This structure is particularly beneficial relative to a forward merger or a basic "A" merger if the target has assets that are difficult to transfer. Additional qualifiers restrict tax-free treatment in reverse triangular mergers, which are beyond the scope of this text. Readers should note, however, that reverse triangular mergers are quite common.

---

[7]WorldCom's celebrated collapse after its stock-financed acquisition of MCI, the largest merger in U.S. history at the time, is probably the most well known example of this phenomenon. Cendant, Loewen, and McKesson are other acquiring firms whose stock prices plunged after stock-financed acquisitions. See for example "Shares of Former High-Flier Cendant Plunge on Accounting Troubles," *Dow Jones Online News,* (April 16, 1998); D. Morse and M. Heinzl, "Laid Low: Funeral-Home Owners Discover the Downside of Sale to Consolidator: Some Find Payments Cease After Heavy Debt Lands Loewen in Chapter 11," *The Wall Street Journal* (September 17, 1999), p. A1; and G. Ceron, "Accounting Snafu at McKesson HBOC Reminiscent of Cendant Fiasco," *Dow Jones News Service* (April 28, 1999).

FIGURE 16.2 Tax-Free Forward Triangular Merger under I.R.C. §368(a)(1)(A)

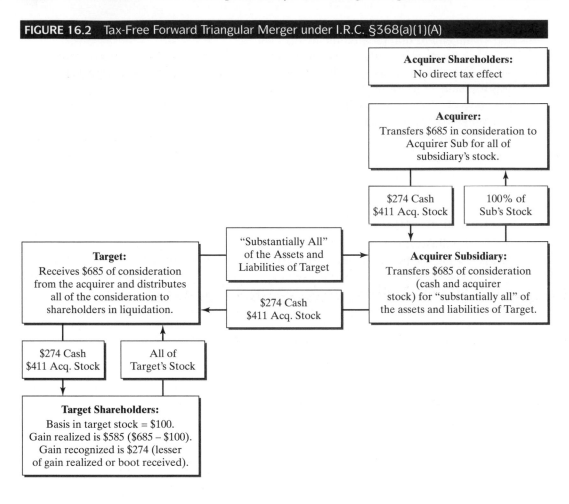

Acquirer Shareholders:
No direct tax effect

Acquirer:
Transfers $685 in consideration to Acquirer Sub for all of subsidiary's stock.

$274 Cash
$411 Acq. Stock

100% of
Sub's Stock

Target:
Receives $685 of consideration from the acquirer and distributes all of the consideration to shareholders in liquidation.

"Substantially All" of the Assets and Liabilities of Target

Acquirer Subsidiary:
Transfers $685 of consideration (cash and acquirer stock) for "substantially all" of the assets and liabilities of Target.

$274 Cash
$411 Acq. Stock

$274 Cash
$411 Acq. Stock

All of
Target's Stock

Target Shareholders:
Basis in target stock = $100.
Gain realized is $585 ($685 − $100).
Gain recognized is $274 (lesser of gain realized or boot received).

Postacquisition Structure:

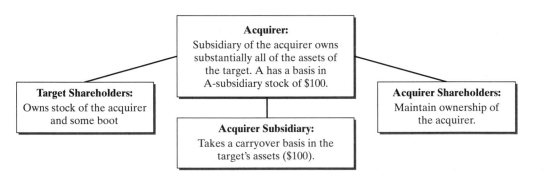

Acquirer:
Subsidiary of the acquirer owns substantially all of the assets of the target. A has a basis in A-subsidiary stock of $100.

Target Shareholders:
Owns stock of the acquirer and some boot

Acquirer Shareholders:
Maintain ownership of the acquirer.

Acquirer Subsidiary:
Takes a carryover basis in the target's assets ($100).

16.3 SECTION 368 "B" REORGANIZATION: STOCK-FOR-STOCK ACQUISITION

The "B" reorganization is a stock acquisition rather than an asset acquisition. The acquirer exchanges its stock directly with that of target shareholders, thereby obtaining ownership of the target's assets through ownership of its stock. Figure 16.3 illustrates a **Section 368 "B" reorganization.** Notice that the target becomes a subsidiary of the acquirer with this structure and therefore maintains its legal identity while the owners of the target's stock change. After the acquisition, this structure looks like a reverse triangular merger under Section 368 "A."

Requirements to Qualify for Tax-Free Treatment under Section 368(a)(1)(B)

As a general rule, this "B" structure is more restrictive than the 368 "A" structure. Unlike an "A" reorganization, a "B" reorganization does not have to be a statutory

FIGURE 16.3 Tax-Free Merger under I.R.C. §368(a)(1)(B)—Stock-for-Stock Merger

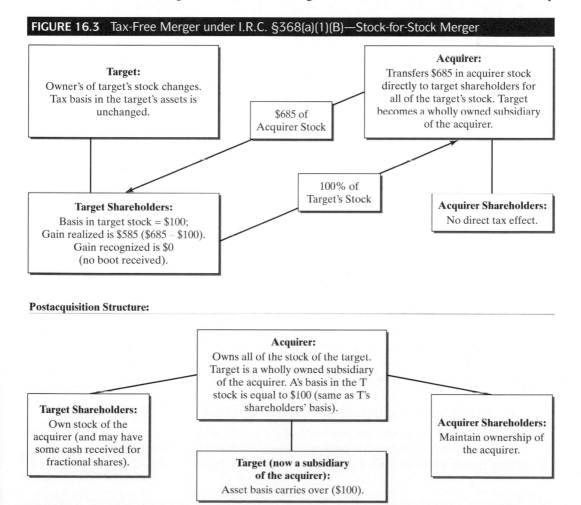

merger. Therefore, acquirer and target shareholders need not provide formal approval via proxy vote. However, target shareholders implicitly vote by tendering their shares for acquiring firm shares.

In order for the transaction to qualify for tax-free treatment under Section 368 "B," 100% of the consideration used in the acquisition must be voting stock of the acquirer. Use of any cash in the transaction disqualifies the deal's tax-free treatment, with the exception of cash paid for fractional shares. Acquirers can use either common or preferred stock as long as the stock has voting rights. Finally, the acquirer must obtain 80% control of the target in order for the transaction to qualify as tax-free. As a result of this last requirement, transactions of this type are typically unwound prior to formal completion of the deal if the acquirer doesn't obtain 80% of the target corporation's stock.

Tax Consequences of a Section 368 "B"

We again use the facts presented in Section 16.2 to illustrate the tax consequences of this structure, with one slight modification related to the percentage of stock received by target shareholders. Under this structure, the acquirer is willing to purchase the target for $685 (100% of the consideration) of its voting common stock.

The shareholders of T will realize a gain of $585 on the acquisition. The realized gain is the difference between the value of the consideration received ($685) and T shareholders' basis in the T stock ($100). T's shareholders will recognize a gain of $0, which is computed as the lesser of the gain realized ($585) or boot received ($0). As a result, T's shareholders will have stock worth $685 after tax, and will take a substituted basis in the acquiring firm stock received in the transaction. Thus they will have a basis in the A stock equal to $100, plus the gain recognized of $0 less the boot received of $0 for a basis of $100. If T shareholders were to sell this A stock for its fair market value ($685), they would recognize a capital gain of $585.

The acquirer will again take a carryover basis in the assets of the target. In this case, the acquirer will have a tax basis in the net assets of the target of $100. Unlike the case in the 368 "A" structure, the acquirer will have a basis in the stock of the target as well. The acquirer takes a carryover basis in the stock of the target equal to the target's shareholder's basis in the target's stock preacquisition, in this case $100. The second column of Table 16.2 illustrates the computations in this section.

The target corporation becomes a subsidiary of the acquirer and we again encounter a situation in which the acquiring firm could have a different basis in the stock and assets of the target, now a subsidiary of the acquirer.[8] For example, if the target shareholder's basis in the stock of the target had been $200 instead of $100, then the acquirer would have had basis in the target's stock and assets of $200 and $100, respectively. The tax attributes of the target will carry over to the acquirer, but they will be limited by **Section 382.**

Nontax Issues Associated with the Section 368 "B" Structure

Because the acquirer obtains the stock of the target with this structure, it also is liable for all the target's liabilities, recorded and unrecorded. This structure therefore subjects the acquirer to potentially significant nontax costs. However, the acquirer's liability is

---

[8] Recall in Chapter 14 that taxable stock acquisitions of freestanding C corporations typically result in the acquirer having a basis in the stock of the target that exceeds the net asset basis of the target. See Table 14.2.

limited to its investment in the target because the target is a subsidiary of the acquirer. Unlike the case in a Section 368 "A" merger, the target corporation now becomes a subsidiary of the acquirer. Therefore, the acquirer indirectly obtains all the assets of the target. Title to the target's assets does not change because the target retains its corporate identity. For this reason, the Section 368 "B" structure can be beneficial if the target has assets that are difficult to transfer. Target shareholders receive stock of the acquirer and are subjected to the same potential costs as mentioned with respect to an "A" structure.

Triangular type structures under 368 "B" are also options, and similar restrictions apply to these structures as noted previously, although the basic restrictions under 368 "B," such as 100% stock, are typically more onerous than those governing triangular mergers, such as 50% stock minimum.

16.4 SECTION 368 "C" REORGANIZATION: STOCK-FOR-ASSETS ACQUISITION

The "C" reorganization, like the "A" is an asset acquisition rather than a stock acquisition. The acquirer exchanges its voting stock, and perhaps some boot, with the target firm in return for substantially all of the target's assets. The target then distributes the acquirer's stock and other consideration received in the acquisition to its shareholders in liquidation. Figure 16.4 illustrates a **Section 368 "C" reorganization.** This structure is similar to the "A" reorganization, with a few notable differences.

Requirements to Qualify for Tax-Free Treatment under Section 368(a)(1)(C)

This structure is more restrictive on some dimensions than the 368 "A" structure but less restrictive in other respects. Unlike an "A," a "C" structure does not have to be a statutory merger. However, the acquirer must purchase substantially all the assets of the target in order for the transaction to qualify as tax-free. Substantially all of the target's assets is defined as 70% of their gross fair market value and 90% of their net fair market value. Unlike the case in the "A" structure, the acquirer is not required to assume all the target's liabilities. Therefore, it is possible to avoid some of the target's liabilities while maintaining a tax-free status.

In a "C" reorganization, at least 80% of the total consideration used must be voting stock of the acquiring firm. If the acquirer uses any boot in the transaction, the liabilities of the target assumed by the acquirer count as boot in the 80% test. For example, if an acquirer used 5% cash in a transaction designed to qualify as a "C," all the target's liabilities assumed by the acquirer would be treated as if the acquirer had paid cash to satisfy those liabilities in the merger. As a result, all the target's liabilities are counted as boot in determining whether 80% or more of the consideration received by the target is stock. As a practical matter, this requirement results in "C"-type mergers frequently using 100% stock of the acquirer as consideration.

Tax Consequences of a Section 368 "C"

We use the same facts familiar from the "B" structure now, but we assume that target shareholders receive 20% cash ($137) and 80% acquiring firm voting stock ($548 worth). Target shareholders still receive $685 of total consideration in the merger.

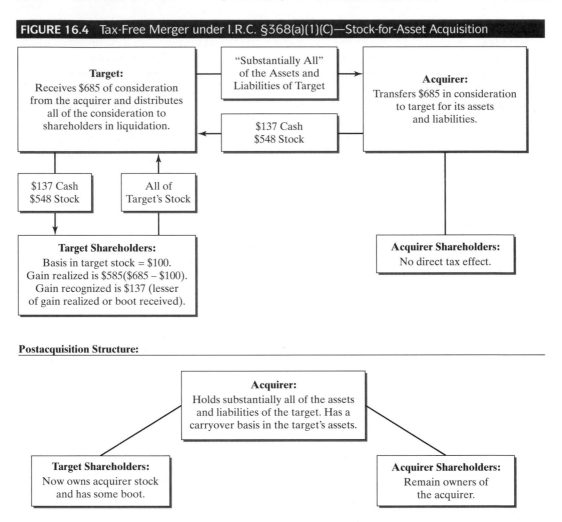

FIGURE 16.4 Tax-Free Merger under I.R.C. §368(a)(1)(C)—Stock-for-Asset Acquisition

Target:
Receives $685 of consideration from the acquirer and distributes all of the consideration to shareholders in liquidation.

"Substantially All" of the Assets and Liabilities of Target

Acquirer:
Transfers $685 in consideration to target for its assets and liabilities.

$137 Cash
$548 Stock

$137 Cash
$548 Stock

All of Target's Stock

Target Shareholders:
Basis in target stock = $100.
Gain realized is $585($685 − $100).
Gain recognized is $137 (lesser of gain realized or boot received).

Acquirer Shareholders:
No direct tax effect.

Postacquisition Structure:

Acquirer:
Holds substantially all of the assets and liabilities of the target. Has a carryover basis in the target's assets.

Target Shareholders:
Now owns acquirer stock and has some boot.

Acquirer Shareholders:
Remain owners of the acquirer.

The shareholders of T will realize a gain of $585 on the acquisition. The realized gain is the difference between the value of consideration received ($685) and T's shareholders' basis in the T stock ($100). T's shareholders will recognize a gain of $137, which is computed as the lesser of the gain realized ($585) or boot received ($137). As a result, T's shareholders will have $109.60 (the tax liability equals $137 × 20%, or $27.40) of cash after tax and acquirer stock worth $548. T's shareholders will take a substituted basis in the acquiring firm stock received in the transaction. With this structure, T's shareholders will take a basis in the A stock equal to $100 ($100 substituted basis plus the gain recognized of $137 less the boot received of $137). If T's shareholders were to sell the A stock for its fair market value ($548), they would recognize a capital gain of $448. Table 16.2 illustrates these computations.

The acquirer will again take a carryover basis in the assets of the target, and will have a tax basis in the net assets of the target of $100. The stock of the target is not acquired, and therefore, the acquirer does not have a basis in the target's stock. The tax attributes of the target will carry over to the acquirer, but they will be limited by **Section 382.**

Triangular Section 368 "C" mergers must meet similar requirements as Section 368 "A" triangular mergers. The tax and nontax effects of these triangular Section 368 "C" mergers are nearly identical to those described with respect to triangular Section 368 "A" triangular mergers. The nontax consequences of "C" reorganizations are similar to those described for "A" reorganizations, with the exception of issues relating to statutory mergers.

16.5 TAX-FREE REORGANIZATIONS UNDER SECTION 351

For a variety of reasons, it is often impractical to structure a transaction to qualify as tax-free under the various provision of Section 368. For example, target shareholders may demand more than 60% of the purchase price in cash, making it essentially impossible to qualify an acquisition as tax-free under the continuity of interest principle. It may be the case that the other shareholders of the target demand tax-free treatment and will not participate in a merger that does not provide tax-free treatment. Section 351 has no continuity of interest requirement.

For those deals that cannot qualify as tax-free under Section 368, Section 351 provides a vehicle to achieve tax-free status.[9] For those readers who are unfamiliar with Section 351, it governs corporate formation transactions. We provide a brief overview of it here to assist with the discussion of Section 351 mergers.

Requirements for Tax-Free Treatment under Section 351

When a new corporation is formed, the founding shareholders generally contribute property, including cash, to the new entity in return for ownership interests (stock). To the extent that shareholders contribute appreciated property, they could be forced to recognize a gain on the exchange of stock for property. Such gain recognition would have undesirable macroeconomic consequences because many viable endeavors would be foregone due to the initial start-up-related tax cost. Section 351 allows the contribution of property to a corporation, tax-free, if certain conditions are met. Specifically, after the contribution, all the contributors must have control of the newly formed entity, which we will call NEWCO. **Control** is defined as ownership of 80% of NEWCO. The contributors can receive NEWCO common or preferred stock and transferors may receive different classes and types of stock.

Contributors who receive stock in NEWCO do so tax-free while those who transfer property to NEWCO in exchange for debt or cash must recognize a taxable gain equal to the lesser of the gain realized on the transfer or the boot received.[10] Contributors who receive stock in NEWCO take a substituted basis in the stock of NEWCO, that is, a basis equal to the basis in the property transferred, which is adjusted for gains recognized and boot received. NEWCO takes a carryover basis in the property transferred increased by any gains recognized by transferring shareholders.

---

[9]Section 351 may also be used in the creation of a joint venture enterprise.
[10]Prior to 1990, debt of NEWCO could be received by the transferor tax-free. Gain recognition was deferred until the transferor received interest and principal payments on the NEWCO debt.

Tax Consequences of a Section 351 Merger

Figure 16.5 provides an illustration of a merger under Section 351. Under this structure, NEWCO is formed by the acquirer. The shareholders of the acquirer (A) contribute their stock in A to NEWCO in return for NEWCO voting stock. A's shareholders have a basis in their A stock of $500 (fair market value of $10,000) and A's net asset tax

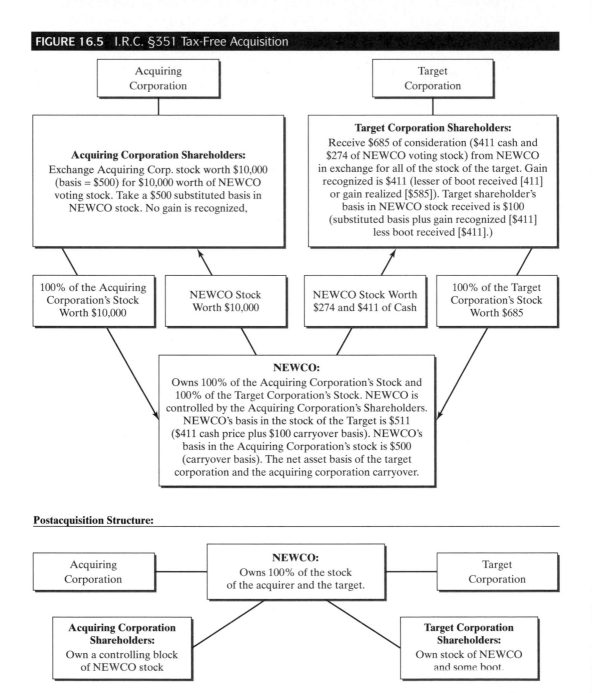

FIGURE 16.5 I.R.C. §351 Tax-Free Acquisition

Acquiring Corporation

Target Corporation

Acquiring Corporation Shareholders:
Exchange Acquiring Corp. stock worth $10,000 (basis = $500) for $10,000 worth of NEWCO voting stock. Take a $500 substituted basis in NEWCO stock. No gain is recognized,

Target Corporation Shareholders:
Receive $685 of consideration ($411 cash and $274 of NEWCO voting stock) from NEWCO in exchange for all of the stock of the target. Gain recognized is $411 (lesser of boot received [411] or gain realized [$585]). Target shareholder's basis in NEWCO stock received is $100 (substituted basis plus gain recognized [$411] less boot received [$411].)

100% of the Acquiring Corporation's Stock Worth $10,000

NEWCO Stock Worth $10,000

NEWCO Stock Worth $274 and $411 of Cash

100% of the Target Corporation's Stock Worth $685

NEWCO:
Owns 100% of the Acquiring Corporation's Stock and 100% of the Target Corporation's Stock. NEWCO is controlled by the Acquiring Corporation's Shareholders. NEWCO's basis in the stock of the Target is $511 ($411 cash price plus $100 carryover basis). NEWCO's basis in the Acquiring Corporation's stock is $500 (carryover basis). The net asset basis of the target corporation and the acquiring corporation carryover.

Postacquisition Structure:

Acquiring Corporation

NEWCO:
Owns 100% of the stock of the acquirer and the target.

Target Corporation

Acquiring Corporation Shareholders:
Own a controlling block of NEWCO stock

Target Corporation Shareholders:
Own stock of NEWCO and some boot.

basis is $200. A's shareholders will receive NEWCO stock worth $10,000 in exchange for their A stock. The target (T) corporation's shareholders contribute their T stock to NEWCO in return for NEWCO voting stock.

After the contribution of A and T stock for NEWCO stock, the shareholders of the acquirer and the target control more than 80% of NEWCO. Therefore, the exchange of property (stock) for NEWCO stock is tax-free under Section 351. Under the structure in Figure 16.5, the target and acquirer become wholly owned subsidiaries of NEWCO. As a practical matter, after the Section 351 transaction, NEWCO will likely be restructured using **Section 332.**[11] NEWCO will also be renamed, perhaps with a similar name to that of the acquirer.

In order to illustrate the tax consequences of the Section 351 structure, let us once again return to our facts (see Table 16.2). NEWCO is willing to purchase the stock of T for $685 in total consideration, in other words $411 of cash and $274 of NEWCO voting common stock. (Assume that NEWCO borrows the $411.) Notice that T's shareholders will receive 60% cash and 40% stock of NEWCO.

The shareholders of T will realize a gain of $585 on the merger. The realized gain is the difference between the value of consideration received ($685) and T shareholder's basis in the T stock ($100). T's shareholders will recognize a gain of $411, which is computed as the lesser of the gain realized ($585) or boot received ($411). After tax, they will have stock worth $274 and cash of $328.80 ($411 less tax of $82.20), and they will take a substituted basis in the NEWCO stock received in the transaction. In this case, T's shareholders take a basis in the NEWCO stock equal to $100, plus the gain recognized of $411 less the boot received of $411 for a basis of $100.

A's shareholders will realize a gain on the Section 351 transaction equal to $9,500, but they will not recognize a gain for tax purposes. They will have a substituted basis in the NEWCO stock received equal to $500.

NEWCO will take a cost basis in the stock of T acquired for cash and a carryover basis in the stock of T acquired for stock. In this case, NEWCO's basis in the T stock acquired will be $411 (cost basis) plus $100 (carryover basis) for a total of $511.[12] If NEWCO sold the stock of T for its fair market value ($274), a gain of $174 would be recognized. T becomes a subsidiary of NEWCO and the net asset basis of T carries over and is therefore $100. The tax attributes of T will likely be limited by Section 382. NEWCO will take a carryover basis in the stock of A ($500) and a carryover basis in A's net assets ($200), and A will become a wholly owned subsidiary of NEWCO as a result of the Section 351 exchange.

Although our simple facts readily allow comparison of the basic tax-free acquisition structures, the preceding example doesn't adequately illustrate the potential benefits of a Section 351 merger. Assume that the target has two shareholders (T1 and T2). T1 owns 60% of T and is a tax-exempt institution with a basis in its T stock of $99. T2 owns 40% of T and is an individual investor with a tax basis in her T stock of $1. Further, T2 is elderly and had planned to hold her T stock until death at which point her heirs will obtain a step-up in the basis of the stock to fair market value, tax-free.[13]

---

[11]Section 332 allows a corporation to liquidate wholly owned subsidiaries in a tax-free manner. Such corporate liquidations are common in various types of acquisitions.

[12]Readers should again notice that the acquirer's (NEWCO's) tax basis of the stock and net assets of the target are different ($511 and $100) with this structure.

[13]We are ignoring estate tax consequences in this chapter.

T1 wants to receive cash in the merger, while T2 wants to receive tax-free consideration. The Section 351 structure permits T's shareholders to satisfy their tax preferences when a Section 368 structure likely would not because too much of the consideration is cash due to the continuity of interest rules. This result is one of the primary benefits of the Section 351 structure relative to the more restrictive Section 368 mergers. In this case, T2 is able to defer (avoid) a taxable gain of $273 ($274 of consideration, which is 40% of $685, less a basis of $1) and a tax liability of $54.60. Hence, in this scenario, the Section 351 structure generates incremental tax benefits relative to a taxable structure of $54.60, which increases T2's after-tax wealth by about 25%.

Many other alternatives are available under Section 351. For example, various types of NEWCO stock can be issued to T shareholders. Some T shareholders may prefer stock that pays dividends while others' tax preferences are for zero dividend securities. In general, the forms of consideration paid to T shareholders' can be designed with T's shareholders' tax status and or tax clientele in mind in order to maximize their after-tax wealth and minimize the net after-tax cost to the acquiring firm and NEWCO.

Comparison of Tax-Free Acquisition Structures

In the previous sections, we presented the salient features of basic tax-free acquisition structures. Here we compare and contrast tax and nontax differences across types of **tax-free acquisition structures.**

Nontax Dimensions

Table 16.1 compares and contrasts differences in the tax and nontax implications of various tax-free acquisition structures discussed in this chapter. Understanding these differences is paramount to being an effective tax planner. In particular, it is important to understand the requirements of the different tax-free transactions in order to anticipate opportunities and constraints associated with a sale or acquisition. When then is each of these structures most beneficial, ignoring pricing issues? Readers can use Table 16.1 to identify which acquisition tax structure is functional given the nontax constraints present in the transaction.

The Section 368 "A" structure provides a great degree of flexibility in terms of the types of consideration that can be offered while maintaining tax-free treatment. This structure may be particularly preferable when the acquirer is sensitive to dilution of voting control because target shareholders can be given nonvoting stock without disqualifying the transaction's tax-free status.

A primary benefit of the Section 368 "B" structure is that it avoids the complexities associated with qualifying the transaction as a statutory merger. It also provides a degree of liability protection because the target becomes a subsidiary of the acquirer. One of the most significant benefits of a "B" reorganization is that it allows the acquirer to obtain all the target's assets, even those that are not transferable to another entity.

The Section 368 "C" structure can be used when the transaction cannot meet the requirements of a "B" reorganization and is similarly unable to qualify as a statutory merger as required for a valid "A" reorganization. A Section 351 structure allows target shareholders to receive tax-free consideration when Section 368 transactions would not.

Tax Dimensions

As Table 16.2 illustrated, the tax-free acquisition structures discussed in Sections 16.2 through 16.5 have differing wealth effects for target shareholders.[14] Notice that the net after-tax cost of the acquisition to the acquirer is $685 in each of our examples. Target shareholders should prefer the Section 368 "B" transaction because their after-tax wealth is highest with this alternative when considering only tax consequences.

However, target shareholders may be indifferent between the Section 368 "B" and "A" structures if they are sufficiently averse to holding acquirer stock. That is, target shareholders may demand a premium for receiving relatively more acquirer stock because acquirer stock is riskier than cash. In particular, cash can be invested in a diversified portfolio of assets while acquirer stock cannot, absent significant transaction costs[15]. We return to a comparison of the tax consequences of tax-free, and taxable, acquisition structures under more realistic assumptions in Section 16.7.

16.6 LIMITATIONS ON TARGET FIRM TAX ATTRIBUTES

After 1986, any transaction that results in a 50% change in ownership of a corporation triggers a limitation on the firm's net operating losses under Section 382.[16] Other limitations apply to the use of other target firm tax attributes, such as capital loss carryforwards and excess tax credits, as specified in Sections 381, 383, and 384. We focus on the limitations on a target's net operating losses as defined under Section 382.[17] The Section 382 limitation is computed as a function of the market value of the subject firm's stock at the time of the ownership change and the **long-term tax-exempt rate.** Specifically, an annual limitation on the amount of the subject firm's tax attributes, such as NOLs, that can be used is computed as the market value of the subject firm's equity at the date of the ownership change multiplied by the long-term tax-exempt rate of return.[18] The long-term tax-exempt rate of return is defined and reported periodically by the U.S. government.

Consider a target firm with NOLs of $100 that is purchased for $200 in a taxable stock acquisition without a Section 338 election, when the long-term tax-exempt rate is 5%. Each year postacquisition, the acquiring firm can use $10 (5% multiplied by $200 equity value at the time of the ownership change) of T's NOLs to offset taxable income.

---

[14]The differential wealth effects are a function of the portion of consideration received by target shareholders that is acquirer stock. If target shareholders received 100% acquirer stock across transaction tax structure, their wealth would be identical.

[15]For example, target shareholders could borrow against acquirer shares and use the loan proceeds to purchase a diversified basket of securities. The transactions cost of such a strategy may be high.

[16]The definition of a qualifying ownership change is quite complex. It is sufficient for readers to understand that in essentially any acquisition, taxable or tax-free, an ownership change as defined under Section 382 occurs.

[17]Section 381 provides the general rules regarding the postacquisition use of target tax attributes in carryover basis transactions while Section 382 deals primarily with limitations on acquirer use of target preacquisition NOLs. Section 383 controls limitations on capital loss carryforwards and target preacquisition tax credits. Section 384 provides restrictions on the use of the acquirer's losses to offset built-in gains of the target.

[18]Prior to the Tax Reform Act of 1986, the limitation on a target's NOLs differed across carryover basis taxable and tax-free transactions. Since 1986, the limitations on a target's tax attributes are essentially identical in taxable and tax-free transactions.

If the combined entity had $20 of income in the year following the acquisition, only $10 of the income could be offset by the NOL. If the combined entity has $5 of taxable income in a particular year postacquisition, the $5 of unused NOL for that year can be carried forward to the following year. The same limitations apply to capital losses, tax credits, and so-called built-in losses.[19] To the extent that a target firm—a subsidiary of the acquirer postacquisition—generates losses *postacquisition,* however, these losses can be offset by profits of the acquirer without limitation.

As noted in Chapter 14, in taxable transactions in which the tax basis of the target's assets are stepped-up, the target firm's NOLs can be used to offset the corporate-level gain on the actual or deemed asset sale. For this reason, it is most common to see transactions structured to result in a step-up of a freestanding C corporation's assets when the target has large NOLs. However, any of the target's NOLs and other valuable tax attributes that are not used to offset the gain on the step-up are lost. Therefore, the decision to step-up the tax basis of the target's assets, which results in the loss of the target's NOLs, is optimal only if the loss of tax savings from the target's tax attributes does not exceed the net tax benefits of the step-up.

How does the acquirer determine whether to structure the acquisition to preserve the target's NOLs? Table 16.3 presents an analysis of the tax costs and benefits of preserving a target's NOLs in a carryover basis transaction relative to using the NOLs to offset the gain on a step-up in the target's assets. In this table, we compare a taxable stock acquisition of a freestanding C corporation in which no Section 338 election is made to a taxable stock acquisition in which the Section 338 election is made. We choose to compare two taxable acquisition structures rather than a taxable and tax-free acquisition in order to avoid the differences in shareholder tax effects.[20] Returning to our example, notice that target shareholders are indifferent between the two structures, both with $648 after tax, and therefore the structuring choice turns on target corporation NOL-related tax effects.

Given the facts in Table 16.3, the target corporation has NOLs of $450, the net basis in the target's assets is $100, and the price that an acquirer is willing to pay for the stock of the target is $685. The corporate tax rate is 35%, the shareholder capital gains tax rate is 20%, and the after-tax discount rate is 10%. We assume that any step-up in the tax basis of the target's assets is amortized over 10 years on a straight-line basis. We also assume that the appropriate long-term tax-exempt rate applicable to target NOLs under Section 382 is 5% and that the target's NOLs expire in exactly 20 years.

Under these assumptions, the aggregate deemed sale price (*ADSP*) in a Section 338 transaction is $757.69, and the target corporate-level gain is $657.69 ($757.69 *ADSP* less $100 target asset basis).[21] The target's NOLs can be used to offset $450 of the $657.69 gain on the step-up. The target corporation (now a subsidiary of the acquirer)

---

[19]A built-in loss occurs when the target corporation has assets with a tax basis greater than fair market value at the time of the acquisition. If the acquirer sells these assets postacquisition, it is realizing tax losses that were derived from the preacquisition target. Hence, these losses are also limited.

[20]A similar analysis could be performed comparing a tax-free carryover basis transaction with a taxable acquisition that resulted in a step-up in the target's assets. We leave such an analysis as an exercise for readers.

[21]The *ADSP* computation (previously discussed in Chapter 14) when the target had NOLs can be represented in general as:

$$ADSP = P + L + t_c(ADSP - \text{BASIS} - \text{NOL})$$

The NOL variable in the equation cannot be larger than *P* less Basis, however.

TABLE 16.3 Comparison of Tax Effects on Target Tax Attributes of Various Acquisition Structures

Fact Pattern:

Purchase price	$685.00
Target shareholder's stock basis	500.00
Net tax basis in the target's assets	100.00
$ADSP^{(1)}$	757.69
Pre-acquisition target NOLs	450.00
$t_c =$	35%
$t_{cg} =$	20%
$r =$	10%
Long-term tax-exempt rate $=$	5%
Amortization period (n) $=$	10

	Taxable Stock Acquisition with a §338 Election	Taxable Stock Acquisition without a §338 Election
Target Shareholder Effects:		
Cash received	$685.00	$685.00
Tax on stock sale[2]	37.00	37.00
After-tax cash[3]	$648.00	$648.00
Target Corporation Tax Effects:		
Gain on step-up[4]	$657.69	$0.00
Less: NOLs	450.00	n/a
Taxable gain on step-up[5]	$207.69	n/a
Tax on gain[6]	$72.69	n/a
Tax Benefits:		
From Carryover of NOLs:		
Gross NOL carryovers	$0.00	$450.00
Annual limitation[7]	0.00	34.25
Annual tax savings[8]	0.00	11.99
Present value of tax savings[9]	0.00	85.59
From a Step-up in Target's Assets:		
Gross step-up[10]	$657.69	n/a
Annual deduction[11]	65.77	n/a
Annual tax savings[12]	23.02	n/a
Present value of tax savings[13]	141.44	n/a
Computation of Net Tax Benefits:		
Gross tax benefits (9) & (12)	$141.44	$85.59
Incremental tax cost[6]	72.69	0.00
Net tax benefits[14]	$68.75	$85.59

[1]$ADSP$ is computed as $G + L + t_c(ADSP - \text{Basis} - NOL)$. In this case, $G = \$685$, $L = \$0$, Basis $= \$100$, NOL $= \$450$ and $t_c = 35\%$. [2]Tax on stock sale is equal to the gain ($685 less $500 stock basis) multiplied by the capital gains tax rate. [3]Purchase price less tax. Notice that target shareholder's are indifferent between these two structures as their after-tax cash is identical. The structure decision therefore turns on the incremental corporate tax effects on the target corporation. [4]Gain on the step-up is computed as $ADSP$ less the net tax basis in the target's assets. This amount is zero when the §338 election is not made. [5]Taxable gain on step-up is the gain on step-up less the NOL. NOLs reduce the gain dollar for dollar. [6]Tax on the gain is the corporate tax rate multiplied by the taxable gain (5). [7]The annual amount of the target's NOLs available to offset taxable income of the target as defined by I.R.C. §382. Computed as the total value of the target's stock at the date of acquisition ($685) multiplied by the long term tax-exempt rate of return (5%). [8]The annual limitation (7) multiplied by the corporate tax rate. [9]The present value of reducing the combined firm's tax liability by $11.99 for 13.1 years discounted at the after-tax discount rate (10%). [10]The gross step-up is equal to the difference between $ADSP$ and the net tax basis of the target's assets preacquisition. [11]The gross step-up ($657.69) divided by the estimated amortization period (10 years) for the step-up. [12](11) multiplied by the corporate tax rate. [13]The present value of depreciation deductions from the step-up discounted at the after-tax discount rate of 10%. [14]Net tax benefits are the gross tax benefits resulting from stepping up the target's assets less the incremental cost of doing so and tax benefits from preserving the target's NOLs, respectively.

will therefore face a tax liability of $72.69 on the gain on step-up. The step-up in the target's assets is $657.69 and under our assumptions, the step-up will generate $65.77 ($657.69/10 years) of additional depreciation deductions each year. The present value of the tax deductions from the step-up under the preceding assumptions is $141.44. The tax cost of obtaining the step-up is $72.69 ($207.69 taxable gain after NOL utilization multiplied by 35%), so the net tax benefit from the step-up is $68.75 ($141.44 incremental tax benefit less $72.69 incremental tax cost).

If the Section 338 election is not made, the NOLs of the target carry over. The annual limitation on the target's NOLs under our scenario is $34.25 and is computed as the long-term tax-exempt rate (5%) multiplied by the purchase price of the target's equity ($685). The target's NOLs then will generate $11.99 ($34.25 multiplied by the tax rate of 35%) worth of tax savings a year for approximately 13.1 years ($450 of NOLs divided by $34.25 per year).[22] The present value of the tax savings from these NOLs is $85.59 (discounted again at a 10% after-tax rate).

In the example presented here, it would be optimal not to make the Section 338 election because the net benefit under the Section 338 structure is $68.75, while the net tax benefit of preserving the target's NOLs is $85.59. However, it is a close call. The estimates in Table 16.3 are sensitive to the useful life applied to any step-up in the target's assets and the number of years remaining before the target's NOLs expire. As the useful life of the target's assets increases, the present value of additional depreciation-related tax deductions declines. Similarly, as the remaining carryforward years for the target's NOLs declines, the present value of preserving those tax attributes also declines because some of the NOLs will expire unused.

In any event, the computations in Table 16.3 provide a basic financial model to compare the tax implications for a target's tax attributes of various acquisition structures. Additional complexity can obviously be added.

Limitations on Acquiring Firm Tax Attributes

The change of ownership rules of Section 382 can also affect the tax attributes of an acquirer in a stock-financed acquisition. A large stock issue by the acquirer has the potential to trigger the 50% ownership change rule under Section 382 and therefore an acquirer needs likewise to consider the impact of the structure of an acquisition on its tax attributes.

Consider WorldCom's 1997 acquisition of MCI, which was a stock-financed acquisition. Because MCI's market value preacquisition was approximately the same as WorldCom's value, a Section 382 ownership change was likely to occur as a result of that transaction. WorldCom had more than $1 billion of NOLs prior to the MCI acquisition, so the limitations under Section 382 were potentially onerous.[23]

Taking Advantage of Expiring NOLs: Sale/Leaseback

Assume that a profitable acquirer recently acquired a target firm that has $100 million of NOLs due to expire within the next 2 years. Further assume that these $100 million

---

[22]It is possible that the target's NOLs may expire in less than 13 years. In such a scenario, the estimation must be modified accordingly.

[23]As a practical matter, most of WorldCom's NOLs were already restricted due to Section 382. That is, WorldCom's NOLs were primarily derived from previously acquired targets and hence these NOLs were already limited due to the previous acquisition. See the tax footnote from WorldCom's 1997 10-K.

of NOLs are subject to a Section 382 limitation of $10 million per year. Can the acquirer construct a strategy that prevents the valuable NOLs from expiring unused?

In one option, NOLs that are limited by Section 382 can be used by the acquirer to offset gains triggered from the sale of assets that had a **built-in gain** at the time of the acquisition. That is, if this target had assets with a basis of $1 million and a fair market value of $76 million at the time of the acquisition, it had a built-in gain of $75 million.[24] If the acquirer, who now owns the target, were to sell the built-in gain assets, the gain on the sale would be shielded by the expiring NOLs. Specifically, if these assets were sold for $76 million, a corporate level gain of $75 million would be recognized, but $75 million of the acquired target's NOLs would offset this gain, leaving the taxable gain on the sale at $0.

Although the gain on this sale doesn't trigger a tax, the selling firm now may be without productive assets that it needs. In addition, the selling firm was seeking a strategy that would utilize the acquired target's NOLs as a tax shield for the firm's taxable income. The sale doesn't really accomplish this objective.

The acquirer in our example can meet this latter objective with one additional modification in the sale strategy. It can sell the built-in gain assets to a financial firm and then lease them back. In this way, the acquirer can maintain use (and perhaps effective ownership) of the built-in gain assets while at the same time generating a recurring tax deduction from the lease payments and perhaps depreciation deductions on the assets. Essentially what this strategy does is convert the expiring NOLs into rental and/or depreciation deductions, which are not limited by Section 382.

16.7 QUANTIFYING PRICING DIFFERENCES BETWEEN TAXABLE AND TAX-FREE ACQUISITIONS OF FREESTANDING C CORPORATIONS

As we have emphasized throughout this text, it is critical to consider the tax implications of a contract to both (or all) parties. In this chapter and in Chapter 14, we have introduced the major tax implications of various structures for buying and selling freestanding C corporations. But how do a buyer and seller arrive at a decision regarding the tax structure and pricing for a transaction? In this section, we illustrate the effect of the tax status and preferences of the acquirer, the target corporation, and the target's shareholders on a transaction's structure (taxable or tax-free) and price.

Table 16.4 presents a financial model from which the analysis follows. We make a number of assumptions for purposes of this illustration:

- Tax basis of the target's net assets = $100
- Target shareholder stock basis = $10
- t_c (corporate tax rate) = 35%
- t_{cg} (shareholder capital gains rate) = 20%
- r (after-tax discount rate) = 10%
- Value of the target's stock = $685

---

[24]Readers may wonder why the acquirer didn't step up the tax basis of the target's assets in the acquisition when there was such a large built-in gain and potential for increased depreciation benefits. Recall from Chapter 14 that a step-up would not typically be viable when the target was a freestanding C corporation. In this scenario, the built-in gain assets could be a small fraction of the target's total assets.

TABLE 16.4 Comparison of Tax Implications of Tax-Free Acquisitions of Freestanding C Corporations

Fact Pattern:

Purchase price	$685.00
Target shareholder stock basis	10.00
Net tax basis of target's assets	100.00
$t_c =$	35%
$t_{cg} =$	20%
$r =$	10%

	Tax-Free Acquisition Structures				Taxable Structure
	§368 "A"[1]	*§368 "B"*[2]	*§368 "C"*[3]	*§351*[4]	*Stock Sale without a §338 Election*
Purchase Price:	$685.00	$685.00	$685.00	$685.00	$685.00
Cash	274.00	0.00	137.00	411.00	685.00
Stock	411.00	685.00	548.00	274.00	0.00
Target corporation tax liability[5]	0.00	0.00	0.00	0.00	0.00
Target shareholder gain recognized[6]	274.00	0.00	137.00	411.00	685.00
Target shareholder tax liability[7]	54.80	0.00	27.40	82.20	135.00
Target Shareholder After-Tax Wealth:					
Cash[8]	$219.20	$0.00	$109.60	$328.80	$550.00
Stock[9]	411.00	685.00	548.00	274.00	0.00
Total	$630.20	$685.00	$657.60	$602.80	$550.00
Acquirer Net After-Tax Cost:					
Pretax cost	$685.00	$685.00	$685.00	$685.00	$685.00
Less: incremental tax savings	0.00	0.00	0.00	0.00	0.00
Net after-tax cost	$685.00	$685.00	$685.00	$685.00	$685.00
Pretax price to leave target shareholders indifferent[10]	$597.83	$550.00	$572.92	$625.00	$685.00

[1]Assumes that the mix of consideration is 60% stock and 40% cash.

[2]The acquirer purchases the target for 100% stock as required by this structure.

[3]Assumes that the mix of consideration is 80% stock and 20% cash.

[4]Assumes that the mix of consideration is 40% stock and 60% cash.

[5]Tax liability at the target corporation level.

[6]Gain recognized by target shareholders is equal to the lesser of boot received or gain realized.

[7]Tax liability at the target shareholder level. Computed as the lesser of the gain realized or boot received multiplied by the capital gains tax rate.

[8]Cash received in the transaction less tax liability associated with any recognized gains.

[9]Assumes that target shareholders hold acquirer stock until death.

[10]The pretax price that leaves target shareholders with the same after-tax wealth as a taxable stock acquisition at a price of $685.

- Target shareholder holds acquirer stock received in the merger until death.
- The target corporation is a C corporation.
- The target is owned by individual investors.
- The target corporation has no liabilities.
- The acquirer's stock does not pay dividends, and the acquirer does not intend to pay dividends anytime in the future.

The acquiring firm is a C corporation, and it is considering purchasing the target using one of the following acquisition structures.[25]

- Taxable stock acquisition without a Section 338 election (100% cash)[26]
- Tax-free asset acquisition under Section 368 "A" (40% cash, 60% stock)
- Tax-free stock acquisition under Section 368 "B" (100% stock)
- Tax-free asset acquisition under Section 368 "C" (20% cash, 80% stock)
- Tax-free stock acquisition under Section 351 (60% cash, 40% stock)

Table 16.4 compares and contrasts the tax implications of each of these structures on the target's shareholders, the target corporation, and the acquirer. Notice that the purchase price for all the structures is $685, and that the purchase price selected leaves the acquirer's after-tax cost equivalent across transaction structures ($685). In all the tax-free acquisitions, we assume that target shareholders hold the acquiring firm stock received in the merger until death so target shareholders never face a tax liability on the transaction to the extent of acquirer stock received. We later relax this assumption in Table 16.5.

The first four columns of Table 16.4 present the tax implications of various tax-free structures. At a pretax price of $685, target shareholders after-tax wealth is highest under the Section 368 "B" structure because target shareholders incur no current tax liabilities with this structure. All the tax-free structures leave the target's shareholders relatively better off than the taxable transaction structure because of the deferral (avoidance under our assumptions) of the capital gains taxes associated with the sale of target shares in a taxable transaction.

In the lower portion of Table 16.4, we compute the pretax acquisition price that leaves the target corporation's shareholders indifferent between a taxable stock acquisition at $685 and a tax-free structure at the determined price. As we did in Chapter 14, we can formally define the prices at which an acquirer and seller are indifferent across transaction tax structures. Such an analysis allows us to enumerate with some precision the optimal structure for an acquisition.[27] We specify target shareholders' indifference

---

[25]In this text, we focus on the differential tax consequences of various acquisition structures. As a practical matter, the tax structure for an acquisition may be determined in part by the attitude of an acquisition (friendly vs. hostile). The less friendly the transaction, the more likely that at least some cash will be used to acquire control of the target. The analyses here provide a technique to quantify the wealth effects associated with mixed consideration (stock and cash) acquisitions.

[26]We omit taxable acquisitions that result in a step-up in the target's assets from this analysis because those structures are quite rare for the reasons illustrated in Chapter 14.

[27]It is important for readers to note that the subsequent analysis ignores target shareholder tax attributes (capital loss carryforwards), target corporation tax attributes (such as NOLs and capital loss carryforwards), and that we assume that all involved parties face the maximum individual or corporate tax rate. After working through the logic, readers should be convinced that such complications could be added quite easily. We omit them here for ease of illustration.

TABLE 16.5 Comparison of Tax Implications of Tax-Free Acquisitions of Freestanding Companies: Advanced Example

Fact Pattern:

Purchase price	$685.00	Estimated holding period for	
Net tax basis of target's assets	100.00	acquiring firm stock	
Target shareholder's basis in target stock =	10.00	obtained in the merger =	2 years
t_c =	35%	Estimated pretax appreciation	
t_{cg} =	20%	in acquirer stock	
r =	10.114%	postacquisition	12.500%

	Tax-Free Acquisition Structures				Taxable Structure
	§368 "A"(1)	§368 "B"(2)	§368 "C"(3)	§351(4)	Stock Sale without a §338 Election
Purchase Price:	$685.00	$685.00	$685.00	$685.00	$685.00
Cash	274.00	0.00	137.00	411.00	685.00
Stock	411.00	685.00	548.00	274.00	0.00
Target corporation tax liability(5)	0.00	0.00	0.00	0.00	0.00
Target shareholder gain recognized at date of acquisition(6)	274.00	0.00	137.00	411.00	675.00
Target shareholder tax liability at date of acquisition(7)	54.80	0.00	27.40	82.20	135.00
Target Shareholder After-Tax Wealth (Assuming 2-Year Holding Period for the Acquiring Firm's Stock):					
Cash(8)	$219.20	$0.00	$109.60	$328.80	$550.00
Stock(9)	344.85	573.66	459.25	230.45	0.00
Total	$564.05	$573.66	$568.85	$559.25	$550.00
Acquirer Net After-Tax Cost:					
Pretax cost	$685.00	$685.00	$685.00	$685.00	$685.00
Incremental tax savings	0.00	0.00	0.00	0.00	0.00
Net after-tax cost	$685.00	$685.00	$685.00	$685.00	$685.00
Pretax price to leave target shareholders indifferent(10)	$667.89	$656.67	$662.23	$673.64	$685.00

(1)Assumes that the mix of consideration is 60% stock and 40% cash.

(2)The acquirer purchases the target for 100% stock as required by this structure.

(3)Assumes that the mix of consideration is 80% stock and 20% cash.

(4)Assumes that the mix of consideration is 40% stock and 60% cash.

(5)Tax liability at the target corporation level.

(6)Computed as the lesser of the gain realized or boot received.

(7)Tax liability at the target shareholder level multiplied by the capital gains tax rate.

(8)Cash received in the transaction less tax liability associated with any recognized gains.

(9)Assumes that target shareholders hold acquirer stock for two years and then sell. Computation also assumes that the acquirer stock appreciates at the pretax rate of return of 12.5% from the date of the acquisition until the date of the final sale. The taxable gain on the sale is computed as the value of the acquirer's stock two years from the acquisition less the basis in that stock. The after-tax proceeds from the stock sale are discounted using the after-tax rate of return (10.114%).

(10)The pretax price that leaves target shareholders with the same after-tax wealth as a taxable stock acquisition, with no §338 election, at a price of $685.

price in a tax-free acquisition as the right-hand side of equation (16.1), given their after-tax wealth in a taxable stock acquisition:[28]

$$ATAX_{\text{taxablestock}} = \text{Price}_{\text{tax-free}} - \text{Tax}$$

$$ATAX_{\text{taxablestock}} = \{[\text{Price}_{\text{stock}\%}(1 + R)^n] - [(\text{Price}_{\text{stock}\%}(1 + R)^n - \text{Stock})t_{\text{cg}}]\}/$$
$$(1 + r)^n + \text{Price}_{\text{boot}\%} - \text{Price}_{\text{boot}\%}t_{\text{cg}}$$

$$ATAX_{\text{taxablestock}} = \{[\text{Price}_{\text{stock}\%}(1 + R)^n] - [\text{Price}_{\text{stock}\%}(1 + R)^n - \text{Stock}]t_{\text{cg}}\}/$$
$$(1 + r)^n + \text{Price}_{\text{boot}\%}(1 - t_{\text{cg}}) \tag{16.1}$$

where

$ATAX_{\text{taxablestock}}$ = target shareholders' after-tax wealth in a taxable stock transaction

$\text{Price}_{\text{tax-free}}$ = the total pretax consideration received by target shareholders in a tax-free transaction

$\text{Price}_{\text{stock}\%}$ = the value of consideration paid to target shareholders in stock

$\text{Price}_{\text{boot}\%}$ = the value of consideration paid to target shareholders that is boot (cash or debt securities)

Stock = target shareholder's basis in the stock of the target

R = the *pretax* rate of return on the acquirer's stock

r = the *after-tax* rate of return

t_{cg} = the shareholder capital gains tax rate

n = the holding period for the acquirer stock

The first term on the right-hand side of equation (16.1) is the future value of the acquirer's stock received in the acquisition n periods in the future. The second term is the value of the tax incurred by target shareholders when they sell the acquirer stock received in the acquisition, n periods in the future. The difference between these two terms is discounted to present value. The last term in equation (16.1) produces the after-tax wealth of target shareholders associated with boot received at the date of the acquisition.[29] If target shareholders intend to hold acquirer stock until death, the second term in the equation becomes zero.[30] Similarly, if no boot is used in the acquisition, the third term is zero. We assume that target shareholders invest any after-tax cash (boot) in securities that earn the same pretax return (R) as yielded by the acquirer's stock.

For a Section 368 "A" structure, the pretax price that leaves target shareholders indifferent is approximately $597.83 while a 100% stock deal under Section 368 "B" could be priced at $550 and target shareholders would be indifferent after tax relative to a taxable stock acquisition at $685. At those pretax prices, target shareholders have the same after-tax wealth as they have under the taxable structure ($550). For example, at $597.83 under the Section 368 "A" structure, target shareholders receive $239.13 of cash and $358.70 of stock (40% cash, 60% stock). Target shareholders again

---

[28]The left-hand side of equation (16.1) is defined by equation (14.4) in Chapter 14.

[29]In deriving equation (16.1) we explicitly assumed that the gain realized would exceed boot received. That is, we assume that the all boot received is immediately taxable. This assumption could be relaxed of course, but equation (16.1) would become less tractable.

[30]We are ignoring any estate tax–related costs and the interaction between income taxes and estate taxes.

face taxable gains equal to the lesser of the gain realized or the boot received. The gain realized is $497.83, which is computed as the difference between the value of consideration received ($597.83) and shareholder basis in the target's stock ($100). Boot received is $239.13, so the gain recognized is $239.13. Capital gains taxes for individual investors are 20%, and the capital gains tax liability on this transaction would therefore be $47.83, or $239.13 × 20%. Target shareholders would then have $358.70 of acquirer stock and $191.30 of cash after tax for total wealth of $550.

Would the acquirer rather pay $685 (cash) in a taxable stock acquisition or $550 (in stock) in a tax-free stock transaction? Ignoring nontax considerations, the acquirer would obviously prefer to pay less and would therefore prefer the Section 368 "B" structure at $550. If the acquirer pays the target $551 of its stock in a Section 368 "B" transaction, it is better off by $134, or $685 − $551, relative to the taxable stock deal priced at $685. This point is profound, and one that we have seen several times throughout this text. Why can the acquirer pay 19.7% less *pretax,* or ($685 − $550)/$685, when using a different tax structure? Because the seller receives consideration that is tax-favored (deferred taxation). The seller will take less of this tax-favored consideration because it is equally well or better off after tax than when it receives a tax-disfavored consideration.[31]

Essentially this conclusion reduces to the fact that considering the tax preferences and attributes of all contracting parties can result in structures that are beneficial to both parties. From a seller's (target shareholder) perspective, a price of $685 in a Section 368 "B" transaction leaves the acquirer's net after-tax cost the same as the taxable stock acquisition without a Section 338 election. So a seller could offer to take $684 (or less) in acquirer stock, thereby leaving the acquirer better off after tax than under the taxable acquisition structure, while the target's shareholders are better off by $134.

The bottom line then is that, with clever tax planning, an acquirer might be able to purchase a target firm for less or a seller may be able to sell it for relatively more. "Clever tax planning" is defined here as considering the tax preferences of one's counterparty and exploiting those preferences.

Our simple illustration ignores some important nontax consequences of these alternate structures that influence transaction structures and prices. Tax-free transactions require the use of acquirer stock, typically a great quantity of acquirer stock. Such a large stock issue dilutes the control of existing acquiring firm shareholders, particularly manager shareholders. As a result, the acquiring firm may prefer, for nontax reasons, not to issue its stock to target shareholders. Furthermore, if the acquirer uses stock, earnings-per-share consequences will be associated with the acquisition. If the earnings-per-share consequences of a stock deal are more adverse than a cash deal, the acquirer may choose not to pay for the target with its stock.[32]

Finally, acquirer stock fluctuates in value, unlike cash, and it therefore subjects target shareholders to additional risk beyond what they would face if they received cash. Target shareholders may thus prefer to receive cash rather than stock when the purchase price is the same. On the other hand, acquirers may prefer to use stock when

---

[31]Ignoring the nontax costs of receiving acquiring firm stock.
[32]This factor can be analyzed, quite precisely, using a financial model like the one in Table 16.4. See for example, "Modeling the effects of alternative acquisitions structures." University of Chicago M&A modeling case, H. Sapra (2003).

they believe that stock is the least expensive way to finance an acquisition. Or they may prefer to forego a tax-free structure and incur the additional costs of a taxable structure when the costs of stock financing are significantly greater than the costs of debt financing. The analysis in Table 16.4 does not consider these factors.

Additional Complexities

The analysis in Table 16.4 also does not address the impact of sales of acquirer stock by target shareholders postacquisition. Such an outcome is likely, of course, and therefore *quantifying* the impact of those subsequent sales on a seller's wealth is important. Sale of the stock will trigger a tax liability for these shareholders, which they should consider when evaluating the structure and pricing of a transaction.

Table 16.5 presents an analysis similar to that shown in Table 16.4, but we now assume that target shareholders sell the acquirer stock received in the acquisition 2 years after the acquisition. We also assume that the acquirer's stock price appreciates postacquisition at a rate of 12.5% pretax and that the after-tax discount rate is 10.114%.[33]

The first four columns of Table 16.5 compute the present value of target shareholder tax liabilities associated with the various tax-free structures assuming that target shareholders sell the acquirer stock 2 years after the acquisition while maintaining the same assumptions employed in Table 16.4. The tax-free structures continue to leave the target's shareholders with more wealth after tax than the taxable structure, but the spread is much narrower than in Table 16.4. For example, target shareholders' after-tax wealth under the Section 368 "B" structure is $573.66 in Table 16.5, while in Table 16.4 the same structure left target shareholders with $685 after tax.

The difference between Table 16.4 and 16.5 is the benefit of permanent tax deferral in the first table. The present value of the *tax liability* associated with the Section 368 "B" structure in Table 16.5 is $111.34. Stated another way, the present value of permanently deferring shareholder capital gains in a Section 368 "B" transaction is $135 ($685 after-tax wealth in a Section 368 "B" with permanent deferral less $550 after-tax cash in a taxable stock acquisition). So the net tax savings with the "B" structure in Table 16.5 is $23.66 ($135 tax liability with a taxable stock acquisition less $111.34 present value tax liability with the tax-free "B" structure). Notice as well that the pretax price required to leave target shareholders indifferent in Table 16.5 is dramatically more than it was in Table 16.4. For example, in Table 16.5, the target shareholders' indifference price in a "C" reorganization is $662.23, while in Table 16.4, the comparable figure is $572.92.

When performing an analysis like that in Table 16.5, we should identify the impact of changes in the key input variables—for example, target shareholder basis in the target's stock—on the indifference price. For example, as the target shareholders' stock

---

[33]These computations are very sensitive to assumptions about the relation between pretax and after-tax rates of returns. Various legitimate assumptions can be made about the pretax return to acquirer stock relative to the pretax return available to shareholders receiving cash. Differences in pretax and after-tax returns could arise from, among other factors, differences in the timing of taxation (deferral vs. current taxation). Financial models like the ones in Table 16.4 and Table 16.5 can be used to analyze the sensitivity of target shareholder after-tax wealth to various pretax rates of appreciation or depreciation. The analyses presented in Chapter 3 dealing with the returns for various investment vehicles relate closely to these estimates and analyses.

basis declines, they are willing to take relatively less total consideration in a transaction that provides tax deferral. Similarly, the 1997 reduction in individual investor capital gains tax rates from 28% to 20% increased the amount of tax-favored consideration that must be provided to target shareholders relative to tax-disfavored consideration.[34] A shareholder, with a zero basis in the target stock, who receives $1 of taxable consideration before 1997 would have $.72 after tax. The same shareholder receiving $1 of taxable consideration after 1997 will have $.80 after tax. Therefore, an acquirer will have to offer a larger quantity of tax-favored consideration pretax after 1997, relative to before 1997, to leave the target shareholder as well off after tax.

We cannot provide a concrete decision rule to determine which acquisition structure is optimal. However, in conjunction with an understanding of the nontax differences in acquisition structure (see Tables 14.1 and 16.1), the analyses in this section provide a good starting point to begin such a task. Overall, the analyses in Tables 16.4 and 16.5 provide a framework from which to analyze the optimal tax structure for an acquisition. Further realistic complications to a model like the one presented here could include incorporation of target NOLs, various types of target shareholders, changing tax rates, and structure-related earnings effects. We leave such analyses to readers as an exercise.

Implications for Corporate Valuation

Although this text does not focus on valuation, our analyses in this chapter and the prior two chapters have some potentially important consequences for valuation. In particular, the simple models in Tables 16.4 and 16.5 suggest that the pricing of corporate acquisitions is related to the tax structure selected in the transaction. A standard preacquisition analysis employed by investment bankers compares the terms and price of a proposed acquisition to the terms and price of historical acquisitions that are deemed similar to the pending transaction. Such procedures are broadly called **comparable analysis.**

Figure 16.6 presents an example of a fairness opinion from an investment bank. A fairness opinion is prepared in most acquisition transactions. The purpose of the opinion is to provide assurance to shareholders of the acquirer and/or the target that the pending acquisition is priced fairly. Point 11 of the investment banker's letter refers to a comparable analysis. A comparable company analysis compares the acquisition price and the acquisition premium associated with the acquisition of companies similar to the target company. This kind of exercise may illustrate important differences between a subject company and comparable companies that materially affected the price of comparable companies. For example, a comparable target firm's shareholder tax basis may have been higher or lower than that of the subject company. Such tax differences may therefore influence the negotiated price for the pending transaction as illustrated in Tables 16.4 and 16.5. Executives, advisors, and tax planners, as part of their overall planning for a merger or acquisition, should consider how tax factors such as selling shareholder tax basis, transaction tax structure, target firm tax attributes, and acquiring firm tax rates affected acquisition prices and premiums in comparable company analyses.

---

[34]Tax-favored consideration would be consideration (form of payment) that provides tax deferral. Tax-disfavored consideration on the other hand would lead to immediate taxation or less tax deferral.

FIGURE 16.6

Fogel, Lucas, Miller & Co.

295 Park Avenue
New York, NY 10107
(212) 494-9000

November 13, 1995

The Brantingham Company
900 South Buena Vista Street
Burbank, CA 91521

Dear Sirs:

We understand that The Brantingham Company ("Brantingham") and North Drop Inc. ("North Drop") have entered into an Amended and Restated Agreement and Plan of Reorganization, dated as of July 31, 1995, (the "Reorganization Agreement") pursuant to which (i) a new holding company will be formed, which will be renamed "The Brantingham Company" ("New Brantingham"). (ii) newly formed subsidiaries of New Brantingham will be merged with and into each of Brantingham and North Drop, (iii) each share of Brantingham common stock will be converted into one share of New Brantingham common stock and (iv) each share of North Drop common stock will be converted into either New Brantingham common stock or cash, or a combination thereof, based on each stockholder's election and subject to certain proration provisions, such that in the aggregate North Drop stockholders will receive the value equivalent of one share of Brantingham common stock plus $65 in cash per share of North Drop (the "Transaction"). You have provided us with the joint Proxy Statement/Prospectus, which includes the Reorganization Agreement, in substantially the form to be sent to the shareholders of Brantingham and North Drop, respectively (the "Proxy Statement").

You have asked us to render our opinion as to whether the Transaction is fair, from a financial point of view, to the stockholders of Brantingham.

In the course of our analysis for rendering this opinion, we have:

1. reviewed the Proxy Statement:
2. reviewed North Drop's Annual Reports to Shareholders and Annual Reports on Form 10-K for the fiscal years ended December 31, 1992 through 1994, and its Quarterly Reports on Form 10-Q for the periods ended April 2, July 2 and October 1, 1995:
3. reviewed certain historical financial statements and certain budget financial statements by business segments of North Drop. Provided to us by North Drop management:
4. reviewed Brantingham's Annual Reports to Stockholders and Annual Reports on Form 10-K for the fiscal years ended September 30, 1992 through 1994 and its Quarterly Reports on Form 10-Q for the periods ended December 31, 1994 and March 31 and June 30, 1995:
5. reviewed certain operating and financial information provided to us by Brantingham management relating to Brantingham's and North Drop's businesses and prospects, including financial forecasts of Brantingham and North Drop, respectively, prepared by Brantingham management:
6. met with North Drop's Chief Financial Officer to discuss North Drop's historical and certain budget financial statements by business segment:
7. met with certain members of Brantingham's senior management to discuss its operations, historical financial statements and future prospects:
8. reviewed the pro forma financial impact of the Transaction on the stockholders of Brantingham:

(continued)

FIGURE 16.6 *(continued)*

9. reviewed the historical prices and trading volumes of the common stock of North Drop and Brantingham:
10. reviewed certain publicly available financial data and stock market performance data of companies which we deemed generally comparable to North Drop and/or Brantingham:
11. reviewed the terms of certain other recent acquisitions of companies and businesses which we deemed generally comparable to North Drop and its component businesses and
12. conducted such other studies, analyses, inquiries and investigations as we deemed appropriate.

In the course of our review, we have relied upon and assumed without independent verification the accuracy and completeness of the financial and other information provided to us by North Drop and Brantingham as well as the completeness of the financial and other information provided to us by SEC filings of North Drop and Brantingham respectively. With respect to the financial forecasts provided to us by North Drop and Brantingham we have assumed that they have been reasonably prepared on bases reflecting the best currently available estimates and judgments of the managements of North Drop and Brantingham as to the expected future performance of North Drop and Brantingham, respectively. We have not assumed any responsibility for the information or financial forecasts provided to us and we have further relied upon the assurances of the managements for North Drop and Brantingham that they are unaware of any facts that would make the information or financial forecasts provided to us incomplete or misleading. In arriving at our opinion, we have not performed or obtained any appraisals of the assets of North Drop or Brantingham and except as described in paragraphs 3, 5 and 6 above, we have not had discussions with management or employees of North Drop regarding North Drop's operations, historical financial statements and future prospects or had access to financial forecasts of North Drop prepared by North Drop. Our opinion is necessarily based on economic, market and other conditions, and the information made available to us as of the date hereof.

Based on the foregoing, it is our opinion that as of this date, the Transaction is fair, from a financial point of view to the stockholders of Brantingham.

We have acted as financial advisor to Brantingham in connection with the Transaction and will receive a fee for such services.

Very truly yours,

Fogel, Lucas, Miller & Co. Inc.

By /s/ Elizabeth Anne Erickson
Managing Director

Trends in Acquisition Volume and Structure Across Time

Several sources contain information about trends in the structure of acquisitions of freestanding corporations and the pricing (premium) associated with those deals. *Mergerstat Review* and Securities Data Corporation are two sources that provide relatively comprehensive acquisition information. Readers may find such data useful, particularly with respect to the issues already discussed. That is, these sources provide summary information on purchase price premiums and deal structures across time and, to a lesser extent, industry. Such data is potentially useful in planning the structure and pricing of a pending transaction. Transaction-by-transaction merger and acquisition data (for example, deal structure, form of payment, premium, target industry) are available from the same sources, among others, in electronic and hard copy form.

16.8 COMPARISON OF TAXABLE AND TAX-FREE ACQUISITIONS OF FREESTANDING C CORPORATIONS

You should now be armed with a solid understanding of the tax and nontax issues associated with various types of acquisitions. But how do we use this knowledge when planning for the acquisition of a freestanding company? In this section, we briefly synthesize the differences in taxable and tax-free acquisitions and introduce a more complex tax-deferred technique with which to acquire a freestanding C corporation.

Table 16.6 compares various tax and nontax factors associated with seven tax structures commonly used to acquire freestanding C corporations. Three of the structures are taxable and four are tax-free. Of these seven structures, the methods presented in the last five columns are the most common. These five structures are actually quite similar in many respects. Notice that in each of these transactions, the target's assets are not stepped up, the tax attributes of the target survive, and tax-based goodwill is not created. The structures do differ in terms of what is acquired (stock or assets), the status of the target's liabilities, the acquirer's source of deal financing, and whether an immediate gain is recognized by target shareholders on the transaction.

Whether to obtain the stock or the assets of the target is an important decision for an acquirer, because when the target's stock is acquired all its liabilities are likewise preserved and obtained by the acquirer. When a target is subject to substantial contingent liability, an acquirer may want to consider an asset acquisition structure (subject to the aforementioned caveats). As we saw in Chapter 14, a taxable asset acquisition results in substantial incremental tax costs. Therefore, in such a situation, a tax-free asset acquisition structure is likely the best choice.

In Table 16.4 and Table 16.5 and the associated text, we provide a method to *quantify* the impact of target shareholder capital gains taxes on target shareholder after-tax wealth and on pretax indifference prices across transaction structures. As Table 16.6 illustrates, a major difference between acquisition methods relates to the tax treatment at the target shareholder level. When target shareholders hold highly appreciated stock, they are going to prefer to receive a tax-free consideration. Stated another way, these types of shareholders will demand a higher pretax price in a taxable deal relative to a tax-free deal.

From the acquirer's perspective, the tax structure of the deal influences the manner in which the transaction is financed. For example, if the transaction is a taxable cash deal, the acquirer will most likely obtain the cash from debt-type borrowings. On the other hand, if the transaction is tax-free, the acquirer must purchase the target with its stock and therefore the deal will be primarily or totally stock financed. The acquirer's tax status and relative stock price influences the acquirer's after-tax financing costs associated with each of the tax structures presented in Table 16.6. The acquirer's relative resistance to diluting its ownership will also influence the viability of a tax-free structure. Conversely, target shareholders may prefer to receive

TABLE 16.6 Overview of Tax and Nontax Features of Various Taxable and Tax-Free Acquisition Structures: Freestanding C Corporations

Tax or Structural Factor	Taxable Structures			Tax-Free Structures			
	Asset Acquisition Followed by a Liquidation	Stock Acquisition With a §338 Election	Stock Acquisition Without a §338 Election	I.R.C. §368 "A"	I.R.C. §368 "B"	I.R.C. §368 "C"	I.R.C. §351
Consideration/method of payment	Cash	Cash	Cash	Stock/cash	Stock	Stock	Mixed but some stock
Consideration required to be tax-free	n/a	n/a	n/a	50% stock	100% stock	80% stock	Varied
Taxable gain recognized by target shareholders?	Yes	Yes	Yes	Partially	No	No	Partially
Step-up in the target's assets	Yes	Yes	No	No	No	No	No
Target's tax attributes survive?(1)	No	No	Yes	Yes	Yes	Yes	Yes
What is acquired? (stock or assets)	Assets	Stock	Stock	Assets	Stock	Assets	Stock or assets
Acquirer obtains all of the target's liabilities?	No	Yes	Yes	Yes	Yes	No	No
Tax-based goodwill?(2)	Yes	Yes	No	No	No	No	No
Acquirer's finance the acquisition with(3):	Debt	Debt	Debt	Stock/debt	Stock	Stock	Stock/debt
Target shareholders ultimately have?	Cash	Cash	Cash	Stock/cash	Stock	Stock	Stock/boot
Primary benefit of the structure	Target shareholders get cash which provides diversification(4)	Target shareholders get cash which provides diversification(4)	Target shareholders get cash which provides diversification(4)	Tax deferral of target shareholder gains(5)	Tax deferral of target shareholder gains(5)	Tax deferral of target shareholder gains(5)	Tax deferral of target shareholder gains(5)

(1)Target tax attributes include net operating loss carryforwards and various types of tax credits among others.

(2)This row indicates whether any goodwill recorded in the acquisition, for financial accounting purposes, would also be recorded on the tax-basis balance sheet. Tax-based goodwill only occurs when the tax basis of the target's assets are stepped-up.

(3)In taxable transactions, acquirers almost always pay cash for the target. It is common in these transactions for acquirers to obtain a large portion of the cash from debt related borrowings although recently, some acquirers have issued stock to the public and used the cash proceeds from the stock issue to purchase target companies. In tax-free acquisitions, the acquirer by definition must use its stock as payment for the target. These deals are therefore by definition stock financed.

(4)When shareholders receive cash in an acquisition, they have the ability to invest the after-tax proceeds from the transaction in a diversified basket of securities. In a tax-free acquisition in which target shareholders receive stock of the acquiring firm instead of cash, they do not have this option.

(5)Target shareholders defer gains on their exchange of target stock for acquirer stock until they sell the acquirer stock. When acquirer stock is sold, target shareholders recognize the taxable gain associated with the acquisition (assuming that acquirer stock has at least retained its value postacquisition).

cash instead of acquiring firm stock if they are averse to holding acquirer stock postacquisition.[35]

In summary, many important tax and nontax differences characterize transaction structure. Many of the differences are quantifiable and measurable as we have demonstrated.

Advanced Techniques to Provide Diversification and Tax-Free Treatment

A major advantage to a taxable transaction, as illustrated at the bottom of Table 16.6, is the ability to diversify one's holdings with the consideration received in the acquisition. That is, when a seller receives cash, this cash is most likely reinvested in a diversified basket of securities. Stated another way, the receipt of cash is not the objective, simply an *interim step* on the road to reinvestment and diversification. The major advantage to a tax-free transaction structure is the ability to defer capital gains on the sale of target shares. Unfortunately, tax deferral comes at the cost of a loss of diversification relative to the receipt of cash, because target shareholders must hold acquirer stock in order to obtain and maintain tax deferral.

From a tax planning perspective, an ideal transaction structure would be one in which target shareholders receive a tax-free consideration that simultaneously provided diversification. This objective would be met if the acquirer could purchase the target with a security that tracked, for example, the Standard & Poor's 500 Index while simultaneously providing tax deferral. Is this scenario possible? Through the use of derivatives and an **exchange fund,** such an outcome is possible, but at fairly substantial transactions costs. Specifically, target shareholders can receive the right to obtain the return from a diversified basket of securities such as the S&P 500 Index in return for their ownership in the target.

Consider the founding owner of a privately held corporation, which is currently worth $1 billion, whose basis in the stock of the firm is $0. The owner's objective is to monetize her ownership in the target corporation in a tax-minimizing manner. A taxable transaction structure would trigger a taxable gain of $1 billion and a capital gains tax of $200 million. The seller's after-tax proceeds that could be invested in a diversified basket of assets would be about $800 million. A traditional tax-free transaction under Section 368 would defer the $200 million of tax, but the owner would have to assume the risks associated with holding the acquirer's stock instead of a diversified portfolio of assets.

An exchange fund derivative transaction could provide significant benefits to the seller of this privately held corporation.[36] For example, if the seller received $900 million worth of "securities" whose value tracked a well-diversified set of assets—stocks, bonds, real estate—in a tax-free exchange, the seller's after-tax wealth would be higher by $100 million ($900 million less $800 million after tax in a taxable deal priced at $1 billion). An acquirer could benefit from such a structure because it is able to purchase the

---

[35]See A. Rappaport and M. Sirower, "Stock or Cash? The Trade-offs for Buyers and Sellers in Mergers and Acquisitions," *Harvard Business Review* (November–December 1999), p. 147–158, for additional discussion of these issues.

[36]Periodic proposed changes in the taxation of exchange funds could eliminate the viability of the use of this specific technique. Of course, the tax planning strategy is not affected by legislative changes, only the execution of the strategy changes.

target corporation at a lower *after-tax cost* than would be possible in a taxable cash transaction (see Tables 16.4 and 16.5). In this scenario, the acquirer could purchase the target for $100 million less after tax than it could in a taxable cash deal ($1 billion purchase price in a taxable cash deal less $900 million in a derivative-based tax-free deal). With this acquisition structure variant, the acquirer and seller can divide the tax benefits derived from tax deferral/avoidance.[37]

Essentially, of course, this example is just a sophisticated illustration of the same premise you have seen throughout the book—tax planning that considers the tax preferences of the buyer and seller can increase the after-tax wealth of both parties.

Summary of Key Points

1. The most common of tax-free reorganization structures are so-called Section 368 A, B, and C reorganizations. "A" reorganizations are statutory mergers, "B" reorganizations involve an acquisition of at least 80% of the target company's stock solely in exchange for the purchaser's stock, and "C" reorganizations involve an acquisition of substantially all the target company's assets primarily in exchange for the purchaser's stock.
2. Conditions that must be met to qualify as a tax-free reorganization include a business purpose, continuity of shareholder interest, and continuity of the business.
3. Financial accounting consequences (balance sheet and income statement) of reorganizations can differ significantly from their tax consequences and are often alleged to influence the form, whether cash or stock, such transactions take.
4. Corporate reorganization is an area in which nontax factors often dominate tax factors. But the legal form that many transactions take could simply not be explained were it not for tax considerations.
5. Tax-free structures provide tax benefits but are also associated with substantial nontax costs. Specifically, the stock issue associated with a tax-free deal may dilute the control of acquirer shareholders. Target shareholders may resist receiving payment in the form of acquirer stock due to real or perceived risks associated with holding the acquirer's stock.
6. Any type of acquisition that results in a carryover basis in the target's assets, taxable or tax-free, triggers limitations on the target's tax attributes. These limitations can substantially reduce the value of the target's tax attributes postacquisition.
7. The tax costs and benefits that are traded off in the acquisition of a freestanding company include target shareholder capital gains taxes, target corporation capital gains taxes, target corporation tax attributes, and incremental benefits from stepping up the tax basis of the target's assets.

Discussion Questions

1. Why might two corporations wish to combine tax-free? How could tax costs inhibit an otherwise efficient combination?
2. Why might an acquirer want to maintain a target company as a separate legal entity and not merge the target into one of its own subsidiaries or buy the target's assets?

---

[37]See "Barry Diller, Vivendi, and Mixing Bowl Partnerships," J. Robinson, in *Cases in Tax Strategy*, 3rd edition (2003, Pearson/Prentice Hall) for a complex illustration of this type of transaction.

3. What are the tax benefits of using a Section 351 transfer of property to a controlled corporation? In what ways is it superior to a Section 368 reorganization?
4. Why might you expect a cash merger to fetch a higher price for the target's shares than one in which the purchaser's stock is exchanged for the target's stock?
5. What factors might cause you to expect the cash merger and the stock acquisition to be consummated at the same or similar prices?
6. Why would a tax-free stock-for-stock merger be priced higher than a taxable cash acquisition?
7. What are the primary tax and nontax benefits of a:
   a. Section 368 A tax-free reorganization
   b. Section 368 B tax-free reorganization
   c. Section 368 C tax-free reorganization
   d. Section 351 tax-free acquisition
8. What are the primary tax and nontax costs of a:
   a. Section 368 A tax-free reorganization
   b. Section 368 B tax-free reorganization
   c. Section 368 C tax-free reorganization
   d. Section 351 tax-free acquisition
9. Under what general circumstances is a taxable acquisition structure preferable? Consider specifically the tax attributes and tax status of the target corporation and the target's shareholders. Also consider the tax preferences and nontax circumstances of the acquiring corporation.
10. Under what general circumstances is a tax-free acquisition structure preferable? Consider specifically the tax attributes and tax status of the target corporation and the target's shareholders. Also consider the tax preferences and nontax circumstances of the acquiring corporation.

Tax Planning Problems

1. Assume the following factors in assessing the value of preserving NOLs in the acquisition of a target:
   • The target corporation has NOLs of $675.
   • The net basis in the target's assets is $200.
   • The cash price that an acquirer is willing to pay for the stock of the target is $900.
   • Target shareholders have a basis in the stock of the target of $400.
   • The corporate tax rate is 35%.
   • The shareholder capital gains tax rate is 20%.
   • The after-tax discount rate is 10%.
   • Any step-up in the tax basis of the target's assets is amortized over 10 years on a straight-line basis.
   • The appropriate long-term tax-exempt rate applicable to target NOLs under Section 382 is 4%. The target's NOLs will expire in 20 years.
   a. Should the acquirer make a Section 338 election and use the target's NOLs to offset any gain on the step-up, or should it forego the election and preserve the target's NOLs?
   b. What if the step-up in the tax basis of the target's assets is amortized straight-line over a 15-year period, and the long-term tax-exempt rate applicable to target NOLs under Section 382 is 4.75%? Should the acquirer make a Section 338 election and use the target's NOLs to offset any gain on the step-up, or should it forego the election and preserve the target's NOLs?

2. Here is a set of facts about the pending acquisition of Baja, Inc. (the target) by Calstar, Inc. (the acquirer).
   - Baja, Inc. is owned by Smith and Calegari. Smith owns 30% of Baja's common stock and has a basis in his Baja, Inc. stock of $10. Calegari owns the remaining 70% of Baja stock and has a basis in his stock of $1,000.
   - Calstar, Inc. wants to acquire Baja and is willing to pay $100,000.
   - Calstar's outstanding common stock is currently worth $50,000. Calstar management owns approximately 45% of the currently outstanding common stock.
   - Baja possesses valuable patents, licenses, and other intangible assets that cannot be sold and has assets with titles that are nontransferable.
   - Baja does not have substantial contingent liabilities.
   - Calegari will not sell unless he receives only cash for his Baja stock.
   - Smith will not sell unless he receives consideration that is tax-free.
   - Calstar's management will not purchase Baja with its common stock, which would significantly reduce its voting control.

   What acquisition structure would you recommend for this transaction (please mention the Tax Code section)? Diagram the structure and provide details and description as necessary. Be concise.

3. It was announced today that Matrix Inc. will acquire Cajun Systems. Cajun Systems has assets with a tax basis of $5 billion and has $1 billion of liabilities. Prior to being acquired, Cajun Systems had no goodwill on its tax books, although it had approximately $2 billion of goodwill on its financial statements. Cajun's identifiable assets, which include intangible assets other than goodwill, are estimated by Matrix to have a fair market value of $9 billion and its liabilities have a fair market value of $1 billion.

   Cajun has two primary classes of shareholders. The first consists of taxable investors, who own 15 million of Cajun Systems outstanding shares with an aggregate basis of $2 billion. For simplicity, assume these stockholders have all held Cajun stock more than 18 months and all purchased the stock at the same price. The second consists of various nontaxable entities, including pension funds and certain foreign investors, who own the remaining 5 million of Cajun's outstanding shares and have an aggregate basis of $1 billion.

   Neither Matrix nor Cajun Systems has any net operating loss carryovers, and both face a 35% tax rate. Assume any boot is taxable at capital gains rates of 20%. Except for the facts given, assume the transaction otherwise meets the requirements for pooling of interests accounting.

   Matrix gives voting stock in itself in exchange for all of the outstanding stock of Cajun Systems (a Section 368 "B" structure). Cajun becomes a wholly owned subsidiary of Matrix. At the time of the exchange, the Matrix stock given has a market value of $10 billion.

   a. What tax basis will Matrix take in the stock of Cajun Systems acquired?
   b. What tax basis will Cajun (and Matrix through its ownership of Cajun) have in its net assets, or assets less liabilities, following the acquisition?

   Instead, assume Matrix gives voting stock in itself of $7.5 billion and cash of $2.5 billion, and Cajun is merged under state law into a newly created, wholly owned acquisition subsidiary of Matrix called Newco, a Section 368 "A" structure.

   c. Assuming that the cash portion of the purchase price all goes to the nontaxable investors, and the entire stock portion of the purchase price goes to the taxable investors. How much tax will the Cajun shareholders pay in aggregate at the time of the sale?

d. Now assume instead that the cash and stock portions of the purchase price are prorated, so that each Cajun shareholder gets a package of cash and Matrix stock. That is, every share of Cajun stock is exchanged for $125 cash and $375 of Matrix stock. How much tax will Cajun shareholders pay in aggregate at the time of the sale?

e. Assuming the structure outlined in part (b), what tax basis will Newco have in the net assets of Cajun?

f. Assuming the structure outlined in part (b), how much tax-deductible goodwill will Matrix/Cajun have postacquisition?

4. The following table contains the facts for this problem. You are working for Cabo (the acquirer) who wants to purchase Golden Gate. Cabo is considering a taxable stock purchase at a price of $150,000 or some type of tax-free acquisition.

Fact Pattern for Problem 4

Purchase price	$150,000.00
Net tax basis of target's assets	20,000.00
Target shareholder's basis in target stock	5,000.00
t_c	35%
t_{cg}	20%
Estimated holding period for acquiring firm stock obtained in the merger	4 years
Estimated pretax appreciation in acquirer stock postacquisition	12.500%
r	10.324%

	Tax-Free Acquisition Structures			Taxable Structure
	Section 368 "A" (1)	Section 368 "B" (2)	Section 351 (4)	Stock Sale without a Section 338 Election
Purchase price:	$150,000.00	$150,000.00	$150,000.00	$150,000.00
Cash component	60,000.00	0.00	90,000.00	150,000.00
Stock component	90,000.00	150,000.00	60,000.00	0.00

Based on the facts and the data in the table directly above:

a. What is Golden Gate shareholders' after-tax wealth under a Section 368 "A" structure based on the terms presented in the table?

b. What is Golden Gate shareholders' after-tax wealth under a Section 368 "B" structure based on the terms presented in the table?

c. What is Golden Gate shareholders' after-tax wealth under a Section 351 structure based on the terms presented in the table?

d. At what pretax purchase price in a Section 368 "A" will the shareholders of Golden Gate be indifferent, relative to a taxable stock purchase at $150,000?

e. At what pretax purchase price in a Section 368 "B" will the shareholders of Golden Gate be indifferent, relative to a taxable stock purchase at $150,000?

f. At what pretax purchase price in a Section 351 are the shareholders of Golden Gate indifferent, relative to a taxable stock purchase at $150,000?

g. Ignoring nontax costs, will Cabo prefer one of the tax-free structures relative to the taxable stock acquisition at $150,000? Why?

h. How large would the nontax costs of a Section 368 B have to be to cause Cabo to prefer the taxable stock acquisition at a price of $150,000 relative to the Section 368 B at the pretax price computed in part (f)?

5. It was announced today that Florida, Inc., will acquire Menlo Park, Inc. Menlo Park has assets with a gross tax basis of $6 million and has $1.5 million of liabilities. Prior to being acquired, Menlo Park had no goodwill on its tax books, although it had approximately $2 million of goodwill on its financial statements. Menlo Park's identifiable assets, which include intangible assets other than goodwill, are estimated by Florida to have a fair market value of $22 million, and its liabilities have a fair market value of $1.5 million.

Menlo Park has two primary classes of shareholders. The first consists of taxable investors, who own 1,200 of Menlo Park's outstanding shares with an aggregate basis of $10 million. For simplicity, assume these stockholders have all held Menlo Park stock more than 12 months and all purchased the stock at the same price. The second consists of various nontaxable entities such as pension funds and certain foreign investors that own the remaining 800 outstanding Menlo Park shares. These stockholders have an aggregate basis of $1 million.

Neither Florida nor Menlo Park has any net operating loss carryovers, and both face a 35% tax rate. Assume any boot is taxable at capital gains rates of 20%.

Florida gives voting common stock in itself in exchange for all of the outstanding stock of Menlo Park, a Section 368 "B" structure. Menlo Park becomes a wholly owned subsidiary of Florida. At the time of the exchange, the Florida stock given has a market value of $20 million.

a. What tax basis will Florida take in the stock of Menlo Park acquired?

b. What tax basis will Menlo Park and Florida through its ownership of Menlo Park have in its net assets following the acquisition?

Instead, assume Florida gives voting stock in itself of $16 million and $5 million in cash, and Menlo Park is merged under state law into a newly created, wholly owned acquisition subsidiary of Florida, called Biscayne, Inc., which is a triangular 368 "A" structure.

c. Assume that the cash and stock portions of the purchase price are prorated so that each Menlo Park shareholder gets a package of cash and Florida stock. That is, every share of Menlo Park stock is exchanged for $2,500 cash and $8,000 of Florida stock ($10,500 of consideration per share of stock multiplied by 2,000 shares outstanding is $21 million). How much tax will Menlo Park's shareholders pay in aggregate at the time of the sale?

d. What tax basis will Florida's Biscayne subsidiary have in the net assets of Menlo Park?

e. How much tax-deductible goodwill will Florida/Menlo Park have postacquisition?

6. Assume the following factors in assessing the sensitivity of the optimal acquisition structure when the target has NOLs:
   - The target corporation (a freestanding C corporation) has NOLs of $16,500.
   - The net basis in the target's assets is $1,800.
   - The cash price that an acquirer is willing to pay for the stock of the target is $19,275.
   - Target shareholders have a basis in the stock of the target of $4,000.
   - The corporate tax rate is 35%.
   - The shareholder capital gains tax rate is 20%.
   - The after-tax discount rate is 7%.
   - Any step-up in the tax basis of the target's assets is amortized over 15 years on a straight-line basis.
   - The appropriate long-term tax-exempt rate applicable to target NOLs under Section 382 is 5%. The target's NOLs will expire in 12 years.

   a. Should the acquirer make a Section 338 election and use the target's NOLs to offset any gain on the step-up, or should it forego the election and preserve the target's NOLs?

   b. Now instead assume that the after-tax discount rate is 9%. What structure—to make or forego the Section 338 election—do you recommend?

   c. Starting with the part (a) assumptions, assume instead that the target's NOLs expire in 17 years and the after-tax discount rate is 7%. What structure—to make or forego the Section 338 election—do you recommend?

   d. Starting with the part (a) assumptions, assume instead that the step-up in the tax basis of the target's assets is amortized over 20 years and the after-tax discount rate is 11%. What structure—to make or forego the Section 338 election—do you recommend?

References and Additional Readings

Cases:

Erickson, M., 2003. "Comparing the Proposed Acquisitions of MCI by British Telecom, GTE and WorldCom," in *Cases In Tax Strategy,* edited by M. Erickson. Upper Saddle River, NJ: Pearson Prentice Hall.

Robinson, J. 2003. "Barry Diller and Vivendi's Mixing Bowl Partnership," in *Cases In Tax Strategy,* edited by M. Erickson. Upper Saddle River, NJ: Pearson Prentice Hall.

See list at the end of Chapter 13.

17 TAX PLANNING FOR DIVESTITURES

After completing this chapter, you should be able to:

1. Understand the various types of taxable and tax-free divestiture methods.

2. Explain when a Section 338(h)(10) election should be made in the sale of a subsidiary.

3. Compute the price at which a divesting parent and an acquirer are indifferent between different subsidiary sale tax structures.

4. Explain the requirements under which a divestiture qualifies for tax-free treatment.

5. Understand the tax implications of tax-free divestitures for the distributing corporation and its shareholders.

Corporations seek to restructure through divestiture for a variety of reasons. Some conglomerates are unable to effectively and efficiently manage far-flung unrelated businesses. For this reason, they may choose to divest unrelated businesses or separate the conglomerate into distinct portions. However, firms often feel that the market doesn't appropriately price the various divergent portions of the company.[1] They therefore believe that separating it into several standalone businesses will result in appropriate, and presumably higher, prices for the separate underpriced businesses.

From a tax perspective, several structural divestiture alternatives are available. Several methods are tax-free while others are taxable. Tax-free divestiture methods include spin-offs, tax-free subsidiary sales (under Section 368), and equity carve-outs. Taxable divestiture methods include taxable asset sales and taxable stock sales.

In general, a tax-free divestiture method does not result in a taxable gain or loss at the divesting parent corporation level. It also does not usually result in the recognition of a financial accounting gain or loss, although certain balance sheet accounts are affected. Under certain tax-free divestiture structures, the historical shareholders of the parent retain ownership of the divested subsidiary.

---

[1]See for example, E. Nelson, "J. C. Penney, Amid Slumping Sales at Stores, May Be Better Off Dividing into Several Stocks," *The Wall Street Journal* (April 9, 1999), p. C2; and "Monsanto Feels Pressure from The Street," *The Wall Street Journal* (October 21, 1999), p. C1.

In a taxable divestiture, the divesting parent recognizes a taxable gain or loss and will also typically recognize a financial accounting gain or loss. Generally, a taxable divestiture results in a change in ownership of the divested business—that is, historical shareholders of the divesting parent do not retain control of the divested business. In this chapter, we introduce and analyze the tax and nontax implications of various divestiture methods.

17.1 SUBSIDIARY SALES[2]

In Chapters 14 and 16, we analyzed several ways to acquire freestanding C corporations using either taxable or tax-free structures. Some of the same principles apply to acquisitions of subsidiaries of freestanding companies, although several differences are notable. In particular, the seller of a subsidiary is a corporation and not an individual shareholder or a group of various types of shareholders. We focus on taxable subsidiary sales because they are most common, but we begin with a brief analysis of tax-free subsidiary sales. Table 17.1 provides a summary of the tax consequences of various subsidiary sale structures.

Tax-Free Subsidiary Sales

In a tax-free subsidiary sale, the divesting parent exchanges the stock or assets of the subsidiary for the stock of the acquiring firm. The same principles that applied in tax-free reorganizations of freestanding companies generally apply in nontaxable subsidiary sales as well. For ease of exposition, we illustrate with an example of a tax-free subsidiary stock sale. In this case, the divesting parent sells the stock of the subsidiary to an acquirer in exchange for the acquirer's stock.

Figure 17.1 illustrates this transaction. Assuming that the transaction is structured to qualify as a Section 368(a)(1)(B) reorganization, the divesting parent will not recognize a taxable gain or loss on the exchange. The selling parent will take a substituted basis in the acquiring-firm stock received equal to its basis in the sold subsidiary's stock. The sold subsidiary becomes a wholly owned subsidiary of the acquirer and the net asset basis of the sold subsidiary carries over. The sold subsidiary's tax attributes survive and remain with the sold subsidiary, but they are limited under **Section 382.** The acquirer takes a basis in the sold subsidiary's stock equal to the divesting parent's basis in the sold subsidiary's stock, a so-called carryover basis.

This structure is generally undesirable for several reasons. First, the seller holds a large block of acquirer stock after the transaction and therefore the seller has not truly divested its holding in the sold subsidiary. Furthermore, the seller will hold a relatively illiquid block of the acquirer. Finally, if the fair market value of the subsidiary is greater than the seller's tax basis in the subsidiary's stock, the acquirer and the seller will both hold financial positions with a built-in gain after consummation of the transaction.[3] For these reasons, tax-free subsidiary sales are fairly unusual.

---

[2]This section is based on "The Effect of Transaction Structure on Price: Evidence from Subsidiary Sales," M. Erickson and S. Wang, *Journal of Accounting and Economics* (2000), v. 30.

[3]Essentially, the parent's built-in gain presale is duplicated in the acquirer's hands while being preserved in the divesting parent's hands, thereby leaving both parties facing a tax liability when they sell the acquirer or divested subsidiary's stock.

TABLE 17.1 Tax Implications of Various Subsidiary Sale Tax Structures

	Tax Structure			
Factors Influenced by Structure	**Tax-Free Stock Sale**	**Taxable Asset Sale**	**Taxable Stock Sale without an I.R.C. §338(h)(10) Election[1]**	**Taxable Stock Sale with an I.R.C. §338(h)(10) Election[1]**
What is acquired?	Stock	Assets	Stock	Stock
Consideration used:	Acquirer stock	Usually cash[1]	Usually cash[1]	Usually cash[1]
Effect on the Divesting Parent:				
Gain or loss recognized:	No	Yes	Yes	Yes
Gain computed as:	No gain recognized	Price less basis in subsidiary's *net assets*	Price less basis in subsidiary's *stock*	Price less basis in subsidiary's *net assets*
Character of gain:	n/a	Ordinary income and capital gain[2]	Capital gain	Ordinary income and capital gain[2]
Sold Subsidiary's NOLs	Remain with subsidiary, but limited by §382	Remain with divesting parent, and can offset gain on sale; not limited by §382	Remain with subsidiary, but limited by §382	Remain with divesting parent, and can offset gain on sale; not limited by §382
Effect on the Acquirer:				
Basis in subsidiary's assets:	Carryover	Step-up to purchase price paid	Carryover	Step-up to purchase price paid
Basis in subsidiary's stock:	Carryover	n/a[3]	Purchase price	Purchase price
Tax benefits from additional depreciation and amortization deductions:	No	Yes	No	Yes

[1]Consideration can be cash, debt securities, acquiring-firm stock, or some combination. Most often, however, the acquirer uses primarily cash in these transactions.

[2]Ordinary income arises from recaptured depreciation while capital gain is the difference between the purchase price and the historical cost of the assets. The top corporate statutory federal tax rate on ordinary income and capital gain income is currently 35%.

[3]The stock of the subsidiary is not acquired and therefore the acquirer does not have a basis in the acquired subsidiary's stock.

FIGURE 17.1 Tax-Free Subsidiary Stock Sale under I.R.C. §368(a)(1)(B)

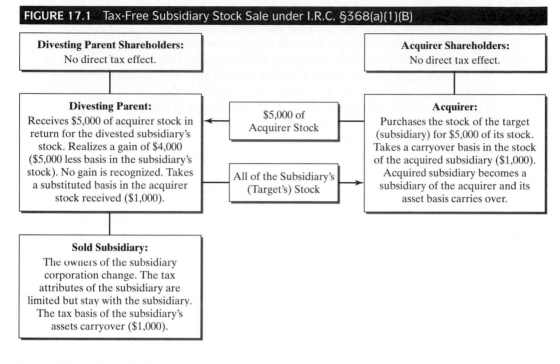

Divesting Parent Shareholders:
No direct tax effect.

Acquirer Shareholders:
No direct tax effect.

Divesting Parent:
Receives $5,000 of acquirer stock in return for the divested subsidiary's stock. Realizes a gain of $4,000 ($5,000 less basis in the subsidiary's stock). No gain is recognized. Takes a substituted basis in the acquirer stock received ($1,000).

$5,000 of
Acquirer Stock

Acquirer:
Purchases the stock of the target (subsidiary) for $5,000 of its stock. Takes a carryover basis in the stock of the acquired subsidiary ($1,000). Acquired subsidiary becomes a subsidiary of the acquirer and its asset basis carries over.

All of the Subsidiary's
(Target's) Stock

Sold Subsidiary:
The owners of the subsidiary corporation change. The tax attributes of the subsidiary are limited but stay with the subsidiary. The tax basis of the subsidiary's assets carryover ($1,000).

Postacquisition Ownership Structure:

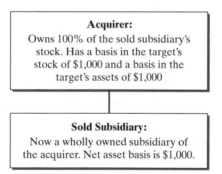

Acquirer:
Owns 100% of the sold subsidiary's stock. Has a basis in the target's stock of $1,000 and a basis in the target's assets of $1,000

Sold Subsidiary:
Now a wholly owned subsidiary of the acquirer. Net asset basis is $1,000.

Taxable Subsidiary Sales

The three basic taxable structures in which a corporation can sell a subsidiary are (1) a taxable asset sale, (2) a taxable stock sale, and (3) a taxable stock sale accompanied by a Section 338(h)(10) election. The latter results in the stock sale being taxed as if the divesting parent sold the assets of the subsidiary instead of the subsidiary's stock. As in the analyses presented in Chapter 14, we work through the mechanics of these structures with the help of a simple numerical example.

TAXABLE ASSET SALE

In a taxable subsidiary asset sale, the acquirer—typically, a corporation—purchases the assets of the target subsidiary corporation, usually for cash, from the divesting parent. The target corporation recognizes a gain or loss equal to the difference between the purchase price and the net tax basis of the assets. To the extent that the gain is recaptured depreciation (or arises from the sale of inventory), the gain will be ordinary. The difference between the purchase price of the target's assets and their historical cost will be a capital gain. Because the target is a subsidiary of the divesting parent, the taxable gain or loss passes through to the parent. The divesting parent corporation may or may not liquidate the sold subsidiary, but generally liquidation of the sold subsidiary occurs.

If the parent liquidates the target corporation, no gain or loss is recognized under **Section 332.**[4] The tax attributes of the subsidiary, such as its net operating losses or NOLs, survive and are available to the parent corporation without incurring the limitations under Section 382. If the target or parent has NOLs, these NOLs can be used to offset the gain on the subsidiary asset sale. The acquiring corporation will take a basis in the assets of the acquired subsidiary equal to the purchase price, and the step-up in basis of the target's assets will be equivalent to the amount of the gain—purchase price less net asset basis—recognized by the target corporation. The purchase price will be allocated to tangible and intangible assets, including goodwill,[5] as prescribed by the residual method, as discussed in Chapter 14.

Figure 17.2 presents the structure of a taxable subsidiary asset acquisition followed by a liquidation of the target subsidiary. For purposes of illustration assume the following basic facts for our taxable subsidiary asset sale:

- The target corporation has assets with a net basis of $1,000 (historical cost equals $1,000 with $0 of accumulated depreciation) and no liabilities.
- The parent corporation has a basis in the stock of the target of $1,000 and the subsidiary is 100% owned by the parent.
- The subsidiary has no NOLs nor has the divesting parent.
- The acquirer pays the parent $5,000 for all the target's assets and the sold subsidiary is liquidated by the parent after the sale.

Given these facts, the target corporation recognizes a gain on the sale of its assets of $4,000 ($5,000 less $1,000 basis) and the character of the gain is capital in nature. A $4,000 capital gain taxed at 35% results in a tax liability of $1,400 for the target corporation. After tax, the target corporation has $3,600, which is distributed to the parent in exchange for all the target's stock in liquidation. Table 17.2 provides the details of these computations and those that follow. The parent corporation does not recognize a gain on the liquidation under Section 332. The shareholders of the parent corporation do not recognize a gain or loss unless the parent corporation distributes the proceeds of the asset sale, which is unusual.

---

[4]Section 332 allows a corporation to liquidate wholly owned subsidiaries in a tax-free manner. Such corporate liquidations are common in various types of acquisitions.

[5]The amortization associated with these intangible assets is tax deductible under Section 197.

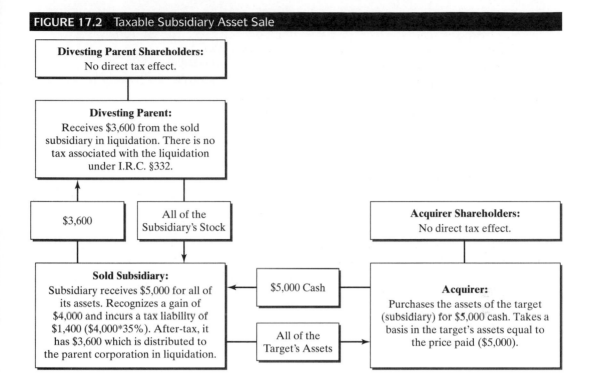

FIGURE 17.2 Taxable Subsidiary Asset Sale

The acquiring corporation takes a basis in the assets of the target equal to the purchase price ($5,000), so the step-up in the tax basis of the target's assets is $4,000. A portion of the $4,000 step-up may be allocated to goodwill and other intangibles. For financial accounting purposes, the acquirer would account for this transaction using the purchase method. As in the case of asset acquisitions of freestanding companies, some of the target subsidiary's liabilities may remain with it. This treatment is a potential benefit for the acquirer, but a divesting parent should price the costs of liability retention. As we noted in Chapter 14, asset acquisitions are potentially costly in terms of transaction costs, such as title transfer, and some assets may not be transferable. On the other hand, this structure may be particularly useful when selling pieces of a business or selected assets rather than an entire incorporated subsidiary.

TAXABLE STOCK SALE WITHOUT A SECTION 338(H)(10) ELECTION
The divesting parent may sell the stock of the subsidiary rather than the assets. Under this structure, the acquirer purchases the stock of the target corporation from the parent for cash.[6] The parent corporation recognizes a

---

[6]In some cases, acquirers use their stock in a taxable stock acquisition. The transaction is typically structured to fail to qualify for tax-free treatment under Section 368(a)(1)(B) making the transaction a taxable stock acquisition. See WorldCom's acquisition of CompuServe from H&R Block, for example.

TABLE 17.2 Tax Implications of Various Taxable Subsidiary Sale Structures

Fact Pattern:

Purchase price	$5,000.00
Target's tax net asset basis	1,000.00
Divesting parent's tax basis in target's stock	1,000.00
$t_c =$	35%
$r =$	10%
Amortization period (n) =	10

	Subsidiary Sale Structure		
	Taxable Asset Sale	*Taxable Stock Sale without a §338(h)(10) Election*	*Taxable Stock Sale with a §338(h)(10) Election*
Purchase price	$5,000.00	$5,000.00	$5,000.00
Tax Effect for Divesting Parent:			
Gain on sale[1]	$4,000.00	$4,000.00	$4,000.00
Cash received	$5,000.00	$5,000.00	$5,000.00
Tax on gain[2]	1,400.00	1,400.00	1,400.00
After-tax cash	$3,600.00	$3,600.00	$3,600.00
Acquirer Cost:			
Purchase price	$5,000.00	$5,000.00	$5,000.00
Less: incremental tax savings[3]	860.24	0.00	860.24
Net after-tax cost	$4,139.76	$5,000.00	$4,139.76
Acquirer's Tax Basis in Target's:			
Stock	n/a	5,000.00	5,000.00
Net assets	$5,000.00	$1,000.00	$5,000.00
Step-up in the tax basis of the target's assets	4,000.00	0.00	4,000.00

[1]Computed as the purchase price less the divesting parent's basis in the sold subsidiary's stock or net assets, depending on the transaction's structure.

[2]Corporate tax liability on the subsidiary sale. The tax is computed based on the nature of the gain (capital or ordinary) and the appropriate tax rate. We assume here that ordinary and capital gains rates are identical for divesting parents.

[3]The present value of the tax savings resulting from stepping-up the tax basis of the target's assets assuming that the step-up is amortized/depreciated straight-line over a 10-year period, the applicable tax rate is 35% and the after-tax discount rate is 10%.

gain or loss on the sale of the subsidiary's stock equal to the difference between the purchase price and its basis in the subsidiary's stock. The gain or loss will be capital in nature because *stock* is a capital asset.

The acquiring firm will take a basis in the target subsidiary's stock equal to the purchase price, and it will take a carryover basis in the assets of the target. The acquirer obtains all the assets and liabilities of the target, and the target becomes a subsidiary of the acquirer postacquisition. Figure 17.3

FIGURE 17.3   Taxable Subsidiary Stock Sale without a §338(h)(10) Election

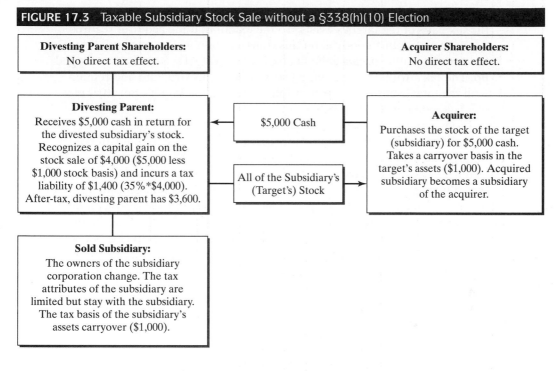

Postacquisition Ownership Structure:

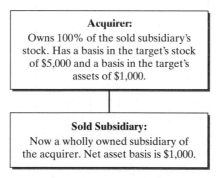

illustrates the mechanics of a taxable subsidiary stock sale without a Section 338(h)(10) election.

Returning to our numerical example, we make the same assumptions here. The acquirer is willing to pay $5,000 for the stock of the target. The selling parent will recognize a capital gain on the stock sale equal to $4,000, which is $5,000 purchase price less stock basis of $1,000, and faces a tax liability of $1,400. After tax, the divesting parent will have $3,600. The acquirer will take a basis in the target's stock of $5,000 and will have a basis in the target's assets of $1,000 (carryover).

Notice that, with this structure, the acquirer does not obtain a step-up in the tax basis of the target's assets. To the extent that the acquirer records financial accounting goodwill on this transaction, it will be goodwill that is not tax deductible, because the tax basis of the target's assets is not stepped-up. The tax attributes of the target survive with this structure and remain with the target subsidiary corporation. However, the target's tax attributes will be limited by Section 382.

From a nontax perspective, a stock sale is often cheaper than an asset sale in terms of transaction costs. In most cases, the divesting parent will hold a minimal number of shares (e.g., 100) that possess 100% of the voting control of the divested subsidiary. As a result, the cost of transferring these shares is typically much lower than the cost of transferring title in the subsidiary's numerous assets. A stock sale preserves the identity of the target with it all its liabilities—recorded and unrecorded. However, the acquirer does obtain some degree of liability protection, because the target corporation becomes a wholly owned subsidiary of the acquirer. On the other hand, if the target has assets that are difficult to transfer, a stock sale facilitates ownership transfer of these assets to the acquirer.

TAXABLE STOCK SALE WITH A SECTION 338(H)(10) ELECTION

An acquirer and divesting parent can structure the divestiture to be completed as a stock sale, while being taxed like an asset sale. The acquirer may prefer to obtain a stepped-up basis in the target's assets, but the nontax costs of an asset sale may be prohibitive. In Section 338(h)(10), the tax law provides a vehicle to facilitate the potentially favorable tax treatment of an asset sale without incurring the nontax costs of an asset sale.

Under Section 338(h)(10), a subsidiary stock sale can be taxed as an asset sale if both the buyer and seller agree to such tax treatment. In a qualifying stock purchase with at least 80% of the target's stock obtained during a 12-month period, the acquirer and divesting parent can jointly agree to make a Section 338(h)(10) election. This election will cause a taxable subsidiary stock sale to be taxed as if the divesting parent had sold the subsidiary's assets to the acquirer rather than the subsidiary's stock. The taxable gain or loss on the transaction is computed as the purchase price less the divesting parent's basis in the *net assets* of the target. No tax is assessed on the stock sale.

Returning to our hypothetical numbers, we illustrate the case in Figure 17.4. With this structure, the stock sale is taxed as if the target sold its assets for $5,000. Hence the parent corporation recognizes a gain on the sale of $4,000 equal to the difference between the purchase price ($5,000) and its basis in the target's *net assets* ($1,000). The gain is capital in nature because the target has no accumulated depreciation. The divesting parent faces a tax liability of $1,400 on the sale and has $3,600 after tax. If the divesting parent or the target subsidiary had NOLs, they could serve to offset the gain on the deemed asset sale. The divesting parent retains the tax attributes of the target.

The acquiring firm takes a basis in the stock of the target equal to the purchase price paid ($5,000) and takes a basis in the net assets of the target also equal to $5,000. The acquirer obtains a stepped-up basis in the target's assets

FIGURE 17.4 Taxable Subsidiary Stock Sale with a §338(h)(10) Election

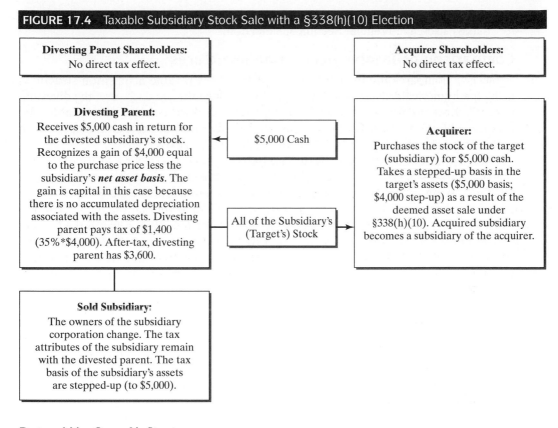

Divesting Parent Shareholders:
No direct tax effect.

Acquirer Shareholders:
No direct tax effect.

Divesting Parent:
Receives $5,000 cash in return for the divested subsidiary's stock. Recognizes a gain of $4,000 equal to the purchase price less the subsidiary's **net asset basis**. The gain is capital in this case because there is no accumulated depreciation associated with the assets. Divesting parent pays tax of $1,400 (35%*$4,000). After-tax, divesting parent has $3,600.

$5,000 Cash

Acquirer:
Purchases the stock of the target (subsidiary) for $5,000 cash. Takes a stepped-up basis in the target's assets ($5,000 basis; $4,000 step-up) as a result of the deemed asset sale under §338(h)(10). Acquired subsidiary becomes a subsidiary of the acquirer.

All of the Subsidiary's (Target's) Stock

Sold Subsidiary:
The owners of the subsidiary corporation change. The tax attributes of the subsidiary remain with the divested parent. The tax basis of the subsidiary's assets are stepped-up (to $5,000).

Postacquisition Ownership Structure:

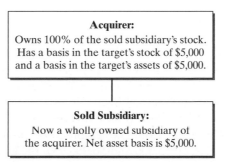

Acquirer:
Owns 100% of the sold subsidiary's stock. Has a basis in the target's stock of $5,000 and a basis in the target's assets of $5,000.

Sold Subsidiary:
Now a wholly owned subsidiary of the acquirer. Net asset basis is $5,000.

because the transaction was taxed like an asset sale (a gain at the target *corporation* level was triggered). The step-up in the target's assets is $4,000, and purchase price will be allocated to the sold subsidiary's assets under Tax Code Section 1060 (residual method).

It is important to note that a valid Section 338(h)(10) election can occur only when both the acquirer and the divesting parent jointly make the election. Without the seller's explicit cooperation, the acquirer cannot obtain a step-up in the tax basis of the target's assets in a stock sale. Recall that in a taxable stock acquisition of a freestanding company, the acquirer unilaterally makes a so-called regular Section 338 election.

Comparison of Taxable Acquisition Structures

Table 17.2 compares the tax implications of the three taxable acquisition structures using the numerical examples we just described. Notice that, in each case, the divesting parent's after-tax wealth is $3,600. In the first and third column of the table, the acquirer obtains a step-up in the tax basis of the divested subsidiary's assets while, in the middle column, the tax basis of the target's assets carry over.

It is important to note that, in step-up basis transactions under a fact pattern like this one *only,* the incremental cost of the step-up in the tax basis of the target's assets is $0. The reason is that the tax basis of the target's net assets is exactly equal to the divesting parent's tax basis in the target's stock. Therefore, whether the parent sells the stock or assets of the target, the gain on the sale will be the same, because the basis in the property sold is identical whether the property is assets or stock. Recall that the incremental cost of obtaining a step-up in the assets of a freestanding C corporation was not $0. This point is a major difference between subsidiary sales and sales of freestanding C corporations.

Returning to the numerical example illustrated in Table 17.2, we see that the optimal structure is either a taxable asset sale or a taxable stock sale with a Section 338(h)(10) election. Those structures result in the lowest after-tax cost to the acquirer ($4,139.76), while the seller is indifferent between structures. From the acquirer's perspective, making the Section 338(h)(10) election is worth $860.24.[7] That is, the acquirer is better off after taxes by $860.24 when the election is made. Because the election cannot be made without the seller's cooperation, the acquirer should be willing to pay the seller up to $860.24 more than $5,000 in order to get the seller to join in making the Section 338(h)(10) election. Actually, the acquirer is willing to pay up to $6,095.93 as illustrated in Table 17.3.

The acquirer is willing to pay more than $860.24 because as the purchase price rises so does the tax benefit from a step-up in the tax basis of the target's assets. Any price between $5,000 and $6,095.93 when the election is made leaves both the buyer and the seller better off after tax than a taxable stock acquisition at $5,000 with no election. The step-up election generates a net tax benefit that increases the wealth of both the divesting parent and the acquirer.

As the price of the sale approaches $5,000 ($6,095.93), the acquirer (divesting parent) captures relatively more of the tax benefits. For example, at a purchase price of $5,547.97 (midpoint between $5,000 and $6,095.93), the acquirer's net after-tax cost is $430.12 lower than it is if the election is not made and the deal is priced at $5,000. Similarly, the divesting parent's after-tax wealth is $356.18 higher if the election is made and the deal is priced at $5,547.97. Table 17.3 contains these computations. You should now see a pattern developing. Note once again how important it is to consider the tax implications of a transaction to both parties.

---

[7]The same is true of the taxable asset sale structure, but we focus on the stock sale with the election here for ease of exposition and because the nontax costs of the stock sale with the election are the same as those without the election.

TABLE 17.3 Tax Implications of Various Taxable Subsidiary Sale Structures

Fact Pattern:

Purchase price—without the §338(h)(10) election	$5,000.00
Purchase price—with the §338(h)(10) election	$6,095.93
Target's tax net asset basis	1,000
Divesting parent's tax basis in target's stock	1,000
$t_c =$	35%
$r =$	10%
Amortization period $(n) =$	10

	Subsidiary Sale Structure		Tax Benefit Split[1]	
	Taxable Stock Sale without a §338(h)(10) Election	**Taxable Stock Sale with a §338(h)(10) Election**	**Midpoint Price with a §338(h)(10) Election**	**Incremental Difference**
Purchase price—base case	$5,000.00			
Acquirer indifference price[2]		$6,095.93		
Purchase price—tax benefit split[1]			$5,547.97	
Tax Effect for Divesting Parent:				
Gain on sale[3]	$4,000.00	$5,095.93	$4,547.97	
Cash received	$5,000.00	$6,095.93	$5,547.97	
Tax on gain[4]	1,400.00	1,783.58	1,591.79	
After-tax cash	$3,600.00	$4,312.35	$3,956.18	$356.18
Acquirer Cost:				
Purchase price	$5,000.00	$6,095.93	$5,547.97	
Less: incremental tax savings[5]	0.00	1,095.93	978.08	
Net after-tax cost	$5,000.00	$5,000.00	$4,569.88	$430.12
Acquirer's Tax Basis in Target's:				
Stock	$5,000.00	$6,095.93	$5,547.97	
Net assets	$1,000.00	$6,095.93	$5,547.97	
Step-up in the tax basis of the target's assets	$0.00	$5,095.93	$4,547.97	

[1]This column presents the split in the net tax benefits from the step-up election assuming a price that is between the divesting parent's and acquirer's indifference price in a step-up transaction [relative to a taxable stock sale without a §338(10)(h) election at a price of $5,000].

[2]Price at which the acquirer is indifferent between making the §338(h)(10) election and a purchase without the election at a price of $5,000.

[3]Computed as the purchase price less the divesting parent's basis in the sold subsidiary's stock or net assets, depending on the transaction's tax structure.

[4]Corporate tax liability on the subsidiary sale. The tax is computed based on the nature of the gain (capital or ordinary) and the appropriate tax rate. We assume here that ordinary and capital gains rates are identical for divesting parents.

[5]The present value of the tax savings resulting from stepping-up the tax basis of the target's assets assuming that the step-up is amortized/depreciated straight-line over a 10-year period, the applicable tax rate is 35% and the after-tax discount rate is 10%.

When Should the Section 338(h)(10) Election Be Made?

Assuming that a divesting parent has decided to sell a subsidiary in a taxable transaction, what structure should be employed? We restrict our analysis to taxable subsidiary stock sales for ease of illustration.

Because the seller and the buyer jointly make a Section 338(h)(10) election, the buyer cannot unilaterally determine the structure of the transaction but requires the seller's cooperation in defining the transaction's tax structure. Consequently, the differential tax effects of the Section 338(h)(10) election on the seller influence the election decision. The seller's tax cost in the absence of a Section 338(h)(10) election is computed as the difference between the sale price and the seller's basis in the sold subsidiary's stock multiplied by the tax rate. On the other hand, the seller's tax cost when a Section 338(h)(10) election is made is the difference between the purchase price and the seller's basis in the net assets of the sold subsidiary, multiplied by the corporate tax rate. The seller will be indifferent between a Section 338(h)(10) election and no election when both choices leave it equally well off. More formally, the seller is indifferent if the price with an election meets the following condition,

$$\text{Price}_{338h10} - t_c(\text{Price}_{338h10} - \text{Asset}) = \text{Price}_{NO338h10} - t_c(\text{Price}_{NO338h10} - \text{Stock}) \quad \textbf{(17.1)}$$

where

$$\text{Price}_{338h10} = \text{the price when a Section 338(h)(10) election is made}$$
$$\text{Price}_{NO338h10} = \text{the purchase price if the election is not made}$$
$$t_c = \text{the corporate tax rate}$$
$$\text{Stock} = \text{seller's basis is the sold subsidiary's stock}$$
$$\text{Asset} = \text{seller's basis in the sold subsidiary's net assets}$$

Assume that $\text{Price}_{NO338h10}$ is the price of the subsidiary, ignoring any change in its asset basis, and that the seller and the acquirer agree on this price. The *minimum* price demanded by the seller to make the Section 338(h)(10) election can be expressed by simplifying equation (17.1) as:

$$\text{Price}_{338h10} = \text{Price}_{NO338h10} + [t_c/(1 - t_c)](\text{Stock} - \text{Asset}) \quad \textbf{(17.2)}$$

As equation (17.2) indicates, the minimum price demanded by the seller in a Section 338(h)(10) transaction can be greater or less than the price without the election. The relationship between the price under the differing structures is a function of the seller's basis in the subsidiary's stock and net assets. If the seller has an equivalent basis in the stock and the assets of the subsidiary, then it will be equally well off after tax, at any price, whether or not the election is made.[8] If the seller's basis in the subsidiary's stock is greater than its basis in the subsidiary's net assets, as is often the case, then the seller will have the same wealth after tax only when Price_{338h10} exceeds $\text{Price}_{NO338h10}$.[9]

If the parties make the Section 338(h)(10) election and the purchase price exceeds the subsidiary's net asset basis, the acquirer will obtain tax benefits from a step-up in

---

[8]This point was illustrated numerically in Table 17.2.
[9]Net asset basis exceeds stock basis relatively infrequently.

the tax basis of the acquired subsidiary's assets. Like a seller, an acquirer is indifferent between tax structures when it is equally well off after tax, as when the after-tax *cost* of the acquisition is the same. Because the acquirer obtains incremental tax benefits with the Section 338(h)(10) election, it is equally well or better off after tax with the election even if the *pretax* purchase price of the subsidiary is higher.

As a result of the tax benefits from the basis step-up, the acquirer should be willing to pay a higher purchase price if the Section 338(h)(10) election is made. Assuming that the acquirer uses straight-line depreciation and amortization after purchasing the subsidiary, we can express the maximum price that the acquiring firm will pay in a Section 338(h)(10) transaction as:

$$\text{Acqprice}_{338h10} = \text{Price}_{\text{NO338h10}} + t_c \times PVANN[(\text{Acqprice}_{338h10} - \text{Asset})/n] \qquad \textbf{(17.3)}$$

where

$\text{Acqprice}_{338h10} =$ the maximum purchase price that the acquiring company is willing to pay in a Section 338(h)(10) transaction

$PVANN =$ the present value of an annuity

$n =$ the average useful life of the acquired subsidiary's assets

$\text{Price}_{\text{NO338h10}}$, Asset, and t_c are defined above.

The second term on the right-side of equation (17.3) is the present value of the tax benefits from stepping up the tax basis of the acquired subsidiary's assets. Rearranging, substituting, and simplifying equation (17.3) yields:

$$\text{Acqprice}_{338h10} = (\text{Price}_{\text{NO338h10}} - t_c\text{Factor} \times \text{Asset})/(1 - t_c\text{Factor}) \qquad \textbf{(17.4)}$$

where Factor is $PVANN/n$, and all other terms are as previously defined. In general, equation (17.3) shows that the acquirer is willing to pay a higher price in order to persuade the seller to make the Section 338(h)(10) election if the subsidiary's net asset basis is less than the purchase price without the election ($\text{Price}_{\text{NO338h10}}$).[10] If the purchase price is less than the net tax basis of the subsidiary's assets, equation (17.4) indicates that the price paid by the acquirer in a Section 338(h)(10) election would be lower than if the election were not made. The election would therefore result in a step-down in the asset basis of the subsidiary.

A Section 338(h)(10) election will be made in a subsidiary sale when the maximum price that the acquirer is willing to pay in a Section 338(h)(10) transaction (Acqprice_{338h10}) is greater than or equal to the minimum price that the seller is willing to accept (Price_{338h10}) in a transaction with the election, or when $\text{Acqprice}_{338h10} - \text{Price}_{338h1070}$. The difference between Acqprice_{338h10} and Price_{338h10} is the difference between equations (17.2) and (17.4). After rearrangement and substitution,

$$\text{Acqprice}_{338h10} - \text{Price}_{338h10} = \left[t_c \bigg/ \left(\frac{1}{\text{Factor}} - t_c \right) \right] (\text{Price}_{\text{NO338h10}} - \text{Asset})$$
$$- [t_c/(1 - t_c)](\text{Stock} - \text{Asset}) \qquad \textbf{(17.5)}$$

If the right-hand side of equation (17.5) is greater (less) than zero, a Section 338(h)(10) election will (will not) be made. Therefore, the Section 338(h)(10)

---

[10]This point was illustrated numerically in Table 17.3.

election decision depends in large part on the difference between the seller's basis in the subsidiary's stock (Stock) and the seller's basis in the subsidiary's net assets (Asset). Specifically, a Section 338(h)(10) election becomes less likely as the difference between the tax basis of the subsidiary's net assets and stock increases.[11]

What Determines a Parent's Basis in a Subsidiary's Stock and Net Assets?

A divesting parent's tax basis in a subsidiary's stock and net assets is determined by the manner in which the subsidiary was created or acquired.

- If the divesting parent internally generated the subsidiary, the parent's tax basis in the stock and net assets of the subsidiary will be the same.
- If the sold subsidiary was previously acquired by the divesting parent, that is, the divested subsidiary was previously a freestanding target that was acquired by the divesting parent, then the parent's tax basis in the subsidiary's stock and assets will be determined by the tax structure used to acquire the target.
- If the target, now the sold subsidiary, was acquired in a taxable stock acquisition, the parent's tax basis in the stock of the sold subsidiary will likely be much higher than its basis in the sold subsidiary's assets. Most taxable stock acquisitions of freestanding C corporations are structured in a manner that results in a carryover basis in the target's assets. At the same time, acquirers take a basis in the stock acquired equal to the purchase price, which usually exceeds the net asset basis of the acquired target by a substantial amount.
- If the target, now the sold subsidiary, was acquired using a tax-free structure, then the divesting parent's basis in the stock and net assets of the sold subsidiary are also not likely to be equal. The parent's basis in the stock of the sold subsidiary is likely to be greater than the net asset basis of the sold subsidiary in this scenario as well.

Additional Complexities: Subsidiary Sale

Let's consider a more complex subsidiary sale example that illustrates the concepts laid out in equations (17.1) through (17.5). Our objective is to determine whether the hypothetical subsidiary stock sale should be accompanied by a Section 338(h)(10) election. Assume the following facts relating to the pending sale of Richard Stevens, Inc.

- Richard Stevens, Inc., an investment bank, is a subsidiary of York Securities, and the net tax basis of Richard Steven's assets is $1,500 (historical cost equals basis).
- York's tax basis in the stock of Richard Stevens is $3,500.[12]
- Chicago Bank wants to purchase Richard Stevens and believes that the value of Richard Stevens is $5,000, if the tax basis of Richard Steven's assets carryover.

---

[11]This conclusion ignores a divesting parent's tax status. For example, if the divesting parent had large capital loss carryforwards, its relative preference for a stock sale without the election would be much greater.
[12]York acquired Richard Stevens in a taxable stock acquisition 3 years ago.

- Chicago Bank wants to pay cash to acquire Richard Stevens.
- The corporate tax rate is 35%, any step-up in the tax basis of Richard Steven's assets will be amortized straight-line over a 10-year period, and the appropriate after-tax discount rate is 10%.

Table 17.4 provides the particulars of the following computations. In a taxable stock sale without the election, York Securities would have $4,475 after tax, which is $5,000 price less $525 tax, or $5,000 minus $3,500 times 35%. Therefore, York would need to receive a pretax price in a Section 338(h)(10) transaction that left it with $4,475 after tax.

Equation (17.2) provided the minimum price demanded by York Securities to make the election ($PRICE_{338h10}$).

$$
\begin{aligned}
Price_{338h10} &= Price_{NO338h10} + [t_c/(1-t_c)](Stock - Asset) \\
&= \$5,000 + (.35/.65)(\$3,500 - \$1,500) \\
&= \$6,076.93
\end{aligned}
\tag{17.2}
$$

Would Chicago Bank be willing to pay $6,076.93 in a transaction that results in a Section 338(h)(10) election if it will pay $5,000 (and York will accept) in a non-Section 338(h)(10) transaction? The acquirer's net after-tax cost in a transaction in which the election is not made, at a price of $5,000, is $5,000. At a pretax price of $6,076.93 in a Section 338(h)(10) transaction, the present value of tax benefits from stepping up the target's assets is $984.11.[13] The acquirer's net after-tax cost is therefore $5,091.83 if the election is made, which is greater than the acquirer's net after-tax cost if the election was not made. Equation (17.4) provided the maximum price that Chicago Bank will pay ($Acqprice_{338h10}$) to purchase Richard Stevens if the election is made.

$$
Acqprice_{338h10} = (Price_{NO338h10} - t_c Factor \times Asset)/(1 - t_c Factor)
\tag{17.4}
$$

Factor is equal to $.6145(n = 10, r = 10\%)$.

$$
\begin{aligned}
Aprice_{338h10} &= [\$5,000 - .35(.6145) \times 1,500]/[1 - .35(.6145)] \\
&= \$5,959.03
\end{aligned}
$$

Given these numbers, the election should not be made, because $Acqprice_{338h10}$ is less than $Price_{338h10}$. That is, the *maximum* price that the acquirer will pay if the election is made is less than the *minimum* price that the seller will accept if the election is made. The incremental cost of making the election is more than the incremental tax benefits associated with the election.[14] Stated another way, the acquirer's net after-tax cost in a Section 338(h)(10) transaction is higher than its net after-tax cost if the election is not made and the deal is priced at $5,000.

---

[13]Assuming that the step-up is amortized straight-line over a 10-year period, the tax rate is 35%, and the appropriate after-tax discount rate is 10%.

[14]The incremental tax benefit of the election at a price of $5,000 is equal to $752. The incremental tax cost to the seller at a price of $5,000 is $700, or $3,500 stock basis less $1,500 asset basis multiplied by 35%. In order to compensate the seller for this additional $700 of taxes, the buyer must pay the seller an additional $1,076.92 pretax, or $1,076.92(1 − t) = $700, where t = 35%. A buyer is unwilling to pay an additional $1,076.92 to obtain $752 of tax benefits, as illustrated by equations (17.2) and (17.4).

TABLE 17.4 Tax Implications of Various Taxable Subsidiary Sale Structures

Fact Pattern:

Purchase price—without a §338(h)(10) election	$5,000.00
Target's tax net asset basis	1,500
Divesting parent's tax basis in target's stock	3,500
$t_c =$	35%
$r =$	10%
Amortization/depreciation period (n) =	10

	Subsidiary Sale Structure		
	Taxable Stock Sale without a §338(h)(10) Election	*Taxable Stock Sale with a §338(h)(10) Election*	*Taxable Stock Sale with a §338(h)(10) Election*
Purchase price	$5,000.00		
Divesting parent indifference price[1]		$6,076.92	
Acquirer indifference price[2]			$5,958.94
Tax Effect for Divesting Parent:			
Gain on sale[3]	1,500.00	4,576.92	4,458.94
Cash received	$5,000.00	$6,076.92	$5,958.94
Tax on gain[4]	525.00	1,601.92	1,560.63
After-tax cash	$4,475.00	$4,475.00	$4,398.31
Acquirer Cost:			
Purchase price	$5,000.00	$6,076.92	$5,958.94
Less: incremental tax savings[5]	0.00	984.31	958.94
Net after-tax cost	$5,000.00	$5,092.61	$5,000.00
Acquirer's Basis in Target's:			
Stock	5,000.00	6,076.92	5,958.94
Net assets	$1,500.00	$6,076.92	$5,958.94
Step-up in the target's assets	0.00	4,576.92	4,458.94

[1]Price at which the divesting parent is indifferent between making the §338(h)(10) election and a purchase without the election at a price of $5,000.

[2]Price at which the acquirer is indifferent between making the §338(h)(10) election and a purchase without the election at a price of $5,000.

[3]Computed as the purchase price less the divesting parent's basis in the sold subsidiary's stock or net assets, depending on the transaction's structure.

[4]Corporate tax liability on the subsidiary sale. The tax is computed based on the nature of the gain (capital or ordinary) and the appropriate tax rate. We assume here that ordinary and capital gains rates are identical for divesting parents.

[5]The present value of the tax savings resulting from stepping-up the target's assets assuming that the step-up is amortized/depreciated straight-line over a 10-year period, the applicable tax rate is 35% and the after-tax discount rate is 10%.

Difference between Subsidiary Sales and Sales of Freestanding C Corporations

Subsidiary sales are often structured to result in a step-up in the tax basis of the target subsidiary's assets, while in acquisitions of freestanding C corporations, the target's assets almost always carry over. Why the disparity between the two transaction types? In the sale of a subsidiary, the incremental cost of the step-up is a function of the difference between the divesting parent's basis in the stock and assets of the sold subsidiary. In many but not all cases, the incremental cost of the step-up in a subsidiary sale is less than the incremental tax benefits from the step-up.

On the other hand, in an acquisition of a freestanding company, the incremental tax cost of obtaining $.35 of tax benefits in the future is $.35. With a nonzero discount rate, the incremental cost of the step-up is therefore always greater than the incremental tax benefits from the step-up. The only exception occurs when the freestanding target has large NOLs. As we illustrated in Chapter 16 (see Table 16.3), in some cases, even when the target has NOLs, a carryover basis transaction is still optimal.

When Is a Section 338(h)(10) Election Optimal?

Assuming that tax rates are constant, a Section 338(h)(10) election is wealth maximizing when the stock and asset basis of the target subsidiary are identical and the purchase price exceeds the net asset basis. In such a case, the incremental cost of the step-up election is $0, as we discussed and illustrated in Table 17.2. The election also makes sense when the tax basis of the target's assets exceeds the tax basis of the target's stock. Although such a circumstance is unusual, in this situation, the tax costs associated with the election are actually *less than* the tax costs if the election is not made. With changing tax rates, these generalizations can change. Equation (17.5) presented formally the case in which the step-up decision is optimal from a tax perspective.

When Is a Section 338(h)(10) Election Suboptimal?

Again, assuming that tax rates are constant, the step-up election doesn't make sense when the divesting parent's tax basis in the sold subsidiary's stock substantially exceeds the net tax basis of the subsidiary's assets. Readers may wonder when such a circumstance is likely to arise. Recall the analyses in Chapters 14 and 16. If the divested subsidiary was previously acquired in a taxable stock acquisition, the divesting parent's basis in the stock of the sold subsidiary is likely to exceed the tax basis of the sold subsidiary's net assets. Because carryover basis transactions are the most common structure used to acquire freestanding companies, in a significant number of situations, the Section 338(h)(10) election will not be viable.

Valuation Effects

The computations and illustrations in the preceding section and in Tables 17.2, 17.3, and 17.4 indicate that a subsidiary's *pretax* selling price varies with the tax bases of the sold subsidiary.[15] As a result, when performing valuations, we must account for the incremental tax costs and tax benefits associated with the tax structure of a subsidiary

---

[15]M. Erickson, and S. Wang, (2000), "The Effect of Transaction Structure on Price: Evidence from Subsidiary Sales," *Journal of Accounting and Economics* provide evidence that pretax prices are higher in subsidiary sales that include a Section 338(h)(10) election.

sale. For example, in comparable **company analyses,** controlling for the tax structure used in the acquisition of comparable companies is critical (see Figure 16.6). Perhaps more importantly, those involved in the purchase (sale) of subsidiaries should consider the ramifications of tax structure on the minimum (maximum) price at which a subsidiary can be acquired (sold). Clever planning on this dimension can have significant wealth effects.

17.2 TAX-FREE DIVESTITURE METHODS

Although taxable subsidiary sales are the most common form of divestiture, in many cases a tax-free divestiture method may be preferable. We focus on two tax-free divestiture methods: equity carve-outs and spin-offs. An equity carve-out is essentially a subsidiary IPO that is tax-free to the divesting parent and its shareholders. The divesting parent gets cash from its sale of the subsidiary's shares. A spin-off on the other hand is much like a large stock dividend. Shareholders of the divesting parent receive stock of the spun-off subsidiary, tax-free, in proportion to their ownership of the divesting parent. In a spin-off, the divesting parent does not obtain cash as part of the transaction, although it is common for the spun-off division to pay a debt-financed dividend to the divesting parent prior to the spin-off.

Equity Carve-Outs

Figure 17.5 illustrates an equity carve-out. The divesting parent firm issues shares in the subsidiary to investors for cash. If the shares are held by the subsidiary, no gain or loss is recognized on the stock issue. This tax treatment is associated with any stock issue by a corporation.

On the other hand, if the shares sold to the public are the parent's shares of the subsidiary, then the sale gives rise to a taxable gain or loss because the parent's stock ownership of the subsidiary constitutes a capital asset in the parent's hands. When this asset is sold, a gain or loss on the sale of the capital asset occurs. If the parent firm wants or needs cash, the subsidiary can pay cash to the divesting parent in the form of a tax-free dividend prior to the stock issue.[16]

For this reason, an equity carve-out can be a tax-free source of cash for the divesting parent. As an empirical fact, equity carve-outs typically involve the issue of a small portion, or less than 20%, of the stock of the subsidiary. Divesting parents are believed to complete these relatively small stock issues because it allows them to ascertain the fair market value of the subsidiary with a complete divestiture likely subsequent to the carve-out. By issuing less than 20% of the subsidiary's stock, the parent retains the ability to either complete a tax-free spin-off or sell the entire subsidiary in a qualifying taxable stock acquisition that can be followed by a Section 338(h)(10) election.[17] For

---

[16]This point is only true if the parent's ownership of the subsidiary is greater than 80%. Ownership of greater than 80% results in a dividends received deduction of 100%.

[17]A qualifying stock purchase is one that results in acquisition of 80% of the voting power of the target. A tax-free spin-off must involve the distribution of at least 80% of the divested subsidiary's stock. In some instances, divesting parents have carved out more than 20% of a subsidiary, but still qualified subsequently for tax-free spin-off treatment. The desired tax treatment was accomplished by the clever use of different classes of stock with different voting rights. See R. Willens, "DuPont's Enlightened Divestiture Plan," Lehman Brothers (October 23, 1998.)

FIGURE 17.5 Equity Carve-Out

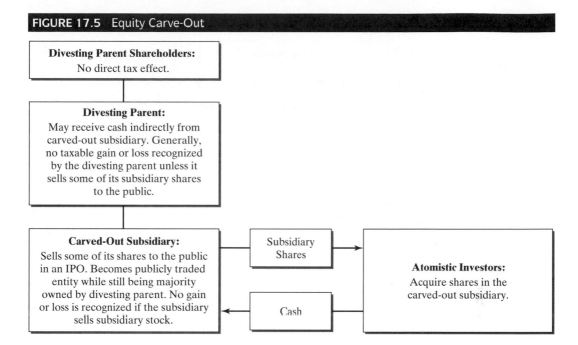

accounting purposes, the divesting parent does not recognize any gain or loss on the equity carve-out.[18]

Tax-Free Spin-Offs

In a spin-off, the divesting parent divides its operations into two (or more) distinct corporate entities. If the parent's business is operated as two subsidiaries, restructuring prior to the spin-off is unnecessary. In either case, the parent firm distributes the stock of the divested subsidiary to its shareholders pro rata. Figure 17.6 illustrates the structure of a spin-off. Essentially, the parent pays a large stock dividend but uses stock of a *subsidiary* for the dividend. After the distribution, shareholders hold interest in two separate businesses: the old parent less the spun-off subsidiary and the spun-off subsidiary. If the transaction qualifies as tax-free under Section 355, the distribution is tax-free to the parent's shareholders and to the divesting parent firm.

In order for such a distribution to qualify for tax-free treatment under Section 355, several general requirements must be met:

- The distributing corporation must have control of the divested subsidiary prior to the distribution. Control is defined as 80% ownership of the subsidiary.
- The divesting parent must distribute a controlling block of subsidiary's stock to shareholders. Control is defined as 80% of the divested subsidiary's stock.

---

[18]If the divesting parent sells some of its subsidiary stock, an accounting gain or loss is recognized. In addition, a divesting parent can elect to recognize a gain on an equity carve-out under SEC *Staff Accounting Bulletin* (SAB) 51. See J. Hand, and T. Skantz, "The Economic Determinants of Accounting Choices: The Unique Case of Equity Carve-Outs Under SAB 51," *Journal of Accounting and Economics* (December 1997), pp. 175–204, for additional details.

FIGURE 17.6   Illustration of a Tax-Free Spin-Off

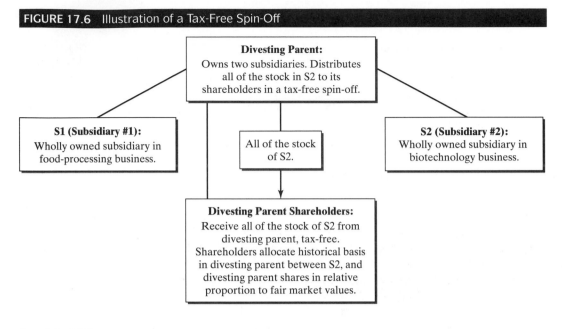

Post-Spin-Off Structure:

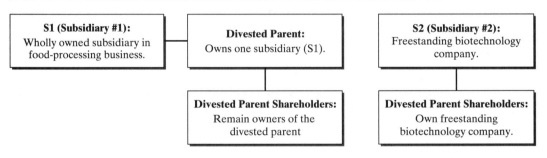

- After the distribution, both the parent and the divested subsidiary must be involved in an active trade or business.
- The transaction cannot be designed as a device for distributing the earnings and profits to the shareholders of the parent.
- The historical shareholders of the divesting parent must maintain a continuity of interest in the parent and spun-off subsidiary.
- The divesting parent cannot have acquired the divested subsidiary during the previous 5 years in a taxable transaction.
- The divestiture must have a valid business purpose and the shareholders of the divesting parent must maintain control of the parent and the divested subsidiary post-spin-off.
- The divesting parent or the spun-off entity cannot be acquired within 2 years of or 2 years after the spin-off.

In a spin-off, the divesting parent's shareholders allocate their basis in the stock of the parent to the stock of the divested subsidiary and to the "new" parent in proportion to the fair market values of the two separate businesses at the date of the spin-off.

For example, consider a shareholder that had a tax basis in a divesting parent's stock of $100 per share prior to the spin-off. At the date of the spin-off, assume that the fair market value of the spun-off business was $200 per share and the value of the remaining parent business (old parent less the divested subsidiary) was $50. The shareholder would have a basis in the stock of the spun-off subsidiary of $80 [(200/($200 + $50)] × $100 basis and a basis in the stock of the parent of $20. The tax basis of the net assets of the remaining parent and the divested subsidiary carry over, that is they are the same as they were for the combined business.

A spin-off is accounted for in the same manner as a stock dividend. Retained earnings are debited in an amount equal to the fair market value of the spun-off subsidiary. Unlike the case in an equity carve-out, there is no direct cash infusion for the parent or the divested subsidiary.

How Can a Spin-Off Be Used to Distribute Earnings and Profits?

We can use an example to illustrate this concept. Consider a publicly traded corporation (BREAKUP) that is owned by ten shareholders. These ten shareholders have a basis in their stock of $1,000. BREAKUP has two subsidiaries: GREEN and RED. BREAKUP's tax basis in the stock and assets of GREEN is $10 and its tax basis in the stock and assets of RED is $500. BREAKUP's market value is $2,000, and investment bankers believe that GREEN is worth $1,500 and RED is worth $500.

BREAKUP decides to do a spin-off of GREEN. After the spin-off, BREAKUP's shareholders own the stock of GREEN and BREAKUP, which is now essentially just RED. Their basis in the stock of GREEN will be equal to $750, or $1,500 fair market value of GREEN divided by the fair market value of BREAKUP ($2,000) multiplied by preshareholder spin-off basis ($1,000), and their basis in BREAKUP will be $250. As a result of the spin-off, the shareholders of BREAKUP obtained a tax-free step-up in the basis of the stock of GREEN from $10 to $750. Hence, if they sell the GREEN stock post-spin-off, they will have more cash after tax because less tax was paid in total than if BREAKUP sold GREEN for cash and then distributed the proceeds to them in redemption of their shares.

Specifically, if GREEN were sold for $1,500, BREAKUP would incur a tax liability of $521.50, or $1,490 × 35%. After tax, BREAKUP could distribute $978.50 to shareholders. If this distribution were taxed as a dividend,[19] shareholders would face a tax on the dividend of $387.48, or $978.50 times 39.6% ordinary income rate, and would have $591.01 after tax. (Dividend tax rates are 15% after 2003 but as high as 39.6% before 2003.) On the other hand, if BREAKUP shareholders were to sell the stock of GREEN after the spin-off for $1,500, they would incur a capital gain of $750 ($1,500 less basis in GREEN stock of $750). This gain would give rise to a capital gains tax of $150, or $750 times 20% capital gains rate, which would leave BREAKUP's shareholders with $1,350 after tax. The result is $758.99 more than if GREEN were sold directly by BREAKUP and the proceeds were distributed to shareholders.[20] We present the specifics of these computations in Table 17.5.

---

[19]Such a distribution could be structured in a manner that resulted in capital gain taxation under Section 302(b)(4).

[20]Note that, as shown in Chapter 14 and in this chapter, the price of a corporation is affected by any tax benefits generated in the transaction. In this case, when GREEN is a subsidiary of BREAKUP, the sale could be structured to provide a step-up in the tax basis of GREEN's assets. The acquirer could be expected to pay for these tax benefits. On the other hand, when GREEN is a freestanding corporation, post-spin-off, a step-up in its assets would not be viable. Hence the sale price of GREEN could be different with and without the spin-off.

TABLE 17.5 Illustration of the Use of a Spin-Off as a Device to Distribute Earnings and Profits

	Base Case: Sale of Appreciated Subsidiary			Spin-Off Scenario		
	BREAKUP (Parent)	RED (Subsidiary)	GREEN (Subsidiary)	BREAKUP (Parent)	RED (Subsidiary)	GREEN (Subsidiary)
Fair market value	$2,000.00	500.00	$1,500.00	$2,000.00	500.00	$1,500.00
Net asset basis	510.00	500.00	10.00	510.00	500.00	10.00
Shareholder basis in BREAKUP stock	1,000.00	n/a	n/a	1,000.00	n/a	n/a
Sale price of GREEN			$1,500.00			
Less: net asset basis			10.00			
Taxable gain to BREAKUP[1]			$1,490.00			
BREAKUP's tax on gain on sale of GREEN[2]			521.50			
After-tax cash from sale of GREEN distributed to shareholders as a dividend[3]			$978.50			
Shareholder tax on dividend[4]			387.49			
Shareholders after-tax cash from sale of GREEN[5]			$591.01			
Sale price of GREEN[6]						$1,500.00
Shareholder basis in GREEN post-spin-off[7]						750.00
Taxable gain to GREEN shareholders on sale of GREEN shares post-spin-off[8]						$750.00
Shareholder-level tax on gain on sale of GREEN[9]						150.00
After-tax cash to shareholders from the sale of GREEN (post-spin-off)[10]						$1,350.00

[1]Taxable gain to BREAKUP corporation on sale of GREEN computed as the sale price less the net asset basis of GREEN.   [2]Corporate tax on the sale of GREEN computed as the taxable gain (1) multiplied by the corporate tax rate (35%).   [3]After-tax cash from sale of GREEN computed as sale price less tax on gain (2).   [4]Shareholder-level tax on cash distributed by assuming the distribution is taxed as a dividend and the appropriate shareholder ordinary income tax rate is 39.6%.   [5]BREAKUP's shareholders' after-tax cash from the sale of GREEN. Computed as the dividend (4) less shareholder level dividend taxes (5).   [6]Sale price of GREEN post-spin-off. The price is assumed to be the same as when BREAKUP sold the assets of the subsidiary. This assumption is unlikely to be true as illustrated in Section 17.1 of this chapter and in various sections of Chapter 14. That is, the purchase price of GREEN will likely be less in the spin-off case than in the asset sale case because there will not be a step-up in the tax basis of GREEN's assets in such a sale (GREEN is a freestanding C corporation post-spin-off).   [7]Shareholder basis in GREEN post-spin-off is computed as the fair market value of GREEN at the spin-off ($1,500) divided by the total fair market value of BREAKUP at the spin-off ($2,000) multiplied by the total shareholder basis in the stock of BREAKUP ($1,000).   [8]Taxable gain to GREEN's shareholders on the sale of GREEN stock. Computed as the difference in the sale price and shareholder's basis in their GREEN stock post-spin-off (8).   [9]Shareholder level tax on the sale of GREEN stock is computed as the taxable gain on the sale (8) multiplied by the long term capital gains tax rate (20%).   [10]Computed as the sale proceeds from the GREEN stock sale less the capital gains taxes on the sale (9).

494

What Are the Consequences of a Spin-Off That Is Disqualified as Tax-Free?

If a spin-off for any of several reasons fails to qualify for tax-free treatment, or if after the spin-off some disqualifying event occurs, the spin-off will be a taxable event. If the spin-off is deemed to fail to qualify for tax-free treatment, the distribution of the subsidiary's stock to the divesting parent's shareholders is taxed as a **property dividend.** That is, the distributing parent corporation must recognize a gain equal to the difference between the fair market value of the property distributed and the parent's net tax basis in the assets of the divested subsidiary.

Notice that the tax is levied on the distributing parent corporation and not on the spun-off corporation. Shareholders receiving stock in a **disqualified spin-off** must recognize a dividend, taxable at ordinary income rates, equal to the fair market value of the property received, that is, the fair market value of the spun-off business. If a spin-off will fail to qualify for tax-free treatment, the distributing corporation typically will cancel the divestiture.

The disqualification issue is also important in those transactions in which an event occurs subsequent to the spin-off. In particular, the acquisition of the divesting parent *postacquisition* can lead to the violation of the continuity of ownership requirements under **Section 355.** Specifically if the ownership of the parent changes by more than 50% within 2 years after the spin-off, the spin-off's tax-free status can be disqualified.[21] In such a situation, the distribution of the spun-off stock to the parent's shareholders becomes a taxable dividend to the distributing parent.[22] As a result, the parent will face a potentially ominous tax liability.

Several conglomerates have used a pending spin-off to fend off a hostile suitor by using this peculiarity of spin-off taxation. That is, a target corporation (divesting parent) can create a tax "poison pill" by completing a spin-off prior to its acquisition by an unwanted suitor. A freestanding target that spins off a division with highly appreciated assets (low basis, high fair market value) will cause an acquirer to pay the tax associated with disqualifying the spin-off's tax-free status. Such disqualification occurs when the hostile suitor acquires the target (divesting parent).[23] The requirements under Section 355 thereby provide targets with a tax-related takeover defense mechanism.

Other Variants of the Spin-Off: Split-Ups, Split-Offs, and Tracking Stock

A spin-off involves the pro rata distribution of the stock of the divested subsidiary to shareholders of the parent. A **split-up** occurs when the divesting parent forms two subsidiary companies and distributes the stock in these two companies to its shareholders

---

[21]These rules were created in part to prevent so-called "monetizing Morris Trust" transactions. A Morris Trust transaction typically involves the spin-off of assets that the parent wishes to retain followed by an acquisition of the remaining, unwanted, assets in a tax-free transaction by a third party. See A. Sloan, "The Loophole King," *Newsweek* (March 31, 1997), p. 55, for additional discussion of monetizing Morris Trust transactions.

[22]Essentially, the divesting parent corporation is treated as if it sold the spun-off business's assets in a taxable transaction.

[23]ITT threatened to use this defensive tactic, preacquisition, to halt Hilton's unwanted takeover attempts. See "ITT Plans to Split into Three Companies: Firm to Take on New Debt, Buy Back Stock in Move to Thwart Hilton Offer," *The Wall Street Journal* (July 17, 1997), p. A3.

in liquidation of the divesting parent. After the transaction is complete, the historical parent corporation no longer exists and shareholders hold stock in two separate businesses. The distribution of the stock of the two subsidiary companies may or may not be pro rata.

In a **split-off,** the divesting parent corporation distributes the stock of the divested subsidiary to its shareholders in redemption for some of their stock in the parent. After the transaction has been completed, the parent's shareholders own stock of the parent and the new subsidiary. The distribution may or may not be pro rata. In either case, the distribution is tax-free to the divesting parent and its shareholders as long as it meets the requirements of **Section 355.**[24]

These spin-off alternatives provide flexibility to shareholders with respect to satisfying their demands for the stock of the divested subsidiary and divesting parent corporation.

In the late 1990s and early 2000s, tracking stocks became a popular divestiture variant. With the typical **tracking stock,** the parent firm creates a stock whose value is designed to track the value of one of the parent company's subsidiaries. In many cases, the tracking stock pays a cash dividend related to the financial performance of the tracked subsidiary. Shareholders of the parent corporation receive the tracking stock in a stock dividend transaction in a procedure similar to a spin-off. However, with a tracking stock, the parent corporation does not distribute a controlling share of the tracked subsidiary to shareholders. Rather, the parent retains control of the tracked subsidiary. For this reason, tracking stock is significantly different from a spin-off. With the bear market of the recent past, tracking stocks seems to have lost much of their luster.

Factors That Influence Divestiture Method Choice

In this chapter, we have provided a mathematical framework from which to quantify the tax and cash flow effects of various divestiture methods. In order to effectively structure a divestiture, however, we need to consider a number of other factors. Table 17.6 provides an overview of the major tax and nontax consequences of the divestiture methods described and analyzed in this chapter. How does a tax planner determine which of these methods is optimal, given a pending divestiture?

Of course, the choice of method will be a function of the tax and nontax preferences of the divesting parent, and the tax and nontax attributes of the subsidiary to be divested. If the parent is in need of cash, it could select one of the methods that generates cash, such as a stock sale or equity carve-out. If the subsidiary to be divested has a market value that greatly exceeds the tax basis of the subsidiary's net assets, the divesting parent may want to consider a spin-off rather than a subsidiary sale structure.

Conversely, if the subsidiary to be divested has a basis that exceeds its fair market value, the divesting parent may want to consider a sale to capture the taxable loss on the sale. Similarly, if the divesting parent has capital loss or operating loss carryforwards, the sale of an appreciated subsidiary may allow the use of the divesting parent's tax attributes in a relatively tax-efficient manner. If the divesting parent is interested in generating accounting gains in order to "smooth" its earnings, a taxable subsidiary sale—or in some cases an equity carve-out—could provide the needed accounting gains.

---

[24]Because split-off distributions can be non-pro-rata, when the shareholders of the parent disagree about the operation of the components of the combined entity, a split-off allows for a tax-free divestiture of the operations of the parent.

TABLE 17.6 Overview of Tax and Nontax Implications of Various Divestiture Methods

Tax or Structural Factor	Tax-Free Subsidiary Sale	Taxable Subsidiary Asset Sale	Taxable Subsidiary Stock Sale without a §338(h)(10) Election	Taxable Subsidiary Stock Sale with a §338(h)(10) Election[1]	Tax-Free Spin-Off	Equity Carve-Out
Divesting parent receives cash	No	Yes	Yes	Yes	No[2]	Yes
Divesting parent maintains control of divested subsidiary	No	No	No	No	No	Yes[3]
Taxable gain or loss at the divesting parent level	No	Yes	Yes	Yes	No	No[4]
Taxable gain for divesting parent shareholders	No	No	No	No	No	No
Step-up in the *tax basis* of the divested subsidiary's assets	No	Yes	No	Yes	No	No
Accounting gain or loss recognized by divesting parent	Possibly	Yes	Yes	Yes	No	Possibly

[1] Subsidiary stock sale that is taxed as if the divesting parent sold the assets of the subsidiary, rather than subsidiary stock.

[2] In some cases, the spun-off subsidiary pays a debt-financed dividend to the divesting parent pre-spin-off.

[3] A carve-out can involve less than or more than enough equity to constitute control of the divested subsidiary.

[4] If the subsidiary sells the shares in the IPO, there is no taxable gain. If the shares sold are shares owned by the divesting parent, a taxable gain or loss results.

To a large extent, the divestiture method chosen is a function of the relative demand for the divested subsidiary. That is, does the subsidiary have willing buyers? Conversely, the spin-off of a poorly performing subsidiary may not be well received by the parent's shareholders, making it a wealth reducing divestiture mechanism.

17.3 ADVANCED DIVESTITURE TECHNIQUES

Other mechanisms can be used to accomplish a divestiture, some of which may provide a divesting parent with cash tax-free. The liquidity provided by these techniques does come at additional transaction costs, however. We briefly introduce such divestiture strategies in this section.

Tax-Free Subsidiary Sale under Section 351 Followed by Secured Borrowing

In some cases, a divesting firm is averse to taxable treatment for a divestiture, but still wants to **monetize** a subsidiary. We saw this situation in Section 16.8 of Chapter 16, but the target was a freestanding C corporation in that case. What divestiture technique might provide a divesting parent with tax-free treatment in the sale of a highly appreciated asset, while at the same time providing cash on the sale?

Recall from Chapter 16 the analysis of tax-free acquisitions through **Section 351.** In that type of tax-free acquisition, the acquirer and target contributed stock or assets to a new corporation in a tax-free corporate formation transaction. A similar technique can be used in the acquisition of a subsidiary.

Consider a divesting parent that owns a subsidiary (BIGGAIN) with a fair market value of $1 billion. The divesting parent's tax basis in the stock and net assets of BIGGAIN are $10 million. Hence, a taxable subsidiary sale would give rise to a $990 million taxable gain and a tax liability to the divesting parent of $346.50 million, or 35% of $990 million.

If an acquirer offered to acquire BIGGAIN in a Section 351 transaction, the divesting parent could defer the $346.50 million of tax liability. Consider the following structure. The acquirer and the divesting parent form NEWCO with the acquirer contributing acquirer stock worth $2 billion and $500 million of cash in return for $2.5 billion of NEWCO voting common stock. The NEWCO common stock has voting rights of two votes per share. Further assume that the divesting parent contributes the stock of BIGGAIN in return for $1 billion of NEWCO voting preferred stock. The preferred stock has voting power equal to one vote per share. The transaction qualifies for tax-free treatment under Section 351 because the contributors have control of NEWCO postcontribution. Figure 17.7 illustrates the structure of this transaction.

While this Section 351 transaction does provide the divesting parent with gain deferral on the sale of BIGGAIN, it does not provide it with cash. Solving this problem is relatively simple. The divesting parent can borrow cash from a financial intermediary using the NEWCO preferred stock as collateral. As a practical matter, the financial intermediary that assisted with consummating the transaction could also provide the secured borrowing. Of course, such a loan will result in nontrivial transaction costs.

As with other tax planning strategies described and analyzed in this text, the net tax savings from the strategy (deferral of $346.50 million of taxes here) must be compared with the nontax costs (transaction costs) in determining the viability of the strategy. It is

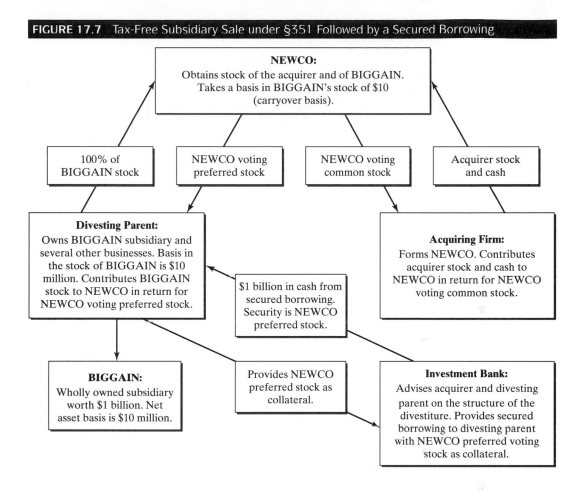

FIGURE 17.7 Tax-Free Subsidiary Sale under §351 Followed by a Secured Borrowing

also important to incorporate the lower purchase price that would accompany this transaction, relative to a taxable sale, due to the lack of a step-up in the divested subsidiary's assets. Financial models like those presented throughout the last three chapters, especially Table 16.3, Table 16.5, and Table 17.4 provide a mechanism for quantifying the incremental benefits and costs (tax and nontax) of such a tax strategy.

Derivative-Based Divestiture Techniques

As we discussed briefly in Chapter 16, derivatives can provide significant tax benefits to buyers and sellers in acquisitions and sales of freestanding corporations. The same is true in divestitures.

Consider a corporation (SMARTBUYER) that acquired a block of five million shares of **restricted stock** of an Internet company (BIGGROWTH.com) for $1 per share. Further assume that this stock appreciated in value to $100 per share, making the total value of the position $500 million, and SMARTBUYER wants to monetize its position in BIGGROWTH, preferably in a tax-deferred manner. SMARTBUYER cannot sell the stock of BIGGROWTH because the stock is restricted. In addition, a sale would generate a large taxable gain.

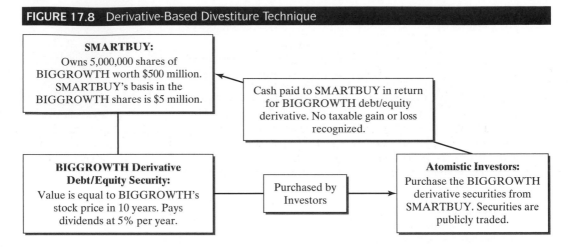

FIGURE 17.8 Derivative-Based Divestiture Technique

One potential solution for SMARTBUYER is to create a new security that contractually is a **derivative,** which it can sell in the capital markets. This new security will carry the right to receive the value of BIGGROWTH in cash in 10 years. Alternatively, holders of the security could receive the stock of BIGGROWTH in 10 years based on some conversion metric. In the interim, assume that this derivative security provides holders with an annual dividend of 5%. Essentially, the security contains the features of a convertible debt instrument. In some ways, the issuance of the derivative is similar to an equity carve-out. Figure 17.8 illustrates this divestiture technique.

What is the tax treatment for SMARTBUYER of the issue of this derivative-type security? If structured correctly, the sale of the security does not give rise to a taxable gain or loss because the issuance is treated much like any stock or debt issue. That is, an issuing firm doesn't recognize a taxable gain or loss when it issues debt or stock. In addition, in some cases firms issuing this type of derivative were able to obtain an interest deduction for the recurring "dividend" payments to holders of the derivative. When SMARTBUYER redeems the derivative or closes out its position in BIGGROWTH, its action would trigger a taxable gain or loss.

This technique has been used by a number of companies. In one of the more notable examples Times Mirror issued a derivative called a premium equity participating security, or PEPS, tied to its position in Netscape.[25] Times Mirror acquired the Netscape stock for about $2 per share, and it appreciated in value rapidly thereafter, leading Times Mirror to seek this derivative-based divestiture solution.

Summary of Key Points

1. A corporation can divest a subsidiary or division in several ways. The most common divestiture methods are subsidiary sales, spin-offs, and equity carve-outs.
2. A sale of the entire subsidiary is typically structured in a manner that gives rise to a taxable gain or loss. An equity carve-out or a spin-off is typically tax-free; the former generates cash flow for the divesting parent firm while the latter does not.

---

[25]See for example T. Pratt, "At Last, Morgan Monetizes Times Mirror/Netscape Stake; Sweetens Terms of 'Peps' Deal to Counter Bad News," *Investment Dealers' Digest* (March 18, 1996); and R. Atlas, "Netscape, for Less," *Forbes* (May 20, 1996).

3. A subsidiary sale can be taxed as a stock sale or an asset sale. Asset sale tax treatment results in a step-up in the tax basis of the sold subsidiary's assets. A stock sale may be preferable due to the costs of title transfer associated with an asset sale. Certain types of stock sales can be taxed under Section 338(h)(10) as if the subsidiary had sold its assets.

4. If an acquirer purchases 80% or more of a subsidiary's stock within a 12-month period, the acquirer and seller can jointly elect to have the stock sale taxed as an asset sale under Section 338(h)(10).

5. Subsidiary sales are often structured in a manner that results in a step-up in the tax basis of the sold subsidiary's assets. As we noted in Chapter 14, sales of freestanding C corporations rarely result in a step-up in the tax basis of the target's assets.

6. In a subsidiary sale, the tax attributes of the sold subsidiary always survive. The tax attributes of the subsidiary stay with the divesting parent in a taxable asset sale or in a taxable stock sale followed by a Section 338(h)(10) election and remain with the subsidiary in a taxable stock sale without a Section 338(h)(10) election.

Discussion Questions

1. If a corporation wishes to divest a subsidiary and needs cash, what possible alternative methods can it consider?

2. If a corporation wishes to divest a subsidiary in a tax-free manner and wants its historical shareholders to maintain a direct ownership in the divested subsidiary, what technique should it employ?

3. Why are tax-free subsidiary sales relatively uncommon?

4. In general, when should a Section 338(h)(10) election be made in a subsidiary sale? Consider the relationship between purchase price, subsidiary stock basis, and subsidiary net asset basis.

5. In general, when should a Section 338(h)(10) election not be made in a subsidiary sale? Consider the relationship between purchase price, subsidiary stock basis, and subsidiary net asset basis.

6. Name four requirements for a spin-off to qualify as tax-free.

7. In a taxable subsidiary stock sale without a Section 338(h)(10) election, do the sold subsidiary's tax attributes such as NOLs survive? If so, who obtains/maintains these attributes?

Tax Planning Problems

1. You are a summer associate at a large Wall Street investment bank and your direct supervisor has informed you that the Sunglass Hut (the acquirer) has engaged your firm to analyze the prospect of acquiring RK, Inc., a wholly owned subsidiary of Consumer Devices, Inc. Consider the following relevant facts:
   - RK has assets with net tax basis of $800 million and fair market value of $1.9 billion. RK has no liabilities.
   - RK is 100% owned by Consumer Devices.
   - Consumer Devices has a tax basis in RK stock of $1 billion. Consumer Devices acquired this stock 5 years ago.
   - Sunglass Hut wants to acquire the stock of RK from Consumer Devices for $1.9 billion in cash.
   - RK, Consumer Devices, and Sunglass Hut are all C corporations.

   Assume that the transaction is structured as a taxable stock sale without a Section 338(h)(10) election.

   a. What tax basis in the assets of RK will Sunglass Hut have postacquisition?

    b. How much cash after tax will Consumer Devices have from the transaction? Assume that Consumer Devices' marginal tax rate is 35%.

Now assume that the transaction is structured as a taxable stock sale with a Section 338(h)(10) election.

    c. What tax basis in the assets of RK will Sunglass Hut have postacquisition?

    d. How much cash after tax will Consumer Devices have? Assume that Consumer Devices' marginal tax rate is 35%.

    e. At what price is Consumer Devices indifferent between a stock sale with a Section 338(h)(10) and a stock sale without a Section 338(h)(10) election at a $1.9 billion purchase price?

    f. At what price is Sunglass Hut indifferent between a stock sale with a Section 338(h)(10) and a stock sale without a Section 338(h)(10) election at a $1.9 billion purchase price? Assume that any basis step-up in RK's assets in a Section 338(h)(10) transaction is depreciated/amortized over 10 years and that the appropriate discount rate for any tax savings from these additional deductions is 10%. Assume that Sunglass Hut's tax rate is 35%.

    g. Should the Section 338(h)(10) election be made? Why?

    h. If Sunglass Hut captured all the net tax benefits associated with the Section 338(h)(10) election (assuming that your answer to part (g) is yes), how much *lower* would its net *after-tax* cost be relative to a sale without a Section 338(h)(10) election at a $1.9 billion purchase price?

    i. If Consumer Devices captured all the net tax benefits associated with the Section 338(h)(10) election (assuming that your answer to part (g) is yes), how much higher would its after-tax wealth be relative to a sale without a Section 338 (h)(10) election at a $1.9 billion purchase price?

2. Consider only circumstances involving the sale of a subsidiary of a C corporation.

    a. Under what circumstances does a Section 338(h)(10) election make sense?

    b. When is a Section 338(h)(10) election suboptimal in the sale of a subsidiary of a C corporation? Be concise.

3. You are a newly hired analyst at a large Wall Street investment bank and your direct supervisor has informed you that Arnie's Army (the acquirer) has engaged your firm to analyze the prospect of acquiring JM, Inc., a wholly owned subsidiary of Nicklaus. Consider the following relevant facts.

- JM has assets with net tax basis of $300 million and fair market value of $900 million. JM has no liabilities.
- JM is 100% owned by Nicklaus.
- Nicklaus has a tax basis in JM stock of $600 million. Nicklaus acquired this stock 5 years ago.
- Arnie's Army wants to acquire the stock of JM from Nicklaus for $900 million in cash.
- JM, Nicklaus, and Arnie's Army are all C corporations.

Assume that the transaction is structured as a taxable stock sale without a Section 338(h)(10) election.

    a. What tax basis in the assets of JM will Arnie's Army have postacquisition?

    b. How much cash after tax will Nicklaus' have from the transaction? Assume that Nicklaus' marginal tax rate is 40%.

Assume that the transaction is structured as a taxable stock sale with a Section 338(h)(10) election.

    c. What tax basis in the assets of JM will Arnie's Army have postacquisition?

    d. How much cash after tax will Nicklaus have? Assume that Nicklaus' marginal tax rate is 40%.

e. At what price (*P*) is Nicklaus indifferent between a stock sale with a Section 338(h)(10) and a stock sale without a Section 338(h)(10) election at a $900 million purchase price?

f. Given the price (*P*) that you computed in part (e), which structure does Arnie's Army prefer: a taxable stock sale without a Section 338(h)(10) election for a price of $900 million or a taxable stock sale with a Section 338(h)(10) election at price (*P*)? Assume that any basis step-up in JM's assets in a Section 338(h)(10) transaction is depreciated/amortized over 12 years and that the appropriate discount rate for any tax savings from these additional deductions is 7%. Assume that Arnie's Army's tax rate is 40%.

g. Should the Section 338(h)(10) election be made? Why?

h. If Arnie's Army captured all the net tax benefits associated with the Section 338(h)(10) election (assuming that your answer to part (g) is yes), how much *lower* would its net *after-tax* cost be relative to a sale without a Section 338(h)(10) election at a $900 million purchase price?

i. If Nicklaus captured all the net tax benefits associated with the Section 338(h)(10) election (assuming that your answer to part (g) is yes), how much higher would its after-tax wealth be relative to a sale without a Section 338(h)(10) election at a $900 million purchase price?

4. Figure 17.9 contains a diagram of two companies, each of which has three subsidiaries. The subsidiaries are identical in terms of risk and lines of business. That is, subsidiary C of Pisces is identical to subsidiary C of Steinbrenner from both an operational standpoint and in terms of asset (inside) tax basis. Assume that the value of each subsidiary is ten times operating cash flow if no step-up is taken in the tax basis of its assets. The corporate tax rate is 35%, the personal ordinary income rate is 40%, and the personal capital gains rate is 20%.

a. What is the pretax liquidation value (or cash received in the sale) of subsidiary A of these two companies? Is it the same or different? Be concise.

b. What is the after-tax liquidation value (or cash received on the sale) of subsidiary A of these two companies? Is it the same or different? Be concise. Assume that the seller can induce the acquirer into paying its maximum indifference price relative to a taxable stock acquisition with no Section 338(h)(10) election.

c. Do the answers to questions in parts (a) and (b) have any implication in the valuation assigned to a conglomerate (a firm with many divisions and subsidiary corporations) in an acquisition?

5. Neptune, Inc., is interested in acquiring the Blackfin, Inc., subsidiary of Bertram, Inc. Here are the facts related to this pending transaction:

- Bertram has a tax basis in the stock and assets of Blackfin of $10 million.
- The fair market value of Blackfin is $500 million.
- Bertram's tax rate is 35%.
- Neptune's tax rate is 35%.
- The after-tax rate of return is 6.5% and any step-up in the basis of Blackfin's assets will be amortized straight-line over 15 years.
- Neptune is offering to acquire Blackfin from Bertram in a Section 351 transaction in which Bertram will receive $500 million of voting preferred stock of NEWCO (formed by Neptune). The NEWCO preferred stock pays dividends at 10%.
- Further, Neptune has arranged for an investment bank to provide a $500 million loan, secured by the NEWCO preferred stock, to Bertram. The loan has an interest rate of 10%.

FIGURE 17.9 The Effect of Stock and Asset Basis on Subsidiary Liquidation Value

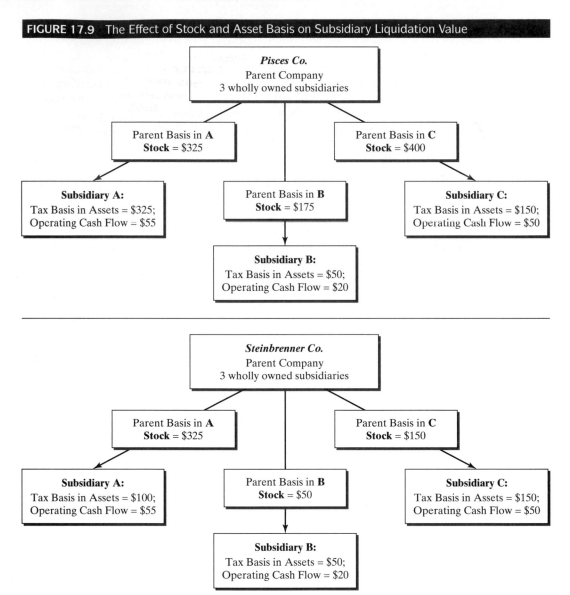

- The investment bank will charge a fee of $2.5 million per year on the loan.
- Bertram will hold the NEWCO preferred for 20 years when it will be sold to pay off the loan.
- Ignore the tax effects of interest deductions and preferred stock dividends in your computations.
  a. What is the present value of deferring the capital gains tax on the subsidiary sale using Section 351 relative to a taxable stock sale at a price of $500 million? That is, how much tax savings will Bertram realize from deferring the capital gain that would be triggered in a taxable sale?
  b. What is the present value after-tax cost of the loan fee to Bertram $(n = 20, r = 6.5\%, t_c = 35\%)$?

    c. What is the maximum price that Neptune would pay in a taxable stock sale with a Section 338(h)(10) election, assuming that it is willing to pay $500 million in a transaction (taxable or tax-free) that does not step-up the tax basis of Blackfin's assets?

    d. At the maximum price that Neptune will pay computed in part (c), how much is the incremental after-tax increase in Bertram's wealth resulting from the Section 338(h)(10) election, relative to a taxable transaction with no election?

    e. The amount computed in part (a) can be considered, for purposes of this problem only, as the gross tax savings from this tax strategy. The sum of the amounts computed in parts (b) and (d) can be considered the costs of the strategy. Given your computations, what is the net tax saving (cost) of this strategy?

6. Briefly explain the uses and/or restrictions of each of the following Tax Code sections:

- Section 351
- Section 332
- Section 338
- Section 338(h)(10)
- Section 368 "A"
- Section 368 "B"
- Section 368 "C"
- Section 355
- Section 382
- Section 197
- Section 1060
- Section 1231
- General Utilities

References and Additional Readings

Cases:

Erickson, M., 2003. "Analyzing Quaker Oats' Sale of Snapple to Triarc," in *Cases In Tax Strategy,* edited by M. Erickson. Upper Saddle River, NJ: Pearson Prentice Hall.

Erickson, M., 2003. "Tax Benefits in Triarc's Sale of Snapple to Cadbury Schwepps," in *Cases In Tax Strategy,* edited by M. Erickson. Upper Saddle River, NJ: Pearson Prentice Hall.

See list at the end of Chapter 13.

18 ESTATE AND GIFT TAX PLANNING

After studying this chapter, you should be able to:

1. Use the vocabulary of estate and gift taxation.

2. Explain the fundamentals of estate and gift taxation.

3. Describe the most common estate-planning techniques.

4. Understand how to monetize appreciated property without triggering taxation.

5. Analyze the tax advantages of charitable giving.

6. Quantify the trade-off between gifts and bequests.

Suppose that you, a relative, or a client has accumulated a substantial amount of wealth. You would like to ensure that family members, friends, and favorite causes are the beneficiaries of your good fortune: the taxing authority is *not* a desired beneficiary. Once you decide to transfer wealth, however, whether by gift or bequest, several forms of taxation can arise: gift taxes on the value of the assets given away, income taxes on the earnings generated by the transferred assets, and estate taxes on your death. Moreover, generation-skipping transfer taxes might await you if you make transfers, whether through gift or bequest, that skip over one or more successive generations of beneficiaries.

Family tax planning for estate and gifts is linked with family income tax planning. A reduction in estate and gift taxes for one family member could lead to higher income taxes for the family as a whole. For example, the transfer of assets from an elderly parent to a child in his or her prime earning years who faces a higher income tax rate might reduce the estate tax but increase income taxes for the family.

Like other tax planning problems, estate and gift tax planning involves a repackaging of assets among taxpayers, and many of the same issues discussed in previous chapters also arise here. Efficient tax planning trades off tax and nontax considerations among transferors and transferees of accumulated wealth. Nontax considerations loom large when parents give away assets to children: parents do not always have complete trust that their children will employ the assets in the desired way, which can make certain tax planning strategies costly. Taxpayers have long tried to "give" away assets to relatives and to charity to reduce the size of their estate while at the same time retaining control over the use of these assets.

For the most part in this chapter we take a tax planner's point of view, leaving aside the broader question of whether the current estate tax is fair, efficient, or in need of reform. We should note, however, that the estate tax is perhaps the most controversial provision of the Internal Revenue Code and one over which commentators' views are highly polarized. On one side of the debate, the estate tax—or "death tax" as it is sometimes called—is perceived as the purest form of the "grabbing hand" of government: The government taxes income once as it is earned then effectively taxes it again by taxing accumulated wealth bequeathed to the next generation. The estate tax is seen as a disruptive penalty on those individuals who build successful businesses and create jobs, acting as a disincentive to innovate and an incentive to engage in excessive consumption during one's retirement. On the other side, the estate tax is seen as a critical tool to combat the formation of powerful dynasties, in which vast fortunes are amassed and passed through the generations. Large concentrations of wealth that can be passed on ad infinitum, the argument goes, create the potential for a ruling aristocracy that threatens democratic society.[1]

The estate tax is therefore highly controversial, and surveys have shown that most individuals believe their estates will wind up paying estate taxes. It appears, however, that most individuals are either overly optimistic about their prospects for future wealth accumulation, misinformed about the law, or both. The vast majority of people die with estates far too small to be subject to estate taxation. The estate tax effectively exempts estates smaller than $1.5 million from taxation (for 2004–2005). Government data show that only about 1.85% of deaths result in an estate tax return being filed.[2] The top 1% of families are quite wealthy, however, holding an estimated 34% of the total household net worth in the United States.[3] Even though good estate-planning techniques are available, the estate tax generated about $24 billion in revenue in 1998, representing about 1.4% of all federal receipts.[4] That may sound small compared with other taxes that are spread across much larger segments of the population, such as FICA and individual income taxes, but the estate tax is concentrated on the small proportion of taxpayers with large wealth accumulations, and it is quite important to them. Readers of this book are much more likely than the average person to face potential estate taxation.

The estate tax is currently in a state of uncertainty. Under the 2001 Tax Act, the estate tax is to be phased out over the years 2002–2009. By 2010 the estate tax is to be repealed. However, for budgetary reasons, the 2001 Tax Act contains a sunset provision

---

[1]See I. Fisher, "Some Impending National Problems," *Journal of Political Economy* (1916). Numerous articles have been written on both sides of the debate: E. McCaffery, "The Uneasy Case for Wealth Transfer Taxation," *Yale Law Journal* (1994); J. Repetti, "The Case for the Estate Tax," *Tax Notes* (March 13, 2000); and L. Kaplow, "Arguments For and Against Estate and Gift Taxation," *Harvard Law School,* working paper (2000).

[2]1997 data. See Staff of the Joint Committee on Taxation "Present Law and Background on Federal Tax Provisions Relating to Retirement Savings Incentives, Health and Long-Term Care, and Estate and Gift Taxes" (June 15, 1999).

[3]1998 data. See M. Sullivan, "For Richest Americans, Two-Thirds of Wealth Escapes Estate Tax," *Tax Notes* (April 17, 2000).

[4]See note 2.

causing the law to expire after 2010. Thus, as currently written, the estate tax will only be repealed for a single year, 2010, after which it returns in full force as if the 2001 Tax Act never existed.

With the shifting sands of political power and variations in the economy, it seems unlikely that Congress will be able to resist modifying the estate tax provisions over the rest of this decade. When Congress passed the 2001 Tax Act, the federal government was in the enviable position of running unprecedented budgetary surpluses. With the downturn in the economy and increased spending on national defense and anti-terrorism, the federal government is again running budget deficits. In short, while estate and gift tax burdens are scheduled to decrease over the rest of the decade, we have likely not seen the last legislation on estate taxation.

This chapter begins with a description of the general structure of estate and gift tax rules, including the unified credit, the annual gift exclusion, treatment of life insurance, the marital deduction, and the Generation-Skipping Transfer Tax. We then describe a set of techniques that we broadly refer to as **monetization techniques,** which are often not thought of as estate-planning techniques but that, in fact, involve both income and estate taxes. We then discuss the most common and most effective estate-planning techniques, beginning with techniques that can be used to eliminate estate taxes on small and moderate-sized estates and progressing to techniques used to reduce estate taxes on large estates. The techniques we discuss include gifting to use the annual gift tax exclusion, bypass trusts, qualified terminable interests property trusts (QTIP trusts), irrevocable life insurance trusts, family limited partnerships (FLPs), charitable remainder trusts, and grantor retained trusts.

We then discuss the substantial incentives provided by the tax law to engage in charitable giving. We show that such incentives are even larger than is commonly believed, and that it generally pays to transfer wealth while alive rather than through the estate at death. We then demonstrate that taxpayers have similar incentives to make noncharitable gifts early, to "freeze" the accumulation of wealth that is taxed in the estate. We present a model that considers both tax and nontax factors, which often conflict, to assess the trade-offs between gifting now and making a bequest.

18.1 FUNDAMENTALS OF ESTATE AND GIFT TAXATION

Estate and gift tax rates in the United States can be in excess of 40%. The maximum rates are scheduled to change over time as follows:

Year	Maximum Estate and Gift Tax Rate
2003	49%
2004	48%
2005	47%
2006	46%
2007–2009	45%
2010	Estate tax repealed, gift tax at maximum 35%

Estate and gift taxes have been integrated in the United States since 1976 so that lifetime taxable gifts increase the marginal tax rate on the estate. The purpose behind the gift tax is to prevent taxpayers from gifting property before their death to avoid paying estate tax. A common misconception is that the recipient of a gift (the donee) pays gift tax or income tax upon receipt of a gift. Not so on both counts. First, gifts are by definition not income and therefore not subject to income tax. Second, the giver (the donor) pays any gift taxes due on the gift, although the IRS can take part of the gift from the donee if the donor is unable to pay.

The donor pays a gift tax on gifts exceeding $11,000 per donee per year, or a limit of $22,000 for married couples because each donor can give $11,000 to each donee. Gifts to charities are generally not subject to gift tax. Although a gift tax is paid as gifts are made, the estate and gift taxes are integrated in that the value of any taxable gifts above the $11,000 annual exemption and gifts not made to charities is added back into the taxable estate at death, and any gift tax paid during the decedent's lifetime is credited against the estate tax liability. What is the effect of adding lifetime taxable gifts to the taxable estate and then giving a credit for gift taxes paid? The effect is to increase the marginal tax rate on the estate and to prevent taxpayers from getting more than one "trip" through the lower tax estate and gift tax brackets. The estate and gift tax schedule that is in effect at the date of death is used to compute the tax credit for previously taxed gifts.

The gift tax exemption and the estate tax exemption are scheduled to increase according to the following schedule:

Year	Gift Tax Exemption	Estate Tax Exemption
2003	$1 million	$1 million
2004 and 2005	$1 million	$1.5 million
2006, 2007, and 2008	$1 million	$2 million
2009	$1 million	$3.5 million

Note that the estate and gift taxes are levied on the *fair market value* of the assets transferred, not their tax bases. Normally the fair market value for tax purposes is the value on the date of transfer, although special rules, such as the "alternate valuation date" 6 months after death, provide some relief when bequested assets decline in value after death. More importantly, fair market values are often subjective, especially in the case of real estate and closely held businesses. A significant strategy of estate and gift planning is to reduce the fair market values of gifted and bequested assets for estate and gift purposes. Family limited partnerships, which are discussed later in the chapter, are a prime example of such techniques.

Specifics of the Gift Tax

As already mentioned, a donor can give a donee $11,000 of gifts per year exempt from gift tax. Note that the $11,000 exclusion is per donee; no provision requires that the donor and donee be related. A billionaire could, for example, give $11,000 to each of 100,000 people in a given year completely free of gift taxes. The $11,000 exemption is indexed for inflation, so it will slowly increase over time. Gifts to one's spouse are completely exempt from gift tax, as are gifts to qualified charities. Gifts to charity have the added benefit of generally being deductible for income tax purposes. Some of the estate- and gift-planning techniques described later in the chapter make use of lifetime giving to charities, such as the charitable remainder trust. Contributions to political organizations are also not subject to gift tax. Neither are payments for educational or medical expenses on behalf of another or to satisfy a legal obligation of support, including child support.

Some things we would not normally think of as gifts are, in fact, gifts for tax purposes. Below-market loans are the prime example. Suppose a mother lends $150,000 to a child, interest-free, to start a business or make a down payment on a house. The mother has in effect made a gift to the extent she does not charge a market rate of interest on the loan. Each year that the child retains the money, the mother is deemed to have made a gift to the child to the extent the interest charged is below market. Further, the mother will have taxable imputed interest income, as if she had collected interest from her child and then made a gift of the same amount to the child.[5]

Note that, while most states impose inheritance taxes, most states do not impose gift taxes. For residents of states that do not have gift taxes but do have inheritance taxes, this provision gives an incentive to gift property rather than bequesting it. Gifting property also has advantages at the federal level, as we will discuss later in the chapter.

Even though gifts generally do not create taxable income for the donee, they do have income tax consequences. Specifically, the tax basis of property received by gift is generally equal to the donor's basis in the property.[6] The donor's holding period also carries over to the donee. Special rules for gifted property later sold at a loss are designed to prevent shifting of deductions from low-tax donors to high-tax donees. In contrast to gifted assets, bequeathed assets get a free step-up in basis at death. The heir takes bequeathed property with a tax basis equal to the fair market value of the property at death. The decedent's unrealized gains, or the excess of fair market value over the decedent's tax basis, go untaxed. Consider an elderly parent who is deciding between giving each of her children $10,000 in cash or giving them $10,000 in appreciated stock with a tax basis in the stock of $500, where whatever is not gifted will be bequeathed. She is better off giving the cash and bequeathing the stock. Giving the stock causes the children to face eventual tax on $9,500 of gain in the stock, while bequeathing it eliminates the $9,500 unrealized gain by virtue of the tax-free step-up at death.

Not all gifts qualify for the $11,000 annual exclusion. For example, a gift of a remainder interest in a piece of land, where the donor retained the life interest, would not generally qualify for the annual exclusion.[7] The gift would be valued at the present value of the future interest, but the annual exclusion would generally not shelter the gift because the donee does not have an unrestricted immediate right to possession of the property. That rule would present a problem for parents gifting to their young children. Accordingly, Congress allows an exception for gifts made under the **Uniform Gifts for Minors Act** (UGMA). Even though a minor doesn't have an unrestricted right to the assets until he or she reaches the age of majority (the particular age depends on the state of residence, but is often 21), the gift can qualify for the annual

---

[5]Special de minimus rules and rules for loans of $100,000 and less apply.

[6]The donee can also add to basis any gift tax that was paid by the donor attributable to the unrealized gain in the property at the time of the gift, where the unrealized gain is the fair market value less the donor's tax basis in the property.

[7]Technically, a remainder interest is one type of a future interest and gifts of future interests are generally not eligible for the annual exclusion. For specifics of what constitutes a future interest consult the additional readings at the end of the chapter.

exclusion.[8] A trap exists for the unwary, however. If the donor is also the custodian of the account and dies before the minor takes control of the assets, the assets are included in the donor's gross estate. This unfortunate scenario can be avoided by having someone other than the donor serve as the custodian.[9]

Specifics of the Estate Tax

The starting point of the estate tax is the computation of the gross estate. Generally, you can think of the **gross estate** as including more assets than the **probate estate.** The probate estate consists of the assets that are administered by the executor of the estate when the deceased died "testate" and left a will or the administrator of the estate when the person died "intestate" leaving no will. The vast majority of decedents whose estates are subject to tax die testate.

What assets does the gross estate commonly include besides those in the probate estate? In most cases, the gross estate includes the following:

1. The proceeds from life insurance policies owned by the decedent
2. Annuities
3. Income in respect of a decedent, such as assets in retirement accounts
4. The full value of property that the decedent had gifted but in which he or she retained either a remainder interest or power of appointment and adjustments for certain gifts made within 3 years of death
5. A portion of jointly held property
6. Property over which the decedent had a general power of appointment
7. Incomplete and/or revocable transfers

What are the common exclusions and deductions from the gross estate to arrive at the taxable estate? In most cases, the following can be excluded and/or deducted from the gross estate:

1. Indebtedness of the decedent and claims against the estate, such as unpaid property taxes
2. Expenses of administering the estate, such as funeral expenses and attorney's fees[10]
3. Bequests to the spouse
4. Charitable bequests
5. Exclusion for certain qualified family-owned businesses

We next discuss the most important inclusions in the gross estate and subtractions from the gross estate.

Life Insurance

The tax treatment of life insurance is commonly misunderstood. It is true that proceeds on life insurance policies are generally exempt from income tax. However, life

---

[8]The so-called "Kiddie Tax" may cause the income from the gifted property to be taxed at the parent's marginal tax rate if the child is under age 14.

[9]Some parents may worry that even a 21-year-old child is not responsible enough to handle a potentially large windfall from a UGMA account. To avoid having the child gain unrestricted control of the assets upon reaching 21 years of age, parents can set up a special trust called a "Crummey" trust, which is beyond the scope of this chapter.

[10]Attorney's fees and executor commissions are often each about 1–2% the value of the estate.

insurance proceeds can be subject to *estate* tax unless careful planning is done. Specifically, the proceeds from a life insurance policy on the decedent are included in the decedent's gross estate if *either* of the following conditions holds: (1) the decedent's estate is the beneficiary on the policy or (2) the decedent possessed any of the "incidents of ownership" in the policy. Beyond outright ownership, incidents of ownership include the power to change a beneficiary, the power to cancel the policy, and the like.

To avoid having life insurance on the decedent become included in the gross estate of the decedent, it is common to have someone other than the decedent, usually a child, own the life insurance policy. The decedent can even make annual gifts to the holder of the policy to cover the premiums. We will have more to say about this subject when we discuss life insurance trusts in Section 18.2.

Income in Respect of a Decedent

Income in respect of a decedent (IRD) is income that generally would have been reported on the decedent's final tax return (or before) had the decedent been using the accrual basis of accounting. The most common examples are unpaid earnings of a cash basis taxpayer—nearly all individuals are cash method taxpayers—and the untaxed buildups in IRAs and other retirement accounts. In each of these cases, the decedent died with something of value that had not yet passed through the income tax.

IRD is included in the gross estate at fair market value. For income tax purposes, no step-up is taken in basis for IRD, so the estate or heirs that realize the income will pay income tax on the IRD. For example, the basis in a regular deductible IRA account inherited by an heir would be zero, so any payout would be taxable to the heir, just as it would have been taxable to the decedent. However, an often overlooked income tax deduction applies for the incremental estate tax that was generated by the IRD.[11]

Marital Deduction and Deduction for Charitable Bequests

The estate tax generally grants deductions for unlimited amounts bequested to the spouse and amounts bequested to qualified charities. The **marital deduction** and **charitable deduction** are the two most significant estate tax deductions. The total gross estate of estates filing returns in 1997 was $162 billion, while the total taxable estate was $89 billion. Of the $73 billion difference, the marital deduction accounts for $49 billion and the charitable deduction accounts for $14 billion.[12] Some of the most common estate-planning techniques described later in the chapter use the marital deduction to ensure that the unified credit and lower brackets of both spouses are used to shelter the estate from taxation.

Unlimited amounts may be bequested to charities and deducted from the gross estate. However, charitable donations are only deductible if they are required by the will. If the charitable donations are left up to the discretion of the executor, their deductible tax status will be disallowed. The will can allow the executor to choose which charities to give to and the amount to give to each, but it must not leave the total amount of charitable bequests to the executor's discretion.

---

[11]Tax Code Section 691(c). See also, L. Asinof, "Estate-Tax Break: Obscure and Powerful," *The Wall Street Journal* (March 29, 2000).
[12]See B. Johnson and J. Mikow, "Federal Estate Tax Returns, 1995–1997," *Statistics of Income Bulletin* (2000).

Credits Against Estate Tax

Several credits are allowed against the estate tax, in addition to the credit for prior gift taxes paid, including the following:

1. The unified transfer credit discussed earlier.
2. State death taxes, subject to some limitations.
3. Credits for certain estate taxes paid by prior decedents, as when a father dies and pays estate tax, and later his son dies and pays estate tax on same property, unless the son dies within 10 years of the father, in which case some relief from double taxation may be available.
4. Credits for certain foreign death taxes.

Generation-Skipping Transfer Tax

Suppose you give or bequest a portion of your assets to your grandchildren or to your great-grandchildren. You pay gift or estate tax on the transfer, but your sons and daughters pay no transfer taxes on their death. The idea is that by skipping one or more generations you also avoid one or more layers of estate and gift tax.

That effectively defeats the estate tax system, and Congress does not like that. To curb such activities, Congress imposed the **Generation-Skipping Transfer Tax** (GSTT) in 1986. The GSTT is an additional tax levied on such transfers at the maximum estate tax rate.

While the details are beyond the scope of our discussion, in brief, the GSTT rules include an exemption for generation-skipping transfers aggregating up to $1.5 million, which is the 2004 figure, indexed for inflation. A married couple can transfer $3 million without being subject to the GSTT. Once the GSTT exemption has been exhausted, the transfer is subject to a flat GSTT rate equal to the maximum rate under the estate and gift tax rate schedule in addition to any normal estate and gift tax that might apply. Because of the generous exemption, however, one strategy is for a married couple to make generation-skipping transfers to grandchildren up to the exemption amount, assuming of course that leaves enough in the estate to provide for the spouse and children.

18.2 ESTATE- AND GIFT-PLANNING STRATEGIES

Now we will discuss the most common and most effective estate- and gift-planning strategies. We order the strategies according to the frequency of their use by most planners. That is, we put the simplest and lowest-cost strategies first and move to progressively more complicated and costly strategies. For most moderate-sized estates, say around $3–$4 million, a few relatively simple strategies should be able to eliminate all gift and estate taxes even without any charitable bequests. For larger estates, the exercise usually becomes one of reducing gift and estate taxes using strategies that maximize the deduction for charitable giving and strategies that reduce the fair market value of the gifted or bequested property for tax purposes.

Making Full Use of the Annual Gift Tax Exclusion

For most families the practice of regular, sustained giving can be an effective estate tax planning strategy. Recall that a husband and wife can each give $11,000 to each donee each year free of gift and estate taxes. For example, a couple with three children could gift $66,000 per year to their kids free of estate and gift tax. It has been estimated, however, that even among high net worth, elderly households, only 45% engage in tax-free giving. Moreover, researchers have estimated that roughly one-fourth of all estate taxes could be avoided by sustained maximum giving to descendents, but that actual use of the gift exclusion reduced estate taxes by less than 4% of the amount that could be saved.[13]

Another benefit of gifting rather than bequesting is that while most states have inheritance taxes, most states do not have gift taxes. Therefore, gifting often avoids state-level transfer taxes. A handful of states do have a gift tax. In those states gifting is put at a disadvantage because state gift taxes are not creditable at federal estate tax level, whereas state inheritance taxes are creditable to some extent.

Why don't people avoid estate and gift taxes by making more extensive use of the annual exclusion? Probably several nontax costs explain the reluctance to give while one is alive. By giving, the donor loses control of the assets. The parent may not trust his or her children with the money, particularly if they are young. A parent may be worried about adverse effects on the children's incentive to work and study. Finally, the parent may be concerned at outliving their remaining assets and having to ask for the money back from their children, which could be humiliating or even fruitless if the children have spent the money.

Gifting in Excess of the Annual Exclusion

In some cases, gifting above the annual exemption is preferred over bequesting. The trade-offs are many and are formally modeled in Section 18.5, but we briefly discuss some trade-offs here. Gifting is one way to "freeze" the value of the estate, in that the gift tax is levied based on the value of the gifted property at the time of the gift. Consequently, if the donor expects the property to appreciate in future, gifting avoids paying transfer tax on appreciation. For example, suppose the value at the time of the gift is $30,000 so that is the value for gift tax purposes. If the property increases in value to $100,000 by the time of death, by gifting the estate saves transfer taxes on $70,000 of appreciation.

An additional benefit of gifting is that the gift taxes themselves are not included in the taxable gift. For example, assume the estate and gift tax rate was 25% and a taxpayer had $1,000,000 to either gift or bequest before paying estate and gift taxes. One option is to make an $800,000 gift and pay $200,000 in gift tax, or 25%($800,000). Another option would be to bequest the $1,000,000, but that would result in $250,000 of estate tax, or 25%($1,000,000) and an after-tax bequest of $750,000. Thus, from the perspective of a pre-estate and gift tax transfer of $1,000,000, gift taxes are, in effect, deductible for gift and estate tax purposes whereas estate taxes are not.

An income tax consequence of gifting, however, is that the donor's basis transfers over to the donee. In contrast, heirs receive a basis stepped up to fair market value for bequested property. If the donor is deciding between gifting cash and gifting appreciated property, he or she may be better off gifting the cash and holding the appreciated property until death, at which time the unrealized tax gain is essentially forgiven by virtue of the step-up in basis at death.[14]

---

[13]See J. Poterba, "The Estate Tax and After-Tax Investment Returns" in *Does Atlas Shrug: The Economic Consequences of Taxing the Rich* (2000); and J. Poterba, "Estate and Gift Taxes and Incentives for Inter Vivos Giving in the United States," *Journal of Public Economics* (2000).

[14]For the year 2010 the fair market value basis rules for inherited property are scheduled to be replaced with a modified carryover basis, similar in many respects with the current carryover basis rules for gifts.

On the other hand, if the donor knows the property is going to be sold shortly, he or she may be better off gifting it to a relative who has a lower marginal tax rate. Caution must be exercised with gifts to young children, however, as unearned income of children under 14 is usually taxed at the parent's marginal tax rate under the so-called "Kiddie Tax."

Using Each Spouse's Unified Credit and Lower Brackets

Suppose John and Jane are married and are each worth $2 million. John dies in 2006 leaving his entire estate of $2 million to Jane. No estate tax is assessed because of the unlimited marital deduction. Jane dies shortly thereafter and bequeaths $4 million (her original $2 million plus the $2 million she inherited from John) to her son, Chip. Only the first $2 million of Jane's estate is offset by her exemption equivalent (recall the exemption equivalent rises to $2 million by 2006), and Jane's estate will pay estate taxes.

The estate taxes could have been avoided. One option would be for John to bequest his $2 million directly to Chip, using up John's exemption equivalent. When Jane dies she bequests her $2 million to Chip, again paying no estate tax on the transfer.

But some people do not want to give their children full access to the money and would prefer leaving the money to their spouse. A **credit shelter trust,** also called a **bypass trust,** can help. John can have his estate leave his $2 million to a bypass trust with his son Chip or other nonspouse heirs as the beneficiary. The "bypass" comes from the fact that the bequest bypasses the spouse's estate.

If John is worried that Jane will not have enough income to live on, he can set up the trust with Jane as the income beneficiary of the trust during her life, with Chip having the remainder interest. Even though some of the value of the trust will accrue to Jane, the entire amount is included in John's gross estate, using up his unified credit as intended. Because Jane's interest in the trust terminates at her death, the remainder passes to Chip without being included in Jane's gross estate.

Because the estate and gift tax is progressive, it can sometimes make sense to structure one's estate to use up not only the exemption equivalent but also the lower brackets.

Using the Marriage Deduction to Defer Estate Taxation

Another type of trust that is quite popular is the **qualified terminable interest property (QTIP) trust** which is often used once the exemption equivalent has been fully utilized by direct bequest or through a bypass trust. The strategy with a QTIP is to defer the estate tax until the death of the second spouse. Actually, the taxpayer does not need a QTIP per se to take advantage of this strategy. Continuing with our example, suppose John is worth $5 million and has already provided for the first $2 million to be put into a bypass trust, using up his exemption equivalent. John could simply bequest the remaining $3 million to Jane and take a $3 million marital deduction. John's estate would pay no estate tax. When Jane dies, the $3 million would be taxable to Jane's estate, assuming she still had the money.

John's real intent, however, may be to provide Jane with income during her life but guarantee that his children will inherit something upon her death. He may be particularly concerned about a direct bequest to Jane if he has children from a prior marriage for whom he wants to provide. A direct bequest to Jane runs the risk that Jane will not include John's other children in her will.

With a QTIP trust, the $3 million is bequested to a trust where Jane has a life interest in the trust's income with the remainder going to John's children, including perhaps his children from the prior marriage. Assuming John's executor makes the proper election at death, the entire $3 million will qualify for the marital deduction on John's estate, even though some of the value winds up accruing to his children. The cost, however, is that Jane's estate will include the entire trust assets at whatever value they have at her death.[15] To qualify for a QTIP, the spouse must be entitled to a life interest in all or a portion of the trust's income, paid at annual or more frequent intervals.

Keeping Life Insurance Out of the Gross Estate

Recall that life insurance is included in the gross estate if the decedent had any of the incidents of ownership such as the ability to change beneficiaries. For young professionals with families and high earnings prospects, it is quite common to have $1 to $2 million of life insurance. If one has other assets that use up the exemption equivalent, allowing the life insurance to enter the gross estate can trigger estate taxes. For older persons, it is common to have whole life or universal life policies with substantial cash buildups in the policies.

Several strategies can be used to keep life insurance out of the gross estate. The first is to continue to own the policy but have one's spouse as the sole beneficiary. While the life insurance would still be included in the gross estate, it would also be deductible under the unlimited marital deduction and thus would avoid estate tax for the time being. When the spouse passes away, of course, any remaining proceeds from the life insurance would be included in the spouse's gross estate.

Another strategy is to have one's spouse or children be the owner of the policy. As long as the decedent had no incidents of ownership and the beneficiary is not the decedent's estate, then the life insurance will not be included in the gross estate. The decedent could even have made annual gifts to the holder of the policy to cover the premiums. Unless the policy is quite large, the annual gift exclusion should be sufficient to make such gifts nontaxable. If the policies are whole or universal life policies with a large buildup, a disadvantage of having one's spouse own them is the risk that the spouse dies first; in that case the buildup value of the policy (but not the face value) is included in the spouse's gross estate.

A parent may not want his or her children to have ownership of a whole or universal life policy. A rebellious child might cash out the policy and squander the money. An **irrevocable life insurance trust** can be used to avoid such problems. The life insurance trust is the owner of the policy and the insured makes annual contributions to the trust to fund the premiums.[16]

Family Limited Partnerships

A strategy to reduce the estate tax is to give away or bequeath a minority interest in the family business to several children. Either way, the courts allow the shares to be

---

[15]Contrast the QTIP with the bypass trust, in which the trust assets were not included in the estate of the second spouse. For this reason, a bypass trust is usually the first line of defense against the estate tax, with the QTIP coming into play after the bypass trust has used up the exemption equivalent and perhaps the lower brackets.

[16]To have the contributions count as gifts of a "present interest" and therefore be eligible for the annual gift exclusion, one can structure the trust to qualify as a "Crummey" trust, which is beyond the scope of this chapter.

valued at a healthy discount relative to a majority interest in the company due to the lack of control. The courts have permitted valuation discounts of 25% to 40% for minority interests. This device was used by the founder of Hallmark Cards to save more than $200 million in estate taxes. It was also used by newspaper magnate Samuel Newhouse, Sr., who built the largest privately held newspaper fortune in the United States. His plan saved more than half a billion dollars in estate taxes. It was litigated by the IRS, the largest estate tax case ever at the time, and was found in the Newhouses' favor in 1990. These discounts reduce the estate tax but transfer a built-in capital gain to the children.

A popular method of reducing the value of the gifted property for tax purposes is the **family limited partnership (FLP).** In an FLP the donor contributes his or her property (often a business) to a limited partnership while retaining the general partnership interest. The donor then gifts the limited partnership interests away, usually to his or her children, valuing them at a substantial discount. The discounts arise because the limited partnership interests are minority interests in the firm and lack marketability. The courts have blessed discounts in the 30% range and higher in certain cases. One reason the limited partnership interests obtain large minority interest discounts is that, for gift tax purposes, gifts are valued in isolation from all other gifts at the value to a hypothetical unrelated buyer. So the donor can split an entity into parts and gift the parts over a period of time, obtaining discounts for each part in isolation.[17]

The gifts are potentially subject to gift tax, but the donor can string the gifts out over several years to make maximum use of the annual exclusion. By retaining general interest, the donor retains control over the business, which may have significant nontax advantages. However, recently the IRS has been winning a number of court cases involving FLPs in which the donor retained what was considered too much control.[18] Gifting the limited partnership interest can also have the income tax advantage of shifting some or all of the income from the business from the parents to the children, who likely have lower marginal tax rates.

Another reason why FLPs have become increasingly popular has to do with changes in the statute of limitations for gift tax returns. Before the 1997 Tax Act, the valuations put on gift tax returns could be challenged by the IRS up to the time when the estate tax return of the decedent was filed. Because this could result in audits of decades-old gifts, Congress changed the statute of limitations to 3 years. Unfortunately for the government, however, the IRS lacks the resources to audit most gift tax returns, so aggressive taxpayers are said to be putting unreasonably low values on their gift tax returns, knowing full well that the statute of limitations will likely pass before the IRS has a chance to audit the return. The IRS does, however, require taxpayers to attach a description to their gift tax return disclosing any gifts for which the taxpayer is applying a valuation discount and the amount of such discount.

In 1999, of the 255,000 gift tax returns filed for gifts of less than $600,000, only 658 were audited—a rate of about 1 return in 400. For gift tax returns of $600,000 to

---

[17]See L. Cunningham, "Remember the Alamo: The IRS Needs Ammunition in Its Fight Against FLPs," *Tax Notes* (March 13, 2000). See also Reg. 25.2512-1 and *Estate of Andrews v. Commissioner*, 79 T.C. 938, 955–56 (1982).
[18]See S. Kalinka, "Estate of Stangi II: IRS Wins Another Battle in Its War Against FLPs," *Tax Notes* (July 28, 2003).

$1 million, the audit rate increases to 1 in 55, and for gift tax returns in excess of $1 million the audit rate jumps to 3 in 4. The average understatement for gift tax returns that were audited was $303,000, resulting in $167,000 of gift taxes due per audited return.[19]

Transfers of Knowledge, Information, and Services

One way to avoid the gift tax is to transfer information or knowledge to children. For example, the parent might inform the child, free of charge, of a good investment opportunity. In effect, it is a nontaxed gift. The IRS cannot tax this activity effectively. Another example is book royalties: it is common for an author to assign the rights or partial rights to a book to a beneficiary just prior to the publisher's acceptance of the book. Before any royalties are earned, the book is given a low value for gift tax purposes. The same type of transfer is effected for venture capital undertakings or for investment knowledge. It is difficult to tax the advice that parents give to children as a gift, even though it could be extremely valuable advice. It is hard to assess a gift tax on the value of baby-sitting services provided by grandparents to their children. Parents cosign notes for mortgages and business ventures; they provide shelter and other services, all of which transfer wealth to their children.

Charitable Remainder Trusts and Grantor Retained Trusts

In **charitable remainder trusts,** the donor takes a lead annuity from a charitable trust, and the charity receives a remainder interest in the assets at a specified future date or upon the death of the donor. This allows the donor to get a charitable deduction for the difference between the fair market value of the property donated and the present value of the annuity the donor retains.

Another set of planning devices includes the **grantor retained trusts:** the grantor retained income trust (GRIT), the grantor retained annuity trust (GRAT), and the grantor retained unit trusts (GRUT). With the GRIT the grantor retains the income from the property but loses working control over the assets, and the grantor's beneficiaries (usually children) receive the remainder interest in the property at the end of a specified period of time, which could coincide with the grantor's death. The old game used to be that the annuity tables specified in the Tax Code could yield artificially low values on the remainder interest, reducing gift taxes. Tax law changes in 1990 reduced the attractiveness of grantor retained trusts by valuing the remainder interest at zero in many cases.

Another major drawback of grantor retained trusts is that, if the grantor dies during the term of the trust, the appreciation in value of the trust assets must be included in the grantor's estate. Grantors can establish a series of trusts, say one for 4 years, another for 8 years, and so on, to hedge against the possibility of early death. Grantor retained trusts are still active, however, and some observers have recently expressed concerns that they are being combined with family limited partnerships to engage in improper tax avoidance.

---

[19]See D. Johnston, "IRS Sees Rise in the Evasion of Gift Taxes," *The New York Times* (April 2, 2000).

18.3 MONETIZING APPRECIATED ASSETS WITHOUT TRIGGERING TAXATION: A CASE STUDY

A problem faced by many today that involves both income and estate tax planning could be called the "low basis problem." Entrepreneurial individuals have founded companies with small amounts of capital, built the companies up, and often taken them public. If the stock is held until death, the unrealized gains escape income taxation, although the value of the stock will be subject to estate taxation. The problem is that it is not always feasible or desirable to have the bulk of one's wealth tied up in the stock of a single, potentially risky, firm. Individuals may wish to diversify their investment or otherwise hedge their risk. Further, many may want to convert a portion of their stock holdings into cash to fund consumption activities such as big houses, travel, and the like.

In some sense the problem faced by these successful individuals is not new; it is simply larger and more widespread than it has been in the past. Consider, for example, the clever tax planning of a family in the decidedly low-technology industry of cosmetics. The facts of the case follow.[20]

Estee Lauder ("Estee") and her late husband, Joseph, founded the cosmetics company known as Estee Lauder in 1946. The company grew to become a cosmetics giant and remained privately held until late 1995. Estee held a large portion of the outstanding Estee Lauder stock and her sons and daughters held the rest. For nontax reasons, Estee wanted to liquidate part of her holdings in Estee Lauder and also wanted to take the company public. Specifically, she wanted to sell 13.8 million of her 23.8 million shares of Estee Lauder as part of the IPO.[21] At this time Estee Lauder was estimated to be at least 87 years old.

The problem was that Estee had a large unrealized gain in her Estee Lauder stock, so selling the stock would trigger a massive capital gains tax. Estee's tax basis in her Estee Lauder stock was equal to what she originally paid for the stock. Since the company was founded more than 50 years ago we can safely assume her basis was quite low, and for simplicity we will assume it was zero. With a stock price of about $24 per share, selling the 13.8 million shares outright would have generated about $330 million of taxable gain and about $120 million or so of federal and state taxes.

Taxation of Short Sales

To understand what Estee did, we need to know what short sales are and how they are taxed. Briefly, in a **short sale** you borrow stock and sell the borrowed stock in the open market. Sometime in the future, you close out the short position by replacing the borrowed stock. A short sale will produce a gain when the stock price declines before you replace it through a "sell high, buy low" strategy. For example, you might sell GE short at $100. Later, GE stock might fall to $75, allowing you to close out the short sale with a $25 gain. Shorting a stock that you do not own is called a **"naked" short sale,** and it is

---

[20]For a teaching case on this topic, see E. Maydew, "Turning a Tax Liability into a Tax Refund: The Case of Estee Lauder," University of North Carolina teaching case (February 2000).

[21]Actually the 13.8 million shares represented sales by both Estee and her son Ronald and the 23.8 million shares figure is assumed. See A. Sloan, "Lauder Family's Stock Maneuvers Could Make a Tax Accountant Blush," *Washington Post* (November 28, 1995).

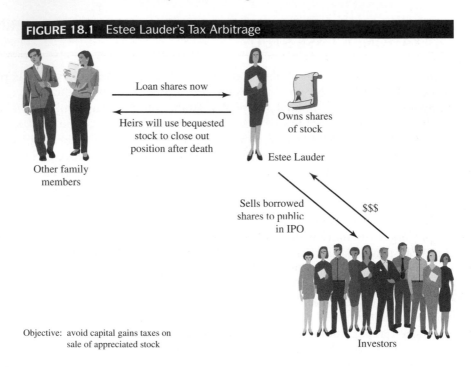

FIGURE 18.1 Estee Lauder's Tax Arbitrage

Loan shares now

Heirs will use bequested stock to close out position after death

Other family members

Owns shares of stock

Estee Lauder

Sells borrowed shares to public in IPO

$$$

Investors

Objective: avoid capital gains taxes on sale of appreciated stock

quite risky. Shorting a stock that you already own, then borrowing additional stock and selling it is called a **short-sale-against-the-box.**

To understand how short sales are taxed, first recall how normal sales are taxed. Suppose you buy (go long in) a share of IBM stock for $15 and later sell the stock for $20. You have a $5 gain based on the difference between the proceeds of $20 and your basis in the stock of $15. Gains on short sales are taxed the same way, but the timing is reversed. Suppose you sell (borrowed) GE stock for $100, the price later falls to $75, and you purchase GE stock to close out the short sale, for a $25 gain.[22] In the case of Estee Lauder, the proceeds from the short sale were fixed at $330 million when Estee initiated the short sale. The gain or loss on the short sale depends on the basis of the stock her estate would use to close out the short sale, which could be well higher than $330 million with future appreciation in the stock and the step-up in basis at her death.

The Strategy

The solution was for Estee to borrow 13.8 million shares of Estee Lauder stock from her sons and daughters (who are also her heirs) and to sell this borrowed stock in the November 1995 IPO. The transaction is illustrated in Figure 18.1. Essentially, it was a very large short-sale-against-the-box. Assume that at her death Estee has three and only three items in her estate: (1) the cash from the short sale, (2) her original "long" position of 23.8 million shares in Estee Lauder, and (3) her obligation to her sons and

---

[22]Special tax rules are designed to prevent investors from using short sales against the box to convert short-term capital gains to long-term capital gains. You should be aware that such rules exist, though they do not come into play in this case.

daughters to replace 13.8 million shares of borrowed Estee Lauder stock. Upon her eventual death, Estee's estate would close out the 13.8 million share short position with 13.8 million shares from her long position. After estate taxes had been paid, the remaining 10 million Estee Lauder shares and any cash in the estate would then be distributed among her sons and daughters in accordance with her will.

The outcome of the strategy was that Estee Lauder effectively sold her stock without triggering tax on the gain. She received the $330 million from the short sale. She had no potential for gain or risk of loss on 13.8 million of her 23.8 million shares because she was short by 13.8 million shares. Because all the 23.8 million shares would receive the step-up in tax basis at her death, the $330 gain would go untaxed, permanently wiping out the potential $120 million tax liability.

But the Estee Lauder strategy went even further, turning the potential tax liability into a potential tax *refund*. How so? If the Estee Lauder stock traded above $24 at her death, as it likely would with normal returns, when Estee's estate closed out the short position with the newly stepped-up stock from her long position, her estate would generate an artificial but perfectly legal tax *loss*. It turns out her heirs would be able to inherit the tax loss and use it to offset other capital gains they might have in their own stockholdings. Essentially, the Estee Lauder strategy was designed to turn a tax liability into a tax refund.

What about estate tax consequences? The 13.8 million short shares effectively cancel out 13.8 million of the long shares for estate tax purposes, leaving only the 10 million net long shares and whatever proceeds from the short sale that remain at death as the gross estate. Actually, the strategy increases Estee's estate taxes relative to an outright sale of the stock because, by avoiding capital gains taxes, Estee dies with more wealth. But it turns out that the income tax savings are about twice as big as the increased estate taxes, even without factoring in the tax benefit from any artificial tax losses inherited by Estee's heirs.

Congress Takes Action

Unfortunately for the Lauder family, this transaction attracted a great deal of public scrutiny and Congress took action against such deferral techniques, although it took a couple years. As part of the so-called Taxpayer Relief Act of 1997, Congress created the "constructive sale" rules of Section 1259. The **constructive sale rules** require taxpayers to recognize gain (but not loss) upon entering into a "constructive sale" of an "appreciated financial position" as if the taxpayer had sold the security for fair market value on the date of the constructive sale and then immediately repurchased the security.

An **appreciated financial position** is defined as any "position" with respect to a stock, debt instrument, or partnership interest that would generate gain if sold for fair market value. "Position" includes long positions, short sales, futures, forwards, and options.

A **constructive sale** is said to exist if the taxpayer enters into any of the following with respect to the appreciated financial position that eliminates all or substantially all of the appreciated position's potential for gain and risk of loss:

- A short sale of substantially identical property
- An offsetting notional principal contract with respect to substantially identical property, such as an equity swap

- A futures or forward contract to deliver substantially identical property
- Other transactions (to be specified in Treasury Regulations) having substantially the same effect as the preceding

Section 1259 applies to any constructive sale taking place after June 8, 1997, which is *after* the date Estee Lauder executed her short sale. However, Section 1259 also contains a provision stating that any grandfathered constructive sales will not be eligible for the tax-free basis step-up at death. It appears that the latter provision was aimed directly at the Lauder family. Shortly after the constructive sale rules were enacted, the Lauder family executed in a series of transactions to unwind their former positions and engage in new tax strategies. But that is another story.

Avoiding the Constructive Sale Rules

Constructive sale rules can be avoided in a number of ways. The strategies may impose somewhat larger transactions costs than the short-sale-against-the-box strategy, but they are still useful for monetizing and hedging appreciated assets. One of the most common techniques is to effectively sell the stock by borrowing money and buying a **cashless collar** around the stock (sell a call and buy a put) with a spread of 5–10% around the stock price. By maintaining some nontrivial risk of loss, investors avoid the constructive sale provisions. In another technique, investors can simply short a different but highly correlated stock. Someone with an appreciated position in Microsoft today, for instance, might short Intel stock, assuming the two are highly correlated. This strategy does involve some risk of loss and potential for gain, to be sure, but if the stocks are highly correlated the investor likely has less risk with the strategy than by simply holding a long position. Other strategies for monetizing appreciated positions without triggering gain recognition have included exchange funds, issuing securities called DECS (debt exchangeable for common stock), and selling stock of a closely held corporation to an ESOP. Many of these techniques, as well as others, are in active use today. It is difficult for Congress to combat such strategies short of taxing all financial assets, or at least those that are publicly traded, on a mark-to-market basis where securities would be treated as if they were sold at year-end at market value.

18.4 THE TAX SUBSIDY TO CHARITABLE GIVING

The tax law encourages charitable giving, and the subsidy is generally greater the earlier the gift. Gifts to qualified charities are exempt from estate and gift taxes, whether made while living or at death. Beyond this exemption, however, two important tax advantages characterize charitable giving during the donor's lifetime: (1) unlike bequests, gifts made to qualified charities while alive yield income tax deductions; and (2) charities, because they are tax exempt, can, in principle, invest funds at a higher after-tax rate of return than the donor can.

To illustrate how the tax rules encourage charitable giving, suppose that you are considering whether to make a bequest to your daughter or a gift to a charity. If you are in a 30% marginal tax bracket, or $t_p = 30\%$, each $1 gift to charity costs you only $.70. Ignoring interest for the moment, you must decide then between making a $1 gift to charity and increasing the size of your taxable estate by $.70. If the estate tax, t_e, is 60%, $.70 added to your estate will give rise to $.42 of estate tax, leaving only $.28 to be passed on to your daughter. So each $1 of gift to charity reduces your daughter's bequest by $1(1 - t_p)(1 - t_e)$ or only $.28. This difference is impressive. You must value leaving an extra dollar to your daughter more than three and one half times as much as a dollar to charity. The income and estate tax rules create a significant incentive to make charitable gifts.

If the charity is going to use the gift in n years, charitable giving has further tax advantages because charities are tax exempt and in theory can earn interest at a higher rate than can the benefactor. Moreover, giving early yields an income tax deduction while bequests do not. The benefit of making a $1 after-tax gift now versus setting aside $1 to leave as a bequest in n years, depends on whether

$$[1/(1 - t_{p0})](1 + R_{ch})^n > [1 + R_p(1 - t_{pn})]^n$$

where t_{p0} and t_{pn} are the donor's marginal tax rates now and in the future over the n years, respectively, R_{ch} is the before-tax return earned by the charity, and R_p is the before-tax return earned on personal account by the donor.

Suppose current (t_{p0}) and future (t_{pn}) income tax rates are 30% that both the charity (R_{ch}) and the taxpayer (R_p) can earn 10% before tax, and that the future bequest will be made in $n = 15$ years when the estate tax rate is 60%. One dollar set aside now for a bequest in 15 years grows to $2.76 given an *after-tax* rate of return of 7% and, after the estate tax, leaves $1.10 for your daughter.

A tax deductible gift of $1.4286 today to a charity has an after-tax cost of $1, that is, $1.4286(1 - .3) = 1. It accumulates to $5.97, or $1.4286(1 + .1)^{15}$ in 15 years, or 5.4 times the value of a gift to your daughter. Giving to charity now versus at death yields a 116% advantage ($5.97 versus $2.76). The reason is that, if you give at death, you lose the income tax deduction and the opportunity to accumulate at the before-tax rate.

Future tax rates would have to increase dramatically to justify deferral of the charitable gift. Moreover, with increases in tax rates, the investment return advantage of the tax-exempt charity over the donor would likely increase.

Of course, nontax factors must be considered as well. Perhaps you will want to change your mind between now and the date of your death as to which charity should be your beneficiary. Alternatively, your tastes or economic circumstances could change over the coming years, such that you decide you would prefer to have the resources for your own consumption.

Donors can take a tax deduction equal to the fair market value of securities contributed to charity; if the stock has been held 12 months or less, the deduction effectively is limited to the cost basis of the stock. Moreover, they do not pay a capital gains tax on the appreciation in the value of assets contributed. Donating toward year-end allows taxpayers to determine whether their tax rates are high, giving them an option to contribute, and to select stocks that have appreciated in value.

18.5 A MODEL OF THE TRADE-OFFS BETWEEN GIFTING NOW VERSUS BY BEQUEST

Giving away assets during one's lifetime, even to noncharitable entities, can be tax-advantageous. How? First, each dollar of the annual $11,000 gift exemption per donee ($22,000 for married couples) given this way removes more than a dollar, tax-free, from the estate. It essentially removes the future appreciation from the estate or "freezes" the estate. That is, the estate is reduced by $(1 + r)^n$, where r is the after-tax rate of return that would have been earned on the assets, and n is the number of years until bequest. The same logic applies to gifts up to the equivalent of the unified estate and gift tax exemption.

For gifts above the annual plus overall exemption equivalent, the benefactor pays a gift tax now and will receive a tax credit later (without interest), for the tax paid. The advantage of the gift is that the benefactor keeps the appreciation on the gifted assets given out of the estate. In special cases, this turns out to be equivalent to obtaining an estate tax deduction for the gift tax paid plus interest on the gift tax. As a result, in a wide variety of circumstances, giving early offers tax advantages. Let us take a closer look.

Suppose a $1 current gift triggers a gift tax today of t_{e0}. The marginal estate tax rate, in n years, at death is t_{en}. Let R_k and R_p denote the before-tax rates of return on investments for the children and their parents, respectively. Let t_k and t_p denote the income tax rates of the children and their parents, respectively.

Notice that a $1 gift requires a present outlay of $1 + t_{e0}$ dollars and triggers a gift tax of t_{e0}. So a comparison of the after-tax accumulations of a current gift and a future bequest requires that, for bequests, $1 + t_{e0}$ dollars be set aside currently, for each dollar of current gift.

Gift: $\qquad [1 + R_k(1 - t_k)]^n - (t_{en} - t'_{e0})$ $\qquad$ **(18.1)**

Bequest: $\quad (1 + t_{e0})[1 + R_p(1 - t_p)]^n(1 - t_{en})$ $\qquad$ **(18.2)**

Because the gift tax credit is based on the schedule in place at death, t'_{e0} might differ from t_{e0}. The term $(t_{en} - t'_{e0})$ represents the difference between the estate tax at time n on $1 of additional taxable gifts that were added back to the estate and the gift tax that can be used as a credit against this tax. If the tax rate schedule is the same at time n as it was at the time of the gift, then t'_{e0} is equal to the actual tax that was paid on the gift initially, t_{e0}. To simplify the analysis, we assume in what follows that the tax rate schedule remains unchanged.

To illustrate how the integration of the estate and gift tax could increase the benefits of early gifting, assume that the parent and child invest in assets that earn the same after-tax rate, r, and that the gift and estate tax rates are constant across time $t_e = t_{e0} = t_{en}$. In this case,

Gift now: $\quad (1 + r)^n$ $\qquad$ **(18.3)**

Bequest: $\quad (1 + t_e)(1 + r)^n(1 - t_e) = (1 - t_e^2)(1 + r)^n$ $\qquad$ **(18.4)**

So the family is better off with a current gift by $t_e^2(1 + r)^n$. Alternatively stated,

$$\frac{\text{Gift now}}{\text{Bequest}} = \frac{1}{1 - t_e^2}$$

If, for example, $t_e = 50\%$, then

$$\frac{\text{Gift now}}{\text{Bequest}} = 1.333$$

that is, the family is 33% better off with a current gift than a bequest. What is going on here? The family effectively achieves not only a tax credit for the gift tax paid earlier but also an estate tax deduction for the gift tax paid earlier with interest. That is, the size of the taxable estate is reduced by the gift taxes paid, plus any income that would have been earned from investing the additional funds.

Suppose a benefactor gave a $1 million gift to a relative and paid the $.5 million tax due on the gift the day before she died. Although the estate includes the value of the gift, $1 million, absent any special rule it would not include the $.5 million gift tax. At a 50% tax rate, this gift saves $250,000 in tax by removing $500,000 from the taxable estate. Recognizing the tax planning incentive to make deathbed gifts, the tax law requires that the gift tax paid be added back to the estate if the gift is made within 3 years of death.

The Trade-Offs Between Gifting and Losing the Step-Up in Basis on Bequests

We next expand the model to account for the fact that many assets transferred from a donor to a donee may have a built-in capital gain or may produce one in the future. This feature favors bequests because of the tax-free step-up in the basis of the assets transferred by bequest. Beneficiaries retain their benefactor's original basis in assets that are gifted prior to death. The trade-off, then, comes between obtaining a step-up in the basis of assets on a bequest (an *income* tax benefit) versus the *estate* tax benefits of early gifts.

Assume that a parent has owned an unincorporated business for m years. The initial basis in the business was b dollars, the initial value of the business was V dollars, and the business has been increasing in value at after-tax rate r_p per year. The parent is now contemplating a gift of the business to his children. He has n years left until his death. Each year, the business pays out distribution, d. For simplicity, assume the distribution paid is that amount that leaves the income tax basis unchanged at amount b. The excess of r_p over d, then, represents the appreciation rate on the value of the business that is not *currently* subject to taxation.

A sale of the business, however, would trigger a capital gains tax. If control of the business is transferred to the children, we assume that the parent receives the same compensation and "dividends" that would have been received had control *not* been transferred. Similarly, the children's compensation is assumed to be the same as if control had *not* been transferred. To make the model simple, we assume a constant rate of return through time, but we allow for the possibility that the parent and children do not operate the business with equal efficiency. In other words, we allow r_p to differ from r_k. We also assume a constant dividend yield, d, each year. At the date of the potential gift, the value of the business is

$$A = V(1 + r_p - d)^m$$

which would attract a gift tax of At_{em}. At death, the estate must pay the differential estate tax on the gift, or $A(t_{em+n} - t_{em})$. If a gift is made, we assume that the business is sold when the parent dies. The children must then pay income tax at a rate of t_{im+n} on the total appreciation of the business in excess of its basis of b. The children retain

$$A(1 + r_k - d)^n - A(t_{em+n} - t_{em}) - t_{im+n}[A(1 + r_k - d)^n - b] \qquad \textbf{(18.5)}$$

Comparing gifting with the parent's decision to retain the business until death, a bequest would yield

$$A(1 + t_{em})(1 + r_p - d)^n(1 - t_{em+n}) \qquad \textbf{(18.6)}$$

If we assume $r_k - d = r_p - d = r$; $t_{em} = t_{em+n} = t_e$; and b = 0 and d = 0 (which most favors a bequest), we find

$$\text{Gift:} \qquad A(1+r)^n(1 - t_{im+n})$$
$$\text{Bequest:} \qquad A(1+r)^n\left(1 - t_e^2\right)$$

For example, if $t_{im+n} = 30\%$ and $t_e = 50\%$, then a bequest is superior to a gift by 75/70 or 7.1%. If, on the other hand, the appreciated asset will be retained by the donee beyond the death of the donor, so that the effective capital gains tax rate is lower (say, 20%), then the *gift* is better by 80/75 = 6.1%. The higher b, the more favorable is the gift. The intuition is that as b becomes smaller, the greater becomes the benefit of the free step-up in tax basis from bequesting the property.

Beyond these tax considerations, nontax costs to gifting early must be considered. A benefactor might not be willing to relinquish control of the assets for personal reasons. Children have been known to squander their newfound wealth, or they might turn against their benefactors (the King Lear Syndrome). Gifting entails transferring assets to children who may be less skillful in managing them, which also exacts a cost. Moreover, it is not uncommon for donors to claim that their donees are doing a poor job in managing the transferred assets. Such tensions can be painful for both parties. Finally, many parents resist transferring wealth to their children out of fear of removing incentives for them to succeed on their own.

Summary of Key Points

1. Income tax planning strategies and estate and gift tax planning strategies sometimes conflict. Most estate plans have important income tax consequences. Substantial conflicts may also arise between the tax and the nontax aspects of estate and gift tax planning.
2. The constructive sale rules of Section 1259 are designed to prevent taxpayers from monetizing appreciated financial positions by, say, executing a short-sale-against-the-box transaction. A number of strategies avoid the constructive sale rules, such as borrowing and executing a cashless collar around the appreciated security.
3. Giving away assets during one's lifetime freezes an estate. Under U.S. tax laws, gifts can be made tax-free in the amount of $11,000 per donee per year, and an additional $1 million in gifts can be made tax-free over each donor's lifetime. Each dollar of exemption used removes more than a dollar, tax-free, from the estate: it also removes the income that can be earned on these assets.
4. By gifting early, the family achieves an estate tax deduction (plus interest) for the gift tax paid at the time the gift was made. A nontax cost of early giving, however, is the donor's loss of control over the assets.
5. The credit shelter or bypass trust is used to take full advantage of each spouse's exemption equivalent and lower estate and gift tax brackets.
6. The qualified terminable interests property (QTIP) trust is often used after a bypass trust has been used to the fullest extent. In a QTIP a spouse essentially bequests the value of some of his estate to his children and some to his spouse while deferring estate tax on the entire transfer until the death of his spouse.
7. Life insurance owned by the decedent is included in her taxable estate. Life insurance trusts are used to keep life insurance out of the gross estate of the decedent.
8. Family limited partnerships are used to reduced the value for gift and estate tax purposes of limited partnership interests transferred to heirs.

9. A charitable remainder trust is particularly tax-advantageous for a grantor who owns an asset that has appreciated substantially in value. No capital gains tax is paid when the asset is transferred to the trust, and the grantor earns income for the life of the trust. Moreover, the grantor receives a current deduction for the value of the remainder interest in the asset that will be transferred to a charitable beneficiary at a future date.

10. Making charitable gifts during one's lifetime has two important tax advantages: (1) unlike bequests, gifts to charity over one's lifetime provide income tax deductions; and (2) the earnings on the assets given to the charity are tax exempt.

11. Many factors are involved in the decision between a bequest and a current gift of assets that have appreciated in value. On death, the beneficiary receives the assets with a tax-free step-up in basis to fair market value. If received as a gift, on the other hand, the beneficiary retains the original basis of the donor. Gifting early removes the assets from the estate and reduces the estate tax. The greater the basis in the assets and the more liberal the dividend policy and therefore the lower the future appreciation, the more likely it is that gifting the asset dominates bequeathing the asset.

Discussion Questions

1. In what sense are the estate and gift taxes "unified"?
2. What is the Generation-Skipping Transfer Tax (GSTT), and why does it exist?
3. What are constructive sales and why is Congress worried about them?
4. How is life insurance treated for income tax and estate tax purposes? Can estate taxation on life insurance proceeds be avoided? If so, how?
5. What are family limited partnerships (FLPs) and how are they used as a tax planning strategy?
6. Under what circumstances is it more tax-advantageous to give to charity during your lifetime rather than on bequest? What nontax factors might influence your decision?
7. What are the advantages of gifting rather than bequeathing assets? What are the nontax costs of doing so?
8. If the basis in an asset is low relative to its current market value, why might bequeathing the asset be more efficient than giving it as a gift? Under what conditions will the gift route be preferred?
9. Apart from the exclusion equivalent, should tax planners recommend that all estate assets be transferred to the surviving spouse, if the goal is to transfer resources to successive generations? What nontax issues arise in the planning problem?
10. If a taxpayer has appreciated property to donate to charity, how can the use of a charitable remainder trust be more efficient than an outright gift?

Exercises

1. Carlos passes away in 2006, bequesting all $400,000 of his property to his wife, Sandra. Carlos also owned a $2,000,000 life insurance policy on himself, with his kids, Juan and Roberto, as equal beneficiaries. Will Carlos's estate owe estate tax?
2. Paula makes the following gifts in the current year: $20,000 to the United Way; $15,000 to her brother, Skip, who is a compulsive gambler; $45,000 to her husband, Larry, to fund a new boat; and $32,000 to a UGMA account for her son, Philip. To what extent will these be taxable gifts? That is, to what extent do they exceed the annual exclusion and begin to offset the unified credit?

Tax Planning Problems

1. Suppose your parents founded a wildly successful business in which they still own 90% of the outstanding stock, which is the source of most of their wealth. The basis in their stock is close to zero. Your parents are nearing retirement age and are considering their options. They would like to buy a house on Mercer Island and a winter home in Cabo San Lucas. They also would like to have sufficient money to travel extensively each year. They want to contribute half their wealth to charity although they have not decided which charities they want to support, with the remainder of their wealth being divided equally between you and your sister. You have recently graduated with your MBA while your sister is about to enter college. Prepare a plan for your parents' consideration and carefully explain each part of the plan.

2. A 65-year-old recently retired engineer is discussing with you, over coffee, whether to gift $500,000 today to his only daughter or invest the $500,000 and bequest the $500,000 plus earnings to his daughter in his will. The engineer expects to live another 10 years. What would you advise the engineer to do? Carefully explain your reasoning and make explicit any assumptions you make, such as taxes, earnings rates, spending patterns, and so on.

3. Following graduation, you meet Mr. Big at a country club. Mr. Big is a venture capitalist who has a sizeable stock portfolio concentrated in a single firm, Red Hat. After several weeks of golfing together, Mr. Big confides in you regarding his financial situation. He owns $30 million of Red Hat stock ($100 per share, 300,000 shares) with a basis of $20 per share. Mr. Big has one child, Big Jr. Mr. Big, who is 75 years old and in poor health, tells you that he just put in an online trade order to sell one-half his Red Hat stock and that he will invest the after-tax proceeds in T-bills because he thinks the market is overvalued. The gains from the sale are taxed at the 15% long-term capital gains rate.

    One year later, Mr. Big passes away, leaving his entire estate to Big Jr. Because of changes in short-term interest rates, the T-bill portfolio he had purchased with the stock sold has produced no after-tax return. At the date of death, Red Hat is trading at $150 per share. Mr. Big's estate pays for any estate taxes by first liquidating a portion of the T-bill portfolio and then, if necessary, a portion of the Red Hat stock.

    Consider these two reminders about estate taxation: First, estates pay an estate tax on the fair market value of the net estate (assets less liabilities). For large estates, such as the one in this question, assume the estate tax will be approximately 45%. Second, it often takes some time for an estate to pay off the debts of the decedent and distribute the net assets to the heirs. In the meantime the assets of the estate may generate income. To prevent this income from going untaxed, estates are required to pay income tax on their earnings. Assume that large estates, such as the one in this question, face income tax rates of approximately 40%. Sometimes estates have negative taxable income. If an estate reports net losses on its final tax return, those losses pass through to the heirs, otherwise they would be lost.

    a. How much will Big Jr. inherit, after all estate taxes have been paid?

    b. Later in the year after Mr. Big's death, Big Jr. recognizes $5 million in long-term capital gains from the sale of other stock from his personal portfolio. How much tax will Big Jr. pay on the sale, net of any capital losses he may have inherited from Mr. Big?

    c. With the same facts as part (a), and instead of selling his Red Hat stock, Mr. Big sells short $15 million of Blue Hat stock, which Mr. Big figures is somewhat correlated with Red Hat stock. Federal Reserve rules on short sales prevent Mr. Big from selling short more than 50% of the value of his long position. The proceeds from the short sale are invested in T-bills. The short sale is held open until Mr. Big's death. Mr. Big's estate liquidates enough T-bill and Red Hat stock (T-bills first) to close out the short sale of Blue Hat and any estate taxes. Any remaining Red Hat stock is distributed to Big Jr. At the date of death, Red Hat stock has increased in price to $150 per share. Blue Hat stock has also increased in value and the short position requires $22.5 million to close out. What will be the current market value of the Red Hat stock that Big Jr. gets from the estate?

d. Later in the year after Mr. Big's death and given the circumstances in part (c), Big Jr. recognizes $5 million in long-term capital gains from the sale of other stock from his personal portfolio. How much tax will Big Jr. pay on the sale, net of any capital losses he may have inherited from Mr. Big?

References and Additional Readings

A sampling of research on the economics of estate and gift taxation.

Gale W., and M. Perozek, 2001. "Do Estate Taxes Reduce Saving?" in *Rethinking Estate and Gift Taxation*. Washington, DC: Brookings Institution. pp. 216–247.

Joulfaian, D., 2000. "Estate Taxes and Charitable Giving," *National Tax Journal,* (Part 2, Sept. 2000), pp. 743–763.

Kopczuk, W., and J. Slemrod, 2001. "The Impact of the Estate Tax on the Wealth Accumulation and Avoidance Behavior of Donors," in *Rethinking Estate and Gift Taxation*. Washington, DC: Brooking Institution Press. pp. 299–343.

Mitchell, O., J. Poterba, M. Warshawsky, and J. Brown, 1999. "New Evidence on the Money's Worth of Individual Annuities," *American Economic Review* (December).

Poterba, J., 2000. "The Estate Tax and After-Tax Returns," in *Does Atlas Shrug: The Economic Consequences of Taxing the Rich* edited by J. Slemrod. Boston: Harvard University Press.

Poterba, J., 2001. "Estate and Gift Taxes and Incentives for Inter Vivos Giving in the United States," *Journal of Public Economics* (January), pp. 237–264.

Poterba J., and S. Weisbenner, 2001. "The Distributional Burdens of Taxing Estates and Unrealized Capital Gains at the Time of Death," in *Rethinking Estate and Gift Taxation*. Washington, DC: Brooking Institution Press, pp. 422–449.

A teaching case on monetizing appreciated assets.

Maydew, E., 2000. "Turning a Tax Liability into a Tax Refund: The Case of Estee Lauder." Teaching case. University of North Carolina.

GLOSSARY

A reorganization—see "Section 368 A reorganization."

Accrual accounting—the method of accounting used to report the results of business operations. A system of accounting that recognizes revenues when net assets (not just cash) increase and expenses when net assets (not just cash) decrease as a result of the firm's operating activities. Net assets are defined as total assets less total liabilities.

Accumulated earnings and profits—see "earnings and profits."

Acquiring company—entity that purchases the target in an acquisition.

Acquisition structure—method of payment (cash or stock) and tax treatment (taxable or tax-free) used in an acquisition. May also apply to method used to acquire a subsidiary of another corporation in which case other tax issues are also relevant.

Adaptive tax planning—type of tax planning that is designed to offset the cost of being in the wrong clientele following unexpected changes in tax status where reversibility is impossible or impractical. See also "reversibility of tax plans."

Adjusted tax basis—the tax version of "adjusted book value." Adjusted basis is equal to historical cost less accumulated tax depreciation. See also "tax basis."

Advance pricing agreements—occur when a firm submits a transfer pricing methodology to the IRS for approval. If the IRS approves, then, in principle, the firm's transfer pricing should not be challenged as long as the firm adheres to the agreement. See also "Section 482," "arm's length pricing," and "transfer prices."

Adverse selection—see "hidden-information problem."

Aggregate deemed sale price (ADSP)—the price at which the target's assets are deemed sold to the acquirer in a Section 338 election transaction.

Arbitrage techniques—an activity that generates positive after-tax returns by buying one asset while simultaneously selling another asset such that the taxpayer has a zero net investment position and bears zero risk.

Arm's length pricing—transfer prices used by related parties are required under the Tax Code to approximate the prices that would have been used between unrelated parties, that is, parties at "arm's length." See also "transfer prices," "Section 482," and "advance pricing agreements."

Asset sale—transaction in which the acquirer purchases the assets of the target or the assets of the sold subsidiary from the seller.

Assignment of income—the taxpayer instructs one party to pay income on the taxpayer's behalf to a third party, transferring the tax liability to the third party as well (the third party is presumably in a lower tax bracket). The assignment of income doctrine requires that the taxpayer must give away the income-generating asset to be successful in shifting taxable income.

Average tax rate—the present value of current plus deferred income taxes (both explicit plus implicit taxes) divided by the present value of taxable income (where taxable income is grossed up to include implicit taxes paid). This measure captures a taxpayer's tax burden better than do conventional measures such as effective tax rates.

B reorganization—see "Section 368 B reorganization."

Basis—gains (and losses) on the sale of an asset are computed as the difference between the sale price and the basis of the asset (usually the purchase price less accumulated depreciation, if any). See also "adjusted tax basis."

Basket of income—where the foreign tax credit limitation must be computed separately for different types or "baskets" of income. The United States uses this approach. See also "foreign tax credit limitation" and "country-by-country limitation."

Before-tax rates of return—the rate of return earned from investing in an asset before any taxes are paid to domestic and foreign federal, state, and local taxing authorities.

Benchmark asset—the calculation of implicit taxes for any given asset requires a benchmark asset against which to compare pretax returns. Unless otherwise noted, we use a fully taxable corporate bond as the benchmark asset because the income is taxed at ordinary tax rates each period and the investment uses after-tax dollars. See also "tax-favored treatment."

Black–Tepper tax arbitrage strategy—corporate pension funds have traditionally held nearly 50% of their assets in common stocks that bear high implicit taxes even though pension funds, because tax exempt, form a natural tax clientele for taxable bonds. One explanation is that fund managers want to invest in riskier projects that have risk premiums and, thus, higher expected returns. Black and Tepper argue that firms would be better off holding bonds in their pension funds and purchasing risky stocks outside the fund with corporate debt.

Book-tax differences—where the financial accounting treatment and tax treatment of the same transaction result in different effects on income. Some book-tax differences are permanent differences, such as municipal bond interest, while others are temporary differences, such as depreciation.

Boot—property (cash) that, when received, can trigger gain recognition in an otherwise nontaxable transaction, such as corporate formation or nontaxable acquisitions.

Branch profits tax—a special tax levied on U.S. branches of foreign corporations to put them on equal footing with U.S. subsidiaries of foreign corporations, which are subject to withholding taxes. Like withholding taxes, taxes on branch profits are often reduced by tax treaties. See "withholding taxes."

Built-in gain—arises when an asset is acquired in a carryover basis transaction and the fair market value of the asset is in excess of the acquired asset's tax basis. See also "carryover basis," "carryover basis transaction," and "adjusted tax basis."

Business-purpose doctrine—see "valid business purpose."

Bypass trust—same as a credit shelter trust. See also "credit shelter trust."

C corporation—an organizational form in which the entity's taxable income is taxed at the corporate level. Owners (shareholders) do not face taxation until dividends are paid or the stock is sold. Shareholders enjoy limited liability and generally do not actively participate in the management of the entity. C corporations can be subsidiaries of other corporations or freestanding.

C reorganization—see "Section 368 C reorganization."

Capital asset—assets whose sale gives rise to capital gains and losses. Examples of capital assets generally include stocks, bonds, puts, and calls. See also "Section 1231 assets."

Capital asset pricing model—model used to estimate expected security returns for individual stocks.

Capital gains—income or gains from the sale of capital assets such as securities. Gains may be taxed at capital gains rates.

Capital loss—loss on the sale of capital assets. Loss can generally offset only capital gains.

Carryover basis—a basis in the property received that is the same as the basis that the transferor had in the property that was transferred. See also "substituted basis."

Carryover basis transaction—transaction in which the tax basis of the target's assets carry over, that is, the target's assets are not stepped up. See also "step-up."

Cashless collar—a risk reduction strategy in which the investor buys a put and sells a call around a security that she is long in to minimize the potential for gain and the risk of loss to a small band or "collar" around the current market price. Cashless collars use the proceeds from the sale of the call to purchase the put. See also "constructive sale."

Centralized management—organizational arrangement in which the top management makes most of the decisions for the organization. See also "decentralized management."

Charitable deduction—gifts and bequests to qualified charities are not subject to gift and estate tax by virtue of the unlimited charitable deduction. Gifts to charities may also yield income tax deductions.

Charitable remainder trust—a trust that allows one to gift appreciated property to a charitable organization and potentially retain more after-tax value than would have been possible by simply selling the property and making the charitable gift.

Check-the-box regulations—a set of Treasury Regulations that allow eligible entities not automatically treated as a corporation to elect (check-the-box) to be treated as a corporation for federal tax purposes; basically an election that applies to unincorporated businesses. Those not electing corporate tax treatment are treated as flow-through entities (see "conduits"). Allows firms to elect, in some cases, to have their foreign operations taxed as either foreign branches or foreign subsidiaries for U.S. purposes. See also "foreign branch" and "foreign subsidiary."

Clientele-based arbitrage—type of arbitrage. The nature of clientele-based arbitrage depends on whether the taxpayer starts out with a relatively high or a relatively low marginal tax rate. For the high-tax-rate taxpayer, clientele-based arbitrage is taking a long position in a relatively tax-favored asset (one that bears a relatively high degree of implicit tax) and a short

position in a tax-disfavored asset (one that bears relatively more explicit tax). For the low-tax-rate taxpayer, clientele-based arbitrage is taking a long position in a tax-disfavored asset and a short position in a tax-favored asset.

Closely held corporations—corporations owned by just a few shareholders, which is common in family or small business concerns. Relative to widely held firms, considerable trust tends to exist among the owners and employees of closely held firms. In fact, closely held firms are typically managed by their owner. By paying themselves generous salaries and bonuses, owner-managers can avoid part of the corporate-level tax. Thus the Treasury keeps close watch on these firms for non-arm's length transactions structured with a primary motivation to avoid tax.

Comparable company analysis—valuation technique, commonly used in acquisitions, in which similar companies' valuation is compared with the valuation of the subject firm, typically in terms of some accounting benchmark (e.g., price to earnings).

Conduits—earnings for these organizations, also known as pass-through entities, are not taxed at the entity level but rather are passed though to the entity's owners and taxed at the owner level. Examples of pass-through entities are partnerships, proprietorships, S corporations, LLCs, and LLPs. For example, partners record their share of partnership profits and losses on their own tax returns, whether the profits are distributed or not.

Constructive dividends—occur when shareholders receive some benefit from the corporation without the corporation declaring a dividend. Constructive dividends are taxed the same as other dividends.

Constructive receipt—even though the taxpayer has not received the income, she is treated as having received it if she has already earned and easily could collect it. Examples include (1) interest credited on bank accounts where funds are available for withdrawal at any time and (2) year-end paychecks that can be picked up at the payroll department.

Constructive sale—a set of antiabuse rules in Section 1259 that tax investors on unrealized gains in securities that they have effectively sold, say through a short-sale-against-the-box transaction. See also "short-sale-against-the-box."

Continuity of business interest—requirement for tax-free treatment in a Section 368 reorganization. The acquirer must use the assets of the target in a productive capacity postacquisition.

Contractual perspective—contracts specify the rights of various parties to make decisions and to receive cash flows in differing circumstances. The tax-related cash flows specified by contracts affect the prices at which assets are traded and the ways in which production is organized by business units.

Control—definition used in various tax-law-related tests. Control relates to the proportion of the entity that is owned by a particular party. In many cases, control is defined as 80% ownership, although it is a definition subject to exceptions.

Controlled foreign corporation (CFC)—most foreign corporations owned more than 50% by U.S. corporations or individuals are CFCs. Subpart F income of CFCs is deemed to be repatriated as earned. See also "Subpart F income."

Convex tax schedule—see "progressive income tax system."

Corporate formation—transaction that creates a corporation, generally governed by Section 351.

Cost basis—basis in property that is equal to cost or purchase price.

Country-by-country limitation—where the foreign tax credit limitation must be computed separately on income from each country in which the firm does business. The United States does not use this system. See also "foreign tax credit limitation" and "basket of income."

Credit shelter trust—a trust designed to use up both spouses' exemption equivalents for estate and gift tax purposes. Same as a bypass trust.

Current earnings and profits—see "earnings and profits."

Decentralized management—organizational arrangement in which lower-level management makes many of the decisions for the organization. See also "centralized management."

Deemed asset sale—transaction that is structured contractually as a stock sale but that is taxed as an asset sale. The target's assets are "deemed" to have been sold even though the target's stock was actually sold.

Deferred compensation contract—a contract between an employer and an employee. An employee can arrange to save for future consumption by agreeing to defer the receipt of current compensation until some future date. The employer deducts the compensation when paid in the later period and the employee includes it in taxable income in the later period when received.

Defined benefit corporate pension plan—type of corporate pension plan that promises the employee a stated benefit at retirement, often based on salary and/or years of service, usually in the form of an annuity.

Defined contribution corporate pension plan—type of corporate pension plan in which the employer and, in some cases, the employee make contributions into an account that will accumulate pension benefits on behalf of the employee. As its name implies, a defined contribution plan specifies contributions into the plan. For example, employees might be required to contribute 5% of their compensation to receive a matching 10% contribution by their employer. The employee's ultimate pension benefit depends on the amounts contributed into the plan and on investment performance.

Demand loans—type of interest-free loan provided by employer to employee. Repayable on employer demand. Loan may be made for a specified term if repayment is required on termination of employment.

Derivative—a contract or asset that provides returns based on the return or payment stream of another asset or group of assets.

Direct foreign tax credit—a tax credit for foreign taxes directly paid by the U.S. taxpayer, e.g., on earnings from a foreign branch. See also "indirect foreign tax credit" and "foreign branch."

Discount—when a bond is issued at less than its face (par) value. The discount represents deferred interest and is amortized over the life of the bond, creating interest income for the holder and interest expense for the issuer. See also "premium," "original issue discount," and "market discount."

Disqualified spin-off—a spin-off that fails to qualify for tax-free treatment. See also "spin-offs."

Disqualifying disposition—term used to describe the situation when the incentive stock option-holder disposes of the stock within 12 months of exercise of the incentive stock option. The disqualification means that the incentive stock option is then taxed as a nonqualified stock option. See also "employee stock options," "incentive stock options," and "nonqualified stock options."

Distribution—occurs when a corporation pays cash or property to its shareholders. Distributions are normally taxed as dividends but, in some cases, can be taxed as a return of capital or capital gain.

Divestiture methods—modes that can be used to sell or separate a component of a company from the remainder of the company. The most common types include subsidiary sales, spin-offs, and equity carve-outs.

Dividend—occurs when a distribution is treated as having been paid from the corporation's "earnings and profits" and is taxable as ordinary income to the recipient at reduced rates post 2002. See also "earnings and profits" and "distribution."

Dividend tax imputation—a system where the shareholders receiving a corporate dividend also receive a credit for corporate taxes already paid on the corporate earnings from which the dividend is declared. The intent is to mitigate the double taxation of corporate dividends (once at the corporate level and again at the shareholder level). Also known as a corporate-tax or dividend-tax integrated system. See also "tax-imputation corporations."

Dividends received deduction (DRD)—allows a corporation receiving a dividend from another corporation to a deduction so that the dividend is only partially taxable. The DRD exists to mitigate the potential for triple taxation of corporate profits. See also "double taxation."

Double taxation—a phrase used to describe the situation where an entity's earnings (for example, corporate profits) are taxed first at the entity level and then again at the owner level (either when distributed as dividends or when the owner sells his ownership share). In contrast, partners and sole proprietors are subject to only one level of taxation, at their own personal rates.

Earnings and profits (E&P)—a tax attribute that relates to the accumulated earnings of an enterprise less payments to owners (dividends); determines whether a distribution is taxable as a dividend or as a return of capital and capital gain. Accumulated earnings and profits are the tax analog to retained earnings, while current earnings and profits are the tax analog to net income.

Effective annualized tax rate on shares—(denoted t_s) if shareholders paid tax at rate t_s each year on their total stock returns (dividends plus capital gains), they would end up with the same after-tax accumulation as they actually achieve.

Effective tax planning—involves considering not only the role of taxes when implementing the decision rule of maximizing after-tax returns, but also consideration of other costs that arise in a world of costly contracting where implementation of tax-minimizing strategies may introduce significant costs along nontax dimensions.

Effective tax rates—(1) for financial reporting purposes it is the sum of taxes currently payable and deferred tax expense divided by net income before tax. Both the numerator and the denominator exclude implicit taxes. Moreover, the tax expense figure is insensitive to the timing of tax payments (that is, a dollar of taxes paid currently is treated no differently than a dollar of taxes to be paid many years into the future). (2) For "tax reformer" (for example, Citizens for Tax Justice) purposes, the effective tax rate is defined as taxes paid currently divided by net income before tax. The numerator excludes not only implicit taxes but also tax deferrals (that is, timing differences in calculating income for tax purposes and for financial reporting purposes). See also "implicit taxes."

Employee stock options (ESOs)—type of equity-based compensation. A stock option is a right to acquire stock at a specified price (exercise price) for a specified period of time (until the expiration date of the contract). Employee stock options are typically granted with an expiration date of 5 to 10 years and at an exercise price equal to the price of the underlying stock at the date of grant.

Employee stock ownership plan (ESOP)—is a special type of defined contribution corporate pension plan. Unlike most defined contribution plans, the ESOP is required to invest primarily in the stock of the company establishing the plan, which is commonly taken to mean that the ESOP must hold at least 50% of its assets in the sponsoring company's stock. Just like other defined contribution plans, the corporation makes tax-deductible annual contributions to the ESOP, which are generally used to buy company stock or to pay down a loan that was used to acquire company stock when the program was initiated. Do not confuse with "employee stock options (ESOs)." See also "defined contribution corporate pension plan."

Entity-level tax—tax levied on the income of the entity at the entity level and before any distributions to the owners of the entity. For example, regular U.S. corporations (see "C corporation") must pay an entity-level tax on their taxable income. They file tax returns and pay tax on corporate taxable income in ways very similar to individuals.

Equity carve-out—transaction in which a corporation sells stock in a subsidiary to the public, also known as a subsidiary IPO.

Excess credit—when a firm's foreign taxes paid are greater than its foreign tax credit limitation. See also "excess limitation" and "foreign tax credit."

Excess limitation—when a firm's foreign tax credit limitation is greater than its foreign taxes paid. See also "excess credit" and "foreign tax credit."

Exchange fund—partnership-type arrangement in which the owner of assets or securities contributes those assets to the fund in return for a share of the returns derived from all of the assets in the fund. Contribution to the fund is typically tax-free and the fund provides owners of appreciated assets with diversification.

Exemption equivalent—same as the unified tax credit. See also "unified tax credit."

Explicit tax rate—the rate of explicit tax paid to the taxing authorities on a given asset, R_a; algebraically, $(R_a - r^*)/R_b)$, where r^* is the after-tax rate of return required on all assets, and R_b is the pretax return on the benchmark asset.

Explicit taxes—tax dollars paid directly to taxing authorities (federal, foreign, state and local).

Family limited partnership (FLP)—occurs when property is placed in a limited partnership and the donor gifts minority limited partnership interests in the business, usually to his or her children. The limited partnership interests are discounted for estate and gift tax purposes because of their lack of marketability and their lack of control.

FASB (Financial Accounting Standards Board)—the body that sets financial accounting regulations in the United States. Major rules are distributed as Statements of Financial Accounting Standards (SFASs).

Financial accounting basis—value assigned to the assets and liabilities of a firm for financial accounting purposes. Often varies from tax basis due to differences in accounting procedures used for financial reporting and tax purposes.

Financial reporting costs—are those costs to the organization arising from reporting lower book income or a higher debt-equity ratio. Such costs arise from explicit contracts with, for example, lenders and employees and from implicit contracts with other stakeholders.

Financing policies—how the firm structures the funding (debt and equity) side of its economic balance sheet. A firm is said to make a "capital structure decision" when it decides how it will finance its activities.

Foreign branch—a firm that does business abroad directly and not through a foreign subsidiary. For tax purposes, income from foreign branches is generally taxable to the domestic parent as earned, regardless of whether the earnings are repatriated. See also "foreign subsidiary" and "check-the-box regulations."

Foreign sales corporation (FSC)—a special type of corporation under the tax laws that provides tax benefits to exporting firms.

Foreign subsidiary—a subsidiary of a domestic firm operating under foreign jurisdiction. For tax purposes, income from foreign subsidiaries is generally not taxable to the domestic parent until repatriated to the domestic parent. See also "foreign branch" and "check-the-box regulations."

Foreign tax credit (FTC)—a credit to a firm operating in a country with a worldwide tax system by which foreign taxes paid mitigate double taxation of their foreign earnings. See also "worldwide system," "foreign tax credit limitation," "direct foreign tax credit," and "indirect foreign tax credit."

Foreign tax credit limitation—rules that limit the foreign tax credits a firm can claim. See also "foreign tax credit," "excess credit," and "excess limitation."

Forward triangular merger—merger in which the acquirer forms a subsidiary and merges the target corporation into the acquiring firm subsidiary.

401(k) plan—type of pension plan set up by employers for their employees. The employer often matches the employee's pretax contributions dollar for dollar. Contributions are tax deductible, and earnings are tax-deferred until withdrawn.

Freestanding C corporation—C corporation that is a standalone entity and not a subsidiary of another corporation.

Frictions—transaction costs incurred by taxpayers in the marketplace that make implementation of certain tax planning strategies costly. It is these frictions and tax rule restrictions that make the potential returns to tax planning so high. See also "tax-rule restrictions."

Fringe benefits—benefits provided by the employer such as employer-provided term life insurance or business meals that are tax deductible to the employer but not taxable to the employee.

FTC limitation—see "foreign tax credit limitation."

General partners—type of partner in a partnership who manages the business and faces unlimited liability, making the partner personally liable for all the debts of the partnership.

General Utilities doctrine—prior to 1986, this rule allowed the capital gain associated with the sale or deemed sale of a corporation's assets to escape taxation.

Generation-Skipping Transfer Tax (GSTT)—a special additional tax levied on gifts and bequests that skip one generation, such as a bequest to a grandchild.

Grantor retained trusts—a trust in which the grantor retains the income from the property, loses control over the assets, and the remainder interest goes to someone other than the grantor.

Gross assets—total asset basis, equal to the sum of liabilities and shareholders' equity.

Gross estate—usually includes assets in the probate estate plus other bequests of the decedent such as life insurance owned by the decedent. See also "probate estate."

Hedging—an activity that reduces the volatility (or spread) in expected cash flow outcomes. For corporations facing progressive tax schedules, the reduction in volatility in cash flows and taxable income can lower expected tax liabilities. Hedging can be undertaken via financial instruments such as options, swaps, and other derivatives.

Hidden-action problem—a type of strategic uncertainty. Arises when one contracting party has control over an action choice that affects future cash flows and where the action choice is *unobservable* to other contracting parties; also known as moral hazard. See also "strategic uncertainty."

Hidden-information problem—a type of strategic uncertainty. Arises when one contracting party has observed a characteristic of the production function he or she cannot control that affects future cash flows and that characteristic is only imperfectly observable by the other contracting parties, also known as adverse selection. See also "strategic uncertainty."

Historical cost—original cost of acquired property.

Identification problem—when a contractual relationship is consistent with more than one economic explanation and observers cannot tell which economic force is responsible for it.

Implicit tax rate (t_{Ia})—the difference in pre-tax returns on a given asset, a, and the benchmark asset, b; algebraically, $t_{Ia} = (R_b - R_a)/R_b$.

Implicit taxes—arise because the before-tax investment returns available on tax-favored assets are less than those available on tax-disfavored assets. Taxpayers wishing to obtain the tax-favored treatment offered by the investment bid up the price of the investment lowering the pretax rate of return.

Incentive stock options (ISOs)—type of employee stock option with no tax to employee at exercise date. Employee is taxed at capital gains tax rate at stock sale date on the difference between the stock sale price and option exercise price. No deduction to corporation at either date.

Income in respect of a decedent (IRD)—is income that has accrued to the decedent but was not subject to income tax by the time the decedent passed away. Accumulations in retirement accounts are commonly IRDs.

Indirect foreign tax credit—arises when dividends are received or deemed to be received from a foreign corporation. The recipient of the dividend gets an indirect foreign tax credit for the foreign taxes paid on the earnings from which the dividend is paid. See also "direct foreign tax credit" and "foreign subsidiary."

Information asymmetry—see "strategic uncertainty."

Inframarginal investors—investors that prefer to invest in one asset over another asset because the after-tax rate of the first asset

is higher. See also "tax clienteles" and "marginal investors."

Installment sale—sale in which the buyer pays the seller in periodic payments (installments) that include a principal and interest component.

Intangible assets—assets that are not tangible. Examples of intangible assets include customer lists, trained workforce, and goodwill.

Investment strategies—how the firm structures the asset side of its economic balance sheet, which includes not only the actively managed assets the firm uses to run its business, but also passive assets such as bonds, stocks, and direct investments in other entities.

Irrevocable life insurance trust—a trust set up to hold one's life insurance to make sure it stays out of one's gross estate.

Keogh plans—type of pension plan available to individuals with self-employment income; contributions are tax deductible; earnings are tax-deferred until withdrawn. Self-employment income includes income earned as a sole proprietorship or from a partnership, income earned as an independent contractor or as a consultant, and book royalties.

Last-in, first-out (LIFO)—an inventory cost system in which the cost of items sold are considered to have come from the newest (last-in) inventory. Contrast with first-in, first-out (FIFO), inventory cost system in which the cost of items sold are considered to have come from the oldest (first-in) inventory.

Limited liability—the investor is at risk for only the amount he or she has invested in the business. Corporate shareholders and limited partners have limited liability.

Limited liability companies (LLCs)—hybrid entities that, under state law, are neither partnerships nor corporations. Under state law, they offer shareholders limited liability while, under current federal tax law, these entities can elect to be taxed as a partnership.

Limited liability partnerships (LLPs)—modified general partnership designed specifically for professional service organizations, such as the Big 4 accounting firms, to operate as a partnership with some personal liability protection. The partners are not protected for breaches of professional responsibility. Many but not all states recognize LLPs, which offer advantages similar to the LLC—namely limited liability with a single level of taxation.

Limited partner—type of partner in a partnership. The liability of limited partners for the partnership's debts is limited to the amount the partner has invested in the business. They face no personal liability for the debts of the partnership. As with most shareholders in widely held corporations, a limited partner typically does not participate actively in the operations of the business.

Liquidating distribution—transaction in which the corporation distributes all of its assets to shareholders in return for all of the stock (ownership interests) in the corporation.

Long-term tax-exempt rate—interest rate used to compute the limitation on a target's tax attributes postacquisition under Tax Code Section 382. The U.S. government publishes this rate periodically.

Marginal explicit tax rate—the effect on the present value of explicit taxes of earning another dollar of taxable income in the current period. See also "explicit taxes" and "marginal tax rate."

Marginal implicit tax rate—the effect on the present value of implicit taxes of earning another dollar of income in the current period. See also "implicit taxes" and "marginal tax rate."

Marginal investors—investors who are indifferent between two or more assets because the (risk-adjusted) after-tax return is the same across the assets. The marginal investors determine the price at which the asset trades because the prices are set such that the after-tax rates of return are the same across the assets. See also "tax clienteles" and "inframarginal investors."

Marginal tax rate—the effect on the present value of total taxes of earning another dollar of income. More formally, the present value of current plus deferred income

taxes (both explicit plus implicit) to be paid per dollar of additional (or marginal) taxable income (where taxable income is grossed up to include implicit taxes paid). This calculation includes the effect of a current dollar of taxable income on future period tax liabilities and includes both implicit taxes as well explicit taxes. See also "explicit taxes" and "implicit taxes."

Marital deduction—gifts and bequests to spouses are not subject to estate and gift tax by virtue of the unlimited marital deduction.

Market discount—occurs if the price of the bond falls after issuance. Market discounts are amortized over the life of the bond and reclassify what would otherwise be capital gains into ordinary income. See also "original issue discount."

Master limited partnerships (MLPs)—are basically partnerships with two types of partner: general partners and limited partners. Provided the limited partners do not actively participate in the management of the partnership, their liability for partnership debts is limited to their invested capital. General partners manage the partnership and have unlimited liability for the partnership's debts.

Monetization techniques—are methods by which an asset is converted into cash without actually selling the asset itself and often without triggering taxation of the unrealized gain on the asset. Monetization strategies often involve some sort of borrowing against the asset or the income from the asset.

Monetize—to convert a nonliquid asset to cash.

Money market savings account—an investment funded with after-tax dollars, the income (interest) from which is taxed each period as ordinary income.

Moral hazard—see "hidden-action problem."

"Naked" short sale—occurs when the short-seller does not have a long position in the security sold short. The downside risk from a naked short sale is unlimited. Contrast with a "short-sale-against-the-box."

Net asset basis—gross asset basis less liabilities; also generally equivalent to shareholders' equity.

Net operating losses (NOLs)—when a firm's taxable income is negative (or deductions exceed gross income). With NOLs, a corporation does not pay tax currently. Under current tax law, an NOL can be carried back 2 years to claim a refund of prior taxes paid or carried forward for up to 20 years to be claimed as a deduction against future taxable income.

Nondeductible IRAs—if the taxpayer does not or cannot make (because of the income limitations) a deductible contribution to an IRA or Roth account, the taxpayer may make nondeductible contributions. The earnings in the pension account are tax-deferred until the taxpayer makes withdrawals in retirement. It receives tax treatment similar to a "single premium deferred annuity."

Nonqualified stock options (NQOs)—type of employee stock option. Employee pays tax on gain at the exercise date at ordinary income rates and employer-corporation is allowed corporate deduction for the amount of the gain. Any subsequent stock price appreciation between exercise date and stock sale date is taxed as capital gains to the employee.

Not-for-profit corporation—a tax-exempt entity that can produce certain goods and services and avoid the corporate tax on the earnings. Prominent examples include not-for-profit hospitals, universities, and religious organizations.

Ordinary income—income derived in the normal course of business from, for example, the sale of goods and/or services. Wages and salaries are classified as ordinary income. See also "capital gains."

Ordinary loss—loss on the sale of goods or services in the ordinary course of business. The loss may offset ordinary income.

Organizational-form arbitrage—is the taking of a long position in an asset or a productive activity through a *favorably* taxed organizational form and a short position in an asset or a productive activity through an *unfavorably* taxed organizational form.

Original issue discount (OID)—the tax term for when a bond is issued at less than its face (par) value. OID is amortized over the life of the bond, creating taxable interest income for the holder and interest deductions for the issuer. See also "premium" and "market discount."

Overfunded—term used to describe the funding status of a defined benefit corporate pension plan. Defined benefit pension plans are funded according to actuarial formulae and an overfunded plan is one that is funded by an amount that exceeds the present value of the firm's expected liability to its employees. See also "defined benefit corporate pension plan."

Partnership—legal organizational form that serves as a tax conduit between the business and its partners. The partnership files its own information tax return, including an income statement, a balance sheet, and a schedule of specific allocations to each of the partners. The partnership entity does not pay any income tax.

Pass-through entities—see "conduits."

Passive activity losses—losses arising from activities in which the taxpayer does not play an active role. Passive activity losses can only be deducted against other passive income and cannot be deducted against other types of (nonpassive) income until the underlying investments are sold.

Pension plan reversions—when a corporation terminates its defined benefit corporate pension plan and reclaims the excess assets; that is, the excess of the value of the plan assets over the present value of the firm's expected liability to its employees. Also known as a "pension plan termination." See also "defined benefit corporate pension plan."

Pension plan termination—see "pension plan reversions."

Perfect capital market—a hypothetical market in which there are no transaction costs, taxes, and no frictions and restrictions.

Permanent difference—difference in financial accounting and tax accounting treatment that is permanent. An example is goodwill that might be recorded for financial accounting purposes but not for tax purposes. Another example is tax-exempt municipal bond interest—excluded from taxable income but included in financial accounting income.

Pooling of interests accounting—financial accounting method used in mergers and acquisitions. Requires the acquirer to record the target on its books at the target's preacquisition financial accounting value.

Premium—when a bond is issued at more than its face (par) value. Amortization of premiums reduce the issuer's interest expense and reduce the holder's interest income. See also "discount."

Primary authority—highest level of authoritative support for the proper tax treatment of a particular transaction. The Tax Code provides *statutory* authority. Other primary authorities include Treasury Regulations, judicial decisions, IRS administrative pronouncements, and Congressional Committee Reports.

Private letter rulings—similar to Revenue Rulings but not considered to be of sufficient general interest to publish as Revenue Rulings. Private rulings are available to the public under *The Freedom of Information Act,* but they cannot be cited as precedent in a court of law. Still, they may be valuable as an indication of IRS policy.

Probate estate—that part of the estate that is administered by an executor (if the decedent had a will) or by the administrator (if the decedent died without a will). Some bequests, like life insurance, are not part of the probate estate. See also "gross estate."

Progressive income tax system—a schedule of marginal tax rates that increases as taxable income increases. Contrast with a flat tax system where the same tax rate is applied to all levels of income. Progressiveness can also arise because tax losses do not give rise to immediate refunds if they have to be carried forward. Also known as a convex tax schedule.

Property distributions—occur when the firm distributes property to shareholders instead of cash. Property distributions are taxed like cash distributions with a special rule so that corporations cannot recognize a loss on a property distribution.

Property dividend—payment to shareholders that is in the form of property rather than cash.

Publicly traded partnerships (PTPs)—in the early 1980s, some partnerships, especially oil and gas entities, listed their partnership interests on organized stock exchanges, which made it easier for partners to sell or expand their partnership holdings. However, with the 1987 Tax Act, easy transferability of partnership interests (for example, interests traded on an organized exchange such as the New York Stock Exchange) results, with some exceptions, in the partnership being taxed as a corporation.

Purchase accounting financial accounting method used in mergers and acquisitions. Requires the acquirer to record the target on its books at the purchase price.

Qualified stock purchase—stock purchase in which the acquirer purchases at least 80% of the target's stock during a 12-month period.

Qualified terminable interest property (QTIP) trust—a trust that makes use of the unlimited marital deduction to defer estate tax until the death of the spouse, while ensuring that the remainder interest in the trust goes to someone other than the spouse, usually the children.

Real estate investment trusts (REITs)—a business entity organized as a trust or corporation that receives most of its earnings from real estate activities. If all of the earnings are distributed each year to beneficiaries or shareholders, the REIT avoids an entity-level tax. To qualify for pass-through treatment, the REIT must satisfy such constraints as having a minimum of 100 shareholders, no significant concentration of ownership, and at least 75% of its assets and income in qualified real estate.

Real Estate Mortgage Investment Conduits (REMICs)—another pass-through entity. Substantially all of the REMIC assets must consist of qualified mortgages and mortgage-related assets. REMICs have two classes of owners: owners of "regular" interests and owners of "residual" interests. The former are like bondholders and the latter are like stockholders (except that REMICs do not pay an entity-level tax).

Realization principle—basis on which income is recognized so that it can be taxed. Income is not typically taxed until certain types of exchanges take place. For example, income from the appreciation of most assets is not taxed until the assets are sold.

Recaptured depreciation—depreciation taken previously that is now recognized as ordinary income because the associated asset has been sold for a price in excess of adjusted basis (historical cost less accumulated depreciation).

Redemption—occurs when a corporation pays cash or property to its shareholders in exchange for a portion of their stock in the firm. Redemptions can be taxed as sales or as dividends.

Related parties—parties that are not economically independent (such as families, affiliated companies and businesses). The IRS worries much less about substance-over-form problems in contracts between parties with opposing interests (arm's length transactions) than it does between related parties because parties with opposing interests cannot always afford to write a contract in which the legal form differs much from the economic substance.

Residual method—see "residual valuation approach."

Residual valuation approach—method used to assign value to the various assets, tangible and intangible, of a target after an acquisition. Value is first assigned to tangible assets based on an appraisal and the remainder or residual is assigned to intangible assets, including goodwill.

Restricted stock—stock that is contractually restricted in some way. Typically recipients of restricted stock cannot sell the stock for a specified period of time from the date of grant.

Revenue Rulings—result from a request for rules clarification from a taxpayer with a particular set of actual or proposed transactions and published as Revenue Rulings provided the IRS believes it is of sufficient general interest. Revenue Rulings represent official IRS policy. See also "private letter rulings."

Reverse triangular merger—merger in which the acquirer forms a subsidiary and merges the acquiring firm subsidiary into the target corporation with the target corporation surviving as a subsidiary of the acquirer.

Reversibility of tax plans—situations in which, if tax rates or tax rules change in ways that make existing agreements inefficient, the contracts can be voided. If the contract can be voided when specified tax-related contingencies occur, then the contract allows for the reversibility of tax plans.

Risk-adjusted—term used to indicate that we are comparing the returns on alternative investments after adjusting for risk differences. Holding taxes constant, the required rate of return on a risky bond exceeds that of a less risky bond because, for the same amount of promised coupons and principal repayment, the prices of bonds with a high risk of default are lower than the prices of bonds with a low risk of default. Thus, to isolate the effects of differential tax treatments on required before-tax rates of return, we must adjust the before-tax rates of return on bonds and other assets for differences in risk.

Roth IRA—eligible taxpayers may contribute up to $3,000 after tax per year. Contributions are not tax deductible but withdrawals are tax-free. That is, earnings in a Roth IRA are not tax-deferred but tax-exempt, provided the withdrawals meet certain conditions.

S corporations—limited liability corporations that are taxed as pass-through entities. Stockholders report their pro rata share of income (loss) on their own income tax return just as if they were taxed as partners. See also "limited liability companies."

Savings incentive match plan for employees (SIMPLE)—an employee benefit for small employers wishing to avoid the complexities of other pension plans. Can be adopted by firms with fewer than 100 employees and can be set up as an IRA for each employee. Employees are allowed to make elective contributions of up to $6,000 per year (pretax) which must then be matched by the employer.

Secondary authorities—second level of authority, after primary authority, for proper tax treatment of a particular transaction: consist primarily of tax professionals (for example, accountants and lawyers), commercial tax services, and tax journals. See also "primary authority."

Section 83(b) election—allows the recipient (a corporate employee) of restricted stock to elect to be taxed at the grant date on the value of the stock as opposed to waiting until the future period in which the restriction lapses. In either case, the value of the stock is taxed as ordinary income. Subsequent gains or losses are taxed as capital gains (with the rate depending on the holding period).

Section 162(m)—regulation that limits corporate tax deductions for compensation to $1 million per individual. Firms can avoid the limitation by qualifying their compensation plan as performance-based or by deferring the excess compensation to a time period in which it is deductible.

Section 197—provides for the tax deductibility of amortization associated with intangible assets such as goodwill; prior to 1993, when this Code Section was enacted, goodwill amortization was not tax deductible.

Section 332—provides for the tax-free liquidation of corporate subsidiaries; allows a corporation to liquidate a subsidiary in a tax-free manner.

Section 338—Tax Code Section giving acquirers and sellers the ability to have a stock sale taxed as if the target's assets were sold. See also "Section 338 election" and "Section 338(h)(10) election."

Section 338 election—election made after the acquisition of the stock of a freestanding C corporation that results in the transaction being taxed as if the acquirer purchased the target's assets instead of its stock.

Section 338(h)(10) election—election made after the acquisition of the stock of a subsidiary of a C corporation or the stock of an S corporation; the election results in the transaction being taxed as if the acquirer purchased the target's assets instead of its stock.

Section 351—specifies the rules required for a corporate formation transaction to qualify for tax-free treatment; also applies to certain types of tax-free acquisition structures. Allows most corporate formations to be nontaxable events to the extent that shareholders do not receive cash (boot) from the corporation. See also "boot."

Section 355—stipulates the conditions under which a spin-off transaction will qualify as tax-free to the divesting parent and its shareholders. See also "spin-offs."

Section 368—Code Section that governs tax-free reorganizations.

Section 368 A reorganization—a tax-free reorganization under Section 368—a statutory stock-for-assets merger.

Section 368 B reorganization—a tax-free reorganization under Section 368—a stock-for-stock merger.

Section 368 C reorganization—a tax-free reorganization under Section 368—a stock-for-asset merger.

Section 382—limits the usage of a target firm's tax attributes postacquisition.

Section 482—gives the IRS authority to combat abusive transfer pricing schemes. See also "transfer prices," "arm's length pricing," and "advance pricing agreements."

Section 1060—governs the allocation of the purchase price to a target's assets.

Section 1231 assets—noninventory assets used in a trade or business that have been held for more than 1 year. Gains from sales of 1231 assets are treated as long-term capital gains while losses are treated as ordinary losses. See also "capital asset."

Short sale—occurs when an investor sells a borrowed security and promises to replace the borrowed security in the future. The short-seller hopes the price of the security will decline so that she can replace the borrowed security at a lower price than for which she sold it.

Short-sale-against-the-box—occurs when an investor shorts a security that he already owns, so that she is long and short in the same security at the same time.

Simplified employee pension plan (SEP)—for small employers wishing to avoid the complexities of other pension plans, a SEP is a program in which the employer opens IRAs for its employees (limited to 25 or fewer employees) and can contribute, similar to regular corporate pension plans, up to the maximum of the lesser of $30,000 a year or 15% of the employee's income.

Single premium deferred annuity (SPDA)—an investment that is funded using after-tax dollars with the income on the account taxed as ordinary income when the funds are withdrawn (as an annuity). That is, the earnings in the account are not taxed each period but tax is deferred until the earnings are withdrawn. See also "nondeductible IRAs."

Small Business Corporations (Section 1244)—original stockholders that collectively contribute up to $1,000,000 of equity in such an entity are permitted to deduct realized capital losses against their other income without regard to the usual annual limitation that applies to the sale of regular stock (currently $3,000). The annual Section 1244 deduction limit is $50,000 per taxpayer ($100,000 for a joint return). To qualify, the corporation must be an operating company rather than engaging primarily in passive investment.

Socially undesirable economic activity—an activity, undertaken in response to the tax laws by taxpayers, that was unanticipated or not intended by legislators. These activities are undertaken with the major (or sole) purpose of reducing the taxpayers' tax bills without any real positive nontax benefits to society.

Sourcing of income—the rules by which income is determined to be U.S. source or foreign source.

Spin-offs—transaction in which a corporation splits into two or more separate companies, typically in a tax-free manner. Shareholders of the divesting corporation own two complete separate corporations post-spin-off.

Split-off—variation on a spin-off, but may involve a non-pro-rata distribution of the stock of the divested firm to parent shareholders. See also "spin-offs."

Split-up—variation on a spin-off, but involves breaking the parent into two corporations and the subsequent distribution, possibly non-pro-rata, of stock in the two new companies to parent shareholders.

Statutory merger—a valid merger under state law.

Step-up—an increase in basis of acquired assets to fair market value or to the purchase price.

Step-up election—in certain types of stock acquisitions, an election (the step-up election) can be made to step up the tax basis of the target's assets. See also "step-up."

Step-up in the tax basis—a step-up in tax basis occurs when the tax (depreciable) basis of assets acquired is increased to the price paid.

Step-up transaction—transaction in which the tax basis of the target's assets are stepped-up. See also "step-up."

Stock appreciation rights (SARs)—type of equity-based compensation that provides employees with cash payments equal to the change in market value of the firm's stock over some specified period of time. Taxation occurs when the employee exercises the right to receive the appreciation on the stock that has occurred since the date of grant. As with stock options, the employee does not make a payment to the firm in the event that the stock price declines below its value at the grant date.

Stock dividends—corporate distribution of additional stock to its existing shareholders. Stock dividends are generally nontaxable events.

Stock rights (warrants)—are options in the corporation that the corporation distributes to its shareholders. Distributions of stock rights are generally nontaxable.

Stock sale—transaction in which the acquirer purchases the stock of the target or the sold subsidiary from the seller.

Straight-line depreciation/amortization—depreciation method under which the asset basis is depreciated in an equal amount each period over the estimated useful life of the asset.

Strategic uncertainty—a situation also known as information asymmetry in which the contracting parties are not equally well informed about what the future investment cash flows might be.

Strategy-dependent—situations in which the taxpayer's marginal tax rate is affected by the very decisions that the taxpayer undertakes to alter its investment and financing activities. For example, if clientele-based arbitrage activities alter a firm's marginal tax rate, it cannot rely on its initial calculation to make an optimal decision. Strategy-dependence increases the complexity of tax planning. Also referred to as the marginal tax rate being endogenous to the decision. See also "clientele-based arbitrage."

Subpart F income—generally passive income from a foreign subsidiary that is deemed for tax purposes to be repatriated to the domestic parent as it is earned. See also "controlled foreign corporation."

Subsidiary sale—transaction in which a parent corporation sells the stock or assets of a subsidiary to another entity.

Substance-over-form doctrine—allows the IRS to look through the legal form of transactions to their economic substance and to reclassify the transaction to reflect its economic substance.

Substituted basis—where the basis of property *received* in a nontaxable transaction is determined by the basis of the property *exchanged* in the transaction. See also "carryover basis."

Symmetric uncertainty—a situation where all contracting parties are equally well informed, but still uncertain, about what the future cash flows from an investment might be.

Tangible assets—assets that are tangible in nature such as buildings, equipment, vehicles, and so on.

Target company—entity that is acquired in an acquisition.

Target firm's tax attributes—see "tax attributes."

Tax arbitrage—is the purchase of one asset (a "long" position) and the sale of another (a "short" position) to create a sure profit despite a zero level of net investment. See also "organizational-form arbitrage" and "clientele-based arbitrage."

Tax attributes—tax-related characteristics of an entity such as net operating loss carryforwards, tax credits, and asset tax basis.

Tax basis—the value assigned to property or assets for *tax* purposes. A factor in the determination of the gain/loss on a sale. Generally the tax basis of an asset equals its cost. The tax basis of assets acquired in nontaxable transactions and by gift or bequest are subject to special rules. See also "adjusted tax basis."

Tax clienteles—taxpayers facing similar marginal tax rates are attracted to the same investments because they offer the highest after-tax rate of return to these taxpayers. Thus certain taxpayers are more likely than others to own various kinds of assets or to organize production in particular ways. See also "marginal investors" and "inframarginal investors."

Tax exemption—when the returns to an activity escape explicit taxation. Tax exemption means that the after-tax rate of return equals the before-tax rate of return.

Tax indemnities—where the other party to the transaction (for example, the issuer of a security) indemnifies (insures) the taxpayer against less favorable tax treatment than that promised.

Tax law ambiguity—often the tax rules are far too general to indicate clearly how particular transactions are to be taxed. Aggressive exploiting of tax law ambiguity can lead to socially undesirable economic activities. See also "Treasury Regulations," "Revenue Rulings," and "private letter rulings."

Tax minimization—involves simply minimizing taxes without consideration of other dimensions of the transaction or business problem. The simplest way to minimize taxes is to earn zero income, which is not considered an effective tax plan.

Tax structure—manner in which a transaction is structured for tax purposes.

Tax treaty shopping—where firms attempt to route transactions though countries that have a favorable tax treaty with their home country.

Taxable acquisitions—transactions in which the seller recognizes a taxable gain or loss.

Taxable asset sale—transaction in which the target's assets are sold for cash or other taxable consideration.

Taxable stock sale—transaction in which the target's stock is sold for cash or other taxable consideration.

Tax-exempt organizations—entities that are not taxed. Examples of such entities include pension funds, universities, hospitals, charities, and religious organizations.

Tax-favored treatment—when an activity receives favorable tax treatment defined relative to immediate full taxation on current income at ordinary tax rates. Tax-favored treatment can arise if the investment is immediately deductible, if taxation on income is deferred until future periods, or if income is taxed at lower capital gains rates. See also "implicit taxes."

Tax-free acquisition structure—method or technique used to acquire a target that is tax-free. Sellers who receive cash nonetheless recognize taxable gains.

Tax-free acquisitions—acquisition in which the *transaction* qualifies as tax-free. Sellers receiving tax-free consideration (e.g., stock) experience tax deferral while sellers receiving cash must recognize a taxable gain.

Tax-free subsidiary sale—sale of a subsidiary in a manner that results in tax deferral of any gain or loss on the sale.

Tax-imputation corporations—a number of countries have a "tax imputation" system that converts part of the corporate-level tax into a partnership-level tax. By imputation we mean that, if the corporation pays a dividend to its stockholders from its after-tax corporate income, stockholders (a) receive a credit (as compensation for the corporate taxes that are imputed to have been paid by them) equal to some fraction of the dividend they receive and (b) declare as dividend income (on which ordinary tax rates are levied) the dividend received plus the tax credit amount. Tax imputation is also known as corporate tax integration.

Tax-rule restrictions—restraints imposed by the taxing authority that prevent taxpayers from using certain tax arbitrage techniques to reduce taxes in socially undesirable ways. See also "frictions."

Technical advice memoranda—a published form of "letter ruling" issued by the IRS national office in response to a request for technical advice from an IRS district or appeals office that is auditing a complex tax matter.

Temporary differences—difference between financial accounting and tax accounting treatment that is temporary in nature. The difference will ultimately reverse itself. An example of a temporary difference is different depreciation methods for financial accounting and tax purposes.

Term loan—type of interest-free loan provided by employer to employee. Repayable at a specified future date, whether employed by the firm at that time or not.

Territorial system—a tax system whereby a country taxes only income that was earned within its borders. See also "worldwide system."

Total tax rate—the sum of the implicit tax rate and the explicit tax rate. See also "explicit tax rate" and "implicit tax rate."

Tracking stock—stock that pays dividends based on the performance of a division or corporate subsidiary.

Traditional deductible IRA—eligible taxpayers may contribute up to $3,000 pretax (or 100% of compensation if less than $3,000) per year. Contributions are tax deductible and, as with most other pension plans, earnings in the pension account are tax-deferred until the taxpayer makes withdrawals in retirement. Withdrawals are taxed as ordinary income.

Transfer prices—prices at which goods and services are transferred between related parties such as a parent and its subsidiary. Transfer prices can be used to shift income from high tax jurisdictions to low tax jurisdictions. Tax authorities try to prevent abuse of transfer prices. See also "Section 482," "arm's length pricing," and "advance pricing agreements."

Treasury Regulations—issued by the Treasury Department to provide general interpretations of newly passed tax bills. Interested parties (such as tax lawyers, tax accountants, and other affected taxpayers) can request hearings of proposed regulations.

Triangular mergers—transaction in which a subsidiary of the acquirer mergers with the target corporation.

Trust preferred stock—stock treated by the issuer as debt for tax purposes but treated as quasi-equity on the balance sheet, reported between the equity and debt sections. Trust preferred stock is popular with banks, for which it counts as Tier 1 regulatory capital.

Unified tax credit—an estate and gift tax credit that effectively exempts the first $1 million of gifts and bequests from tax. Scheduled to increase to $3 million by 2006.

Uniform Gifts to Minors Act (UGMA)—Gifts made to minors under this act qualify for the annual gift exclusion even though the minors do not have unrestricted access to the gifts until they reach age 21.

Valid business purpose—transaction must be motivated by some reason other than tax avoidance. Some valid business purpose must characterize the structure of the transaction otherwise the IRS can recharacterize the transaction, leading to a less favorable tax treatment. A requirement for tax-free treatment in a Section 368 reorganization.

Withholding taxes—taxes levied on payments of dividends, interest, rents, royalties to foreign entities. Withholding taxes are often reduced by tax treaties. See also "tax treaty shopping" and "branch profits tax."

Worldwide system—a tax system whereby a country taxes its citizens, permanent residents, and resident corporations on their worldwide income, providing foreign tax credits to mitigate double taxation. The United States has a worldwide tax system. See also "territorial system" and "foreign tax credit."

INDEX

Court cases are grouped under "court cases." Entries referring to footnotes contain an *n*.

547